WORD PICTURES
IN THE
NEW TESTAMENT

WORD PICTURES
IN THE
NEW TESTAMENT

BY

ARCHIBALD THOMAS ROBERTSON
A. M., D. D., LL. D., Litt. D.
PROFESSOR OF NEW TESTAMENT INTERPRETATION
IN THE
SOUTHERN BAPTIST THEOLOGICAL SEMINARY
OF
LOUISVILLE, KENTUCKY

VOLUME III
THE ACTS OF THE APOSTLES

BAKER BOOK HOUSE
Grand Rapids, Michigan 49516

BY WAY OF INTRODUCTION

But for the Acts we should know nothing of the early apostolic period save what is told in the Epistles. There are various apocryphal "Acts," but they are without historical worth. Hence the importance of this book.

Luke the Author

It ought to be possible to assume this as a fact since the work of Ramsay and Harnack on various phases of the problems concerning the Acts. Harnack, in particular, has covered the ground with his accustomed thoroughness and care in his two volumes (*The Acts of the Apostles*, English Translation by Rev. J. R. Wilkinson, 1909; *The Date of the Acts and the Synoptic Gospels*, English Translation by Rev. J. R. Wilkinson, 1911). Ramsay's view may be found in Chapter I of *St. Paul the Traveller and the Roman Citizen*, Chapter XII of *Pauline and Other Studies*. A good summary of the matter appears in Part V of *The Synoptic Gospels and the Book of Acts* by Dr. D. A. Hayes, in Robertson's *Luke the Historian in the Light of Research*, and in the introduction to the various commentaries by Knowling, Rackham, Furneaux, Rendall, Hackett, Meyer-Wendt, Zahn, Blass, Campbell-Morgan, Stokes. In Part I of *The Acts of the Apostles*, Vol. II of *The Beginnings of Christianity*, edited by Foakes-Jackson and Kirsopp Lake both sides are ably presented: *The Case for the Tradition* by C. W. Emmet, *The Case against the Tradition* by H. Windisch. *The Internal Evidence of Acts* is discussed by the Editors, Foakes-Jackson and Lake, with an adverse conclusion against Luke. Henry J. Cadbury surveys *The Tradition* (the external evidence) and draws a negative conclusion likewise

on the ground that the early writers who ascribe Acts to
Luke were not critical scholars. A similar position is taken
by Cadbury in his more recent volume, *The Making of
Luke—Acts* (1927). But all the same the traditional view
that Luke is the author of the Acts holds the field with
those who are not prejudiced against it. The view of Baur
that Acts is a *Tendenz* writing for the purpose of healing
the breach between Peter and Paul and showing that the
two factions came together had great influence for a while.
In fact both Ramsay and Harnack at first held it. Ramsay
broke away first and he was followed by Harnack. Both were
influenced to change their views by the accumulation of
evidence to the effect that the author of both the Gospel and
Acts is Luke the Physician and Friend of Paul. Part of this
evidence has already been given in the Introduction to the
Gospel according to Luke.

The Author of the Gospel Also

The author of the Acts expressly states that he wrote
"the first treatise (*ton prōton logon*) concerning all things,
O Theophilus, that Jesus began both to do and to teach
until which day he gave command through the Holy Spirit
to the apostles whom he had chosen and was received up"
(Acts 1:1f.). There is no room for dispute that the reference
is directly to the Gospel according to Luke as we have it
now. Like the Gospel the book is dedicated to Theophilus.
And, what is even more important, the same style appears
in both Gospel and Acts. This fact Harnack has shown with
great pains and conclusiveness. There is the same interest
in medical matters and even Cadbury, who denies by implication the Lukan authorship, admits identity of authorship
for both books.

The Unity of the Acts

There are some scholars who are willing to admit the
Lukan authorship of the "we" sections when the author

uses "we" and "us" as in chapter 16:10–40 and 20:6–28:31. It has been argued that Luke wrote a travel-document or diary for these sections, but that this material was used by the editor or redactor of the whole book. But, unfortunately for that view, the very same style appears in the Acts as a whole and in the Gospel also as Harnack has proven. The man who said "we" and "us" in the "we" sections wrote "I" in 1:1 and refers to the Gospel as his work. The effort to disprove the unity of the Acts has failed. It stands as the work of the same author as a whole and the same author who wrote the Gospel.

SOURCES OF THE ACTS

Beyond a doubt Luke employed a variety of sources for this great history as he did for the Gospel (Luke 1:1–4). In fact, Cadbury argues that this Prologue was meant to apply to the Acts also as Volume II whether he intended to write a third volume or not. Certainly we are entitled to say that Luke used the same historical method for Acts. Some of these sources are easy to see. Luke had his own personal experience for the "we" sections. Then he had the benefit of Paul's own notes or suggestions for all that portion where Paul figures from chapters 8 to 28, since Luke was apparently with Paul in Rome when he finished the Book. This would include Paul's sermons and addresses which Luke gives unless one wishes to say, as some do, that Luke followed the style of Thucydides and composed the kind of addresses that he thought Paul would make. I see no evidence of that for each address differs from the others and suits precisely the occasion when it was delivered. The ancients frequently employed shorthand and Paul may have preserved notes of his addresses. Prof. C. C. Torrey, of Yale University, argues in his *Composition and Date of Acts* (1916) that Luke used an Aramaic document for the first fifteen chapters of the Acts. There is an Aramaic element in certain portions of these chapters, but nothing like so pronounced as in Luke 1 and 2 after 1:1–4. It cannot be said that Torrey has made out his case for such a single document. Luke may have had several such documents besides access to others familiar with the early days of the work in Jerusalem. There was Simon Peter whom Paul visited for two weeks in Jerusalem (Gal. 1:18) besides other points of contact with him in Jerusalem and Antioch (Acts 15 and Gal. 2). There was also Barnabas who was early Paul's friend (Acts 9:27) and who knew the beginnings as few did (Acts 4:36f.). Besides many others it is to be observed that Paul with Luke made a special visit to Caesarea where he spent a week with the gifted Philip and his daughters with the gift of prophecy (Acts 21:8f.). But with all the inevitable variety of sources for the information needed to cover the wide field of the Book of Acts the same mind has manifestly worked through it and it is the same style all through that appears in the "we" sections where the writer is confessedly a companion of Paul. No other companion of Paul carries this claim for the authorship and no other was a physician and no author has the external evidence from early writers.

THE DATE

There are three views about the date of the Acts. Baur and his Tübingen School held the second century to be the date of this late pamphlet as they termed it after the fashion of the Clementine Homilies. But that view is now practically abandoned save by the few who still strangely oppose the Lukan authorship. Probably the majority of those who accept the Lukan authorship place it in the latter part of the first century for two reasons. One is that the Gospel according to Luke is dated by them after the destruction of Jerusalem because of the prophecy by Jesus of the encompassing of the city by armies. Predictive prophecy that

would be and so it is considered a prophecy *post eventum.*
The other reason is the alleged use of the *Antiquities* of
Josephus by Luke. Josephus finished this work A.D. 93 so
that, if Luke did use it, he must have written the Acts
after that date. Usually this argument is made to show that
Luke could not have written it at all, but some hold that he
may have lived to an age that would allow it. But it cannot
be assumed that Luke used Josephus because of his mention
of Theudas and Judas the Galilean. They differ so widely
(Acts 5:36f. and Josephus, *Ant.* XX. v, 1, 2) that Von Dob-
schütz (*Dictionary of the Apostolic Church,* art. Josephus)
argues that the two accounts are entirely independent of
each other. So Luke (Lu. 13:1f.) alludes to a Galilean revolt
not mentioned by Josephus and Josephus records three
revolts under Pilate not referred to by Luke. A comparison
of the accounts of the death of Agrippa I in Acts 12:20–23
and *Ant.* XIX. viii, 2 redounds to the credit of Luke. The
Josephus phase of the argument may be brushed to one
side. The third view, held by Harnack and adopted here,
is that Luke wrote the Acts while with Paul in Rome and
finished the book before Paul's release, that is by A.D. 63.
This is the obvious and natural way to take the language of
Luke at the close of Acts. Events had gone no farther and
so he ends the narrative right there. It is argued against
this that Luke contemplated a third volume and for this
reason closed with the arrival of Paul in Rome. But the
use of *prōton* (first) in Acts 1:1 is a common *Koinē* idiom and
does not imply three volumes any more than first and second
stories with us means that the house has three. Of course
this date for the Acts puts the date of the Gospel further
back either in Caesarea (57 to 59) or in Rome (60 to 62).
And that means that Mark's Gospel is still earlier since
Luke used it for his Gospel and the Logia (Q) earlier still.
But all these dates are probable in the light of all the known
facts.

The Historical Value

It was once a fad with a certain school of critics to decry Luke in the Acts as wholly untrustworthy, not above the legendary stage. But the spade has done well by Luke for inscriptions and papyri have brought remarkable confirmation for scores of points where Luke once stood all alone and was discounted because he stood alone. These will be duly noted in the proper places as they occur. Ramsay has done most in this restoration of the rank of Luke as a credible historian, as shown in particular in his *St. Paul the Traveller and the Roman Citizen* and in *The Bearing of Recent Discovery on the Trustworthiness of the New Testament*. In every instance where discoveries have been made they have confirmed the testimony of Luke as concerning *politarchs* in Thessalonica, *proconsul* in Cyprus, etc. The result is that the balance of evidence is now in favour of Luke even when he still stands alone or seems to be opposed by Josephus. Luke, as it stands today, is a more credible historian than Josephus. Ramsay dares to call Luke, all things considered, the greatest of all historians, even above Thucydides. An interesting book on this phase of the subject is Chase's *The Credibility of the Acts of the Apostles* (1902).

The Purpose of the Acts

It is not easy to say in a word precisely the object of Luke in writing this book. It is not the Acts of all the apostles. Outside of Peter and John little is told of any of them after chapter 3. And all the acts of Peter and John are not given for Peter disappears from the narrative after chapter 15, though he has been the central figure through chapter 11. Paul is not one of the twelve apostles, but Luke follows Paul's career mainly after chapter 8. Stephen and Barnabas come in also. Still (*St. Paul on Trial*, 1923) argues that Luke meant the book as an apology to be used in Paul's trial at Rome or at any rate to put Paul in the right light with the Jews in Rome. Hence the full account of Paul's series of defences in Jerusalem, Caesarea, Rome. There may be an element of truth in this idea, but it clearly does not cover the whole purpose of Luke. Others hold that Luke had a dramatic plan to get Paul to Rome as the climax of his campaign to win the Roman Empire to Christ. The book is not a history of all early Christianity. Peter and Paul dominate the atmosphere of the book with Paul as the great hero of Luke. But one can easily see that the work is done with consummate skill. The author is a man of culture, of Christian grace, of literary power. The book pulses with life today.

THE TEXT OF THE ACTS

A special problem arises concerning the text of Acts inasmuch as the Codex Bezae (D) with some other Western support presents a great many additions to the Neutral-Alexandrian text of Aleph A B C. Blass has even proposed the idea that Luke himself issued two editions of the book, an attractive hypothesis that is not generally accepted. J. M. Wilson has published *The Acts of the Apostles from Codex Bezae*. The whole subject is elaborately treated by J. H. Ropes in Vol. III, *The Text of Acts* in Part I of *The Beginnings of Christianity*. Besides thorough discussion of all the problems of text involved Ropes gives the text of the Vatican Codex (B) on the left page and that of Codex Bezae (D) on the right, making comparison easy. Blass's ideas appear in his *Acta Apostolorum*.

CONTENTS

THE ACTS OF THE APOSTLES

xvi   CONTENTS

THE ACTS OF THE APOSTLES

CHAPTER I

The Title is simply *Acts* (*Praxeis*) in Aleph, Origen, Tertullian, Didymus, Hilary, Eusebius, Epiphanius. *The Acts of the Apostles* (*Praxeis apostolōn*) is the reading of B D (Aleph in subscription) Athanasius, Origen, Tertullian, Cyprian, Eusebius, Cyril of Jerusalem, Theodoret, Hilary. *The Acts of the Holy Apostles* (*Praxeis tōn hagiōn apostolōn*) is read by A² E G H A K Chrysostom. It is possible that the book was given no title at all by Luke, for it is plain that usage varied greatly even in the same writers. The long title as found in the Textus Receptus (Authorized Version) is undoubtedly wrong with the adjective "Holy." The reading of B D, "*The Acts of the Apostles*," may be accepted as probably correct.

1. *The former treatise* (*ton men prōton*). Literally, the first treatise. The use of the superlative is common enough and by no means implies, though it allows, a third volume. This use of *prōtos* where only two are compared is seen between the Baptist and Jesus (John 1:15), John and Peter (John 20:4). The idiom is common in the papyri (Robertson, *Grammar*, pp. 662, 669). The use of *men solitarium* here, as Hackett notes, is common in Acts. It is by no means true that *men* requires a following *de* by contrast. The word is merely a weakened form of *mēn* = surely, indeed. The reference is to the "first treatise" and merely emphasizes that. The use of *logos* (*word*) for treatise or historical narrative is common in ancient Greek as in Herodotus 6 and 9. Plato (*Phaedo*, p. 61 B) makes a contrast between *muthos* and *logos*. *I made* (*epoiēsamēn*). Aorist middle indicative, the middle being the usual construction for mental acts with *poieō*. *O Theophilus* (*O Theophile*). The interjection

3

Ō here as is common, though not in Luke 1:3. But the adjective *kratiste* (most excellent) is wanting here. See remarks on Theophilus on Luke 1:3. Hackett thinks that he lived at Rome because of the way Acts ends. He was a man of rank. He may have defrayed the expense of publishing both Luke and Acts. Perhaps by this time Luke may have reached a less ceremonious acquaintance with Theophilus. *Which Jesus began* (*hōn ērxato Iēsous*). The relative is attracted from the accusative *ha* to the genitive *hōn* because of the antecedent *pantōn* (all). The language of Luke here is not merely pleonastic as Winer held. Jesus "began" "both to do and to teach" (*poiein te kai didaskein*). Note present infinitives, linear action, still going on, and the use of *te—kai* binds together the life and teachings of Jesus, as if to say that Jesus is still carrying on from heaven the work and teaching of the disciples which he started while on earth before his ascension. The record which Luke now records is really the Acts of Jesus as much as the Acts of the Apostles. Dr. A. T. Pierson called it "The Acts of the Holy Spirit," and that is true also. The Acts, according to Luke, is a continuation of the doings and teachings of Jesus. "The following writings appear intended to give us, and do, in fact, profess to give us, that which Jesus *continued* to do and teach after the day in which he was taken up" (Bernard, *Progress of Doctrine in the N.T.*).

2. *Until the day in which* (*achri hēs hēmeras*). Incorporation of the antecedent into the relative clause and the change of case *hēi* (locative) to *hēs* (genitive). *Was received up* (*anelēmpthē*). First aorist passive indicative of *analambanō*. Common verb to lift anything up (Acts 10:16) or person as Paul (Acts 20:13). Several times of the Ascension of Jesus to heaven (Mark 16:19; Acts 1:2, 11, 22; I Tim. 3:16) with or without "into heaven" (*eis ton ouranon*). This same verb is used of Elijah's translation to heaven in the LXX (II Kings 2:11). The same idea, though not this word, is in

Luke 24:51. See Luke 9:51 for *analēmpsis* of the Ascension. *Had given commandment (enteilamenos).* First aorist middle participle of *entellō* (from *en* and *tellō*, to accomplish), usually in the middle, old verb, to enjoin. This special commandment refers directly to what we call the commission given the apostles before Christ ascended on high (John 20:21-23; Matt. 28:16-20 = Mark 16:15-18 = I Cor. 15:6; Luke 24:44-49). He had given commands to them when they were first chosen and when they were sent out on the tour of Galilee, but the immediate reference is as above. *Through the Holy Spirit (dia pneumatos hagiou).* In his human life Jesus was under the guidance of the Holy Spirit. This applies to the choice of the apostles (Luke 6:13) and to these special commands before the Ascension. *Whom he had chosen (hous exelexato).* Aorist middle indicative, not past perfect. The same verb (*eklexamenos*) was used by Luke in describing the choice of the twelve by Jesus (Luke 6:13). But the aorist does not stand "for" our English pluperfect as Hackett says. That is explaining Greek by English. The Western text here adds: "And ordered to proclaim the gospel."

3. *To whom also (hois kai).* He chose them and then also manifested himself to these very same men that they might have personal witness to give. *Shewed himself alive (parestēsen heauton zōnta).* To the disciples the first Sunday evening (Mark 16:14 = Luke 24:36-43 = John 20:19-25), the second Sunday evening (John 20:26-29), at the Sea of Tiberias (John 21:1-23), on the mountain in Galilee (Matt. 28:16-20 = Mark 16:15-18 = I Cor. 15:6), to the disciples in Jerusalem and Olivet (Luke 24:44-53; Mark 16-19f. = Acts 1:1-11). Luke uses this verb *paristēmi* 13 times in the Acts both transitively and intransitively. It is rendered by various English words (present, furnish, provide, assist, commend). The early disciples including Paul never doubted the fact of the Resurrection, once they were convinced by personal experience. At first some doubted like Thomas (Mark 16:14;

Luke 24:41; John 20:24f.; Matt. 28:17). But after that they never wavered in their testimony to their own experience with the Risen Christ, "whereof we are witnesses" Peter said (Acts 3:15). They doubted at first, that we may believe, but at last they risked life itself in defence of this firm faith. *After his passion* (*meta to pathein auton*). Neat Greek idiom, *meta* with the articular infinitive (second aorist active of *paschō*) and the accusative of general reference, "after the suffering as to him." For *pathein* used absolutely of Christ's suffering see also Acts 17:3; 26:23. *By many proofs* (*en pollois tekmēriois*). Literally, "in many proofs." *Tekmērion* is only here in the N.T., though an old and common word in ancient Greek and occurring in the *Koiné* (papyri, etc.). The verb *tekmairō*, to prove by sure signs, is from *tekmar*, a sign. Luke does not hesitate to apply the definite word "proofs" to the evidence for the Resurrection of Christ after full investigation on the part of this scientific historian. Aristotle makes a distinction between *tekmērion* (proof) and *sēmeion* (sign) as does Galen the medical writer. *Appearing* (*optanomenos*). Present middle participle from late verb *optanō*, late *Koiné* verb from root *optō* seen in *opsomai*, *ōphthēn*. In LXX, papyri of second century B.C. (Deissmann, *Light from the Ancient East*, p. 83). Only here in the N.T. For *optasia* for vision see Acts 26:19; Luke 1:22; 24:23. *By the space of forty days* (*di' hēmerōn tesserakonta*). At intervals (*dia*, between) during the forty days, ten appearances being known to us. Jesus was not with them continually now in bodily presence. The period of forty days is given here alone. The Ascension was thus ten days before Pentecost when the Holy Spirit came. Moses was in the mount forty days (Ex. 24:18) and Jesus fasted forty days (Matt. 4:2). In the Gospel of Luke 24 this separation of forty days between the Resurrection and the Ascension is not drawn. *The things concerning the Kingdom of God* (*ta peri tēs basileias tou theou*). This phrase appears 33 times in Luke's Gospel, 15 times in Mark, 4 times in Matthew who elsewhere has "the kingdom of heaven," once in John, and 6 times in Acts. No essential distinction is to be drawn between the two for the Jews often used "heaven" rather than "God" to avoid using the Tetragrammaton. But it is noticeable how the word kingdom drops out of Acts. Other words like gospel (*euaggelion*) take the place of "kingdom." Jesus was fond of the word "kingdom" and Luke is fond of the idiom "the things concerning" (*ta peri*). Certainly with Jesus the term "kingdom" applies to the present and the future and covers so much that it is not strange that the disciples with their notions of a political Messianic kingdom (Acts 1:6) were slow to comprehend the spiritual nature of the reign of God.

4. *Being assembled together with them* (*sunalizomenos*). Present passive participle from *sunalizō*, an old verb in Herodotus, Xenophon, etc., from *sun*, with, and *halizō*, from *halēs*, crowded. The margin of both the Authorized and the Revised Versions has "eating with them" as if from *sun* and *hals* (salt). Salt was the mark of hospitality. There is the verb *halisthēte en autōi* used by Ignatius *Ad Magnes.* X, "Be ye salted in him." But it is more than doubtful if that is the idea here though the Vulgate does have *convescens illis* "eating with them," as if that was the common habit of Jesus during the forty days (Wendt, Feine, etc.). Jesus did on occasion eat with the disciples (Luke 24:41–43 =Mark 16:14). *To wait for the promise of the Father* (*perimenein tēn epaggelian tou patros*). Note present active infinitive, to keep on waiting for (around, *peri*). In the Great Commission on the mountain in Galilee this item was not given (Matt. 28:16–20). It is the subjective genitive, the promise given by the Father (note this Johannine use of the word), that is the Holy Spirit ("the promise of the Holy Spirit," objective genitive). *Which ye heard from me* (*hēn ēkousate mou*). Change from indirect discourse (com-

mand), infinitives *chōrizesthai* and *perimenein* after *parēg-geilen* to direct discourse without any *ephē* (said he) as the English (Italics). Luke often does this (*oratio variata*). Note also the ablative case of *mou* (from me). Luke continues in verse 5 with the direct discourse giving the words of Jesus.

5. *Baptized with water* (*ebaptisen hudati*) *and with the Holy Ghost* (*en pneumati baptisthēsesthe hagiōi*). The margin has "in the Holy Ghost" (Spirit, it should be). The American Standard Version renders "in" both with "water" and "Holy Spirit" as do Goodspeed (American Translation) and Mrs. Montgomery (Centenary Translation). John's own words (Matt. 3:11) to which Jesus apparently refers use *en* (in) both with water and Spirit. There is a so-called instrumental use of *en* where we in English have to say "with" (Rev. 13:10 *en machairēi*, like *machairēi*, Acts 12:2). That is to say *en* with the locative presents the act as located in a certain instrument like a sword (Robertson, *Grammar*, pp. 589f.). But the instrumental case is more common without *en* (the locative and instrumental cases having the same form). So it is often a matter of indifference which idiom is used as in John 21:8 we have *tōi ploiariōi* (locative without *en*). They came *in* (locative case without *en*) the boat. So in John 1:31 *en hudati baptizōn* baptizing in water. No distinction therefore can be insisted on here between the construction *hudati* and *en pneumati* (both being in the locative case, one without, one with *en*). Note unusual position of the verb *baptisthēsesthe* (future passive indicative) between *pneumati* and *hagiōi*. This baptism of the Holy Spirit was predicted by John (Matt. 3:11) as the characteristic of the Messiah's work. Now the Messiah himself in his last message before his Ascension proclaims that in a few days the fulfilment of that prophecy will come to pass. The Codex Bezae adds here "which ye are about to receive" and "until the Pentecost" to verse 5. *Not many days hence* (*ou meta pollas tautas hēmeras*). A neat Greek

idiom difficult to render smoothly into English: "Not after many days these." The litotes (not many = few) is common in Luke (7:6; 15:13; Acts 17:27; 19:11; 20:12; 21:39; 28:14; 28:2). The predicate use of *tautas* (without article) is to be noted. "These" really means as a starting point, "from these" (Robertson, *Grammar*, p. 702). It was ten days hence. This idiom occurs several times in Luke (24:21; Acts 24:21), as elsewhere (John 4:18; II Pet. 3:1). In Luke 2:12 the copula is easily supplied as it exists in Luke 1:36; 2:2.

6. *They therefore (hoi men oun)*. Demonstrative use of *hoi* with *men oun* without any corresponding *de* just as in 1:1 *men* occurs alone. The combination *men oun* is common in Acts (27 times). Cf. Luke 3:18. The *oun* is resumptive and refers to the introductory verses (1:1–5), which served to connect the Acts with the preceding Gospel. The narrative now begins. *Asked (ērōtōn)*. Imperfect active, repeatedly asked before Jesus answered. *Lord (kurie)*. Here not in the sense of "sir" (Matt. 21:30), but to Jesus as Lord and Master as often in Acts (19:5, 10, etc.) and in prayer to Jesus (7:59). *Dost thou restore (ei apokathistaneis)*. The use of *ei* in an indirect question is common. We have already seen its use in direct questions (Matt. 12:10; Luke 13:23 which see for discussion), possibly in imitation of the Hebrew (frequent in the LXX) or as a partial condition without conclusion. See also Acts 7:1; 19:2; 21:37; 22:25. The form of the verb *apokathistanō* is late (also *apokathistaō*) ōmega form for the old and common *apokathistēmi*, double compound, to restore to its former state. As a matter of fact the Messianic kingdom for which they are asking is a political kingdom that would throw off the hated Roman yoke. It is a futuristic present and they are uneasy that Jesus may yet fail to fulfil their hopes. Surely here is proof that the eleven apostles needed the promise of the Father before they began to spread the message of the Risen Christ. They still yearn for a political kingdom for Israel even after faith and hope

have come back. They need the enlightenment of the Holy Spirit (John 14–16) and the power of the Holy Spirit (Acts 1:4 f.).

7. *Times or seasons* (*chronous ē kairous*). "Periods" and "points" of time sometimes and probably so here, but such a distinction is not always maintained. See Acts 17:26 for *kairous* in the same sense as *chronous* for long periods of time. But here some distinction seems to be called for. It is curious how eager people have always been to fix definite dates about the second coming of Christ as the apostles were about the political Messianic kingdom which they were expecting. *Hath set* (*etheto*). Second aorist middle indicative, emphasizing the sovereignty of the Father in keeping all such matters to himself, a gentle hint to people today about the limits of curiosity. Note also "his own" (*idiāi*) "authority" (*exousiāi*).

8. *Power* (*dunamin*). Not the "power" about which they were concerned (political organization and equipments for empire on the order of Rome). Their very question was ample proof of their need of this new "power" (*dunamin*), to enable them (from *dunamai*, to be able), to grapple with the spread of the gospel in the world. *When the Holy Ghost is come upon you* (*epelthontos tou hagiou pneumatos eph' humas*). Genitive absolute and is simultaneous in time with the preceding verb "shall receive" (*lēmpsesthe*). The Holy Spirit will give them the "power" as he comes upon them. This is the baptism of the Holy Spirit referred to in verse 5. *My witnesses* (*mou martures*). Correct text. "Royal words of magnificent and Divine assurance" (Furneaux). Our word martyrs is this word *martures*. In Luke 24:48 Jesus calls the disciples "witnesses to these things" (*martures toutōn*, objective genitive). In Acts 1:22 an apostle has to be a "witness to the Resurrection" of Christ and in 10:39 to the life and work of Jesus. Hence there could be no "apostles" in this sense after the first generation. But here

the apostles are called "my witnesses." "His by a direct personal relationship" (Knowling). The expanding sphere of their witness when the Holy Spirit comes upon them is "unto the uttermost part of the earth" (*heōs eschatou tēs gēs*). Once they had been commanded to avoid Samaria (Matt. 10:5), but now it is included in the world program as already outlined on the mountain in Galilee (Matt. 28:19 = Mark 16:15). Jesus is on Olivet as he points to Jerusalem, Judea, Samaria, the uttermost (last, *eschatou*) part of the earth. The program still beckons us on to world conquest for Christ. "The Acts themselves form the best commentary on these words, and the words themselves might be given as the best summary of the Acts" (Page). The events follow this outline (Jerusalem till the end of chapter 7, with the martyrdom of Stephen, the scattering of the saints through Judea and Samaria in chapter 8, the conversion of Saul, chapter 9, the spread of the gospel to Romans in Caesarea by Peter (chapter 10), to Greeks in Antioch (chapter 11), finally Paul's world tours and arrest and arrival in Rome (chapters 11 to 28).

9. *As they were looking* (*blepontōn autōn*). Genitive absolute. The present participle accents the fact that they were looking directly at Jesus. *He was taken up* (*epērthē*). First aorist passive indicative of *epairō*, old and common verb meaning to lift up. In Luke 24:51 we have "he was borne up" (*anephereto*) and in Acts 1:2, 1:11; I Tim. 3:6 "was received up" (*anelēmpthē*). Received (*hupelaben*). Second aorist active indicative of *hupolambanō*, literally here "took under him." He seemed to be supported by the cloud. "In glory" Paul adds in I Tim. 3:16. *Out of their sight* (*apo tōn ophthalmōn autōn*). From their eyes (*apo* with ablative case).

10. *Were looking steadfastly* (*atenizontes ēsan*). Periphrastic imperfect active of *atenizō*, a late intensive verb (intensive *a* and *teinō*, to stretch). Common in Acts and also

in Luke 4:20 and 22:56 as well as Acts 10:4, which see. *As he went* (*poreuomenou autou*). Genitive absolute of present middle participle. They saw him slipping away from their eyes as the cloud bore him away. *Stood by them* (*pareistēkeisan autois*). Past perfect active indicative of *paristēmi* and intransitive (note *i* in B instead of *ei* for augment, mere itacism).

11. *Who also* (*hoi kai*). Common use of *kai* pleonastic to show that the two events were parallel. This is the simplest way from Homer on to narrate two parallel events. *Why?* (*ti*). Jesus had told them of his coming Ascension (John 6:62; 20:17) so that they should have been prepared. *This Jesus* (*houtos ho Iēsous*). *Qui vobis fuit eritque semper Jesus, id est, Salvator* (Corn. a Lapide). The personal name assures them that Jesus will always be in heaven a personal friend and divine Saviour (Knowling). *So in like manner* (*houtōs hon tropon*). Same idea twice. "So in which manner" (incorporation of antecedent and accusative of general reference). The fact of his second coming and the manner of it also described by this emphatic repetition.

12. *Olivet* (*Elaiōnos*). Genitive singular. Vulgate *Olivetum*. Made like *ampelōn*. Here only in the N.T., usually *to oros tōn Elaiōn* (the Mount of Olives), though some MSS. have Olivet in Luke 19:29; 21:37. Josephus (*Ant.* VII. 9, 2) has it also and the papyri (Deissmann, *Light from the Ancient East*, p. 170). *A sabbath day's journey off* (*Sabbatou echōn hodon*). Luke only says here that Olivet is a Sabbath day's journey from Jerusalem, not that Jesus was precisely that distance when he ascended. In the Gospel Luke (24:50) states that Jesus led them "over against" (*heōs pros*) Bethany (about two miles or fifteen furlongs). The top of Olivet is six furlongs or three-fourths of a mile. The Greek idiom here is "having a journey of a Sabbath" after "which is nigh unto Jerusalem" (*ho estin eggus Ierousalēm*), note the periphrastic construction. Why Luke mentions this

item for Gentile readers in this form is not known, unless
it was in his Jewish source. See Ex. 16:29; Numb. 35:5;
Josh. 3:4. But it does not contradict what he says in Luke
24:50, where he does not say that Jesus led them all the way
to Bethany.

13. *Into the upper chamber* (*eis to huperōion*). The upstairs
or upper room (*huper* is upper or over, the adjective *huper-
ōios*), the room upstairs where the women staid in Homer,
then a room up under the flat roof for retirement or prayer
(Acts 9:37, 39), sometimes a large third story room suitable
for gatherings (Acts 20:9). It is possible, even probable,
that this is the "large upper room" (*anōgeon mega*) of
Mark 14:15 = Luke 22:12. The Vulgate has *coenaculum* for
both words. The word is used in the N.T only in Acts.
It was in a private house as in Luke 22:11 and not in the
temple as Luke 24:53 might imply, "continually" (*dia
pantos*) these words probably meaning on proper occasions.
They were abiding (*ēsan katamenontes*). Periphrastic imperfect active. Perfective use of *kata*, to abide permanently.
It is possible that this is the house of Mary the mother of
John Mark where the disciples later met for prayer (Acts
12:12). Here alone in the N.T., though old compound.
Some MSS. here read *paramenontes*. This could mean constant residence, but most likely frequent resort for prayer
during these days, some being on hand all the time as they
came and went. *Simon the Zealot* (*Simon ho Zēlōtēs*). Called
Simon the Cananaean (*ho Cananaios*) in Matt. 10:4, Mark
3:18, but Zealot in Luke 6:16 as here giving the Greek
equivalent of the Aramaic word because Luke has Gentiles
in mind. The epithet (member of the party of Zealots)
clung to him after he became an apostle and distinguishes
him from Simon Peter. See Vol. I on the Gospel of Matthew
for discussion of the four lists of the apostles. *Judas the son
of James* (*Joudas Iakōbou*). Literally, Judas of James,
whether son or brother (cf. Jude 1:1) we do not really know.

"Of James" is added to distinguish him from Judas Iscariot (John 14:22). However we take it, he must be identified with the Thaddaeus (= Lebbaeus) of Mark and Matthew to make the list in the third group identical. No name appears in Acts for that of Judas Iscariot.

14. *With one accord* (*homothumadon*). Old adverb in -*don* from adjective *homothumos* and that from *homos*, same, and *thumos*, mind or spirit, with the same mind or spirit. Common in ancient Greek and papyri. In the N.T. eleven times in Acts and nowhere else save Rom. 15:6. See Matt. 18:19. *Continued* (*ēsan proskarterountes*). Periphrastic imperfect active of *proskartereō*, old verb from *pros* (perfective use) and *kartereō* from *karteros*, strong, steadfast, like the English "carry on." Already in Mark 3:9 which see and several times in Acts and Paul's Epistles. They "stuck to" the praying (*tēi proseuchēi*, note article) for the promise of the Father till the answer came. *With the women* (*sun gunaixin*). Associative instrumental case plural of *gunē* after *sun*. As one would expect when praying was the chief work on hand. More women certainly included than in Luke 8:2; Mark 15:40f. = Matt. 27:55f. = Luke 23:49; Mark 15:47 = Matt. 27:61 = Luke 23:55f.; Mark 16:1 = Matt. 28:1; Luke 24:1f. = John 20:1, 11–18; Matt. 28:9f. There were probably other women also whose testimony was no longer scouted as it had been at first. Codex Bezae adds here "and children." *And Mary the mother of Jesus* (*kai Mariam tēi mētri tou Iēsou*). A delicate touch by Luke that shows Mary with her crown of glory at last. She had come out of the shadow of death with the song in her heart and with the realization of the angel's promise and the prophecy of Simeon. It was a blessed time for Mary. *With his brethren* (*sun tois adelphois autou*). With his brothers, it should be translated. They had once disbelieved in him (John 7:5). Jesus had appeared to James (I Cor. 15:7) and now it is a happy family of believers including the

mother and brothers (half-brothers, literally) of Jesus. They continue in prayer for the power from on high.

15. *Brethren* (*adelphōn*). Codex Bezae has "disciples." *Multitude of persons* (*ochlos onomatōn*). Literally, multitude of names. This Hebraistic use of *onoma* = person occurs in the LXX (Numb. 1:2; 18:20; 3:40, 43; 26:53) and in Rev. 3:4; 11:13. *Together* (*epi to auto*). The word "gathered" is not in the Greek here, but it does occur in Matt. 22:34 and that is undoubtedly the idea in Luke 17:35 as in Acts 2:1, 44, 47; I Cor. 11:20; 14:23. So also here. They were in the same place (*to auto*). *About a hundred and twenty* (*hōs hekaton eikosi*). A crowd for "the upper room." No special significance in the number 120, just the number there.

16. *Brethren* (*andres adelphoi*). Literally, men, brethren or brother men. More dignified and respectful than just "brethren." Demosthenes sometimes said *Andres Athēnaioi*. Cf. our "gentlemen and fellow-citizens." Women are included in this address though *andres* refers only to men. *It was needful* (*edei*). Imperfect tense of the impersonal *dei* with the infinitive clause (first aorist passive) and the accusative of general reference as a loose subject. Peter here assumes that Jesus is the Messiah and finds scripture illustrative of the treachery of Judas. He applies it to Judas and quotes the two passages in verse 20 (Psa. 69:25; Psa. 109:8). The Holy Spirit has not yet come upon them, but Peter feels moved to interpret the situation. He feels that his mind is opened by Jesus (Luke 24:45). It is a logical, not a moral, necessity that Peter points out. Peter here claims the Holy Spirit as speaking in the scriptures as he does in II Peter 1:21. His description of Judas as "guide" (*hodēgou*) to those who seized (*sullabousin*) Jesus is that of the base traitor that he was. This very verb occurs in Luke 22:54 of the arrest of Jesus.

17. *Was numbered* (*katērithmenos ēn*). Periphrastic past

perfect passive indicative of *katarithmeō*, old verb, but here only in the N.T. (perfective use of *kata*). *Received his portion* (*elachen ton klēron*). Second aorist active indicative of *lagchanō*, old verb, to obtain by lot as in Luke 1:9 and John 19:24, especially by divine appointment as here and II Peter 2:1. *Klēros* also means lot, an object used in casting lots (Acts 1:26), or what is obtained by lot as here and 8:21, of eternal salvation (Acts 26:18; Col. 1:12), of persons chosen by divine appointment (I Peter 5:3). From this latter usage the·Latin *cleros*, *clericus*, our clergy, one chosen by divine lot. So Peter says that Judas "obtained by lot the lot of this ministry" (*diakonias*) which he had when he betrayed Jesus. The Master chose him and gave him his opportunity.

18. *Now this man* (*Houtos men oun*). Note *men oun* again without a corresponding *de* as in 1:6. Verses 18 and 19 are a long parenthesis of Luke by.way of explanation of the fate of Judas. In verse 20 Peter resumes and quotes the scripture to which he referred in verse 16. *Obtained* (*ektē-sato*). First aorist middle indicative of *ktaomai*, to acquire, only in the middle, to get for oneself. With the covenant money for the betrayal, acquired it indirectly apparently according to Matt. 26:14-16; 27:3-8 which see. *Falling headlong* (*prēnēs genomenos*). Attic form usually *pranēs*. The word means, not "headlong," but "flat on the face" as opposed to *huptios* on the back (Hackett). Hackett observes that the place suits admirably the idea that Judas hung himself (Matt. 27:5) and, the rope breaking, fell flat on his face and *burst asunder in the midst* (*elakēsen mesos*). First aorist active indicative of *laskō* old verb (here only in the N.T.), to clang, to crack, to crash, like a falling tree. Aristophanes uses it of crashing bones. *Mesos* is predicate nominative referring to Judas. *Gushed out* (*exechuthē*). First aorist passive indicative of *ekcheō*, to pour out.

19. *Language* (*dialektōi*). Not a dialect of the Greek, but a different language, the Aramaic. So also in 2:6; 21:40.

Dialektos is from *dialegomai*, to converse, to speak between two (*dia*). *Akeldama* (*Hakeldamach*). This Aramaic word Peter explains as "the field of blood." Two traditions are preserved: one in Matt. 27:7 which explains that the priests purchased this potter's field with the money which Judas flung down as the price of the blood of Jesus. The other in Acts describes it as the field of blood because Judas poured out his blood there. Hackett and Knowling argue that both views can be true. "The ill-omened name could be used with a double emphasis" (Hackett).

20. *For it is written* (*gegraptai gar*). Luke here returns to the address of Peter interrupted by verses 18 and 19. Perfect passive indicative, the usual idiom in quoting scripture, stands written. Psalm 69 is often quoted as Messianic in Matthew and John. *His habitation* (*hē epaulis autou*). Only here in the N.T., a country house, cottage, cabin. *His office* (*tēn episkopēn autou*). Our word bishopric (Authorized Version) is from this word, office of bishop (*episcopos*). Only that is not the idea here, but over-seership (*epi, skopeō*) or office as in I Peter 2:12. It means to visit and to inspect, to look over. The ecclesiastical sense comes later (I Tim. 3:1).

21. *Must* (*dei*). Present necessity corresponding to the old necessity (*edei*) about Judas (verse 16). This sentence in verses 21 and 22 begins with *dei*. *That* (*hōi*). Locative case of the relative attracted to the case of the antecedent. *Went in and went out* (*eisēlthen kai exēlthen*). Constative aorist active. *With us* (*eph' hēmas*). Over us, the margin has it. But the full phrase would be *eph' hēmas kai aph' hēmōn*. He came to us and went from us (Knowling).

22. *Beginning* (*arxamenos*). Aorist middle participle of *archō*, agreeing (*nominative*) with *ho kurios Iēsous* (the Lord Jesus). The ministry of Jesus began with the ministry of John. Strictly speaking *arxamenos* should be the accusative and agree with *martura* (witness) in verse 22, but the con-

struction is a bit free. The ministry of Jesus began with the baptism of John and lasted until the Ascension. *A witness with us of his resurrection (martura tēs anastaseōs autou sun hēmin).* This Peter considers the essential thing in a successor to Judas. The one chosen should be a personal witness who can speak from his own experience of the ministry, resurrection, and ascension of the Lord Jesus. One can easily see that this qualification will soon put an end to those who bear such personal testimony.

23. *They put forward two (estēsan duo).* First aorist active indicative (transitive) of *histēmi* (not intransitive second aorist, though same form in the third person plural). Somebody nominated two names, Justus and Matthias.

24. *Show us the one whom thou hast chosen (anadeixon hon exelexō).* First aorist active imperative of *anadeiknumi*, to show up, make plain. First aorist middle indicative second person singular of *eklegō*, to pick out, choose, select. In this prayer they assume that God has made a choice. They only wish to know his will. They call God the *heart-searcher* or *heart-knower (kardiognōsta,* vocative singular), a late word, here and Acts 15:8 only in the N.T. Modern physicians have delicate apparatus for studying the human heart.

25. *Apostleship (apostolēs).* Jesus had called the twelve apostles. An old word for sending away, then for a release, then the office and dignity of an apostle (Acts 1:25; Rom. 1:5; I Cor. 9:2; Gal. 2:8). *To his own place (eis ton topon ton idion).* A bold and picturesque description of the destiny of Judas worthy of Dante's *Inferno.* There is no doubt in Peter's mind of the destiny of Judas nor of his own guilt. He made ready his own berth and went to it.

26. *He was numbered (sunkatepsēphisthē).* To the Jews the lot did not suggest gambling, but "the O.T. method of learning the will of Jehovah" (Furneaux). The two nominations made a decision necessary and they appealed to God

in this way. This double compound *sunkatapsēphizō* occurs here alone in the N.T. and elsewhere only in Plutarch (*Them.* 21) in the middle voice for condemning with others. *Sunpsēphizō* occurs in the middle voice in Acts 19:19 for counting up money and also in Aristophanes. *Psēphizō* with *dapanēn* occurs in Luke 14:28 for counting the cost and in Rev. 13:18 for "counting" the number of the beast. The ancients used pebbles (*psēphoi*) in voting, black for condemning, white (Rev. 2:17) in acquitting. Here it is used in much the same sense as *katarithmeō* in verse 17.

CHAPTER II

1. *Was now come* (*en tōi sunplērousthai*). Luke's favourite idiom of *en* with the articular present infinitive passive and the accusative of general reference, "in the being fulfilled completely (perfective use of *sun-*) as to the day of Pentecost." Common verb, but only in Luke in N.T. In literal sense of filling a boat in Luke 8:23, about days in Luke 9:51 as here. Whether the disciples expected the coming of the Holy Spirit on this day we do not know. Blass holds that the present tense shows that the day had not yet come. It is a Hebrew idiom (Ex. 7:25) and Luke may mean that the day of Pentecost was not yet over, was still going on, though Hackett takes it for the interval (fifty days) between Passover and Pentecost. Apparently this day of Pentecost fell on the Jewish Sabbath (our Saturday). It was the feast of first fruits. *All together in one place* (*pantes homou epi to auto*). All together in the same place. Note *homou* here (correct text), not *homothumadon* as in 1:14, and so a bit of tautology.

2. *Suddenly* (*aphnō*). Old adverb, but in the N.T. only in Acts (2:2; 16:26; 28:6). Kin to *exaiphnēs* (Acts 22:61). *A sound* (*ēchos*). Our *echo*. Old word, already in Luke 4:37 for rumour and Luke 21:25 for the roar of the sea. It was not wind, but a roar or reverberation "as of the rushing of a mighty wind" (*hōsper pheromenēs pnoēs biaias*). This is not a strict translation nor is it the genitive absolute. It was "an echoing sound as of a mighty wind borne violently" (or rushing along like the whirr of a tornado). *Pnoē* (wind) is used here (in the N.T. only here and 17:25 though old word) probably because of the use of *pneuma* in verse 4 of the Holy Spirit. In John 3:5-8 *pneuma* occurs for both wind

and Spirit. *Filled* (*eplērōsen*). "As a bath is filled with water, that they might be baptized with the Holy Ghost, in fulfilment of Acts 1:5" (Canon Cook). *They were sitting* (*ēsan kathēmenoi*). Periphrastic imperfect middle of *kathēmai*.

3. *Parting asunder* (*diamerizomenai*). Present middle (or passive) participle of *diamerizō*, old verb, to cleave asunder, to cut in pieces as a butcher does meat (aorist passive in Luke 11:17f.). So middle here would mean, parting themselves asunder or distributing themselves. The passive voice would be "being distributed." The middle is probably correct and means that "the fire-like appearance presented itself at first, as it were, in a single body, and then suddenly parted in this direction and that; so that a portion of it rested on each of those present" (Hackett). The idea is not that each tongue was cloven, but each separate tongue looked like fire, not real fire, but looking like (*hōsei*, as if) fire. The audible sign is followed by a visible one (Knowling). "Fire had always been, with the Jews, the symbol of the Divine presence (cf. Ex. 3:2; Deut. 5:4). No symbol could be more fitting to express the Spirit's purifying energy and refining energy" (Furneaux). The Baptist had predicted a baptizing by the Messiah in the Holy Spirit and in fire (Matt. 3:11). *It sat* (*ekathisen*). Singular verb here, though plural *ōpthēsan* with tongues (*glōssai*). A tongue that looked like fire sat upon each one.

4. *With other tongues* (*heterais glōssais*). Other than their native tongues. Each one began to speak in a language that he had not acquired and yet it was a real language and understood by those from various lands familiar with them. It was not jargon, but intelligible language. Jesus had said that the gospel was to go to all the nations and here the various tongues of earth were spoken. One might conclude that this was the way in which the message was to be carried to the nations, but future developments disprove it.

This is a third miracle (the sound, the tongues like fire, the untaught languages). There is no blinking the fact that Luke so pictures them. One need not be surprised if this occasion marks the fulfilment of the Promise of the Father. But one is not to confound these miraculous signs with the Holy Spirit. They are merely proof that he has come to carry on the work of his dispensation. The gift of tongues came also on the house of Cornelius at Caesarea (Acts 10:44–47; 11:15–17), the disciples of John at Ephesus (Acts 19:6), the disciples at Corinth (I Cor. 14:1–33). It is possible that the gift appeared also at Samaria (Acts 8:18). But it was not a general or a permanent gift. Paul explains in I Cor. 14:22 that "tongues" were a sign to unbelievers and were not to be exercised unless one was present who understood them and could translate them. This restriction disposes at once of the modern so-called tongues which are nothing but jargon and hysteria. It so happened that here on this occasion at Pentecost there were Jews from all parts of the world, so that some one would understand one tongue and some another without an interpreter such as was needed at Corinth. The experience is identical in all four instances and they are not for edification or instruction, but for adoration and wonder and worship. *As the Spirit gave them utterance (kathōs to pneuma edidou apophtheggesthai autois).* This is precisely what Paul claims in I Cor. 12:10, 28, but all the same without an interpreter the gift was not to be exercised (I Cor. 14:6–19). Paul had the gift of tongues, but refused to exercise it except as it would be understood. Note the imperfect tense here (*edidou*). Perhaps they did not all speak at once, but one after another. *Apophtheggesthai* is a late verb (LXX of prophesying, papyri). Lucian uses it of the ring of a vessel when it strikes a reef. It is used of eager, elevated, impassioned utterance. In the N.T. only here, verse 14 and 26:25. *Apophthegm* is from this verb.

5. *Were dwelling* (*ēsan katoikountes*). Periphrastic imperfect active indicative. Usually *katoikeō* means residence in a place (4:16; 7:24; 9:22, 32) as in verse 14 (Luke 13:4). Perhaps some had come to Jerusalem to live while others were here only temporarily, for the same word occurs in verse 9 of those who dwell in Mesopotamia, etc. *Devout* (*eulabeis*). Reverent (*eu*, well, *lambanō*, to take). See on Luke 2:25 like Simeon waiting for the consolation of Israel or hoping to die and be buried in the Holy City and also Acts 8:2.

6. *When this sound was heard* (*genomenēs tēs phōnēs tautēs*). Genitive absolute with aorist middle participle. Note *phōnē* this time, not *ēcho* as in verse 1. *Phōnē* originally meant sound as of the wind (John 3:8) or an instrument (I Cor. 14:7, 8, 10), then voice of men. The meaning seems to be that the excited "other tongues" of verse 4 were so loud that the noise drew the crowd together. The house where the 120 were may have been (Hackett) on one of the avenues leading to the temple. *Were confounded* (*sunechuthē*). First aorist passive indicative of *suncheō* or *sunchunō*, to pour together precisely like the Latin *confundo*, to confound. The Vulgate has it *mente confusa est*. It is an old verb, but in the N.T. only in Acts five times (2:6; 9:22; 19:32; 21:27, 31). *In his own language* (*tēi idiāi dialektōi*). Locative case. Each one could understand his own language when he heard that. Every one that came heard somebody speaking in his native tongue.

7. *Were amazed* (*existanto*). Imperfect middle of *existēmi*, to stand out of themselves, wide-open astonishment. *Marvelled* (*ethaumazon*). Imperfect active. The wonder grew and grew. *Galileans* (*Galilaioi*). There were few followers of Jesus as yet from Jerusalem. The Galileans spoke a rude Aramaic (Mark 14:70) and probably crude Greek vernacular also. They were not strong on language and yet these are the very people who now show such remarkable linguistic powers. These people who have come together are all Jews

and therefore know Aramaic and the vernacular *Koinê*,
but there were various local tongues "wherein we were
born" (*en hēi egennēthēmen*). An example is the Lycaonian
(Acts 14:11). These Galilean Christians are now heard
speaking these various local tongues. The lists in verses
9–11 are not linguistic, but geographical and merely illustrate how widespread the Dispersion (*Diaspora*) of the
Jews was as represented on this occasion. Jews were everywhere, these "Jews among the nations" (Acts 21:21). Page
notes four main divisions here: (1) The Eastern or Babylo-
nian, like the Parthians, Medes, Elamites, Mesopotamians.
(2) The Syrian like Judea, Cappadocia, Pontus, Asia,
Phrygia, Pamphylia. (3) The Egyptian like Egypt, Libya,
Cyrene. (4) The Roman. *Jews and proselytes* (*prosēlutoi*).
These last from *proserchomai*, to come to, to join, Gentile
converts to Judaism (circumcision, baptism, sacrifice).
This proselyte baptism was immersion as is shown by I.
Abrahams (*Studies in Pharisaism and the Gospels*, p. 38).
Many remained uncircumcised and were called proselytes
of the gate.

11. *Cretes and Arabians.* These two groups "seem to have
been added to the list as an afterthought" (Knowling).
Crete is an island to itself and Arabia was separate also
though near Judea and full of Jews. The point is not that
each one of these groups of Jews spoke a different language,
but that wherever there was a local tongue they heard men
speaking in it. *We do hear them speaking* (*akouomen lalountōn autōn*). Genitive case *autōn* with *akouō* the participle
lalountōn agreeing with *autōn*, a sort of participial idiom of
indirect discourse (Robertson, *Grammar*, pp. 1040ff.). *The
mighty works* (*ta megaleia*). Old adjective for magnificent. In
LXX, but only here (not genuine in Luke 1:49) in the N.T.
Cf. II Peter 1:16 for *megaleiotēs* (majesty).

12. *Were perplexed* (*diēporounto*). Imperfect middle of
diaporeō (*dia*, a privative, *poros*) to be wholly at a loss. Old

verb, but in N.T. only in Luke and Acts. They continued amazed (*existanto*) and puzzled. *What meaneth this?* (*Ti thelei touto einai*). Literally, what does this wish to be?

13. *Mocking* (*diachleuazontes*). Old verb, but only here in the N.T., though the simple verb (without *dia*) in 17:32. *Chleuē* means a joke. *With new wine* (*gleukous*). Sweet wine, but intoxicating. Sweet wine kept a year was very intoxicating. Genitive case here after *memestōmenoi eisin* (periphrastic perfect passive indicative), old verb *mestoō*, only here in the N.T. Tanked up with new wine, state of fulness.

14. *Standing up with the eleven* (*statheis sun tois hendeka*). Took his stand with the eleven including Matthias, who also rose up with them, and spoke as their spokesman, a formal and impressive beginning. The Codex Bezae has "ten apostles." Luke is fond of this pictorial use of *statheis* (first aorist passive participle of *histēmi*) as seen nowhere else in the N.T. (Luke 18:11, 40; 19:8; Acts 5:20; 17:22; 27:21). *Lifted up his voice* (*epēren tēn phōnēn autou*). This phrase only in Luke in the N.T. (Luke 11:29; Acts 2:14; 14:11; 22:22), but is common in the old writers. First aorist active indicative of *epairō*. The large crowd and the confusion of tongues demanded loud speaking. "This most solemn, earnest, yet sober speech" (Bengel). Codex Bezae adds "first" after "voice." Peter did it to win and hold attention. *Give ear unto my words* (*enōtisasthe ta rhēmata mou*). Late verb in LXX and only here in the N.T. First aorist middle from *enōtizomai* (*en, ous*, ear) to give ear to, receive into the ear. People's ears differ greatly, but in public speech they have to be reached through the ear. That puts an obligation on the speaker and also on the auditors who should sit where they can hear with the ears which they have, an obligation often overlooked.

15. *As ye suppose* (*hōs humeis hupolambanete*). Note use of *humeis* (ye) for decided emphasis. *The third hour* (*hōra tritē*). Three o'clock in the day Jewish time, nine Roman.

Drunkenness belongs to the night (I Thess. 5:7). It was a quick, common sense reply, and complete answer to their suspicion.

16. *This is that which hath been spoken by the prophet Joel* (*touto estin to eirēmenon dia tou prophētou Iōēl*). Positive interpretation of the supernatural phenomena in the light of the Messianic prophecy of Joel 2:28-32. Peter's mind is now opened by the Holy Spirit to understand the Messianic prophecy and the fulfilment right before their eyes. Peter now has spiritual insight and moral courage. The *power* (*dunamis*) of the Holy Spirit has come upon him as he proceeds to give the first interpretation of the life and work of Jesus Christ since his Ascension. It is also the first formal apology for Christianity to a public audience. Peter rises to the height of his powers in this remarkable sermon. Jesus had foretold that he would be a Rock and now he is no longer shale, but a solid force for aggressive Christianity. He follows here in verses 17 to 21 closely the LXX text of Joel and then applies the passage to the present emergency (22-24).

17. *In the last days* (*en tais eschatais hēmerais*). Joel does not have precisely these words, but he defines "those days" as being "the day of the Lord" (cf. Isa. 2:2; Micah 4:1). *I will pour forth* (*ekcheō*). Future active indicative of *ekcheō*. This future like *edomai* and *piomai* is without tense sign, probably like the present in the futuristic sense (Robertson, *Grammar*, p. 354). Westcott and Hort put a different accent on the future, but the old Greek had no accent. The old Greek had *ekcheusō*. This verb means to pour out. *Of my Spirit* (*apo tou pneumatos*). This use of *apo* (of) is either because of the variety in the manifestations of the Spirit (I Cor. 12) or because the Spirit in his entirety remains with God (Holtzmann, Wendt). But the Hebrew has it: "I will pour out my Spirit" without the partitive idea in the LXX. *And your daughters* (*kai hai thugateres hūmōn*).

Anna is called a prophetess in Luke 2:36 and the daughters
of Philip prophesy (Acts 21:9) and verse 18 (handmaidens).
See also I Cor. 11:5 (*prophētousa*). *Visions (horaseis)*.
Late word for the more common *horama*, both from *horaō*,
to see. In Rev. 4:3 it means appearance, but in Rev. 9:17
as here an ecstatic revelation or vision. *Dream dreams (enu-
pniois enupniasthēsontai)*. Shall dream with (instrumental
case) dreams. First future passive of *enupniazō* from *en-
upnios (en* and *hupnos*, in sleep), a common late word.
Only here in the N.T. (this from Joel as all these verses 17 to
21 are) and Jude 8. *Yea and (kai ge)*. Intensive particle *ge*
added to *kai* (and), an emphatic addition (= Hebrew *vegam*).
Servants (doulous), *handmaidens (doulas)*. Slaves, actual
slaves of men. The humblest classes will receive the Spirit
of God (cf. I Cor. 1:26–31). But the word "prophesy"
here is not in the LXX (or the Hebrew).

19. *Wonders (terata)*. Apparently akin to the verb *tēreō*,
to watch like a wonder in the sky, *miracle (miraculum)*,
marvel, portent. In the New Testament the word occurs
only in the plural and only in connection with *sēmeia* (signs)
as here and in verse 43. But *signs (sēmeia)* here is not in the
LXX. See on Matt. 11:20. In verse 22 all three words
occur together: powers, wonders, signs *(dunamesi, terasi,
sēmeiois)*. *Above (anō)*. This word is not in the LXX nor is
"beneath" *(katō)*, both probably being added to make
clearer the contrast between heaven and earth. *Blood and
fire and vapour of smoke (haima kai pur kai atmida kapnou)*.
A chiasm as these words illustrate bloodshed and destruction
by fire as signs here on earth.

20. *Shall be turned (metastraphēsetai)*. Second future
passive of *metastrephō*, common verb, but only three times
in the N.T. (Acts 2:20 from Joel; James 4:9; Gal. 1:7).
These are the "wonders" or portents of verse 19. It is
worth noting that Peter interprets these "portents" as
fulfilled on the Day of Pentecost, though no such change of

the sun into darkness or of the moon into blood is recorded.
Clearly Peter does not interpret the symbolism of Joel in
literal terms. This method of Peter may be of some service
in the Book of Revelation where so many apocalyptic symbols occur as well as in the great Eschatological Discourse
of Jesus in Matt. 24 and 25. In Matt. 24:6, 29 Jesus had
spoken of wars on earth and wonders in heaven. *Before
the day of the Lord come, that great and notable day (prin
elthein hēmeran kuriou tēn megalēn kai epiphanē)*. The use
of *prin* with the infinitive and the accusative of general
reference is a regular Greek idiom. The use of the adjectives with the article is also good Greek, though the article
is not here repeated as in 1:25. The Day of the Lord is a
definite conception without the article. *Notable (epiphanē)*
is the same root as epiphany *(epiphaneia)* used of the Second
Coming of Christ (II Thess. 2:8; I Tim. 6:14; II Tim. 4:1;
Tit. 2:13). It translates here the Hebrew word for "terrible." In the Epistles the Day of the Lord is applied (Knowling) to the Coming of Christ for judgment (I Thess. 5:2;
I Cor. 1:8; II Cor. 1:14; Phil. 1:10).

21. *Shall call on (epikalesētai)*. First aorist middle subjunctive of *epikaleō*, common verb, to call to, middle voice
for oneself in need. Indefinite relative clause with *ean* and so
subjunctive, punctiliar idea, in any single case, and so aorist.

22. *Hear these words (akousate tous logous toutous)*. Do it
now (aorist tense). With unerring aim Peter has found the
solution for the phenomena. He has found the key to God's
work on this day in his words through Joel. *As ye yourselves know (kathōs autoi oidate)*. Note *autoi* for emphasis.
Peter calls the audience to witness that his statements are
true concerning "Jesus the Nazarene." He wrought his
miracles by the power of God in the midst of these very
people here present.

23. *Him (touton)*. "This one," resumptive and emphatic
object of "did crucify and slay." *Being delivered up (ekdo-*

ton). Verbal adjective from *ekdidōmi*, to give out or over. Old word, but here only in the N.T. Delivered up by Judas, Peter means. *By the determinate counsel and foreknowledge of God* (*tēi hōrismenēi boulēi kai prognōsēi tou theou*). Instrumental case. Note both purpose (*boulē*) and foreknowledge (*prognōsis*) of God and "determined" (*hōrismenē*, perfect passive participle, state of completion). God had willed the death of Jesus (John 3:16) and the death of Judas (Acts 1:16), but that fact did not absolve Judas from his responsibility and guilt (Luke 22:22). He acted as a free moral agent. *By the hand* (*dia cheiros*). Luke is fond of these figures (hand, face, etc.) very much like the Hebrew though the vernacular of all languages uses them. *Lawless men* (*anomōn*). Men without law, who recognize no law for their conduct, like men in high and low stations today who defy the laws of God and man. Old word, very common in the LXX. *Ye did crucify* (*prospēxantes*). First aorist active participle of *prospēgnumi*, rare compound word in Dio Cassius and here only in the N.T. One must supply *tōi staurōi* and so it means "fastened to the cross," a graphic picture like Paul's "nailed to the cross" (*proselōsas tōi staurōi*) in Col. 2:14. *Did slay* (*aneilate*). Second aorist active indicative with first aorist vowel *a* instead of *o* as is common in the *Koinē*. This verb *anaireō*, to take up, is often used for kill as in Acts 12:2. Note Peter's boldness now under the power of the Holy Spirit. He charges the people to their faces with the death of Christ.

24. *God raised up* (*ho theos anestēsen*). *Est hoc summum orationis* (Blass). Apparently this is the first public proclamation to others than believers of the fact of the Resurrection of Jesus. "At a time it was still possible to test the statement, to examine witnesses, to expose fraud, the Apostle openly proclaimed the Resurrection as a fact, needing no evidence, but known to his hearers" (Furneaux). *The pangs of death* (*tas ōdinas tou thanatou*). Codex Bezae has

"Hades" instead of death. The LXX has *ōdinas thanatou* in Psa. 18:4, but the Hebrew original means "snares" or "traps" or "cords" of death where sheol and death are personified as hunters laying snares for prey. How Peter or Luke came to use the old Greek word *ōdinas* (birth pangs) we do not know. Early Christian writers interpreted the Resurrection of Christ as a birth out of death. "Loosing" (*lusas*) suits better the notion of "snares" held a prisoner by death, but birth pangs do bring deliverance to the mother also. *Because* (*kathoti*). This old conjunction (*kata, hoti*) occurs in the N.T. only in Luke's writings. *That he should be holden* (*krateisthai auton*). Infinitive present passive with accusative of general reference and subject of *ēn adunaton*. The figure goes with "loosed" (*lusas*) above.

25. *Concerning him* (*eis auton*). Peter interprets Psa. 16:8–11 as written by David and with reference to the Messiah. There is but one speaker in this Psalm and both Peter here and Paul in Acts 13:36 make it the Messiah. David is giving his own experience which is typical of the Messiah (Knowling). *I beheld* (*proorōmēn*). Imperfect middle without augment of *prooraō*, common verb, but only twice in the N.T., to see beforehand (Acts 21:29) or to see right before one as here. This idea of *pro-* is made plainer by "before my face" (*enōpion mou*). *On my right hand* (*ek dexiōn mou*). The Lord Jehovah like a defender or advocate stands at David's right hand as in trials in court (Psa. 109:31). *That* (*hina*) here is almost result. *Moved* (*saleuthō*). First aorist passive subjunctive of *saleuō*, to shake like an earthquake.

26. *Was glad* (*ēuphranthē*). First aorist (timeless here like the Hebrew perfect) passive indicative of *euphrainō* (cf. Luke 15:32. Timeless also is "rejoiced" (*ēgalliasato*). *Shall dwell* (*kataskēnōsei*). Shall tabernacle, pitch a tent, make one's abode (cf. Matt. 13:32). See on Matt. 8:20 about *kataskēnōseis* (nests). *In hope* (*ep' elpidi*). On hope, the hope of the resurrection.

27. *In Hades* (*eis Hāidēn*). Hades is the unseen world, Hebrew Sheol, but here it is viewed as death itself "considered as a rapacious destroyer" (Hackett). It does not mean the place of punishment, though both heaven and the place of torment are in Hades (Luke 16:23). "Death and Hades are strictly parallel terms: he who is dead is in Hades" (Page). The use of *eis* here = *en* is common enough. The Textus Receptus here reads *eis Hāidou* (genitive case) like the Attic idiom with *domon* (abode) understood. "Hades" in English is not translation, but transliteration. The phrase in the Apostles' Creed, "descended into hell" is from this passage in Acts (Hades, not Gehenna). The English word "hell" is Anglo-Saxon from *helan*, to hide, and was used in the Authorized Version to translate both Hades as here and Gehenna as in Matt. 5:22. *Thy Holy One* (*ton hosion sou*). Peter applies these words to the Messiah. *Corruption* (*diaphthoran*). The word can mean destruction or putrefaction from *diaphtheirō*, old word, but in N.T. only here and Acts 13:34-37. The Hebrew word in Psa. 16 can mean also the pit or the deep.

28. *The ways of life* (*hodous zōēs*). Though dead God will show him the ways back to life.

29. *I may say* (*exon eipein*). Supply *estin* before *exon*, periphrastic present indicative of *exeimi*, to allow, permit. The Authorized Version has "Let me speak," supplying *esto* present imperative. *Freely* (*meta parrēsias*). Telling it all (*pan, rhēsia* from *eipon*, to speak), with fulness, with boldness. Luke is fond of the phrase (as in 4:13). It is a new start for Simon Peter, full of boldness and courage. *The patriarch* (*tou patriarchou*). Transliteration of the word, from *patria*, family, and *archō*, to rule, the founder of a family. Late word in LXX. Used of Abraham (Heb. 7:4), of the twelve sons of Jacob as founders of the several tribes (Acts 7:8), and here of David as head of the family from whom the Messiah comes. *Was buried* (*etaphē*). Second aorist passive indicative of *thaptō*. His tomb was on Mt. Zion where most of the kings were buried. The tomb was said to have fallen into ruins in the time of the Emperor Hadrian. Josephus (*Ant.* XVI. 7,1) attributes most of the misfortunes of Herod's family to the fact that he tried to rifle the tomb of David.

31. *Foreseeing* (*proidōn*). Second aorist active participle. Did it as a prophet. *Of the Christ* (*tou Christou*). Of the Messiah. See under verse 32. This is a definite statement by Peter that David knew that in Psalm 16 he was describing the resurrection of the Messiah.

32. *This Jesus* (*touton ton Iēsoun*). Many of the name "Jesus," but he means the one already called "the Nazarene" (verse 22) and foretold as the Messiah in Psa. 16 and raised from the dead by God in proof that he is the Messiah (2:24, 32), "this Jesus whom ye crucified" (verse 36). Other terms used of him in the Acts are the Messiah, verse 31, the one whom God "anointed" (Acts 10:38), as in John 1:41, Jesus Christ (9:34). In 2:36 God made this Jesus Messiah, in 3:20 the Messiah Jesus, in 17:3 Jesus is the Messiah, in 18:5 the Messiah is Jesus, in 24:24 Christ Jesus. *Whereof* (*hou*). Or "of whom." Either makes sense and both are true. Peter claims the whole 120 as personal witnesses to the fact of the Resurrection of Jesus from the dead and they are all present as Peter calls them to witness on the point. In Galilee over 500 had seen the Risen Christ at one time (I Cor. 15:6) most of whom were still living when Paul wrote. Thus the direct evidence for the resurrection of Jesus piles up in cumulative force.

33. *By the right hand of God* (*tēi dexiāi tou theou*). This translation makes it the instrumental case. The margin has it "at" instead of "by," that is the locative case. And it will make sense in the true dative case, "to the right hand of God." These three cases came to have the same form in Greek. Rom. 8:24 furnishes another illustration of like

ambiguity (*tēi elpidi*), saved by hope, in hope, or for hope.
Usually it is quite easy to tell the case when the form is
identical. *Exalted* (*hupsōtheis*). First aorist passive participle of *hupsoō*, to lift up. Here both the literal and tropical
sense occurs. Cf. John 12:32. *The promise of the Holy Spirit*
(*tēn epaggelian tou pneumatos tou hagiou*). The promise
mentioned in 1:4 and now come true, consisting in the Holy
Spirit "from the Father" (*para tou patros*), sent by the
Father and by the Son (John 15:26; 16:7). See also Gal.
3:14. *He hath poured forth* (*execheen*). Aorist active indicative of *ekcheō* the verb used by Joel and quoted by Peter
already in verses 17 and 18. Jesus has fulfilled his promise.
This which ye see and hear (*touto ho humeis kai blepete kai
akouete*). This includes the sound like the rushing wind, the
tongues like fire on each of them, the different languages
spoken by the 120. "The proof was before their eyes in
this new energy from heaven" (Furneaux), a culminating
demonstration that Jesus was the Messiah.

34. *Ascended not* (*ou—anebē*). It is more emphatic than
that: For not David ascended into the heavens. Peter quotes
Psa. 110:1 as proof. No passage in the O.T. is so constantly
quoted as Messianic as this. "St. Peter does not demand
belief upon his own assertion, but he again appeals to the
Scriptures, and to words which could not have received a
fulfilment in the case of David" (Knowling). *Sit thou*
(*kathou*). Late *Koinē* form for earlier *katheso*, present middle
imperative second singular of *kathēmai*.

35. *Till I make* (*heōs an thō*). Second aorist active subjunctive of *tithēmi* with *an* after *heōs* for the future, a common Greek idiom. This dominion of Christ as Mediator
will last till the plan of the kingdom is carried out (I Cor.
15:23–28). Complete subjugation will come, perhaps referring to the custom of victorious kings placing their feet
upon the necks of their enemies (Josh. 10:24). *Therefore
assuredly* (*Asphalōs oun*). Assuredly therefore, without any

slip or trip (*asphalēs* from *a* privative and *sphallō*, to trip, to slip. Peter draws a powerfully pungent conclusion by the use of the adverb *asphalōs* and the inferential conjunction *oun*. Peter's closing sentence drives home the point of his sermon: "This very Jesus whom ye crucified (note *humeis*, strongly emphatic *ye*), him God made both Lord and Messiah" (*kai kurion kai Christon*), as David foretold in Psa. 110 and as the events of this day have confirmed. The critics are disturbed over how Luke could have gotten the substance of this masterful address spoken on the spur of the moment with passion and power. They even say that Luke composed it for Peter and put the words in his mouth. If so, he made a good job of it. But Peter could have written out the notes of the address afterwards. Luke had plenty of chances to get hold of it from Peter or from others.

37. *They were pricked in their heart* (*katenugēsan tēn kardian*). Second aorist indicative of *katanussō*, a rare verb (LXX) to pierce, to sting sharply, to stun, to smite. Homer used it of horses dinting the earth with their hoofs. The substantive *katanuxis* occurs in Rom. 11:8. Here only in the N.T. It is followed here by the accusative of the part affected, the heart. *What shall we do?* (*Ti poiēsōmen*). Deliberative subjunctive first aorist active. The sermon went home, they felt the sting of Peter's words, compunction (*compungo*). Codex Bezae adds: "Show us."

38. *Repent ye* (*metanoēsate*). First aorist (ingressive) active imperative. Change your mind and your life. Turn right about and do it now. You *crucified* this Jesus. Now *crown* him in your hearts as Lord and Christ. This first. *And be baptized every one of you* (*kai baptisthētō hekastos hūmōn*). Rather, "And let each one of you be baptized." Change of number from plural to singular and of person from second to third. This change marks a break in the thought here that the English translation does not preserve. The first thing to do is make a radical and complete change of

heart and life. Then let each one be baptized after this change has taken place, and the act of baptism be performed "in the name of Jesus Christ" (*en tōi onomati Iēsou Christou*). In accordance with the command of Jesus in Matt. 28:19 (*eis to onoma*). No distinction is to be insisted on between *eis to onoma* and *en tōi onomati* with *baptizō* since *eis* and *en* are really the same word in origin. In Acts 10:48 *en tōi onomati Iēsou Christou* occurs, but *eis to onoma* in 8:16 and 19:5. The use of *onoma* means in the name or with the authority of one as *eis onoma prophētou* (Matt. 10:41) as a prophet, in the name of a prophet. In the Acts the full name of the Trinity does not occur in baptism as in Matt. 28:19, but this does not show that it was not used. The name of Jesus Christ is the distinctive one in Christian baptism and really involves the Father and the Spirit. See on Matt. 28:19 for discussion of this point. "Luke does not give the form of words used in baptism by the Apostles, but merely states the fact that they baptized those who acknowledged Jesus as Messiah or as Lord" (Page). *Unto the remission of your sins (eis aphesin tōn hamartiōn hūmōn).* This phrase is the subject of endless controversy as men look at it from the standpoint of sacramental or of evangelical theology. In themselves the words can express aim or purpose for that use of *eis* does exist as in I Cor. 2:7 *eis doxan hēmōn* (for our glory). But then another usage exists which is just as good Greek as the use of *eis* for aim or purpose. It is seen in Matt. 10:41 in three examples *eis onoma prophētou, dikaiou, mathētou* where it cannot be purpose or aim, but rather the basis or ground, on the basis of the name of prophet, righteous man, disciple, because one is, etc. It is seen again in Matt. 12:41 about the preaching of Jonah (*eis to kērugma Iōnā*). They repented because of (or at) the preaching of Jonah. The illustrations of both usages are numerous in the N.T. and the *Koiné* generally (Robertson, *Grammar*, p. 592). One will decide the use here according as he believes that baptism is essential to the remission of sins or not. My view is decidedly against the idea that Peter, Paul, or any one in the New Testament taught baptism as essential to the remission of sins or the means of securing such remission. So I understand Peter to be urging baptism on each of them who had already turned (repented) and for it to be done in the name of Jesus Christ on the basis of the forgiveness of sins which they had already received. *The gift of the Holy Ghost (tēn dōrean tou hagiou pneumatos).* The gift consists (Acts 8:17) in the Holy Spirit (genitive of identification).

39. *The promise (hē epaggelia).* The promise made by Jesus (1:4) and foretold by Joel (verse 18). *To you (humin).* You Jews. To your descendants, sons and daughters of verse 17. *To all that are afar off (pāsin tois eis makran .* The horizon widens and includes the Gentiles. Those "afar off" from the Jews were the heathen (Isa. 49:1; 57:19; Eph. 2:13, 17). The rabbis so used it. *Shall call (an proskalesētai).* First aorist middle subjunctive with *an* in an indefinite relative clause, a perfectly regular construction. The Lord God calls men of every nation anywhere whether Jews or Gentiles. It may be doubted how clearly Peter grasped the significance of these words for he will have trouble over this very matter on the housetop in Joppa and in Caesarea, but he will see ere long the full sweep of the great truth that he here proclaims under the impulse of the Holy Spirit. It was a great moment that Peter here reaches.

40. *With many other words (heterois logois pleiosin).* Instrumental case. Not necessarily "different" (*heterois*), but "further," showing that Luke does not pretend to give all that Peter said. This idea is also brought out clearly by *pleiosin* ("more," not "many"), more than these given by Luke. *He testified (diemarturato).* First aorist middle of *diamarturomai*, old verb, to make solemn attestation or call to witness (perfective use of *dia*), while *martureō* is to bear witness. Page insists that here it should be translated "pro-

tested solemnly" to the Jews as it seems to mean in Luke 16:28; Acts 20:23; I Tim. 5:21; II Tim. 2:14; 4:1. *And exhorted (kai parekalei)*. Imperfect active, kept on exhorting. *Save yourselves (sōthēte)*. First aorist passive of *sōzō*. Literally, Be ye saved. *Crooked (skolias)*. Old word, opposite of *orthos*, straight. *Pravus* the opposite of *rectus*, a perversity for turning off from the truth. Cf. Luke 9:41; Phil. 2:15.

41. *They then (Hoi men oun)*. A common phrase in Acts either without antithesis as in 1:6; 5:41; 8:4, 25; 9:31; 11:19; 16:5; or with it as here, 8:25; 13:4; 14:3; 17:17; 23:31; 25:4. *Oun* connects with what precedes as the result of Peter's sermon while *men* points forward to what is to follow. *Were baptized (ebaptisthēsan)*. First aorist passive indicative, constative aorist. Note that only those who had already received the word and were converted were baptized. *There were added (prosetethēsan)*. First aorist passive indicative of *prostithēmi*, old verb to add, to join to. Luke means that the 3,000 were added to the 120 already enlisted. It is not stated they were all baptized by Peter or the twelve or all on the same day, though that is the natural implication of the language. The numerous pools in Jerusalem afforded ample opportunity for such wholesale baptizing and Hackett notes that the habit of orientals would place no obstacle in the way of the use of the public reservoirs. Furneaux warns us that all the 3,000 may not have been genuine converts and that many of them were pilgrims at the passover who returned home. *Souls (psuchai)*. Persons as in verse 43.

42. *They continued steadfastly (ēsan proskarturountes)*. Periphrastic active imperfect of *proskartureō* as in Acts 1:14 (same participle in verse 46). *Fellowship (koinōniāi)*. Old word from *koinōnos* (partner, sharer in common interest) and this from *koinos* what is common to all. This partnership involves participation in, as the blood of Christ (Phil. 2:1) or co-operation in the work of the gospel (Phil. 1:5) or contri-

bution for those in need (II Cor. 8:4; 9:13). Hence there is
wide diversity of opinion concerning the precise meaning of
koinōnia in this verse. It may refer to the distribution of
funds in verse 44 or to the oneness of spirit in the community
of believers or to the Lord's Supper (as in I Cor. 10:16) in
the sense of communion or to the fellowship in the common
meals or *agapae* (love-feasts). *The breaking of bread (tēi
klasei tou artou).* The word *klasis* is an old word, but used
only by Luke in the N.T. (Luke 24:35; Acts 2:42), though
the verb *klaō* occurs in other parts of the N.T. as in verse 46.
The problem here is whether Luke refers to the ordinary
meal as in Luke 24:35 or to the Lord's Supper. The same
verb *klaō* is used of breaking bread at the ordinary meal
(Luke 24:30) or the Lord's Supper (Luke 22:19). It is generally supposed that the early disciples attached so much
significance to the breaking of bread at the ordinary meals,
more than our saying grace, that they followed the meal
with the Lord's Supper at first, a combination called *agapai*
or love-feasts. "There can be no doubt that the Eucharist
at this period was preceded uniformly by a common repast,
as was the case when the ordinance was instituted" (Hackett). This led to some abuses as in I Cor. 11:20. Hence it is
possible that what is referred to here is the Lord's Supper
following the ordinary meal. "To simply explain *tēi klasei
tou artou* as = 'The Holy Communion' is to pervert the plain
meaning of words, and to mar the picture of family life,
which the text places before us as the ideal of the early
believers" (Page). But in Acts 20:7 they seem to have
come together especially for the observance of the Lord's
Supper. Perhaps there is no way to settle the point conclusively here. *The prayers (tais proseuchais).* Services where
they prayed as in 1:14, in the temple (Acts 3:1), in their
homes (4:23).

43. *Came (egineto).* Imperfect middle, kept on coming.
Were done (egineto). Same tense. Awe kept on coming on all

and signs and wonders kept on coming through the apostles. The two things went on *pari passu*, the more wonders the more fear.

44. *Were together* (*ēsan epi to auto*). Some MSS. *ēsan kai* (were and). But they were together in the same place as in 2:1. *And had* (*kai eichon*). Imperfect active, kept on having, a habit in the present emergency. *Common* (*koina*). It was not actual communism, but they held all their property ready for use for the common good as it was needed (4:32). This situation appears nowhere else except in Jerusalem and was evidently due to special conditions there which did not survive permanently. Later Paul will take a special collection for the poor saints in Jerusalem.

45. *Sold* (*epipraskon*). Imperfect active, a habit or custom from time to time. Old and common verb, *pipraskō*. *Parted* (*diemerizon*). Imperfect again of *diamerizō*, old verb for dividing or distributing between (*dia*) people. *According as any man had need* (*kathoti an tis chreian eichen*). Regular Greek idiom for comparative clause with *an* and imperfect indicative corresponding precisely with the three preceding imperfects (Robertson, *Grammar*, p. 967).

46. *With one accord in the temple* (*homothumadon en tōi hierōi*). See on 1:14 for *homothumadon*. They were still worshipping in the temple for no breach had yet come between Christians and Jews. Daily they were here and daily breaking bread at home (*kat' oikon*) which looks like the regular meal. *They did take their food* (*metelambanon trophēs*). Imperfect tense again and clearly referring to the regular meals at home. Does it refer also to the possible *agapai* or to the Lord's Supper afterwards as they had common meals "from house to house" (*kat' oikon*)? We know there were local churches in the homes where they had "worship rooms," the church in the house. At any rate it was "with singleness" (*aphelotēti*) of heart. The word occurs only here in the N.T., though a late *Koiné* word (papyri). It comes from *aphelēs,*

free from rock (*phelleus* is stony ground), smooth. The old form was *apheleia*.

47. *Having favor* (*echontes charin*). Cf. Luke 2:52 of the Boy Jesus. *Added* (*prosetithei*). Imperfect active, kept on adding. If the Lord only always "added" those who join our churches. Note verse 41 where same verb is used of the 3,000. *To them* (*epi to auto*). Literally, "together." Why not leave it so? "To the church" (*tēi ekklēsiāi*) is not genuine. Codex Bezae has "in the church." *Those that were being saved* (*tous sōzomenous*). Present passive participle. Probably for repetition like the imperfect *prosetithei*. Better translate it "those saved from time to time." It was a continuous revival, day by day. *Sōzō* like *sōtēria* is used for "save" in three senses (beginning, process, conclusion), but here repetition is clearly the point of the present tense.

CHAPTER III

1. *Were going up (anebainon).* Descriptive imperfect active. They were ascending the terraces to the temple courts. *The ninth (tēn enatēn).* Our three o'clock in the afternoon, the time of the evening sacrifice. Peter and John like Paul later kept up the Jewish worship, but not as a means of sacramental redemption. There were three hours of prayer (third, sixth, ninth).

2. *Was carried (ebastazeto).* Imperfect passive, picturing the process as in verse 1. *Laid daily (etithoun kath' hēmeran).* Imperfect again describing their custom with this man. *Beautiful (Hōraian).* This gate is not so called elsewhere. It may have been the Gate of Nicanor on the east side looking towards Kidron described by Josephus (*Ant.* XV. 11, 3; *War* V. 5, 3) as composed chiefly of Corinthian brass and very magnificent.

3. *Asked (ērōtā).* Began to ask, inchoative imperfect. It was his chance.

4. *Fastening his eyes (atenisas).* First aorist (ingressive) active participle of *atenizō.* For this verb see on Luke 4:20 and Acts 1:10. Peter fixed his eyes on the beggar and invited him to look (*blepson*) on them.

5. *Gave heed unto them (epeichen autois).* Imperfect active of *epechō*, to hold to. For the idiom with *ton noun* understood see 7:14; I Tim. 4:16. He held his eyes right on Peter and John with great eagerness "expecting to receive something" (*prosdokōn ti labein*). He took Peter's invitation as a promise of a large gift.

6. *In the name (en tōi onomati).* The healing power is *in* that name (Page) and Peter says so. Cf. Luke 9:49; 10:17; Acts 4:7, 10; 19:27; 16:18. *Walk (peripatei).* Present im-

perative, inchoative idea, begin to walk and then go on walking. But the beggar does not budge. He knows that he cannot walk.

7. *Took him by the right hand* (*piasas auton tēs dexiās cheiros*). Doric form *piazō* for *piezō*. Genitive of the part affected. Peter had to pull him up on his feet before he would try to walk.

8. *Leaping up* (*exallomenos*). Present middle participle, leaping out repeatedly after Peter pulled him up. Only here in the N.T. *He stood* (*estē*). Second aorist active. *Walked* (*periepatei*). Went on walking, imperfect active. He came into the temple repeating these new exercises (walking, leaping, praising God).

10. *They took knowledge of him* (*epeginōskon*). Imperfect active, inchoative, began to perceive. *Were filled* (*eplēsthēsan*). Effective first aorist passive. *At that which had happened* (*tōi sumbebēkoti*). Perfect active participle of *sumbainō*.

11. The Codex Bezae adds "as Peter and John went out." *As he held* (*kratountos autou*). Genitive absolute of *krateō*, to hold fast, with accusative rather than genitive to get hold of (Acts 27:13). Old and common verb from *kratos* (strength, force). Perhaps out of gratitude and partly from fear (Luke 8:38). *In the porch that is called Solomon's* (*epi tēi stoāi tēi kaloumenēi Solomōntos*). The adjective Stoic (*stoikos*) is from this word *stoa* (porch). It was on the east side of the court of the Gentiles (Josephus, *Ant.* XX. 9, 7) and was so called because it was built on a remnant of the foundations of the ancient temple. Jesus had once taught here (John 10:23). *Greatly wondering* (*ekthamboi*). Wondering out of (*ek*) measure, already filled with wonder (*thambous*, verse 10). Late adjective. Construction according to sense (plural, though *laos* singular) as in 5:16; 6:7; 11:1, etc.

12. *Answered* (*apekrinato*). First aorist middle indicative. The people looked their amazement and Peter answered

that. *Ye men of Israel* (*Andres Israēleitai*). Covenant name
and so conciliatory, the stock of Israel (Phil. 3:5). *At this
man* (*epi toutōi*). Probably so, though it could be "at this
thing." *Fasten you your eyes* (*atenizete*). The very verb
used about Peter in verse 4. *On us* (*hēmin*). Dative case,
emphatic proleptical position before *ti atenizete*. *On us why
do ye fasten your eyes? As though* (*hōs*). *Hōs* with the participle gives the alleged reason, not always the true one. *Power*
(*dunamei*). Instrumental case, *causa effectiva*. *Godliness*
(*eusebeiāi*). *Causa meritoria*. *Had made* (*pepoiēkosin*).
Perfect active participle of *poieō*. *To walk* (*tou peripatein*).
Articular infinitive in the genitive case of result, purpose
easily shading off into result (ecbatic infinitive) as here as
is true also of *hina*.

13. *His servant Jesus* (*ton paida Iēsoun*). This phrase
occurs in Isa. 42:1; 52:13 about the Messiah except the name
"Jesus" which Peter adds, the first part of the quotation
is from Ex. 3:6; 5:30. The LXX translated the Hebrew
ebhedh by *pais*, the servant of Jehovah being a Messianic
designation. But the phrase "servant of God" (*pais theou*)
is applied also to Israel (Luke 1:54) and to David (Luke
1:69; Acts 4:25). Paul terms himself *doulos theou* (Tit. 1:1).
Pais is just child (boy or girl), and it was also used of a
slave (Matt. 8:6, 8, 13). But it is not here *huios* (son) that
Peter uses, but *pais*. Luke quotes Peter as using it again
in this Messianic sense in Acts 3:26; 4:27, 30. *Whom ye
delivered up* (*hon humeis men paredōkate*). Note emphatic
use of *humeis* (*ye*). No *de* to correspond to *men*. First aorist
active (*k* aorist) plural indicative of *paradidōmi* (usual form
paredote, second aorist). *When he* (*ekeinou*). Emphatic
pronoun, that one, in contrast with "ye" (*humeis*), genitive
absolute with *krinantos*, here the nearest word (Pilate), the
latter.

14. *But ye* (*humeis de*). In contrast with Pilate (*ekeinou*).
Murderer (*andra phonea*). A man a murderer. In contrast

with "the Holy and Righteous One." *To be granted* (*char-isthēnai*). As a favour (*charis*). First aorist passive infinitive of *charizomai;.* So also 25:11, 27:24.

15. *But the Prince of life ye killed* (*ton de archēgon tēs zōēs apekteinate*). "The magnificent antithesis" (Bengel) Peter here draws between their asking for a murderer and killing the Prince (or Author) of life. Peter pictures Jesus as the source of all life as is done in John 1:1–18 and Col. 1:14–20 and Heb. 1:2f. *Archēgos* (*archē*, beginning, *agō*, to lead) is an adjective "furnishing the first cause or occasion" in Euripides, Plato. Thence substantive, the originator, the leader, the pioneer as of Jesus both Beginner and Finisher (Heb. 12:2). See also Heb. 2:10 and Acts 5:31 where it is applied to Jesus as "Prince and Saviour." But God raised him from the dead in contrast to what they had done. *Whereof we are witnesses* (*hou hēmeis martures esmen*). Of which fact (the resurrection) or of whom as risen, *hou* having the same form in the genitive singular for masculine or neuter. Peter had boldly claimed that all the 120 have seen the Risen Christ. There is no denial of that claim.

16. *By faith in his name* (*tēi pistei tou onomatos autou*). Instrumental case of *pistei* (Aleph and B do not have *epi*) and objective genitive of *onomatos*. *His name* (*to onoma autou*). Repeats the word name to make the point clear. Cf. verse 6 where Peter uses "the name of Jesus Christ of Nazareth" when he healed the man. *Made strong* (*estereō-sen*). Same verb used in verse 7 (and 16:5). Nowhere else in the N.T. Old verb from *stereos*, firm, solid. *Through him* (*di' autou*). Through Jesus, the object of faith and the source of it. *Perfect soundness* (*holoklērian*). Perfect in all its parts, complete, whole (from *holos*, whole, *klēros*, allotment). Late word (Plutarch) once in LXX (Isa. 1:6) and here alone in the N.T., but adjective *holoklēros*, old and common (James 1:4; I Thess. 5:23).

17. *And now* (*kai nun*). Luke is fond of these particles

of transition (7:34; 10:5; 20:25; 22:16) and also *kai ta nun*
(4:29; 5:38; 22:32; 27:22), and even *kai nun idou* (13:11;
20:22). *I wot* (*oida*). Old English for "I know." *In ignorance* (*kata agnoian*). This use of *kata* occurs in the *Koiné*.
See also Philemon 14. One may see Luke 23:34 for the words
of the Saviour on the Cross. "They had sinned, but their
sin was not of so deep a dye that it could not have been still
more heinous" (Hackett). If they had known what they
were doing, they would not knowingly have crucified the
Messiah· (I Cor. 2:8).

18. *Foreshewed* (*prokatēggeilen*). First aorist active indicative of *prokataggellō*, late compound to announce fully
beforehand. Only twice in the N.T. in the critical text
(Acts 3:18; 7:52). *That his Christ should suffer* (*pathein ton
Christon autou*). Accusative of general reference with the
aorist active infinitive (*pathein* of *paschō*) in indirect discourse (predictive purpose of God). Their crime, though
real, was carrying out God's purpose (2:23; John 3:16).
See the same idea in Acts 17:3; 26:23. This "immense paradox" (Page) was a stumbling block to these Jews as it is yet
(I Cor. 1:23). Peter discusses the sufferings of Christ in
I Peter 4:13; 5:1.

19. *Repent therefore* (*metanoēsate oun*). Peter repeats to
this new crowd the command made in Acts 2:38 which see.
God's purpose and patience call for instant change of attitude on their part. Their guilt does not shut them out if
they will turn. *And turn again* (*kai epistrepsate*). Definitely
turn to God in conduct as well as in mind. *That your sins
may be blotted out* (*pros to exaliphthēnai humōn tas hamartias*).
Articular infinitive (first aorist passive of *exaleiphō*, to wipe
out, rub off, erase, smear out, old verb, but in the N.T. only
here and Col. 2:14) with the accusative of general reference
and with *pros* and the accusative to express purpose. *That so*
(*hopōs an*). Final particle with *an* and the aorist active
subjunctive *elthōsin* (come) and not "when" as the Author-

ized Version has it. Some editors put this clause in verse
20 (Wescott and Hort, for instance). *Seasons of refreshing*
(*kairoi anapsuxeōs*). The word *anapsuxis* (from *anapsuchō*,
to cool again or refresh, II Tim. 1:16) is a late word (LXX)
and occurs here alone in the N.T. Surely repentance will
bring "seasons of refreshing from the presence of the Lord."

20. *And that he may send the Christ who hath been ap-*
pointed for you, even Jesus (*kai aposteilēi ton prokecheiris-*
menon humin Christon Iēsoun). First aorist active subjunctive with *hopōs an* as in 15:17 and Luke 2:35. There is
little real difference in idea between *hopōs an* and *hina an*.
There is a conditional element in all purpose clauses. The
reference is naturally to the second coming of Christ as
verse 21 shows. Knowling admits "that there is a spiritual
presence of the enthroned Jesus which believers enjoy as a
foretaste of the visible and glorious Presence of the *Par-*
ousia." Jesus did promise to be with the disciples all the
days (Matt. 28:20), and certainly repentance with accompanying seasons of refreshing help get the world ready for the
coming of the King. The word *prokecheirismenon* (perfect
passive participle of *procheirizō*, from *procheiros*, at hand,
to take into one's hands, to choose) is the correct text here,
not *prokekērugmenon*. In the N.T. only here and Acts 22:
14; 26:16. It is not "Jesus Christ" here nor "Christ Jesus,"
but "the Messiah, Jesus," identifying Jesus with the Messiah. See the Second Epiphany of Jesus foretold also in
I Tim. 6:15 and the First Epiphany described in I Pet. 1:20.

21. *Restoration* (*apokatastaseōs*). Double compound (*apo,*
kata, histēmi), here only in the N.T., though common in
late writers. In papyri and inscriptions for repairs to temples
and this phrase occurs in Jewish apocalyptic writings, something like the new heaven and the new earth of Rev. 21:1.
Paul has a mystical allusion also to the agony of nature in
Rom. 8:20-22. The verb *apokathistēmi* is used by Jesus of
the spiritual and moral restoration wrought by the Baptist

as Elijah (Matt. 17:11 = Mark 9:12) and by the disciples
to Jesus in Acts 1:6. Josephus uses the word of the return
from captivity and Philo of the restitution of inheritances
in the year of jubilee. As a technical medical term it means
complete restoration to health. See a like idea in *palin-
genesia* (renewal, new birth) in Matt. 19:28 and Tit. 3:5.
This universalism of Peter will be clearer to him after Joppa
and Caesarea.

22. *Like unto me* (*hōs eme*). As me, literally; Moses (Deut.
18:14-18) claims that God raised him up as a prophet and
that another and greater one will come, the Messiah. The
Jews understood Moses to be a type of Christ (John 1:21).
God spoke to Moses face to face (Ex. 33:11) and he was the
greatest of the prophets (Deut. 34:10).

23. *That prophet* (*tou prophētou ekeinou*). Emphasizes
the future prophet as on "him" (*autou*) before "hearken."
They had refused to "hearken" to Moses and now, alas,
many had refused to "hearken" to Christ. *Shall be utterly
destroyed* (*exolethreuthēsetai*). First future passive of *exole-
(o) threuō*, a late verb, to destroy utterly (*ex*), only here in
the N.T., common in the LXX.

24. *From Samuel* (*apo Samouēl*). Schools of prophets
arose in his time, few before him (I Sam. 3:1).

25. *Ye* (*Humeis*). Emphatic position. *The covenant which
God made* (*tēs diathēkēs hēs ho theos dietheto*). Literally,
"the covenant which God covenanted." *Diathēkē* and *dietheto* (second aorist middle indicative of *diathēmi*) are the
same root. See on Matt. 26:28. The covenant (agreement
between two, *dia, tithēmi*) was with Abraham (Gen. 12:1-3)
and repeated at various times (Gen. 18:18; 22:18; 26:4,
etc.). In Heb. 9:15-18 the word is used both for covenant
and will. The genitive relative *hēs* attracted to case of the
antecedent.

26. *Unto you first* (*Humin prōton*). The Jews were first
in privilege and it was through the Jews that the Messiah

was to come for "all the families of the earth." *His servant*
(*ton paida autou*).   As in verse 13, the Messiah as God's
Servant.   *To bless you* (*eulogounta humas*).   Present active
participle to express purpose, blessing you (Robertson,
Grammar, p. 991).   *In turning away* (*en tōi apostrephein*).
Articular infinitive in the locative case, almost preserved in
the English.

CHAPTER IV

1. *The captain of the temple* (*ho stratēgos tou hierou*). Twenty-four bands of Levites guarded the temple, one guard at a time. They watched the gates. The commander of each band was called captain (*stratēgos*). Josephus names this captain of the temple police next to the high priest (*War*. VI. 5, 3). *The Sadducees* (*hoi Saddoukaioi*). Most of the priests were Sadducees now and all the chief priests since John Hyrcanus I deserted the Pharisees (Josephus, *Ant*. XVII. 10, 6; XVIII. 1, 4; XX. 9, 1). The Sadducees were slow to line up with the Pharisees against Jesus, but they now take the lead against Peter and John. *Came upon them* (*epestēsan autois*). Second aorist active indicative (intransitive). Burst upon them suddenly or stood by them in a hostile attitude here (Luke 20:1; 24:4; Acts 6:12; 17:5; 22:20; 23:11).

2. *Being sore troubled* (*diaponoumenoi*). Present passive participle of old verb *diaponeō* (perfective use of *dia*) to be worked up, indignant. In the N.T. only here and 16:8. *Because* (*dia to*). The articular infinitive with two accusatives, one the object (the people), the other ("they") of general reference. *In Jesus* (*en Iēsou*). In the case of Jesus, an actual instance of resurrection which the Sadducees denied (Matt. 22:23). This same use of *en* appears in I Cor. 4:6 (in us). The Sadducees were also aristocrats and political ecclesiastics who disliked popular disturbances. In particular, they resented the claim about Jesus whom they had helped crucify.

3. *In ward* (*eis tērēsin*). Probably in one of the chambers of the temple. In safe keeping (from *tēreō*, to guard). Old word, in the N.T. only here and Acts 5:18; I Cor. 7:19. So

in papyri. *Now eventide* (*hespera ēdē*). Hence no trial could take place before the next day, a regulation violated in the case of Jesus.

4. *Men* (*andrōn*). Strictly, men and not women, for *anthrōpos* is the term for both men and women. But in Luke 11:31 *andres* seems to include both men and women and that is possible here, though by no means certain, for see Matt. 14:21 where the women and children are expressly excepted.

5. *Rulers and elders and scribes* (*tous archontas kai tous presbuterous kai tous grammateis*). The three classes composing the Sanhedrin (rulers = chief priests who were Sadducees, the scribes usually Pharisees, the elders not in either class: 24 priests, 24 elders, 22 scribes). *Were gathered together* (*sunachthēnai*). First aorist passive infinitive of *sunagō* with accusative of general reference and the subject of *egeneto*.

6. *Annas* (*Hannas*). One of the rulers or chief priests, ex-high priest (A.D. 7–14) and father-in-law of *Caiaphas* (*Kaiaphas*) who was actual high priest at that time, though the title clung to Annas as here (both so called in Luke 3:2), Caiaphas so by Roman law, Annas so in the opinion of the Jews. They with John and Alexander are the leaders among the Sadducees in pressing the case against Peter and John.

7. *In the midst* (*en tōi mesōi*). The Sanhedrin sat in a semicircle. *They inquired* (*epunthanonto*). Imperfect middle, began to inquire. *Or in what name* (*ē en poiōi onomati*). As if by some magical formula such as exorcists practised (Acts 19:13) as if to catch them by (Deut. 13:1). *Have ye done this* (*epoiēsate touto humeis*). Note emphatic use of *humeis* (ye).

8. *Filled with the Holy Spirit* (*plēstheis pneumatos hagiou*). For this occasion and so above all fear as in verse 31 and as in 2:4.

9. *Concerning a good deed done to an impotent man* (*epi*

euergesiāi anthrōpou asthenous). Objective genitive. Note *euergesia* (old word, in the N.T. only here and I Tim. 6:2), as a benefactor, not a malefactor. Skilful turn made by Peter. *Is made whole* (*sesōstai*). Perfect passive indicative of *sōzō*, stands whole.

10. *Be it known* (*gnōston estō*). Imperative present active third singular of *eimi*, to be, and the verbal adjective *gnōston*. *Whom ye crucified* (*hon humeis estaurōsate*). Too good a chance to miss, and so Peter boldly charges the Sanhedrin with responsibility for the death of Jesus. Note *humeis* (ye) again. *Whom God raised from the dead* (*hon ho theos ēgeiren ek nekrōn*). Note repetition of *hon* (*whom*). This is God's answer to their act of crucifixion. *In him doth this man stand* (*en toutōi houtos parestēken*). Rather (note play on *houtos*), "In this one (*hon, hon*) this one stands (present perfect active indicative, intransitive)." In Jesus this man stands before you whole (*hugiēs*). It was a centre shot.

11. *Of you the builders* (*huph' humōn tōn oikodomōn*). The experts, the architects, had rejected Jesus for their building (Psa. 118:22) as Jesus himself had pointed out (Matt. 21:42 = Luke 21:17). This very Rejected Stone God had made the head of the corner (either the highest corner stone right under the roof or the corner stone under the building, Isa. 28:16) as Jesus showed, as Peter here declares and repeats later (I Peter 2:6f.).

12. *Salvation* (*hē sōtēria*). The Messianic salvation as in 5:31; 17:11 and as Jesus meant in John 4:22. It is amazing to see Peter speaking thus to the Sanhedrin and proclaiming the necessity of salvation (*dei sōthēnai*) in the name of Jesus Christ and in no other. If this was true then, it is true today. There is no second (*heteron*) name to go beside that of Jesus in India, China, Japan, or America.

13. *The boldness* (*tēn parrēsian*). Telling it all (*pan, rēsia*). See also verses 29, 31. Actually Peter had turned the table on the Sanhedrin and had arraigned them before the bar

of God. *Had perceived* (*katalabomenoi*). Second aorist middle participle of *katalambanō*, common verb to grasp strongly (*kata*), literally or with the mind (especially middle voice), to comprehend. The rulers recalled Peter and John from having seen them often with Jesus, probably during the temple teaching, etc. *They were unlearned* (*agrammatoi eisin*). Present indicative retained in indirect discourse. Unlettered men without technical training in the professional rabbinical schools of Hillel or Shammai. Jesus himself was so regarded (John 7:15, "not having learned letters"). *And ignorant* (*kai idiōtai*). Old word, only here in the N.T. and I Cor. 14:24; II Cor. 11:6. It does not mean "ignorant," but a layman, a man not in office (a private person), a common soldier and not an officer, a man not skilled in the schools, very much like *agrammatos*. It is from *idios* (one's own) and our "idiosyncracy" is one with an excess of such a trait, while "idiot" (this very word) is one who has nothing but his idiosyncracy. Peter and John were men of ability and of courage, but they did not belong to the set of the rabbis. *They marvelled* (*ethaumazon*). Imperfect (inchoative) active, began to wonder and kept it up. *Took knowledge of them* (*epeginōskon autous*). Imperfect (inchoative) active again, they began to recognize them as men that they had seen with Jesus.

14. *They could say nothing against it* (*ouden eichon anteipein*). Imperfect again, they kept on having nothing to say against it. The lame man was standing there before their eyes in proof of what Peter had said.

15. *They conferred among themselves* (*suneballon pros allēlous*). Imperfect active again. With Peter and John and the lame man outside, they began to compare (*sun, ballō*) notes and take stock of their predicament.

16. *What shall we do?* (*Ti poiēsōmen*). Deliberative aorist active subjunctive (ingressive and urgent aorist). *Notable miracle* (*gnōston sēmeion*). Or sign. It was useless to deny it

with the man there. *We cannot deny it* (*ou dunametha arneisthai*). That is, it will do no good.

17. *That it spread no further* (*hina mē epi pleion dianemē-thēi*). First aorist passive subjunctive of *dianemō*, to distribute with *hina mē*, negative purpose. *Let us threaten them* (*apeilēsōmetha autois*). Hortatory aorist middle subjunctive of *apeileō*, old verb (note middle voice). In the N.T. only here and I Peter 2:23. *That they speak henceforth to no man in this name* (*mēketi lalein epi tōi onomati toutōi mēdeni anthrō-pōn*). Indirect command with the infinitive and double negative (*mēketi, mēdeni*). They will not say "Jesus," but make a slur at "this name," contemptuous use of *houtos*, though they apparently do mention the name "Jesus" in verse 18.

18. *Not to speak at all* (*katholou mē phtheggesthai*). Same construction as above, infinitive in indirect command with negative *mē* (and *mēde*).

20. *For we cannot but speak* (*ou dunametha gar hēmeis—mē lalein*). Both negatives hold here, "For we (note emphatic *hēmeis*) are not able not to speak" (what we saw and heard). This is defiance of the civil and ecclesiastical authorities that was justified, for the temple authorities stepped in between the conscience and God. Peter and John were willing to pay the price of this defiance with their lives. This is the courage of martyrs through all the ages.

21. *When they had further threatened them* (*prosapeilēsa-menoi*). The "further" is in "*pros*" (in addition), *Finding nothing how they might punish them* (*mēden heuriskontes to pōs kolasōntai autous*). Note the article "*to*" before *pōs* (*how*), "the how." Aorist middle deliberative subjunctive *kolasōntai* in indirect question after *pōs* from *kolazō*, to lop (*kolos*, lopped), to curb, to prune, to correct, to punish. Old verb, in the N.T. only here and II Pet. 2:9. *Glorified God* (*edoxazon ton theon*). Imperfect active, kept on glorifying God while the Sanhedrin were threatening Peter and John. It was to laugh at the helplessness of the Sanhedrin.

22. *Was wrought* (*gegonei*). Second past perfect active without augment from *ginomai*.

23. *To their own company* (*pros tous idious*). Their own people as in John 1:11; 13:1; Acts 24:23; I Tim. 5:8; Tit. 3:14, not merely the apostles (all the disciples). In spite of Peter's courageous defiance he and John told the brotherhood all that had been said by the Sanhedrin. They had real apprehension of the outcome.

24. *With one accord* (*homothumadon*). A concert of voices as already seen by the word in 1:14; 2:46 and later in 5:12; 7:57; 15:25. *O Lord* (*Despota*). Our word despot. Old word for relation of master to slaves or household servants (I Tim. 6:1; II Tim. 2:21; Tit. 2:9; I Peter 2:18). Simeon thus addressed God (Luke 2:29). So in II Peter 2:1; Jude 4; 6:10. See "slaves" in verse 29.

25. *By the mouth of our father David* (*tou patros hēmōn dia pneumatos hagiou stomatos Daueid*). From Psa. 2:1f. here ascribed to David. Baumgarten suggests that the whole company sang the second Psalm and then Peter applied it to this emergency. The Greek MSS. do not have *dia* (by) here before *stomatos*, but only *dia* before *pneumatos hagiou* (the Holy Spirit). Hort calls this a "primitive error" perhaps due to an early scribe who omitted this second *dia* so close to the first *dia* (Robertson, *Introduction to the Textual Criticism of the N.T.*, p. 238). A small list of such primitive errors is there given as suggested by Dr. Hort. *Why* (*hina ti*). This Greek idiom calls for *genētai* (second aorist middle subjunctive), *That what may happen*. *The Gentiles* (*ethnē*). So always in LXX, while *laoi* (peoples) can include Jews. *Did rage* (*ephruaxan*). First aorist active indicative of *phruassō*, late word, to neigh like a horse, to prance or stamp the ground, to put on lofty airs. Only here in the N.T. in this quotation from Psa. 2:1. *Imagine* (*emeletēsan*). First aorist active indicative of *meletaō*. Old verb from *meletē* (care), to practise, to cau-

tion, as orators and rhetoricians. Only here in the N.T. in this quotation.

26. *Set themselves in array* (*parestēsan*). Literally, stood by. *Against his Anointed* (*kata tou Christou autou*). Against his Messiah, his Christ.

27. *Both Herod and Pontios Pilate* (*Hērōidēs te kai Pontius Peilatos*). Luke alone (Luke 23:12) tells of the reconciliation between Herod and Pilate at the trial of Jesus. So Peter and the rest interpret this prophecy as directly fulfilled in their conduct towards Jesus Christ. *Whom thou didst anoint* (*hon echrisas*). As in verse 26 (cf. Luke 4:18 and Isa. 61:1). Inaugurated as King Messiah.

28. *Foreordained* (*proōrisen*). First aorist active indicative of *proorizō*, "They rise above sight and seem to see the Hand which 'shapes men's ends, rough hew them how they will'" (Furneaux).

29. *And now* (*kai ta nun*). "And as to (accusative of general reference) the now things (the present situation)." Only in the Acts in the N.T. (5:38; 17:30; 20:32; 27:22). *Grant* (*dos*). Second aorist active imperative of *didōmi*, urgency of the aorist, Do it now. *To speak thy word with all boldness* (*meta parrēsias pasēs lalein ton logon sou*). Literally, "with all boldness to go on speaking (present active infinitive) thy word." Peter and John had defied the Sanhedrin in verse 20, but all the same and all the more they pray for courage in deed to live up to their brave words. A wholesome lesson.

30. *While thou stretchest forth thy hand* (*en tōi tēn cheira ekteinein se*). Luke's favourite idiom, "In the stretching out (articular present active infinitive) the hand as to thee" (accusative of general reference), the second allusion to God's "hand" in this prayer (verse 28). *To heal* (*eis iasin*). For healing. See verse 22. *And that signs and wonders may be done* (*kai sēmeia kai terata ginesthai*). Either to be taken as in the same construction as *ekteinein* with *en tōi* as Re-

vised Version has it here or to be treated as subordinate purpose to *en tōi ekteinein* (as Knowling, Page, Wendt, Hackett). The latter most likely true. They ask for a visible sign or proof that God has heard this prayer for courage to be faithful even unto death.

31. *The place was shaken* (*esaleuthē ho topos*). By an earthquake most likely as in 16:26, but none the less a token of God's presence and power (Psa. 114:7; Isa. 2:19, 21; Heb. 12:26f.). *Were gathered together* (*ēsan sunēgmenoi*). Periphrastic past perfect passive of *sunagō*. *They spake* (*elaloun*). Imperfect active indicative, began to speak, after being filled (*eplēsthēsan*, aorist passive indicative) with the Holy Spirit. Luke uses the very words of the prayer in verse 29 to describe their conduct.

32. *Of one heart and soul* (*kardia kai psuchē mia*). It is not possible to make sharp distinction between heart and soul here (see Mark 12:30), only that there was harmony in thought and affection. But the English translation is curiously unlike the Greek original. "There was one heart and soul (nominative case, not genitive as the English has it) in the multitude (*tou plēthous*, subjective genitive) of those who believed." *Not one of them* (*oude heis*). More emphatic than *oudeis*, "not even one." *Common* (*koina*). In the use of their property, not in the possession as Luke proceeds to explain. The word *koinos* is kin to *sun* (together with) = *xun* (Epic) and so *xunos* = *koinos*. See this word already in 2:44. The idea of unclean (Acts 10:15) is a later development from the original notion of common to all.

33. *Gave their witness* (*apedidoun to marturion*). Imperfect active of *apodidōmi*, old verb to give back, to pay back a debt (Luke 7:42), but a late omega form instead of the usual *apedidosan*. They kept on giving their witness with power after the answer to their prayer (verse 31). *Of the resurrection* (*tēs anastaseōs*). It was on this issue that the Sadducees had arrested them (4:1-3).

34. *That lacked* (*endeēs*). Literally, in need, old adjective, here only in the N.T. *Were* (*hupērchon*). Imperfect active of *huparchō*, to exist. *Sold them and brought* (*pōlountes epheron*). Present active participle and imperfect active indicative. Selling they brought from time to time, as there was occasion by reason of need. Hence the wants were kept supplied. *Laid them* (*etithoun*). Imperfect active again, *repetition*, of *tithēmi*, late omega form for the usual *etithesan*.

35. *Distribution was made* (*diedideto*). Imperfect passive of *diadidōmi*, late omega form for *diedidoto* (the stem vowel *o* displaced by *e*). Impersonal use of the verb here. *According as any one had need* (*kathoti an tis chreian eichen*). Imperfect active of *echō* with *kathoti* and *an* with the notion of customary repetition in a comparative clause (Robertson, *Grammar*, p. 967).

36. *Barnabas* (*Barnabas*). His name was Joseph (correct text, and not Jesus) and he is mentioned as one illustration of those in verse 34 who selling brought the money. The apostles gave him the nickname Barnabas by which later he was known because of this noble deed. This fact argues that all did not actually sell, but were ready to do so if needed. Possibly Joseph had a larger estate than some others also. The meaning of the nickname is given by Luke as "son of consolation or exhortation" (*huios paraklēseōs*). Doubtless his gifts as a preacher lay along this same line. Rackham thinks that the apostles gave him this name when he was recognized as a prophet. In Acts 11:23 the very word *parekalei* (exhorted) is used of Barnabas up at Antioch. He is the type of preacher described by Paul in I Cor. 14:3. Encouragement is the chief idea in *paraklēsis* though exhortation, comfort, consolation are used to render it (Acts 9:31; 13:15; 15:31). See also 16:9; 20:12. It is not necessary to think that the apostles coined the name Barnabas for Joseph which originally may have come from *Barnebous* (Deissmann, *Bible Studies*, pp. 308–10), son of Nebo, or even the

Hebrew *Bar Nebi* (son of a prophet). But, whatever the origin, the popular use is given by Luke. He was even called apostle along with Paul (Acts 14:14) in the broad sense of that word.

37. *Having a field* (*huparchontos autōi agrou*). Genitive absolute with present active participle of *huparchō* and dative of possession. *Sold it and brought* (*pōlēsas ēnegken*). Aorist active párticiple of *pōleō* and second aorist active indicative of *pherō* because a single definite instance. So also with *ethēken* (laid), first aorist active.

CHAPTER V

1. *Sold (epōlēsen)*. Aorist active indicative again, for a single case.

2. *Kept back (enosphisato)*. First aorist middle indicative of *nosphizō*, old verb from *nosphi*, afar, apart, and so to set apart, to separate for oneself, but only here, verse 3 and Tit. 2:10 in the N.T. *His wife also being privy to it (suneiduiēs kai tēs gunaikos)*. Genitive absolute with second perfect participle of *sunoida*, to know together with one, "his wife also knowing it together with him." *Brought a certain part (enegkas meros ti)*. Aorist active participle of *pherō*, for a definite act. The praise of Joseph was too much for Ananias, but he was not willing to turn over all. He wanted praise for giving all and yet he took care of himself by keeping some. Thus he started the Ananias Club that gave a new meaning to his lovely name (God is gracious).

3. *Filled (eplērōsen)*. The very verb used of the filling by the Holy Spirit (4:31). Satan the adversary is the father of lies (John 8:44). He had entered into Judas (Luke 22:3; John 13:27) and now he has filled the heart of Ananias with a lie. *To lie to the Holy Spirit (pseusasthai se to pneuma to hagion)*. Infinitive (aorist middle) of purpose with accusative of general reference *(se)* and the accusative of the person (object) as often in Greek writers, though here only in the N.T. with this verb. Usual dative of the person in verse 4 *(anthrōpois,* men, *tōi theōi,* God). The Holy Spirit had been given them to guide them into truth (John 15:13).

4. *Whiles it remained (menon)*. Present active participle of *menō*, unsold, Peter means. *After it was sold (prathen)*. First aorist passive of *pipraskō*, to sell. *How is that thou hast conceived (Ti hoti ethou)*. *Quid est quod*. See Luke 2:49.

See also Acts 5:9. Second aorist middle indicative **second** person singular of *tithēmi*. The devil filled his heart (verse 3), but all the same Ananias did it too and is wholly responsible.

5. *Hearing* (*akouōn*). Present active participle of *akouō*, while hearing. *Fell down* (*pesōn*). Second aorist active participle of *piptō*, fell all of a sudden while listening. *Gave up the ghost* (*exepsuxen*). First aorist active indicative of *ekpsuchō*, late verb in LXX and Hippocrates, to breathe out, to expire. In the N.T. only here, verse 10, and 12:23. It is needless to blame Peter for the death of Ananias. He had brought the end upon himself. It was the judgment of God. Physically the nervous shock could have caused the collapse.

6. *The young men* (*hoi neōteroi*). Literally the younger men (contrast with *hoi presbuteroi*, the elder men). Same as *neaniskoi* in verse 10 and so no order in the young church. Perhaps these young men were acting as ushers or actual pallbearers. *Wrapped him round* (*sunesteilan*). First aorist active indicative of *sustellō*, old verb, to draw together, or contract (I Cor. 7:29), to roll together, to wrap with bandages, to enshroud as here. Nowhere else in the N.T. Frequent in medical writers. They may have used their own mantles. The time for burial was short in Jerusalem for sanitary reasons and to avoid ceremonial defilement.

7. *And it was about the space of three hours after* (*egeneto de hōs hōrōn triōn diastēma*). Literally "Now there came an interval (*diastēma*, distance, space between) of about (*hōs*) three hours." *When* (*kai*). This use of *kai* after *egeneto* is characteristic of Luke's style in the Gospel. *Not knowing* (*mē eiduia*). Feminine singular of second perfect active participle of *oida*. *Mē* usual negative of the participle in the *Koinē*.

8. *For so much* (*tosoutou*). Genitive of price. Perhaps Peter pointed to the pile of money at the feet of the apostles (verse 2). The use of *ei* in direct questions appears in Luke

(13:23; 22:49) as in the LXX like the Hebrew *im* and in Acts 1:6; 19:2, etc.

9. *Ye have agreed together* (*sunephōnēthē humin*). First aorist passive indicative of *sumphōneō* (to voice together, symphony), impersonal with dative; It was agreed together by you (or for you). "Your souls were allured together respecting this deceit" (Vincent). *To tempt the Spirit of the Lord* (*peirasai to pneuma kuriou*). Like "Thou shalt not tempt the Lord thy God." It was close to the unpardonable sin which was attributing the manifest work of the Holy Spirit to Beelzebub. *The feet* (*hoi podes*). Graphic picture by Peter as he heard the steps of the young men at the door.

10. *Immediately* (*parachrēma*). Hence her death was regarded as supernatural like that of Ananias. *By her husband* (*pros ton andra autēs*). Face to face to her husband.

11. *Upon the whole church* (*eph' holēn tēn ekklēsian*). Here *ekklēsia* for the first time in Acts of the believers in Jerusalem. Twice already in the Gospels, once of the whole body of believers or the Kingdom (Matt. 16:18), the other of the local body (Matt. 18:17). In Acts 7:38 it is used of the whole congregation of Israel while in 19:32 it is used of a public assembly in Ephesus. But already in Acts 8:3 it is applied to the church which Saul was persecuting in their homes when not assembled. So here the etymological meaning of "assembly" disappears for "the church" were now the scattered saints hiding in their separate homes. The whole body of believers in Jerusalem and all who heard of the fate of Ananias and Sapphira (beautiful, her name means) were in awe and dread. It was already a dangerous thing to be a follower of Christ unless one was willing to walk straight.

12. *Were wrought* (*egineto*). Imperfect middle, wrought from time to time. *With one accord* (*homothumadon*). As already in 1:14; 2:46; 4:24 and later 7:57; 8:6; 12:20; 15:25; 18:21; 19:29, old adverb and only in Acts in the N. T. Here "all" is added. In Solomon's Porch again as in 3:11 which see.

13. *Durst* (*etolma*). Imperfect active of *tolmaō*, old verb, not to fear or shun through fear, boldly to take a stand. The fate of Ananias and Sapphira continued to hold many in check. *Join* (*kollasthai*). Present middle infinitive of *kollaō*, old verb to cleave to like glue as in Luke 15:15 which see. Seven times in Acts (9:26; 10:28; 17:34). The outsiders (the rest) preferred, many of them, to remain outside for the present, especially the rulers. *Howbeit the people* (*all'—ho laos*). Probably individuals among the people, the populace as distinct from the rulers and hostile outsiders.

14. *Were the more added* (*mãllon prosetithento*). Rather (*mãllon*) instead of decrease as one might expect. Imperfect passive indicative of *prostithēmi* common *mi* verb, kept on being added. *Both of men and women* (*andrōn te kai gunai-kōn*). The distinction between *andres* and *gunaikes* and to be considered in connection with *andres* in 4:4 which see.

15. *Insomuch that* (*hōste*). With the present infinitive *ekpherein* and *tithenai*, regular Greek idiom for result. *Into the streets* (*eis tas plateias*). Supply *hodous* (ways), into the broad ways. *On beds and couches* (*epi klinariōn kai kra-battōn*). Little beds (*klinaria* diminutive of *klinē*) and camp beds or pallets (see on Mark 2:4, 9, 11). *As Peter came by* (*erchomenou Petrou*). Genitive absolute with present middle participle. *At the least his shadow might overshadow* (*kàn hē skia episkiasei*). Future active indicative with *hina* (common with *hopōs* in ancient Greek) and *kàn* (crasis for *kai ean* = even if), even if only the shadow. The word for shadow (*skia*, like our "sky") is repeated in the verb and preserved in our "overshadow." There was, of course, no virtue or power in Peter's shadow. That was faith with superstition, of course, just as similar cases in the Gospels occur (Matt. 9:20; Mark 6:56; John 9:5) and the use of Paul's handkerchief (Acts 19:12). God honours even superstitious faith if it is real faith in him. Few people are wholly devoid of superstition.

16. *Came together* (*sunērcheto*). Imperfect middle, kept on coming. *Round about* (*perix*). Old adverb, strengthened form of *peri*, only here in the N.T. *Vexed* (*ochloumenous*). Present passive participle of *ochleō*, to excite a mob (*ochlos*) against one, to trouble, annoy. Old word, only here in the N.T., though *enochleō* in Luke 6:18. *Were healed every one* (*etherapeuonto hapantes*). Imperfect passive, were healed one at a time, repetition.

17. *Which is the sect of the Sadducees* (*hē ousa hairesis tōn Saddoukaiōn*). Literally, "the existing sect of the Sadducees" or "the sect which is of the Sadducees," *hē* being the article, not the relative. *Hairesis* means a choosing, from *haireomai*, to take for oneself, to choose, then an opinion chosen or tenet (possibly II Pet. 2:1), then parties or factions (Gal. 5:20; I Cor. 11:19; possibly II Peter 2:1). It is applied here to the Sadducees; to the Pharisees in Acts 15:5; 26:5; to the Christians in 24:5-14 and 28:22. Already Luke has stated that the Sadducees started the persecution of Peter and John (Acts 4:1f.). Now it is extended to "the apostles" as a whole since Christianity has spread more rapidly in Jerusalem than before it began.

18. *With jealousy* (*zēlou*). Genitive case. Old word from *zeō*, to boil, our zeal. In itself it means only warmth, ardour, zeal, but for a bad cause or from a bad motive, jealousy, envy, rivalry results (Acts 13:45). Common in the epistles. *In public ward* (*en tērēsei dēmosiāi*). As in 4:3 only with *dēmosiāi* (public) added, in the public prison, perhaps not the "common" prison, but any prison is bad enough. In verse 19 it is called "the prison" (*tēs phulakēs*), the guardhouse.

20. *And stand* (*kai stathentes*). First aorist passive participle (intransitive, ingressive aorist), take a stand. Bold and pictorial command. *All the words of this life* (*panta ta rhēmata tēs zōēs tautēs*). Not just a Hebraism for "all these words of life." Probably "this life" which the Sadducees

deny and of which the angel is now speaking, this eternal life. (John 6:63, 68; I Cor. 15:19).

21. *About daybreak* (*hupo ton orthron*). From *ornumi*, to stir up, to arouse, so the dawn (Luke 24:1; John 8:2). Old word, but in the N.T. only these three passages. "Under the dawn" or "about dawn." *Sub lucem*. The temple doors would be open for early worshippers and traffickers (John 2:14). *Taught* (*edidaskon*). Imperfect active, began to teach. *The council* (*to sunedrion*). The Sanhedrin. *The senate* (*tēn gerousian*). From *gerōn*, an old man, just as the Latin *senatus* is from *senex*, old. Like the *gerontes* in Homer and the Elder Statesmen in Japan. Apparently the senate of the people were also part of the Sanhedrin and the use of "and" (*kai*) is explanatory and adds this item in particular. Page thinks that this group of elders were not members of the Sanhedrin at all. *To the prison house* (*eis to desmōtērion*), another word for prison (*tērēsis dēmosia* in verse 18, *hē phulakē* in verse 19). See also verses 22, 23, 25. This from *desmos*, bond, and *tēreō*, to keep, place where bound men are kept.

22. *The officers* (*hoi hupēretai*). Under-rowers, literally (Matt. 5:25). The servants or officers who executed the orders of the Sanhedrin. *Shut* (*kekleismenon*). Perfect passive participle of *kleiō*. Shut tight. *Standing at the doors* (*hestōtas epi tōn thurōn*). Graphic picture of the sentinels at the prison doors.

24. *They were much perplexed* (*diēporoun*). Imperfect active of *diaporeō* old verb by Luke only in the N.T. See already on Acts 2:12. They continued puzzled. *Whereunto this would grow* (*ti an genoito touto*). More exactly, *As to what this would become*. Second aorist middle optative of *ginomai* with *an*, the conclusion of a condition of the fourth class (undetermined with less likelihood of determination), the unexpressed condition being "if the thing should be allowed to go on." The indirect question simply retains the optative with *an* (Robertson, *Grammar*, pp. 1021, 1044). If they

had only known how this grain of mustard seed would grow into the greatest tree on earth and how dwarfed the tree of Judaism would be beside it!

26. *Brought* (*ēgen*). Imperfect active of *agō*, was bringing (leading), slowly no doubt, and solemnly. *But without violence* (*ou meta bias*). Literally, not with violence. *For they feared* (*ephobounto gar*). Imperfect middle, still feared, kept on fearing. *Lest they be stoned* (*mē lithasthōsin*). Negative purpose with *mē* (like *hina mē*), probably with "not with violence," though possible with "they feared." They handled the apostles gently for fear of being stoned themselves by the people. First aorist passive subjunctive of *lithazō* (from *lithos*, stone), old verb to pelt with stones (Acts 14:19; John 10:31–33).

27. *They set them* (*estēsan*). First aorist active indicative (transitive) of *histēmi*.

28. *We straitly charged* (*Paraggeliāi parēggeilamen*). Like the Hebrew idiom (common in the LXX), though found in Greek, with charging (instrumental case) we charged (cf. same idiom in Luke 22:15). Somewhat like the cognate accusative. The command referred to occurs in Acts 4:17 and 18 and the refusal of Peter and John in 4:20. *To bring upon us* (*epagagein eph' hēmās*). Note repetition of *epi*. Second aorist active infinitive of *epagō*, old verb, but in the N.T. only here and II Pet. 2:1, 5. The Sanhedrin gladly took the blood of Christ on their heads and their children to Pilate (Matt. 27:25). Paul tried to save the Jews (Acts 18:6; 22:20). "*This man*" (*tou anthrōpou toutou*). Contemptuous slur and refusal to call the name of Jesus as in the Talmud later.

29. *We must* (*dei*). Moral necessity left them no choice. They stood precisely where Peter and John were when before the Sanhedrin before (Acts 4:20). *Obey* (*peitharchein*). Old verb from *peithomai* and *archē*, to obey a ruler. Only by Luke and Paul in the N.T.

30. *Ye slew* (*diecheirisasthe*).   First aorist middle indicative of *diacheirizomai*, old verb from *dia* and *cheir* (hand), to take in hand, manage, to lay hands on, manhandle, kill. In the N.T. only here and Acts 26:21.   *Hanging him upon a tree* (*kremasantes epi xulou*).   First aorist active participle of *kremannumi* (*kremannuō* seen already in Matt. 18:6 and Luke 23:39).   Peter refers to Deut. 21:23 as Paul does in Gal. 3:13, the curse pronounced on every one who "hangs upon a tree."

31. *Exalt* (*upsōsen*).   In contrast to their murder of Christ as in 2:23f.   Peter repeats his charges with increased boldness.   *With his right hand* (*tēi dexiāi autou*).   So instrumental case, or at his right hand (locative case), or even "to his right hand" (dative case) as in 2:33.   *Prince and Saviour* (*archēgon kai sōtēra*).   See on 3:15.   Clearly "Prince" here. *To give* (*tou dounai*).   Genitive of articular infinitive (second aorist active of *didōmi*) of purpose.

32. *We are witnesses* (*hēmeis esmen martures*).   As in 2:32. *Things* (*rhēmatōn*).   Literally, sayings, but like the Hebrew *dabhar* for "word" it is here used for "things."   *And so is the Holy Ghost* (*kai to pneuma to hagion*).   The word for "is" (*estin*) is not in the Greek, but this is plainly the meaning. Peter claims the witness of the Holy Spirit to the raising of Jesus Christ, God's Son, by the Father.

33. *Were cut to the heart* (*dieprionto*).   Imperfect passive of *diapriō* old verb (*dia, priō*), to saw in two (*dia*), to cut in two (to the heart).   Here it is rage that cuts into their hearts, not conviction of sin as in Acts 2:37.   Only here and Acts 7:54 (after Stephen's speech) in the N.T. (cf. Simeon's prophecy in Luke 2:35).   *Were minded* (*eboulonto*).   Imperfect middle of *boulomai*.   They were plotting and planning to kill (*anelein*, as in Acts 2:23 and Luke 23:33 which see) then and there.   The point in 4:7 was whether the apostles deserved stoning for curing the cripple by demoniacal power, but here it was disobedience to the command of the San-

hedrin which was not a capital offence. "They were on the point of committing a grave judicial blunder" (Furneaux).

34. *Gamaliel* (*Gamaliēl*). The grandson of Hillel, teacher of Paul (Acts 22:3), later president of the Sanhedrin, and the first of the seven rabbis termed "Rabban." It is held by some that he was one of the doctors who heard the Boy Jesus in the temple (Luke 2:47) and that he was a secret disciple like Joseph of Arimathea and Nicodemus, but there is no evidence of either position. Besides, he appears here as a loyal Pharisee and "a doctor of the law" (*nomodidaskalos*). This word appears already in Luke 5:17 of the Pharisaic doctors bent on criticizing Jesus, which see. Paul uses it of Judaizing Christians (I Tim. 1:7). Like other great rabbis he had a great saying: "Procure thyself a teacher, avoid being in doubt; and do not accustom thyself to give tithes by guess." He was a man of judicial temper and not prone to go off at a tangent, though his brilliant young pupil Saul went to the limit about Stephen without any restraint on the part of Gamaliel so far as the record goes. Gamaliel champions the cause of the apostles as a Pharisee to score a point against the Sadducees. He acts as a theological opportunist, not as a disciple of Christ. He felt that a temporizing policy was best. There are difficulties in this speech of Gamaliel and it is not clear how Luke obtained the data for the address. It is, of course, possible that Saul was present and made notes of it for Luke afterwards. *Had in honour of all the people* (*timios panti tōi laōi*). Ethical dative. *Timios* from *timē*, old word meaning precious, dear. *The men* (*tous anthrōpous*). Correct text as in verse 35, not "the apostles" as Textus Receptus.

35. *Take heed* (*prosechete heautois*). Hold your mind (*noun*, unexpressed) for or on yourselves (dative case), the usual idiom.

36. *Theudas* (*Theudas*). Luke represents Gamaliel here about A.D. 35 as speaking of a man who led a revolt before

that of Judas the Galilean in connection with the enrolment
under Quirinius (Cyrenius) in A.D. 6. But Josephus (*Ant.*
XX. 5, 1) tells of a Theudas who led a similar insurrection
in the reign of Claudius about A.D. 44 or 45. Josephus (*Ant.*
XVIII. 1, 6; XX. 5, 2; *War* ii. 8, 1 and 17, 8) also describes
Judas the Galilean or Gaulonite and places him about A.D.
6. It is not certain that Josephus and Luke (Gamaliel)
refer to the same Theudas as the name is an abbreviation of
Theodosus, a common name. "Josephus gives an account
of four men named Simon who followed each other within
forty years, and of three named Judas within ten years,
who were all instigators of rebellion" (Hackett). If the same
Theudas is meant, then either Josephus or Luke (Gamaliel)
has the wrong historical order. In that case one will credit
Luke or Josephus according to his estimate of the two as
reliable historians. *To be somebody* (*einai tina*). Indirect
assertion with the infinitive and the accusative of general
reference (*heauton*) and *tina*, predicate accusative. *Tina*
could be "anybody" or "somebody" according to context,
clearly "somebody" of importance here. *Joined themselves*
(*proseklithē*). Correct text and not *prosekollēthē* (Textus
Receptus). First aorist passive indicative of *prosklinō*, old
verb to lean towards, to incline towards. Here only in the
N.T. *Was slain* (*anēirethē*). First aorist passive of *anaireō*
(cf. verse 33). *Obeyed* (*epeithonto*). Imperfect middle, kept
on obeying. *Were dispersed* (*dieluthēsan*). First aorist passive indicative (effective aorist) of *dialuō*, old verb to dis-
solve, to go to pieces. Here only in the N.T.

37. *Of the enrolment* (*tēs apographēs*). Described by
Josephus (*Ant.* XV. 1, 1). The same word used by Luke of
the first enrolment started by Augustus B.C. 8 to 6 (Luke 2:2).
See the discussion on Luke 2:2. This is the second enrolment
in the fourteen year cycle carried on for centuries as shown
by numerous dated papyri. Ramsay (*The Bearing of Recent
Discovery on the Trustworthiness of the N.T.*) has produced

proof from inscriptions that Quirinius was twice in Syria as
Luke reports (Robertson, *Luke the Historian in the Light
of Research*). *Drew away* (*apestēse*). Causative sense of the
first aorist active indicative of *aphistēmi*, made people (*laon*,
no need of "some of the") to revolt (apostatize) with
him. *He also* (*kàkeinos*, crasis for *kai ekeinos*). That one,
also. *Were scattered abroad* (*dieskorpisthēsan*). First aorist
(effective) passive indicative of *diaskorpizō*, old verb to
disperse. Used of sheep (Mark 14:27), of property (Luke
15:13). Aorist here after imperfect (*epeithonto*) as in verse 36.

38. *Refrain from* (*apostēte apo*). Second aorist (ingressive)
active imperative of *aphistēmi* of verse 37. Do ye stand off
from these men. "Hands off" was the policy of Gamaliel.
For if—be (*hoti ean—ēi*). *Hoti* gives the reason for the advice.
Gamaliel presents two alternatives in terms of two conditional clauses. The first one is stated as a condition of the
third class, *ean* with the present subjunctive *ēi*, undetermined with prospect of determination. Assuming that it is
from men, "it will be overthrown" (*kataluthēsetai*, first
future passive of *kataluō*, to loosen down like a falling house)
as was true of the following of Theudas and Judas the
Galilean.

39. *But if it is of God* (*ei de ek theou estin*). The second alternative is a condition of the first class, determined as fulfilled, *ei* with the present indicative. By the use of this idiom
Gamaliel does put the case more strongly in favor of the
apostles than against them. This condition *assumes* that the
thing is so without *affirming* it to be true. On the basis of
this alternative Gamaliel warns the Sanhedrin that they
cannot "overthrow" (*katalusai*) these men for they in that
case must "overthrow" God, *lest haply ye be found* (*mē
pote—hurethēte*, negative purpose with first aorist passive
subjunctive) *even to be fighting against God* (*kai theomachoi*,
late adjective from *theos* and *machomai*, in LXX and here
only in the N.T.).

40. *To him they agreed* (*epeisthēsan autōi*).   First aorist passive indicative of *peithō*, to persuade, the passive to be persuaded by, to listen to, to obey.   Gamaliel's shrewd advice scored as against the Sadducaic contention (verse 17). *Not to speak* (*mē lalein*).   The Sanhedrin repeated the prohibition of 4:18 which the apostles had steadily refused to obey.   The Sanhedrin stood by their guns, but refused to shoot.   It was a "draw" with Gamaliel as tactical victor over the Sadducees.   Clearly now the disciples were set free because only the Sadducees had become enraged while the Pharisees held aloof.

41. *They therefore* (*hoi men oun*).   No answering *de*. *They were counted worthy to suffer dishonour for the Name* (*katēxiōthēsan huper tou onomatos atimasthēnai*).   First aorist passive indicative of *kataxioō*, old verb to count worthy. Three times in N.T. (Luke 20:35; Acts 5:41; II Thess. 1:5). First aorist passive infinitive of *atimazō*, old verb to make one dishonoured (*atimos*).   Forms here an oxymoron (*oxus*, sharp, *moros*, foolish) pointedly foolish saying "which is witty or impressive through sheer contradiction or paradox as laborious idleness, sublime indifference" (Vincent).   The apostles felt honoured by dishonour.   Note the same use of "the Name" as in James 2:7; III John 7.   With the Jews this absolute use of "the Name" meant Jehovah.   The Christians now apply it to Jesus.

42. *Every day* (*pāsan hēmeran*).   Accusative of extent of time, all through every day. *In the temple and at home* (*en tōi hierōi kai kat' oikon*).   This was a distinct triumph to go back to the temple where they had been arrested (verse 25) and at home or from house to house, as it probably means (cf. 2:46).   It was a great day for the disciples in Jerusalem. *They ceased not* (*ouk epauonto*).   Imperfect middle.   They kept it up. *Jesus as the Christ* (*ton Christon Iēsoun*).   Jesus is the direct object of the participles *didaskontes* (teaching) and *euaggelizomenoi* (preaching or evangelizing) while "the

Christ" (*ton Christon*) is the predicate accusative. These words give the substance of the early apostolic preaching as these opening chapters of Acts show, that Jesus of Nazareth is the Messiah of promise. Gamaliel had opened the prison doors for them and they took full advantage of the opportunity that now was theirs.

CHAPTER VI

1. *When the number of the disciples was multiplying (plē-thunontōn tōn mathētōn).* Genitive absolute of *plēthunō*, old verb from *plēthos*, fulness, to increase. The new freedom from the intercession of Gamaliel was bearing rich fruit. *A murmuring of the Grecian Jews (goggusmos tōn Hellēnistōn).* Late onomatopoetic word (LXX) from the late verb *gogguzō*, to mutter, to murmur. The substantive occurs also in John 7:12; Phil. 2:14; I Peter 4:9. It is the secret grumblings that buzz away till they are heard. These "Grecian Jews" or Hellenists are members of the church in Jerusalem who are Jews from outside of Palestine like Barnabas from Cyprus. These Hellenists had points of contact with the Gentile world without having gone over to the habits of the Gentiles, the Jews of the Western Dispersion. They spoke Greek. *Against the Hebrews (pros tous Ebraious).* The Jewish Christians from Jerusalem and Palestine. The Aramaean Jews of the Eastern Dispersion are usually classed with the Hebrew (speaking Aramaic) as distinct from the Grecian Jews or Hellenists. *Were neglected (paretheōrounto).* Imperfect passive of *paratheōreō*, old verb, to examine things placed beside (*para*) each other, to look beyond (*para* also), to overlook, to neglect. Here only in the N.T. These widows may receive daily (*kathēmerinēi*, late adjective from *kath' hēmeran*, only here in the N.T.) help from the common fund provided for all who need it (Acts 4:32–37). The temple funds for widows were probably not available for those who have now become Christians. Though they were all Christians here concerned, yet the same line of cleavage existed as among the other Jews (Hebrew or Aramaean Jews and Hellenists). It is not here said that the murmuring arose

72

THE ACTS OF THE APOSTLES

among the widows, but because of them. Women and money
occasion the first serious disturbance in the church life. There
was evident sensitiveness that called for wisdom.

2. *The multitude* (*to plēthos*). The whole church, not just
the 120. *Fit* (*areston*). Pleasing, verbal adjective from
areskō, to please, old word, but in the N.T. only here and
Acts 12:3; John 8:29; I John 3:22. *Non placet. Should forsake* (*kataleipsantas*). Late first aorist active participle for
usual second aorist *katalipontas* from *kataleipō*, to leave
behind. *Serve tables* (*diakonein trapezais*). Present active
infinitive of *diakoneō* from *diakonos* (*dia* and *konis*, dust),
to raise a dust in a hurry, to serve, to minister either at
table (John 12:20), or other service (John 12:25f.), to serve as
deacon (I Tim. 3:10, 13). "Tables" here hardly means
money-tables as in John 2:15, but rather the tables used in
the common daily distribution of the food (possibly including
the love-feasts, Acts 2:43-47). This word is the same root
as *diakonia* (ministration) in verse 1 and *deacon* (*diakonos*)
in Phil. 1:1 and I Tim. 3:8-13. It is more frequently used in
the N.T. of ministers (preachers) than of deacons, but it is
quite possible, even probable, that the office of deacon as
separate from bishop or elder grew out of this incident in
Acts 6:1-7. Furneaux is clear that these "seven" are not
to be identified with the later "deacons" but why he does
not make clear.

3. *Of good report* (*marturoumenous*). Present passive participle of *martureō*, to bear witness to. Men with a good reputation as well as with spiritual gifts (the Holy Spirit and
wisdom). *We may appoint* (*katastēsomen*). Future active
indicative of *kathistēmi*, we shall appoint. The action of the
apostles follows the choice by the church, but it is promised
as a certainty, not as a possibility. The Textus Receptus has
a first aorist active subjunctive here (*katastēsōmen*).

4. *But we* (*hemeis de*). In contrast to the work given the
seven. *The ministry of the word* (*tēi diakoniāi tou logou*). The

same word *diakoniāi* employed in verse 1, but here about preaching as the special ministry with which the apostles were concerned. For "continue steadfastly" (*proskarterēsomen*) see on 2:42.

5. *Pleased* (*ēresen*). Aorist active indicative of *areskō* like Latin *placuit* when a vote was taken. The use of *enōpion* before "the whole multitude" is like the LXX. *They chose* (*exelexanto*). First aorist middle indicative of *eklegō*, to pick out for oneself. Each one of the seven has a Greek name and was undoubtedly a Hellenist, not an Aramaean Jew. Consummate wisdom is here displayed for the murmuring had come from the Hellenists, seven of whom were chosen to take proper care of the widows of Hellenists. This trouble was settled to stay settled so far as we know. Nothing is here told of any of the seven except Stephen who is "a man full of faith and the Holy Spirit" and Nicolas "a proselyte of Antioch" (who was not then born a Jew, but had come to the Jews from the Greek world).

6. *They laid their hands on them* (*epethēkan autois tas cheiras*). First aorist active indicative of *epitithēmi*. Probably by the apostles who ratified the choice (verse 3). The laying on of hands "was a symbol of the impartation of the gifts and graces which they needed to qualify them for the office. It was of the nature of a prayer that God would bestow the necessary gifts, rather than a pledge that they were actually conferred" (Hackett).

7. *Increased* (*ēuxanen*). Imperfect active, kept on growing all the more because the apostles were now relieved from the daily ministration of the food. *Multiplied* (*eplēthuneto*). Imperfect passive. The two imperfects kept pace with each other. *Of the priests* (*tōn hierōn*). Who were usually Sadducees. It was a sad day for Annas and Caiaphas and all the sect of the Sadducees (5:17). *Were obedient to* (*hupēkouon*). Imperfect active of *hupakouō*, repetition, one after another. *The faith* (*tēi pistei*). Here meaning the gospel,

the faith system as in Rom. 1:5; Gal. 1:23; Jude 3, etc. Here the word means more than individual trust in Christ.

8. *Wrought* (*epoiei*). Imperfect active, repeatedly wrought. Evidently a man like Stephen would not confine his "ministry" to "serving tables." He was called in verse 5 "full of faith and the Holy Spirit." Here he is termed "full of grace (so the best MSS., not faith) and power." The four words give a picture of remarkable attractiveness. The grace of God gave him the power and so "he kept on doing great wonders and signs among the people." He was a sudden whirlwind of power in the very realm of Peter and John and the rest.

9. *The synagogue of the Libertines* (*ek tēs sunagōgēs tēs legomenēs Libertinōn*). The Libertines (Latin *libertinus*, a freedman or the son of a freedman) were Jews, once slaves of Rome (perhaps descendants of the Jews taken to Rome as captives by Pompey), now set free and settled in Jerusalem and numerous enough to have a synagogue of their own. Schuerer calls a Talmudic myth the statement that there were 480 synagogues in Jerusalem. There were many, no doubt, but how many no one knows. These places of worship and study were in all the cities of the later times where there were Jews enough to maintain one. Apparently Luke here speaks of five such synagogues in Jerusalem (that of the Libertines, of the Cyrenians, of the Alexandrians, of Cilicia, and of Asia). There probably were enough Hellenists in Jerusalem to have five such synagogues. But the language of Luke is not clear on this point. He may make only two groups instead of five since he uses the article *tōn* twice (once before *Libertinōn kai Kurēnaiōn kai Alexandreōn*, again before *apo Kilikias kai Asias*). He also changes from the genitive plural to *apo* before Cilicia and Asia. But, leaving the number of the synagogues unsettled whether five or two, it is certain that in each one where Stephen appeared as a Hellenist preaching Jesus as the

Messiah he met opposition. Certain of them "arose" (*anestēsan*) "stood up" after they had stood all that they could from Stephen, "disputing with Stephen" (*sunzētountes tōi Stephanōi*). Present active participle of *sunzēteō*, to question together as the two on the way to Emmaus did (Luke 24:15). Such interruptions were common with Jews. They give a skilled speaker great opportunity for reply if he is quick in repartee. Evidently Stephen was fully equipped for the emergency. One of their synagogues had men from Cilicia in it, making it practically certain that young Saul of Tarsus, the brilliant student of Gamaliel, was present and tried his wits with Stephen. His ignominious defeat may be one explanation of his zest in the stoning of Stephen (Acts 8:1).

10. *They were not able to withstand* (*ouk ischuon antistēnai*). Imperfect active of *ischuō*, to have strength, and ingressive second aorist active (intransitive) infinitive of *anthistēmi*. They continued unable (without strength enough) to take a stand against. Stephen knocked them down, Saul included, as fast as they got up. Stephen was like a battery charged and in action. *The wisdom and spirit* (*tēi sophiāi kai pneumati*). Dative case. They stood up against Stephen's wisdom and the Holy Spirit "by whom he spoke" (*hōi elalei*). Instrumental case and the relative agrees with "Spirit." He kept on speaking so (*elalei*, imperfect active). It was a desperate situation.

11. *Then they suborned men* (*tote hupebalon andras*). Second aorist active indicative of *hupoballō*, old verb, but here only in the N.T., to put under like a carpet, to bring men under one's control by suggestion or by money. One recalls the plight of Caiaphas in the trial of Jesus when he sought false witnesses. *Subornaverunt.* They put these men forward in an underhand way for fraud. *Blasphemous words against Moses and God* (*blasphēma eis Mōusēn kai ton theon*). The punishment for blasphemy was stoning to

death. See Matt. 12:31 for discussion of the word *blasphē-mia, blasphēmeō, blasphēmos*, all in the N.T. from *blaptō*, to harm, and *phēmē*, speech, harmful speech, or *blax*, stupid, and *phēmē*. But the charge against Stephen was untrue. Please note that Moses is here placed before God and practically on a par with God in the matter of blasphemy. The purpose of this charge is to stir the prejudices of the people in the matter of Jewish rights and privileges. It is the Pharisees who are conducting this attack on Stephen while the Sadducees had led them against Peter and John. The position of Stephen is critical in the extreme for the Sadducees will not help him as Gamaliel did the apostles.

12. *They stirred up the people (sunekinēsan ton laon).* They shook the people together like an earthquake. First aorist active indicative of *sunkineō*, to throw into commotion. Old verb, but here only in the N.T. The elders and the scribes (Pharisees) are reached, but no word about the Sadducees. This is the first record of the hostility of the masses against the disciples (Vincent). *Came upon him (epistantes).* Second aorist (ingressive) active participle of *ephistēmi*. Rushed at him. *Seized (sunērpasan).* Effective aorist active of *sunarpazō* as if they caught him after pursuit.

13. *False witnesses (marturas pseudeis).* Just as Caiaphas did with Jesus. *Ceaseth not (ou pauetai).* Wild charge just like a false witness that Stephen talks in the synagogues against the law and the holy temple.

14. *We have heard him say (akēkoamen autou legontos).* The only direct testimony and evidently wrong. Curiously like the charge brought against Jesus before Caiaphas that he would destroy the temple and build it again in three days. Undoubtedly Stephen had said something about Christianity before as meant for others besides Jews. He had caught the spirit of Jesus about worship as shown to the woman at Sychar in John 4 that God is spirit and to be worshipped

by men anywhere and everywhere without having to come
to the temple in Jerusalem. It was inflammable material
surely and it was easy to misrepresent and hard to clear up.
This Jesus of Nazareth (*Iēsous ho Nazōraios houtos*). With
contempt.

15. *As if the face of an angel* (*hōsei prosōpon aggelou*).
Even his enemies saw that, wicked as they were. See Ex.
34:30 for the face of Moses when he came down from Sinai
(II Cor. 3:7). Page quotes Tennyson: "God's glory smote
him on the face." Where were Peter and John at this crisis?
Apparently Stephen stands alone before the Sanhedrin as
Jesus did. But he was not alone for he saw Jesus standing
at the right hand of God (Acts 7:56). There was little that
Peter and John could have done if they had been present.
Gamaliel did not interpose this time for the Pharisees were
behind the charges against Stephen, false though they were
as Gamaliel could have found out.

CHAPTER VII

1. *Are these things so?* (*ei tauta houtōs echei*). On this use of *ei* in a direct question see on 1:6. Literally "Do these things hold thus?" A formal question by the high priest like our "Do you plead guilty, or not guilty?" (Furneaux). The abrupt question of the high priest would serve to break the evident spell of the angelic look on Stephen's face. Two charges had been made against Stephen (1) speaking against the holy temple, (2) changing the customs which Moses had delivered. Stephen could not give a yes or no answer to these two charges. There was an element of truth in each of them and a large amount of error all mixed together. So he undertakes to explain his real position by the historical method, that is to say, by a rapid survey of God's dealing with the people of Israel and the Gentiles. It is the same method adopted by Paul in Pisidian Antioch (Acts 13:16ff.) after he had become the successor of Stephen in his interpretation of the universal mission of Christianity. If one is disposed to say that Luke made up this speech to suit Stephen's predicament, he has to explain how the style is less Lukan than the narrative portions of Acts with knowledge of Jewish traditions that a Greek would not be likely to know. Precisely how Luke obtained the data for the speech we do not know, but Saul heard it and Philip, one of the seven, almost certainly. Both could have given Luke help about it. It is even possible that some one took notes of this important address. We are to remember also that the speech was interrupted at the end and may not include all that Stephen meant to say. But enough is given to give us a good idea of how Stephen met the first charge "by showing that the worship of God is not confined to Jerusalem or the Jewish

temple" (Page).   Then he answers the second charge by
proving that God had many dealings with their fathers
before Moses came and that Moses foretold the coming of
the Messiah who is now known to be Jesus.   It is at this
point (verse 51) that Stephen becomes passionate and so
powerful that the wolves in the Sanhedrin lose all self-
control.   It is a great and masterful exposition of the world-
wide mission of the gospel of Christ in full harmony with
the Great Commission of Christ.   The apostles had been so
busy answering the Sadducees concerning the Resurrection
of Christ and maintaining their freedom to teach and preach
that they had not pushed the world-wide propaganda of the
gospel as Jesus had commanded after they had received the
Promise of the Father.   But Stephen had proclaimed the
same message of Christ and was now facing the same fate.
Peter's mind had been enlightened by the Holy Spirit so
that he could rightly interpret Joel and David in the light
of Pentecost.   "So Stephen read the history of the Old
Testament with new eyes in the light of the life and death of
Jesus" (Furneaux).

2. *Brethren and fathers* (*andres adelphoi kai pateres*).
The spectators (brethren) and members of the Sanhedrin
(fathers) as Paul in Acts 22:1.   *Hearken* (*akousate*).   First
aorist (ingressive) active imperative, Give me your attention
now.   *The God of glory* (*Ho theos tēs doxēs*).   The God characterized by glory (genitive case, genus or kind) as seen in
the Shekinah, the visible radiance of God.   Jesus is also
called "the Glory" = the Shekinah in James 2:1.   Cf. Ex.
25:22; 40:34; Lev. 9:6; Heb. 9:5.   By these words Stephen
refutes the charge of blasphemy against God in Acts 6:11.
Appeared (*ōphthē*).   First aorist passive indicative of *horaō*.
See on Luke 23:43.   Before there was temple or tabernacle
and away over in Mesopotamia (Ur of the Chaldees, Gen.
11:31), even before (*prin ē* with the infinitive) he dwelt in
Haran (*Charran*, or Carrae not far from Edessa, where

Crassus met death after his defeat by the Parthians b.c. 53).

3. *Which I shall shew thee* (*hēn an soi deixō*). Indefinite relative clause with *an* and the aorist active subjunctive (same form in first person singular as the future active indicative). Abraham followed on as God led him.

4. *When his father was dead* (*meta to apothanein auton*). *Meta* with the accusative of the articular infinitive and the accusative of general reference (*auton*), regular Greek idiom. In Gen. 11:32 it is stated that Terah died at Haran at the age of 205. There are various explanations of the discrepancy, but no one that seems certain. It is possible (Hackett, Felten) that Abraham is mentioned first in Gen. 11:26 because he became the most prominent and was really younger than Haran his brother who died before the first migration who was really sixty years older than Abraham. According to this view Terah was 130 years old at the birth of Abraham, leaving Abraham 75 at the death of Terah (205). *Wherein ye now dwell* (*eis hēn humeis nun katoikeite*). Note *eis* in the sense of *en* as often. Note also emphatic use of *humeis* (ye) and now (*nun*).

5. *Not so much as to set his foot on* (*oude bēma podos*). From Deut. 2:5. Old word from *bainō*, to go, to step. "Stepping of a foot," only instance of this original meaning in the N.T. From this it comes to mean a platform reached by steps, official seat of a judge (Matt. 27:19). The field purchased by Abraham (Gen. 23:9–17) was not a gift from God. *Promised* (*epēggeilato*). First aorist middle indicative of *epaggellō*, common verb. See Gen. 12:7; 17:8; 48:4 for this promise. So God appeared again to Abraham in a strange land. *In possession* (*eis kataschesin*). Late word, in LXX, and in N.T. only here and verse 45. From *katechō*, to hold back, then to hold fast (*or down*), to possess. It was fulfilled in the descendants of Abraham. *When as yet he had no child* (*ouk ontos autōi teknou*). Genitive absolute with negative *ouk* rather than *mē* to emphasize actual absence of a

child. He had only the promise of God about the land and
the child.

6. *On this wise* (*houtōs*). A free quotation from Gen. 15:
13. *Should sojourn* (*estai paroikon*). Shall be a sojourner,
Paroikos (*para*, beside, *oikos*, home), one dwelling near one's
home, but not of it, so a stranger, foreigner, old word, often
in LXX, temporary residence without full rights of citizenship (7:29; 13:17), and descriptive of Christians (Eph. 2:19;
I Peter 1:17; 2:11). *In a strange land* (*en gēi allotriāi*). In a
land not one's own, that belongs to another, alien as in Matt.
17:25f., which see. *Four hundred years* (*etē tetrakosia*). Accusative of duration of time. As in Gen. 15:13, but a round
number as in Ex. 12:40 the time is 430 years. But in Gal.
3:17 Paul, following the LXX in Ex. 12:40, takes the 430
years to cover the period in Canaan and the stay in Egypt,
cutting the sojourn in Egypt to about half. Josephus gives
it both ways. Hackett suggests two solutions, one that
there were two ways of reckoning the period among the Jews
with no way of settling it, the other that by the 430 years in
Egypt the writers meant to include Canaan also as merely
the preliminary to the period in Egypt.

7. *Will I judge* (*krinō egō*). Future (accent on *ō*) active
indicative of *krinō* and *egō* (I) expressed is emphatic. *In
this place* (*en tōi topōi toutōi*). Quoted from Ex. 3:12 and
referring to Sinai or Horeb, but Stephen applies it to the
Promised Land.

8. *The covenant of circumcision* (*diathēkēn peritomēs*). A
covenant marked by (genitive) circumcision (no article) of
which circumcision is the sign (Rom. 4:11) as set forth in
Gen. 17:9-14. In the ancient Greek *diathēkē* was usually will
(Latin, *testamentum*) and *sunthēkē* was used for covenant
(*sun*, together, rather than *dia*, between). But the LXX and
the N.T. use *diathēkē* for covenant (will in Heb. 9:15f.) as
Lightfoot on Gal. 3:16 says: "The LXX translation and
New Testament writers probably preferred *diathēkē* as

better expressing the *free grace* of God than *sunthēkē.*"
And so (*kai houtōs*). After the covenant was made and as a
sign and seal of it.

9. *Moved with jealousy* (*zēlōsantes*). First aorist active
participle of *zēloō*, old verb from *zēlos* (Acts 5:17), to burn
or boil with zeal, and then with envy as here (17:5, etc.) and
Gen. 37:11.

10. *Delivered him out* (*exeilato auton ek*). First aorist
middle indicative of *exaireō*, old verb to take out, snatch out.
Note repetition of *ek*. *Pharaoh King of Egypt* (*Pharaō
basileōs Aiguptou*). Pharaoh is not a name, but a title, the
Egyptian *peraā* meaning great house.

11. *Found no sustenance* (*ouch hēuriskon chortasmata*). Imperfect active, kept on not finding. *Chortasmata* is from
chortazō, originally to feed with grass (*chortos*) or herbs. Old
word, but only here in the N.T. and includes food for both
men and animals. In Gen. 24:25, 32 it is fodder for the
cattle, a first necessity for owners of herds of cattle.

12. *That there was corn* (*onta sitia*). Participle (present
active of *eimi*) in indirect discourse, after *akousas*, "heard of
corn being in Egypt." *Sitia* is diminutive of *sitos* and means
grain (wheat, barley, not our maize or Indian corn), old
word also for provisions, victuals, here only in the N.T.
The first time (*prōton*). While Jacob himself remained in
Canaan before he went down to Egypt and died there
(verse 15f.).

13. *At the second time* (*en tōi deuterōi*). This expression
only here in the N.T. This second visit is recorded in Gen.
45:1ff. *Became manifest* (*phaneron egeneto*). In Gen. 41:12 the
fact that Joseph was a Hebrew had been incidentally mentioned to Pharaoh, but now it was made clear to him.

14. *Three-score and fifteen souls* (*en psuchais hebdomēkonta
pente*). Stephen follows the LXX which counts some grand-
children of Joseph and so makes it 75 whereas Gen. 46:26
has 66 and then the next verse makes it 70 including Jacob

and Joseph with his two sons. The use of *en* means "consisting in."

16. *They were carried over unto Shechem* (*metetethēsan eis Suchem*). First aorist passive of *metatithēmi*, only here in the N.T. in this sense of changing places. Jacob was buried in the cave of Machpelah (Gen. 50:13). The O.T. does not say where the sons of Jacob were buried save that Joseph was buried in Shechem (Josh. 24:32). Possibly only "our fathers" without Jacob is the subject of "were carried." *Which Abraham bought* (*hōi ōnēsato Abraam*). Hackett is sure that our present text is wrong. Hort notes some sixty "primitive errors" in the critical text of the N.T. It is possible that this is also one. If "Jacob" is substituted for "Abraham," the matter is cleared up. "It is quite as likely, judging *a priori*, that the word producing the error escaped from some early copyist as that so glaring an error was committed by Stephen" (Hackett). At any rate Abraham bought a burying-place, the cave of Machpelah, from Ephron the Hittite at Hebron (Gen. 23:16), while Jacob bought a field from the sons of Hamor at Shechem (Gen. 33:19; Josh. 24:32). Abraham had built an altar at Shechem when he entered Canaan (Gen. 12:6f.). It is possible, of course, that Abraham also bought the ground on which the altar stood. *In Shechem* (*en Suchem*). This is the reading of Aleph B C instead of the Textus Receptus *tou Suchem* which makes it "Hamar the father of Sichem." "In Shechem" is the true reading.

17. *Drew nigh* (*ēggizen*). Imperfect active, was drawing nigh.

18. *Another king* (*basileus heteros*). A different kind of king also, probably a king of the new dynasty after the shepherd kings had been expelled from Egypt. *Who knew not Joseph* (*hos ouk ēidei ton Iōsēph*). Second past perfect of *oida* used like an imperfect. Joseph's history and services meant nothing to the new king. "The previous dynasty

had been that of the Hyksos: the new king was Ahmes who drove out the Hyksos" (Knobel).

19. *Dealt subtilly* (*katasophisamenos*). First aorist middle participle of *katasophizomai*, late compound (*kata* and *sophizō*, old verb, to make wise, to become wise, then to play the sophist), perfective use of *kata*. In the LXX, but here only in the N.T. To use fraud, craft, deceit. *That they should cast out their babes* (*tou poiein ta brephē ektheta*). *Tou poiein* (genitive of the articular present infinitive)can be either design or result. The Revised Version here takes it as purpose while the Authorized as result. In either case Pharaoh required the Israelites to expose their children to death, a possible practice done voluntarily in heathen China and by heathen in so-called Christian lands. But the Israelites fought against such an iniquity. The word *ektheta* (exposed, cast out) is a verbal adjective from *ektithēmi*. It is an old word, but here only in the N.T. and not in the LXX. *To the end they might not live* (*eis to mē zōogoneisthai*). Purpose with *eis* and the articular infinitive (present middle). This compound verb is from *zōogonos* (from *zōos*, alive, and *genō*, to bear) and is used by late writers and the LXX. It is three times in the N.T. (here, Luke 17:33; I Tim. 6:13) in the sense to preserve alive.

20. *Exceeding fair* (*asteios tōi theōi*). Ethical dative, fair to God (as God looked at him). *Asteios* is from *astu*, city, and so means "of the city," with city manners and polish. Old word, only twice in the N.T. (here and Heb. 11:23) and both times about Moses and taken from Ex. 2:2. *He was nourished* (*anetraphē*). Second aorist passive indicative of *anatrephō*. He was brought up at home for three months in defiance of the new Pharaoh.

21. *When he was cast out* (*ektethentos autou*). Genitive absolute with first aorist passive participle cf *ektithēmi*. *Took up* (*aneilato*). Second aorist middle indicative (with first aorist vowel *a* instead of *e* as often in the *Koinē*) of

anaireō, common in the N.T. in the sense of take up and make away with, to kill as in verse 28, but here only in the N.T. in the original sense of taking up from the ground and with the middle voice (for oneself). Quoted here from Ex. 2:5. The word was used of old for picking up exposed children as here. Vincent quotes Aristophanes (*Clouds,* 531): "I exposed (the child), and some other women, having taken it, adopted (*aneileto*) it." Vulgate has *sustulit.* "Adopted" is the idea here. "After the birth of a child the father took it up to his bosom, if he meant to rear it; otherwise it was doomed to perish" (Hackett). *Nourished him for her own son (anethrepsato auton heautēi eis huion).* Literally, "she nursed him up for herself (*heautēi* besides middle voice) as a son." This use of *eis* = as occurs in the old Greek, but is very common in the LXX as a translation of the Hebrew *le.* The tradition is that she designed Moses for the throne as the Pharaoh had no son (Josephus, *Ant.* ii. 9, 7).

22. *Was instructed (epaideuthē).* First aorist passive indicative of *paideuō,* to train a child (*pais*), the usual idea in ancient Greek as here. The notion of chastisement (Heb. 12:6) is also in the old Greek and especially in the LXX and the N.T. Here with instrumental case (*pasēi sophiāi*) or the locative. The accusative would usually be retained after this verb. The priestly caste in Egypt was noted for their knowledge of science, astronomy, medicine, and mathematics. This reputation was proverbial (I Kings 4:30). Modern discoveries have thrown much light on the ancient civilization of Egypt. Moses, like Paul, was a man of the schools. *Mighty in his words and works (dunatos en logois kai ergois autou).* The same phrase used of Jesus in Luke 24:19. The adjective *dunatos* is employed of Apollos as an interpreter of the Scriptures (Acts 18:24). Moses did not have the rhetorical skill or eloquence of Aaron (Ex. 4:10), but his words like his deeds carried weight and power.

23. *When he was well-nigh forty years old* (*Hōs eplērouto autōi tessarakontaetēs chronos*). A rather awkward Greek idiom for the English: "When a forty year old time (same idiom in Acts 13:18 and only twice in the N.T.) was being fulfilled (*eplērouto,* imperfect passive) for him (dative case)." The life of Moses is divided into three periods of forty years each (in Egypt 40 years, in Midian 40, governed Israel 40, 120 when he died, Deut. 34:7). *It came into his heart* (*anebē epi tēn kardian autou*). Second aorist active indicative of *anabainō,* common verb. Came up as if from the lower deeps of his nature. This Hebrew image occurs in Jer. 3:16; Isa. 65:17; I Cor. 2:9. *To visit* (*episkepsasthai*). First aorist middle infinitive of *episkeptomai,* old verb to go to see for oneself, with his own eyes, to help if possible. Used of God visiting his people (Luke 7:16). Our "visit" is from Latin *video,* to see, *visito,* to go to see. During the Welsh mining troubles the Prince of Wales made a sympathetic visit to see for himself the actual condition of the coal miners. Moses desired to know first hand how his kinsmen were faring.

24. *Suffer wrong* (*adikoumenon*). Present passive participle of *adikeō.* By blows (Ex. 2:11). *Avenged* (*epoiēsen ekdikēsin*). First aorist active indicative of *poieō.* This idiom occurs in Luke 18:7 with *ekdikēsin* (this from *ekdikeō* and that from *ekdikos* without right or law *dikē* and then exacting law of right out of *ek* one, exacting vengeance). *Him that was oppressed* (*tōi kataponoumenōi*). Present passive articular participle in the dative case of *kataponeo,* to tire down with toil, to treat roughly, common in late Greek, in the N.T. only here and II Pet. 2:7 (sore distressed). The man was on the point of being overcome. *Smiting* (*pataxas*). First aorist active participle of *patassō,* in the old Greek the beat of the heart, only in the LXX and N.T. to smite a deadly blow as here like *plēssō.*

25. *He supposed* (*enomizen*). Imperfect active of *nomizō.* He was supposing, Stephen explains, when he smote the

Egyptian. *That his brethren understood* (*sunienai tous adelphous*). Present active infinitive of *suniēmi*, to send (put) together, to grasp, to comprehend, in indirect discourse with the accusative of general reference. *By his hand was giving them deliverance* (*dia cheiros autou didōsin sotērian autois*). Picturesque use of "hand" as in 2:23, present active indicative of *didōmi* retained in indirect discourse after imperfect *enomizen*. *But they understood not* (*hoi de ou sunēkan*). Page notes "the rhetorical power of these words" from Stephen. *Sunēkan* (first aorist indicative, *k* aorist) refers to *sunienai* just before.

26. *The day following* (*tēi epiousēi hēmerāi*). Locative case, "on the following day" (from *epeimi*, to come upon, to approach, present active participle *epiōn -ousa, -on*). Common phrase in old Greek both with *hēmera* (day) as here and without as 16:11. Only in Acts in the N.T. *Appeared* (*ōphthē*). First aorist passive indicative of *horaō* not with idea that only a vision but rather that it was sudden or unexpected. *As they strove* (*machomenois*). Present middle participle of *machomai*, actually fighting. *Would have set them at one again* (*sunēllassen autous eis eirēnen*). Better, he tried to reconcile them (or change them into peace). It is the conative imperfect active as in Matt. 3:14 of *sunallassō*, only here in the N.T. though common in the old Greek. Vulgate has *reconciliabat*. The usual word in the N.T. for reconcile is *katallassō*. *Do ye wrong one to another* (*adikeite allēlous*). The same word used in verse 24 of the wrong done one of the Hebrews by the Egyptian, but here both are "brethren."

27. *Thrust him away* (*apōsato auton*). First aorist middle indicative (*Koiné* for Attic *apeōsato*) of *apōtheō*, to push away from oneself in middle voice as here, common in old Greek. Again in verse 39; 13:46; Rom. 11:1; I Tim. 1:19. It is always the man who is doing the wrong who is hard to reconcile.

28. *Wouldest thou kill me?* (*mē anelein me su theleis*). Expecting the answer no, but a thrust direct at Moses, Do you wish to kill me (note *me su* right together, *me thou*). See Ex. 2:14 quoted by Stephen.

29. *Sojourner* (*paroikos*). Temporary dweller (cf. Abraham in verse 6) in Midian though for forty years.

30. Sentence begins with genitive absolute again. *In a flame of fire in a bush* (*en phlogi puros batou*). Horeb in Ex. 3:1; but Sinai and Horeb were "probably peaks of one mountain range" (Page), Horeb "the mountain of the dried-up ground," Sinai "the mountain of the thorns." Literally, "in the flame of fire of a bush" (two genitives, *puros* and *batou* dependent on *phlogi*, flame). Descriptive genitives as in 9:15; II Thess. 1:8. *Batos* (bush) is the wild acacia (*mimosa nilotica*). In Ex. 3:20 it is Jehovah who speaks. Hence "angel" here with Stephen is understood to be the Angel of the Presence, the Eternal Logos of the Father, the Angel of Jehovah.

31. *The sight* (*to horama*). Used of visions in the N.T. as in Matt. 17:9. *As he drew near* (*proserchomenou autou*). Genitive absolute with present middle participle of *proserchomai*. *A voice of the Lord* (*phōnē kuriou*). Here the angel of Jehovah of verse 30 is termed Jehovah himself. Jesus makes powerful use of these words in his reply to the Sadducees in defence of the doctrine of the resurrection and the future life (Mark 12:26, Matt. 22:32; Luke 20:37f.) that God here describes himself as the God of the living. *Trembled* (*entromos genomenos*). Literally, becoming tremulous or terrified. The adjective *entromos* (*en*, *tromos* from *tremō*, to tremble, to quake) occurs in Plutarch and the LXX. In the N.T. only here and Acts 16:29. *Durst not* (*ouk etolma*). Imperfect active, was not daring, negative conative imperfect.

33. *Holy ground* (*gē hagia*). The priests were barefooted when they ministered in the temple. Moslems enter their mosques barefooted today. Cf. Josh. 5:15. *Sandal* (*hup-*

odēma, bound under) is here "a distributive singular" (Hackett). Even the ground near the bush was "holy," a fine example for Stephen's argument.

34. *I have surely seen (idōn eidon)*. Imitation of the Hebrew infinitive absolute, (Ex. 3:7) "Seeing I saw" (cf. Heb. 6:14). *The affliction (tēn kakōsin)*. From *kakoō*, to treat evilly (from *kakos*, evil). Old word, here only in the N.T. and from Ex. 3:7. *Groaning (stenagmou)*. Old word from *stenazō*, to sigh, to groan. In the N.T. only here and Rom. 8:26. Root *sten* in our word stentorian. *I am come down (katebēn)*. Second aorist active indicative of *katabainō*, I came down. *To deliver (exelesthai)*. Second aorist middle infinitive of *exaireō*, to take out for myself. *I will send (aposteilō)*. First aorist active subjunctive (hortatory of *apostellō*, "Let me send").

35. *This Moses (Touton ton Mōusēn)*. Rhetorical repetition follows this description of Moses (five times, anaphora, besides the use here, six cases of *houtos* here about Moses: verse 35 twice, 36, 37, 38, 40). Clearly Stephen means to draw a parallel between Moses and Jesus. They in Egypt *denied (ērnēsanto)* Moses as now you the Jews denied (*ērnēsasthe*, 3:13) Jesus. Those in Egypt scouted Moses as "ruler and judge" (verses 27 and 35, *archonta kai dikastēn*) and God "hath sent" (*apestalken*, perfect active indicative, state of completion) Moses "both a ruler and a deliverer" (*archonta kai lutrōtēn*) as Jesus was to be (Luke 1:68; 2:38; Heb. 9:12; Tit. 2:14). "Ransomer" or "Redeemer" (*lutrōtēs*) is not found elsewhere, *lutron* (ransom), *lutroō*, to ransom, and *lutrōsis*, ransoming or redemption, are found often. In Acts 5:31 Christ is termed "Prince and Saviour." *With the hand (sun cheiri)*. So the correct text. The Pharisees had accused Stephen of blaspheming "against Moses and God" (6:11). Stephen here answers that slander by showing how Moses led the people out of Egypt in co-operation (*sun*) with the hand of the Angel of Jehovah.

37. *Like unto me* (*hōs eme*). This same passage Peter quoted to the crowd in Solomon's Porch (Acts 3:22). Stephen undoubtedly means to argue that Moses was predicting the Messiah as a prophet like himself who is no other than Jesus so that these Pharisees are in reality opposing Moses. It was a neat turn.

38. *In the church in the wilderness* (*en tēi ekklēsiāi en tēi erēmōi*). Better rendered "congregation" here as in Heb. 2: 12 (Psa. 22:22), the people of Israel gathered at Mt. Sinai, the whole nation. Moses is here represented as receiving the law from an angel as in Heb. 2:2; Gal. 3:19 (Deut. 33:2, LXX) and so was a mediator (*mesitēs*) or middle man between the angel and the people whereas Jesus is the Mediator of a better covenant (Heb. 8:6). But Exodus does not speak of an angel. *Living oracles* (*logia zōnta*). A *logion* is a little word (diminutive of *logos*). Common in the old Greek, LXX, Philo, in ecclesiastical writers for sayings of Christ, Papias (for instance) saying that Matthew wrote in Hebrew (Aramaic) "Logia of Jesus." Oxyrhynchus papyri fragments called "Logia of Jesus" are of much interest though only fragments. The Greeks used it of the "oracles" or brief sayings from Delphi. In the N.T. the word occurs only four times (Acts 7:38; Rom. 3:2; Heb. 5:12; I Pet. 4:11). Here the participle *zōnta*, living, is the same used by Peter (I Peter 2:4f.), stone (*lithos*) of Christ and Christians. The words from God to Moses are still "living" today. In I Peter 4:11 the word is applied to one who speaks *logia theou* (oracles of God). In Rom. 3:2 Paul refers to the substance of the law and of prophecy. In Heb. 5:12 the writer means the substance of the Christian religious teaching.

39. *To whom* (*hōi*). That is Moses, this Moses. *Would not be* (*ouk ēthelēsan genesthai*). Aorist active, negative aorist, were unwilling to become (*genesthai*) obedient. *Thrust him from them* (*apōsanto*). Indirect middle of the very verb used of the man (verse 27) who "thrust" Moses away from

him. *Turned back* (*estraphēsan*). Second aorist passive indicative of *strephō*, to turn. They yearned after the fleshpots of Egypt and even the gods of Egypt. It is easy now to see why Stephen has patiently led his hearers through this story. He is getting ready for the home-thrust.

40. *Gods which shall go before us* (*theous hoi proporeusontai hēmōn*). Ex. 32:1. As guides and protectors, perhaps with some allusion to the pillar of fire and of cloud that had gone before them (Ex. 13:21). The future indicative here with *hoi* (relative) expresses purpose. *We wot not* (*ouk oidamen*). We do not know. How quickly they had forgotten both God and Moses while Moses was absent in the mount with God. *Become of him* (*egeneto autōi*). Happened to him. "This" (*houtos*) here is a contemptuous allusion to Moses by the people.

41. *They made a calf* (*emoschopoiēsan*). First aorist active indicative of *moschopoieō*, here only in the N.T. and unknown elsewhere. The LXX (Ex. 32:3) has *epoiēse moschon* from which phrase the word is evidently made. Aaron made the calf, but so did the people (Ex. 32:35). *The idol* (*tōi eidōlōi*). Stephen calls it by the right name. The people said it was their way of worshipping Jehovah! So the Egyptians worshipped the bull Apis at Memphis as the symbol of Osiris (the sun). They had another sacred bull Mnevis at Leontopolis. *Eidōlon* (from *eidos*, form or figure) is the image or likeness of anything. The heathen worship the god through the image or idol. *Rejoiced* (*euphrainonto*). Imperfect, middle, kept on rejoicing (Ex. 32:6, 18) or making merry.

42. *Gave them up* (*paredōken*). First aorist active indicative of *paradidōmi*. This same form occurs three times like clods on a coffin in a grave in Rom. 1:24, 26, 28 where Paul speaks of God giving the heathen up to their lusts. *To serve the host of heaven* (*latreuein tēi stratiāi tou ouranou*). The verb *latreuō* is used of the worship of God (Matt. 4:10) as well as of idols as here (from *latron*, hire, *latris*, hireling, then

to serve). But the worship of the host of heaven (Deut. 17:3; II Kings 17:16; 21:3; II Chron. 33:3, 5; Jer. 8:2; 19:13) is Sabaism or worship of the host (*stratia*) of heaven (sun, moon, and stars) instead of the Lord of hosts. This star-worship greatly injured the Jews. *In the book of the prophets* (*en biblōi tōn prophētōn*). That is the twelve minor prophets which the Jews counted as one book (cf. Acts 13:40). This quotation is from Amos 5:25-27. The greater prophets were Isaiah, Jeremiah, Ezekiel. *Slain beasts* (*sphagia*). Here only in the N.T. (from Amos 5:25) *sphagē*, slaughter, *sphazō*, to slay.

43. *The tabernacle of Moloch* (*tēn skēnēn tou Moloch*). Or tent of Moloch which they took up after each halt instead of the tabernacle of Jehovah. Moloch was the god of the Amorites to whom children were offered as live sacrifices, an ox-headed image with arms outstretched in which children were placed and hollow underneath so that fire could burn underneath. *The star of the god Rephan* (*to astron tou theou Rompha*). Spelled also Romphan and Remphan. Supposed to be Coptic for the star Saturn to which the Egyptians, Arabs, and Phoenicians gave worship. But some scholars take the Hebrew *Kiyyoon* to mean statues and not a proper name at all, "statues of your gods" carried in procession, making "figures" (*tupous*) with both "tabernacle" and "star" which they carried in procession. *I will carry* (*metoikiō*). Attic future of *metoikisō* from *metoikizō*. *Beyond Babylon* (*epekeina Babulōnos*). The Hebrew and the LXX have "beyond Damascus." An adverbial preposition (*ep' ekeina* with *merē* understood) used in the old Greek and the LXX with the ablative case and meaning "beyond." Here only in the N.T. in quotation from Amos. 5:27.

44. *The tabernacle of the testimony* (*hē skēnē tou marturiou*). Probably suggested by the mention of "the tabernacle of Moloch" (verse 43). See on Matt. 17:4 for discussion of *skēnē* (from *skia*, shadow, root *ska*, to cover). This first sanctuary was not the temple, but the tent in the

wilderness. "Stephen passes on from the conduct of the Israelites to his other argument that God is not necessarily worshipped in a particular spot" (Page). *According to the figure* (*kata ton tupon*). According to the type or pattern. *Tupos* is from *tupto*, to strike, to smite, and is the print of the blow (John 20:25), then the figure formed by a blow or impression like our type, a model or example. Quoted from Ex. 25:40. Common word in the old Greek. *That he had seen* (*hon heōrakei*). Past perfect active of *horaō*, to see (double reduplication).

45. *Which* (*hēn*). Agreeing with *skēnēn*, not with *tupon*. *In their turn* (*diadexamenoi*). First aorist middle participle of *diadechomai*, to receive through another, to receive in sucession or in turn. Late Greek, only here in N.T. Deissmann (*Bible Studies*, p. 115) argues from a second century B.C. papyrus that *diadochos* means rather deputy or court official than successor. *With Joshua* (*meta Iēsou*). With Jesus, the Greek form of Joshua (contracted from Jehoshua, Matt. 1:21), as in Heb. 4:8. *When they entered on the possession of the nations* (*en tēi kataschesei tōn ethnōn*). Literally "in (or at the time of) the possession of the nations." See on 7:5 for the only other N.T. instance of *kataschesis*. *Which* (*hōn*). The nations, genitive by attraction to case of *ethnōn*. *Thrust out* (*exōsen*). First aorist active indicative of *exōtheō*, to push out, common verb, here, only in N.T. save some MSS. in Acts 27:39.

46. *Asked* (*eitēsato*). Aorist middle (indirect) indicative, asked for himself (as a favour to himself). Cf. II Sam. 7:2f. *A habitation* (*skēnōma*). Like Psa. 132:5, but it was a house that David proposed to build (II Sam. 7:2), not a tent (*skēnē*) which already existed. *Skēnōma* here means a more permanent abode (*oikon*, house, in verse 47), though from the same root as *skēnē*.

48. *Howbeit* (*all'*). By contrast with what Solomon did and David planned. Note emphatic position of "not"

(*all' ouch*), "But not does the Most High dwell." The presence of the Most High is not confined in any building, even one so splendid as Solomon's Temple as Solomon himself foresaw and acknowledged in his prayer (I Kings 8:27; II Chron. 6:18). *In houses made with hands* (*en cheiropoiētois*). No word here for "houses" or "temples" in correct text (*naois* temples in Textus Receptus). Literally, "In things made with hands" (*cheir*, hand, *poiētos*, verbal adjective of *poieō*). It occurs in Mark 14:58 of the temple and of the sanctuary of Moab (Isa. 16:12). It occurs also in Acts 17:24; Heb. 9:11, 24; Eph. 2:11. Common in the old Greek. *The prophet* (*ho prophētēs*). Isa. 66:1. Isaiah taught plainly that heaven is God's throne.

49. *What manner of house* (*Poion oikon*). What sort of a house? This interrogative is sometimes scornful as in 4:7 and Luke 6:32ff. (Page). So Stephen shows by Isaiah that Solomon was right that the temple was not meant to "confine" God's presence and that Jesus had rightly shown that God is a spirit and can be worshipped anywhere by any individual of any race or land. It is a tremendous argument for the universality and spirituality of Christianity free from the shackles of Jewish racial and national limitations, but its very strength only angered the Sanhedrin to desperation.

51. *Stiffnecked* (*sklērotrachēloi*). From *sklēros* (hard) and *trachēlos*, neck, both old words, but this compound only in the LXX and here alone in the N.T. Critics assume that Stephen was interrupted at this point because of the sharp tone of the speech. That may be true, but the natural climax is sufficient explanation. *Uncircumcised in heart* (*aperitmētoi kardiais*). Late adjective common in LXX and here only in the N.T. Verbal of *peritemnō*, to cut around and *a* privative. Both of these epithets are applied to the Jews in the O.T. (Ex. 32:9; 33:3, 5; 34:9; Lev. 26:41; Deut. 9:6; Jer. 6:10). *Kardiais* is locative plural like *ōsin* (ears),

but some MSS. have genitive singular *kardias* (objective genitive). No epithet could have been more galling to these Pharisees than to be turned "uncircumcised in heart" (Rom. 2:29). They had only the physical circumcision which was useless. *Ye always* (*humeis aei*). Emphatic position of *humeis* and "always" looks backward over the history of their forefathers which Stephen had reviewed. *Resist* (*antipiptete*). Old word to fall against, to rush against. Only here in the N.T., but used in the O.T. which is here quoted (Numb. 27:14). Their fathers had made "external worship a substitute for spiritual obedience" (Furneaux). Stephen has shown how God had revealed himself gradually, the revelation sloping upward to Christ Jesus. "And as he saw his countrymen repeating the old mistake—clinging to the present and the material, while God was calling them to higher spiritual levels—and still, as ever, resisting the Holy Spirit, treating the Messiah as the patriarchs had treated Joseph, and the Hebrews Moses—the pity of it overwhelmed him, and his mingled grief and indignation broke out in words of fire, such as burned of old on the lips of the prophets" (Furneaux). Stephen, the accused, is now the accuser, and the situation becomes intolerable to the Sanhedrin.

52. *Which of the prophets* (*tina tōn prophētōn*). Jesus (Luke 11:47 and Matt. 23:29-37) had charged them with this very thing. Cf. II Chron. 36:16. *Which shewed before* (*prokataggeilantas*). The very prophets who foretold the coming of the Messiah their fathers killed. *The coming* (*tēs eleuseōs*). Not in ancient Greek or LXX and only here in the N.T. (in a few late writers). *Betrayers* (*prodotai*). Just like Judas Iscariot. He hurled this old biting word at them. In the N.T. only here and Luke 6:16; II Tim. 3:4. It cut like a knife. It is blunter than Peter in Acts 3:13. *Murderers* (*phoneis*). The climax with this sharp word used of Barabbas (3:14).

53. *Ye who* (*hoitines*). The very ones who, *quippe qui*,

often in Acts when the persons are enlarged upon (8:15; 9:35; 10:41, 47). *As it was ordained by angels* (*eis diatagas aggelōn*). About angels see on 7:38. *Diatagē* (from *diatassō*, to arrange, appoint) occurs in late Greek, LXX, inscriptions, papyri, Deissmann, *Light from the Ancient East*, pp. 89ff., and in N.T. only here and Rom. 13:2. At (or as) the appointment of angels (cf. Matt. 10:41; 12:41 for this use of *eis*). *And kept it not* (*kai ouk ephulaxate*). Like a whip-cracker these words cut to the quick. They gloried in possessing the law and openly violated it (Rom. 2:23).

54. *When they heard* (*akouontes*). Present active participle of *akouō*, while hearing. *They were cut to the heart* (*dieprionto tais kardiais*). See 5:33 where the same word and form (imperfect passive of *diapriō*) is used of the effect of Peter's speech on the Sadducees. Here Stephen had sent a saw through the hearts of the Pharisees that rasped them to the bone. *They gnashed on him with their teeth* (*ebruchon tous odontas ep' auton*). Imperfect (inchoative) active of *bruchō* (Attic *brukō*), to bite with loud noise, to grind or gnash the teeth. Literally, They began to gnash their teeth at (*ep'*) him (just like a pack of hungry, snarling wolves). Stephen knew that it meant death for him.

55. *And Jesus standing* (*kai Iēsoun hestōta*). Full of the Holy Spirit, gazing steadfastly into heaven, he saw God's glory and Jesus "standing" as if he had risen to cheer the brave Stephen. Elsewhere (save verse 56 also) he is pictured as sitting at the right hand of God (the Session of Christ) as in Matt. 26:64; Mark 16:19; Acts 2:34; Eph. 1:20; Col. 3:1; Heb. 1:3.

56. *Opened* (*diēnoigmenous*). Perfect passive predicate participle of *dianoignumi* (cf. Matt. 3:16 = Luke 3:21). *The son of man* (*ton huion tou anthrōpou*). Elsewhere in the N.T. in Christ's own words. Here Stephen may refer to the words of Jesus as preserved in Matt. 26:64.

57. *Stopped their ears* (*suneschon ta ōta autōn*). Second

aorist active of *sunechō*, to hold together. They held their ears together with their hands and affected to believe Stephen guilty of blasphemy (cf. Matt. 26:65). *Rushed upon him with one accord (hōrmēsan homothumadon ep' auton)*. Ingressive aorist active indicative of *hormaō*, to rush impetuously as the hogs did down the cliff when the demons entered them (Luke 8:33). No vote was taken by the Sanhedrin. No scruple was raised about not having the right to put him to death (John 8:31). It may have taken place after Pilate's recall and before his successor came or Pilate, if there, just connived at such an incident that did not concern Rome. At any rate it was mob violence like modern lynching that took the law into the hands of the Sanhedrin without further formalities. *Out of the city (ek tēs poleōs)*. To keep from defiling the place with blood. But they sought to kill Paul as soon as they got him out of the temple area (Acts 21:30f.). *Stoned (elithoboloun)*. Imperfect active indicative of *lithoboleō*, began to stone, from *lithobolos* (*lithos*, stone, *ballō*, to throw), late Greek verb, several times in the N.T. as Luke 13:34. Stoning was the Jewish punishment for blasphemy (Lev. 24:14–16). *The witnesses (hoi martures)*. The false testifiers against Stephen suborned by the Pharisees (Acts 6:11, 13). These witnesses had the privilege of casting the first stones (Deut. 13:10; 17:7) against the first witness for Christ with death (*martyr* in our modern sense of the word). *At the feet of a young man named Saul (para tous podas neaniou kaloumenou Saulou)*. Beside (*para*) the feet. Our first introduction to the man who became the greatest of all followers of Jesus Christ. Evidently he was not one of the "witnesses" against Stephen, for he was throwing no stones at him. But evidently he was already a leader in the group of Pharisees. We know from later hints from Saul (Paul) himself that he had been a pupil of Gamaliel (Acts 22:3). Gamaliel, as the Pharisaic leader in the Sanhedrin, was probably on hand to hear the accusations against Stephen by the Pharisees. But, if so, he does not raise his voice against this mob violence. Saul does not seem to be aware that he is going contrary to the views of his master, though pupils often go further than their teachers.

59. *They stoned* (*elithoboloun*). Same verb and tense repeated, they kept on stoning, they kept it up as he was calling upon the Lord Jesus and making direct prayer to him as "Lord Jesus" (*Kurie Iēsou*). *Receive my spirit* (*dexai to pneuma mou*). Aorist middle imperative, urgency, receive it now. Many have followed Stephen into death with these words upon their dying lips. Sec. 9:14, 21, 22:16.

60. *Kneeled down* (*theis ta gonata*). Second aorist active participle of *tithēmi*, placing the knees (on the ground). This idiom is not in the old Greek for kneeling, but Luke has it five times (Luke 22:41; Acts 7:60; 9:40; 22:36; 21:5) and Mark once (15:19). Jesus was standing at the right hand of God and Stephen knelt before him in worship and called on him in prayer. *Lay not this sin to their charge* (*mē stēsēis autois tautēn tēn hamartian*). First aorist (ingressive) active subjunctive with *mē*, regular Greek idiom, Place not to them or against them (dative *autois*) this sin. The very spirit of Jesus towards his enemies as he died upon the Cross (Luke 23:34). *He fell asleep* (*ekoimēthē*). First aorist passive indicative of *koimaō*, to put to sleep. Old verb and the metaphor of sleep for death is common in all languages, but it is peculiarly appropriate here as Jesus used it of Lazarus. See also Acts 13:36; I Cor. 15:18, etc. Our word cemetery (*koimētērion*) is the sleeping place of the dead. Knowling calls *ekoimēthē* here "a picture word of rest and calmness which stands in dramatic contrast to the rage and violence of the scene."

CHAPTER VIII

1. *Was consenting (ēn suneudokōn)*. Periphrastic imperfect of *suneudokeō*, a late double compound (*sun, eu, dokeō*) that well describes Saul's pleasure in the death (*anairesis*, taking off, only here in the N.T., though old word) of Stephen. For the verb see on Luke 23:32. Paul himself will later confess that he felt so (Acts 22:20), coolly applauding the murder of Stephen, a heinous sin (Rom. 1:32). It is a gruesome picture. Chapter VII should have ended here. *On that day (en ekeinēi tēi hēmerāi)*. On that definite day, that same day as in 2:41. *A great persecution (diōgmos megas)*. It was at first persecution from the Sadducees, but this attack on Stephen was from the Pharisees so that both parties are now united in a general persecution that deserves the adjective "great." See on Matt. 13:21 for the old word *diōgmos* from *diōkō*, to chase, hunt, pursue, persecute. *Were all scattered abroad (pantes diesparēsan)*. Second aorist passive indicative of *diaspeirō*, to scatter like grain, to disperse, old word, in the N.T. only in Acts 8:1, 4; 11:19. *Except the apostles (plēn tōn apostolōn)*. Preposition *plēn* (adverb from *pleon*, more) with the ablative often in Luke. It remains a bit of a puzzle why the Pharisees spared the apostles. Was it due to the advice of Gamaliel in Acts 5:34–40? Or was it the courage of the apostles? Or was it a combination of both with the popularity of the apostles in addition?

2. *Devout (eulabeis)*. Only four times in the N.T. (Luke 2:25; Acts 2:5; 8:2; 22:12). Possibly some non-Christian Jews helped. The burial took place before the Christians were chiefly scattered. *Buried (sunekomisan)*. Aorist active indicative of *sunkomizō*, old verb to bring together, to collect, to join with others in carrying, to bury (the whole

funeral arrangements). Only here in the N.T. *Lamentation* (*kopeton*). Late word from *koptomai*, to beat the breast, in LXX, Plutarch, etc., only here in the N.T.

3. *Laid waste* (*elumaineto*). Imperfect middle of *lumainomai*, old verb (from *lumē*, injury), to dishonour, defile, devastate, ruin. Only here in the N.T. Like the laying waste of a vineyard by a wild boar (Psa. 79:13). Picturesque description of the havoc carried on by Saul now the leader in the persecution. He is victor over Stephen now who had probably worsted him in debate in the Cilician synagogue in Jerusalem. *Into every house* (*kata tous oikous*). But Luke terms it "the church" (*tēn ekklēsian*). Plainly not just an "assembly," but an organized body that was still "the church" when scattered in their own homes, "an unassembled assembly" according to the etymology. Words do not remain by the etymology, but travel on with usage. *Haling* (*surōn*). Literally, dragging forcibly (=hauling). Present active participle of *surō*, old verb. *Men and women* (*andras kai gunaikas*). A new feature of the persecution that includes the women. They met it bravely as through all the ages since (cf. 9:2; 22:4). This fact will be a bitter memory for Paul always. *Committed* (*paredidou*). Imperfect active of *paradidōmi*, old verb, kept on handing them over to prison.

4. *They therefore* (*hoi men oun*). Demonstrative *hoi* as often (1:6, etc.) though it will make sense as the article with the participle *diasparentes*. The general statement is made here by *men* and a particular instance (*de*) follows in verse 5. The inferential particle (*oun*) points back to verse 3, the persecution by young Saul and the Pharisees. Jesus had commanded the disciples not to depart from Jerusalem till they received the Promise of the Father (1:4), but they had remained long after that and were not carrying the gospel to the other peoples (1:8). Now they were pushed out by Saul and began as a result to carry out the Great Commission for world conquest, that is those "scattered abroad"

(*diasparentes*, second aorist passive participle of *diaspeirō*). This verb means disperse, to sow in separate or scattered places (*dia*) and so to drive people hither and thither. Old and very common verb, especially in the LXX, but in the N.T. only in Acts 8:1, 4; 11:19. *Went about* (*diēlthon*). Constative second aorist active of *dierchomai*, to go through (from place to place, *dia*). Old and common verb, frequent for missionary journeys in the Acts (5:40; 8:40; 9:32; 11:19; 13:6). *Preaching the word* (*euaggelizomenoi ton logon*). Evangelizing or gospelizing the word (the truth about Christ). In 11:19 Luke explains more fully the extent of the labours of these new preachers of the gospel. They were emergency preachers, not ordained clergymen, but men stirred to activity by the zeal of Saul against them. The blood of the martyrs (Stephen) was already becoming the seed of the church. "The violent dispersion of these earnest disciples resulted in a rapid diffusion of the gospel" (Alvah Hovey).

5. *Philip* (*Philippos*). The deacon (6:5) and evangelist (21:8), not the apostle of the same name (Mark 3:18). *To the city of Samaria* (*eis tēn polin tēs Samarias*). Genitive of apposition. Samaria is the name of the city here. This is the first instance cited of the expansion noted in verse 4. Jesus had an early and fruitful ministry in Samaria (John 4), though the twelve were forbidden to go into a Samaritan city during the third tour of Galilee (Matt. 10:5), a temporary prohibition withdrawn before Jesus ascended on high (Acts 1:8). *Proclaimed* (*ekērussen*). Imperfect active, began to preach and kept on at it. Note *euaggelizomenoi* in verse 4 of missionaries of good news (Page) while *ekērussen* here presents the preacher as a herald. He is also a teacher (*didaskalos*) like Jesus. Luke probably obtained valuable information from Philip and his daughters about these early days when in his home in Caesarea (Acts 21:8).

6. *Gave heed* (*proseichon*). Imperfect active as in verses 10 and 11, there with dative of the person (*autōi*), here with

the dative of the thing (*tois legomenois*). There is an ellipse of *noun* (*mind*). They kept on giving heed or holding the mind on the things said by Philip, spell-bound, in a word. *When they heard* (*en tōi akouein autous*). Favourite Lukan idiom, *en* and the locative case of the articlar infinitive with the accusative of general reference "in the hearing as to them." *Which he did* (*ha epoiei*). Imperfect active again, which he kept on doing from time to time. Philip wrought real miracles which upset the schemes of Simon Magus.

7. *For many* (*polloi gar*). So the correct text of the best MSS., but there is an anacoluthon as this nominative has no verb with it. It was "the unclean spirits" that "came out" (*exērchonto*, imperfect middle). The margin of the Revised Version has it "came forth," as if they came out of a house, a rather strained translation. The loud outcry is like the demons cast out by Jesus (Mark 3:11; Luke 4:41). *Palsied* (*paralelumenoi*, perfect passive participle). Luke's usual word, loosened at the side, with no power over the muscles. Furneaux notes that "the servant was reaping where the Master had sown. Samaria was the mission field white for the harvest (John 4:35)." The Samaritans who had been bewitched by Simon are now carried away by Philip.

9. *Simon* (*Simōn*). One of the common names (Josephus, *Ant.* XX. 7, 2) and a number of messianic pretenders had this name. A large number of traditions in the second and third centuries gathered round this man and Baur actually proposed that the Simon of the Clementine Homilies is really the apostle Paul though Paul triumphed over the powers of magic repeatedly (Acts 13:6–12; 19:11–19), "a perfect absurdity" (Spitta, *Apostelgeschichte*, p. 149). One of the legends is that this Simon Magus of Acts is the father of heresy and went to Rome and was worshipped as a god (so Justin Martyr). But a stone found in the Tiber A.D. 1574 has an inscription to *Semoni Sanco Deo Fidio Sacrum* which is (Page) clearly to Hercules, Sancus being a Sabine name

for Hercules. This Simon in Samaria is simply one of the many magicians of the time before the later gnosticism had gained a foothold. "In his person Christianity was for the first time confronted with superstition and religious imposture, of which the ancient world was at this period full" (Furneaux). *Which beforetime used sorcery* (*proüpērchen mageuōn*). An ancient idiom (periphrastic), the present active participle *mageuōn* with the imperfect active verb from *proüparchō*, the idiom only here and Luke 23:12 in the N.T. Literally "Simon was existing previously practising magic." This old verb *mageuō* is from *magos* (a *magus*, seer, prophet, false prophet, sorcerer) and occurs here alone in the N.T. *Amazed* (*existanōn*). Present active participle of the verb *existanō*, later form of *existēmi*, to throw out of position, displace, upset, astonish, chiefly in the Gospels in the N.T. Same construction as *mageuōn*. *Some great one* (*tina megan*). Predicate accusative of general reference (infinitive in indirect discourse). It is amazing how gullible people are in the presence of a manifest impostor like Simon. The **Magi** were the priestly order in the Median and Persian empires and were supposed to have been founded by Zoroaster. The word *magoi* (*magi*) has a good sense in Matt. 2:1, but here and in Acts 13:6 it has the bad sense like our "magic."

10. *That power of God which is called Great* (*hē Dunamis tou theou hē kaloumenē Megalē*). Apparently here already the oriental doctrine of emanations or aeons so rampant in the second century. This "power" was considered a spark of God himself and Jerome (*in Matt. c. 24*) quotes Simon (Page) as saying: *Ego sum sermo Dei, . . . ego omnipotens, ego omnia Dei.* Simon claimed to *impersonate God.*

11. *Because that of long time he had amazed them with his sorceries* (*dia to hikanōi chronōi tais magiais exestakenai autous*). Causal use of *dia* with the accusative articular infinitive (perfect active Koiné form and transitive, *exestakenai*). Same verb as in verse 9 participle *existanōn* and in

verse 13 imperfect passive *existato* (cf. also 2:7 already). *Chronōi* is associative instrumental and *magiais* instrumental case.

12. *They were baptized* (*ebaptizonto*). Imperfect passive (repetition, from time to time), while *believed* (*episteusan*) is constative aorist antecedent to the baptism. Note dative case of Philip with *episteusan*. Note the gospel of Philip "concerning the kingdom of God, and the name of Jesus Christ."

13. *And Simon also himself believed* (*Ho de Simōn kai autos episteusen*). Note the same verb in the aorist tense *episteusen*. What did he believe? Evidently that Jesus was this "power of God" not himself (Simon). He saw that the miracles wrought by Philip in the name of Christ were genuine while he knew that his own were frauds. He wanted this power that Philip had to add to his own pretensions. "He was probably half victim of self-delusion, half conscious impostor" (Furneaux). He was determined to get this new "power," but had no sense of personal need of Jesus as Saviour for his sins. So he submitted to baptism (*baptistheis*, first aorist passive participle of *baptizō*), clear proof that baptism does not convey salvation. *He continued with Philip* (*ēn proskarterōn tōi Philippōi*). Periphrastic imperfect of the verb *proskartereō* (see on 2:46). He stuck to Philip (dative case) to find out the secret of his power. *Beholding* (*theōrōn*). Watching the signs and miracles (powers, *dunameis* that threw his "power" in the shade) as they were wrought (*ginomenas*, present middle participle of *ginomai*). The more he watched the more the wonder grew (*existato*). He had "amazed" (verse 9) the people by his tricks and he was himself more "amazed" than they by Philip's deeds.

14. *That Samaria had received* (*hoti dedektai hē Samaria*). The district here, not the city as in verse 5. Perfect middle indicative of *dechomai* retained in indirect discourse. It was a major event for the apostles for now the gospel was going

into Samaria as Jesus had predicted (1:8).   Though the Samaritans were nominally Jews, they were not held so by the people.   The sending of Peter and John was no reflection on Philip, but was an appropriate mission since "many Christian Jews would be scandalized by the admission of Samaritans" (Furneaux).   If Peter and John sanctioned it, the situation would be improved.   John had once wanted to call down fire from heaven on a Samaritan village (Luke 9:54).

15. *That they might receive* (*hopōs labōsin*).   Second aorist active subjunctive of *lambanō*, final clause with *hopōs*.   Did they wish the Samaritan Pentecost to prove beyond a doubt that the Samaritans were really converted when they believed?   They had been baptized on the assumption that the Holy Spirit had given them new hearts.   The coming of the Holy Spirit with obvious signs (cf. 10:44-48) as in Jerusalem would make it plain.

16. *He was fallen* (*ēn epipeptōkos*).   Periphrastic past perfect active of *epipiptō*, old verb.   The participle is neuter here because of the grammatical gender of *pneuma*, but the translation should be "he" (natural gender), not "it."   We should not use "it" for the Holy Spirit.   *Only they had been baptized* (*monon de babaptismenoi huperchon*).   Periphrastic past perfect passive of *baptizō* with *huparchō* (see verse 9 *proüpērchon*), instead of *ēsan*.   *Into the name* (*eis to onoma*).   Better, in the name (see on 2:38).

17. *Laid they their hands* (*epetithesan tas cheiras*).   Imperfect active, repetition.   The laying on of hands did not occur at the great Pentecost (2:4, 33) nor in 4:31; 10:44 nor is it mentioned in I Corinthians 12 and 14.   It is mentioned in Acts 6:7 about the deacons and in 13:3 when Barnabas and Saul left Antioch.   And in Saul's case it was Ananias who laid his hands on him (9:17).   Hence it cannot be concluded that the Holy Spirit was received only by the laying on of the hands of the apostles or by the hands of anyone.

The so-called practice of "confirmation" appeals to this passage, but inconclusively. *They received (elambanon).* Imperfect active, repetition as before and *pari passu* with the laying on of the hands.

18. *When Simon saw (Idōn de ho Simōn).* This participle (second aorist active of *horaō*) shows plainly that those who received the gift of the Holy Spirit spoke with tongues. Simon now saw power transferred to others. Hence he was determined to get this new power. *He offered them money (prosēnegken chrēmata).* Second aorist active indicative of *prospherō.* He took Peter to be like himself, a mountebank performer who would sell his tricks for enough money. Trafficking in things sacred like ecclesiastical preferments in England is called "Simony" because of this offer of Simon.

19. *Me also (kàmoi).* This is the whole point with this charlatan. He wants the power to pass on "this power." His notion of "The Holy Spirit" was on this low level. He regarded spiritual functions as a marketable commodity. Money "can buy diamonds, but not wisdom, or sympathy, or faith, or holiness" (Furneaux).

20. *Perish with thee (sun soi eiē eis apōleian).* Literally, Be with thee for destruction. Optative for a future wish. The use of *eis* with the accusative in the predicate is especially common in the LXX. The wish reveals Peter's indignation at the base offer of Simon. Peter was no grafter to accept money for spiritual power. He spurned the temptation. The natural meaning of Peter's language is that Simon was on the road to destruction. It is a warning and almost a curse on him, though verse 22 shows that there was still room for repentance. *To obtain (ktāsthai).* To acquire. Usual meaning of the present tense (infinitive middle) of *ktaomai.*

21. *Lot (klēros).* Same idea as "part" (*meris*), only as a figure. *Matter (logoi).* Literally, word or subject (as in Luke 1:4; Acts 15:6), the power of communicating the Holy

Spirit. This use of *logos* is in the ancient Greek. *Straight* (*eutheia*). Quotation from Psa. 78:37. Originally a mathematically straight line as in Acts 9:11, then moral rectitude as here.

22. *Wickedness* (*kakias*). Only here in Luke's writings, though old word and in LXX (cf. I Pet. 2:1, 16). *If perhaps* (*ei ara*). *Si forte.* This idiom, though with the future indicative and so a condition of the first class (determined as fulfilled), yet minimizes the chance of forgiveness as in Mark 11:13. Peter may have thought that his sin was close to the unpardonable sin (Matt. 12:31), but he does not close the door of hope. *The thought* (*hē epinoia*). Old Greek word from *epinoeō*, to think upon, and so purpose. Only here in the N.T.

23. *That thou art* (*se onta*). Participle in indirect discourse after *horō* (I see). *In the gall of bitterness* (*eis cholēn pikrias*). Old word from *cholas* either from *cheō*, to pour, or *chloē*, yellowish green, bile or gall. In the N.T. only in Matt. 27:34 and here. In LXX in sense of wormwood as well as bile. See Deut. 29:18; 32:32; Lam. 3:15; Job 16:14. "Gall and bitterness" in Deut. 29:18. Here the gall is described by the genitive *pikrias* as consisting in "bitterness." In Heb. 12:15 "a root of bitterness," a bitter root. This word *pikria* in the N.T. only here and Heb. 12:15; Rom. 3:14; Eph. 4:31. The "bond of iniquity" (*sundesmon adikias*) is from Isa. 58:6. Paul uses this word of peace (Eph. 4:3), of love (Col. 3:14), of the body (Col. 2:19). Peter describes Simon's offer as poison and a chain.

24. *Pray ye for me* (*Deēthēte humeis huper emou*). Emphasis on *humeis* (you). First aorist passive imperative. Simon is thoroughly frightened by Peter's words, but shows no sign of personal repentance or change of heart. He wants to escape the penalty for his sin and hopes that Peter can avert it. Peter had clearly diagnosed his case. He was an unconverted man in spite of his profession of faith and baptism.

There is no evidence that he ever changed his life at all. *Which* (*hōn*). Genitive by attraction of the accusative relative *ha* to case of the unexpressed antecedent *toutōn* (of those things), a common Greek idiom.

25. *They therefore* (*hoi men oun*). Demonstrative *hoi* with *men* (no following *de*) and the inferential *oun* (therefore) as often in Acts (1:6, etc.). *Returned* (*hupestrephon*). Imperfect active picturing the joyful journey of preaching (*euēggelizonto*, imperfect middle) to the Samaritan villages. Peter and John now carried on the work of Philip to the Samaritans. This issue was closed.

26. *Toward the South* (*kata mesēmbrian*). Old word from *mesos* and *hēmera*, midday or noon as in Acts 22:16, the only other example in the N.T. That may be the idea here also, though "towards the South" gets support from the use of *kata liba* in Acts 27:12. *The same is desert* (*hautē estin erēmos*). Probably a parenthetical remark by Luke to give an idea of the way. One of the ways actually goes through a desert. Gaza itself was a strong city that resisted Alexander the Great five months. It was destroyed by the Romans after war broke out with the Jews.

27. *A eunuch of great authority* (*eunouchos dunastēs*). Eunuchs were often employed by oriental rulers in high posts. *Dynasty* comes from this old word *dunastēs* used of princes in Luke 1:52 and of God in I Tim. 6:15. Eunuchs were not allowed to be Jews in the full sense (Deut. 23:1), but only proselytes of the gate. But Christianity is spreading to Samaritans and to eunuchs. *Candace* (*Kandakēs*). Not a personal name, but like Pharaoh and Ptolemy, the title of the queens of Ethiopia. This eunuch apparently brought the gospel to Ethiopia. *Treasure* (*gazēs*). Persian word, common in late Greek and Latin for the royal treasure, here only in the N.T. *For to worship* (*proskunēsōn*). Future active participle expressing purpose, a common idiom in

the ancient Greek, but rare in the N.T. (Robertson, *Grammar*, p. 1128).

28. *Was reading* (*aneginōsken*).   Imperfect active descriptive, not periphrastic like the two preceding verbs (was returning and sitting).   He was reading aloud as Philip "heard him reading" (*ēkousen auton anaginōskontos*), a common practice among orientals.   He had probably purchased this roll of Isaiah in Jerusalem and was reading the LXX Greek text.   See imperfect again in verse 32.

29. *Join thyself* (*kollēthēti*).   See this vivid word (be glued to, first aorist passive imperative) already in 5:13 and Luke 10:11; 15:15.   Philip probably jumped on the running board on the side of the chariot.

30. *Understandest thou what thou readest?* (*Ara ge ginōskeis ha anaginōskeis?*)   The interrogative particle *ara* and the intensive particle *ge* indicate doubt on Philip's part.   The play (*paranomasia*) upon the words in the Greek is very neat: *Do you know what you know again (read)?*   The verb for read (*anaginōsko*) means to know the letters again, recognize, read.   The famous comment of Julian about the Christian writings is often quoted: *Anegnōn, egnōn, kategnōn* (I read, I understood, I condemned).   The keen retort was: *Anegnōs, all' ouk egnōs, ei gar egnōs, ouk an kategnōs* (You read, but did not understand; for if you had understood, you would not have condemned).

31. *How can I, except some one shall guide me?* (*Pōs gar an dunaimēn ean me tis hodēgēsei me?*).   This is a mixed condition, the conclusion coming first belongs to the fourth class (undetermined with less likelihood of being determined) with *an* and the optative, but the condition (*ean*, instead of the usual *ei*, and the future indicative) is of the first class (determined or fulfilled.   Robertson, *Grammar*, p. 1022), a common enough phenomenon in the *Koiné*.   The eunuch felt the need of some one to guide (*hodēgeō* from *hodēgos*, guide, and that from *hodos*, way, and *hegeomai*, to lead).

32. *The place (hē periochē).* See the verb *periechei* so used in I Pet. 2:6. The word is used either of the section as in Codex A before the beginning of Mark or the contents of a passage. He was here reading one particular passage (Isa. 53:7f.). The quotation is from the LXX which has some variations from the Hebrew.

33. *Was taken away (ērthē).* First aorist passive indicative of *airō*, to take away. It is not clear what the meaning is here either in the Hebrew or the LXX. Knowling suggests that the idea is that justice was withheld, done away with, in his death, as it certainly was in the death of Christ.

34. *Of whom (peri tinos).* Concerning whom, a pertinent inquiry surely and one that troubles many critics today.

35. *Beginning from this scripture (arxamenos apo tēs graphēs tautēs).* As a text. Philip needed no better opening than this Messianic passage in Isaiah. *Preached unto him Jesus (euēggelisato autōi ton Iēsoun).* Philip had no doubt about the Messianic meaning and he knew that Jesus was the Messiah. There are scholars who do not find Jesus in the Old Testament at all, but Jesus himself did (Luke 24:27) as Philip does here. Scientific study of the Old Testament (historical research·) misses its mark if it fails to find Christ the Center of all history. The knowledge of the individual prophet is not always clear, but after events throw a backward light that illumines it all (I Pet. 1:11f.; II Pet. 1:19–21).

36. *What doth hinder me to be baptized? (Ti kōluei me baptisthēnai?).* Evidently Philip had said something about baptism following faith and conversion. Verse 37 is not a genuine part of Acts, a western addition. Later baptismal liturgies had it.

39. *Out of the water (ek tou hudatos).* Not from the edge of the water, but up out of the water as in Mark 1:10. *Caught away (hērpasen).* Suddenly and miraculously, for *harpazō*, like the Latin *rapio*, means to carry off. Cf. II Cor.

12:2; I Thess. 4:17. *Went on his way* (*eporeueto*). Kept on going, imperfect active.

40. *He preached the gospel* (*euēggelizeto*). Imperfect middle describing the evangelistic tour of Philip "till he came to Caesarea" (*heōs tou elthein auton*, genitive articular infinitive with the preposition *heōs* and the accusative of general reference) where he made his home and headquarters thereafter (Acts 21:28) and was known as the Evangelist.

CHAPTER IX

1. *Yet* (*eti*). As if some time elapsed between the death of Stephen as is naturally implied by the progressive persecution described in 8:3. The zeal of Saul the persecutor increased with success. *Breathing threatening and slaughter* (*enpneōn apeilēs kai phonou*). Present active participle of old and common verb. Not "breathing out," but "breathing in" (inhaling) as in Aeschylus and Plato or "breathing on" (from Homer on). The partitive genitive of *apeilēs* and *phonou* means that threatening and slaughter had come to be the very breath that Saul breathed, like a warhorse who sniffed the smell of battle. He breathed on the remaining disciples the murder that he had already breathed in from the death of the others. He exhaled what he inhaled. Jacob had said that "Benjamin shall ravin as a wolf" (Gen. 49:27). This greatest son of Benjamin was fulfilling this prophecy (Furneaux). The taste of blood in the death of Stephen was pleasing to young Saul (8:1) and now he revelled in the slaughter of the saints both men and women. In 26:11 Luke quotes Paul as saying that he was "exceedingly mad against them."

2. *Asked* (*ēitēsato*). First aorist middle indicative, the indirect middle, asked for himself (as a favour to himself). Felten notes that "Saul as a Pharisee makes request of a Sadducee" (the high priest) either Caiaphas if before A.D. 35, but if in 36 Jonathan, son of Caiaphas or if in 37 Theophilus, another son of Caiaphas. *Letters* (*epistolas*). Julius Ceasar and Augustus had granted the high priest and Sanhedrin jurisdiction over Jews in foreign cities, but this central ecclesiastical authority was not always recognized in every local community outside of Judea. Paul says that he received his authority to go to Damascus from the priests

(Acts 26:10) and "the estate of the elders" (22:5), that is the Sanhedrin. *To Damascus (eis Damaskon)*. As if no disciples of importance (outside the apostles in Jerusalem) were left in Judea. Damascus at this time may have been under the rule of Aretas of Arabia (tributary to Rome) as it certainly was a couple of years later when Saul escaped in a basket (II Cor. 11:32). This old city is the most enduring in the history of the world (Knowling). It is some 150 miles Northeast from Jerusalem and watered by the river Abana from Anti-Lebanon. Here the Jews were strong in numbers (10,000 butchered by Nero later) and here some disciples had found refuge from Saul's persecution in Judea and still worshipped in the synagogues. Paul's language in Acts 26:11 seems to mean that Damascus is merely one of other "foreign cities" to which he carried the persecution. *If he found (ean heurēi)*. Third class condition with aorist subjunctive retained after secondary tense (asked). *The Way (tēs hodou)*. A common method in the Acts for describing Christianity as the Way of life, absolutely as also in 19:9, 23; 22:4; 24:14, 22 or the way of salvation (16:17) or the way of the Lord (18:25). It is a Jewish definition of life as in Isa. 40:3 "the way of the Lord," Psa. 1:6 "the way of the righteous," "the way of the wicked." Jesus called himself "the way" (John 14:6), the only way to the Father. The so-called Epistle of Barnabas presents the Two Ways. The North American Indians call Christianity the Jesus Road. *That he might bring them bound (hopōs dedemenous agagēi)*. Final clause with *hopōs* (less common than *hina*) and aorist (effective) subjunctive (*agagēi*, reduplicated aorist of *agō*, common verb) and perfect passive participle (*dedemenous*) of *deō*, in a state of sheer helplessness like his other victims both men and women. Three times (8:3; 9:2; 22:4) this fact of persecuting women is mentioned as a special blot in Paul's cruelty (the third time by Paul himself) and one of the items in his being chief of sinners (I Tim. 1:15).

3. *As he journeyed (en tōi poreuesthai).* Luke's common idiom for a temporal clause (in the journeying), *en* with the locative articular middle infinitive. *Drew nigh (eggizein).* Present active infinitive, was drawing nigh. *Shone round about him (auton periēstrapsen).* First aorist (ingressive) active indicative of *periastraptō*, late compound verb common in LXX and Byzantine writers, here and 22:6 alone in the N.T. "A light from heaven suddenly flashed around him." It was like a flash of lightning. Paul uses the same verb in 22:5, but in 26:13 he employs *perilampsan* (shining around). There are numerous variations in the historical narrative of Saul's conversion in 9:3-18 and Luke's report of Paul's two addresses, one on the steps of the Tower of Antonia facing the murderous mob (22:6-16), the other before Festus and Agrippa (26:12-20). A great deal of capital has been made of these variations to the discredit of Luke as a writer as if he should have made Paul's two speeches conform at every point with his own narrative. This objection has no weight except for those who hold that Luke composed Paul's speeches freely as some Greek writers used to do. But, if Luke had notes of Paul's speeches or help from Paul himself, he naturally preserved the form of the two addresses without trying to make them agree with each other in all details or with his own narrative in chapter 9. Luke evidently attached great importance to the story of Saul's conversion as the turning point not simply in the career of the man, but an epoch in the history of apostolic Christianity. In broad outline and in all essentials the three accounts agree and testify to the truthfulness of the account of the conversion of Saul. It is impossible to overestimate the worth to the student of Christianity of this event from every angle because we have in Paul's Epistles his own emphasis on the actual appearance of Jesus to him as the fact that changed his whole life (I Cor. 15:8; Gal. 1:16f.). The variations that appear in the three accounts

do not mar the story, when rightly understood, as we shall see. Here, for instance, Luke simply mentions "a light from heaven," while in 22:6 Paul calls it "a great (*hikanon*) light" "about noon" and in 26:13 "above the brightness of the sun," as it would have to be "at midday" with the sun shining.

4. *He fell upon the earth* (*pesōn epi tēn gēn*). Second aorist active participle. So in 22:7 Paul says: "I fell unto the ground" (*epesa eis to edaphos*) using an old word rather than the common *gēn*. In 26:14 Paul states that "we were all fallen to the earth" (*pantōn katapesontōn hēmōn eis tēn gēn*, genitive absolute construction). But here in verse 7 "the men that journeyed with him stood speechless" (*histēkeisan eneoi*). But surely the points of time are different. In 26:14 Paul refers to the first appearance of the vision when all fell to the earth. Here in verse 7 Luke refers to what occurred after the vision when both Saul and the men had risen from the ground. *Saul, Saul* (*Saoul, Saoul*). The Hebrew form occurs also in 22:7 and 26:14 where it is expressly stated that the voice was in the Hebrew (Aramaic) tongue as also in 9:17 (Ananias). Deissmann (*Bible Studies*, p. 316) terms this use of *Saoul* "the historian's sense of liturgical rhythm." For the repetition of names by Jesus note Luke 10:41 (Martha, Martha), Luke 22:31 (Simon, Simon). *Me* (*me*). In persecuting the disciples, Saul was persecuting Jesus, as the words of Jesus in verse 5 made plain. Christ had already spoken of the mystic union between himself and his followers (Matt. 10:40; 25:40, 45; John 15:1–5). The proverb (Pindar) that Jesus quotes to Saul about kicking against the goad is genuine in 26:14, but not here.

5. *Lord* (*kurie*). It is open to question if *kurie* should not here be translated "Sir" as in 16:30 and in Matt. 21:29 (30); John 5:7; 12:21; 20:15; and should be so in John 9:36. It is hardly likely that at this stage Saul recognized Jesus as

Lord, though he does so greet him in 22:10 "What shall I
do, Lord?" Saul may have recognized the vision as from
God as Cornelius says "Lord" in 10:4. Saul surrendered
instantly as Thomas did (John 20:28) and as little Samuel
(I Sam. 3:9). This surrender of the will to Christ was the
conversion of Saul. He saw a real Person, the Risen Christ,
to whom he surrendered his life. On this point he never
wavered for a moment to the end.

6. The best MSS. do not have "trembling and astonished," and "What wilt thou have me to do, Lord?" The
Textus Receptus put these words in here without the authority of a Greek codex. See 22:10 above for the genuine text.
It shall be told thee (*lalēthēsetai*). Future passive indicative
of *laleō*. It is hardly likely that Luke records all that Jesus
said to Saul, but more was to come on his arrival in Damascus. Saul had received all that he could bear just now
(John 16:12). *What* (*hoti*). Rare in *Koinē* use of this indefinite neuter relative in an indirect question, the only example
in the N.T. (Robertson, *Grammar*, p. 731). Human agents
like Ananias can finish what Jesus by supernatural manifestation has here begun in Saul.

7. *That journeyed with him* (*hoi sunodeuontes autōi*). Not
in the older Greek, but in the *Koinē*, with the associative
instrumental. *Speechless* (*eneoi*). Mute. Only here in N.T.,
though old word. *Hearing the voice, but beholding no man*
(*akouontes men tēs phōnēs, mēdena de theōrountes*). Two
present active participles in contrast (*men, de*). In 22:9
Paul says that the men "beheld the light" (*to men phōs
etheasanto*), but evidently did not discern the person. Paul
also says there, "but they heard not the voice of him that
spake to me" (*tēn de phōnēn ouk ēkousan tou lalountos moi*).
Instead of this being a flat contradiction of what Luke says
in 9:7 it is natural to take it as being likewise (as with the
"light" and "no one") a distinction between the "sound"
(original sense of *phōnē* as in John 3:8) and the separate

words spoken. It so happens that *akouō* is used either with the accusative (the extent of the hearing) or the genitive (the specifying). It is possible that such a distinction here coincides with the two senses of *phōnē*. They heard the sound (9:7), but did not understand the words (22:9). However, this distinction in case with *akouō*, though possible and even probable here, is by no means a necessary one for in John 3:8 where *phōnēn* undoubtedly means "sound" the accusative occurs as Luke uses *ēkousen phōnēn* about Saul in Acts 9:4. Besides in 22:7 Paul uses *ēkousa phōnēs* about himself, but *ēkousa phōnēn* about himself in 26:14, interchangeably.

8. *He saw nothing* (*ouden eblepen*). Imperfect active indicative, was seeing nothing. "The glory of that light" (22:11) when he saw Jesus had blinded his eyes now wide open (*aneōigmenōn*, perfect passive participle of *anoigō* with double reduplication). The blindness was proof that something had happened to him and that it was no hallucination that he had seen the Risen Christ. Saul arose after the others were on their feet. *They led him by the hand* (*cheiragōgountes*). From *cheiragōgos* (*cheir*, hand and *agō*, to lead). Only here in the N.T., but in LXX and late writers though not in the old Greek. It was a pathetic picture to see the masterful Saul, victorious persecutor and conqueror of the disciples, now helpless as a child.

9 *Not seeing* (*mē blepōn*). The usual negative *mē* of the participle. It was a crisis for Saul, this sudden blindness for three days (*hēmeras treis*, accusative of extent of time). Later (Gal. 4:15) Paul has an affection of the eyes which may have been caused by this experience on the road to Damascus or at least his eyes may have been predisposed by it to weakness in the glare of the Syrian sun in the land where today so much eye trouble exists. He neither ate nor drank anything, for his appetite had gone as often happens in a crisis of the soul. These must have been days of terrible stress and strain.

10. *Ananias* (*Hananias*). Name common enough (cf. 5:1 for another Ananias) and means "Jehovah is gracious." *Nomen et omen* (Knowling). This Ananias had the respect of both Jews and Christians in Damascus (22:12). *In a vision* (*en horamati*). Zeller and others scout the idea of the historicity of this vision as supernatural. Even Furneaux holds that "it is a characteristic of the Jewish Christian sources to point out the Providential ordering of events by the literary device of a vision," as "in the early chapters of Matthew's and Luke's Gospels." He is content with this "beautiful expression of the belief" with no interest in the actual facts. But that is plain illusion, not to say delusion, and makes both Paul and Luke deceived by the story of Ananias (9:10–18; 22:12–16, 26). One MS. of the old Latin Version does omit the vision to Ananias and that is basis enough for those who deny the supernatural aspects of Christianity.

11. *To the street* (*epi tēn rhumēn*). See on Luke 14:21. A run way (from *rheō*, to run) between the houses. So were the narrow lanes or alleys called streets and finally in later Greek the word is applied to streets even when broad. *Straight* (*eutheian*). Most of the city lanes were crooked like the streets of Boston (old cow-paths, people say), but this one still runs "in a direct line from the eastern to the western gate of the city" (Vincent). Since the ancients usually rebuilt on the same sites, it is probable that the line of the street of that name today is the same, though the actual level has been much raised. Hence the identification of the house of Ananias and the house of Judas are very precarious.

12. *Coming in and laying* (*eiselthonta kai epithenta*). Second aorist (ingressive) active participles picturing the punctiliar act as a sort of indirect discourse after verbs of sensation (Robertson, *Grammar*, pp. 1040–2). Some ancient documents do not have "in a vision" here. *Receive his sight* (*anablepsei*). First aorist active subjunctive with *hopōs* (purpose). See again as in 9:17.

13. *How much evil* (*hosa kaka*). How many evil things.
Saul's reputation (26:10) as a persecutor had preceded him.
To thy saints (*tois hagiois*). Dative of disadvantage. "Used
here for the first time as a name for the Christians" (Knowling), but it came to be the common and normal (Hackett)
term for followers of Christ (9:32, 41; 26:10; I Cor. 1:2, etc.).
This common word is from *to hagos*, religious awe or reverence
and is applied to God's name (Luke 1:49), God's temple
(Matt. 24:15), God's people as set apart for God (Luke
1:70; 2:23; Rom. 1:7, etc.). Ananias in his ignorance saw in
Saul only the man with an evil reputation while Jesus saw in
Saul the man transformed by grace to be a messenger of
mercy.

14. *Hath authority* (*echei exousian*).   Probably Ananias
had received letters from the Christians left in Jerusalem
warning him of the coming of Saul. The protest of Ananias
to Jesus against any dealing with Saul is a fine illustration
of our own narrow ignorance in our rebellious moods against
the will of God.

15. *A chosen vessel* (*skeuos eklogēs*).   A vessel of choice
or selection. The genitive of quality is common in the Hebrew, as in the vernacular *Koinê*. Jesus chose Saul before
Saul chose Jesus. He felt of himself that he was an earthen
vessel (II Cor. 4:7) unworthy of so great a treasure. It was a
great message that Ananias had to bear to Saul. He told it
in his own way (9:17; 22:14f.) and in 26:16f. Paul blends
the message of Jesus to Ananias with that to him as one.
Before the Gentiles (*enōpion tōn ethnōn*). This was the chief
element in the call of Saul. He was to be an apostle to the
Gentiles (Eph. 3:6–12).

16. *I will shew* (*hupodeixō*).   Beforehand as a warning as
in Luke 3:7 and from time to time. *He must suffer* (*dei
auton pathein*). Constative aorist active infinitive (*pathein*,
from *paschō*) covering the whole career of Saul. Suffering
is one element in the call that Saul receives. He will learn

"how many things" (*hosa*) are included in this list by degrees and by experience. A glance at II Cor. 10-12 will show one the fulfilment of this prophecy. But it was the "gift" of Christ to Paul to go on suffering (*paschein*, present infinitive, Phil. 1:39).

17. *Laying his hands on him* (*epitheis ep' auton tas cheiras*). As in the vision Saul saw (verse 12). *Brother Saul* (*Saoul adelphe*). All suspicion has vanished and Ananias takes Saul to his heart as a brother in Christ. It was a gracious word to Saul now under suspicion on both sides. *The Lord, even Jesus* (*ho kurios, Iēsous*). Undoubted use of *kurios* as Lord and applied to Jesus. *Who appeared* (*ho ophtheis*). First aorist passive participle of *horaō*, was seen as in 26:16 and with the dative also (*soi*). *Thou camest* (*ērchou*). Imperfect indicative middle, "thou wert coming." *Be filled with the Holy Spirit* (*plēstheis pneumatos hagiou*). This enduement of special power he will need as an apostle (Hackett) and as promised by Jesus (1:8; Gal. 2:7).

18. *Fell off* (*apepesan*). Second aorist active indicative (note—an ending like first aorist) of *apopiptō*, old verb, but here alone in the N.T. *As if it were scales* (*hōs lepides*). Chiefly late word (LXX) from *lepō*, to peel, and only here in the N.T. See Tobit 11:13, "The white film peeled from his eyes" (*elepisthē*). Luke does not say that actual "scales" fell from the eyes of Saul, but that it felt that way to him as his sight returned, "as if" (*hōs*). Medical writers use the word *lepis* for pieces of the skin that fall off (Hobart, *Medical Language of St. Luke*, p. 39). Luke may have heard Paul tell of this vivid experience. *Was baptized* (*ebaptisthē*). First aorist passive indicative. Apparently by Ananias (22:16) as a symbol of the new life in Christ already begun, possibly in the pool in the house of Judas as today water is plentiful in Damascus or in Abana or Pharpar (Furneaux), better than all the waters of Israel according to Naaman (II Kings 5:12).

19. *Was strengthened* (*enischuthē*).   First aorist passive indicative of *enischuō*, to receive strength (*ischus*), comparatively late verb and here only in the N.T. save Luke 22:43 where it is doubtful.   Poor verse division.   This clause belongs in sense to verse 18.   *Some days* (*hēmeras tinas*).   An indefinite period, probably not long, the early period in Damascus before Saul left for Arabia (Gal. 1:13-24).

20. *He proclaimed Jesus* (*ekērussen ton Iēsoun*).   Imperfect indicative, inchoative, began to preach.   Jesus, not Christ, is the correct text here.   He did this first preaching in the Jewish synagogues, a habit of his life when possible, and following the example of Jesus.   *That he is the Son of God* (*hoti houtos estin ho huios tou theou*).   This is Paul's platform as a Christian preacher, one that he always occupied to the very end.   It was a complete reversal of his previous position.   Jesus had turned him completely around.   It is the conclusion that Saul now drew from the vision of the Risen Christ and the message through Ananias.   By "the Son of God" Saul means the Messiah of promise and hope, the Messianic sense of the Baptist (John 1:34) and of Nathanael (John 1:49) for Saul is now proclaiming his faith in Jesus in the very synagogues where he had meant to arrest those who professed their faith in him.   Peter laid emphasis on the Resurrection of Jesus as a glorious fact and proclaimed Jesus as Lord and Christ.   Paul boldly calls Jesus the Son of God with full acknowledgment of his deity from the very start.   Thomas had come to this place slowly (John 20:28).   Saul begins with this truth and never leaves it.   With this faith he can shake the world.   There is no power in any other preaching.

21. *Were amazed* (*existanto*).   Imperfect middle indicative of *existēmi*.   They continued to stand out of themselves in astonishment at this violent reversal in Saul the persecutor. *Made havock* (*porthēsas*).   First aorist active participle of *portheō*, to lay waste, an old verb, but only here and Gal.

1:13, 23 by Paul, an interesting coincidence. It is the old proverb about Saul among the prophets (I Sam. 10:12) revived with a new meaning (Furneaux). *Had come (eleluthei)*. Past perfect indicative active. *Might bring (agagēi)*. Second aorist (effective) active subjunctive of *agō* with *hina* (purpose). *Bound (dedemenous)*. Perfect passive participle of *deō*. Interesting tenses.

22. *Increased the more (mallon enedunamouto)*. Imperfect passive indicative of *endunamoō*, to receive power (late verb), progressive increase in strength as opposition grew. Saul's recantation stirred controversy and Saul grew in power. See also Paul in Phil. 4:13; I Tim. 1:12; II Tim. 2:1; 4:17; Rom. 4:20. Christ, the dynamo of spiritual energy, was now pouring power (Acts 1:8) into Paul who is already filled with the Holy Spirit (Acts 9:17). *Confounded (sunechunnen)*. Imperfect active indicative of *sunchunnō* (late form of *suncheō*, to pour together, commingle, make confusion. The more Saul preached, the more the Jews were confused. *Proving (sunbibazōn)*. Present active participle of *sunbibazō*, old verb to make go together, to coalesce, to knit together. It is the very word that Luke will use in 16:10 of the conclusion reached at Troas concerning the vision of Paul. Here Saul took the various items in the life of Jesus of Nazareth and found in them the proof that he was in reality "the Messiah" (*ho Christos*). This method of argument Paul continued to use with the Jews (Acts 17:3). It was irresistible argument and spread consternation among the Jews. It was the most powerful piece of artillery in the Jewish camp that was suddenly turned round upon them. It is probable that at this juncture Saul went into Arabia for several years (Gal. 1:12–24). Luke makes no mention of this important event, but he leaves ample room for it at this point.

23. *When many days were fulfilled (Hōs eplērounto hēmerai hikanai)*. Imperfect passive indicative of *plēroō*, old and

common verb, were in process of being fulfilled. How "many" (considerable, *hikanai*, common word for a long period) Luke does not say nor does he say that Saul spent all of this period in Damascus, as we know from Gal. 1:16–18 was not the case. Paul there states definitely that he went away from Damascus to Arabia and returned there before going back to Jerusalem and that the whole period was about "three years" which need not mean three full years, but at least portions of three. Most of the three years was probably spent in Arabia because of the two explosions in Damascus (before his departure and on his return) and because he was unknown in Jerusalem as a Christian on his arrival there. It cannot be argued from the frequent lacunae in the Acts that Luke tells all that was true or that he knew. He had his own methods and aims as every historian has. We are at perfect liberty to supplement the narrative in the Acts with items from Paul's Epistles. So we must assume the return of Saul from Arabia at this juncture, between verses 22 and 23, when Saul resumed his preaching in the Jewish synagogues with renewed energy and grasp after the period of mature reflection and readjustment in Arabia. *Took counsel together* (*sunebouleusanto*). First aorist (effective) middle indicative of *sunbouleuō*, old and common verb for counselling (*bouleuō*) together (*sun*). Things had reached a climax. It was worse than before he left for Arabia. Paul was now seeing the fulfilment of the prophecy of Jesus about him (9:16). *To kill him* (*anelein auton*). Second aorist (effective) active infinitive of *anaireō*, to take up, to make away with, to kill (Luke 23:32; Acts 12:1, etc.). The infinitive expresses purpose here as is done in verse 24 by *hopōs* and the aorist active subjunctive of the same verb (*anelōsin*). Saul now knew what Stephen had suffered at his hands as his own life was in peril in the Jewish quarter of Damascus. It was a picture of his old self. He may even have been scourged here (II Cor. 11:24).

24. *Plot* (*epiboulē*). Old word for a plan (*boulē*) against (*epi*) one. In the N.T. only in Acts (9:24; 20:3, 19; 23:30). *They watched* (*paretērounto*). Imperfect middle indicative of *paratēreō*, common verb in late Greek for watching beside (*para*) or insidiously or on the sly as in Luke 6:7, they kept on watching by day and night to kill him. In II Cor. 11:32 Paul says that the Ethnarch of Aretas "kept guard" (*ephrourei*, imperfect active of *phroureō*) to seize him. Probably the Jews obtained the consent of the Ethnarch and had him appoint some of them as guards or watchers at the gate of the city.

25. *Through the wall* (*dia tou teichous*). Paul in II Cor. 11:33 explains *dia tou teichous* as being *dia thuridos* (through a window) which opened into the house on the inside of the wall as is true today in Damascus as Hackett saw there. See Joshua 2:15f. (cf. I Sam. 19:12) for the way that Rahab let out the spies "by a cord through the window." *Lowering him* (*auton chalasantes*). First aorist active participle of *chalaō*, old and common verb in a nautical sense (Acts 27:17, 30) as well as otherwise as here. Same verb used by Paul of this experience (II Cor. 11:33). *In a basket* (*en sphuridi*). The word used when the four thousand were fed (Mark 8:8 = Matt. 15:37). A large basket plaited of reeds and distinguished in Mark 8:19f. (=Matt. 16:9f.) from the smaller *kophinos*. Paul uses *sarganē*, a basket made of ropes. This escape by night by the help of the men whom he had come to destroy was a shameful memory to Paul (II Cor. 11:33). Wendt thinks that the coincidences in language here prove that Luke had read II Corinthians. That, of course, is quite possible.

26. *He assayed* (*epeirazen*). Imperfect active of conative action. *To join himself* (*kollasthai*). Present middle (direct) infinitive of conative action again. Same word *kollaō* in Luke 15:15 and Acts 10:28. See on Matt. 19:5 for discussion. *Were all afraid of him* (*pantes ephobounto auton*). They were

fearing him.   Imperfect middle picturing the state of mind of the disciples who had vivid recollections of his conduct when last here.   What memories Saul had on this return journey to Jerusalem after three years.   He had left a conquering hero of Pharisaism.   He returns distrusted by the disciples and regarded by the Pharisees as a renegade and a turncoat.   He made no effort to get in touch with the Sanhedrin who had sent him to Damascus.   He had escaped the plots of the Jews in Damascus only to find himself the object of suspicion by the disciples in Jerusalem who had no proof of his sincerity in his alleged conversion.   *Not believing (mē pisteuontes).*   They had probably heard of his conversion, but they frankly disbelieved the reports and regarded him as a hypocrite or a spy in a new rôle to ruin them.   *Was (estin).*   The present tense is here retained in indirect discourse according to the common Greek idiom.

27.   *Took him (epilabomenos).*   Second aorist middle (indirect) participle of *epilambanō*, common verb to lay hold of. Barnabas saw the situation and took Saul to himself and listened to his story and believed it.   It is to the credit of Barnabas that he had the insight and the courage to stand by Saul at the crucial moment in his life when the evidence seemed to be against him.   It is a pleasing hypothesis that this influential disciple from Cyprus had gone to the University of Tarsus where he met Saul.   If so, he would know more of him than those who only knew his record as a persecutor of Christians.   That fact Barnabas knew also, but he was convinced that Jesus had changed the heart of Saul and he used his great influence (Acts 4:36; 11:22) to win the favour of the apostles, Peter in particular (Gal. 1:19) and James the half-brother of Jesus.   The other apostles were probably out of the city as Paul says that he did not see them.   *To the apostles (pros tous apostolous).*   Both Barnabas and James are termed apostles in the general sense, though not belonging to the twelve, as Paul did not, though himself

later a real apostle. So Barnabas introduced Saul to Peter and vouched for his story, declared it fully (*diēgēsato*, in detail) including Saul's vision of Jesus (*eiden ton kurion*) as the vital thing and Christ's message to Saul (*elalēsen autōi*) and Saul's bold preaching (*ēparrēsiasato*, first aorist middle indicative of *parrēsiazō* from *pan—rēsia* telling it all as in Acts 2:29). Peter was convinced and Saul was his guest for two weeks (Gal. 1:18) with delightful fellowship (*historēsai*). He had really come to Jerusalem mainly "to visit" (to see) Peter, but not to receive a commission from him. He had that from the Lord (Gal. 1:1f.). Both Peter and James could tell Saul of their special experiences with the Risen Christ. Furneaux thinks that Peter was himself staying at the home of Mary the mother of John Mark (Acts 12:12) who was a cousin of Barnabas (Col. 4:10). This is quite possible. At any rate Saul is now taken into the inner circle of the disciples in Jerusalem.

28. *Going in and going out (eisporeumenos kai ekporeuomenos)*. Barnabas and Peter and James opened all the doors for Saul and the fear of the disciples vanished.

29. *Preaching boldly (parrēsiazomenos)*. For a while. Evidently Saul did not extend his preaching outside of Jerusalem (Gal. 1:22) and in the city preached mainly in the synagogues of the Hellēnists (*pros tous Hellenistas*) as Stephen had done (Acts 8:9). As a Cilician Jew he knew how to speak to the Hellenists. *Disputed (sunezētei)*. Imperfect active of *sunzēteō*, the very verb used in 6:9 of the disputes with Stephen in these very synagogues in one of which (Cilicia) Saul had probably joined issue with Stephen to his own discomfort. It was intolerable to these Hellenistic Jews now to hear Saul taking the place of Stephen and using the very arguments that Stephen had employed. *But they went about to kill him (Hoi de epecheiroun anelein auton)*. Demonstrative *hoi* with *de* and the conative imperfect of *epicheireō*, to put the hand to, to try, an old verb used in

the N.T. only three times (Luke 1:1; Acts 9:29; 19:3). They offer to Saul the same conclusive answer that he gave to Stephen, death. Paul tells how the Lord Jesus appeared to him at this juncture in a vision in the temple (Acts 22:17–21) with the distinct command to leave Jerusalem and how Paul protested that he was willing to meet the fate of Stephen in whose death he had a shameful part. That is to Saul's credit, but the Lord did not want Saul to be put to death yet. His crown of martyrdom will come later.

30. *Knew it* (*epignontes*). Second aorist active participle of *epiginōskō*, to know fully. The disciples saw it clearly, so they *conducted* (*katēgagon*, effective second aorist active indicative of *katagō*). *Sent forth* (*exapesteilan*). Double compound (*ex*, out, *apo*, away or off). Sent him out and off *to Tarsus* (*eis Tarson*). Silence is preserved by Luke. But it takes little imagination to picture the scene at home when this brilliant young rabbi, the pride of Gamaliel, returns home a preacher of the despised Jesus of Nazareth whose disciples he had so relentlessly persecuted. What will father, mother, sister think of him now?

31. *So the church* (*Hē men oun ekklēsia*). The singular *ekklēsia* is undoubtedly the true reading here (all the great documents have it so). By this time there were churches scattered over Judea, Galilee, and Samaria (Gal. 1:22), but Luke either regards the disciples in Palestine as still members of the one great church in Jerusalem (instance already the work of Philip in Samaria and soon of Peter in Joppa and Caesarea) or he employs the term *ekklēsia* in a geographical or collective sense covering all of Palestine. The strictly local sense we have seen already in 8:1 and 3 (and Matt. 18:17) and the general spiritual sense in Matt. 16:18. But in Acts 8:3 it is plain that the term is applied to the organization of Jerusalem Christians even when scattered in their homes. The use of *men oun* (so) is Luke's common way of gathering up the connection. The obvious meaning is

that the persecution ceased because the persecutor had been converted. The wolf no longer ravined the sheep. It is true also that the effort of Caligula A.D. 39 to set up his image in the temple in Jerusalem for the Jews to worship greatly excited the Jews and gave them troubles of their own (Josephus, *Ant.* XVIII. 8, 2–9). *Had peace* (*eichen eirēnēn*). Imperfect active. Kept on having peace, enjoying peace, because the persecution had ceased. Many of the disciples came back to Jerusalem and the apostles began to make preaching tours out from the city. This idiom (*echō eirēnēn*) occurs again in Rom. 5:1 (*eirēnēn echōmen*, present active subjunctive) where it has been grievously misunderstood. There it is an exhortation to keep on enjoying the peace with God already made, not to make peace with God which would be *eirēnēn schōmen* (ingressive aorist subjunctive). *Edified* (*oikodomoumenē*). Present passive participle, linear action also. One result of the enjoyment of peace after the persecution was the continued edification (Latin word *aedificatio* for building up a house), a favourite figure with Paul (I Cor. 14; Eph. 3) and scattered throughout the N.T., old Greek verb. In I Peter 2:5 Peter speaks of "the spiritual house" throughout the five Roman provinces being "built up" (cf. Matt. 16:18). *In the comfort of the Holy Spirit* (*tēi paraklēsei tou hagiou pneumatos*). Either locative (*in*) or instrumental case (*by*). The Holy Spirit had been promised by Jesus as "another Paraclete" and now this is shown to be true. The only instance in Acts of the use of *paraklēsis* with the Holy Spirit. The word, of course, means calling to one's side (*parakaleō*) either for advice or for consolation. *Was multiplied* (*eplēthuneto*). Imperfect middle passive. The multiplication of the disciples kept pace with the peace, the edification, the walking in the fear of the Lord, the comfort of the Holy Spirit. The blood of the martyrs was already becoming the seed of the church. Stephen had not borne his witness in vain.

32. *Lydda* (*Ludda*). In O.T. Lod (I Chron. 8:12) and near Joppa. Later Diospolis.

33. *Aenias* (*Ainean*). Old Greek name and so probably a Hellenistic Jew. He was apparently a disciple already (the saint, verse 32). Luke the physician notes that he had been bed ridden for eight years. See on 5:15 for "bed" (*krabattou*) and 8:7 and Luke 5:18 for "paralyzed" (*paralelumenos*, perfect passive participle of *paraluō* with *ēn*, periphrastic past perfect passive).

34. *Healeth* (*iātai*). Aoristic present middle indicative, heals here and now. *Make thy bed* (*strōson seautōi*). First aorist (ingressive) active imperative of *strōnnumi* (-*uō*). Old word with "bed" (*krabatton*) understood as the object. Literally, spread thy bed for thyself (dative case), what others for eight years have done for thee.

35. *Sharon* (*Sarōna*). The Plain of Sharon, not a town. Thirty miles long from Joppa to Caesarea.

36. *At Joppa* (*En Ioppēi*). The modern Jaffa, the port of Jerusalem (II Chron. 2:16). *Disciple* (*mathētria*). Feminine form of *mathētēs*, a learner from *manthanō*, to learn, a late word and only here in the N.T. *Tabitha* (*Tabeitha*). Aramaic form of the Hebrew *Tsebi* and, like the Greek word *Dorcas* (*Dorkas*), means Gazelle, "the creature with the beautiful look" (or eyes), from *derkomai*. The gazelle was a favourite type for beauty in the orient (Song of Solomon 2:9, 17; 4:5; 7:3). She may have had both the Aramaic and the Greek name, Tabitha Dorcas like John Mark. There is nothing said about a husband and so she was probably unmarried. She is the second woman mentioned by name after Pentecost (Sapphira the other). She did her beautiful deeds by herself. She did not have a Dorcas society. *Did* (*epoiei*). Imperfect active, her habit.

37. *In an upper chamber* (*en huperōiōi*). See on 1:13. Also in verse 39. In that house. This service was rendered by the women, though Luke has *lousantes* (masculine plural

aorist active participle of *louō*), a general way of saying "they washed." The interment was not hurried as in Jerusalem (Ananias and Sapphira) and the upper room is where the body was usually placed.

38. *Delay not* (*mē oknēseis*). Ingressive aorist active subjunctive in prohibition. Direct discourse and not indirect as late MSS. have (aorist active infinitive, *oknēsai*). Possibly the two messengers started before Dorcas was quite dead, though we do not know. Peter had recently healed Aeneas and the disciples may have had faith enough to believe that he could raise the dead by the power of Christ. W. M. Ramsay doubts if Dorcas was really dead, but why see legends in these supernatural events?

39. *Stood by him* (*parestēsan autōi*). Second aorist active indicative, intransitive, of *paristēmi*). Vivid picture of this group of widows as they stood around Peter, weeping (*klaiousai*) and showing (*epideiknumenai*, present middle as belonging to themselves, pointing with pride to) the very inner garments (*chitōnas*) and outer garments (*himatia*), like the Latin *tunica* and *toga*, which she made from time to time (*epoiei*, imperfect active, repeated action). It was a heart-breaking scene.

40. *Put them all forth* (*ekbalōn exō pantas*). Second aorist (effective) active participle of *ekballō*, a rather strong word, perhaps with some difficulty. Cf. Mark 5:40 which incident Peter may have recalled. The words are not genuine in Luke 8:54. Peter's praying alone reminds one of Elijah (I Kings 17:20) and the widow's son and Elisha for the Shunammite's son (II Kings 4:33). *Tabitha, arise* (*Tabeitha, anastēthi*). With sublime faith like *Taleitha koum* of Jesus in Mark 5:41. *She sat up* (*anekathisen*). Effective aorist active indicative of *anakathizō*. Often in medical writers, only here in the N.T. and Luke 7:15 where Westcott and Hort have in the margin the uncompounded form *ekathisen*. Vivid picture.

41. *Raised her up* (*anestēsen autēn*). First aorist active indicative, transitive, of *anistēmi*. *Presented* (*parestēsen*). First aorist active indicative, transitive of *paristēmi* (cf. intransitive second aorist in verse 39 above). It was a joyful time for Peter, the widows, all the saints, and for Dorcas.

43. *Many days* (*hēmeras hikanas*). See on verse 23. Luke is fond of the phrase and uses it for time, number, size. It might be "ten days, ten months, or ten years" (Page). *With one Simon a tanner* (*para tini Simōni bursei*). The use of *para* is usual for staying with one (by his side). "The more scrupulous Jews regarded such an occupation as unclean, and avoided those who pursued it. The conduct of Peter here shows that he did not carry his prejudices to that extent" (Hackett). One of the rabbis said: "It is impossible for the world to do without tanners; but woe to him who is a tanner." A Jewess could sue for divorce if she discovered that her husband was a tanner. And yet Peter will have scruples on the housetop in the tanner's house about eating food considered unclean. "The lodging with the tanner was a step on the road to eating with a Gentile" (Furneaux).

CHAPTER X

1. *Cornelius* (*Kornēlios*). The great Cornelian family of
Rome may have had a freedman or descendant who is
centurion (*hekaton-tarchēs*, leader of a hundred, Latin *cen-
turio*). See on Matt. 8:5. These Roman centurions always
appear in a favourable light in the N.T. (Matt. 8:5; Luke
7:2; 23:47; Acts 10:1; 22:25; 27:3). Furneaux notes the
contrasts between Joppa, the oldest town in Palestine, and
Caesarea, built by Herod; the Galilean fisherman lodging
with a tanner and the Roman officer in the seat of govern-
mental authority. *Of the band called the Italian* (*ek speirēs
tēs kaloumenēs Italikēs*). A legion had ten cohorts or "bands"
and sixty centuries. The word *speirēs* (note genitive in *-ēs*
like the Ionic instead of *-as*) is here equal to the Latin
cohors. In the provinces were stationed cohorts of Italic
citizens (volunteers) as an inscription at Carnuntum on the
Danube (Ramsay) has shown (epitaph of an officer in the
second Italic cohort). Once more Luke has been vindicated.
The soldiers could, of course, be Roman citizens who lived
in Caesarea. But the Italian cohorts were sent to any part
of the empire as needed. The procurator at Caesarea would
need a cohort whose loyalty he could trust, for the Jews were
restless.

2. *Devout* (*eusebēs*). Old word from *eu* (well) and *sebomai*
(to worship, to reverence), but rare in the N.T. (Acts 10:
2, 7; II Peter 2:1). It might refer to a worshipful pagan (Acts
17:23, *sebasmata*, objects of worship), but connected with
"one that feared God" (*phoboumenos ton theon*) Luke describes "a God-fearing proselyte" as in 10:22, 35. This is
his usual term for the Gentile seekers after God (13:16, 26;
17:4, 17, etc.), who had come into the worship of the syna-

gogue without circumcision, and were not strictly proselytes, though some call such men "proselytes of the gate"
(cf. Acts 13:43); but clearly Cornelius and his family were
still regarded as outside the pale of Judaism (10:28, 34;
11:1, 8; 15:7). They had seats in the synagogue, but were
not Jews. *Gave much alms* (*poiōn eleemosunas pollas*).
Doing many alms (the very phrase in Matt. 6:2), a characteristic mark of Jewish piety and from a Gentile to the
Jewish people. *Prayed* (*deomenos*). Begging of God. Alms-
giving and prayer were two of the cardinal points with the
Jews (Jesus adds fasting in his picture of the Pharisee in
Matt. 6:1–18).

3. *Coming in* (*eiselthonta*). Ingressive second aorist active
participle, not present. So punctiliar, "saw come," not
"saw coming." So also "say" or "speak," not "saying."
Luke repeats the account of this vision to Cornelius twice
(10:30; 11:13) and also the story of the vision to Peter
(10:1–16, 28; 11:5).

4. *Lord* (*kurie*). Cornelius recognizes the angel of God
(verse 3) as God's messenger. *Are gone up* (*anebēsan*).
Timeless second aorist active indicative of *anabainō*. Gone
up like the smoke of incense in sacrifices. *For a memorial*
(*eis mnēmosunon*). Old word from *mnēmōn*. The only other
instance in the N.T. is by Jesus about the act of Mary of
Bethany (Matt. 26:13; Mark 14:9). His prayers and his
alms proved his sincerity and won the ear of God.

5. *Fetch* (*metapempsai*). First aorist middle (indirect,
for one's self) imperative of *metapempō*, usual voice in
ancient Greek with this verb in sense of sending another for
one's own sake. Only in Acts in the N.T. See also 10:22.

6. *Lodgeth* (*xenizetai*). Present passive indicative of
xenizō old verb from *xenos*, a stranger as a guest. So to entertain a guest as here or to surprise by strange acts (Acts
17:20; I Peter 4:4). *Whose* (*hōi*). To whom, dative of possession. *By the seaside* (*para thalassan*). Along by the sea.

Note accusative case. Outside the city walls because a
tanner and to secure water for his trade. Some tanneries
are by the seashore at Jaffa today.

8. *Rehearsed* (*exēgēsamenos*). See on Luke 24:35. All
the details about the vision. The soldier was "devout" like
Cornelius and would protect the two household servants
(*oiketōn*).

9. *On the morrow* (*tēi epaurion*). Locative case of article
with the compound adverb (*hēmerāi* day being understood),
the second day after leaving Caesarea, 28 miles from Joppa.
The third day (the next morrow, verse 23) they start back
home and the fourth day (on the morrow again, verse 24)
they reach Caesarea. *As they* (*ekeinōn*). The party of three
from Caesarea. Genitive absolute with present participle
hodoiporountōn (journeying) and *eggizontōn* (drew nigh).
The housetop (*to dōma*). Old word and in Gospels (Luke
3:19, etc.), but only here in Acts. From *demō*, to build, and
so any part of the building (hall, dining room, and then roof).
The roof was nearly flat with walls around and so was a
good place for meditation and prayer and naps.

10. *Hungry* (*prospeinos*). Only instance of the word
known, a *hapax legomenon*. Probably "very hungry"
(*pros* = besides, in addition). *Desired* (*ēthelen*). Imperfect
active. Was longing to eat. It was about twelve o'clock
noon and Peter may even have smelt the savory dishes,
"while they made ready" (*paraskeuazontōn*). "The natural
and the supernatural border closely on one another, with no
definable limits" (Furneaux). *He fell into a trance* (*egeneto ep' auton ekstasis*). More exactly, "An ecstasy came
upon him," in which trance he passed out of himself (*ekstasis*,
from *existēmi*) and from which one came to himself (12:11).
Cf. also 11:5 and 22:17. It is thus different from a vision
(*horama*) as in verse 3.

11. *Beholdeth* (*theōrei*). Vivid historical present and
change from past time. *Opened* (*aneōigmenon*, perfect

passive participle with double reduplication, state of completion). *Descending (katabainon)*. Present active participle
describing the process. *Sheet (othonēn)*. Old word for linen
cloth and only here in the N.T. Accusative case in apposition with *skeuos* (vessel). *Let down (Kathiemenon)*. Present
passive participle of *Kathiēmi*. Old verb, but in the N.T.
only here and Luke 5:19 and Acts 9:25. Linear action here
picturing the process, "being let down." *By four corners
(tessarsin archais)*. Instrumental case of *archē*, beginning.
We say "end" or extremity for this use of the word. The
picture is the sheet held up by four cords to which the sheet
is fastened. Isa. 11:12 had said that Israel would be gathered
from the four corners of the earth. Knowling follows Hobart
in taking the four corners of the sheet to be a medical phrase
for bandage (the end of a bandage).

12. *Were (hupērchen)*. Imperfect of *huparchō* in sense of
ēn, to exist, be. Fish are not mentioned, perhaps because the
sheet had no water, though they were clean and unclean
also (Lev. 11:9; Deut. 14:9). *All manner of (panta)*. Literally, all, but clearly all varieties, not all individuals. Both
clean and unclean animals are in the sheet.

14. *Not so, Lord (Mēdamōs, kurie)*. The negative *mēdamōs* calls for the optative *eiē* (may it not be) or the imperative *estō* (let it be). It is not *oudamōs*, a blunt refusal (I
shall not do it). And yet it is more than a mild protest as
Page and Furneaux argue. It is a polite refusal with a reason given. Peter recognizes the invitation to slay *(thuson)*
the unclean animals as from the Lord *(kurie)* but declines
it three times. *For I have never eaten anything (hoti oudepote
ephagon pan)*. Second aorist active indicative, I never did
anything like this and I shall not do it now. The use of *pan*
(everything) with *oudepote* (never) is like the Hebrew *(lo—
kōl)* though a like idiom appears in the vernacular Koiné
(Robertson, *Grammar*, p. 752). *Common and unclean (koinon
kai akatharton)*. *Koinos* from epic *xunos (xun, sun, together*

with) originally meant common to several (Latin *communis*)
as in Acts 2:44; 4:32; Tit. 1:4; Jude 3. The use seen here
(also Mark 7:2, 5; Rom. 14:14; Heb. 10:29; Rev. 21:27;
Acts 10:28; 11:8), like Latin *vulgaris* is unknown in ancient
Greek. Here the idea is made plain by the addition of
akatharton (unclean), ceremonially unclean, of course. We
have the same double use in our word "common." See on
Mark 7:18f. where Mark adds the remarkable participle
katharizōn (making all meats clean), evidently from Peter
who recalls this vision. Peter had been reared from childhood to make the distinction between clean and unclean
food and this new proposal even from the Lord runs against
all his previous training. He did not see that some of God's
plans for the Jews could be temporary. This symbol of the
sheet was to show Peter ultimately that Gentiles could be
saved without becoming Jews. At this moment he is in
spiritual and intellectual turmoil.

15. *Make not thou common (su mē koinou)*. Note emphatic
position of *su* (thou). Do thou stop making common what
God cleansed (*ekatharisen*). The idiom of *mē* with the present active imperative *koinou* means precisely this. Peter
had just called "common" what God had invited him to
slay and eat.

16. *Thrice (epitris)*. For three times. Peter remained unconvinced even by the prohibition of God. Here is a striking illustration of obstinacy on the part of one who acknowledges
the voice of God to him when the command of the Lord
crosses one's preferences and prejudices. There are abundant
examples today of precisely this thing. In a real sense Peter
was maintaining a pose of piety beyond the will of the Lord.
Peter was defiling what God had cleansed. *Was received up*
(*anelēmphthē*). First aorist passive indicative of *analambanō*,
to take up. The word used of the Ascension (1:22).

17. *Was much perplexed in himself (en heautōi diēporei)*.
Imperfect active of *diaporeō*, intensive compound (*dia*,

thoroughly, and *a* privative and *poros*, way), to be completely
at a loss to know what road to take. Old verb, but in N.T.
only in Luke and Acts. Page notes that Luke is singularly
fond of verbs compounded with *dia*. See on Luke 9:7 and
Acts 2:12. When out of the ecstasy he was more puzzled than
ever. *Might be* (*an eiē*). Optative with *an* in indirect question simply retained from the direct (Robertson, *Grammar*,
pp. 1021, 1044). See Acts 17:18, for the direct ano Luke
1:62 for the indirect (*an theloi* both times). It is the conclusion of a fourth class condition. *Having made inquiry*
(*dierōtēsantes*). First aorist active participle of *dierōtaō*,
another compound of *dia*, to ask one after another, to ask
through, old verb, but only here in the N.T. It took diligent
inquiry to find the obscure house of Simon the tanner.
Stood before the gate (*epestēsan epi ton pulōna*). Second aorist
active indicative of *ephistēmi*, intransitive. Note repetition
of *epi*. The messengers stopped right at the folding gates of
the passage (*pulōna*) which led from the street to the inner
court or house.

18. *Called* (*phōnēsantes*). In a loud voice that those inside
the house might hear. *Asked* (*epunthanonto*). Imperfect
middle of *punthanomai*, old verb to make inquiry especially
with an indirect question as here. Kept on inquiring. Westcott and Hort follow B C here and read *eputhonto* (second
aorist middle, effective aorist). Either makes sense, though
the imperfect is more picturesque. *Were lodging* (*xenizetai*).
Present middle indicative retained in indirect question.
See on verse 6 for the verb.

19. *Thought* (*dienthumoumenou*). Genitive absolute of
present middle participle of *dienthumeomai*, a double compound (*dia* and *en-* with *thumos*) and another *hapax legomenon* save in ecclesiastical writers, though *enthumeomai* is
common enough and Textus Receptus so reads here. Peter
was revolving in his mind, through and through, in and out,
to find the meaning of the strange vision.

20. *But (alla)*. So usually, though it is open to question whether *alla* is adversative here and not rather, "Now then." *Get thee down (katabēthi)*. Second aorist active imperative, at once. *Go (poreuou)*. Present middle imperative, go on. *Nothing doubting (mēden diakrinomenos)*. Another compound of *dia*, old and common verb for a divided mind (*dia* like *duo*, two). Note usual negative of the present middle participle, the subjective *mēden*. The notion of wavering (James. 1:6) is common with this verb in the middle voice. In Acts 11:12 the aorist active (*mēden diakrinanta*) is used perhaps with the idea of conduct towards others rather than his own internal doubt as here (Page). *For I (hoti egō)*. The Holy Spirit assumes responsibility for the messengers from Cornelius and thus connects their mission with the vision which was still troubling Peter. Peter had heard his name called by the man (verse 19).

21. *Cause (aitia)*. Or reason. Common in this sense. See on Matt. 19:3.

22. *Righteous (dikaios)*. In the Jewish sense as in Luke 1:6; 2:25. *Well reported of (marturoumenos)*. Present passive participle as in 6:3. Cf. the other centurion in Luke 7:4. *Nation (ethnous)*. Not *laou*, for the speakers are Gentiles. *Was warned (echrēmatisthē)*. First aorist passive of *chrēmatizō*, old word for doing business, then consulting an oracle, and here of being divinely (word God not expressed) warned as in Matt. 2:12, 22; Luke 2:26; Heb. 11:7. Then to be called or receive a name from one's business as in Acts 11:26; Rom. 7:3.

23. *Lodged them (exenisen)*. Active voice here rather than passive as in 10:6. *Accompanied him (sunēlthan autōi)*. Associative instrumental case after verb. The wisdom of having these half dozen Jewish Christians from Joppa with Peter in the house of Cornelius in Caesarea becomes manifest in Jerusalem (11:12).

24. *Was waiting (ēn prosdokōn)*. Periphrastic imperfect

active, in eager expectation and hope, directing the mind (*dokaō*) towards (*pros*) anything. Old and common verb. *Near* (*anagkaious*). Only instance in the N.T. of this sense of *anagkaios* from *anagkē*, necessity, what one cannot do without, necessary (I Cor. 12:22), duty (Acts 13:46), or blood relations as here. The ancient Greek writers combined these two words (*suggeneis*, kinsmen, *anagkaious*, necessary friends) as here. It was a homogeneous group of Gentiles close to Cornelius and predisposed to hear Peter favourably.

25. *That Peter entered* (*tou eiselthein ton Petron*). This is a difficult construction, for the subject of *egeneto* (it happened) has to be the articular genitive infinitive *tou eiselthein* with the accusative of general reference *ton Petron*. Most commentators consider it inexplicable. It is probably an extension of the ordinary articular infinitive under the influence of the Hebrew infinitive construct without regard to the case, regarding it as a fixed case form and so using it as nominative. Precisely this construction of *tou* and the infinitive as the subject of a verb occurs in the LXX (II Chron. 6:7, etc.). See Robertson, *Grammar*, pp. 1067f. for full discussion of this obvious Hebraism. Somewhat similar examples appear in Acts 20:3; 27:1. But the Codex Bezae avoids this awkward idiom by the genitive absolute (*proseggizontos tou Petrou*) and some additional details (one of the servants ran forward and announced that he was come). *Worshipped him* (*prosekunēsen*). "Cornelius was not an idolator and would not have honoured Peter as a god" (Furneaux). The word probably means here reverence like old English usage (Wycliff) and not actual worship, though Peter took it that way (verse 26). Jesus accepted such worship (Matt. 8:2; Luke 5:8 by Peter).

27. *As he talked with him* (*sunomilōn autōi*). Present active participle of *sunomileō*, rare compound and here alone in the N.T., with associative instrumental case. The uncompounded verb is common enough though in the N.T.

only in Luke 24:14 which see and Acts 20:11; 24:26. *Findeth* (*heuriskei*). Vivid historical present indicative active. *Come together* (*sunelēluthotas*). Second perfect active participle of *sunerchomai*. It was an expectant group of Gentiles eager for Peter's interpretation of the vision of Cornelius.

28. *How that it is an unlawful thing* (*hōs athemiton estin*). The conjunction *hōs* is sometimes equivalent to *hoti* (that). The old form of *athemitos* was *athemistos* from *themistos* (*themizō*, *themis*, law custom) and *a* privative. In the N.T. only here and I Peter 4:3 (Peter both times). But there is no O.T. regulation forbidding such social contact with Gentiles, though the rabbis had added it and had made it binding by custom. There is nothing more binding on the average person than social custom. On coming from the market an orthodox Jew was expected to immerse to avoid defilement (Edersheim, *Jewish Social Life*, pp. 26–28; Taylor's *Sayings of the Jewish Fathers*, pp. 15, 26, 137, second edition). See also Acts 11:3; Gal. 2:12. It is that middle wall of partition between Jew and Gentile (Eph. 2:14) which Jesus broke down. *One of another nation* (*allophulōi*). Dative case of an old adjective, but only here in the N.T. (*allos*, another, *phulon*, race). Both Juvenal (*Sat.* XIV. 104, 105) and Tacitus (*History*, V. 5) speak of the Jewish exclusiveness and separation from Gentiles. *And yet unto* (*kamoi*). Dative of the emphatic pronoun (note position of prominence) with *kai* (*crasis*) meaning here "and yet" or adversative "but" as often with *kai* which is by no means always merely the connective "and" (Robertson, *Grammar*, pp. 1182f.). Now Peter takes back both the adjectives used in his protest to the Lord (verse 14) "common and unclean." It is a long journey that Peter has made. He here refers to "no one" (*mēdena*), not to "things," but that is great progress.

29. *Without gainsaying* (*anantirrhētōs*). *A* privative with compound adverb from *anti* (back, in return, against) and

verbal *rhētos* (from *errhēthēn,* to speak). Late and rare and here only in the N.T., but the adjective in 19:36. *Without answering back.* That is true after the Holy Spirit expressly told Peter to go with the messengers of Cornelius (10:19–23). Peter's objections were made to the Lord in the vision which he did not understand. But that vision prepared him for this great step which he had now taken. He had stepped over the line of Jewish custom. *With what intent (tini logōi).* More exactly, "for what reason" as in Plato, *Gorgias* 512 C.

30. *Four days ago (apo tetartēs hēmeras).* From the fourth day, reckoning backwards from this day. *I was keeping the ninth hour of prayer (ēmēn tēn enatēn proseuchomenos).* Periphrastic middle imperfect and accusative of extension of time (all the ninth hour).

31. *Is heard (eisēkousthē).* Sort of timeless first aorist passive indicative as is "are had in remembrance" (*emnēsthēsan.* See verse 4 "are gone up for a memorial").

32. *In the house of Simon (en oikiāi Simōnos).* See 9:43 for *para Simōni* with same idea.

33. *And thou hast well done that thou art come (su te kalōs epoiēsas paragenomenos).* "And thou didst well in coming." A regular formula for expressing thanks as in Phil. 4:14; III John 6; II Peter 1:19. The participle completes the idea of *kalōs poieō* neatly. Cornelius commends Peter for his courage in breaking away from Jewish custom and takes no offence at the implied superiority of the Jews over the Gentiles. Cornelius and his circle of kinsmen and close friends are prepared soil for a new era in the history of Christianity. The Samaritans were now nominal Jews and the Ethiopian eunuch was a single case, but here Peter the chief apostle, not Philip the preaching deacon (evangelist), was involved. It was a crisis. Cornelius reveals an open mind for the message of God through Peter. *Commanded thee (prostetagmena soi).* Perfect passive participle with the dative case (*soi*). Cornelius is a military man and he employs a military

term (*prostassō*, old word to command). He is ready for
orders from the Lord.

34. *Opened his mouth* (*anoixas to stoma*). Solemn formula
for beginning his address (8:35; 18:14; Matt. 5:2; 13:35).
But also good elocution for the speaker. *I perceive* (*katal-
ambanomai*). Aoristic present middle of *katalambanō*, to take
hold of, the middle noting mental action, to lay hold with
the mind (Acts 4:13; 10:34; 25:25; Eph. 3:18). It had been
a difficult thing for Peter to grasp, but now "of a truth"
(*ep' alētheias*) the light has cleared away the fogs. It was
not until Peter had crossed the threshold of the house of
Cornelius in the new environment and standpoint that he
sees this new and great truth. *Respecter of persons* (*prosō-
polēmptēs*). This compound occurs only here and in Chrysostom. It is composed of *prosōpon* face or person (*pros* and
ops, before the eye or face) and *lambanō*. The abstract form
prosōpolēmpsia occurs in James 2:1 (also Rom. 2:11; Eph.
6:9; Col. 3:25) and the verb *prosōpolempteō* in James 2:9.
The separate phrase (*lambanein prosōpon*) occurs in Luke
20:21 and Gal. 2:6. The phrase was already in the LXX
(Deut. 10:17; II Chron. 19:7; Psa. 82:6). Luke has simply
combined the two words into one compound one. The idea
is to pay regard to one's looks or circumstances rather than
to his intrinsic character. The Jews had come to feel that
they were the favourites of God and actually sons of the
kingdom of heaven because they were descendants of Abraham. John the Baptist rebuked them for this fallacy.

35. *Acceptable to him* (*dektos autōi*). Verbal adjective
from *dechomai*. *Acceptabilis*. That is to say, a Gentile
would not have to become a Jew in order to become a Christian. Evidently Peter had not before perceived this fact.
On the great Day of Pentecost when he spoke of the promise
"to all those afar off" (2:39) Peter understood that they
must first become Jews and then Christians. The new idea
that now makes a revolution in Peter's outlook is precisely

this that Christ can and will save Gentiles like this Cornelius group without their becoming Jews at all.

36. *The word which he sent (ton logon hon apesteilen).* Many ancient MSS. (so Westcott and Hort) read merely *ton logon apesteilen* (he sent the word). This reading avoids the anacoluthon and inverse attraction of *logon* to the case of the relative *hon* (which). *Preaching good tidings of peace through Jesus Christ (euaggelizomenos eirēnēn dia Iēsou Christou).* Gospelizing peace through Jesus Christ. There is no other way to have real peace between individuals and God, between races and nations, than by Jesus Christ. Almost this very language occurs in Eph. 2:17 where Paul states that Jesus on the cross "preached (gospelized) peace to you who are afar off and peace to you who are near." Peter here sees what Paul will see later with great clearness. *He is Lord of all (houtos estin pantōn kurios).* A triumphant parenthesis that Peter throws in as the reason for his new truth. Jesus Christ is Lord of all, both Jews and Gentiles.

37. *Ye know (humeis oidate).* Peter reminds his Gentile audience that the main facts concerning Jesus and the gospel were known to them. Note emphatic expression of *humeis* (you). *Beginning (arxamenos).* The Textus Receptus has *arxamenon* (accusative), but the nominative is given by Aleph A B C D E H and is certainly correct. But it makes a decided anacoluthon. The accusative would agree with *rhēma* used in the sense of message or story as told by the disciples. The nominative does not agree with anything in the sentence. The same phrase occurs in Luke 23:5. Here is this aorist middle participle almost used like an adverb. See a similar loose use of *arxamenos* in the same sense by Peter in Acts 1:22. The baptism of John is given as the *terminus a quo.* The story began with a skip to Galilee after the baptism just like the Gospel of Mark. This first message of Peter to the Gentiles (10:37-44) corresponds in broad outline with Mark's Gospel. Mark heard Peter preach

many times and evidently planned his Gospel (the Roman Gospel) on this same model. There is in it nothing about the birth and childhood of Jesus nor about the intervening ministry supplied by John's Gospel for the period (a year) between the baptism and the Galilean Ministry. Peter here presents an objective statement of the life, death, and resurrection of Jesus with proof from the Scriptures that he is the Messiah. It is a skilful presentation.

38. *Jesus of Nazareth* (*Iēsoun ton apo Nazareth*). Jesus the one from Nazareth, the article before the city identifying him clearly. The accusative case is here by *prolepsis*, Jesus being expressed for emphasis before the verb "anointed" and the pronoun repeated pleonastically after it. "Jesus transfers the mind from the gospel-history to the personal subject of it" (Hackett). *God anointed him* (*echrisen, auton, ho theos*). First aorist active of the verb *chriō*, to anoint, from which the verbal *Christos* is formed (Acts 2:36). The precise event referred to by Peter could be the Incarnation (Luke 1:35f.), the Baptism (Luke 3:22), the Ministry at Nazareth (Luke 4:14). Why not to the life and work of Jesus as a whole? *Went about doing good* (*diēlthen euergetōn*). Beautiful description of Jesus. Summary (constative) aorist active of *dierchomai*, to go through (*dia*) or from place to place. The present active participle *euergetōn* is from the old verb *euergeteō* (*eu*, well, *ergon*, work) and occurs only here in the N.T. The substantive *euergetēs* (benefactor) was often applied to kings like Ptolemy Euergetes and that is the sense in Luke 22:25 the only N.T. example. But the term applies to Jesus far more than to Ptolemy or any earthly king (Cornelius a Lapide). *And healing* (*kai iōmenos*). And in particular healing. Luke does not exclude other diseases (cf. Luke 13:11, 16), but he lays special emphasis on demoniacal possession (cf. Mark 1:23). *That were oppressed* (*tous katadunasteuomenous*). Present passive articular participle of *katadunasteuō*. A late verb in LXX and papyri.

In the N.T. only here and James 2:6 (best MSS.). One of the compounds of *kata* made transitive. The reality of the devil (the slanderer, *diabolos*) is recognized by Peter. *For God was with him* (*hoti ho theos ēn met' autou*). Surely this reason does not reveal "a low Christology" as some charge. Peter had used the same language in Acts 7:9 and earlier in Luke 1:28, 66 as Nicodemus does in John 3:2.

39. *And we are witnesses* (*kai hēmeis martures*). Compare "ye yourselves know" (verse 37). Peter thus appeals to what the audience know and to what the disciples know. He made the same claim about personal witnesses of the Resurrection of Jesus at Pentecost (2:32). Here Peter affirms full knowledge of the work of Jesus in Judea (for whole country including Galilee and Perea) and Jerusalem (given mainly in John's Gospel). In the Greek *hōn* (which) is attracted into the genitive case to agree with the antecedent *pantōn* (all), a common enough idiom. *Whom also they slew* (*hon kai aneilan*). Second aorist active indicative of *anaireō* with *a* as often in Acts (2:23; 5:30). But note *kai* (also) in the old MSS., not in the Textus Receptus. They "also" slew him, went that far, "this crowning atrocity" (Vincent), *kai* could here be "even." *Hanging him on a tree* (*kremasantes epi xulou*). This same expression used by Peter in 5:30 which see for discussion.

40. *Gave him to be made manifest* (*edōken auton emphanē genesthai*). Peculiar phrase, here only in the N.T. and in Rom. 10:20 (quoted from Isa. 65:1). *Emphanē*, predicate accusative after infinitive *genesthai* agreeing with *auton* object of *edōken*.

41. *Chosen before* (*prokecheirotonēmenois*). Perfect passive participle dative plural from *procheirotoneō*, to choose or designate by hand (*cheirotoneō*, *cheir*, hand, and *teinō*, to stretch, as in Acts 14:23; II Cor. 8:19), beforehand (*pro*), a double compound as old as Plato, but here alone in the N.T. Peter is evidently stating the thing as it happened

and not trying to make a convincing story by saying that
both friends and foes saw him after his resurrection. It is
the "historian's candour" (Paley) in Luke here that adds
to the credibility of the narrative. The sceptical Jews would
not have believed and Jesus was kept from open contact
with the world of sin after his Passion. *To us who did eat
and drink with him* (*hēmin hoitines sunephagomen kai sune-
piomen autōi*). The "who" (*hoitines*) is first person agreeing
with "us" (*hēmin*). Second aorist active indicative of the
common verbs *sunesthiō* and *sumpinō*. *Autōi* is associative
instrumental case. There are difficulties to us in understanding how Jesus could eat and drink after the resurrection as
told here and in Luke 24:41-3, but at any rate Peter makes
it clear that it was no hallucination or ghost, but Jesus himself whom they saw after he rose from the dead, "after the
rising as to him" (*meta to anastēnai auton, meta* with the
accusative articular infinitive second aorist active and the
accusative *auton* of general reference). Furneaux dares to
think that the disciples misunderstood Jesus about eating
after the resurrection. But that is to deny the testimony
merely because we cannot explain the transition state of the
body of Jesus.

42. *He charged* (*parēggeilen*). First aorist active indicative as in 1:4. There Jesus is the subject and so probably
here, though Page insists that *ho theos* (God) is here because
of verse 40. *To testify* (*diamarturasthai*). First aorist middle
infinitive. See on 2:40. *Ordained* (*hōrismenos*). Perfect
passive participle of *horizō*, old verb, to mark out, to limit,
to make a horizon. *Judge* (*kritēs*). The same point made by
Peter in I Peter. 4:5. He does not use the word "Messiah"
to these Gentiles though he did say "anointed" (*echrisen*)
in verse 38. Peter's claim for Jesus is that he is the Judge
of Jew and Gentile (living and dead).

43. *Every one that believeth* (*panta ton pisteuonta*). This
accusative active participle of general reference with the

infinitive in indirect discourse is the usual idiom.   Only
labein (second aorist active infinitive of *lambanō*) is not
indirect statement so much as indirect command or arrangement.   The prophets bear witness to Jesus Christ to this
effect.   It is God's plan and no race distinctions are drawn.
Peter had already said the same thing at Pentecost (2:38),
but now he sees himself that Gentiles do not have to become Jews, but have only to believe in Jesus as Messiah
and Judge as foretold by the prophets.   It was glorious news
to Cornelius and his group.   *Through his name* (*dia tou
onomatos autou*), not as a *title* or magic formula (Acts
18:13), but the power of Christ himself represented by
his name.

44. *While Peter yet spake* (*eti lalountos tou Petrou*).   Genitive absolute of present participle, still going on.   *The Holy
Ghost fell* (*epepesen to pneuma to hagion*).   Second aorist
active indicative of *epipiptō*, old verb to fall upon, to re-
cline, to come upon.   Used of the Holy Spirit in 8:16; 10:44;
11:15.   It appears that Peter was interrupted in his sermon
by this remarkable event.   The Jews had received the Holy
Spirit (2:4), the Samaritans (8:17), and now Gentiles.   But
on this occasion it was before baptism, as was apparently
true in Paul's case (9:17f.).   In 8:16 and in 19:5 the hands
of the apostles were also placed after baptism on those who
received the Holy Spirit.   Here it was unexpected by Peter
and by Cornelius and was indubitable proof of the conversion of these Gentiles who had accepted Peter's message and
had believed on Jesus Christ as Saviour.

45. *They of the circumcision which believed* (*hoi ek peritomēs pistoi*).   The believing ones of the circumcision, more
exactly.   *Were amazed* (*exestēsan*).   Second aorist active
indicative, intransitive, of *existēmi*.   They stood out of
themselves.   *On the Gentiles also* (*kai epi ta ethnē*).   Or, even
upon the Gentiles.   *Was poured out* (*ekkechutai*).   Present
perfect passive retained in indirect discourse of *ekcheō* or

ekchunō, old verb, used metaphorically of the Holy Spirit also in 2:17 (from Joel 2:28f.), 33.

46. *They heard* (*ēkouon*). Imperfect active, were hearing, kept on hearing. *Speak* (*lalountōn*). Present active participle, speaking, for they kept it up. *With tongues* (*glōssais*). Instrumental case as in 2:4, 11 which see. The fuller statement there makes it clear that here it was new and strange tongues also as in 19:6 and I Cor. 14:4-19. This sudden manifestation of the Holy Spirit's power on uncircumcised Gentiles was probably necessary to convince Peter and the six brethren of the circumcision that God had opened the door wide to Gentiles. It was proof that a Gentile Pentecost had come and Peter used it effectively in his defence in Jerusalem (Acts 11:15).

47. *Can any man forbid the water?* (*Mēti to hudōr dunatai kōlūsai tis?*). The negative *mēti* expects the answer *No*. The evidence was indisputable that these Gentiles were converted and so were entitled to be baptized. See the similar idiom in Luke 6:39. Note the article with "water." Here the baptism of the Holy Spirit had preceded the baptism of water (Acts 1:5; 11:16). "The greater had been bestowed; could the lesser be withheld?" (Knowling). *That these should not be baptized* (*tou mē baptisthēnai toutous*). Ablative case of the articular first aorist passive infinitive of *baptizō* with the redundant negative after the verb of hindering (*kōlūsai*) and the accusative of general reference (*toutous*). The redundant negative after the verb of hindering is not necessary though often used in ancient Greek and in the *Koinē* (papyri). Without it see Matt. 19:14; Acts 8:36 and with it see Luke 4:42; 24:16; Acts 14:18. Cf. Robertson, *Grammar*, pp. 1061, 1094, 1171. The triple negatives here are a bit confusing to the modern mind (*mēti* in the question, *kōlūsai*, to hinder or to cut off, *mē* with *baptisthēnai*). Literally, Can any one cut off the water from the being baptized as to these? Meyer: "The water is in

this animated language conceived as the element offering itself for the baptism." *As well as we* (*hōs kai hēmeis*). The argument was conclusive. God had spoken. Note the query of the eunuch to Philip (Acts 8:36).

48. *Commanded* (*prosetaxen*). First aorist active indicative. Peter himself abstained from baptizing on this occasion (cf. Paul in I Cor. 1:14). Evidently it was done by the six Jewish brethren. *Them to be baptized* (*autous baptisthēnai*). Accusative of general reference with the first aorist passive infinitive. *In the name of Jesus Christ* (*en tōi onomati Iēsou Christou*). The essential name in Christian baptism as in 2:38 and 19:5. But these passages give the authority for the act, not the formula that was employed (Alvah Hovey in Hackett's *Commentary*. See also chapter on the Baptismal Formula in my *The Christ of the Logia*). "Golden days" (*aurei dies*, Bengel) were these for the whole group.

CHAPTER XI

1. *In Judea* (*kata tēn Ioudaian*). Throughout Judea (probably all Palestine), distributive use of *kata*. The news from Casearea spread like wildfire among the Jewish Christians. The case of the Samaritans was different, for they were half Jews, though disliked. But here were real Romans even if with Jewish affinities. *Had received* (*edexanto*). First aorist middle indicative. The English idiom requires "had" received, the Greek has simply "received."

2. *They that were of the circumcision* (*hoi ek peritomēs*). Literally, those of circumcision (on the side of circumcision, of the circumcision party). The phrase in 10:46 is confined to the six brethren with Peter in Caesarea (11:12). That can hardly be the meaning here for it would mean that they were the ones who brought the charge against Peter though Hort takes this view. All the disciples in Jerusalem were Jews so that it can hardly mean the whole body. In Gal. 2:12 the phrase has the narrower sense of the Judaizing or Pharisaic wing of the disciples (Acts 15:5) who made circumcision necessary for all Gentile converts. Probably here by anticipation Luke so describes the beginning of that great controversy. The objectors probably did not know of Peter's vision at Joppa, but only of the revolutionary conduct of Peter in Caesarea. These extremists who spoke probably had abundant sympathy in their protest. The apostles are mentioned in verse 1, but are not referred to in verse 2. Apparently they are in contrast with the circumcision party in the church. *Contended* (*diekrinonto*). Imperfect middle of the common verb *diakrinō*, to *separate*. Here to separate oneself apart (*dia*), to take sides against, to make a cleavage (*dia*, two, in two) as in Jude 9. So Peter is at

once put on the defensive as the contention went on. It is plain that Peter was not regarded as any kind of pope or overlord.

3. *Thou wentest in* (*eisēlthes*). Direct form, but Westcott and Hort have it *eisēlthen* (he went in), indirect form. So with *sunephages* (didst eat) and *sunephagen* (did eat). The direct is more vivid. *Men uncircumcised* (*andras akrobustian echontas*). "Men having uncircumcision." It is a contemptuous expression. They did not object to Peter's preaching to the Gentiles, but to his going into the house of Cornelius and eating with them, violating his supposed obligations as a Jew (Hackett). It was the same complaint in principle that the Pharisees had made against Jesus when he ate with publicans and sinners (Luke 15:12). The Jews had not merely the Mosaic regulations about clean and unclean food, but also the fact that at a Gentile table some of the meat may have been an idol sacrifice. And Peter himself had similar scruples when the vision came to him at Joppa and when he entered the house of Cornelius in Caesarea (10:28). Peter had been led beyond the circumcision party.

4. *Began* (*arxamenos*). Not pleonastic here, but graphically showing how Peter began at the beginning and gave the full story of God's dealings with him in Joppa and Caesarea. *Expounded* (*exetitheto*). Imperfect middle of *ektithēmi*, to set forth, old verb, but in the N.T. only in Acts (7:21; 11:4; 18:26; 28:23), a deliberate and detailed narrative "in order" (*kathexēs*). Old word for in succession. In the N.T. only in Luke 1:2; 8:1; Acts 3:24; 11:14; 18:23. Luke evidently considered this defence of Peter important and he preserves the marks of authenticity. It came originally from Peter himself (verses 5, 6, 15, 16). "The case of Cornelius was a test case of primary importance" (Page), "the first great difficulty of the early Church." Part of the story Luke gives three times (10:3–6, 30–32; 11:13f.). See the discussion chapter 10 for details given here.

5. *Let down* (*kathiemenēn*). Here agreeing with the "sheet" (*othonēn*, feminine), not with "vessel" (*skeuos*, neuter) as in 10:11. *Even unto me* (*achri emou*). Vivid detail added here by Peter.

6. *When I had fastened my eyes* (*atenisas*). This personal touch Peter adds from his own experience. See on Luke 4:20; Acts 3:4, 12 for this striking verb *atenizō*, to stretch the eyes towards, first aorist active participle here. *I considered* (*katanoeō*). Imperfect active of *kataneoō* to put the mind down on, to ponder, I was pondering. *And saw* (*kai eidon*). Second aorist active indicative, saw in a flash.

7. *A voice saying* (*phōnēs legousēs*). Genitive case after *ēkousa* (cf. 9:7 and accusative 9:4 which see for discussion). Participle *legousēs* (present active of *legō*) agreeing with *phōnēs*, a kind of indirect disoourse use of the participle.

8. *Came into my mouth* (*eisēlthen eis to stoma mou*). Instead of *ephagon* (I ate) in 10:14. Different phrase for the same idea.

10. *Was drawn up* (*anespasthē*). Instead of *anelēmpthē* (was taken up) in 10:16. First aorist passive indicative of *anaspaō*, old verb, but in N.T. only in Luke 14:5 and here.

12. *Making no distinction* (*mēden diakrinanta*). So Westcott and Hort (first aorist active participle) instead of *mēden diakrinomenon* "nothing doubting" (present middle participle) like 10:20. The difference in voice shows the distinction in meaning. *We entered into the man's house* (*eisēlthomen eis ton oikon tou andros*). Peter confesses it, but shows that the other six went in also. He avoids mention of Cornelius's name and office.

13. *Standing and saying* (*stathenta kai eiponta*). More precisely, "stand and say" (punctiliar act, first aorist passive and second aorist active participles). *Fetch Simon* (*metapempsai Simōna*). First aorist middle imperative. Third time mentioned (10:5, 22; 11:13). Perhaps Peter is anxious to make it plain that he did not go of his own initia-

tive into the house of Cornelius. He went under God's direct orders.

14. *Whereby thou shalt be saved, thou and all thy house* (*en hois sōthēsei su kai pās ho oikos sou*). Future passive indicative of *sōzō*, to save. Clearly Cornelius was unsaved in spite of his interest in Jewish worship. Clearly also the household of Cornelius would likewise be won to Christ by the words of Simon Peter. This is household conversion before the household baptism (10:48; 11:17).

15. *As I began to speak* (*en tōi arxasthai me lalein*). *En* with the locative of the articular aorist infinitive *arxasthai* (punctiliar action simply) and the accusative of general reference. The second infinitive *lalein* (to speak) is dependent on *arxasthai*, "In the beginning to speak as to me." *Even as on us at the beginning* (*hōsper kai eph' hēmās en archēi*). Peter recalls vividly the events at Pentecost, the speaking with tongues and all. It is noteworthy that Peter does not here repeat his sermon. "He rests his defence, not on what he said, but on what God did" (Furneaux).

16. *I remembered* (*emnēsthēn*). First aorist passive indicative of the common verb *mimnēskō*, to remind. Peter recalls the very words of Jesus as reported in Acts 1:5. Peter now understands this saying of Jesus as he had not done before. That is a common experience with us all as new experiences of grace open richer veins in God's truth (John 12:16). Peter clearly sees that the water baptism is merely the symbol or picture of the spiritual baptism in the heart.

17. *The like gift* (*tēn isēn dōrean*). The equal gift, equal in quality, rank, or measure. Common word. *When we believed* (*pisteusasin*). First aorist active participle of *pisteuō* in the dative case. It agrees both with *hēmin* (unto us) and with *autois* (unto them), "having believed on the Lord Jesus Christ." Both classes (Gentiles and Jews) trusted in Christ, and both received the Holy Spirit. *Who was I* (*egō tis ēmēn*). Note order, "I, who was I." "*That I could with-*

stand God" (*dunatos kōlūsai ton theon*). Literally, "able to withstand or hinder God." It is a rhetorical question, really two questions. Who was I? Was I able to hinder God? Peter's statement of the facts made an unanswerable defence. And yet Peter (Gal. 2:11) will later in Antioch play the coward before emissaries from Jerusalem on this very point of eating with Gentile Christians.

18. *Held their peace* (*hēsuchasan*). Ingressive aorist active indicative of *hēsuchazō*, old verb to be quiet, to keep quiet. The wrangling (verse 2) ceased. The critics even "glorified God" (*edoxasan*, ingressive aorist again). *Then to the Gentiles also* (*Ara kai tois ethnesin*). *Ergo* as in Luke 11:20, 48 and like *ara oun* in Rom. 5:18. In ancient Greek inferential *ara* cannot come at the beginning of a clause as here. It was reluctant acquiescence in the undoubted fact that God had "granted repentance unto life" to these Gentiles in Caesarea, but the circumcision party undoubtedly looked on it as an exceptional case and not to be regarded as a precedent to follow with other Gentiles. Peter will see in this incident (Acts 15:8) the same principle for which Paul contends at the Jerusalem Conference. Furneaux suggests that this conduct of Peter in Caesarea, though grudgingly acquiesced in after his skilful defence, decreased his influence in Jerusalem where he had been leader and helped open the way for the leadership of James the Lord's brother.

19. *They therefore that were scattered abroad* (*hoi men oun diasparentes*). Precisely the same words used in 8:4 about those scattered by Saul (which see) and a direct reference to it is made by the next words, "upon the tribulation that arose about Stephen" (*apo tēs thlipseōs tēs genomenēs epi Stephanōi*). As a result of (*apo*), in the case of (*epi*) Stephen. From that event Luke followed Saul through his conversion and back to Jerusalem and to Tarsus. Then he showed the activity of Peter outside of Jerusalem as a result of the cessation of the persecution from the conversion of Saul with

the Gentile Pentecost in Caesarea and the outcome in Jerusalem. Now Luke starts over again from the same persecution by Saul and runs a new line of events up to Antioch
parallel to the other, probably partly following. *Except to
Jews only* (*ei mē monon Ioudaiois*). Clearly these disciples
did not know anything about the events in Caesarea and
at first their flight preceded that time. But it was a wonderful episode, the eager and loyal preaching of the fleeing
disciples. The culmination in Antioch was probably after
the report of Peter about Caesarea. This Antioch by the
Orontes was founded 300 B.C. by Seleucus Nicator and was
one of five cities so named by the Seleucides. It became the
metropolis of Syria though the Arabs held Damascus first.
Antioch ranked next to Rome and Alexandria in size, wealth,
power, and vice. There were many Jews in the cosmopolitan
population of half a million. It was destined to supplant
Jerusalem as the centre of Christian activity.

20. *Spake* (*elaloun*). Inchoative imperfect active, began
to speak. For them it was an experiment. *Unto the Greeks
also* (*kai pros tous Hellēnas*). This is undoubtedly the correct reading in spite of Hellenists (*Hellēnistas*) or Grecian
Jews in B E H L P. *Hellēnas* is read by A and D and a cor-
rector of Aleph. The presence of "also" or "even" (*kai*)
in Aleph A B makes no sense unless "Greeks" is correct.
Hellenists or Grecian Jews as Christians were common
enough as is seen in Acts 2 and 6. Saul also had preached to
the Hellenists in Jerusalem (9:29). Hellenists were merely
one kind of Jews in contrast with those who spoke Aramaic
(Acts 6). It is true that the case of Cornelius was first in
importance, but it is not clear that it was before the work in
Antioch. Probably the report of the work among the Greeks
in Antioch reached Jerusalem after Peter's defence in 11:
1-18. That explains the calm tone about it and also why
Barnabas and not Peter was sent to investigate. Peter and
John (Acts 8) had condoned Philip's work in Samaria and

Peter was the agent in the work among the Romans in Caesarea. His position was now well-known and his services discounted for this new crisis. These Greeks in Antioch were apparently in part pure heathen and not "God-fearers" like Cornelius. A man of wisdom was called for. These preachers were themselves Hellenists (verse 19) and open to the lessons from their environment without a vision such as Peter had at Joppa. "It was a departure of startling boldness" (Furneaux) by laymen outside of the circle of official leaders.

21. *The hand of the Lord was with them (ēn cheir kuriou met' autōn).* This O.T. phrase (Ex. 9:3; Isa. 59:1) is used by Luke (1:66; Acts 4:28, 30; 13:11). It was proof of God's approval of their course in preaching the Lord Jesus to Greeks. *Turned unto the Lord (epestrepsen epi ton kurion).* First aorist active indicative of *epistrephō*, common verb to turn. The usual expression for Gentiles turning to the true God (14:15; 15:3, 19; 26:18, 20; I Thess. 1:9). Here "Lord" refers to "the Lord Jesus" as in verse 20, though "the hand of the Lord" is the hand of Jehovah, clearly showing that the early disciples put Jesus on a par with Jehovah. His deity was not a late development read back into the early history.

22. *Came to the ears (ēkousthē eis ta ōta).* First aorist passive indicative of *akouō*, was heard in the ears. *Of the church which was in Jerusalem (tēs ekklēsias tēs en Ierousalēm).* Not yet was the term "church" applied to the group of disciples in Antioch as it is in 11:26 and 13:1. *They sent forth (exapesteilan).* First aorist active indicative of the double compound verb *ex-apo-stellō*, to send out and away. The choice of Barnabas was eminently wise. He already had a position of leadership in Jerusalem because of his generosity (4:36f.) and his championship of Saul after his conversion (9:27). He was originally from Cyprus and probably had personal friends among some of the leaders in this new move-

ment.   He was to investigate the work of the travelling
preachers (verse 19) all the way to Antioch (*heōs Antiocheias*).

23. *The grace of God, was glad* (*tēn charin tēn tou theou
echarē*).   Note repetition of the article, "the grace that of
God."   The verb (second aorist passive indicative of *chairō*)
has the same root as *charis*.   See the same *suavis parono-
masia* in Luke 1:28.   "Grace brings gladness" (Page).   "A
smaller man would have raised difficulties as to circumcision
or baptism" (Furneaux).   *He exhorted* (*parekalei*).   Imperfect
active, picturing the continuous encouragement from Barnabas.   *With purpose of heart* (*tēi prothesei tēs kardias*).   Placing
before (from *pro-tithēmi*), old word for set plan as in Acts
27:13; Rom. 8:28.   The glow of the first enthusiasm might
pass as often happens after a revival.   Barnabas had a special
gift (4:36) for work like this.   *Cleave unto the Lord* (*pros-
menein* [*en*] *tōi kuriōi*).   Dative case (locative if *en* is genuine)
of *kurios* (here Jesus again) after *prosemenein* to keep on
remaining loyal to (present active infinitive).   Persistence
was needed in such a pagan city.

24. *For* (*hoti*).   Because.   This is the explanation of the
conduct of Barnabas.   The facts were opposed to the natural
prejudices of a Jew like Barnabas, but he rose above such
racial narrowness.   He was a really good man (*agathos*).
See Rom. 5:7 for distinction between *agathos* and *dikaios*,
righteous, where *agathos* ranks higher than *dikaios*.   Besides,
Barnabas was full of the Holy Spirit (like Peter) and of faith
and so willing to follow the leading of God's Spirit and take
some risks.   This is a noble tribute paid by Luke.   One wonders if Barnabas was still living when he wrote this.   Certainly he was not prejudiced against Barnabas though he
will follow the fortunes of Paul after the separation (15:36–
41).   *Was added unto the Lord* (*prosetethē tōi kuriōi*).   First
aorist passive indicative of *prostithēmi*, common verb to add
to.   These people were added to the Lord Jesus before they

were added to the church. If that were always true, what a difference it would make in our churches.

25. *To seek for Saul* (*anazētēsai Saulon*). First aorist (effective) active infinitive of purpose. *Anazēteō* is a common verb since Plato, but in the N.T. only here and Luke 2:44, 45, to seek up and down (*ana*), back and forth, to hunt up, to make a thorough search till success comes. It is plain from Gal. 1:21 that Saul had not been idle in Cilicia. Tarsus was not very far from Antioch. Barnabas probably knew that Saul was a vessel of choice (Acts 9:15) by Christ for the work among the Gentiles. He knew, of course, of Saul's work with the Hellenists in Jerusalem (9:29) and echoes of his work in Cilicia and Syria had probably come to him. So to Tarsus he goes when he saw the need for help. "He had none of the littleness which cannot bear the presence of a possible rival" (Furneaux). Barnabas knew his own limitations and knew where the man of destiny for this crisis was, the man who already had the seal of God upon him. The hour and the man met when Barnabas brought Saul to Antioch. The door was open and the man was ready, far more ready than when Jesus called him on the road to Damascus. The years in Cilicia and Syria were not wasted for they had not been idle. If we only knew the facts, it is probable that Saul also had been preaching to Hellenes as well as to Hellenists. Jesus had definitely called him to work among the Gentiles (9:15). In his own way he had come to the same place that Peter reached in Caesarea and that Barnabas now holds in Antioch. God always has a man prepared for a great emergency in the kingdom. The call of Barnabas was simply the repetition of the call of Christ. So Saul came.

26. *Even for a whole year* (*kai eniauton holon*). Accusative of extent of time, probably the year A.D. 44, the year preceding the visit to Jerusalem (11:30), the year of the famine. The preceding years with Tarsus as headquarters

covered A.D. 37 (39) to 44. *They were gathered together with the church* (*sunachthēnai en tēi ekklēsiāi*). First aorist passive infinitive of *sunagō*, old verb, probably here to meet together as in Matt. 28:12. In Acts 14:27 the verb is used of gathering together the church, but here *en tēi ekklēsiāi* excludes that idea. Barnabas met together "in the church" (note first use of the word for the disciples at Antioch). This peculiar phrase accents the leadership and co-operation of Barnabas and Saul in teaching (*didaxai*, first aorist active infinitive) much people. Both infinitives are in the nominative case, the subject of *egeneto* (it came to pass). *And that the disciples were called Christians first in Antioch* (*chrēmatisai te prōtōs en Antiocheiāi tous mathētas Christianous*). This first active infinitive *chrēmatisai* is also a subject of *egeneto* and is added as a separate item by the use of *te* rather than *kai*. For the word itself in the sense of divine command see on Matt. 2:12, 22; Luke 2:26; Acts 10:22. Here and in Rom. 7:3 it means to be called or named (assuming a name from one's business, *chrēma*, from *chraomai*, to use or to do business). Polybius uses it in this sense as here. *Tous mathētas* (the disciples) is in the accusative of general reference with the infinitive. *Christianous* (Christians) is simply predicate accusative. This word is made after the pattern of *Herodianus* (Matt. 22:16, *Herōidianoi*, followers of Herod), *Caesarianus*, a follower of Caesar (Deissmann, *Light from the Ancient East*, p. 377, gives papyri examples of the genitive *Kaisaros* meaning also "belonging to Caesar" like the common adjective *Caesarianus*). It is made thus like a Latin adjective, though it is a Greek word, and it refers to the Hebrew belief in a Messiah (Page). The name was evidently given to the followers of Christ by the Gentiles to distinguish them from the Jews since they were Greeks, not Grecian Jews. The Jews would not call them Christians because of their own use of *Christos* the Messiah. The Jews termed them Galileans or Nazarenes. The followers of Christ called themselves disciples (learners),

believers, brethren, saints, those of the Way. The three uses
of Christian in the N.T. are from the heathen standpoint
(here), Acts 26:28 (a term of contempt in the mouth of
Agrippa), and I Peter 4:16 (persecution from the Roman
government). It is a clear distinction from both Jews and
Gentiles and it is not strange that it came into use first here
in Antioch when the large Greek church gave occasion for it.
Later Ignatius was bishop in Antioch and was given to the
lions in Rome, and John Chrysostom preached here his
wonderful sermons.

27. *Prophets* (*prophētai*). Christian prophets these were
(cf. 13:1) who came from Jerusalem (the headquarters,
8:15). Judas and Silas are called prophets (14:4; 15:32).
They were not just fore-tellers, but forth-tellers. The prophet
had inspiration and was superior to the speaker with tongues
(I Cor. 14:3). John was a prophet (Luke 7:26). We need
prophets in the ministry today.

28. *Signified* (*esēmainen*). Imperfect active in Westcott
and Hort, but aorist active *esēmānen* in the margin. The verb
is an old one from *sēma* (*sēmeion*) a sign (cf. the symbolic
sign in 21;11). Here Agabus (also in 21:10) does predict a
famine through the Holy Spirit. *Should be* (*mellein esesthai*).
Mellō occurs either with the present infinitive (16:27), the
aorist infinitive (12:6), or the future as here and 24:15;
27:10. *Over all the world* (*eph' holēn tēn oikoumenēn*). Over
all the inhabited earth (*gēn*, understood). Probably a common hyperbole for the Roman empire as in Luke 2:1. Josephus (*Ant.* VIII. 13, 4) appears to restrict it to Palestine.
In the days of Claudius (*epi Klaudiou*). He was Roman
Emperor A.D. 41–44. The Roman writers (Suetonius, Dio
Cassius, Tacitus) all tell of dearths (*assiduae sterilitates*)
during the brief reign of Claudius who was preceded by
Caligula and followed by Nero.

29. *Every man according to his ability* (*kathōs euporeito
tis*). Imperfect middle of *euporeō*, to be well off (from *eu-*

poros), old verb, but here alone in the N.T., "as any one was well off." The sentence is a bit tangled in the Greek from Luke's rush of ideas. Literally, "Of the disciples, as any one was able (or well off), they determined (*hōrisan*, marked off the horizon) each of them to send relief (*eis diakonian*, for ministry) to the brethren who dwelt in Judaea." The worst of the famine came A.D. 45. The warning by Agabus stirred the brethren in Antioch to send the collection on ahead.

30. *Sending* (*aposteilantes*). First aorist active participle of *apostellō*, coincident action with *epoiēsan* (did). *To the elders* (*pros tous presbuterous*). The first use of that term for the Christian preachers. In 20:17 and 28 "elders" and "bishops" are used interchangeably as in Titus 1:5, 7. The term probably arose gradually and holds a position in the church similar to the same term in the synagogue. The apostles were apparently absent from Jerusalem at this time and they were no longer concerned with serving tables. In 21:18 Paul presented the later collection also to the elders. Since Peter and James (till his death) were in Jerusalem during the persecution in chapter 12 it is probable that the visit of Barnabas and Saul to Jerusalem came really after that persecution for Peter left Jerusalem (12:17). The elders here mentioned may include the preachers in Judea also outside of Jerusalem (26:20).

CHAPTER XII

1. *About that time (kat' ekeinon ton kairon)*. Same phrase in Rom. 9:9. That is, the early part of A.D. 44 since that is the date of Herod's death. As already suggested, Barnabas and Saul came down from Antioch to Jerusalem after the persecution by Herod at the end of 44 or the beginning of 45. *Herod the king (Hērōidēs ho basileus)*. Accurate title at this particular time. Herod Agrippa I, grandson of Herod the Great, was King of Palestine A.D. 42 to 44; only for these three years was a Herod king over Palestine since the death of Herod the Great and never afterwards. Archelaus never actually became king though he had the popular title at first (Matt. 2:22). *Put forth his hands (epebalen tas cheiras)*. Second aorist active indicative of *epiballō*, old verb, to cast upon or against. The same idiom with *tas cheiras* (the hands, common Greek idiom with article rather than possessive pronoun) in 4:3 and 5:18. *To afflict (kakōsai)*. First aorist active infinitive of *kakoō*, old word to do harm or evil to (*kakos*), already in 7:6, 19. Outside of Acts in the N.T. only I Peter 5:13. Infinitive of purpose. Probably the first who were afflicted were scourged or imprisoned, not put to death. It had been eight years or more since the persecution over the death of Stephen ceased with the conversion of Saul. But the disciples were not popular in Jerusalem with either Sadducees or Pharisees. The overtures to the Gentiles in Caesarea and Antioch may have stirred up the Pharisees afresh (cf. 6:14). Herod Agrippa I was an Idumean through his grandfather Herod the Great and a grandson of Mariamne the Maccabean princess. He was a favourite of Caligula the Roman Emperor and was anxious to placate his Jewish subjects while retaining the favour

of the Romans. So he built theatres and held games for the Romans and Greeks and slew the Christians to please the Jews. Josephus (*Ant.* XIX. 7, 3) calls him a pleasant vain man scrupulously observing Jewish rites. Here we have for the first time political power (after Pilate) used against the disciples.

2. *James the brother of John* (*Iakōbon ton adelphon Iōanou*). He had been called by Jesus a son of thunder along with his brother John. Jesus had predicted a bloody death for both of them (Mark 10:38ff. = Matt. 20:23). James is the first of the apostles to die and John probably the last. He is not James the Lord's brother (Gal. 1:19). We do not know why Luke tells so little about the death of James and so much about the death of Stephen nor do we know why Herod selected him as a victim. Eusebius (*H.E.* ii. 9) quotes Clement of Alexandria as saying that a Jew made accusations against James and was converted and beheaded at the same time with him.   *Killed with the sword* (*aneilen machairēi*). The verb is a favourite one with Luke (Acts 2:33; 5:33, 36; 7:28; 9:23–29; 10:39, etc.). Instrumental case and Ionic form of *machaira*. The Jews considered beheading a shameful death as in the case of the Baptist (Matt. 14:10).

3. *That it pleased the Jews* (*hoti areston estin tois Ioudaiois*). Indirect assertion with the present tense *estin* retained. *Areston* is the verbal adjective from *areskō* followed by the dative as in John 8:29. *Proceeded to seize* (*prosetheto sullabein*). A patent Hebraism in Luke 20:11f. already, and nowhere else in the N.T. It occurs in the LXX (Gen. 4:2; 8:12; 18:29, etc.). Second aorist middle indicative of *prostithēmi* and the second aorist active infinitive of *sullambanō*. Literally, he added to seize, he seized Peter in addition to James. *The days of unleavened bread* (*hēmerai tōn azumōn*). By this parenthesis Luke locates the time of the year when Peter was arrested, the passover. It was a fine occasion for Agrippa to increase his favour among the crowds of Jews

there by extra zeal against the Christians. It is possible that Luke obtained his information about this incident from John Mark for at his Mother's house the disciples gathered (12:12).

4. *When he had taken him* (*piasas*). See on 3:7 for same form. *He put him in prison* (*etheto eis phulakēn*). Second aorist middle indicative of *tithēmi*, common verb. This is the third imprisonment of Peter (4:3; 5:18). *To four quaternions of soldiers* (*tessarsin tetradiois stratiōtōn*). Four soldiers in each quaternion (*tetradion* from *tetras*, four), two on the inside with the prisoner (chained to him) and two on the outside, in shifts of six hours each, sixteen soldiers in all, the usual Roman custom. Probably Agrippa had heard of Peter's previous escape (5:19) and so took no chances for connivance of the jailors. *After the passover* (*meta to pascha*). The passover feast of eight days. "The stricter Jews regarded it as a profanation to put a person to death during a religious festival" (Hackett). So Agrippa is more scrupulous than the Sanhedrin was about Jesus. *To bring him forth* (*anagagein auton*). Second aorist active infinitive of *anagō*, to lead up, old verb, used literally here. Peter was in the inner prison or lower ward and so would be led up to the judgment seat where Herod Agrippa would sit (cf. John 19:13). *To the people* (*tōi laōi*). Ethical dative, in the presence of and for the pleasure of the Jewish people.

5. *Therefore* (*men oun*). Because of the preceding situation. *Was kept* (*etēreito*). Imperfect passive, continuously guarded, waiting for the feast to be over. *But prayer was made earnestly* (*proseuchē de ēn ektenōs ginomenē*). Probably *de* here is not adversative (but), merely parallel (*and*) as Page argues. It was a crisis for the Jerusalem church. James had been slain and Peter was to be the next victim. Hence "earnestly" (late adverb from *ektenēs*, strained, from *ekteinō*, to stretch. In the N.T. only here, Luke 22:44; I Peter 1:22) prayer was *going up* (*ginomenē*, present middle

participle, periphrastic imperfect with *ēn*). It looked like a desperate case for Peter. Hence the disciples prayed the more earnestly.

6. *Was about to bring him forth* (*ēmellen prosagagein* or *proagagein*). The MSS. vary, but not *anagagein* of verse 4. *The same night* (*tēi nukti ekeinēi*). Locative case, *on that (very) night*. *Was sleeping* (*ēn koimōmenos*). Periphrastic middle imperfect. *Bound with two chains* (*dedemenos halusesin dusin*). Perfect passive participle of *deō*, to bind, followed by instrumental case. One chain was fastened to each soldier (one on each side of Peter). *Kept* (*etēroun*). Imperfect active, were keeping. Two guards outside before the door and two inside, according to Roman rule. Did Peter recall the prophecy of Jesus that he should be put to death in his old age (John 21:18)? Jesus had not said, as Furneaux does, that he would die by crucifixion.

7. *Stood by him* (*epestē*). Ingressive second aorist active indicative of *ephistēmi*, intransitive. This very form occurs in Luke 2:9 of the sudden appearance of the angel of the Lord to the shepherds. Page notes that this second aorist of *ephistēmi* occurs seven times in the Gospel of Luke, eight times in the Acts, and nowhere else in the N.T. Note also the same form *apestē* (departed from, from *aphistēmi*, stood off from) of the disappearance of the angel in verse 10. *In the cell* (*en tōi oikēmati*). Literally, a dwelling place or habitation (from *oikeō*, to dwell, *oikos*, house), but here not the prison as a whole as in Thucydides, but the room in the prison (cell) where Peter was chained to the two guards. Old word, but only here in the N.T. *He smote Peter on the side* (*pataxas tēn pleuran tou Petrou*). More exactly, "smote the side of Peter." Strongly enough to wake Peter up who was sound asleep and yet not rouse the two guards. It was probably between 3 A.M. and 6 A.M., hours when changes in the guards were made. *Rise up* (*anasta*). Short form (*Koiné*) of *anastēthi*, second aorist active imperative of

anistēmi, intransitive. So also Acts 9:11 (Westcott and Hort text); Eph. 5:14. *Fell off (exepesan)*. Second aorist active with *a* ending like first aorist of *expiptō*, old verb. This miracle was necessary if Peter was to escape without rousing the two guards.

8. *Gird thyself (zōsai)*. Direct middle first aorist (ingressive) imperative (Robertson, *Grammar*, pp. 806f.) from *zōnnumi (zōnnuō)*. Old verb, but in the N.T. only here and John 21:18 (twice to Peter) where the active voice and the reflexive pronoun occur in the first example. The girdle was worn round the *chitōn* or undergarment. *Bind on (hupodēsai)*. Indirect middle (by yourself or for yourself) first aorist imperative of *hupodeō*, to bind under, old verb, only three times in the N.T. [Mark 6:9; Acts 12:8; Eph. 6:15 (middle)]. *Sandals (sandalia)*. Persian word common from Herodotus on, a sole made of wood or leather covering the bottom of the foot and bound on with thongs. In the N.T. only here and Mark 6:9. In the LXX used indiscriminately with *hupodēma*. *Cast about thee (peribalou)*. Second aorist middle (indirect) imperative of *periballō*, old and common verb to throw around, especially clothing around the body as here. The *himation* (outer garment) was put over the *chitōn*. It was not a hurried flight. *Follow me (akolouthei moi)*. Present (linear) active imperative, keep on following me (associative instrumental case).

9. *Wist not (ouk ēidei)*. Past perfect of *oida* used as imperfect, did not know. *Followed (ēkolouthei)*. Imperfect active, kept on following as the angel had directed (verse 8). *That it was true (hoti alēthes estin)*. Indirect assertion and so present tense retained. Note "true" (*alēthes*) in the sense of reality or actuality. *Which was done (to ginomenon)*. Present middle participle, that which was happening. *Thought he saw a vision (edokei horama blepein)*. Imperfect active, kept on thinking, puzzled as he was. *Blepein* is the infinitive in indirect assertion without the pronoun (he)

expressed which could be either nominative in apposition with the subject as in Rom. 1:22 or accusative of general reference as in Acts 5:36; 8:9 (Robertson, *Grammar*, pp. 1036–40). Peter had had a vision in Joppa (10:10) which Luke describes as an "ecstasy," but here is objective fact, at least Luke thought so and makes that distinction. Peter will soon know whether he is still in the cell or not as we find out that a dream is only a dream when we wake up.

10. *When they were past* (*dielthontes*). Second aorist active participle of *dierchomai*, transitive with *dia* in composition. *The first and the second ward* (*prōtēn phulakēn kai deuteran*). It is not clear to what this language refers. Some take it to mean single soldiers, using *phulakēn* in the sense of a guard (one before the door, one at the iron gate). But it seems hardly likely that the two soldiers with whom Peter had been stationed are meant. Probably the "first ward" means the two soldiers of the quaternion stationed by the door and the second ward some other soldiers, not part of the sixteen, further on in the prison by the iron gate. However understood, the difficulties of escape are made plain. *Unto the iron gate that leadeth into the city* (*epi tēn pulēn tēn sidērān tēn pherousan eis tēn polin*). Note the triple use of the article (the gate the iron one the one leading into the city). For this resumptive use of the article see Robertson, *Grammar*, pp. 762, 764. This iron gate may have opened from a court out into the street and effectually barred escape. *Opened to them* (*ēnoigē autois*). Second aorist passive indicative of *anoigō*, the usual later form though *ēnoichthē* (first aorist passive) occurs also, was opened. *Of its own accord* (*automatē*). Old compound adjective (*autos*, self, obsolete *maō*, to desire eagerly, feminine form though masculine *automatos* also used as feminine). In the N.T. only here and Mark 4:28. It was a strange experience for Peter. The Codex Bezae adds here "went down the seven steps" (*katebēsan tous hepta bathmous*), an interesting detail that adds to the

picture. *One street* (*rhumēn mian*). The angel saw Peter through one of the narrow streets and then left him. We have no means of knowing precisely the location of the prison in the city. On "departed" (*apestē*) see on verse 7.

11. *Was come to himself* (*en heautōi genomenos*). Second aorist middle participle of *ginomai* with *en* and the locative case, "becoming at himself." In Luke 15:17 we have *eis heauton elthōn* (coming to himself, as if he had been on a trip away from himself). *Now I know of a truth* (*nun oida alēthōs*). There was no further confusion of mind that it was an ecstasy as in 10:10. But he was in peril for the soldiers would soon learn of his escape, when the change of guards came at 6 A.M. *Delivered me* (*exeilato me*). Second aorist middle indicative of *exaireō*. The Lord rescued me of himself by his angel. *Expectation* (*prosdokias*). Old word from *prosdokaō*, to look for. In the N.T. only here and Luke 21:26. James had been put to death and the Jewish people were eagerly waiting for the execution of Peter like hungry wolves.

12. *When he had considered* (*sunidōn*). Second aorist active participle of *suneidon* (for the defective verb *sunoraō*), to see together, to grasp as a whole, old verb, but in the N.T. only here and 14:6, save the perfect indicative *sunoida* (I Cor. 4:4) and participle (Acts 5:2). It is the word from which *suneidēsis* (conscience) comes (Rom. 2:15). Peter's mind worked rapidly and he decided what to do. He took in his situation clearly. *To the house of Mary* (*epi tēn oikian tēs Marias*). Another Mary (the others were Mary the mother of Jesus, Mary of Bethany, Mary Magdalene, Mary wife of Cleopas, Mary the mother of James and Joses). She may have been a widow and was possessed of some means since her house was large enough to hold the large group of disciples there. Barnabas, cousin of John Mark her son (Col. 4:10), was also a man of property or had been (Acts 4:36f.). It is probable that the disciples had been in the habit of meeting in her house, a fact known to Peter and he was

evidently fond of John Mark whom he afterwards calls "my son" (I Peter 5:13) and whom he had met here. The upper room of Acts 1:13 may have been in Mary's house and Mark may have been the man bearing a pitcher of water (Luke 22:10) and the young man who fled in the Garden of Gethsemane (Mark 14:51f.). There was a gate and portress here as in the house of the highpriest (John 18:16). Peter knew where to go and even at this early hour hoped to find some of the disciples. Mary is one of the many mothers who have become famous by reason of their sons, though she was undoubtedly a woman of high character herself. *Were gathered together and were praying* (*ēsan sunēthroismenoi kai proseuchomenoi*). Note difference in the tenses, one periphrastic past perfect passive (*sunathroizō* old verb, in the N.T. here only and 19:25 and the uncompounded *throizō* in Luke 24:33) and the periphrastic imperfect. The praying apparently had been going on all night and a large number (many, *hikanoi*) of the disciples were there. One recalls the time when they had gathered to pray (4:31) after Peter had told the disciples of the threats of the Sanhedrin (4:23). God had rescued Peter then. Would he let him be put to death now as James had been?

13. *When he knocked at the door of the gate* (*krousantos autou tēn thuran tou pulōnos*). Genitive absolute with aorist active participle of *krouō*, common verb to knock or knock at. So from the outside (Luke 13:25). *Pulōn* here is the gateway or passageway from the door (*thura*) that leads to the house. In verse 14 it is still the passageway without the use of *thura* (door, so for both door and passageway). *To answer* (*hupakousai*). To listen under before opening. First aorist active infinitive of *hupakouō*, common verb to obey, to hearken. *A maid* (*paidiskē*). Portress as in John 18:17. A diminutive of *pais*, a female slave (so on an ostracon of second century A.D., Deissmann, *Light from the Ancient East*, p. 200). *Rhoda*. A rose. Women can have such beauti-

ful names like Dorcas (Gazelle), Euodia (Sweet Aroma), Syntyche (Good Luck). Mark or Peter could tell Luke her name.

14. *When she knew* (*epignousa*). Second aorist (ingressive) active participle of *epiginōskō*, to know fully or in addition (*epi*), to recognize. She knew Peter and his voice from his frequent visits there. *For joy* (*apo tēs charās*). From her joy (ablative case), life-like picture of the maid who left Peter standing outside with the door to the passageway unopened. Note the aorist tenses for quick action (*ouk ēnoixen*), *eisdramousa* (from *eistrechō*, defective verb, only here in the N.T.), *apēggeilen*. Stood (*hestanai*). Second perfect active infinitive of *histēmi*, intransitive, in indirect assertion with *ton Petron* (Peter) accusative of general reference. The slave girl acted as if she were a member of the family (Furneaux), but she left Peter in peril.

15. *Thou art mad* (*mainēi*). Present middle indicative second person singular. Old verb, only in the middle voice. Festus used the same word to Paul (26:24). The maid was undoubtedly excited, but it was a curious rebuff from those who had been praying all night for Peter's release. In their defence it may be said that Stephen and James had been put to death and many others by Saul's persecution. *She confidently affirmed* (*diischurizeto*). Imperfect middle of *diischurizomai*, an old word of vigorous and confident assertion, originally to lean upon. Only here in the N.T. The girl stuck to her statement. *It is his angel* (*Ho aggelos estin autou*). This was the second alternative of the disciples. It was a popular Jewish belief that each man had a guardian angel. Luke takes no position about it. No scripture teaches it.

16. *Continued knocking* (*epemenen krouōn*). Imperfect active and present participle. Now all heard the knocking. *When they had opened* (*anoixantes*). First aorist active participle of *anoigō* or *-numi*. The whole group rushed out to the courtyard this time to make sure. *They were amazed*

(*exestēsan*). The frequent second aorist active (intransitive) indicative of *existēmi*.

17. There were probably loud exclamations of astonishment and joy. *Beckoning with the hand* (*kataseisas tēi cheiri*). First aorist active participle of *kataseiō*, old verb to signal or shake down with the hand (instrumental case *cheiri*). In the N.T. only in Acts 12:17; 13:16; 19:33; 21:40. The speaker indicates by a downward movement of the hand his desire for ¨silence (to hold their peace, *sigāin*, present active infinitive, to keep silent). Peter was anxious for every precaution and he wanted their instant attention. *Declared* (*diēgēsato*). First aorist middle of *diēgeomai*, old verb to carry through a narrative, give a full story. See also Acts 9:27 of Barnabas in his defence of Saul. Peter told them the wonderful story. *Unto James and the brethren* (*Iakōbōi kai tois adelphois*). Dative case after *apaggeilate* (first aorist active imperative). Evidently "James and the brethren" were not at this meeting, probably meeting elsewhere. There was no place where all the thousands of disciples in Jerusalem could meet. This gathering in the house of Mary may have been of women only or a meeting of the Hellenists. It is plain that this James the Lord's brother, is now the leading presbyter or elder in Jerusalem though there were a number (11:30; 21:18). Paul even terms him apostle (Gal. 1:19), though certainly not one of the twelve. The twelve apostles probably were engaged elsewhere in mission work save James now dead (Acts 12:2) and Peter. The leadership of James is here recognized by Peter and is due, partly to the absence of the twelve, but mainly to his own force of character. He will preside over the Jerusalem Conference (Acts 15:13). *To another place* (*eis heteron topon*). Probably Luke did not know the place and certainly it was prudent for Peter to conceal it from Herod Agrippa. Probably Peter left the city. He is back in Jerusalem at the Conference a few years later (Acts 15:7) and after the death of Herod Agrippa.

Whether Peter went to Rome during these years we do not know. He was recognized later as the apostle to the circumcision (Gal. 2:7; I Peter 1:1) and apparently was in Rome with John Mark when he wrote the First Epistle (I Peter 5:13), unless it is the real Babylon. But, even if Peter went to Rome during this early period, there is no evidence that he founded the church there. If he had done so, in the light of II Cor. 10:16 it would be strange that Paul had not mentioned it in writing to Rome, for he was anxious not to build on another man's foundation (Rom. 15:20). Paul felt sure that he himself had a work to do in Rome. Unfortunately Luke has not followed the ministry of Peter after this period as he does Paul (appearing again only in chapter 15). If Peter really left Jerusalem at this time instead of hiding in the city, he probably did some mission work as Paul says that he did (I Cor. 9:5).

18. *As soon as it was day* (*Genomenēs hēmeras*). Genitive absolute, day having come. *No small stir* (*tarachos ouk oligos*). Litotes (*ouk oligos*), occurs eight times in the Acts as in 15:2, and nowhere else in the N.T. *Tarachos* (stir) is an old word from *tarassō*, to agitate. In the N.T only here and 19:23. Probably all sixteen soldiers were agitated over this remarkable escape. They were responsible for the prisoner with their lives (cf. Acts 16:27; 27:42). Furneaux suggests that Manaen, the king's foster-brother and a Christian (13:1), was the "angel" who rescued Peter from the prison. That is not the way that Peter looked at it. *What was become of Peter* (*ti ara ho Petros egeneto*). An indirect question with the aorist indicative retained. *Ara* adds a syllogism (therefore) to the problem as in Luke 1:66. The use of the neuter *ti* (as in Acts 13:25) is different from *tis*, though nominative like *Petros*, literally, "what then Peter had become," "what had happened to Peter" (in one idiom). See the same idiom in John 21:21 (*houtos de ti*). *But this one what* (verb *genēsetai* not used).

19. *He examined (anakrinas).* First aorist active participle of *anakrinō*, old verb to sift up and down, to question thoroughly, in a forensic sense (Luke 23:14; Acts 4:9; 12:19; 28:18). *That they should be put to death (apachthēnai).* First aorist passive infinitive (indirect command) of *apagō*, old verb to lead away, especially to execution as in Matt. 27: 31. Here it is used absolutely. This was the ordinary Roman routine and not a proof of special cruelty on the part of Herod Agrippa. *Tarried (dietriben).* Imperfect active. Herod Agrippa made his home in Jerusalem, but he went to Caesarea to the public games in honour of Emperor Claudius.

20. *Was highly displeased (ēn thumomachōn).* Periphrastic imperfect active of *thumomacheō*, late compound of *thumos* (passionate heat) and *machomai*, to fight. Only here in the N.T., to fight desperately, to have a hot quarrel. Whether it was open war with the Phoenicians or just violent hostility we do not know, save that Phoenicia belonged to Syria and Herod Agrippa had no authority there. The quarrel may have been over commercial matters. *They came with one accord (homothumadon parēsan).* The representatives of Tyre and Sidon. See on 1:14 for *homothumadon*. Tyre was a colony of Sidon and had become one of the chief commercial cities of the world by reason of the Phoenician ships. *The king's chamberlain (ton epi tou koitōnos tou basileōs).* The one over the bedchamber (*koitōnos*, late word from *koitē*, bed, here only in the N.T.). *Made their friend (peisantes).* First aorist active participle of *peithō*, to persuade. Having persuaded (probably with bribes as in Matt. 28:14). *They asked for peace (ēitounto eirēnēn).* Imperfect middle of *aiteō*, kept on asking for peace. *Because their country was fed (dia to trephesthai autōn tēn choran).* Causal sentence with *dia* and the articular infinitive (present passive of *trephō*, to nourish or feed) and the accusative of general reference, "because of the being fed as to their country." Tyre and Sidon as large commercial cities on the coast

received large supplies of grain and fruits from Palestine. Herod had cut off the supplies and that brought the two cities to action.

21. *Upon a set day* (*taktēi hēmerāi*). Locative case and the verbal adjective of *tassō*, to arrange, appoint, old word, here only in the N.T. Josephus (*Ant.* XVII. 6, 8; XIX. 8, 2) gives a full account of the occasion and the death of Herod Agrippa. It was the second day of the festival in honour of the Emperor Claudius, possibly his birthday rather than the *Quinquennalia*. The two accounts of Luke and Josephus supplement each other with no contradiction. Josephus does not mention the name of Blastus. *Arrayed himself in royal apparel* (*endusamenos esthēta basilikēn*). First aorist middle (indirect) participle of *endunō* or *enduō*, common verb to put on. Literally, having put royal apparel on himself (a robe of silver tissue, Josephus says). The rays of the sun shone on this brilliant apparel and the vast crowd in the open amphitheatre became excited as Herod began to speak. *Made an oration* (*edēmēgorei*). Imperfect active of *dēmēgoreō*, old verb from *dēmēgoros* (haranguer of the people), and that from *dēmos* (people) and *agoreuō*, to harangue or address the people. Only here in the N.T. He kept it up.

22. *Shouted* (*epephōnei*). Imperfect active, kept on shouting, calling out to him. Old verb, but only four times in the N.T. and all by Luke. The heathen crowd (*dēmos*) repeated their flattering adulation to gain Herod's favour. *The voice of a god* (*theou phōnē*). In the pagan sense of emperor worship, not as the Supreme Being. But it was pleasing to Herod Agrippa's vanity.

23. *Smote him* (*epataxen auton*). Effective aorist active indicative of *patassō*, old verb, used already in verse 7 of gentle smiting of the angel of the Lord, here of a severe stroke of affliction. Like Nebuchadnezzar (Dan. 4:30) pride went before a fall. He was struck down in the very zenith of his glory. *Because* (*anth' hōn*). *Anti* with the genitive of the

relative pronoun, "in return for which things." He accepted
the impious flattery (Hackett) instead of giving God the
glory. He was a nominal Jew. *He was eaten of worms* (*genomenos skōlēkobrōtos*). Ingressive aorist middle participle,
"becoming worm-eaten." The compound verbal adjective
(*skōlēx*, worm, *brōtos*, eaten, from *bibrōskō*) is a late word
(II Macc. 9:9) of the death of Antiochus Epiphanes, used
also of a tree (Theophrastus), here only in the N.T.   The
word *skōlēx* was used of intestinal worms and Herodotus (IV.
205) describes Pheretima, Queen of Cyrene, as having
swarms of worms which ate her flesh while still alive. Josephus (*Ant.* XIX. 8, 2) says that Herod Agrippa lingered
for five days and says that the rotting of his flesh produced
worms, an item in harmony with the narrative in Luke.
Josephus gives further details, one a superstitious sight of an
owl sitting on one of the ropes of the awning of the theatre
while the people flattered him, an omen of his death to him.
Luke puts it simply that God smote him. *Gave up the ghost*
(*exepsuxen*).   Effective aorist active of *ekpsuchō*, to breathe
out, late verb, medical term in Hippocrates, in the N.T.
only in Acts 5:5, 10; 12:23. Herod was carried out of the
theatre a dying man and lingered only five days.

24. *Grew and multiplied* (*ēuxanen kai eplēthuneto*). Imperfect active and passive.   Cf. 6:1.   The reaction from the
death of James and the imprisonment of Peter.

25. *From Jerusalem* (*ex Ierousalēm*).   Probably correct
text, though D has *apo*. Westcott and Hort follow Aleph B
in reading *eis* (*to*) Jerusalem, an impossible reading contradicted by 11:29f. and 13:1. The ministration (*diakonian*)
referred to is that in 11:29f. which may have taken place,
in point of time, after the death of Herod. *Taking with them*
(*sunparalabontes*).   Taking along (*para*) with (*sun*) them,
John Mark from Jerusalem (12:12) to Antioch (13:1). The
aorist participle does not express subsequent action as Rackham here argues (Robertson, *Grammar*, pp. 861–863).

CHAPTER XIII

1. *In the church that was there* (*kata tēn ousan ekklēsian*). Possibly distributed throughout the church (note "in the church" 11:26). Now a strong organization there. Luke here begins the second part of Acts with Antioch as the centre of operations, no longer Jerusalem. Paul is now the central figure instead of Peter. Jerusalem had hesitated too long to carry out the command of Jesus to take the gospel to the whole world. That glory will now belong to Antioch. *Prophets and teachers* (*prophētai kai didaskaloi*). All prophets were teachers, but not all teachers were prophets who were for-speakers of God, sometimes fore-speakers like Agabus in 11:28. The double use of *te* here makes three prophets (Barnabas, Symeon, Lucius) and two teachers (Manaen and Saul). Barnabas heads the list (11:22) and Saul comes last. Symeon Niger may be the Simon of Cyrene who carried the Saviour's cross. Lucius of Cyrene was probably one of the original evangelists (11:20). The name is one of the forms of Luke, but it is certainly not Luke the Physician. Manaen shows how the gospel was reaching some of the higher classes (home of Herod Antipas). *Foster-brother* (*suntrophos*). Old word for nourished with or brought up with one *collactaneus* (Vulgate). These are clearly the outstanding men in the great Greek church in Antioch.

2. *As they ministered to the Lord* (*leitourgountōn autōn toi kuriōi*). Genitive absolute of *leitourgeō*, old verb, used of the Attic orators who served the state at their own cost (*leōs* or *laos*, people, and *ergon*, work or service). Common in the LXX of the priests who served in the tabernacle (Ex. 28:31, 39) like *leitourgia* (Luke 1:23) which see. So in Heb. 10:11. In Rom. 15:27 of aiding others in poverty. Here of

worship (prayer, exhortation, fasting). The word liturgy grows out of this use. *And fasted (kai nēsteuontōn)*. Genitive absolute also. Christian Jews were keeping up the Jewish fast (Luke 18:12). Note fasting also in the choice of elders for the Mission Churches (Acts 14:23). Fasting was not obligatory on the Christians, but they were facing a great emergency in giving the gospel to the Gentile world. *Separate me (aphorisate dē moi)*. First aorist active imperative of *aphorizō*, old verb to mark off boundaries or horizon, used by Paul of his call (Rom. 1:1; Gal. 1:15). The Greek has *dē*, a shortened form of *ēdē* and like Latin *jam* and German *doch*, now therefore. It ought to be preserved in the translation. Cf. Luke 2:15; Acts 15:36; I Cor. 6:20. *Moi* is the ethical dative. As in verse 1 Barnabas is named before Saul. Both had been called to ministry long ago, but now this call is to the special campaign among the Gentiles. Both had been active and useful in such work. *Whereunto (ho)*. Here *eis* has to be repeated from *eis to ergon* just before, "for which" as Jesus sent the twelve and the seventy in pairs, so here. Paul nearly always had one or more companions.

3. *When they had fasted (nēsteusantes)*. Either finishing the same fast in verse 2 or another one (Hackett), but clearly a voluntary fast. *Laid their hands upon them (epithentes tas cheiras autois)*. Second aorist active participle of *epitithēmi*. Not ordination to the ministry, but a solemn consecration to the great missionary task to which the Holy Spirit had called them. Whether the whole church took part in this ceremony is not clear, though in 15:40 "the brethren" did commend Paul and Silas. Perhaps some of them here acted for the whole church, all of whom approved the enterprise. But Paul makes it plain in Phil. 4:15 that the church in Antioch did not make financial contribution to the campaign, but only goodwill. But that was more than the church at Jerusalem would have done as a whole since Peter had been arraigned there for his activities in Caesarea (Acts

11:1–18). Clearly Barnabas and Saul had to finance the tour themselves. It was Philippi that first gave money to Paul's campaigns. There were still heathen enough in Antioch, but the church approved the going of Barnabas and Saul, their very best.

4. *So they* (*autoi men oun*). They themselves indeed therefore. No contrast is necessary, though there is a slight one in verses 5 and 6. Luke again refers to the Holy Spirit as the source of their authority for this campaign rather than the church at Antioch. *Sent forth* (*ekpemphthentes*). Old verb from *ekpempō* and first aorist passive participle, but in the N.T. only here and Acts 17:10. *Sailed* (*apepleusan*). Effective aorist active indicative of *apopleō*, old verb to sail away, depart from. In the N.T. only here and 14:26; 20:15; 27:1. Barnabas was from Cyprus where there were many Jews.

5. *Proclaimed* (*katēggellon*). Imperfect active of *kataggellō*, inchoative, began to proclaim. This was Paul's rule of procedure, "to the Jew first" (Rom. 1:16; Acts 13:46; 17:2; 18:4, 19; 19:8). *They had also* (*eichon de kai*). Imperfect active, descriptive. *As their attendant* (*hupēretēn*). Literally, "under-rower" (*hupo, eretēs*) in the trireme. Probably here minister (*chazzan*) or assistant in the synagogue as in Luke 4:20. Cf. Matt. 5:25. It is not clear what John Mark did, though he was evidently selected by Barnabas as his cousin. He may have helped in the baptizing. There were probably others also in the company (verse 13). The "also" may mean that Mark did some preaching. Barnabas was probably the leader in the work in these Jewish synagogues.

6. *Unto Paphos* (*achri Paphou*). The new Paphos at the other end of the island, reached by a fine Roman road, some eight miles north of the old Paphos famous for the worship of Venus. *A certain sorcerer, a false prophet, a Jew* (*andra tina magon pseudoprophētēn Ioudaion*). Literally, "a certain man" (*andra tina*) with various descriptive epithets. The

word *magon* does not necessarily mean "sorcerer," but only a *magus* (Matt. 2:1, 7, 10 which see). The bad sense occurs in Acts 8:9, 11 (Simon Magus) and is made plain here by "false prophet." In verse 8 here Barjesus (Son of Jesus) is called "Elymas the sorcerer (or Magian)," probably his professional title, as Luke interprets the Arabic or Aramaic word Elymas. These Jewish mountebanks were numerous and had great influence with the uneducated. In Acts 19:13 the seven sons of Sceva, Jewish exorcists, tried to imitate Paul. If one is surprised that a man like Sergius Paulus should fall under the influence of this fraud, he should recall what Juvenal says of the Emperor Tiberius "sitting on the rock of Capri with his flock of Chaldaeans around him."

7. *With the proconsul Sergius Paulus* (*sun tōi anthupatōi Sergiōi Paulōi*). Luke used to be sharply criticized for applying this term to Sergius Paulus on the ground that Cyprus was a province under the appointment of the emperor with the title of propraetor and not under the control of the senate with the title of proconsul. That was true B.C. 30, but five years later it was changed to proconsul by Augustus and put under the control of the Senate. Two inscriptions have been found with the date A.D. 51 and 52 with the names of proconsuls of Cyprus and one is in the Cesnola Collection, an inscription found at Soli with the name of Paulus as Proconsul, undoubtedly this very man, though no date occurs. *A man of understanding* (*andri sunetōi*). All the more amazing that he should be a victim of Barjesus. He had given up idolatry at any rate and was eager to hear Barnabas and Saul.

8. *Withstood them* (*anthistato autois*). Imperfect middle of *anthistēmi*, to stand against (face to face). Dative case (*autois*). He persisted in his opposition and was unwilling to lose his great prize. There may have been a public discussion between Elymas and Saul. *To turn aside* (*diastrepsai*).

First aorist active infinitive of *diastrephō*, old verb to turn or twist in two, to distort, to pervert (cf. Matt. 17:17; Luke 23:2).

9. *But Saul, who is also called Paul* (*Saulos de, ho kai Paulos*). By this remarkably brief phrase Luke presents this epoch in the life of Saul Paul. The "also" (*kai*) does not mean that the name Paul was given now for the first time, rather than he had always had it. As a Jew and a Roman citizen, he undoubtedly had both names all the time (cf. John Mark, Symeon Niger, Barsabbas Justus). Jerome held that the name of Sergius Paulus was adopted by Saul because of his conversion at this time, but this is a wholly unlikely explanation, "an element of vulgarity impossible to St. Paul" (Farrar). Augustine thought that the meaning of the Latin *paulus* (little) would incline Saul to adopt, "but as a proper name the word rather suggested the glories of the Aemilian family, and even to us recalls the name of another Paulus, who was 'lavish of his noble life' " (Page). Among the Jews the name Saul was naturally used up to this point, but from now on Luke employs Paul save when there is a reference to his previous life (Acts 22:7; 26:14). His real career is work among the Gentiles and Paul is the name used by them. There is a striking similarity in sound between the Hebrew Saul and the Roman Paul. Paul was proud of his tribe of Benjamin and so of King Saul (Phil. 3:5). *Filled with the Holy Spirit* (*plēstheis pneumatos hagiou*). First aorist (ingressive) passive participle of *pimplēmi* with the genitive case. A special influx of power to meet this emergency. Here was a cultured heathen, typical of the best in Roman life, who called forth all the powers of Paul plus the special help of the Holy Spirit to expose the wickedness of Elymas Barjesus. If one wonders why the Holy Spirit filled Paul for this emergency rather than Barnabas, when Barnabas was named first in 13:2, he can recall the sovereignty of the Holy Spirit in his choice of agents (I Cor.

12:4–11) and also the special call of Paul by Christ (Acts 9:15; 26:17f.). *Fastened his eyes* (*atenisas*). As already in Luke 4:20; 22:56; Acts 3:4, 12; 6:15; 10:4.

10. *Of all guile* (*pantos dolou*). From *delō*, to catch with bait, old word, already seen in Matt. 26:4; Mark 7:22; 14:1. Paul denounces Elymas as a trickster. *All villainy* (*pāsēs rhāidiourgias*). Late compound from *rhāidiourgos* (*rhāidios*, easy, facile, *ergon*, deed, one who does a thing adroitly and with ease). So levity in Xenophon and unscrupulousness in Polybius, Plutarch, and the papyri. Only here in the N.T., though the kindred word *rhāidiourgēma* occurs in Acts 18:14. With deadly accuracy Paul pictured this slick rascal. *Thou son of the devil* (*huie diabolou*). Damning phrase like that used by Jesus of the Pharisees in John 8:44, a slanderer like the *diabolos*. This use of son (*huios*) for characteristic occurs in Acts 3:25; 4:36, a common Hebrew idiom, and may be used purposely by Paul in contrast with the name Barjesus (son of Jesus) that Elymas bore (13:6). *Enemy of all righteousness* (*echthre pāsēs dikaiosunēs*). Personal enemy to all justice, sums up all the rest. Note triple use of "all" (*pantos, pāsēs, pāsēs*), total depravity in every sense. *Wilt thou not cease?* (*ou pausēi*). An impatient rhetorical question, almost volitive in force (Robertson, *Grammar*, p. 874). Note *ou*, not *mē*, *To pervert* (*diastrephōn*). Present active participle describing the actual work of Elymas as a perverter or distorter (see verse 8). More exactly, Wilt thou not cease perverting? *The right ways of the Lord* (*tas hodous tou kuriou tas eutheias*). The ways of the Lord the straight ones as opposed to the crooked ways of men (Isa. 40:4; 42:16; Luke 3:5). The task of John the Baptist as of all prophets and preachers is to make crooked paths straight and to get men to walk in them. This false prophet was making even the Lord's straight ways crooked. Elymas has many successors.

11. *Upon thee* (*epi se*). The use of *epi* with the accusative

is rich and varied, the precise shade of meaning depending on the content. The "hand of the Lord" might be kindly (Acts 11:21) or hostile (Heb. 10:31), but when God's hand touches one's life (Job 19:21) it may be in judgment as here with Elymas. He has not humbled himself under the mighty hand of God (I Peter 5:6). *Not seeing* (*mē blepōn*). Repeating with negative participle the negative idea in "blind" (*tuphlos*). "It was a judicial infliction; blindness for blindness, darkness without for wilful darkness within" (Furneaux). He was an example of the blind leading the blind that was to cease and Sergius Paulus was to be led into the light. The blindness was to be "for a season" (*achri kairou*, Luke 4:13), if it should please God to restore his sight. Paul apparently recalls his own blindness as he entered Damascus. *A mist* (*achlus*). Especially a dimness of the eyes, old poetic word and late prose, in LXX, only here in N.T. Galen uses it of the opacity of the eye caused by a wound. *He went about seeking some one to lead him by the hand* (*periagōn ezētei cheiragōgous*). A rather free rendering. Literally, "going about (*periagōn*, present active participle of *periagō*) he was seeking (*ezētei*, imperfect active of *zēteō*) guides (*cheiragōgous*, from *cheir*, hand, and *agōgos*, guide, from *agō*, one who leads by the hand)." The very verb *cheiragōgeō*, to lead by the hand, Luke uses of Paul in 9:8, as he entered Damascus.

12. *Believed* (*episteusen*). Ingressive aorist active indicative. Renan considers it impossible that a Roman proconsul could be converted by a miracle. But it was the teaching about the Lord (*tou kuriou*, objective genitive) by which he was astonished (*ekplēssomenos*, present passive participle of *ekplēssō*, see on Matt. 7:28) or struck out as well as by the miracle. The blindness came "immediately" (*parachrēma*) upon the judgment pronounced by Paul. It is possible that Sergius Paulus was converted to Christ without openly identifying himself with the Christians as

his baptism is not mentioned as in the case of Cornelius. But, even if he was baptized, he need not have been deposed from his proconsulship as Furneaux and Rackham argue because his office called for "official patronage of idolatrous worship." But that could have been merely perfunctory as it probably was already. He had been a disciple of the Jewish magician, Elymas Barjesus, without losing his position. Imperial persecution against Christianity had not yet begun. Furneaux even suggests that the conversion of a proconsul to Christianity at this stage would have called for mention by the Roman and Greek historians. There is the name Sergia Paullina in a Christian cemetery in Rome which shows that one of his family was a Christian later. One will believe what he wills about Sergius Paulus, but I do not see that Luke leaves him in the category of Simon Magus who "believed" (8:13) for revenue only.

13. *Paul and his company* .(*hoi peri Paulon*). Neat Greek idiom as in Plato, Cratylus 440 C *hoi peri Herakleiton.* On this idiom see Gildersleeve, *Syntax*, p. 264. It means a man and his followers, "those around Paul." Now Paul ranks first always in Acts save in 14:2; 15:12, 25 for special reasons. Heretofore Saul (Paul) held a secondary position (9:27; 11:30; 13:1f.). "In nothing is the greatness of Barnabas more manifest than in his recognition of the superiority of Paul and acceptance of a secondary position for himself" (Furneaux). *Set sail* (*anachthentes*). First aorist passive participle of *anagō.* Thirteen times in the Acts and Luke 8:22 which see. They sailed up to sea and came down (*katagō, katabainō*) to land. So it looks. *Departed from them* (*apochōrēsas ap' autōn*). First aorist active participle of *apochōreō*, old verb to withdraw, go away from. In the N.T. only here and Matt. 7:23; Luke 9:39. He is called John there as in verse 5 and Mark in 15:39, though John Mark in 12:12, 25. This may be accidental or on purpose (Deiss-

mann, *Bible Studies*, p. 317). Luke is silent on John's reasons
for leaving Paul and Barnabas. He was the cousin of Barnabas and may not have relished the change in leadership.
There may have been change in plans also now that Paul
is in command. Barnabas had chosen Cyprus and Paul
has led them to Perga in Pamphylia and means to go on into
the highlands to Antioch in Pisidia. There were perils of
many sorts around them and ahead (II Cor. 11:26), perils to
which John Mark was unwilling to be exposed. Paul will
specifically charge him at Antioch with desertion of his
post (Acts 15:39). It is possible, as Ramsay suggests, that
the mosquitoes at Perga gave John malaria. If so, they bit
Paul and Barnabas also. He may not have liked Paul's
aggressive attitude towards the heathen. At any rate he
went home to Jerusalem instead of to Antioch, *zu seiner
Mutter* (Holtzmann). It was a serious breach in the work,
but Paul and Barnabas stuck to the work.

14. *Passing through* (*dielthontes*). It is not clear why Paul
and Barnabas left Perga so soon nor why they went to Antioch in Pisidia. Ramsay suggests malaria that spurred them on
to the hills after the desertion of John Mark. They preached
at Perga on the return (14:25) and apparently hurried away
now. Farrar thinks that the hot weather had driven the
population to the hills. At any rate it is not difficult to
imagine the perils of this climb over the rough mountain
way from Perga to Pisidian Antioch to which Paul apparently refers in II Cor. 11:26. *Sat down* (*ekathisan*). Ingressive
aorist active indicative, took their seats as visiting Jews,
possibly in the seats of the rabbis (J. Lightfoot). Whether
they expected to be called on or not, they were given the
opportunity as prominent visitors. The Pisidian Antioch was
really in Phrygia, but towards Pisidia to distinguish it from
Antioch on the Maeander (Ramsay, *Church in the Roman
Empire*, p. 25). It was a colony like Philippi and so a free
city. If Paul is referring to South Galatia and not North

Galatia in Gal. 4:13 when he says that his preaching in Galatia at first was due to illness, then it was probably here at Pisidian Antioch. What it was we have no means of knowing, though it was a temptation in his flesh to them so severe that they were willing to pluck out their eyes for him (Gal. 4:14f.). Opthalmia, malaria, epilepsy have all been suggested as this stake in the flesh (II Cor. 12:7). But Paul was able to preach with power whatever his actual physical condition was.

15. *After the reading of the law and the prophets* (*meta tēn anagnōsin tou nomou kai tōn prophētōn*). The law was first read in the synagogues till B.C. 163 when Antiochus Epiphones prohibited it. Then the reading of the prophets was substituted for it. The Maccabees restored both. There was a reading from the law and one from the prophets in Hebrew which was interpreted into the Aramaic or the Greek *Koiné* for the people. The reading was followed by the sermon as when Jesus was invited to read and to preach in Nazareth (Luke 4:16f.). For the service in the synagogue see Schuerer, *History of the Jewish People*, Div. II, Vol. II, pp. 79ff. It was the duty of the rulers of the synagogue (*archisunagōgoi*) to select the readers and the speakers for the service (Mark 5:22, 35–38; Luke 8:49; 13:14; Acts 13:15; 18:8, 17). Any rabbi or distinguished stranger could be called on to speak. *If ye have any word of exhortation for the people* (*ei tis estin en humin logos paraklēseōs pros ton laon*). Literally, if there is among you any word of exhortation for the people. It is a condition of the first class and assumed to be true, a polite invitation. On "exhortation" (*paraklēsis*) see 9:31. It may be a technical phrase used in the synagogue (Heb. 13:22; I Tim. 4:13).

16. *Paul stood up* (*anastas Paulos*). The Jewish custom was to sit while speaking (Luke 4:20), but the Greek and Roman was to stand (Acts 17:22). It is possible as Lewin (*Life of St. Paul*, Vol. I, p. 141) suggests that here Paul

stepped upon the platform and then took his seat as he began to speak or he may have followed the Greek and Roman custom. Paul is the leader now and the more gifted speaker (Acts 14:12), so that he responds to the courteous invitation of the rulers. *Beckoning* (*kataseisas*). First aorist active participle of *kataseiō*, old verb to shake down, a dramatic gesture for quiet and order like Peter in 12:17 and Paul on the steps of the tower of Antonia (21:40). *And ye that fear God* (*kai hoi phoboumenoi ton theon*). Evidently large numbers of these Gentiles like Cornelius in Caesarea were present. They offered Paul a great opportunity for reaching the purely pagan Gentiles. This (verses 16–41) is the first full report of a sermon of Paul's that Luke has preserved for us. He is now a practised preacher of the gospel that he began proclaiming at Damascus, that Jesus of Nazareth is the Messiah of promise and the Saviour of the whole world both Jew and Gentile if they will only believe on him and be saved. It is possible that Paul here based his sermon on the passages of the law and the prophets that had just been read. He uses two words from the LXX, one in verse 19 from Deut. 1:31 *etrophophorēsen* (as a nursing-father bare he them), the reading of many old MSS. and the one preferred by the American Committee, the other in verse 17 from Isaiah 1:2 *hupsōsen* (exalted). At any rate it is clear that Paul spoke in Greek so that all could understand his sermon. He may have written out notes of this sermon afterwards for Luke. The keynotes of Paul's theology as found in his Epistles appear in this sermon. It is interesting to observe the steady growth of Paul's Christology as he faced the great problems of his day. Here we see Paul's gospel for the Jews and the God-fearers (Gentiles friendly to the Jews).

17. *Chose* (*exelexato*). First aorist middle (indirect), selected for himself. Israel was the chosen people. *Exalted* (*hupsōsen*). From *hupsoō*, late verb from *hupsos* so often

used of Christ. *When they sojourned* (*en tēi paroikiāi*). In the sojourn. Late word from *paroikos* (sojourner, dweller, Acts 7:6) common in LXX. In N.T. only here and I Peter 1:17. *With a high arm* (*meta brachionos hupsēlou*). Vivid picture from the LXX (Ex. 6:1, 6; Deut. 5:15; Psa. 136:12).

18. *Suffered he their manners* (*etropophorēsen*). First aorist active indicative of *tropophoreō*, late word from *tropos*, manner, and *pherō*, reading of Aleph B D and accepted by Westcott and Hort. But A C Sahidic Bohairic read *etrophophorēsen* from *trophophoreō* (*trophos*, a nurse, and *pherō*,) late word (II Macc. 7:27), probably correct word here and Deut. 1:31.

19. *When he had destroyed* (*kathelōn*). Second aorist active participle of *kathaireō*, to tear down, old verb. *He gave them for an inheritance* (*kateklēronomēsen*). First aorist active indicative of the double compound verb *kata-klēro-nomeō*, late verb in LXX (Numb. 34:18; Deut. 3:28; Josh. 14:1) and only here in the N.T., to distribute by lot, to distribute as an inheritance. This is the correct reading and not *kateklērodotēsen* from *kataklērodoteō* of the Textus Receptus. These two verbs were confused in the MSS. of the LXX as well as here. *For about four hundred and fifty years* (*hōs etesin tetrakosiois kai pentēkonta*). Associative instrumental case with an expression of time as in 8:11; Luke 8:29 (Robertson, *Grammar*, p. 527). The oldest MSS. (Aleph A B C Vg Sah Boh) place these figures before "after these things" and so in verse 19. This is the true reading and is in agreement with the notation in I Kings 6:1. The difficulty found in the Textus Receptus (King James Version) thus disappears with the true text. The four hundred and fifty years runs therefore from the birth of Isaac to the actual conquest of Canaan and does not cover the period of the Judges. See on Acts 7:6.

20. *And after these things* (*kai meta tauta*). That is, the time of the Judges then began. Cf. Judges 2:16. *Until*

Samuel the prophet (*heōs Samouēl prophētou*). The *terminus ad quem*. He was the last of the judges and the first of the prophets who selected the first king (Saul) under God's guidance. Note the absence of the Greek article with *prophētou*.

21. *They asked* (*ēitēsanto*). First aorist indirect middle indicative, they asked for themselves. They were tired of a theocracy. Cf. I Sam. 8:5; 10:1. Paul mentions with pride that Benjamin was the tribe of Saul (his name also), but he does not allude to Saul's sin (Furneaux). *For the space of forty years* (*etē tesserakonta*). Accusative of extent of time. Not in the O.T., but in Josephus, *Ant.* VI. 14, 9.

22. *When he had removed him* (*metastēsas auton*). First aorist active participle of *methistēmi*, old verb to transfer, to transpose (note force of *meta*). This verb occurs in Luke 16:4 by the unjust steward about his removal from office. Cf. I Sam. 15:16. *To be* (*eis*). As or for, Greek idiom like the Hebrew *le*, common in the LXX. *A man after my heart* (*andra kata tēn kardian mou*). The words quoted by Paul as a direct saying of God are a combination of Psa. 89:20, 21 and I Sam. 13:14 (the word of the Lord to Samuel about David). Knowling thinks that this free and rather loose quotation of the substance argues for the genuineness of the report of Paul's sermon. Hackett observes that the commendation of David is not absolute, but, as compared with the disobedient Saul, he was a man who did God's will in spite of the gross sin of which he repented (Psa. 51). Note "wills" (*thelēmata*), plural, of God.

23. *Of this man's seed* (*toutou apo tou spermatos*). Emphatic position of *toutou*. Of this one from the (his) seed. *According to promise* (*kat' epaggelian*). This phrase in Gal. 3:29; II Tim. 1:1. See the promise in II Sam. 7:2; Psa. 132:11; Isa. 11:1, 10; Jer. 23:5f.; Zech. 3:8. In Zech. 3:8 the verb *agō* is used of the sending of the Messiah as here. *A Saviour Jesus* (*Sōtēra Iēsoun*). Jesus is in apposition with

Saviour (accusative case) and comes at the end of the sentence in contrast with "this man" (David) at the beginning. Paul goes no further than David because he suggests to him Jesus, descendant in the flesh from David. By "Israel" here Paul means the Jewish people, though he will later enlarge this promise to include the spiritual Israel both Gentile and Jew (Rom. 9:6f.).

24. *When John had first preached* (*prokēruxantos Iōanou*). Literally, John heralding beforehand, as a herald before the king (Luke 3:3). Genitive absolute of first aorist active participle of *prokērussō*, old verb to herald beforehand, here alone in the N.T., though Textus Receptus has it also in Acts 3:20. *Before his coming* (*pro prosōpou tēs eisodou autou*). Literally, before the face of his entering in (here act of entrance as I Thess. 1:9, not the gate as in Heb. 10:19). See Mal. 3:1 quoted in Matt. 11:10 (=Luke 7:27) for this Hebrew phrase and also Luke 1:76. *The baptism of repentance* (*baptisma metanoias*). Baptism marked by, characterized by (genitive case, case of kind or species) repentance (change of mind and life). The very phrase used of John's preaching in Mark 1:4=Luke 3:3. It is clear therefore that Paul understood John's ministry and message as did Peter (Acts 2:38; 10:37).

25. *As John was fulfilling his course* (*hōs eplērou Iōanēs ton dromon*). Imperfect active of *plēroō*, describing his vivid ministry without defining the precise period when John asked the question. Paul uses this word *dromos* (course) of his own race (Acts 20:24; II Tim. 4:7). *What suppose ye that I am?* (*Ti eme huponoeite einai?*) Note *ti* (neuter), not *tina* (masculine), *what* not *who*, character, not identity. It is indirect discourse (the infinitive *einai* and the accusative of general reference). *Huponoeō* (*hupo, noeō*) is to think secretly, to suspect, to conjecture. *I am not he* (*ouk eimi egō*). These precise words are not given in the Gospels, but the idea is the same as the disclaimers by the Baptist

in John 1:19–27 (cf. also Matt. 3:11 = Mark 1:7 = Luke
3:16). Paul had a true grasp of the message of the Baptist.
He uses the very form *lūsai* (first aorist active infinitive of
luō) found in Mark 1:7 and Luke 3:16 and the word for
shoes (*hupodēma*, singular) in all three. His quotation is
remarkably true to the words in the Synoptic Gospels. How
did Paul get hold of the words of the Baptist so clearly?

26. *To us* (*hēmin*). Both Jews and Gentiles, both classes
in Paul's audience, dative of advantage. *Is sent forth* (*ex-
apestalē*). Second aorist passive indicative of the double
compound verb *exapostellō*, common verb to send out (*ex*)
and forth (*apo*). It is a climacteric or culminative aorist
tense. It has come to us in one day, this glorious promise.
The word of this salvation (*ho logos tēs sōtērias tautēs*). The
message of Jesus as Saviour (verse 23), long ago promised
and now come to us as Saviour.

27. *Because they knew him not* (*touton agnoēsantes*). First
aorist active participle (causal) of *agnoeō*, old verb, not to
know. Peter gives "ignorance" (*agnoia*) as the excuse of the
Jews in the death of Christ (3:17) and Paul does the same
about his conduct before his conversion (I Tim. 1:13).
This ignorance mitigated the degree of their guilt, but it did
not remove it, for it was willing ignorance and prejudice.
The voices of the prophets which are read (*tas phōnas tōn
prophētōn tas anaginōskomenas*). Object also of *agnoēsantes*,
though it could be the object of *eplērōsan* (fulfilled) if *kai*
is taken as "also". The "voices" were heard as they were
read aloud each Sabbath in the synagogue. In their ignorant
condemnation they fulfilled the prophecies about the suffering Messiah.

28. *Though they found no cause of death* (*mēdemian aitian
thanatou heurontes*). Second aorist active with usual negative of the participle. As a matter of fact the Sanhedrin did
charge Jesus with blasphemy, but could not prove it (Matt.
26:65; 27:24; Luke 23:22). At this time no Gospel had prob-

ably been written, but Paul knew that Jesus was innocent. He uses this same idiom about his own innocence (Acts 28: 18). *That he should be slain (anairethēnai auton).* First aorist passive infinitive, the accusative case, the direct object of *ēitēsanto* (first aorist middle indicative, asked as a favour to themselves).

29. *From the tree (apo tou xulou).* Not here strictly a tree, but wood as already in 5:30; 10:29 and later in Gal. 3:13. Strictly speaking, it was Joseph of Arimathea and Nicodemus who took the body of Jesus down from the cross, though the Jews had asked Pilate to have the bones of Jesus broken that his body should not remain on the cross during the Sabbath (John 19:31). Paul does not distinguish the details here. *Laid (ethēkan).* First (kappa) aorist active indicative third plural of *tithēmi* in place of *ethesan* the usual second aorist active plural form. *Tomb (mnēmeion).* Memorial, common in the Gospels.

30. *But God raised him from the dead (ho de theos ēgeiren ek nekrōn).* This crucial fact Paul puts sharply as he always did.

31. *Was seen for many days (ōphthē epi hēmeras pleious).* The common verb (first aorist passive indicative of *horaō*, to see) for the appearance of the Risen Christ, the one used by Paul of his own vision of Christ (I Cor. 15:8), which is not reported by Luke here. For more days (than a few), the language means, forty in all (1:3). *Of them that came up with him (tois sunanabāsin autōi).* Dative (after *ōphthē*) articular participle (second aorist active of *sunanabainō*) with associative instrumental case (*autōi*), the very men who knew him best and who could not be easily deceived about the reality of his resurrection. But this fact rules Paul out on this point, for he had not fellowshipped with Jesus from Galilee to Jerusalem. *Who are now his witnesses (hoitines nun eisin martures autou).* The very point that Peter used to clinch his argument with such powerful effect (2:32; 3:15).

32. *We bring you good tidings of the promise* (*hēmeis humās euaggelizometha tēn epaggelian*). Two accusatives here (person and thing), old Greek did not use accusative of the person with this verb as in 16:10; Luke 3:18. Note "we you" together. Here the heart of Paul's message on this occasion.

33. *Hath fulfilled* (*ekpeplērōken*). Hath filled out (*ek*). *Unto our children* (*tois teknois hēmōn*). The MSS. vary greatly here about *hēmōn* (our), some have *autōn*, some *autōn hēmin*. Westcott and Hort consider these readings "a primitive error" for *hēmin* (to us) taken with *anastēsas Iēsoun* (having for us raised up Jesus). This raising up (from *anistēmi*, set up) as in 3:22; 7:37 refers not to resurrection (verse 34), but to the sending of Jesus (two raisings up). *In the second psalm* (*en tōi psalmōi tōi deuterōi*). Psa. 2:7. D has *prōtōi* because the first psalm was often counted as merely introductory.

34. *Now no more to return to corruption* (*mēketi mellonta hupostrephein eis diaphthoran*). No longer about to return as Lazarus did. Jesus did not die again and so is the first fruits of the resurrection (I Cor. 15:23; Rom. 6:9). *He hath spoken* (*eirēken*). Present perfect active indicative, common way of referring to the permanent utterances of God which are on record in the Scriptures. *The holy and sure blessings of David* (*ta hosia Daueid ta pista*). See II Sam. 7:13. Literally, "the holy things of David the trustworthy things." He explains "the holy things" at once.

35. *Because* (*dioti*). Compound conjunction (*dia, hoti*) like our "because that." The reason for the previous statement about "the holy things." *Thou wilt not give thy holy one to see corruption* (*ou dōseis ton hosion sou idein diaphthoran*). Quotation from Psa. 16:10 to show that Jesus did not see corruption in his body, a flat contradiction for those who deny the bodily resurrection of Jesus.

36. *His own generation* (*idiāi geneāi*). Either locative case, "in his own generation" or dative object of *hupēretēsas*

(served). *The counsel of God* (*tēi tou theou boulēi*). So here, either the dative, the object of *hupēretēsas* if *geneāi* is locative, or the instrumental case "by the counsel of God" which again may be construed either with *hupēretēsas* (having served) or after *ekoimēthē* (fell on sleep). Either of the three ways is grammatical and makes good sense. *Koimaomai* for death we have already had (Acts 7:60). So Jesus (John 11:11) and Paul (I Cor. 15:6, 51). *Was laid* (*prosetethē*). Was added unto (first aorist passive indicative of *prostithēmi*). See the verb in 2:47; 5:14. This figure for death probably arose from the custom of burying families together (Gen. 15:15; Judg. 2:10). *Saw corruption* (*eiden diaphthoran*). As Jesus did not (Acts 2:31) as he shows in verse 37.

38. *Through this man* (*dia toutou*). This very man whom the Jews had crucified and whom God had raised from the dead. Remission of sins (*aphesis hamartiōn*) is proclaimed (*kataggelletai*) to you. This is the keynote of Paul's message as it had been that of Peter at Pentecost (2:38; 5:31; 10:43). Cf. 26:18. This glorious message Paul now presses home in his exhortation.

39. *And by him every one that believeth is justified from all things, from which ye could not be justified by the law of Moses* (*kai apo pantōn hōn ouk ēdunēthēte en nomōi Mōuseōs dikaiothēnai en toutōi pās ho pisteuōn dikaioutai*). This is a characteristic Greek sentence with the principal clause at the end and Pauline to the core. A literal rendering as to the order would be: "And from all the things from (*apo* not repeated in the Greek, but understood, the ablative case being repeated) which ye were not able to be justified in this one every one who believes is justified." The climax is at the close and gives us the heart of Paul's teaching about Christ. "We have here the germ of all that is most characteristic in Paul's later teaching. It is the argument of the Epistle to Galatians and Romans in a sentence" (Furneaux). The failure of the Mosaic law to bring the kind of righteousness

that God demands is stated. This is made possible in and by (*en*) Christ alone. Paul's favourite words occur here, *pisteuō*, believe, with which *pistis*, faith, is allied, *dikaioō*, to set right with God on the basis of faith. In Rom. 6:7 Paul uses *apo* also after *dikaioō*. These are key words (*pisteuō* and *dikaioō*) in Paul's theology and call for prolonged and careful study if one is to grasp the Pauline teaching. *Dikaioō* primarily means to make righteous, to declare righteous like *axioō*, to deem worthy (*axios*). But in the end Paul holds that real righteousness will come (Rom. 6–8) to those whom God treats as righteous (Rom. 3–5) though both Gentile and Jew fall short without Christ (Rom. 1–3). This is the doctrine of grace that will prove a stumbling block to the Jews with their ceremonial works and foolishness to the Greeks with their abstract philosophical ethics (I Cor. 1:23–25). It is a new and strange doctrine to the people of Antioch.

40. *Beware therefore* (*blepete oun*). The warning is pertinent. Perhaps Paul noticed anger on the faces of some of the rabbis. *Lest there come upon you* (*mē epelthēi*). Second aorist active subjunctive with the negative final conjunction *mē*. *In the prophets* (*en tois prophētais*). The quotation is from the LXX text of Hab. 1:5. The plural here refers to the prophetic collection (Luke 24:44; Acts 24:14). "The Jews of Habakkuk's day had refused to believe in the impending invasion by the Chaldeans, and yet it had come" (Furneaux).

41. *Ye despisers* (*hoi kataphronētai*). Not in the Hebrew, but in the LXX. It is pertinent for Paul's purpose. *Perish* (*aphanisthēte*). Or vanish away. First aorist passive imperative. Added by the LXX to the Hebrew. *If one declare it unto you* (*ean tis ekdiēgētai humin*). Condition of third class with present middle subjunctive, if one keep on outlining (double compound, *ek-di-ēgeomai*) it unto you. Paul has hurled a thunderbolt at the close.

42. *And as they went out* (*Exiontōn de autōn*). Genitive

absolute with present active participle of *exeimi*, to go out, old verb, in the N.T. only in Acts 12:42; 17:15; 20:7; 27:43. As they (Paul and Barnabas) were going out with all the excitement and hubbub created by the sermon. *They besought* (*parekaloun*). Imperfect active, inchoative, began to beseech. The Textus Receptus inserts wrongly *ta ethnē* (the Gentiles) as if the Jews were opposed to Paul from the first as some doubtless were. But both Jews and Gentiles asked for the repetition of the sermon (*lalēthēnai*, first aorist passive infinitive object of *parekaloun* with accusative of general reference). *The next Sabbath* (*eis to metaxu sabbaton*). Late use (Josephus, Plutarch, etc.) of *metaxu* (*meta* and *xun = sun*) in sense of after or next instead of between (sense of *meta* prevailing). Note use of *eis* for "on" or "by."

43. *When the synagogue broke up* (*lutheisēs tēs sunagōgēs*). Genitive absolute of first aorist passive participle of *luō*. Apparently Paul and Barnabas had gone out before the synagogue was formally dismissed. *Of the devout proselytes* (*tōn sebomenōn prosēlutōn*). Of the worshipping proselytes described in verses 16 and 25 as "those who fear God" (cf. 16:14) employed usually of the uncircumcised Gentiles who yet attended the synagogue worship, but the word *prosēlutoi* (*pros, ēlutos* verbal from *erchomai*, a new-comer) means usually those who had become circumcised (proselytes of righteousness). Yet the rabbis used it also of proselytes of the gate who had not yet become circumcised, probably the idea here. In the N.T. the word occurs only in Matt. 23:15; Acts 2:11 (10); 6:5; 13:43. Many (both Jews and proselytes) followed (*ēkolouthēsan*, ingressive aorist active indicative of *akoloutheō*) Paul and Barnabas to hear more without waiting till the next Sabbath. So we are to picture Paul and Barnabas speaking (*proslalountes*, late compound, in N.T. only here and 28:20) to eager groups. *Urged* (*epeithon*). Imperfect active of *peithō*, either descriptive (were persuading) or conative (were trying to persuade). Paul had great

powers of persuasion (18:4; 19:8, 26; 26:28; 28:23; II Cor. 5:11; Gal. 1:10). These Jews "were beginning to understand for the first time the true meaning of their national history" (Furneaux), "the grace of God" to them.

44. *The next Sabbath* (*tōi erchomenōi sabbatōi*). Locative case, on the coming (*erchomenōi*, present middle participle of *erchomai*) Sabbath. So the best MSS., though some have *echomenōi* (present middle participle of *echō* in sense of near, bordering, following as in Luke 13:33; Acts 29:15)'. *Almost* (*schedon*). Old word, but in N.T. only here, Acts 19:26; Heb. 9:22. *Was gathered together* (*sunēchthē*). First aorist (effective) passive indicative of *sunagō*, old and common verb. The "whole city" could hardly all gather in the synagogue. Perhaps Paul spoke in the synagogue and Barnabas to the overflow outside (see verse 46). It was an eager and earnest gathering "to hear (*akousai*, first aorist active infinitive of purpose) the word of God" and a great opportunity for Paul and Barnabas. The Codex Bezae has it "to hear Paul." It was the new preacher (Paul) that drew the big crowd. It was a crowd such as will later hang on the words of John Wesley and George Whitfield when they preach Jesus Christ.

45. *The Jews* (*hoi Ioudaioi*). Certainly not the proselytes of verse 43. Probably many of the Jews that were then favourably disposed to Paul's message had reacted against him under the influence of the rabbis during the week and evidently on this Sabbath very many Gentiles ("almost the whole city," "the multitudes" *tous ochlous*) had gathered, to the disgust of the stricter Jews. Nothing is specifically stated here about the rabbis, but they were beyond doubt the instigators of, and the ringleaders in, the opposition as in Thessalonica (17:5). No such crowds (*ochlous*) came to the synagogue when they were the speakers. *With jealousy* (*zēlou*). Genitive case of *zēlos* (from *zeō*, to boil) after *eplēsthēsan* (effective first aorist passive indicative of *pimplēmi*). Envy and jealousy arise between people of the same calling

(doctors towards doctors, lawyers towards lawyers, preachers towards preachers). So these rabbis boiled with jealousy when they saw the crowds gathered to hear Paul and Barnabas. *Contradicted* (*antelegon*). Imperfect active of *antilegō*, old verb to speak against, to say a word in opposition to (*anti*, face to face). It was interruption of the service and open opposition in the public meeting. Paul and Barnabas were guests by courtesy and, of course, could not proceed further, when denied that privilege. *Blasphemed* (*blasphēmountes*). Blaspheming. So the correct text without the addition *antilegontes* (repeated from *antelegon* above). Common verb in the Gospels for saying injurious and harmful things. Doubtless these rabbis indulged in unkind personalities and made it plain that Paul and Barnabas were going beyond the limitations of pure Judaism in their contacts with Gentiles.

46. *Spake out boldly* (*parrēsiasamenoi*). First aorist middle participle of *parrēsiazomai*, to use freedom in speaking, to assume boldness. Both Paul and Barnabas accepted the challenge of the rabbis. They would leave their synagogue, but not without a word of explanation. *It was necessary to you first* (*Humin ēn anagkaion prōton*). They had done their duty and had followed the command of Jesus (1:8). They use the very language of Peter in 3:26 (*humin prōton*) "to you first." This position Paul as the apostle to the Gentiles will always hold, the Jew first in privilege and penalty (Rom. 1:16; 2:9 and 10). *Ye thrust it from you* (*apōtheisthe auton*). Present middle (indirect, from yourselves) indicative of *apōtheō*, to push from. Vigorous verb seen already in Acts 7:27, 39 which see. *Judge yourselves unworthy* (*ouk axious krinete heautous*). Present active indicative of the common verb *krinō*, to judge or decide with the reflexive pronoun expressed. Literally, Do not judge yourselves worthy. By their action and their words they had taken a violent and definite stand. *Lo, we turn to the Gentiles* (*idou strephometha*

eis ta ethnē). It is a crisis (*idou*, lo): "Lo, we turn ourselves to the Gentiles." Probably also aoristic present, we now turn (Robertson, *Grammar*, pp. 864–70). *Strephometha* is probably the direct middle (Robertson, *Grammar*, pp. 806–08) though the aorist passive *estraphēn* is so used also (7:39). It is a dramatic moment as Paul and Barnabas turn from the Jews to the Gentiles, a prophecy of the future history of Christianity. In Rom. 9 to 11 Paul will discuss at length the rejection of Christ by the Jews and the calling of the Gentiles to be the real (the spiritual) Israel.

47. *For so hath the Lord commanded us* (*houtōs gar entetaltai hēmin ho kurios*). Perfect middle indicative of *entellō*, poetic (Pindar) and late verb to enjoin (1:2). The command of the Lord Paul finds in Isa. 49:6 quoted by Simeon also (Luke 2:32). The conviction of Paul's mind was now made clear by the fact of the rejection by the Jews. He could now see more clearly the words of the prophet about the Gentiles: The Messiah is declared by God in Isaiah to be "a light to the Gentiles" (*ethnōn*, objective genitive), "a light for revelation to the Gentiles" (*phōs eis apokalupsin ethnōn*, Luke 2:32). So Paul is carrying out the will of God in turning to the Gentiles. He will still appeal to the Jews elsewhere as they allow him to do so, but not here. *That thou shouldest be* (*tou einai se*). Genitive articular infinitive of purpose with the accusative of general reference. This is all according to God's fixed purpose (*tetheika*, perfect active indicative of *tithēmi*). *Unto the uttermost part of the earth* (*heōs eschatou tēs gēs*). Unto the last portion (genitive neuter, not feminine) of the earth. It is a long time from Paul to now, not to say from Isaiah to now, and not yet has the gospel been carried to half of the people of earth. God's people are slow in carrying out God's plans for salvation.

48. *As the Gentiles heard this they were glad* (*akouonta ta ethnē echairon*). Present active participle of *akouō* and im-

perfect active of *chairō*, linear action descriptive of the joy of the Gentiles. *Glorified the word of God* (*edoxazon ton logon tou theou*). Imperfect active again. The joy of the Gentiles increased the fury of the Jews. "The synagogue became a scene of excitement which must have been something like the original speaking with tongues" (Rackham). The joy of the Gentiles was to see how they could receive the higher blessing of Judaism without circumcision and other repellent features of Jewish ceremonialism. It was the gospel of grace and liberty from legalism that Paul had proclaimed. Whether Gal. 4:13 describes this incident or not (the South Galatian theory), it illustrates it when Gentiles received Paul as if he were Christ Jesus himself. It was triumph with the Gentiles, but defeat with the Jews. *As many as were ordained to eternal life* (*hosoi ēsan tetagmenoi eis zōēn aiōnion*). Periphrastic past perfect passive indicative of *tassō*, a military term to place in orderly arrangement. The word "ordain" is not the best translation here. "Appointed," as Hackett shows, is better. The Jews here had voluntarily rejected the word of God. On the other side were those Gentiles who gladly accepted what the Jews had rejected, not all the Gentiles. Why these Gentiles here ranged themselves on God's side as opposed to the Jews Luke does not tell us. This verse does not solve the vexed problem of divine sovereignty and human free agency. There is no evidence that Luke had in mind an *absolutum decretum* of personal salvation. Paul had shown that God's plan extended to and included Gentiles. Certainly the Spirit of God does move upon the human heart to which some respond, as here, while others push him away. *Believed* (*episteusan*). Summary or constative first aorist active indicative of *pisteuō*. The subject of this verb is the relative clause. By no manner of legerdemain can it be made to mean "those who believe were appointed." It was saving faith that was exercised only by those who were appointed unto eternal life, who were ranged on the side of eternal life, who were thus revealed as the subjects of God's grace by the stand that they took on this day for the Lord. It was a great day for the kingdom of God.

49. *Was spread abroad* (*diephereto*). Imperfect passive of *diapherō*, to carry in different directions (*dia*). By the recent converts as well as by Paul and Barnabas. This would seem to indicate a stay of some months with active work among the Gentiles that bore rich fruit. *Throughout all the region* (*di' holēs tēs chōras*). Antioch in Pisidia as a Roman colony would be the natural centre of a Roman *Regio*, an important element in Roman imperial administration. There were probably other *Regiones* in South Galatia (Ramsay, *St. Paul the Traveller and Roman Citizen*, pp. 102–12).

50. *Urged on* (*parōtrunan*). First aorist (effective) active of *par-otrunō*, old verb, but here alone in the N.T., to incite, to stir up. The Jews were apparently not numerous in this city as they had only one synagogue, but they had influence with people of prominence, like "the devout women of honourable estate" (*tas sebomenas gunaikas tas euschē-monas*), the female proselytes of high station, a late use of an old word used about Joseph of Arimathea (Mark 15:43). The rabbis went after these Gentile women who had embraced Judaism (cf. Acts 17:4 in Thessalonica) as Paul had made an appeal to them. The prominence of women in public life here at Antioch is quite in accord with what we know of conditions in the cities of Asia Minor. "Thus women were appointed under the empire as magistrates, as presidents of the games, and even the Jews elected a woman as Archisynagogos, at least in one instance at Smyrna" (Knowling). In Damascus Josephus (*War* II. 20, 21) says that a majority of the married women were proselytes. Strabo (VIII. 2) and Juvenal (VI. 542) speak of the addiction of women to the Jewish religion. *The chief men of the city* (*tous prōtous tēs poleōs*). Probably city officials (the

202 WORD PICTURES IN NEW TESTAMENT

Duumviri, the Praetors, the First Ten in the Greek Cities
of the east) or other "foremost" men, not officials. The
rabbis were shrewd enough to reach these men (not proselytes) through the women who were proselytes of distinction.
Stirred up a persecution (*epēgeiran diōgmon*). First aorist
active indicative of *epegeirō*, old verb, but in the N.T. only
here and 14:2. Paul seems to allude to this persecution in
II Tim. 3:11 "persecutions, sufferings, what things befell
me at Antioch, at Iconium, at Lystra, what persecutions I
endured." Here Paul had perils from his own countrymen
and perils from the Gentiles after the perils of rivers and
perils of robbers on the way from Perga (II Cor. 11:26).
He was thrice beaten with rods (*tris erhabdisthēn*, II Cor.
11:25) by Roman lictors in some Roman colony. If that
was here, then Paul and Barnabas were publicly scourged
by the lictors before they left. Probably the Jews succeeded
in making the Roman officials look on Paul and Barnabas
as disturbers of the public peace. So "they cast them out
of their borders" (*exebalon autous apo tōn horiōn autōn*).
Second aorist active indicative of *ekballō*, forcible expulsion
plainly as public nuisances. Just a few days before they
were the heroes of the city and now!

51. *But they shook off the dust of their feet against them* (*Hoi
de ektinaxamenoi ton koniorton tōn podōn ep' autous*). First
aorist middle (indirect) participle of *ektinassō*, to shake out or
off. Homer uses it for knocking out teeth. In the papyri. The
middle aorist participle occurs again in 18:6 and the active
imperative with the dust of the feet in Mark 6:11 (Luke
10:11 has *apomassometha*). and Matt. 10:14 (command of
Jesus). It is a dramatic gesture that forbids further inter-
course. "As a protest against the injustice which cast them
out. The sandal was taken off and the dust shaken out as a
symbolic token that the very soil of the country was defiling"
(Furneaux). *Unto Iconium* (*eis Ikonion*). About 45 miles
southeast from Antioch in Pisidia, at the foot of the Taurus

mountains. At various times it was reckoned also in Pisidia
or Phrygia as well as Lycaonia, Phrygian in population and
distinguished by Luke (Acts 14:6) from Lystra and Derbe,
cities of Lycaonia. As compared with Antioch (a Roman
colony) it was a native Phrygian town. When the province
of Galatia was divided, Iconium became the capital of Lycaonia and eclipsed Antioch in Pisidia. Strictly speaking at
this time Lystra and Derbe were cities of Lycaonia-Galatica
while Iconium was in Phrygia-Galatica (all three in the
Roman Province of Galatia). It was at the meeting place of
several Roman roads and on the highway from east to west.
It is still a large town Konieh with 30,000 population.

52. *And the disciples* (*hoi te* or *hoi de mathētai*). The Gentile Christians in Antioch in Pisidia. Persecution had precisely the opposite effect to the intention of the Jews for they
"were filled with joy and the Holy Spirit" (*eplērounto
charas kai pneumatos hagiou*). Imperfect passive, they kept
on being filled. It had been so before (Acts 4:31; 8:4; 9:31;
12:24). The blood of the martyrs is still the seed of the
church.

CHAPTER XIV

1. *They entered together (kata to auto eiselthein).* Like *epi to auto* in 3:1. The infinitive *eiselthein* is the subject of *egeneto. So spake that (lalēsai houtōs hōste).* Infinitive again parallel to *eiselthein.* With the result that, actual result here stated with *hōste* and the aorist infinitive *pisteusai* (Robertson, *Grammar*, pp. 999f.) rather than *hōste* and the indicative like John 3:16. It was a tremendous first meeting.

2. *That were disobedient (hoi apeithēsantes).* First aorist active articular participle, not the present *apeithountes* as the Textus Receptus has it. But the meaning is probably the Jews that disbelieved, rather than that disobeyed. Strictly *apeitheō* does mean to disobey and *apisteō* to disbelieve, but that distinction is not observed in John 3:36 nor in Acts 19:9 and 28:24. The word *apeitheō* means to be *apeithēs*, to be unwilling to be persuaded or to withhold belief and then also to withhold obedience. The two meanings run into one another. To disbelieve the word of God is to disobey God. *Made them evil affected (ekakōsan).* First aorist active indicative of *kakoō*, old verb from *kakos*, to do evil to, to ill-treat, then in later Greek as here to embitter, to exasperate as in Psa. 105:32 and in Josephus. In this sense only here in the N.T. Evidently Paul preached the same message as in Antioch for it won both Jews and Gentiles, and displeased the rabbis. Codex Bezae adds here that "the chiefs of the synagogue and the rulers" brought persecution upon Paul and Barnabas just as was argued about Antioch. Outside the synagogue the Jews would poison the minds of the Gentiles against Paul and Barnabas. "The story of Thecla suggests a means, and perhaps the apostles were brought before the magistrates on some charge of interference with family life.

The magistrates however must have seen at once that there was no legal case against them; and by a sentence of acquittal or in some other way the Lord gave peace" (Rackham). As we have it, the story of Paul and Thecla undoubtedly has apocryphal features, though Thecla may very well be an historical character here at Iconium where the story is located. Certainly the picture of Paul herein drawn cannot be considered authentic though a true tradition may underlie it: "bald, bowlegged, strongly built, small in stature, with large eyes and meeting eyebrows and longish nose; full of grace; sometimes looking like a man, sometimes having the face of an angel."

3. *Long time therefore* (*hikanon men oun chronon*). Accusative of duration of time (possibly six months) and note *men oun*. There is an antithesis in *eschisthē de* (verse 4) and in verse 5 (*egeneto de*). After the persecution and vindication there was a season of great opportunity which Paul and Barnabas used to the full, "speaking boldly" (*parrēsiazomenoi* as in 13:46 at Antioch in Pisidia, "in the Lord" (*epi tōi kuriōi*), upon the basis of the Lord Jesus as in 4:17f. And the Lord Jesus "bore witness to the word of his grace" as he always does, "granting signs and wonders to be done by their hands" (*didonti sēmeia kai terata ginesthai dia tōn cheirōn autōn*). Present participle (*didonti*) and present infinitive (*ginesthai*) repetition of both signs and wonders (note both words) just as had happened with Peter and John and the other apostles (2:43; 4:29f.; 5:12; cf. Heb. 2:4). The time of peace could not last forever with such a work of grace as this. A second explosion of persecution was bound to come and some of the MSS. actually have *ek deuterou* (a second time).

4. *But the multitude of the city was divided* (*eschisthē de to plēthos tēs poleōs*). First aorist passive indicative of *schizō*, old verb to split, to make a schism or factions as Sadducees and Pharisees (23:7). This division was within the

Gentile populace. Part held (*hoi men ēsan*), literally "some were with the Jews" (*sun tois Ioudaiois*), part with the apostles (*hoi de sun tois apostolois*). Common demonstrative of contrast (*hoi men, hoi de*, Robertson, *Grammar*, p. 694). The Jewish leaders made some impression on the Gentiles as at Antioch in Pisidia and later at Thessalonica (17:4f.). This is the first time in the Acts that Paul and Barnabas are termed "apostles" (see also verse 14). Elsewhere in the Acts the word is restricted to the twelve. Certainly Luke does not here employ it in that technical sense. To have followed Jesus in his ministry and to have seen the Risen Christ was essential to the technical use (1:22f.). Whether Barnabas had seen the Risen Christ we do not know, but certainly Paul had (I Cor. 9:1f.; 15:8). Paul claimed to be an apostle on a par with the twelve (Gal. 1:1, 16–18). The word originally means simply one sent (John 13:16) like messengers of the churches with the collection (II Cor. 8:23). The Jews used it of those sent from Jerusalem to collect the temple tribute. Paul applies the word to James the Lord's brother (Gal. 1:19), to Epaphroditus (Phil. 2:25) as the messenger of the church in Philippi, to Silvanus and Timothy (I Thess. 2:6; Acts 18:5), apparently to Apollos (I Cor. 4:9), and to Andronicus and Junias (Rom. 16:6f.). He even calls the Judaizers "false apostles" (II Cor. 11:13).

5. *An onset* (*hormē*). A rush or impulse as in James 3:4. Old word, but only twice in the N.T. (here and James). It probably denotes not an actual attack so much as the open start, the co-operation of both Jews and Gentiles (the disaffected portion), "with their rulers" (*sun tois archousin autōn*), that is the rulers of the Jewish synagogue (13:27). The city officials would hardly join in a mob like this, though Hackett and Rackham think that the city magistrates were also involved as in Antioch in Pisidia (13:50). *To entreat them shamefully* (*hubrisai*). First aorist active infinitive of *hubrizō*, old verb to insult insolently. See on Matt. 22:6;

Luke 18:32. *To stone* (*lithobolēsai*). First aorist active infinitive of *lithoboleō*, late verb from *lithobolos* (*lithos*, stone, *ballō*, to throw) to pelt with stones, the verb used of the stoning of Stephen (7:58). See on Matt. 21:35. The plan to stone them shows that the Jews were in the lead and followed by the Gentile rabble. "Legal proceedings having failed the only resource left for the Jews was illegal violence" (Rackham).

6. *They became aware of it* (*sunidontes*). Second aorist (ingressive) active participle of *sunoraō* (*suneidon*), old word to see together, to become conscious of as already in 12:12. In the N.T. only by Luke and Paul. *Fled* (*katephugon*). Second aorist (effective) active indicative of *katapheugō*, old verb, but in the N.T. only here and Heb. 6:18. Paul and Barnabas had no idea of remaining to be stoned (lynched) by this mob. It is a wise preacher who always knows when to stand his ground and when to leave for the glory of God. Paul and Barnabas were following the directions of the Lord Jesus given to the twelve on their special tour of Galilee (Matt. 10:23). Lystra and Derbe, cities of Lycaonia (still part of the Province of Galatia, though in another *Regio*), not far from the base of the Black Mountain. Professor Sterrett has apparently identified Lystra by an inscription about six hours (18 miles) south-southwest from Iconium near the village Khatyn Serai and Derbe probably near the village Losta or Zosta though its location is really not known. Lystra had been made a colony in B.C. 6 and Derbe was the frontier city of the Roman empire in the southeast. These are the only cities mentioned, but they were of importance and show that Paul kept to his plan of going to centres of influence. The new imperial road from Antioch and Iconium reached these cities. The region round about (*tēn perichōron*) was "a high table land, ill-watered, bleak, but suited for sheep pasture" (Page).

7. *And there they preached the gospel* (*kakei euaggelizomenoi*

ēsan). Periphrastic imperfect middle. We are to think of extensive evangelistic work perhaps with the assistance of disciples from Antioch and Iconium since Paul and Barnabas could not speak Lycaonian. *Kakei* is crasis for *kai ekei*.

8. *At Lystra* (*en Lustrois*). Neuter plural as in 16:2; II Tim. 3:11 while feminine singular in 14:6, 21; 16:1. There was apparently no synagogue in Lystra and so not many Jews. Paul and Barnabas had to do open-air preaching and probably had difficulty in being understood by the natives though both Greek and Latin inscriptions were discovered here by Professor Sterrett in 1885. The incident narrated here (verses 8–18) shows how they got a real hearing among these rude heathen. *There sat* (*ekathēto*). Imperfect middle of *kathēmai*. Was sitting. This case is very much like that in 3:1–11, healed by Peter. Possibly outside the gate (verse 13) or some public place. *Impotent in his feet* (*adunatos tois posin*). Old verbal, but only here in the N.T. in this sense except figuratively in Rom. 15:1. Elsewhere it means "impossible" (Matt. 19:26). Locative case. Common in medical writers in the sense of "impotent." So Tobit 2:10; 5:9. *Had walked* (*periepatēsen*). So best MSS., first aorist active indicative "walked," not *periepepatēkei*, "had walked" (past perfect active).

9. *The same* (*houtos*). Just "this one." *Heard* (*ēkouen*). Imperfect active, was listening to Paul speaking (*lalountos*). Either at the gate or in the market place (17:17) Paul was preaching to such as would listen or could understand his Greek (*Koinē*). Ramsay (*St. Paul the Traveller*, pp. 114, 116) thinks that the cripple was a proselyte. At any rate he may have heard of the miracles wrought at Iconium (verse 3) and Paul may have spoken of the work of healing wrought by Jesus. This man was "no mendicant pretender," for his history was known from his birth. *Fastening his eyes upon him* (*atenisas autōi*). Just as in 13:9 of Paul and 1:10 which see. Paul saw a new hope in the man's eyes and face. *He had*

faith (echei pistin). Present active indicative retained in indirect discourse. *To be made whole (tou sōthēnai).* Genitive of articular first aorist passive infinitive (purpose and result combined) of *sōzō*, to make sound and also to save. Here clearly to make whole or well as in Luke 7:50 (cf. Acts 3:16; 4:10).

10. *Upright (orthos).* Predicate adjective. In this sense Galen and Hippocrates frequently use *orthos* (erect, straight). Paul spoke in a loud *(megalēi)* voice so that all could hear and know. *He leaped up and walked (hēlato kai periepatei).* Rather, He leaped up with a single bound and began to walk. The second aorist middle indicative (with first aorist vowel *a*) of *hallomai* (late verb, in papyri) and inchoative imperfect active of *peripateō*, common verb to walk around. This graphic picture is concealed by the usual English rendering. It is possible that Luke obtained the vivid report of this incident from Timothy who may have witnessed it and who was probably converted during Paul's stay here (16:3). His father was a prominent Greek and his mother Eunice, possibly a widow, may have lived here with her mother Lois (II Tim. 1:5).

11. *Lifted up their voice (epēran tēn phōnēn autōn).* First aorist active of *epairō*. In their excitement they elevated their voices. *In the speech of Lycaonia (Lukaonisti).* Adverb from verb *lukaonizō*, to use the language of Lycaonia found here alone, but formed regularly like *Ebraisti* (John 5:2), *Hellēnisti* (Acts 21:37), *Rōmaisti* (John 19:20). Paul was speaking in Greek, of course, but the excitement of the crowd over the miracle made them cry out in their native tongue which Paul and Barnabas did not understand. Hence it was not till preparations for offering sacrifice to them had begun that Paul understood the new rôle in which he and Barnabas were held. *In the likeness of men (homoiōthentes anthrōpois).* First aorist passive participle of *homoiō*, to liken, with the associative instrumental case. In this primitive

state the people hold to the old Graeco-Roman mythology.
The story of Baucis and Philemon tells how Jupiter (Zeus)
and Mercury (Hermes) visited in human form the neighbouring region of Phrygia (Ovid, *Meta.* VIII. 626). Jupiter (Zeus)
had a temple in Lystra.

12. *They called* (*ekaloun*). Inchoative imperfect began to
call. *Barnabas, Jupiter* (*ton Barnaban Dia*). Because Barnabas was the older and the more imposing in appearance.
Paul admits that he was not impressive in looks (II Cor.
10:10). *And Paul, Mercury* (*ton de Paulon Hermēn*). Mercury
(*Hermēs*) was the messenger of the gods, and the spokesman
of Zeus. *Hermēs* was of beautiful appearance and eloquent
in speech, the inventor of speech in legend. Our word her-
meneutics or science of interpretation comes from this word
(Heb. 7:2; John 1:38). *Because he was the chief speaker*
(*epeidē autos ēn ho hēgoumenos tou logou*). Paul was clearly
"the leader of the talk." So it seemed a clear case to the
natives. If preachers always knew what people really think
of them! Whether Paul was alluding to his experience in
Lystra or not in Gal. 4:14, certainly they did receive him as
an angel of God, as if "Mercury" in reality.

13. *Whose temple was before the city* (*tou ontos pro tēs
pōleōs*). The god (Zeus) is identified with his temple. He had
a statue and temple there. *Oxen and garlands* (*taurous kai
stemmata*). Probably garlands to put on the oxen before
they were slain. It was common to sacrifice bullocks to
Jupiter and Mercury. *Would have done sacrifice* (*ēthelen
thuein*). Imperfect indicative, wanted to offer sacrifice. He
was planning to do it, and his purpose now became plain to
Paul and Barnabas.

14. *Having heard* (*akousantes*). Such elaborate preparation "with the multitudes" (*sun tois ochlois*) spread rumours
and some who spoke Greek told Paul and Barnabas. It is
possible that the priest of Jupiter may have sent a formal
request that the visiting "gods" might come out to the

statue by the temple gates to make it a grand occasion. *They rent their garments (diarrēxantes).* First aorist active participle from *diarrēgnumi,* old verb to rend in two. Like the high priest in Matt. 26:65 as if an act of sacrilege was about to be committed. It was strange conduct for the supposed gods! *Sprang forth (exepēdēsan).* First aorist (ingressive) active indicative of *ekpēdaō* (note *ek*), old verb, here only in the N.T. It was all a sign of grief and horror with loud outcries *(krazontes).*

15. *Sirs (andres).* Literally, Men. Abrupt, but courteous. *We also are men of like passions with you (kai hēmeis homoiopatheis esmen humin anthrōpoi).* Old adjective from *homoios* (like) and *paschō,* to experience. In the N.T. only here and James 5:17. It means "of like nature" more exactly and affected by like sensations, not "gods" at all. Their conduct was more serious than the obeisance of Cornelius to Peter (10:25f.). *Humin* is associative instrumental case. *And bring you good tidings (euaggelizomenoi).* No "and" in the Greek, just the present middle participle, "gospelizing you." They are not gods, but evangelists. Here we have Paul's message to a pagan audience without the Jewish environment and he makes the same line of argument seen in Acts 17:21–32 and Rom. 1:18–23. At Antioch in Pisidia we saw Paul's line of approach to Jews and proselytes (Acts 13:16–41). *That ye should turn from these vain things (apo toutōn tōn mataiōn epistrephein).* He boldly calls the worship of Jupiter and Mercury and all idols "vain" or empty things, pointing to the statues and the temple. *Unto the living God (epi theon zōnta).* They must go the whole way. Our God is a live God, not a dead statue. Paul is fond of this phrase (II Cor. 6:16; Rom. 9:26). *Who made (hos epoiēsen).* The one God is alive and is the Creator of the Universe just as Paul will argue in Athens (Acts 17:24). Paul here quotes Psa. 146:6 and has Gen. 1:1 in mind. See also I Thess. 1:9 where a new allegiance is also claimed as here.

16. *In the generations gone by* (*en tais parōichēmenais geneais*). Perfect middle participle from *paroichomai*, to go by, old verb, here alone in the N.T. *Suffered* (*eiasen*). Constative aorist active indicative of *eaō* (note syllabic augment). Paul here touches God in history as he did just before in creation. God's hand is on the history of all the nations (Gentile and Jew), only with the Gentiles he withdrew the restraints of his grace in large measure (Acts 17:30; Rom. 1:24, 26, 28), judgment enough for their sins. *To walk in their ways* (*poreuesthai tais hodois autōn*). Present middle infinitive, to go on walking, with locative case without *en*. This philosophy of history does not mean that God was ignorant or unconcerned. He was biding his time in patience.

17. *And yet* (*kaitoi*). Old Greek compound particle (*kai toi*). In the N.T. twice only, once with finite verb as here, once with the participle (Heb. 4:3). *Without witness* (*amarturon*). Old adjective (*a* privative and *martus*, witness), only here in the N.T. *Left* (*aphēken*). First aorist active (*k* aorist indicative of *aphiēmi*). *In that he did good* (*agathourgōn*). Present active causal participle of *agathourgeō*, late and rare verb (also *agathoergeō* I Tim. 6:18), reading of the oldest MSS. here for *agathopoieō*, to do good. Note two other causal participles here parallel with *agathourgōn*, viz., *didous* ("giving you") present active of *didōmi*, *empiplōn* ("filling") present active of *empimplaō* (late form of *empimplēmi*). This witness to God (his doing good, giving rains and fruitful seasons, filling your hearts with food and gladness) they could receive without the help of the Old Testament revelation (Rom. 1:20). Zeus was regarded as the god of rain (Jupiter Pluvius) and Paul claims the rain and the fruitful (*karpophorous*, *karpos*, and *pherō*, fruit bearing, old word, here alone in N.T.) seasons as coming from God. Lycaonia was often dry and it would be an appropriate item. "Mercury, as the God of merchandise, was also the dispenser of food" (Vincent). Paul does not talk about laws of nature

as if they governed themselves, but he sees the living God
"behind the drama of the physical world" (Furneaux).
These simple country people could grasp his ideas as he
claims everything for the one true God. *Gladness* (*euphro-
sunēs*). Old word from *euphrōn* (*eu* and *phrēn*), good cheer.
In the N.T. only Acts 2:28 and here. Cheerfulness should
be our normal attitude when we consider God's goodness.
Paul does not here mention Christ because he had the single
definite purpose to dissuade them from worshipping Barnabas and himself.

18. *Scarce* (*molis*). Adverb in same sense as old *mogis*,
from *molos*, toil. *Restrained* (*katepausan*). Effective first
aorist active indicative of *katapauō*, old verb in causative
sense to make abstain from. *From doing sacrifice unto them*
(*tou mē thuein autois*). Ablative case of the articular infinitive with redundant negative after *katepausan*, regular
Greek idiom (Robertson, *Grammar*, pp. 1094, 1171). It had
been a harrowing and well-nigh a horrible ordeal, but finally
Paul had won. If only nobody else had interposed!

19. *But there came thither Jews from Antioch and Iconium*
(*Epēlthan de apo Antiocheias kai Ikoniou Ioudaioi*). Came
to or upon them, *epēlthan*, second aorist (ingressive) indicative of *eperchomai*. Whether news of the miracle had reached
those cities we do not know. These may have been travelling grain merchants. At any rate there was an interval in
which Paul and Barnabas won some disciples (verse 22).
There would be a natural reaction, even revulsion, in the
minds of many who had come so near to worshipping Paul
and Barnabas. The pendulum swings easily from one extreme to the other. The hostile Jews from Antioch and
Iconium may even have followed Paul and Barnabas along
the fine Roman road on purpose to keep them on the run.
They had driven them out of Antioch and out of Iconium
and now appear at Lystra at an opportune moment for their
work. *Having persuaded the multitudes* (*peisantes tous och-*

lous). First aorist (effective) active participle of *peithō*. They had complete success with many and struck at the psychological moment. *They stoned Paul (lithasantes ton Paulon)*. First aorist active participle of *lithazō*, late verb from *lithos* for throwing stones (used by Paul referring to this one incident when alone he was stoned, II Cor. 11:25). The wounds inflicted may have left some of the scars (*stigmata*) mentioned in Gal. 6:17. They stoned Paul as the chief speaker (Mercury) and passed by Barnabas (Jupiter). It was a Jewish mode of punishment as against Stephen and these Jews knew that Paul was the man that they had to deal with. Hackett notes that the Jews with two exceptions incited the persecutions which Paul endured. The exceptions were in Philippi (16:16-40) and Ephesus (19:23-41). *Dragged him out of the city (esuron exō tēs poleōs)*. They hurled Stephen outside of the city before stoning him (7:58). It was a hurried and irregular proceeding, but they were dragging (imperfect active of *surō*, old verb) Paul out now. *Supposing that he were dead (nomizontes auton tethnēkenai)*. Present active participle with infinitive (second perfect active of *thnēskō*) in indirect discourse with accusative of general reference. The Jews are jubilant this time with memories of Paul's escape at Antioch and Iconium. The pagan mob feel that they have settled accounts for their narrow escape from worshipping two Jewish renegade preachers. It was a good day's work for them all. Luke does not say that Paul was actually dead.

20. *Stood round about him (kuklōsantōn auton)*. Genitive absolute with first aorist active participle of *kukloō*, old verb from *kuklos* (circle, cycle) to make a circle round, to encircle. The would-be murderers left and a group of disciples gathered round to see if Paul was dead or alive and, if dead, to bury him. In that group Timothy may very well have been along with Eunice and Barnabas. Timothy, a lad of about fifteen, would not soon forget that solemn scene

(II Tim. 3:11). But Paul suddenly (apparently a miraculous recovery) rose up (*anastas*) and entered the city to the surprise and joy of the disciples who were willing to brave persecution with Paul. *With Barnabas* (*sun tōi Barnabāi*). With the assistance of Barnabas. It was plainly unwise to continue in Lystra so that they set out on the next day (*tēi epaurion*, ten times in Acts), shaken and bruised as Paul was. Derbe was some forty miles distant, near the pass to the Cilician Gates.

21. *When they had preached the gospel to that city* (*euaggelisamenoi tēn polin ekeinēn*). Having evangelized (first aorist middle participle) that city, a smaller city and apparently with no trouble from the Jews. *Had made many disciples* (*mathēteusantes hikanous*). First aorist active participle of *mathēteuō* from *mathētēs*, a learner or disciple. Late verb in Plutarch, to be a disciple (Matt. 27:57 like John 19:38) and then to disciple (old English, Spenser), to make a disciple as in Matt. 28:19 and here. Paul and Barnabas were literally here obeying the command of Jesus in discipling people in this heathen city. *They returned to Lystra and to Iconium, and to Antioch* (*hupestrepsan eis tēn Lustran kai eis Ikonion kai eis Antiocheian*). Derbe was the frontier city of the Roman empire. The quickest way to return to Antioch in Syria would have been by the Cilician Gates or by the pass over Mt. Taurus by which Paul and Silas will come to Derbe in the second tour (Acts 15:41–16:1), but difficult to travel in winter. But it was necessary to revisit the churches in Lystra, Iconium, Antioch in Pisidia and to see that they were able to withstand persecution. Paul was a Roman citizen though he had not made use of this privilege as yet for his own protection. Against mob violence it would count for little, but he did not hesitate. Paul had been stoned in Lystra, threatened in Iconium, expelled in Antioch. He shows his wisdom in conserving his work.

22. *Confirming* (*epistērizontes*). Late verb (in LXX), in N.T. only in Acts 14:22; 15:32, 41, to make more firm, to give additional (*epi*) strength. Each time in Acts the word is used concerning these churches. *To continue in the faith* (*emmenein tēi pistei*). To remain in with locative, old verb. It is possible that *pistis* here has the notion of creed as Paul uses it later (Col. 1:23 with *epimenō;* I Tim. 5:8). It seems to be here more than trust or belief. These recent converts from heathenism were ill-informed, were persecuted, had broken family and social ties, greatly needed encouragement if they were to hold out. *We must* (*dei hēmās*). It does not follow from this use of "we" that Luke was present, since it is a general proposition applying to all Christians at all times (II Tim. 3:12). Luke, of course, approved this principle. Knowling asks why Timothy may not have told Luke about Paul's work. It all sounds like quotation of Paul's very language. Note the change of construction here after *parakalountes* (infinitive of indirect command, *emmenein*, but *hoti dei*, indirect assertion). They needed the right understanding of persecution as we all do. Paul frankly warned these new converts in this heathen environment of the many tribulations through which they must enter the Kingdom of God (the culmination at last) as he did at Ephesus (Acts 20:20) and as Jesus had done (John 16:33). These saints were already converted.

23. *And when they had appointed for them elders in every church* (*cheirotonēsantes de autois kat' ekklēsian presbuterous*). They needed also some form of organization, though already churches. Note distributive use of *kata* with *ekklēsian* (2:46; 5:42; Titus 1:5). *Cheirotoneō* (from *cheirotonos*, extending the hand, *cheir*, hand, and *teinō*, to stretch) is an old verb that originally meant to vote by show of the hands, finally to appoint with the approval of an assembly that chooses as in II Cor. 8:19, and then to appoint without regard to choice as in Josephus (*Ant.* XIII. 2, 2) of the ap-

pointment of Jonathan as high priest by Alexander. So in
Acts 10:41 the compound *procheiratoneō* is used of witnesses
appointed by God. But the seven (deacons) were first
selected by the Jerusalem church and then appointed (*katastēsomen*) by the apostles. That is probably the plan
contemplated by Paul in his directions to Titus (1:5) about
the choice of elders. It is most likely that this plan was the
one pursued by Paul and Barnabas with these churches.
They selected the elders in each instance and Paul and
Barnabas "ordained" them as we say, though the word
cheirotoneō does not mean that. "Elders" were mentioned
first in 11:30. Later Paul will give the requirements expected
in these "elders" or "bishops" (Phil. 1:1) as in I Tim. 3:
1-7; Titus 1:5-9. It is fairly certain that these elders were
chosen to correspond in a general way with the elders in
the Jewish synagogue after which the local church was
largely copied as to organization and worship. Paul, like
Jesus, constantly worshipped and spoke in the synagogues.
Already it is plain, as at Antioch in Syria (11:26), that
the Christians can no longer count on the use of the Jewish
synagogue. They must have an organization of their own.
The use of the plural here implies what was true at Philippi
(Phil. 1:1) and Ephesus (Acts 20:17, 28) that each church
(one in each city) "had its college of elders" (Hackett) as
in Jerusalem (21:18). Elder (*presbuteros*) was the Jewish
name and bishop (*episkopos*) the Greek name for the same
office. "Those who are called elders in speaking of Jewish
communities are called bishops in speaking of Gentile communities" (Hackett). Hovey rightly holds against Hackett
that teaching was a normal function of these elders, pastors
or bishops as they were variously called (I Tim. 3:2; Titus
1:9; I Cor. 12:28, 30; Eph. 4:11). *Had prayed with fasting*
(*proseuxamenoi meta nēsteiōn*). It was a serious matter,
this formal setting apart of these "elders" in the churches.
So it was done in a public meeting with prayer and fasting

as when Paul and Barnabas were sent forth from Antioch in Syria (13:3) on this mission tour. *They commended them to the Lord (parethento autous tōi kuriōi).* Second aorist middle indicative of *paratithēmi.* Old and solemn word, to entrust, to deposit as in a bank (I Tim. 1:18; II Tim. 2:2). Cf. *parathēkē* in I Tim. 6:20; II Tim. 1:12, 14. It was all that they could now do, to commit them to the Lord Jesus. Jesus used this word on the cross (Luke 22:32). *On whom they had believed (eis hon pepisteukeisan).* Past perfect indicative (without augment) of *pisteuō.* They had "trusted" in Jesus (II Tim. 1:12) and Paul now "entrusts" them to him with confidence. It was a solemn and serious occasion in each instance as it always is to set apart men for the ministry. These men may not have been ideal men for this service, but they were the only ones available and they were chosen from the actual membership in each instance, men who knew local conditions and problems.

24. *When they had spoken the word in Perga (lalēsantes en Pergēi ton logon).* Now they stopped and preached in Perga which they had apparently not done before (see 13:13f.). After leaving Antioch they passed on through Pisidia, as if Antioch was not strictly in Pisidia (see on 13:14) and into Pamphylia. They crossed from Perga to Attaleia, the port of Perga, sixteen miles down the Cestus, and capital of Pamphylia, to find a ship for Antioch in Syria. It is now called Adala and for long was the chief harbour of the south coast of Asia Minor. We do not know why they did not revisit Cyprus, perhaps because no permanent Gentile churches were founded there.

26. *They sailed away to Antioch (apepleusan eis Antiocheian).* Effective aorist active indicative of *apopleō,* to sail off. They had been gone some eighteen months. *They had been committed (ēsan paradedomenoi).* Periphrastic past perfect passive of *paradidōmi,* old and common verb. High and serious thoughts filled the hearts of these first returned

missionaries as they neared home. The grace of God had been with them. They had fulfilled (*eplērōsan*) the work to which they had been set apart by the Holy Spirit with the prayers of the Antioch church. They now had a wondrous story to tell.

27. *Gathered the church together* (*sunagagontes tēn ekklēsian*). Second aorist active participle of *sunagō*. It "was the first missionary meeting in history" (Furneaux). It was not hard to get the church together when the news spread that Paul and Barnabas had returned. "The suitability of the Gospel to become the religion of the world had not before been put to the test" (Furneaux). Doubtless many "wiseacres" had predicted failure as they did for William Carey and for Adoniram Judson and Luther Rice. *Rehearsed* (*anēggellon*). Imperfect active. It was a long story for they had many things to tell of God's dealings "with them" (*met' autōn*) for God had been "with them" all the while as Jesus had said he would be (Matt. 28:20, *meth' hūmōn*). Paul could recount some of the details given later in II Cor. 11. *And how* (*kai hoti*). Or "and that" in particular, as the upshot of it all. *He had opened a door of faith unto the Gentiles* (*ēnoixen tois ethnesin thuran pisteōs*). Three times in Paul's Epistles (I Cor. 16:9; II Cor. 2:12; Col. 4:3) he employed the metaphor of "door," perhaps a reminiscence of the very language of Paul here. This work in Galatia gained a large place in Paul's heart (Gal. 4:14f.). The Gentiles now, it was plain, could enter the kingdom of God (verse 22) through the door of faith, not by law or by circumcision or by heathen philosophy or mythology.

28. *And they tarried no little time* (*dietribon de chronon ouk oligon*). Imperfect active of *diatribō*, old verb to rub hard, to consume, with accusative of extent of time. It was a happy time of fellowship. The experiment entered upon by the church of Antioch was now a pronounced success. It was at the direct command of the Holy Spirit, but they had

prayed for the absent missionaries and rejoiced at their signal success. There is no sign of jealousy on the part of Barnabas when Paul returns as the chief hero of the expedition. A new corner has been turned in the history of Christianity. There is a new centre of Christian activity. What will Jerusalem think of the new developments at Antioch? Paul and Barnabas made no report to Jerusalem.

CHAPTER XV

1. *And certain men came down from Judea (kai tines katelthontes apo tēs Ioudaias).* Evidently the party of the circumcision in the church in Jerusalem (11:2) had heard of the spread of the gospel among the Gentiles in Cyprus, Pamphylia, and South Galatia (Phrygia, Pisidia, Lycaonia). Possibly John Mark after his desertion at Perga (13:13) told of this as one of his reasons for coming home. At any rate echoes of the jubilation in Antioch in Syria would be certain to reach Jerusalem. The Judaizers in Jerusalem, who insisted that all the Gentile Christians must become Jews also, had acquiesced in the case of Cornelius and his group (11:1–18) after plain proof by Peter that it was the Lord's doing. But they had not agreed to a formal campaign to turn the exception into the rule and to make Christianity mainly Gentile with a few Jews instead of mainly Jewish with a few Gentiles. Since Paul and Barnabas did not come up to Jerusalem, the leaders among the Judaizers decided to go down to Antioch and attack Paul and Barnabas there. They had volunteered to go without church action in Jerusalem for their activity is disclaimed by the conference (Acts 15:24). In Gal. 2:4 Paul with some heat describes these Judaizers as "false brethren, secretly introduced who sneaked in to spy out our liberty." It is reasonably certain that this visit to Jerusalem described in Gal. 2:1–10 is the same one as the Jerusalem Conference in Acts 15:5–29 in spite of the effort of Ramsay to identify it with that in 11:29f. Paul in Galatians is not giving a list of his visits to Jerusalem. He is showing his independence of the twelve apostles and his equality with them. He did not see them in 11:29f., but only "the elders." In Acts 15 Luke gives the

outward narrative of events, in Gal. 2:1–10 Paul shows us
the private interview with the apostles when they agreed
on their line of conduct toward the Judaizers. In Gal. 2:2
by the use of "them" (*autois*) Paul seems to refer to the
first public meeting in Acts before the private interview
that came in between verses 5 and 6 of Acts 15. If we recall
the difficulty that Peter had on the subject of preaching
the gospel to the heathen (10:1–11:18), we can the better
understand the attitude of the Judaizers. They were men
of sincere convictions without a doubt, but they were ob-
scurantists and unable and unwilling to receive new light
from the Lord on a matter that involved their racial and
social prejudices. They recalled that Jesus himself had been
circumcised and that he had said to the Syro-Phoenician
woman that he had come only save to the lost sheep of the
house of Israel (Matt. 15:24ff.). They argued that Christ
had not repealed circumcision. So one of the great religious
controversies of all time was begun, that between spiritual
religion and ritualistic or ceremonial religion. It is with us
yet with baptism taking the place of circumcision. These
self-appointed champions of circumcision for Gentile Christians were deeply in earnest. *Taught the brethren* (*edidaskon
tous adelphous*). Inchoative imperfect active, began to teach
and kept it up. Their attitude was one of supercilious superiority. They probably resented the conduct of Barnabas, who,
when sent by the Church in Jerusalem to investigate the conversion of the Greeks in Antioch (11:20–26), did not return
and report till a strong church had been established there
with the help of Saul and only then with a big collection to
confuse the issue. Paul and Barnabas were on hand, but
the Judaizers persisted in their efforts to force their views
on the church in Antioch. It was a crisis. *Except ye be circumcised after the custom of Moses, ye cannot be saved* (*ean me
peritmēthēte tōi ethei Mōuseōs, ou dunasthe sōthēnai*). There
was the dictum of the Judaizers to the Gentiles. Paul and

Barnabas had been circumcised. This is probably the precise language employed, for they spoke in Greek to these Greeks. It is a condition of the third class (undetermined, but with prospect of being determined, *ean* plus the first aorist passive subjunctive of *peritemnō*). There was thus hope held out for them, but only on condition that they be circumcised. The issue was sharply drawn. The associative instrumental case (*tōi ethei*) is customary. "Saved" (*sōthēnai*) here is the Messianic salvation. This doctrine denied the efficacy of the work of Christ.

2. *When Paul and Barnabas had no small dissension and questioning with them* (*Genomenēs staseōs kai zētēseōs ouk oligēs tōi Paulōi kai Barnabāi pros autous*). Genitive absolute of second aorist middle participle of *ginomai*, genitive singular agreeing with first substantive *staseōs*. Literally, "No little (litotes for much) strife and questioning coming to Paul and Barnabas (dative case) with them" (*pros autous*, face to face with them). Paul and Barnabas were not willing to see this Gentile church brow-beaten and treated as heretics by these self-appointed regulators of Christian orthodoxy from Jerusalem. The work had developed under the leadership of Paul and Barnabas and they accepted full responsibility for it and stoutly resisted these Judaizers to the point of sedition (riot, outbreak in Luke 23:25; Acts 19:40) as in 23:7. There is no evidence that the Judaizers had any supporters in the Antioch church so that they failed utterly to make any impression. Probably these Judaizers compelled Paul to think through afresh his whole gospel of grace and so they did Paul and the world a real service. If the Jews like Paul had to believe, it was plain that there was no virtue in circumcision (Gal. 2:15–21). It is not true that the early Christians had no disagreements. They had selfish avarice with Ananias and Sapphira, murmuring over the gifts to the widows, simony in the case of Simon Magus, violent objection to work in Caesarea, and

now open strife over a great doctrine (grace vs. legalism). *The brethren appointed* (*etaxan*). "The brethren" can be supplied from verse 1 and means the church in Antioch. The church clearly saw that the way to remove this deadlock between the Judaizers and Paul and Barnabas was to consult the church in Jerusalem to which the Judaizers belonged. Paul and Barnabas had won in Antioch. If they can win in Jerusalem, that will settle the matter. The Judaizers will be answered in their own church for which they are presuming to speak. The verb *etaxan* (*tassō*, to arrange) suggests a formal appointment by the church in regular assembly. Paul (Gal. 2:2) says that he went up by revelation (*kat' apokalupsin*), but surely that is not contradictory to the action of the church. *Certain others of them* (*tinas allous*). Certainly Titus (Gal. 2:1, 3), a Greek and probably a brother of Luke who is not mentioned in Acts. Rackham thinks that Luke was in the number. *The apostles and elders* (*tous apostolous kai presbuterous*). Note one article for both (cf. "the apostles and the brethren" in 11:1). "Elders" now (11:30) in full force. The apostles have evidently returned now to the city after the death of Herod Agrippa I stopped the persecution.

3. *They therefore* (*hoi men oun*). Luke's favourite method of resumptive narrative as we have seen (11:19, etc.), demonstrative *hoi* with *men* (indeed) and *oun* (therefore). *Being brought on their way by the church* (*propemphthentes hupo tēs ekklēsias*). First aorist passive participle of *propempō*, old verb, to send forward under escort as a mark of honour as in 20:38; 21:5; III John 6. They were given a grand send-off by the church in Antioch. *Passed through* (*diērchonto*). Imperfect middle describing the triumphal procession through both (*te kai*) Phoenicia and Samaria. *The conversion* (*tēn epistrophēn*). The turning. *They caused great joy* (*epoioun charan megalēn*). Imperfect active. They were raising a constant paean of praise as they proceeded

toward Jerusalem. Probably the Judaizers had gone on or kept still.

4. *Were received* (*paredechthēsan*). First aorist passive indicative of *paradechomai*, old verb, to receive, to welcome. Here it was a public reception for Paul and Barnabas provided by the whole church including the apostles and elders, at which an opportunity was given to hear the story of Paul and Barnabas about God's dealings with them among the Gentiles. This first public meeting is referred to by Paul in Gal. 2:2 "I set before them (*autois*,) the gospel, etc."

5. *But there rose up* (*exanestēsan de*). Second aorist active indicative (intransitive). Note both *ex* and *an*. These men rose up out of the crowd at a critical moment. They were believers in Christ (*pepisteukotes*, having believed), but were still members of "the sect of the Pharisees" (*tēs haireseōs tōn Pharisaiōn*). Evidently they still held to the Pharisaic narrowness shown in the attack on Peter (11:2f.). Note the dogmatism of their "must" (*dei*) after the opposition of Paul and Barnabas to their "except" (*ean me*) at Antioch (15:1). They are unconvinced and expected to carry the elders with them. Codex Bezae says that they had appealed to the elders (15:2, 5). At any rate they have made the issue in open meeting at the height of the jubilation. It is plain from verse 6 that this meeting was adjourned, for another gathering came together then. It is here that the private conference of which Paul speaks in Galatians 2:1–10 took place. It was Paul's chance to see the leaders in Jerusalem (Peter, James, and John) and he won them over to his view of Gentile liberty from the Mosaic law so that the next public conference (Acts 15:6–29) ratified heartily the views of Paul, Barnabas, Peter, James, and John. It was a diplomatic triumph of the first order and saved Christianity from the bondage of Jewish ceremonial sacramentalism. So far as we know this is the only time that Paul and John

met face to face, the great spirits in Christian history after
Jesus our Lord. It is a bit curious to see men saying today
that Paul surrendered about Titus and had him circumcised
for the sake of peace, the very opposite of what he says in
Galatians, "to whom I yielded, no not for an hour." Titus
as a Greek was a red flag to the Judaizers and to the com-
promisers, but Paul stood his ground.

6. *Were gathered together* (*sunēchthēsan*).   First aorist
(effective) passive indicative. The church is not named here
as in verse 4, but we know from verses 12 and 22 that the
whole church came together this time also along with the
apostles and elders. *Of this matter* (*peri tou logou toutou*).
Same idiom in 8:21; 19:38. They realized the importance of
the issue.

7. *When there had been much questioning* (*pollēs zēteseōs
genomenēs*).   Genitive absolute with second aorist middle
participle of *ginomai*. Evidently the Judaizers were given
full opportunity to air all their grievances and objections.
They were allowed plenty of time and there was no effort
to shut off debate or to rush anything through the meeting.
Peter rose up (*anastas Petros*). The wonder was that he had
waited so long. Probably Paul asked him to do so. He was
the usual spokesman for the apostles and his activities in
Jerusalem were well-known.   In particular his experience
at Caesarea (Acts 10) had caused trouble here in Jerusalem
from this very same party of the circumcism (Acts 11:1–18).
It was fitting that Peter should speak. This is the last time
that Peter appears in the Acts. *A good while ago* (*aph'
hēmerōn archaiōn*).   From ancient days. The adjective
archaios is from *archē*, beginning, and its actual age is a matter of relativity. So Mnason (Acts 21:16) is termed "an
ancient disciple." It was probably a dozen years since God
"made choice" (*exelexato*) to speak by Peter's mouth to
Cornelius and the other Gentiles in Caesarea. His point is
that what Paul and Barnabas have reported is nothing new.

The Judaizers made objection then as they are doing now.

8. *Which knoweth the heart* (*kardiognōstēs*). Late word from *kardia* (heart) and *gnōstēs* (known, *ginōskō*). In the N.T. only here and 1:24 which see. *Giving them the Holy Spirit* (*dous to pneuma to hagion*). And before their baptism. This was the Lord's doing. They had accepted (11:18) this witness of God then and it was true now of these other Gentile converts.

9. *He made no distinction between us and them* (*outhen diekrinen metaxu hēmōn te kai autōn*). He distinguished nothing (first aorist active ind.) between (both *dia* and *metaxu*) both (*te kai*) us and them. In the matter of faith and conversion God treated us Jews as heathen and the heathen as Jews. *Cleansing their hearts by faith* (*tēi pistei katharisas tas kardias autōn*). Not by works nor by ceremonies. Peter here has a thoroughly Pauline and Johannine idea of salvation for all both Jew and Greek. Cf. 10:15.

10. *Why tempt ye God?* (*ti peirazete ton theon;*). By implying that God had made a mistake this time, though right about Cornelius. It is a home-thrust. They were refusing to follow the guidance of God like the Israelites at Massah and Meribah (Ex. 17:7; Deut. 6:16; I Cor. 10:9). *That ye should put* (*epitheinai*). Second aorist active infinitive of *epitithēmi*, epexegetic, explaining the tempting. *A yoke upon the neck* (*zugon epi ton trachēlon*). Familiar image of oxen with yokes upon the necks. Paul's very image for the yoke of bondage of the Mosaic law in Gal. 5:1. It had probably been used in the private interview. Cf. the words of Jesus about the Pharisees (Matt. 23:4) and how easy and light his own yoke is (Matt. 11:30). *Were able to bear* (*ischusamen bastasai*). Neither our fathers nor we had strength (*ischuō*) to carry this yoke which the Judaizers wish to put on the necks of the Gentiles. Peter speaks as the spiritual emancipator. He had been slow to see the meaning of God's dealings

with him at Joppa and Caesarea, but he has seen clearly by now. He takes his stand boldly with Paul and Barnabas for Gentile freedom.

11. *That we shall be saved* (*sōthēnai*). First aorist passive infinitive in indirect discourse after *pisteuomen*. More exactly, "We believe that we are saved through the grace of the Lord Jesus in like manner as they also." This thoroughly Pauline note shows that whatever hopes the Judaizers had about Peter were false. His doctrine of grace is as clear as a bell. He has lifted his voice against salvation by ceremony and ritualism. It was a great deliverance.

12. *Kept silence* (*esigēsen*). Ingressive first aorist active of *sigaō*, old verb, to hold one's peace. All the multitude became silent after Peter's speech and because of it. *Hearkened* (*ēkouon*). Imperfect active of *akouō*, descriptive of the rapt attention, were listening. *Unto Barnabas and Paul* (*Barnaba kai Paulou*). Note placing Barnabas before Paul as in verse 25, possibly because in Jerusalem Barnabas was still better known than Paul. *Rehearsing* (*exēgoumenōn*). Present middle participle of *exēgeomai*, old verb, to go through or lead out a narrative of events as in Luke 24:35; Acts 10:8 which see. Three times (14:27; 15:4, 12) Paul is described as telling the facts about their mission work, facts more eloquent than argument (Page). One of the crying needs in the churches is fuller knowledge of the facts of mission work and progress with enough detail to give life and interest. The signs and wonders which God had wrought among the Gentiles set the seal of approval on the work done through (*dia*) Barnabas and Paul. This had been Peter's argument about Cornelius (11:17). This same verb (*exēgēsato*) is used by James in verse 14 referring to Peter's speech.

13. *After they had held their peace* (*meta to sigēsai autous*). Literally, "after the becoming silent (ingressive aorist active of the articular infinitive) as to them (Barnabas and

Paul, accusative of general reference)." *James answered* (*apekrithē Iakōbos*). First aorist passive (deponent) indicative. It was expected that James, as President of the Conference, would speak last. But he wisely waited to give every one an opportunity to speak. The challenge of the Judaizers called for an opinion from James. Furneaux thinks that he may have been elected one of the twelve to take the place of James the brother of John since Paul (Gal. 1:19) calls him apostle. More likely he was asked to preside because of his great gifts and character as chief of the elders.

14. *Hearken unto me* (*akousate mou*). Usual appeal for attention. James was termed James the Just and was considered a representative of the Hebraic as opposed to the Hellenistic wing of the Jewish Christians (Acts 6:1). The Judaizers had doubtless counted on him as a champion of their view and did later wrongfully make use of his name against Peter at Antioch (Gal. 2:12). There was instant attention when James began to speak. *Symeon* (*Sumeōn*). The Aramaic form of Simon as in II Peter 2:1. This little touch would show his affinities with the Jewish Christians (not the Judaizers). This Aramaic form is used also in Luke 2:25, 34 of the old prophet in the temple. Possibly both forms (Symeon, Aramaic, and Simon, Greek) were current in Jerusalem. *How* (*kathōs*). Strictly, "according as," here like *hōs* in indirect discourse somewhat like the epexegetic or explanatory use in III John 3. *First* (*prōton*). Told by Peter in verse 7. James notes, as Peter did, that this experience of Barnabas and Paul is not the beginning of work among the Gentiles. *Did visit* (*epeskepsato*). First aorist middle indicative of *episkeptomai*, old verb to look upon, to look after, provide for. This same verb occurs in James 1:27 and is one of various points of similarity between this speech of James in Acts and the Epistle of James as shown by Mayor in his *Commentary on James*. Somehow Luke may have obtained notes of these various addresses. *To*

take from the Gentiles a people for his name (*labein ex ethnōn laon tōi onomati autou*). Bengel calls this *egregium paradoxon*, a chosen people (*laon*) out of the Gentiles (*ethnōn*). This is what is really involved in what took place at Caesarea at the hands of Peter and the campaign of Barnabas and Paul from Antioch. But such a claim of God's purpose called for proof from Scripture to convince Jews and this is precisely what James undertakes to give. This new Israel from among the Gentiles is one of Paul's great doctrines as set forth in Gal. 3 and Rom. 9–11. Note the use of God's "name" here for "the Israel of God" (Gal. 6:16).

15. *To this agree* (*toutōi sumphōnousin*). Associative instrumental case (*toutōi*) after *sumphōnousin* (voice together with, symphony with, harmonize with), from *sumphōneō*, old verb seen already in Matt. 18:19; Luke 5:36; Acts 5:9 which see. James cites only Amos 9:11 and 12 from the LXX as an example of "the words of the prophets" (*hoi logoi tōn prophētōn*) to which he refers on this point. The somewhat free quotation runs here through verses 16 to 18 of Acts 15 and is exceedingly pertinent. The Jewish rabbis often failed to understand the prophets as Jesus showed. The passage in Amos refers primarily to the restoration of the Davidic empire, but also the Messiah's Kingdom (the throne of David his father," Luke 1:32).

16. *I will build again* (*anoikodomēsō*). Here LXX has *anastēsō*. Compound (*ana*, up or again) of *oikodomeō*, the verb used by Jesus in Matt. 16:18 of the general church or kingdom as here which see. *The tabernacle of David* (*tēn skēnēn Daueid*), a poetical figure of the throne of David (II Sam. 7:12) now "the fallen tent" (*tēn peptōkuian*), perfect active participle of *piptō*, state of completion. *The ruins thereof* (*ta katestrammena autēs*). Literally, "the ruined portions of it." Perfect passive participle of *katastrephō*, to turn down. It is a desolate picture of the fallen, torn down tent of David. *I will set it up* (*anorthōsō*). Old

verb from *anorthoō* (*ana, orthos*), to set upright. See on Luke
13:13 of the old woman whose crooked back was set straight.

17. *That the residue of men may seek after the Lord* (*hopōs
an ekzētēsōsin hoi kataloipoi tōn anthrōpōn ton kurion*). The
use of *hopōs* with the subjunctive (effective aorist active) to
express purpose is common enough and note *an* for an additional tone of uncertainty. On the rarity of *an* with *hopōs*
in the *Koiné* see Robertson, *Grammar*, p. 986. Here the
Gentiles are referred to. The Hebrew text is quite different,
"that they may possess the remnant of Edom." Certainly
the LXX suits best the point that James is making. But
the closing words of this verse point definitely to the Gentiles
both in the Hebrew and the LXX, "all the Gentiles" (*panta
ta ethnē*). Another item of similarity between this speech
and the Epistle of James is in the phrase "my name is called"
(*epikeklētai to onoma mou*) and James 2:7. The purpose of
God, though future, is expressed by this perfect passive indicative *epikeklētai* from *epi-kaleō*, to call on. It is a Jewish
way of speaking of those who worship God.

18. *From the beginning of the world* (*ap' aiōnos*). Or, "from
of old." James adds these words, perhaps with a reminiscence
of Isa. 45:21. His point is that this purpose of God, as set
forth in Amos, is an old one. God has an Israel outside of and
beyond the Jewish race, whom he will make his true "Israel"
and so there is no occasion for surprise in the story of God's
dealings with the Gentiles as told by Barnabas and Paul.
God's eternal purpose of grace includes all who call upon
his name in every land and people (Isa. 2:1; Micah. 4:1).
This larger and richer purpose and plan of God was one of
the mysteries which Paul will unfold in the future (Rom.
16:25; Eph. 3:9). James sees it clearly now. God is making
it known (*poiōn tauta gnōsta*), if they will only be willing
to see and understand. It was a great deliverance that
James had made and it exerted a profound influence on
the assembly.

19. *Wherefore* (*dio*). "Because of which," this plain purpose of God as shown by Amos and Isaiah. *My judgment is* (*egō krinō*). Note expression of *egō*. *I give my judgment.* (*Ego censeo*). James sums up the case as President of the Conference in a masterly fashion and with that consummate wisdom for which he is noted. It amounts to a resolution for the adoption by the assembly as happened (verse 33). *That we trouble not* (*mē parenochlein*). Present active infinitive with *mē* in an indirect command (Robertson, *Grammar*, p. 1046) of *parenochleō*, a common late verb, occurring here alone in the N.T. This double compound (*para, en*) is from the old compound *enochleō* (*en* and *ochlos*, crowd, annoyance) seen in Luke 6:18 and Heb. 12:15, and means to cause trouble beside (*para*) one or in a matter. This is the general point of James which he explains further concerning "those who are turning from the Gentiles unto God," the very kind of people referred to in Amos.

20. *But that we write unto them* (*alla episteilai autois*). By way of contrast (*alla*). First aorist active infinitive of *epistellō*, old verb to send to one (message, letter, etc.). Our word *epistle* (*epistolē* as in verse 30) comes from this verb. In the N.T. only here, Heb. 13:22, and possibly Acts 21:25. *That they abstain from* (*tou apechesthai*). The genitive of the articular infinitive of purpose, present middle (direct) of *apechō*, old verb, to hold oneself back from. The best old MSS. do not have *apo*, but the ablative is clear enough in what follows. James agrees with Peter in his support of Paul and Barnabas in their contention for Gentile freedom from the Mosaic ceremonial law. The restrictions named by James affect the moral code that applies to all (idolatry, fornication, murder). Idolatry, fornication and murder were the outstanding sins of paganism then and now (Rev. 22:15). Harnack argues ably against the genuineness of the word *pniktou* (strangled) which is absent from D Irenaeus, Tertullian, Cyprian. It is a nice point, though the best MSS.

have it in accord with Lev. 17:10–16. The problem is whether the words were added because "blood" was understood as not "murder," but a reference to the Mosaic regulation or whether it was omitted to remove the ceremonial aspect and make it all moral and ethical. The Western text omits the word also in verse 29. But with the word retained here and in verse 29 the solution of James is not a compromise, though there is a wise concession to Jewish feeling. *Pollutions of idols* (*alisgēmatōn*). From *alisgeō* only in the LXX and this substantive nowhere else. The word refers to idolatrous practices (pollutions) and things sacrificed to idols (*eidōluthōn*) in verse 29, not to sacrificial meat sold in the market (I Cor. 10:27), a matter not referred to here. Cf. Lev. 17:1–9. All the four items in the position of James (accepting *pniktou*) are mentioned in Lev. 17 and 18.

21. *For Moses* (*Mōusēs gar*). A reason why these four necessary things (verse 28) are named. In every city are synagogues where rabbis proclaim (*kērussontas*) these matters. Hence the Gentile Christians would be giving constant offence to neglect them. The only point where modern Christian sentiment would object would be about "things strangled" and "blood" in the sense of any blood left in the animals, though most Christians probably agree with the feeling of James in objecting to blood in the food. If "blood" is taken to be "murder," that difficulty vanishes. Moses will suffer no loss for these Gentile Christians are not adherents of Judaism.

22. *Then it seemed good* (*Tote edoxen*). First aorist active indicative of *dokeō*. A regular idiom at the beginning of decrees. This Eirenicon of James commended itself to the whole assembly. Apparently a vote was taken which was unanimous, the Judaizers probably not voting. The apostles and the elders (*tois apostolois kai tois presbuterois*, article with each, dative case) probably all vocally expressed their position. *With the whole church* (*sun holei tēi ekklēsiāi*).

Probably by acclamation. It was a great victory. But James was a practical leader and he did not stop with speeches and a vote. *To choose men out of their company* (*eklexamenous andras ex autōn*). Accusative case, though dative just before (*tois apostolois*, etc.), of first aorist middle participle of *eklegō*, to select. This loose case agreement appears also in *grapsantes* in verse 23 and in MSS. in verse 25. It is a common thing in all Greek writers (Paul, for instance), especially in the papyri and in the Apocalypse of John. *Judas called Barsabbas* (*Ioudan ton kaloumenon Barsabban*). Not otherwise known unless he is a brother of Joseph Barsabbas of 1:23, an early follower of Jesus. The other, Silas, is probably a shortened form of Silvanus (*Silouanos*, I Peter 5:12), the companion of Paul in his second mission tour (Acts 15:32, 41; 16:25). *Chief men* (*hēgoumenous*). Leaders, leading men (participle from *hēgeomai*, to lead).

23. *And they wrote* (*grapsantes*). First aorist active participle of *graphō* and the nominative as if a principal verb *epempsan* had been used instead of *pempsai*, the first aorist active infinitive (anacoluthon). This committee of four (Judas, Silas, Barnabas, Paul) carried the letter which embodied the decision of the Conference. This letter is the writing out of the judgment of James and apparently written by him as the President. *The apostles and the elders, brethren* (*hoi apostoloi kai hoi presbuteroi, adelphoi*). So the oldest and best MSS. without *kai* (and) before "brethren." This punctuation is probably correct and not "elder brethren." The inquiry had been sent to the apostles and elders (verse 2) though the whole church joined in the welcome (verse 4) and in the decision (verse 22). The apostles and elders send the epistle, but call themselves "brothers to brothers," *Fratres Fratibus Salutem.* "The brothers" (*tois adelphois*) addressed (dative case) are of the Gentiles (*ex ethnōn*) and those in Antioch, Syria, and Cilicia, because they were im-

mediately involved. But the decision of this Conference was meant for Gentile Christians everywhere (16:4). *Greeting (Chairein)*. The customary formula in the beginning of letters, the absolute infinitive (usually *chairein*) with the nominative absolute also as in James 1:1; Acts 23:26 and innumerable papyri (Robertson, *Grammar*, pp. 1902f.).

24. *Certain which went from us (tines ex hēmōn*, Aleph B omit *exelthontes*). A direct blow at the Judaizers, put in delicate language (we heard *ēkousamen*) as if only at Antioch (15:1), and not also in Jerusalem in open meeting (15:5). *Have troubled you with words (etaraxan humas logois*). What a picture of turmoil in the church in Antioch, words, words, words. Aorist tense of the common verb *tarassō*, to agitate, to make the heart palpitate (John 14:1, 27) and instrumental case of *logois*. *Subverting your souls (anaskeuazontes tas psuchas humōn)*. Present active participle of *anaskeuazō*, old verb (*ana* and *skeuos*, baggage) to pack up baggage, to plunder, to ravage. Powerful picture of the havoc wrought by the Judaizers among the simple-minded Greek Christians in Antioch. *To whom we gave no commandment (hois ou diesteilametha)*. First aorist middle indicative of *diastellō*, old verb to draw asunder, to distinguish, to set forth distinctly, to command. This is a flat disclaimer of the whole conduct of the Judaizers in Antioch and in Jerusalem, a complete repudiation of their effort to impose the Mosaic ceremonial law upon the Gentile Christians.

25. *It seemed good unto us (edoxen hēmin)*. See statement by Luke in verse 22, and now this definite decision is in the epistle itself. It is repeated in verse 28. *Having come to one accord (genomenois homothumadon)*. On this adverb, common in Acts, see on 1:14. But *genomenois* clearly means that the final unity was the result of the Conference (private and public talks). The Judaizers are here brushed to one side as the defeated disturbers that they really were who had lacked the courage to vote against the majority. *To choose*

out men and send them (*eklexamenois andras pempsai* A B L, though Aleph C D read *eklexamenous* as in verse 22). Precisely the same idiom as in verse 22, "having chosen out to send." *With our beloved Barnabas and Paul* (*sun tois agapē-tois hēmōn Barnabāi kai Paulōi*). The verbal adjective *agapētois* (common in the N.T.) definitely sets the seal of warm approval on Barnabas and Paul. Paul (Gal. 2:9) confirms this by his statement concerning the right hand of fellowship given.

26. *Have hazarded their lives* (*paradedōkosi tas psuchas autōn*). Perfect active participle dative plural of *paradidōmi*, old word, to hand over to another, and with *psuchas*, to hand over to another their lives. The sufferings of Paul and Barnabas in Pisidia and Lycaonia were plainly well-known just as the story of Judson in Burmah is today. On the use of "name" here see on 3:6.

27. *Who themselves also shall tell you the same things by word of mouth* (*kai autous dia logou apaggellontas ta auta*). Literally, "they themselves also by speech announcing the same things." The present participle, as here, sometimes is used like the future to express purpose as in 3:26 *eulogounta* after *apesteilen* and so here *apaggellontas* after *apestalkamen* (Robertson, *Grammar*, p. 1128). Judas and Silas are specifically endorsed (perfect active indicative of *apostellō*) as bearers of the epistle who will also verbally confirm the contents of the letter.

28. *To the Holy Spirit and to us* (*tōi pneumati tōi hagiōi kai hēmin*). Dative case after *edoxen* (third example, verses 22, 25, 28). Definite claim that the church in this action had the guidance of the Holy Spirit. That fact was plain to the church from what had taken place in Caesarea and in this campaign of Paul and Barnabas (verse 8). Jesus had promised that the Holy Spirit would guide them into all truth (John 16:13). Even so the church deliberated carefully before deciding. What a blessing it would be if this were

always true! But even so the Judaizers are only silenced for the present, not convinced and only waiting for a better day to start over again. *No greater burden (mēden pleon baros)*. The restrictions named did constitute some burden (cf. Matt. 20:12), for the old word *baros* means weight or heaviness. Morality itself is a restraint upon one's impulses as is all law a prohibition against license.

29. *Than these necessary things (plēn toutōn tōn epanagkes)*. This old adverb (from *epi* and *anagkē*) means on compulsion, of necessity. Here only in the N.T. For discussion of these items see on verses 20 and 21. In comparison with the freedom won this "burden" is light and not to be regarded as a compromise in spite of the arguments of Lightfoot and Ramsay. It was such a concession as any converted Gentile would be glad to make even if "things strangled" be included. This "necessity" was not a matter of salvation but only for fellowship between Jews and Gentiles. The Judaizers made the law of Moses essential to salvation (15:16). *It shall be well with you (eu praxete)*. Ye shall fare well. A classical idiom used here effectively. The peace and concord in the fellowship of Jews and Gentiles will justify any slight concession on the part of the Gentiles. This letter is not laid down as a law, but it is the judgment of the Jerusalem Christians for the guidance of the Gentiles (16:4) and it had a fine effect at once (15:30–35). Trouble did come later from the Judaizers who were really hostile to the agreement in Jerusalem, but that opposition in no way discredits the worth of the work of this Conference. No sane agreement will silence perpetual and professional disturbers like these Judaizers who will seek to unsettle Paul's work in Antioch, in Corinth, in Galatia, in Jerusalem, in Rome. *Fare ye well (Errōsthe)*. *Valete*. Perfect passive imperative of *rhōnnumi*, to make strong. Common at the close of letters. Be made strong, keep well, fare well. Here alone in the N.T. though some MSS. have it in 23:30.

30. *So they* (*hoi men oun*). As in verse 3. *When they were dismissed* (*apoluthentes*). First aorist passive participle of *apoluō*, common verb to loosen, to dismiss. Possibly (Hackett) religious services were held as in verse 33 (cf. 13:3) and perhaps an escort for part of the way as in verse 3. *The multitude* (*to plēthos*). Public meeting of the church as in verses 1–3. Deissmann (*Bible Studies*, p. 232) gives illustrations from the inscriptions of the use of *plēthos* for official, political, and religious gatherings. The committee formally "delivered" (*epedōkan*) the epistle to the church authorities.

31. *When they had read it* (*anagnontes*). Second aorist active participle of *anaginōskō*. Public reading, of course, to the church. *They rejoiced* (*echarēsan*). Second aorist (ingressive) passive indicative of *chairō*. They burst into exultant joy showing clearly that they did not consider it a weak compromise, but a glorious victory of Gentile liberty. *For the consolation* (*epi tēi paraklēsei*). The encouragement, the cheer in the letter. See *parekalesan* in verse 32. Consolation and exhortation run into one another in this word.

32. *Being themselves also prophets* (*kai autoi prophētai ontes*). As well as Paul and Barnabas and like Agabus (11: 27–30), for-speakers for Christ who justify the commendation in the letter (verse 27) "with many words" (*dia logou pollou*), "with much talk," and no doubt with kindly words concerning the part played at the Conference by Paul and Barnabas. *Confirmed* (*epestērixan*). See on 14:22. It was a glorious time with no Judaizers to disturb their fellowship as in 1–3.

33. *Some time* (*chronon*). Accusative after *poiēsantes*, "having done time." How long we do not know.

34. *But it seemed good unto Silas to abide there* (*edoxe de Silāi epimeinai autou*). This verse is not in the Revised Version or in the text of Westcott and Hort, being absent from Aleph A B Vulgate, etc. It is clearly an addition to

help explain the fact that Silas is back in Antioch in verse
40. But the "some days" of verse 36 afforded abundant
time for him to return from Jerusalem. He and Judas went
first to Jerusalem to make a report of their mission.

35. *Tarried* (*dietribon*). Imperfect active of *diatribo*, old
verb to pass time, seen already in 12:19; 14:3, 28. *With many
others also* (*meta kai heterōn pollōn*). A time of general revival and naturally so after the victory at Jerusalem. It is
at this point that it is probable that the sad incident took
place told by Paul in Gal. 2:11–21. Peter came up to see
how things were going in Antioch after Paul's victory in
Jerusalem. At first Peter mingled freely with the Greek
Christians without the compunctions shown at Caesarea and
for which he had to answer in Jerusalem (Acts 11:1–18).
Rumours of Peter's conduct reached Jerusalem and the Judaizers saw a chance to reopen the controversy on the line
of social customs, a matter not passed on at the Jerusalem
Conference. These Judaizers threaten Peter with a new trial
and he surrenders and is followed by Barnabas and all the
Jewish brethren in Antioch to the dismay of Paul who boldly
rebuked Peter and Barnabas and won them back to his view.
It was a crisis. Some would even date the Epistle to the
Galatians at this time also, an unlikely hypothesis.

36. *Let us return now and visit the brethren* (*epistrepsantes
de episkepsōmetha tous adelphous*). Paul takes the initiative
as the leader, all the more so if the rebuke to Peter and Barnabas in Gal. 2:11–21 had already taken place. Paul is anxious, like a true missionary, to go back to the fields where
he has planted the gospel. He uses the hortatory subjunctive (*episkepsōmetha*) for the proposal (see on 15:14 for this
verb). Note the repeated *epi* (*epi-strepsantes* and *episkepsōmetha*). There is special point in the use of *dē* (shortened form of *ēdē*), now at this juncture of affairs (cf. 13:2).
How they fare (*pōs echousin*). Indirect question, "how they
have it." The precariousness of the life of new converts in

pagan lands is shown in all of Paul's Epistles (Furneaux). So he wanted to go city by city (*kata polin pāsan*).

37. *Was minded to take with them* (*ebouleto sunparalabein*). Imperfect middle (*ebouleto*), not aorist middle *ebouleusato* of the Textus Receptus. Barnabas willed, wished and stuck to it (imperfect tense). *Sunparalabein* is second aorist active infinitive of the double compound *sunparalambanō*, old verb to take along together with, used already about John Mark in 12:25 and by Paul in Gal. 2:1 about Titus. Nowhere else in the N.T. Barnabas used the ingressive aorist in his suggestion.

38. *But Paul thought not good to take with them* (*Paulos de ēxiou—mē sunparalambanein touton*). The Greek is far more effective than this English rendering. It is the imperfect active of *axioō*, old verb to think meet or right and the present active infinitive of the same verb (*sunparalambanō*) with negative used with this infinitive. Literally, "But Paul kept on deeming it wise not to be taking along with them this one." Barnabas looked on it as a simple punctiliar proposal (aorist infinitive), but Paul felt a lively realization of the problem of having a quitter on his hands (present infinitive). Each was insistent in his position (two imperfects). Paul had a definite reason for his view describing John Mark as "him who withdrew from them from Pamphylia" (*ton apostanta ap' autōn apo Pamphulias*). Second aorist active articular participle of *aphistēmi*, intransitive use, "the one who stood off from, apostatized from" (our very word "apostasy"). And also as the one who "went not with them to the work" (*kai mē sunelthonta autois eis to ergon*). At Perga Mark had faced the same task that Paul and Barnabas did, but he flinched and flickered and quit. Paul declined to repeat the experiment with Mark.

39. *A sharp contention* (*paroxusmos*). Our very word *paroxysm* in English. Old word though only twice in the N.T. (here and Heb. 10:24), from *paroxunō*, to sharpen

(*para, oxus*) as of a blade and of the spirit (Acts 17:16; I Cor. 13:5). This "son of consolation" loses his temper in a dispute over his cousin and Paul uses sharp words towards his benefactor and friend. It is often so that the little irritations of life give occasion to violent explosions. If the incident in Gal. 2:11–21 had already taken place, there was a sore place already that could be easily rubbed. And if Mark also joined with Peter and Barnabas on that occasion, Paul had fresh ground for irritation about him. But there is no way to settle differences about men and we can only agree to disagree as Paul and Barnabas did. *So that they parted asunder from one another* (*hōste apochōristhēnai autous ap' allēlōn*). Actual result here stated by *hōste* and the first aorist passive infinitive of *apochōrizō*, old verb to sever, to separate, here only and Rev. 6:4 in the N.T. The accusative of general reference (*autous*) is normal. For construction with *hōste* see Robertson, *Grammar*, pp. 999f. *And Barnabas took Mark with him and sailed away to Cyprus* (*ton te Barnaban paralabonta ton Markon ekpleusai eis Kupron*). Second infinitival clause *ekpleusai* after *hōste* connected by *te*. The same participle is used here minus *sun, paralabonta* (second aorist active). Barnabas and Mark sailed out (*ekpleusai* from *ekpleō*) from the harbour of Antioch. This is the last glimpse that Luke gives us of Barnabas, one of the noblest figures in the New Testament. Paul has a kindly reference to him in I Cor. 9:6. No one can rightly blame Barnabas for giving his cousin John Mark a second chance nor Paul for fearing to risk him again. One's judgment may go with Paul, but one's heart goes with Barnabas. And Mark made good with Barnabas, with Peter (I Peter 5:13) and finally with Paul (Col. 4:10; II Tim. 4:11). See my little book on John Mark (*Making Good in the Ministry*). Paul and Barnabas parted in anger and both in sorrow. Paul owed more to Barnabas than to any other man. Barnabas was leaving the greatest spirit of the time and of all times.

40. *Chose* (*epilexamenos*).   First aorist middle (indirect) participle of *epilegō*, choosing for himself, as the successor of Barnabas, not of Mark who had no place in Paul's plans at this time.   *Commended* (*paradotheis*).   First aorist passive of *paradidōmi*, the same verb employed about Paul and Barnabas (14:26) on their return from the first tour.   It is clear now that the sympathy of the church at Antioch is with Paul rather than with Barnabas in the cleavage that has come.   The church probably recalled how in the pinch Barnabas flickered and went to the side of Peter and that it was Paul who for the moment stood *Paulus contra mundum* for Gentile liberty in Christ against the threat of the Judaizers from Jerusalem.   Silas had influence in the church in Jerusalem (verse 22) and was apparently a Roman citizen (16:37) also.   He is the Silas or Silvanus of the epistles (I Thess. 1:1; II Thess. 1:1; II Cor. 1:19; I Peter 5:12).   It is remarkable that Peter mentions both Mark and Silas as with him (I Peter 5:12f.) at the same time.

41. *Went through* (*diērcheto*).   Imperfect middle.   So Paul went forth on his second mission tour with heart-aches and high hopes mingled together.   *Syria and Cilicia* (*tēn Surian kai tēn Kilikian*).   He took the opposite course from the first tour, leaving Cyprus to Barnabas and Mark.   Probably Paul had established these churches while in Tarsus after leaving Jerusalem (Acts 9:30; Gal. 1:21).   Paul would go "by the Gulf of Issus through the Syrian Gates, a narrow road between steep rocks and the sea, and then inland, probably past Tarsus and over Mt. Taurus by the Cilician gates" (Page).   This second tour will occupy Luke's story in Acts through 18:22.

CHAPTER XVI

1. *And he came also to Derbe and Lystra (katēntēsen de kai eis Derbēn kai eis Lustran).* First aorist active of *katantaō*, late verb to come down to, to arrive at. He struck Derbe first of the places in the first tour which was the last city reached then. *Timothy (Timotheos).* Apparently a native of Lystra ("there," *ekei*), his Hebrew mother named Eunice and grandmother Lois (II Tim. 1:5) and his Greek father's name not known. He may have been a proselyte, but not necessarily so as Timothy was taught the Scriptures by his mother and grandmother (II Tim. 3:15), and, if a proselyte, he would have had Timothy circumcised. It is idle to ask if Paul came on purpose to get Timothy to take Mark's place. Probably Timothy was about eighteen years of age, a convert of Paul's former visit a few years before (I Tim. 1:2) and still young twelve years later (I Tim. 4:12). Paul loved him devotedly (I Tim. 1:3; 5:23; II Tim. 3:15; Phil. 2:19f.). It is a glorious discovery to find a real young preacher for Christ's work.

2. *Was well reported of (emartureito).* Imperfect passive. It was a continuous witness that was borne the young disciple both in his home town of Lystra and in Derbe. Already he had so borne himself that his gifts and graces for the ministry were recognized. It is a wise precaution that the approval of the local church is necessary for the licensing and the ordaining of a preacher. If God has called a man for the work signs of it will be manifest to others.

3. *Him would Paul have to go forth with him (touton ēthelēsen ho Paulos sun autōi exelthein).* This one (note emphatic position) Paul wanted (first aorist active indicative of *thelō* with temporal augment as if from *ethelō* the old form). Here

was a gifted young man who was both Jew and Greek. *He took and circumcised him* (*labōn perietemen auton*). Any one could perform this rite. Paul had stoutly resisted circumcision in the case of Titus, a pure Greek (Gal. 2:3, 5), because the whole principle of Gentile liberty was at stake. But Timothy was both Jew and Greek and would continually give offence to the Jews with no advantage to the cause of Gentile freedom. So here for the sake of expediency, "because of the Jews" (*dia tous Ioudaious*), Paul voluntarily removed this stumbling-block to the ministry of Timothy. Otherwise Timothy could not have been allowed to preach in the synagogues. *Idem non est semper idem.* But Timothy's case was not the case of Titus. Here it was a question of efficient service, not an essential of salvation. Hovey notes that Timothy was circumcised because of Jewish unbelievers, not because of Jewish believers. *Was a Greek* (*Hellēn hupērchen*). Imperfect active in indirect assertion where ordinarily the present *huparchei* would be retained, possibly indicating that his father was no longer living.

4. *They delivered them* (*paredidosan autois*). Imperfect active, kept on delivering to them in city after city. This is a proof of Paul's loyalty to the Jerusalem compact (Knowling). The circumcision of Timothy would indicate also that the points involved were under discussion and that Paul felt no inconsistency in what he did. *The decrees* (*ta dogmata*). Old word from *dokeō*, to give an opinion. It is used of public decrees of rulers (Luke 2:1; Acts 17:7), of the requirements of the Mosaic law (Col. 2:14), and here of the regulations or conclusions of the Jerusalem Conference. Silas was with Paul and his presence gave added dignity to the passing out of the decrees, a charter of Gentile freedom, since he was one of the committee from Jerusalem to Antioch (15:22, 27, 32). *Which had been ordained* (*ta kekrimena*). Perfect passive articular participle of *krinō*, to judge, emphasizing the permanence of the conclusions reached by the apostles

and elders in Jerusalem. *For to keep* (*phulassein*). This present active infinitive likewise accents that it is a charter of liberty for continual living, not a temporary compromise.

5. *Were strengthened* (*estereounto*). Imperfect passive of *stereoō*, old verb to make firm and solid like the muscles (Acts 3:7, 16), these three the only examples in the N.T. *Increased* (*eperisseuon*). Imperfect active of the old and common verb *perisseuō* from *perissos* (overplus). The blessing of God was on the work of Paul, Silas, and Timothy in the form of a continuous revival.

6. *The region of Phrygia and Galatia* (*tēn Phrugian kai Galatikēn chōran*). This is probably the correct text with one article and apparently describes one "Region" or District in The Province of Galatia which was also Phrygian (the old-ethnographic name with which compare the use of Lycaonia in 14:6). Strictly speaking Derbe and Lystra, though in the Province of Galatia, were not Phrygian, and so Luke would here be not resumptive of the record in verses 1–5; but a reference to the country around Iconium and Antioch in Pisidia in North Galatia is not included. This verse is hotly disputed at every point by the advocates of the North Galatian theory as represented by Chase and the South Galatian theory by Ramsay. Whatever is true in regard to the language of Luke here and in 18:23, it is still possible for Paul in Gal. 1:2 to use the term Galatia of the whole province of that name which could, in fact, apply to either South or North Galatia or to both. He could, of course, use it also in the ethnographic sense of the real Gauls or Celts who dwelt in North Galatia. Certainly the first tour of Paul and Barnabas was in the Province of Galatia though touching only the Regions of Pisidia, Phrygia, and Lycaonia, which province included besides the Gauls to the north. In this second tour Lycaonia has been already touched (Derbe and Lystra) and now Phrygia. The question arises why Luke here and in 18:23 adds the

term "of Galatia" (*Galatikēn*) though not in 13:14 (Pisidian Antioch) nor in 14:6 (cities of Lycaonia). Does Luke mean to use "of Galatia" in the same ethnographic sense as "of Phrygia" or does he here add the province (Galatia) to the name of the Region (Phrygia)? In itself either view is possible and it really matters very little except that the question is raised whether Paul went into the North Galatian Region on this occasion or later (18:23). He could have done so and the Epistle be addressed to the churches of South Galatia, North Galatia, or the province as a whole. But the Greek participle *kōluthentes* ("having been forbidden") plays a part in the argument that cannot be overlooked whether Luke means to say that Paul went north or not. This aorist passive participle of *kōluō*, to hinder, can only express simultaneous or antecedent action, not subsequent action as Ramsay argues. No example of the so-called subsequent use of the aorist participle has ever been found in Greek as all Greek grammarians agree (Robertson, *Grammar*, pp. 860–63, 1112–14). The only natural meaning of *kōluthentes* is that Paul with Silas and Timothy "passed through the region of Phrygia and Galatia" because they were hindered by the Holy Spirit from speaking the word in Asia (the Province of Asia of which Ephesus was the chief city and west of Derbe and Lystra). This construction implies that the country called "the region of Phrygia and Galatia" is not in the direct line west toward Ephesus. What follows in verse 7 throws further light on the point.

7. *Over against Mysia* (*kata tēn Musian*). This was an ill-defined region rather north and west of Phrygia. The Romans finally absorbed most of it in the Province of Asia. *They assayed to go into Bithynia* (*epeirazon eis tēn Bithunian poreuthēnai*). Conative imperfect of *peirazō* and ingressive aorist passive infinitive of *poreuomai*. Now Bithynia is northeast of Mysia and north of Galatia (province). Clearly Luke means to say that Paul had, when hindered by the

Holy Spirit from going west into Asia, gone north so as to come in front of Bithynia. This journey would take him directly through Phrygia and the North Galatian country (the real Gauls or Celts). This is, to my mind, the strongest argument for the North Galatian view in these verses 6 and 7. The grammar and the topography bring Paul right up to Bithynia (north of the old Galatia). It is verses 6 and 7 that make me pause before accepting the plausible arguments of Ramsay for the South Galatian theory. In itself the problem is nothing like so important or so determinative as he makes it. But shall we smash Luke's grammar to pieces to bolster up a theory of criticism? *And the* Spirit *of Jesus suffered them not (kai ouk eiasen autous to pneuma Iēsou).* The same Spirit who in verse 6 had forbidden going into Asia now closed the door into Bithynia. This expression occurs nowhere else, but we have the spirit of Christ (Rom. 8:9) and the Spirit of Jesus Christ (Phil. 1:19). *Eiasen* is first aorist active indicative of *eaō*, old verb to allow.

8. *Passing by Mysia (parelthontes tēn Musian).* Literally, passing alongside or skirting Mysia, neglecting it without preaching there. Strictly they passed through part of it to reach Troas. *To Troas (eis Troiada).* This city, named Alexandria Troas after Alexander the Great, was the seaport of Mysia, though a Roman colony and not counted as part of either Asia or Bithynia. New Ilium, on the site of the old Troy, was four miles farther north. It was the place to take ship for Philippi. Twice again Paul will be here (II Cor. 2:12; Acts 20:6).

9. *A vision (horama).* Old word, eleven times in Acts, once in Matt. 17:9. Twice Paul had been hindered by the Holy Spirit from going where he wanted to go. Most men would have gone back home with such rebuffs, but not so Paul. Now the call is positive and not negative, to go "far hence to the Gentiles" (22:21). He had little dreamed of such a call when he left Antioch. Paul's frequent visions

always came at real crises in his life. *A man of Macedonia* (*anēr Makedōn*). Ramsay follows Renan in the view that this was Luke with whom Paul had conversed about conditions in Macedonia. Verse 10 makes it plain that Luke was now in the party, but when he joined them we do not know. Some hold that Luke lived at Antioch in Syria and came on with Paul and Silas, others that he joined them later in Galatia, others that he appeared now either as Paul's physician or new convert. Ramsay thinks that Philippi was his home at this time. But, whatever is true about Luke, the narrative must not be robbed of its supernatural aspect (10:10; 22:17). *Was standing* (*ēn hestōs*). Second perfect active participle of *histēmi*, intransitive, periphrastic imperfect. Vivid picture. *Help us* (*boēthēson hēmin*). Ingressive first aorist active imperative of *boētheō* (*boē, theō*), to run at a cry, to help. The man uses the plural for all including himself. It was the cry of Europe for Christ.

10. *We sought* (*ezētēsamen*). This sudden use of the plural, dropped in 17:1 when Paul leaves Philippi, and resumed in 20:5 when Paul rejoins Luke in Philippi, argues conclusively that Luke, the author, is in the party ("we" portions of Acts) and shows in a writer of such literary skill as Luke that he is not copying a document in a blundering sort of way. Paul told his vision to the party and they were all ready to respond to the call. *Concluding* (*sunbibazontes*). A very striking word, present active participle of *sunbibazō*, old verb to make go together, to coalesce or knit together, to make this and that agree and so to conclude. Already in 9:22 of Paul's preaching. This word here gives a good illustration of the proper use of the reason in connection with revelation, to decide whether it is a revelation from God, to find out what it means for us, and to see that we obey the revelation when understood. God had called them to preach to the Macedonians. They had to go.

11. *Setting sail* (*anachthentes*). Same word in 13:13 which

see. *We made a straight course* (*euthudromēsamen*). First aorist active indicative of compound verb *euthudromeō* (in Philo) from adjective *euthudromos* (in Strabo), running a straight course (*euthus, dromos*). In the N.T. only here and 21:1. It is a nautical term for sailing before the wind. Luke has a true feeling for the sea. *To Samothrace* (*eis Samothrāikēn*). A small island in the Aegean about halfway between Troas and Neapolis. *The day following* (*tēi epiousēi*). Locative case of time with *hēmerāi* (day) to be supplied (7:26; 20:15; 21:18; 23:11). With adverse winds it took five days to make the run of 125 miles (20:6). *To Neapolis* (*eis Nean Polin*). To New Town (Newton, Naples, Neapolis). The port of Philippi ten miles distant, Thracian, but reckoned as Macedonian after Vespasian.

12. *To Philippi* (*eis Philippous*). The plural like *Athēnai* (Athens) is probably due to separate sections of the city united (Winer-Moulton, *Grammar*, p. 220). The city (ancient name Krenides or Wells) was renamed after himself by Philip, the father of Alexander the Great. It was situated about a mile east of the small stream Gangites which flows into the river Strymon some thirty miles away. In this valley the Battle of Philippi was fought B.C. 42 between the Second Triumvirate (Octavius, Antonius, Lepidus) and Brutus and Cassius. In memory of the victory Octavius made it a colony (*kolōnia*) with all the privileges of Roman citizenship, such as freedom from scourging, freedom from arrest save in extreme cases, and the right of appeal to the emperor. This Latin word occurs here alone in the N.T. Octavius planted here a colony of Roman veterans with farms attached, a military outpost and a miniature of Rome itself. The language was Latin. Here Paul is face to face with the Roman power and empire in a new sense. He was a new Alexander, come from Asia to conquer Europe for Christ, a new Caesar to build the Kingdom of Christ on the work of Alexander and Caesar. One need not think that Paul was

conscious of all that was involved in destiny for the world. Philippi was on the Egnatian Way, one of the great Roman roads, that ran from here to Dyrrachium on the shores of the Adriatic, a road that linked the east with the west. *The first of the district* (*prōtē tēs meridos*). Philippi was not the first city of Macedonia nor does Luke say so. That honour belonged to Thessalonica and even Amphipolis was larger than Philippi. It is not clear whether by *meris* Luke means a formal division of the province, though the *Koiné* has examples of this geographical sense (papyri). There is no article with *prōtē* and Luke may not mean to stress unduly the position of Philippi in comparison with Amphipolis. But it was certainly a leading city of this district of Macedonia. *We were tarrying* (*ēmen diatribontes*). Periphrastic imperfect active.

13. *By a river side* (*para potamon*). The little river Gangites (or Gargites) was one mile west of the town. Philippi as a military outpost had few Jews. There was evidently no synagogue inside the city, but "without the gates" (*exō tēs pulēs*) they had noticed an enclosure "where we supposed" (*hou enomizomen*, correct text, imperfect active), probably as they came into the city, "was a place of prayer" (*proseuchēn einai*). Infinitive with accusative of general reference in indirect discourse. *Proseuchē* is common in the LXX and the N.T. for the act of prayer as in Acts 2:42, then for a place of prayer either a synagogue (III Macc. 7:20) or more often an open air enclosure near the sea or a river where there was water for ceremonial ablutions. The word occurs also in heathen writers for a place of prayer (Schürer, *Jewish People*, Div. II, Vol. II, p. 69, Engl. Tr.). Deissmann (*Bible Studies*, p. 222) quotes an Egyptian inscription of the third century B.C. with this sense of the word and one from Panticapaeum on the Black Sea of the first century A.D. (*Light from the Ancient East*, p. 102). Juvenal (III. 296) has a sneering reference to the Jewish *proseucha*.

Josephus (*Ant.* XIV. 10, 23) quotes a decree of Halicarnassus which allowed the Jews "to make their prayers (*proseuchas*) on the seashore according to the custom of their fathers." There was a synagogue in Thessalonica, but apparently none in Amphipolis and Apollonia (Acts 17:1). The rule of the rabbis required ten men to constitute a synagogue, but here were gathered only a group of women at the hour of prayer. In pioneer days in this country it was a common thing to preach under bush arbours in the open air. John Wesley and George Whitfield were great open air preachers. Paul did not have an inspiring beginning for his work in Europe, but he took hold where he could. The conjecture was correct. It was a place of prayer, but only a bunch of women had come together (*tais sunelthousais gunaixin*), excuse enough for not preaching to some preachers, but not to Paul and his party. The "man of Macedonia" turned out to be a group of women (Furneaux). Macedonian inscriptions show greater freedom for women in Macedonia than elsewhere at this time and confirm Luke's story of the activities of women in Philippi, Thessalonica, Berea. *We sat down and spake* (*kathisantes elaloumen*). Having taken our seats (aorist active participle of *kathizō*) we began to speak or preach (inchoative imperfect of *laleō*, often used for preaching). Sitting was the Jewish attitude for public speaking. It was not mere conversation, but more likely conversational preaching of an historical and expository character. Luke's use of the first person plural implies that each of the four (Paul, Silas, Timothy, Luke) preached in turn, with Paul as chief speaker.

14. *Lydia* (*Ludia*). Her birthplace was Thyatira in Lydia. She may have been named after the land, though Lydia is a common female name (see Horace). Lydia was itself a Macedonian colony (Strabo, XIII. 4). Thyatira (note plural form like Philippi and one of the seven churches of Asia here Rev. 2:18) was famous for its purple dyes as old as

Homer (Iliad, IV. 141) and had a guild of dyers (*hoi bapheis*) as inscriptions show. *A seller of purple* (*porphuropōlis*). A female seller of purple fabrics (*porphura*, *pōlis*). Late word, masculine form in an inscription. There was a great demand for this fabric as it was used on the official toga at Rome and in Roman colonies. We still use the term "royal purple." See on Luke 16:19. Evidently Lydia was a woman of some means to carry on such an important enterprise from her native city. She may have been a freed-woman, since racial names were often borne by slaves. *One that worshipped God* (*sebomenē ton theon*). A God-fearer or proselyte of the gate. There was a Jewish settlement in Thyatira which was especially interested in the dyeing industry. She probably became a proselyte there. Whether this was true of the other women we do not know. They may have been Jewesses or proselytes like Lydia, probably all of them employees of hers in her business. When Paul writes to the Philippians he does not mention Lydia who may have died meanwhile and who certainly was not Paul's wife. She was wealthy and probably a widow. *Heard us* (*ēkouen*). Imperfect active of *akouō*, was listening, really listening and she kept it up, listening to each of these new and strange preachers. *Opened* (*diēnoixen*). First aorist active indicative of *dianoigō*, old word, double compound (*dia, ana, oigō*) to open up wide or completely like a folding door (both sides, *dia*, two). Only the Lord could do that. Jesus had opened (the same verb) the mind of the disciples to understand the Scriptures (Luke 24:45). *To give heed* (*prosechein*). To hold the mind (*ton noun* understood), present active infinitive. She kept her mind centred on the things spoken by Paul whose words gripped her attention. She rightly perceived that Paul was the foremost one of the group. He had personal magnetism and power of intellect that the Spirit of God used to win the heart of this remarkable woman to Christ. It was worth coming to Philippi to win this fine personality to the Kingdom of God. She will be the chief spirit in this church that will give Paul more joy and co-operation than any of his churches. It is not stated that she was converted on the first Sabbath, though this may have been the case. "One solitary convert, a woman, and she already a seeker after God, and a native of that very Asia where they had been forbidden to preach" (Furneaux). But a new era had dawned for Europe and for women in the conversion of Lydia.

15. *And when she was baptized* (*hōs de ebaptisthē*). First aorist passive indicative of *baptizō*. The river Gangites was handy for the ordinance and she had now been converted and was ready to make this public declaration of her faith in Jesus Christ. *And her household* (*kai ho oikos autēs*). Who constituted her "household"? The term *oikos*, originally means the building as below, "into my house" and then it includes the inmates of a house. There is nothing here to show whether Lydia's "household" went beyond "the women" employed by her who like her had heard the preaching of Paul and had believed. "Possibly Euodia and Syntyche and the other women, Phil. 4:2, 3, may have been included in the family of Lydia, who may have employed many slaves and freed women in her trade" (Knowling). "This statement cannot be claimed as any argument for infant baptism, since the Greek word may mean her servants or her work-people" (Furneaux). In the household baptisms (Cornelius, Lydia, the jailor, Crispus) one sees "infants" or not according to his predilections or preferences. *If ye have judged me* (*ei kekrikate me*). Condition of the first class, assumed to be true (*ei* and the indicative, here perfect active of *krinō*). She had confessed her faith and submitted to baptism as proof that she was "faithful to the Lord" (*pistēn tōi kuriōi*), believing on the Lord. "If she was fit for that, surely she was fit to be their hostess" (Furneaux). And Paul and his party had clearly no comfortable place to stay while

in Philippi. The ancient hotels or inns were abominable. Evidently Paul demurred for there were four of them and he did not wish to sacrifice his independence or be a burden even to a woman of wealth. *And she constrained us* (*kai parebiasato hēmas*). Effective first aorist middle of *parabiazomai*, late word, in the N.T. only here and Luke 24:29. Some moral force (*bia*) or hospitable persuasion was required (cf. I Sam. 28:23), but Lydia had her way as women usually do. So he accepted Lydia's hospitality in Philippi, though he worked for his own living in Thessalonica (II Thess. 3:8) and elsewhere (II Cor. 11:9). So far only women have been won to Christ in Philippi. The use of "us" shows that Luke was not a householder in Philippi.

16. *A spirit of divination* (*pneuma puthōna*). So the correct text with accusative (apparition, a spirit, a python), not the genitive (*puthōnos*). Hesychius defines it as *daimonion manikon* (a spirit of divination). The etymology of the word is unknown. Bengel suggests *puthesthai* from *punthanomai*, to inquire. Python was the name given to the serpent that kept guard at Delphi, slain by Apollo, who was called *Puthios Apollo* and the prophetess at Delphi was termed Pythia. Certainly Luke does not mean to credit Apollo with a real existence (I Cor. 8:4). But Plutarch (A.D. 50–100) says that the term *puthōnes* was applied to ventriloquists (*eggastrimuthoi*). In the LXX those with familiar spirits are called by this word ventriloquists (Lev. 19:31, 20:6, 27, including the witch of Endor I Sam. 28:7). It is possible that this slave girl had this gift of prophecy "by soothsaying" (*manteuomenē*). Present middle participle of *manteuomai*, old heathen word (in contrast with *prophēteuō*) for acting the seer (*mantis*) and this kin to *mainomai*, to be mad, like the howling dervishes of later times. This is the so-called instrumental use of the circumstantial participles. *Brought* (*pareichen*). Imperfect active of *parechō*, a steady source of income. *Much gain* (*ergasian pollēn*). Work, business, from

ergazomai, to work. *Her masters* (*tois kuriois autēs*). Dative case. Joint owners of this poor slave girl who were exploiting her calamity, whatever it was, for selfish gain, just as men and women today exploit girls and women in the "white slave" trade. As a fortune-teller she was a valuable asset for all the credulous dupes of the community. Simon Magus in Samaria and Elymas Barjesus in Cyprus had won power and wealth as soothsayers.

17. *The Most High God* (*tou theou tou hupsistou*). Pagan inscriptions use this language for the Supreme Being. It looks like supernatural testimony like that borne by the demoniacs to Jesus as "son of the Most High God" (Luke 8:28. Cf. also Mark 1:24; 3:11; Matt. 8:29; Luke 4:41, etc.). She may have heard Paul preach about Jesus as the way of salvation. *The way of salvation* (*hodon sōtērias*). A way of salvation, strictly speaking (no article). There were many "ways of salvation" offered to men then as now.

18. *She did* (*epoiei*). Imperfect active, kept it up for many days. The strange conduct gave Paul and the rest an unpleasant prominence in the community. *Being sore troubled* (*diaponētheis*). First aorist passive of *diaponeō*, old verb, to work laboriously, then in passive to be "worked up," displeased, worn out. In the N.T. only here and 4:2 which see (there of the Sadducees about Peter's preaching). Paul was grieved, annoyed, indignant. He wanted no testimony from a source like this any more than he did the homage of the people of Lystra (14:14). *That very hour* (*autēi tēi hōrāi*). Locative case of time and familiar Lukan idiom in his Gospel, "at the hour itself." The cure was instantaneous. Paul, like Jesus, distinguished between the demon and the individual.

19. *Was gone* (*exēlthen*). Was gone out of the slave girl, second aorist active indicative of *exerchomai*. "The two most important social revolutions worked by Christianity have been the elevation of woman and the abolition of

slavery" (Furneaux). Both are illustrated here (Lydia and this slave girl). "The most sensitive part of 'civilized' man is the pocket" (Ramsay). *Laid hold on* (*epilabomenoi*). Second aorist middle participle of *epilambanō* as in 9:27 and 17:19, but here with hostile intent. *Dragged* (*heilkusan*). First aorist active indicative of *helkuō*, late form of the old verb *helkō* (also in James 2:6) to draw as a sword, and then to drag one forcibly as here and 21:30. It is also used of spiritual drawing as by Jesus in John 12:32. Here it is by violence. *Into the marketplace* (*eis tēn agoran*). Into the Roman forum near which would be the courts of law as in our courthouse square, as in 17:17. Marketing went on also (Mark 7:4), when the crowds collect (Mark 6:56), from *ageirō*, to collect or gather. *Unto the rulers* (*epi tous archontas*). General Greek term for "the magistrates."

20. *Unto the magistrates* (*tois stratēgois*). Greek term (*stratos*, *agō*) for leader of an army or general. But in civic life a governor. The technical name for the magistrates in a Roman colony was *duumviri* or duumvirs, answering to consuls in Rome. *Stratēgoi* here is the Greek rendering of the Latin *praetores* (praetors), a term which they preferred out of pride to the term *duumviri*. Since they represented consuls, the praetors or duumvirs were accompanied by lictors bearing rods (verse 35). *These men* (*houtoi hoi anthrōpoi*). Contemptuous use. *Being Jews* (*Ioudaioi huparchontes*). The people of Philippi, unlike those in Antioch (11:26), did not recognize any distinction between Jews and Christians. These four men were Jews. This appeal to race prejudice would be especially pertinent then because of the recent decree of Claudius expelling Jews from Rome (18:2). It was about A.D. 49 or 50 that Paul is in Philippi. The hatred of the Jews by the Romans is known otherwise (Cicero, *Pro Flacco*, XXVIII; Juvenal, XIV. 96-106). *Do exceedingly trouble* (*ektarassousin*). Late compound (effective use of *ek* in composition) and only here in the N.T.

21. *Customs which it is not lawful for us to receive, or to observe, being Romans* (*ethē ha ouk estin hēmin paradechesthai oude poiein Rōmaiois ousin*).   Note the sharp contrast between "being Jews" in verse 20 and "being Romans" here. This pose of patriotism is all sound and fury. It is love of money that moves these "masters" far more than zeal for Rome. As Roman citizens in a colony they make full use of all their rights of protest. Judaism was a *religio licita* in the Roman empire, only they were not allowed to make proselytes of the Romans themselves. No Roman magistrate would pass on abstract theological questions (18:15), but only if a breach of the peace was made (*ektarassousin hēmōn tēn polin*) or the formation of secret sects and organizations.   Evidently both of these last points are involved by the charges of "unlawful customs" by the masters who are silent about their real ground of grievance against Paul and Silas. *Ethos* (kin to *ēthos*, I Cor. 15:33) is from *ethō*, to be accustomed or used to a thing. The Romans granted toleration to conquered nations to follow their religious customs provided they did not try to win the Romans. But the Jews had made great headway to favour (the God-fearers) with increasing hatred also. Emperor worship had in store grave peril for both Jews and Christians.   The Romans will care more for this than for the old gods and goddesses. It will combine patriotism and piety.

22. *Rose up together* (*sunepestē*). Second aorist (ingressive) active of the double compound *sunephistēmi*, intransitive, old verb, but only here in the N.T. (cf. *katepestēsan* in 18:12). There was no actual attack of the mob as Paul and Silas were in the hands of the officers, but a sudden and violent uprising of the people, the appeal to race and national prejudice having raised a ferment. *Rent their garments off them* (*perirēxantes autōn ta himatia*). First aorist active participle of *perirēgnumi*, old verb, to break off all around, to strip or rend all round. Here only in the N.T. The duumvirs prob-

ably gave orders for Paul and Silas to be stripped of their outer garments (*himatia*), though not actually doing it with their own hands, least of all not stripping off their own garments in horror as Ramsay thinks. That would call for the middle voice. In II Macc. 4:38 the active voice is used as here of stripping off the garments of others. Paul in I Thess. 2:2 refers to the shameful treatment received in Philippi, "insulted" (*hubristhentas*). As a Roman citizen this was unlawful, but the duumvirs looked on Paul and Silas as vagabond and seditious Jews and "acted with the highhandedness characteristic of the fussy provincial authorities" (Knowling). *Commanded* (*ekeleuon*). Imperfect active, repeatedly ordered. The usual formula of command was: "Go, lictors; strip off their garments; let them be scourged." *To beat them with rods* (*rhabdizein*). Present active infinitive of *rhabdizō*, old verb, but in the N.T. = *virgis caedere* only here and II Cor. 11:25 where Paul alludes to this incident and two others not given by Luke (*tris erhabdisthēn*). He came near getting another in Jerusalem (Acts 22:25). Why did not Paul say here that he was a Roman citizen as he does later (verse 37) and in Jerusalem (22:26f.)? It might have done no good in this hubbub and no opportunity was allowed for defence of any kind.

23. *When they had laid* (*epithentes*). Second aorist (constative) active participle of *epitithēmi*, to place upon. *Many stripes* (*pollas plēgas*). The Jewish law was forty stripes save one (II Cor. 11:24). The Roman custom depended on the caprice of the judge and was a terrible ordeal. It was the custom to inflict the stripes on the naked body (back) as Livy 2.5 says: "*Missique lictores ad sumendum supplicium, nudatos virgis caedunt.*" On *plēgas* (from *plēssō*, to strike a blow) see on Luke 10:30; 12:47f. *The jailor* (*tōi desmophulaki*). Late word (*desmos*, *phulax*, keeper of bonds), in the N.T. only here (verses 23, 27, 36). The LXX has the word *archidesmophulax* (Gen. 39:21-23). Chrysostom calls this

jailor Stephanus, he was of Achaia (I Cor. 16:15). *To keep safely* (*asphalōs tērein*). Present active infinitive, to keep on keeping safely, perhaps "as dangerous political prisoners" (Rackham). He had some rank and was not a mere turnkey.

24. *Into the inner prison* (*eis tēn esōteran phulakēn*). The comparative form from the adverb *esō* (within), Ionic and old Attic for *eisō*. In the LXX, but in the N.T. only here and Heb. 6:19. The Roman public prisons had a vestibule and outer prison and behind this the inner prison, a veritable dungeon with no light or air save what came through the door when open. One has only to picture modern cells in our jails, the dungeons in feudal castles, London prisons before the time of Howard, to appreciate the horrors of an inner prison cell in a Roman provincial town of the first century A.D. *Made their feet fast* (*tous podas ēsphalisato autōn*). First aorist (effective) middle of *asphalizō*, from *asphalēs* (safe), common verb in late Greek, in the N.T. only here and Matt. 24:64ff. The inner prison was safe enough without this refinement of cruelty. *In the stocks* (*eis to xulon*). *Xulon*, from *xuō*, to scrape or plane, is used for a piece of wood whether a cross or gibbet (Acts 5:30; 10:39; 13:29; Gal. 3:13; I Peter 2:24) or a log or timber with five holes (four for the wrists and ankles and one for the neck) or two for the feet as here, *xulopedē*, Latin *vervus*, to shackle the feet stretched apart (Job 33:11). This torment was practiced in Sparta, Athens, Rome, and Adonirom Judson suffered it in Burmah. *Xulon* is also used in the N.T. for stick or staff (Matt. 26:47) and even a tree (Luke 23:31). Tertullian said of Christians in the stocks: *Nihil crus sentit in vervo, quum animus in caelo est* (Nothing the limb feels in the stocks when the mind is in heaven).

25. *About midnight* (*kata de mesonuktion*). Middle of the night, old adjective seen already in Mark 13:35; Luke 11:5 which see. *Were praying and singing* (*proseuchomenoi humnoun*). Present middle participle and imperfect active indic-

ative: Praying they were singing (simultaneously, blending together petition and praise). *Humneō* is an old verb from *humnos* (cf. Isa. 12:4; Dan. 3:23). Paul and Silas probably used portions of the Psalms (cf. Luke 1:39f., 67f.; 2:28f.) with occasional original outbursts of praise. *Were listening to them* (*epēkroōnto autōn*). Imperfect middle of *epakroaomai*. Rare verb to listen with pleasure as to a recitation or music (Page). It was a new experience for the prisoners and wondrously attractive entertainment to them.

26. *Earthquake* (*seismos*). Old word from *seiō*, to shake. Luke regarded it as an answer to prayer as in 4:31. He and Timothy were not in prison. *So that the foundations of the prison house were shaken* (*hōste saleuthēnai ta themelia tou desmōtēriou*). Regular construction of the first aorist passive infinitive and the accusative of general reference with *hōste* for actual result just like the indicative. This old word for prison house already in Matt. 11:2; Acts 5:21, 23 which see. *Themelia* is neuter plural of the adjective *themelios*, from *thema* (thing laid down from *tithēmi*). So already in Luke 6:48; 14:29. If the prison was excavated from rocks in the hillside, as was often the case, the earthquake would easily have slipped the bars of the doors loose and the chains would have fallen out of the walls. *Were opened* (*eneōichthēsan*). First aorist passive indicative of *anoigō* (or -*numi*) with triple augment (*ē*, *e*, *ō*), while there is no augment in *anethē* (first aorist passive indicative of *aniēmi*, were loosed), old verb, but in the N.T. only here and 27:40; Eph. 6:9; Heb. 13:5.

27. *Being roused out of sleep* (*exupnos genomenos*). Becoming *exupnos* (rare word, only here in N.T., in LXX and Josephus). An earthquake like that would wake up any one. *Open* (*aneōigmenos*). Perfect passive participle with double reduplication in predicate position, standing open. *Drew his sword* (*spasamenos tēn machairan*). First aorist middle participle of *spaō*, to draw, as in Mark 14:47, drawing his

own sword himself. Our word spasm from this old word. *Was about* (*ēmellen*). Imperfect active of *mellō* with both syllabic and temporal augment and followed here by present infinitive. He was on the point of committing suicide as Brutus had done near here. Stoicism had made suicide popular as the escape from trouble like the Japanese *hari-kari*. *Had escaped* (*ekpepheugenai*). Second perfect active infinitive of *ekpheugō*, old verb with perfective force of *ek*, to flee out, to get clean away. This infinitive and accusative of general reference is due to indirect discourse after *nomizōn*. Probably the prisoners were so panic stricken by the earthquake that they did not rally to the possibility of escape before the jailor awoke. He was responsible for the prisoners with his life (12:19; 27:42).

28. *Do thyself no harm* (*mēden praxēis seautōi kakon*). The usual construction (*mē* and the aorist subjunctive) for a prohibition not to *begin* to do a thing. The older Greek would probably have used *poiēseis* here. The later Greek does not always preserve the old distinction between *poieō*, to do a thing, and *prassō*, to practice, though *prassete* keeps it in Phil. 4:9 and *poieō* is rightly used in Luke 3:10-14. As a matter of fact *prassō* does not occur in Matthew or in Mark, only twice in John, six times in Luke's Gospel, thirteen in Acts, and elsewhere by Paul. *Sprang in* (*eisepēdēsen*). First aorist active of *eispēdaō*, old verb, but here only in the N.T. Cf. *ekpēdaō* in 14:14. The jailor was at the outer door and he wanted lights to see what was inside in the inner prison.

29. *Trembling for fear* (*entromos genomenos*). "Becoming terrified." The adjective *entromos* (in terror) occurs in N.T. only here and 7:32 and Heb. 12:21. *Fell down* (*prosepesen*). Second aorist active indicative of *prospiptō*, old verb. An act of worship as Cornelius before Peter (10:25), when *prosekunēsen* is used.

30. *Brought them out* (*progagōn autous exō*). Second

aorist active participle of *proagō*, to lead forward. He left the other prisoners inside, feeling that he had to deal with these men whom he had evidently heard preach or had heard of their message as servants of the Most High God as the slave girl called them. There may have been superstition behind his fear, but there was evident sincerity.

31. *To be saved* (*hina sōthō*). Final clause with *hina* and first aorist passive subjunctive. What did he mean by "saved"? Certainly more than escape from peril about the prisoners or because of the earthquake, though these had their influences on him. Cf. way of salvation in verse 17. *Believe on the Lord Jesus* (*Pisteuson epi ton kurion Iēsoun*). This is what Peter told Cornelius (10:43). This is the heart of the matter for both the jailor and his house.

32. *They spake the word of God* (*elalēsan ton logon tou theou*). So Paul and Silas gave fuller exposition of the way of life to the jailor "with all that were in his house." It was a remarkable service with keenest attention and interest, the jailor with his warden, slaves, and family.

33. *Washed their stripes* (*elousen apo tōn plēgōn*). Deissmann (*Bible Studies*, p. 227) cites an inscription of Pergamum with this very construction of *apo* and the ablative, to wash off, though it is an old verb. This first aorist active indicative of *louō*, to bathe, succinctly shows what the jailor did to remove the stains left by the rods of the lictors (verse 22). *Niptō* was used for washing parts of the body. *And was baptized, he and all his, immediately* (*kai ebaptisthē autos kai hoi autou hapantes parachrēma*). The verb is in the singular agreeing with *autos*, but it is to be supplied with *hoi autou*, and it was done at once.

34. *He brought them up* (*anagagōn*). Second aorist active participle of *anagō*. It looks as if his house was above the prison. The baptism apparently took place in the pool or tank in which he bathed Paul and Silas (De Wette) or the rectangular basin (*impluvium*) in the court for receiving the

rain or even in a swimming pool or bath (*kolumbēthra*) found within the walls of the prison (Kuinoel). Meyer: "Perhaps the water was in the court of the house; and the baptism was that of immersion, which formed an essential part of the symbolism of the act." *Set meat* (*parethēken trapezan*). Set a "table" before them with food on it. They had probably had no food for a day. *With all his house* (*panoikei*). Adverb, once in Plato, though usually *panoikiāi*. In LXX, but here alone in the N.T. It is in an amphibolous position and can be taken either with "rejoiced" (*ēgalliasato*) or "having believed" (*pepisteukōs*, perfect active participle, permanent belief), coming between them. The whole household (family, warden, slaves) heard the word of God, believed in the Lord Jesus, made confession, were baptized, and rejoiced. Furneaux considers the haste in baptism here "precipitate" as in the baptism of the eunuch. But why delay?

35. *The serjeants* (*tous rhabdouchous*). Fasces-bearers, regular Greek word (*rhabdos, echō*) for Latin *lictores* though Cicero says that they should carry *baculi*, not *fasces*. Was this message because of the earthquake, the influence of Lydia, or a belated sense of justice on the part of the magistrates (praetors)? Perhaps a bit of all three may be true. The Codex Bezae expressly says that the magistrates "assembled together in the market place and recollecting the earthquake that had happened they were afraid."

36. *Now therefore* (*nun. oun*). Note both particles (time and inference). It was a simple matter to the jailor and he was full of glee over this happy outcome.

37. *Unto them* (*pros autous*). The lictors by the jailor. The reply of Paul is a marvel of brevity and energy, almost every word has a separate indictment showing the utter illegality of the whole proceeding. *They have beaten us* (*deirantes hēmas*). First aorist active participle of *derō*, old verb to flay, to skin, to smite. The *Lex Valeria* B.C. 509

and the *Lex Poscia* B.C. 248 made it a crime to inflict blows
on a Roman citizen. Cicero says, "To fetter a Roman citizen
was a crime, to scourge him a scandal, to slay him—parri-
cide." Claudius had "deprived the city of Rhodes of its
freedom for having crucified some citizen of Rome" (Rackham). *Publicly* (*dēmosiāi*). This added insult to injury.
Common adverb (*hodōi*) supplied with adjective, associative
instrumental case, opposed to *idiāi* or *kat' oikous*, Acts 20:20)
Uncondemned (*akatakritous*). This same verbal adjective
from *kata-krinō* with *a* privative is used by Paul in 22:25 and
nowhere else in the N.T. Rare in late Greek like *akatagnōstos*,
but in late *Koinē* (papyri, inscriptions). The meaning is
clearly "without being tried." Paul and Silas were not
given a chance to make a defence. They were sentenced
unheard (25:16). Even slaves in Roman law had a right to
be heard. *Men that are Romans* (*anthrōpous Romaious
huparchontas*). The praetors did not know, of course, that
Paul and Silas were Roman citizens any more than Lysias
knew it in Acts 22:27. Paul's claim is not challenged in
either instance. It was a capital offence to make a false
claim to Roman citizenship. *Have cast us into prison* (*ebalan
eis phulakēn*). Second aorist active indicative of *ballō*, old
verb, with first aorist ending as often in the *Koinē* (-an, not
-on). This was the climax, treating them as criminals. *And
now privily* (*kai nun lathrāi*). Paul balances their recent
conduct with the former. *Nay verily, but* (*ou gar, alla*). No
indeed! It is the use of *gar* so common in answers (*ge+ara*)
as in Matt. 27:23. *Alla* gives the sharp alternative. *Themselves* (*autoi*). As a public acknowledgment that they had
wronged and mistreated Paul and Silas. Let them come
themselves and lead us out (*exagagetōsan*, third person plural
second aorist active imperative of *exagō*). It was a bitter
pill to the proud praetors.

39. *They feared* (*ephobēthēsan*). This is the explanation.
They became frightened for their own lives when they saw

what they had done to Roman citizens. *They asked* (*ērōtōn*). Imperfect active of *erōtaō*. They kept on begging them to leave for fear of further trouble. The colonists in Philippi would turn against the praetors if they learned the facts, proud as they were of being citizens. This verb in the *Koiné* is often used as here to make a request and not just to ask a question.

40. *Into the house of Lydia* (*pros tēn Ludian*). No word in the Greek for "house," but it means the house of Lydia. Note "the brethren" here, not merely Luke and Timothy, but other brethren now converted besides those in the house of the jailor. The four missionaries were guests of Lydia (verse 15) and probably the church now met in her home. *They departed* (*exēlthan*). Paul and Silas, but not Luke and Timothy. Note "they" here, not "we." Note also the *-an* ending instead of *-on* as above. The movements of Timothy are not perfectly clear till he reappears at Beroea (17:15). It seems unlikely that he came to Thessalonica with Paul and Silas since only Paul and Silas obtained security there (17:9) and were sent on to Beroea (17:10). Probably Timothy was sent to Thessalonica from Philippi with gifts of which Paul spoke later (Phil. 4:15f.). Then he followed Paul and Silas to Beroea.

CHAPTER XVII

1. *When they had passed through* (*diodeusantes*). First aorist active participle of *diodeuō*, common verb in the *Koiné* (Polybius, Plutarch, LXX, etc.), but in the N.T. only here and Luke 8:1. It means literally to make one's way (*hodos*) through (*dia*). They took the Egnatian Way, one of the great Roman roads from Byzantium to Dyrrachium (over 500 miles long) on the Adriatic Sea, opposite Brundisium and so an extension of the Appian Way. *Amphipolis* (*tēn Amphipolin*). So called because the Strymon flowed almost around (*amphi*) it, the metropolis of Macedonia Prima, a free city, about 32 miles from Philippi, about three miles from the sea. Paul and Silas may have spent only a night here or longer. *Apollonia* (*tēn Apollōnian*). Not the famous Apollonia in Illyria, but 32 miles from Amphipolis on the Egnatian Way. So here again a night was spent if no more. Why Paul hurried through these two large cities, if he did, we do not know. There are many gaps in Luke's narrative that we have no way of filling up. There may have been no synagogues for one thing. *To Thessalonica* (*eis Thessalonikēn*). There was a synagogue here in this great commercial city, still an important city called Saloniki, of 70,000 population. It was originally called Therma, at the head of the Thermaic Gulf. Cassander renamed it Thessalonica after his wife, the sister of Alexander the Great. It was the capital of the second of the four divisions of Macedonia and finally the capital of the whole province. It shared with Corinth and Ephesus the commerce of the Aegean. One synagogue shows that even in this commercial city the Jews were not very numerous. As a political centre it ranked with Antioch in Syria and Caesarea in Pales-

tine. It was a strategic centre for the spread of the gospel as Paul later said for it sounded (echoed) forth from Thessalonica throughout Macedonia and Achaia (I Thess. 1:8).

2. *As his custom was* (*kata to eiōthos tōi Paulōi*). The same construction in Luke 4:16 about Jesus in Nazareth (*kata to eiōthos autōi*) with the second perfect active participle neuter singular from *ethō*. Paul's habit was to go to the Jewish synagogue to use the Jews and the God-fearers as a springboard for his work among the Gentiles. *For three Sabbaths* (*epi sabbata tria*). Probably the reference is to the first three Sabbaths when Paul had a free hand in the synagogue as at first in Antioch in Pisidia. Luke does not say that Paul was in Thessalonica only three weeks. He may have spoken there also during the week, though the Sabbath was the great day. Paul makes it plain, as Furneaux shows, that he was in Thessalonica a much longer period than three weeks. The rest of the time he spoke, of course, outside of the synagogue. Paul implies an extended stay by his language in I Thess. 1:8. The church consisted mainly of Gentile converts (II Thess. 3:4, 7, 8) and seems to have been well organized (I Thess. 5:12). He received help while there several times from Philippi (Phil. 4:16) and even so worked night and day to support himself (I Thess. 2:9). His preaching was misunderstood there in spite of careful instruction concerning the second coming of Christ (I Thess. 4:13–5:5; II Thess. 2:1-12). *Reasoned* (*dielexato*). First aorist middle indicative of *dialegomai*, old verb in the active to select, distinguish, then to revolve in the mind, to converse (interchange of ideas), then to teach in the Socratic ("dialectic") method of question and answer (cf. *dielegeto* in verse 17), then simply to discourse, but always with the idea of intellectual stimulus. With these Jews and God-fearers Paul appealed to the Scriptures as text and basis (*apo*) of his ideas.

3. *Opening and alleging* (*dianoigōn kai paratithemenos*). Opening the Scriptures, Luke means, as made plain by the

mission and message of Jesus, the same word (*dianoigō*) used by him of the interpretation of the Scriptures by Jesus (Luke 24:32) and of the opening of the mind of the disciples also by Jesus (Luke 24:45) and of the opening of Lydia's heart by the Lord (16:14). One cannot refrain from saying that such exposition of the Scriptures as Jesus and Paul gave would lead to more opening of mind and heart. Paul was not only "expounding" the Scriptures, he was also "propounding" (the old meaning of "allege") his doctrine or setting forth alongside the Scriptures (*para-tithemenos*), quoting the Scripture to prove his contention which was made in much conflict (I Thess. 2:2), probably in the midst of heated discussion by the opposing rabbis who were anything but convinced by Paul's powerful arguments, for the Cross was a stumbling-block to the Jews (I Cor. 1:23). *That it behoved the Christ to suffer* (*hoti ton Christon edei pathein*). The second aorist active infinitive is the subject of *edei* with *ton Christon*, the accusative of general reference. This is Paul's major premise in his argument from the Scriptures about the Messiah, the necessity of his sufferings according to the Scriptures, the very argument made by the Risen Jesus to the two on the way to Emmaus (Luke 24:25-27). The fifty-third chapter of Isaiah was a passage in point that the rabbis had overlooked. Peter made the same point in Acts 3:18 and Paul again in Acts 26:23. The minor premise is the resurrection of Jesus from the dead. *To rise again from the dead* (*anastēnai ek nekrōn*). This second aorist active infinitive *anastēnai* is also the subject of *edei*. The actual resurrection of Jesus was also a necessity as Paul says he preached to them (I Thess. 4:14) and argued always from Scripture (I Cor. 15:3-4) and from his own experience (Acts 9:22; 22:7; 26:8, 14; I Cor. 15:8). *This Jesus is the Christ* (*houtos estin ho Christos, ho Iēsous*). More precisely, "This is the Messiah, viz., Jesus whom I am proclaiming unto you." This is the conclusion of Paul's line of argument and it is

THE ACTS OF THE APOSTLES

logical and overwhelming. It is his method everywhere as in
Damascus, in Antioch in Pisidia, here, in Corinth. He spoke
as an eye-witness.

4. *Some of them (tines ex autōn)*. That is of the Jews who
were evidently largely afraid of the rabbis. Still "some"
were persuaded (*epeisthēsan*, effective first aorist passive
indicative) and "consorted with" (*proseklērōthēsan*). This
latter verb is also first aorist passive indicative of *prosklēroō*,
a common verb in late Greek (Plutarch, Lucian), but only
here in the N.T., from *pros* and *klēros*, to assign by lot. So
then this small group of Jews were given Paul and Silas by
God's grace. *And of the devout Greeks a great multitude (tōn te
sebomenōn Hellēnōn plēthos polu)*. These "God-fearers"
among the Gentiles were less under the control of the jealous
rabbis and so responded more readily to Paul's appeal.
In I Thess. 1:9 Paul expressly says that they had "turned
to God from idols," proof that this church was mainly
Gentile (cf. also I Thess. 2:14). *And of the chief women not a
few (gunaikōn te tōn prōtōn ouk oligai)*. Literally, "And of
women the first not a few." That is, a large number of
women of the very first rank in the city, probably devout
women also like the men just before and like those in 13:50
in Antioch in Pisidia who along with "the first men of the
city" were stirred up against Paul. Here these women were
openly friendly to Paul's message, whether proselytes or
Gentiles or Jewish wives of Gentiles as Hort holds. It is
noteworthy that here, as in Philippi, leading women take
a bold stand for Christ. In Macedonia women had more
freedom than elsewhere. It is not to be inferred that all those
converted belonged to the higher classes, for the industrial
element was clearly large (I Thess. 4:11). In II Cor. 8:2
Paul speaks of the deep poverty of the Macedonian churches,
but with Philippi mainly in mind. Ramsay thinks that Paul
won many of the heathen not affiliated at all with the synagogue. Certain it is that we must allow a considerable

interval of time between verses 4 and 5 to understand what Paul says in his Thessalonian Epistles.

5. *Moved with jealousy* (*zēlōsantes*). Both our English words, *zeal* and *jealousy*, are from the Greek *zēlos*. In 13:45 the Jews (rabbis) "were filled with jealousy" (*eplēsthēsan zēlou*). That is another way of saying the same thing as here. The success of Paul was entirely too great in both places to please the rabbis. So here is jealousy of Jewish preachers towards Christian preachers. It is always between men or women of the same profession or group. In I Thess. 2:3–10 Paul hints at some of the slanders spread against him by these rabbis (deceivers, using words of flattery as men-pleasers, after vain-glory, greed of gain, etc.). *Took unto them* (*proslabomenoi*). Second aorist middle (indirect, to themselves) participle of *proslambanō*, old and common verb. *Certain vile fellows of the rabble* (*tōn agoraiōn andras tinas ponērous*). The *agora* or market-place was the natural resort for those with nothing to do (Matt. 20:4) like the court-house square today or various parks in our cities where bench-warmers flock. Plato (*Protagoras* 347 C) calls these *agoraioi* (common word, but in N.T. only here and 19:38) idlers or good-for-nothing fellows. They are in every city and such "bums" are ready for any job. The church in Thessalonica caught some of these peripatetic idlers (II Thess. 3:10f.) "doing nothing but doing about." So the Jewish preachers gather to themselves a choice collection of these market-loungers or loafers or wharf-rats. The Romans called them *subrostrani* (hangers round the rostrum or *subbasilicari*). *Gathering a crowd* (*ochlopoiēsantes*). Literally, making or getting (*poieō*) a crowd (*ochlos*), a word not found elsewhere. Probably right in the *agora* itself where the rabbis could tell men their duties and pay them in advance. Instance Hyde Park in London with all the curious gatherings every day, Sunday afternoons in particular. *Set the city on an uproar* (*ethoruboun*). Imperfect active of *thorubeō*, from

thorubos (tumult), old verb, but in the N.T. only here and 20:10; Matt. 9:23; Mark 4:39. They kept up the din, this combination of rabbis and rabble. *Assaulting the house of Jason (epistantes tēi oikiāi Iasonos).* Second aorist (ingressive) active of *ephistēmi,* taking a stand against, rushing at, because he was Paul's host. He may have been a Gentile (Jason the name of an ancient king of Thessaly), but the Jews often used it for Joshua or Jesus (II Macc. 1:7). *They sought (ezētoun).* Imperfect active. They burst into the house and searched up and down. *Them (autous).* Paul and Silas. They were getting ready to have a lynching party.

6. *When they found them not (mē heurontes).* Usual negative *mē* with the participle in the *Koinê*, second aorist (effective) active participle, complete failure with all the noise and "bums." *They dragged (esuron).* Imperfect active, vivid picture, they were dragging (literally). See already 8:3; 16:19. If they could not find Paul, they could drag Jason his host and some other Christians whom we do not know. *Before the rulers of the city (epi tous politarchas).* This word does not occur in Greek literature and used to be cited as an example of Luke's blunders. But now it is found in an inscription on an arch in the modern city preserved in the British Museum. It is also found in seventeen inscriptions (five from Thessalonica) where the word or the verb *politarcheō* occurs. It is a fine illustration of the historical accuracy of Luke in matters of detail. This title for city officers in Thessalonica, a free city, is correct. They were burgomasters or "rulers of the city." *Crying (boōntes).* Yelling as if the house was on fire like the mob in Jerusalem (21:28). *These that have turned the world upside down (hoi tēn oikoumenēn anastatōsantes).* The use of *oikoumenēn* (supply *gēn* or *chōran*, the inhabited earth, present passive participle of *oikeō*) means the Roman Empire, since it is a political charge, a natural hyperbole in their excitement, but the phrase occurs for the Roman Empire in Luke 2:1. It is possible that news

had come to Thessalonica of the expulsion of the Jews from Rome by Claudius. There is truth in the accusation, for Christianity is revolutionary, but on this particular occasion the uproar (verse 5) was created by the rabbis and the hired loafers. The verb *anastatoō* (here first aorist active participle) does not occur in the ancient writers, but is in LXX and in Acts 17:6; 21:38; Gal. 5:12. It occurs also in Harpocration (A.D. 4th cent.) and about 100 B.C. *exanastatoō* is found in a fragment of papyrus (Tebtunis no. 2) and in a Paris Magical Papyrus l. 2243f. But in an Egyptian letter of Aug. 4, 41 A.D. (Oxyrhynchus Pap. no. 119, 10) "the bad boy" uses it = "he upsets me" or " he drives me out of my senses" (*anastatoi me*). See Deissmann, *Light from the Ancient East*, pp. 84f. It is not a "Biblical word" at all, but belongs to the current *Koinê*. It is a vigorous and graphic term.

7. *Whom Jason hath received* (*hous hupodedektai Iasōn*). Present perfect middle indicative of *hupodechomai*, to entertain, old verb, but in N.T. only in Luke 10:38; 19:6; Acts 17:7; James 2:25. This is Jason's crime and he is the prisoner before the politarchs. *These all* (*houtoi pantes*). Jason, the "brethren" of verse 6, Paul and Silas, and all Christians everywhere. *Contrary* (*apenanti*). Late compound preposition (*apo, en, anti*) found in Polybius, LXX, here only in the N.T. *The decrees of Caesar* (*tōn dogmatōn Kaisaros*). This was a charge of treason and was a sure way to get a conviction. Probably the Julian *Leges Majestatis* are in mind rather than the definite decree of Claudius about the Jews (Acts 18:2). *Saying that there is another king, one Jesus* (*Basilea heteron legontes einai Iēsoun*). Note the very order of the words in the Greek indirect discourse with the accusative and infinitive after *legontes*. *Basilea heteron* comes first, a different king, another emperor than Caesar. This was the very charge that the smart student of the Pharisees and Herodians had tried to catch Jesus on (Mark 12:14). The Sanhedrin made it anyhow against Jesus to Pilate

(Luke 23:2) and Pilate had to notice it. "Although the emperors never ventured to assume the title *rex* at Rome, in the Eastern provinces they were regularly termed *basileus*" (Page). The Jews here, as before Pilate (John 19:15), renounce their dearest hope of a Messianic king. It is plain that Paul had preached about Jesus as the Messiah, King of the Kingdom of God over against the Roman Empire, a spiritual kingdom, to be sure, but the Jews here turn his language to his hurt as they did with Jesus. As a matter of fact Paul's preaching about the kingdom and the second coming of Christ was gravely misunderstood by the Christians at Thessalonica after his departure (I Thess. 4:13–5:4; II Thess. 2). The Jews were quick to seize upon his language about Jesus Christ to his own injury. Clearly here in Thessalonica Paul had faced the power of the Roman Empire in a new way and pictured over against it the grandeur of the reign of Christ.

8. *They troubled the multitude and the rulers* (etaraxan ton ochlon kai tous politarchas). First aorist active of *tarassō*, old verb to agitate. The excitement of the multitude "agitated" the politarchs still more. To the people it meant a revolution, to the politarchs a charge of complicity in treason if they let it pass. They had no way to disprove the charge of treason and Paul and Silas were not present.

9. *When they had taken security* (labontes to hikanon). A Greek idiom = Latin *satis accipere*, to receive the sufficient (bond), usually money for the fulfilment of the judgment. Probably the demand was made of Jason that he see to it that Paul and Silas leave the city not to return. In I Thess. 2:17f. Paul may refer to this in mentioning his inability to visit these Thessalonians again. The idiom *lambanein to hikanon* now is found in two inscriptions of the second century A.D. (O. G. I. S. 484, 50 and 629, 101). In Vol. III Oxyrhynchus Papyri no. 294 A.D. 22 the corresponding phrase *dounai heikanon* ("to give security") appears. *They*

let them go (*apelusan autous*). The charge was serious but the proof slim so that the politarchs were glad to be rid of the case.

10. *Immediately by night* (*eutheōs dia nuktos*). Paul's work had not been in vain in Thessalonica (I Thess. 1:7f.; 2:13, 20). Paul loved the church here. Two of them, Aristarchus and Secundus, will accompany him to Jerusalem (Acts 20:4) and Aristarchus will go on with him to Rome (27:2). Plainly Paul and Silas had been in hiding in Thessalonica and in real danger. After his departure severe persecution came to the Christians in Thessalonica (I Thess. 2:14; 3:1–5; II Thess. 1:6). It is possible that there was an escort of Gentile converts with Paul and Silas on this night journey to Beroea which was about fifty miles southwest from Thessalonica near Pella in another district of Macedonia (Emathia). There is a modern town there of some 6,000 people. *Went* (*apēiesan*).   Imperfect third plural active of *apeimi*, old verb to go away, here alone in the N.T. A literary, almost Atticistic, form instead of *apēlthon*. *Into the synagogue of the Jews* (*eis tēn sunagōgēn tōn Ioudaiōn*). Paul's usual custom and he lost no time about it. Enough Jews here to have a synagogue.

11. *More noble than those* (*eugenesteroi tōn*). Comparative form of *eugenēs*, old and common adjective, but in N.T. only here and Luke 19:12; I Cor. 1:26. Followed by ablative case *tōn* as often after the comparative. *With all readiness of mind* (*meta pāsēs prothumias*).   Old word from *prothumos* (*pro, thumos*) and means eagerness, rushing forward. In the N.T. only here and II Cor. 8:11–19; 9:2. In Thessalonica many of the Jews out of pride and prejudice refused to listen. Here the Jews joyfully welcomed the two Jewish visitors. *Examining the Scriptures daily* (*kath' hēmeran anakrinontes tas graphas*).   Paul expounded the Scriptures daily as in Thessalonica, but the Beroeans, instead of resenting his new interpretation, examined (*anakrinō* means to sift up and

down, make careful and exact research as in legal processes
as in Acts 4:9; 12:19, etc.) the Scriptures for themselves.
In Scotland people have the Bible open on the preacher
as he expounds the passage, a fine habit worth imitating.
Whether these things were so (*ei echoi tauta houtōs*). Literally,
"if these things had it thus." The present optative in the
indirect question represents an original present indicative
as in Luke 1:29 (Robertson, *Grammar*, pp. 1043f.). This use
of *ei* with the optative may be looked at as the condition
of the fourth class (undetermined with less likelihood
of determination) as in Acts 17:27; 20:16; 24:19; 27:12
(Robertson, *Grammar*, p. 1021). The Beroeans were eagerly
interested in the new message of Paul and Silas but they
wanted to see it for themselves. What a noble attitude.
Paul's preaching made Bible students of them. The duty of
private interpretation is thus made plain (Hovey).

12. *Many therefore* (*Polloi men oun*). As a result of this
Bible study. *Also of the Greek women of honourable estate.*
The word *Hellēnis* means Greek woman, but the word *gunē*
is added. In particular women of rank (*euschēmonōn*, from
eu and *echō*, graceful figure and the honourable standing) as
in 13:50 (Mark 15:43). Probably Luke means by implication
that the "men" (*andrōn*) were also noble Greeks though he
does not expressly say so. So then the Jews were more open
to the message, the proselytes or God-fearers followed suit,
with "not a few" (*ouk oligoi*) real Greeks (both men and
women) believing. It was quick and fine work.

13. *Was proclaimed* (*katēggelē*). Second aorist passive
indicative of *kataggellō*, common late verb as in Acts 16:21.
Of Paul (*hupo Paulou*). By Paul, of course. *Stirring up and
troubling the multitudes* (*saleuontes kai tarassontes tous ochlous*). Shaking the crowds like an earthquake (4:31) and
disturbing like a tornado (17:8). Success at Thessalonica
gave the rabbis confidence and courage. The attack was
sharp and swift. The Jews from Antioch in Pisidia had like-

wise pursued Paul to Iconium and Lystra. How long Paul had been in Beroea Luke does not say. But a church was established here which gave a good account of itself later and sent a messenger (Acts 20:4) with their part of the collection to Jerusalem. This quiet and noble town was in a whirl of excitement over the attacks of the Jewish emissaries from Thessalonica who probably made the same charge of treason against Paul and Silas.

14. *And then immediately* (*eutheōs de tote*). They acted swiftly as in Thessalonica. *Sent forth* (*exapesteilan*). Double compound (*ex, apo*, both out and away) common in late Greek. First aorist active indicative (*exapostellō*, liquid verb). Same form in 9:30. *As far as to the sea* (*heōs epi tēn thalassan*). It is not clear whether Paul went all the way to Athens by land or took ship at Dium or Pydna, some sixteen miles away, and sailed to Athens. Some even think that Paul gave the Jews the slip and went all the way by land when they expected him to go by sea. At any rate we know that Paul was grieved to cut short his work in Macedonia, probably not over six months in all, which had been so fruitful in Philippi, Thessalonica, and Beroea. Silas and Timothy (note his presence) remained behind in Beroea and they would keep the work going. Paul no doubt hoped to return soon. Silas and Timothy in Beroea would also serve to screen his flight for the Jews wanted his blood, not theirs. The work in Macedonia spread widely (I Thess. 1:7f.).

15. *But they that conducted Paul* (*hoi de kathistanontes ton Paulon*). Articular present active participle of *kathistanō* (late form in A B of *kathistēmi* or *kathistaō*), an old verb with varied uses to put down, to constitute, to conduct, etc. This use here is in the LXX (Josh. 6:23) and old Greek also. *To Athens* (*heōs Athēnōn*). To make sure of his safe arrival. *That they should come to him with all speed* (*hina hōs tachista elthōsin pros auton*). Note the neat Greek idiom *hōs tachista* as quickly as possible (good Attic idiom). The indirect com-

mand and purpose (*hina-elthōsin*, second aorist active subjunctive) is also neat Greek (Robertson, *Grammar*, p. 1046). *Departed* (*exēiesan*). Imperfect active of *exeimi*, old Greek word, but rare in N.T.   All in Acts (13:42; 17:15; 20:7; 27:43)

16. *Now while Paul waited for them in Athens* (*En de tais Athēnais ekdechomenou autous tou Paulou*). Genitive absolute with present middle participle of *ekdechomai*, old verb to receive, but only with the sense of looking out for, expecting found here and elsewhere in N.T. We know that Timothy did come to Paul in Athens (I Thess. 3:1, 6) from Thessalonica and was sent back to them from Athens. If Silas also came to Athens, he was also sent away, possibly to Philippi, for that church was deeply interested in Paul. At any rate both Timothy and Silas came from Macedonia to Corinth with messages and relief for Paul (Acts 18:5; II Cor. 11:8f.). Before they came and after they left, Paul felt lonely in Athens (I Thess. 3:1), the first time on this tour or the first that he has been completely without fellow workers. Athens had been captured by Sulla B.C. 86. After various changes Achaia, of which Corinth is the capital, is a separate province from Macedonia and A.D. 44 was restored by Claudius to the Senate with the Proconsul at Corinth. Paul is probably here about A.D. 50. Politically Athens is no longer of importance when Paul comes though it is still the university seat of the world with all its rich environment and traditions. Rackham grows eloquent over Paul the Jew of Tarsus being in the city of Pericles and Demosthenes, Socrates and Plato and Aristotle, Sophocles and Euripides. In its Agora Socrates had taught, here was the Academy of Plato, the Lyceum of Aristotle, the Porch of Zeno, the Garden of Epicurus. Here men still talked about philosophy, poetry, politics, religion, anything and everything. It was the art centre of the world. The Parthenon, the most beautiful of temples, crowned the Acropolis. Was Paul insensible to all this cultural environ-

ment? It is hard to think so for he was a university man of Tarsus and he makes a number of allusions to Greek writers. Probably it had not been in Paul's original plan to evangelize Athens, difficult as all university seats are, but he cannot be idle though here apparently by chance because driven out of Macedonia. *Was provoked* (*parōxuneto*). Imperfect passive of *paroxunō*, old verb to sharpen, to stimulate, to irritate (from *para, oxus*), from *paroxusmos* (Acts 15:39), common in old Greek, but in N.T. only here and I Cor. 13:5. It was a continual challenge to Paul's spirit when he beheld [*theōrountos*, genitive of present participle agreeing with *autou* (his), though late MSS. have locative *theōrounti* agreeing with *en autōi*]. *The city full of idols* (*kateidōlon ousan tēn polin*). Note the participle *ousan* not preserved in the English (either the city being full of idols or that the city was full of idols, sort of indirect discourse). Paul, like any stranger was looking at the sights as he walked around. This adjective *kateidōlon* (perfective use of *kata* and *eidōlon* is found nowhere else, but it is formed after the analogy of *katampelos, katadendron*), full of idols. Xenophon (*de Republ. Ath.*) calls the city *holē bomos, holē thuma theois kai anathēma* (all altar, all sacrifice and offering to the gods). These statues were beautiful, but Paul was not deceived by the mere art for art's sake. The idolatry and sensualism of it all glared at him (Rom. 1:18-32). Renan ridicules Paul's ignorance in taking these statues for idols, but Paul knew paganism better than Renan. The superstition of this centre of Greek culture was depressing to Paul. One has only to recall how superstitious cults today flourish in the atmosphere of Boston and Los Angeles to understand conditions in Athens. Pausanias says that Athens had more images than all the rest of Greece put together. Pliny states that in the time of Nero Athens had over 30,000 public statues besides countless private ones in the homes. Petronius sneers that it was easier to find a god than a man in Athens. Every

gateway or porch had its protecting god. They lined the
street from the Piraeus and caught the eye at every place of
prominence on wall or in the agora.

17. *So he reasoned* (*dielegeto men oun*). Accordingly therefore, with his spirit stirred by the proof of idolatry. Imperfect middle of *dialego*, same verb used in verse 2 which see.
First he reasoned in the synagogue at the services to the
Jews and the God-fearers, then daily in the agora or market-
place (southwest of the Acropolis, between it and the Areopagus and the Pnyx) to the chance-comers, "them that met
him" (*pros tous paratugchanontas*). Simultaneously with
the synagogue preaching at other hours Paul took his stand
like Socrates before him and engaged in conversation with
(*pros*) those who happened by. This old verb, *paratugchano*,
occurs here alone in the N.T. and accurately pictures the
life in the agora. The listeners to Paul in the agora would
be more casual than those who stop for street preaching, a
Salvation Army meeting, a harangue from a box in Hyde
Park. It was a slim chance either in synagogue or in agora,
but Paul could not remain still with all the reeking idolatry
around him. The boundaries of the agora varied, but there
was always the *Poikilē Stoa* (the Painted Porch), over
against the Acropolis on the west. In this *Stoa* (Porch) Zeno
and other philosophers and rhetoricians held forth from
time to time. Paul may have stood near this spot.

18. *And certain also of the Epicurean and Stoic philosophers encountered him* (*tines de kai tōn Epikouriōn kai
Stōikōn philosophōn suneballon autōi*). Imperfect active of
sunballō, old verb, in the N.T. only by Luke, to bring or put
together in one's mind (Luke 2:19), to meet together (Acts
20:14), to bring together aid (18:27), to confer or converse or
dispute as here and already 4:15 which see. These professional philosophers were always ready for an argument and
so they frequented the agora for that purpose. Luke uses
one article and so groups the two sects together in their

attitude toward Paul, but they were very different in fact. Both sects were eager for argument and both had disdain for Paul, but they were the two rival practical philosophies of the day, succeeding the more abstruse theories of Plato and Aristotle. Socrates had turned men's thought inward (*Gnōthi Seauton*, Know Thyself) away from the mere study of physics. Plato followed with a profound development of the inner self (metaphysics). Aristotle with his cyclopaedic grasp sought to unify and relate both physics and metaphysics. Both Zeno and Epicurus (340-272 B.C.) took a more practical turn in all this intellectual turmoil and raised the issues of everyday life. Zeno (360-260 B.C.) taught in the *Stoa* (Porch) and so his teaching was called Stoicism. He advanced many noble ideas that found their chief illustration in the Roman philosophers (Seneca, Epictetus, Marcus Aurelius). He taught self-mastery and hardness with an austerity that ministered to pride or suicide in case of failure, a distinctly selfish and unloving view of life and with a pantheistic philosophy. Epicurus considered practical atheism the true view of the universe and denied a future life and claimed pleasure as the chief thing to be gotten out of life. He did not deny the existence of gods, but regarded them as unconcerned with the life of men. The Stoics called Epicurus an atheist. Lucretius and Horace give the Epicurean view of life in their great poems. This low view of life led to sensualism and does today, for both Stoicism and Epicureanism are widely influential with people now. "Eat and drink for tomorrow we die," they preached. Paul had doubtless become acquainted with both of these philosophies for they were widely prevalent over the world. Here he confronts them in their very home. He is challenged by past-masters in the art of appealing to the senses, men as skilled in their dialectic as the Pharisaic rabbis with whom Paul had been trained and whose subtleties he had learned how to expose. But, so far as we know, this is a new expe-

rience for Paul to have a public dispute with these philosophical experts who had a natural contempt for all Jews and for
rabbis in particular, though they found Paul a new type at
any rate and so with some interest in him. "In Epicureanism, it was man's sensual nature which arrayed itself against
the claims of the gospel; in Stoicism it was his self-righteous-
ness and pride of intellect" (Hackett). Knowling calls the
Stoic the Pharisee of philosophy and the Epicurean the Sadducee of philosophy. Socrates in this very agora used to try
to interest the passers-by in some desire for better things.
That was 450 years before Paul is challenged by these
superficial sophistical Epicureans and Stoics. It is doubtful
if Paul had ever met a more difficult situation. *What would
this babbler say?* (*Ti an theloi ho spermologos houtos legein?*).
The word for "babbler" means "seed-picker" or picker up of
seeds (*sperma*, seed, *legō*, to collect) like a bird in the agora
hopping about after chance seeds. Plutarch applies the
word to crows that pick up grain in the fields. Demosthenes
called Aeschines a *spermologos*. Eustathius uses it of a man
hanging around in the markets picking up scraps of food
that fell from the carts and so also of mere rhetoricians and
plagiarists who picked up scraps of wisdom from others.
Ramsay considers it here a piece of Athenian slang used to
describe the picture of Paul seen by these philosophers who
use it, for not all of them had it ("some," *tines*). Note the
use of *an* and the present active optative *theloi*, conclusion
of a fourth-class condition in a rhetorical question (Robertson, *Grammar*, p. 1021). It means, What would this picker
up of seeds wish to say, if he should get off an idea? It is a
contemptuous tone of supreme ridicule and doubtless Paul
heard this comment. Probably the Epicureans made this
sneer that Paul was a charlatan or quack. *Other some* (*hoi
de*). But others, in contrast with the "some" just before.
Perhaps the Stoics take this more serious view of Paul. *He
seemeth to be a setter forth of strange gods* (*xenōn daimoniōn*

dokei kataggeleus einai). This view is put cautiously by *dokei* (seems). *Kataggeleus* does not occur in the old Greek, though in ecclesiastical writers, but Deissmann (*Light from the Ancient East*, p. 99) gives an example of the word "on a marble stele recording a decree of the Mitylenaens in honour of the Emperor Augustus," where it is the herald of the games. Here alone in the N.T. *Daimonion* is used in the old Greek sense of deity or divinity whether good or bad, not in the N.T. sense of demons. Both this word and *kataggeleus* are used from the Athenian standpoint. *Xenos* is an old word for a guest-friend (Latin *hospes*) and then host (Rom. 16:23), then for foreigner or stranger (Matt. 25:31; Acts 17:21), new and so strange as here and Heb. 13:9; I Peter 4:12, and then aliens (Eph. 2:12). This view of Paul is the first count against Socrates: Socrates does wrong, introducing new deities (*adikei Sōkratēs, kaina daimonia eispherōn*, Xen. *Mem.* 1). On this charge the Athenians voted the hemlock for their greatest citizen. What will they do to Paul? This Athens was more sceptical and more tolerant than the old Athens. But Roman law did not allow the introduction of a new religion (*religio illicita*). Paul was walking on thin ice though he was the real master philosopher and these Epicureans and Stoics were quacks. Paul had the only true philosophy of the universe and life with Jesus Christ as the centre (Col. 1:12–20), the greatest of all philosophers as Ramsay justly terms him. But these men are mocking him. *Because he preached Jesus and the resurrection* (*hoti ton Iēsoun kai tēn anastasin euēggelizato*). Reason for the view just stated. Imperfect middle indicative of *euaggelizō*, to "gospelize." Apparently these critics considered *anastasis* (Resurrection) another deity on a par with Jesus. The Athenians worshipped all sorts of abstract truths and virtues and they misunderstood Paul on this subject. They will leave him as soon as he mentions the resurrection (verse 32). It is objected that Łuke would not use the word in this sense here for his readers would not understand him. But Luke is describing the misapprehension of this group of philosophers and this interpretation fits in precisely.

19. *And they took hold of him* (*epilabomenoi de autou*). Second aorist middle participle of *epilambanō*, old verb, but in the N.T. only in the middle, here with the genitive *autou* to lay hold of, but with no necessary sense of violence (Acts 9:27; 23:27; Mark 8:23), unless the idea is that Paul was to be tried before the Court of Areopagus for the crime of bringing in strange gods. But the day for that had passed in Athens. Even so it is not clear whether "*unto the Areopagus* (*epi ton Areion Pagon*") means the Hill of Mars (west of the Acropolis, north of the agora and reached by a flight of steps in the rock) or the court itself which met elsewhere as well as on the hills, usually in fact in the Stoa Basilica opening on the agora and near to the place where the dispute had gone on. Raphael's cartoon with Paul standing on Mars Hill has made us all familiar with the common view, but it is quite uncertain if it is true. There was not room on the summit for a large gathering. If Paul was brought before the Court of Areopagus (commonly called the Areopagus as here), it was not for trial as a criminal, but simply for examination concerning his new teaching in this university city whether it was strictly legal or not. Paul was really engaged in proselytism to turn the Athenians away from their old gods to Jesus Christ. But "the court of refined and polished Athenians was very different from the rough provincial magistrates of Philippi, and the philosophers who presented Paul to their cognizance very different from the mob of Thessalonians" (Rackham). It was all very polite. *May we know?* (*Dunametha gnōnai*). Can we come to know (ingressive second aorist active infinitive). *This new teaching* (*hē kainē hautē didachē*). On the position of *hautē* see Robertson, *Grammar*, pp. 700f. The question was

prompted by courtesy, sarcasm, or irony.   Evidently no definite charge was laid against Paul.

20. *For thou bringest certain strange things* (*xenizonta gar tina eisphereis*).   The very verb used by Xenophon (*Mem.* 1) about Socrates.   *Xenizonta* is present active neuter plural participle of *xenizō* and from *xenos* (verse 18), "things surprising or shocking us."   *We would know therefore* (*boulometha oun gnōnai*).   Very polite still, we wish or desire, and repeating *gnōnai* (the essential point).

21. *Spent their time* (*ēukairoun*).   Imperfect active of *eukaireō*.   A late word to have opportunity (*eu, kairos*) from Polybius on.   In the N.T. only here and Mark 6:31.   They had time for, etc.   This verse is an explanatory parenthesis by Luke.   *Some new thing* (*ti kainoteron*).   Literally "something newer" or "fresher" than the new, the very latest, the comparative of *kainos*.   Demosthenes (*Philipp.* I. 43) pictures the Athenians "in the agora inquiring if anything newer is said" (*punthanomenoi kata tēn agoran ei ti legetai neōteron*).   The new soon became stale with these itching and frivolous Athenians.

22. *Stood in the midst of the Areopagus* (*statheis en mesōi tou Areiou Pagou*).   First aorist passive of *histēmi* used of Peter in 2:14.   Majestic figure whether on Mars Hill or in the Stoa Basilica before the Areopagus Court.   There would be a crowd of spectators and philosophers in either case and Paul seized the opportunity to preach Christ to this strange audience as he did in Caesarea before Herod Agrippa and the crowd of prominent people gathered by Festus for the entertainment.   Paul does not speak as a man on trial, but as one trying to get a hearing for the gospel of Christ.   *Somewhat superstitious* (*hōs deisidaimonesterous*).   The Authorized Version has "too superstitious," the American Standard "very religious."   *Deisidaimōn* is a neutral word (from *deidō*, to fear, and *daimōn*, deity).   The Greeks used it either in the good sense of pious or religious or the bad sense of

superstitious.   Thayer suggests that Paul uses it "with kindly ambiguity." Page thinks that Luke uses the word to represent the religious feeling of the Athenians (*religiosus*) which bordered on superstition.   The Vulgate has *superstitiosiores*.   In 25:19 Festus uses the term *deisidaimonia* for "religion."   It seems unlikely that Paul should give this audience a slap in the face at the very start.   The way one takes this adjective here colours Paul's whole speech before the Council of Areopagus.   The comparative here as in verse 21 means more religions than usual (Robertson, *Grammar*, pp. 664f.), the object of the comparison not being expressed. The Athenians had a tremendous reputation for their devotion to religion, "full of idols" (verse 16).

23. *For* (*gar*).   Paul gives an illustration of their religiousness from his own experiences in their city.   *The objects of your worship* (*ta sebasmata humōn*).   Late word from *sebazomai*, to worship.   In N.T. only here and II Thess. 2:4. The use of this word for temples, altars, statues, shows the conciliatory tone in the use of *deisidaimonesterous* in verse 22. *An altar* (*bōmon*).   Old word, only here in the N.T. and the only mention of a heathen altar in the N.T. *With this inscription* (*en hōi epegegrapto*).   On which had been written (stood written), past perfect passive indicative of *epigraphō*, old and common verb for writing on inscriptions (*epigraphē*, Luke 23:38).   *To an Unknown God* (*AGNŌSTŌ THEŌ*). Dative case, dedicated to.   Pausanias (I. 1, 4) says that in Athens there are "altars to gods unknown" (*bōmoi theōn agnōstōn*).   Epimenides in a pestilence advised the sacrifice of a sheep to the befitting god whoever he might be.   If an altar was dedicated to the wrong deity, the Athenians feared the anger of the other gods.   The only use in the N.T. of *agnōstos*, old and common adjective (from *a* privative and *gnōstos* verbal of *ginōskō*, to know).   Our word agnostic comes from it.   Here it has an ambiguous meaning, but Paul uses it though to a stern Christian philosopher it may be the

"confession at once of a bastard philosophy and of a bastard religion" (Hort, *Hulsean Lectures*, p. 64). Paul was quick to use this confession on the part of the Athenians of a higher power than yet known to them. So he gets his theme from this evidence of a deeper religious sense in them and makes a most clever use of it with consummate skill. *In ignorance* (*agnoountes*). Present active participle of *agnoeō*, old verb from same root as *agnōstos* to which Paul refers by using it. *This set I forth unto you* (*touto ego kataggellō humin*). He is a *kataggeleus* (verse 18) as they suspected of a God, both old and new, old in that they already worship him, new in that Paul knows who he is. By this master stroke he has brushed to one side any notion of violation of Roman law or suspicion of heresy and claims their endorsement of his new gospel, a shrewd and consummate turn. He has their attention now and proceeds to describe this God left out of their list as the one true and Supreme God. The later MSS. here read *hon—touton* (whom—this one) rather than *ho—touto* (what—this), but the late text is plainly an effort to introduce too soon the personal nature of God which comes out clearly in verse 24.

24. *The God that made the world* (*Ho theos ho poiēsas ton kosmon*). Not a god for this and a god for that like the 30,000 gods of the Athenians, but the one God who made the Universe (*kosmos* on the old Greek sense of orderly arrangement of the whole universe). *And all things therein* (*kai panta ta en autōi*). All the details in the universe were created by this one God. Paul is using the words of Isa. 42:5. The Epicureans held that matter was eternal. Paul sets them aside. This one God was not to be confounded with any of their numerous gods save with this "Unknown God." *Being Lord of heaven and earth* (*ouranou kai gēs huparchōn kurios*). *Kurios* here owner, absolute possessor of both heaven and earth (Isa. 45:7), not of just parts. *Dwelleth not in temples made with hands* (*ouken cheiropoiētois naois katoikei*). The

old adjective *cheiropoiētos* (*cheir*, *poieō*) already in Stephen's speech (7:48). No doubt Paul pointed to the wonderful Parthenon, supposed to be the home of Athene as Stephen denied that God dwelt alone in the temple in Jerusalem.

25. *As though he needed anything* (*prosdeomenos tinos*). Present middle participle of *prosdeomai*, to want besides, old verb, but here only in the N.T. This was strange doctrine for the people thought that the gods needed their offerings for full happiness. This self-sufficiency of God was taught by Philo and Lucretius, but Paul shows that the Epicurean missed it by putting God, if existing at all, outside the universe. *Seeing he himself giveth to all* (*autos didous pasin*). This Supreme Personal God is the source of life, breath, and everything. Paul here rises above all Greek philosophers.

26. *And he made of one* (*epoiēsen te ex henos*). The word *haimatos* (blood) is absent from Aleph A B and is a later explanatory addition. What Paul affirms is the unity of the human race with a common origin and with God as the Creator. This view runs counter to Greek exclusiveness which treated other races as barbarians and to Jewish pride which treated other nations as heathen or pagan (the Jews were *laos*, the Gentiles *ethnē*). The cosmopolitanism of Paul here rises above Jew and Greek and claims the one God as the Creator of the one race of men. The Athenians themselves claimed to be *antochthonous* (indigenous) and a special creation. Zeno and Seneca did teach a kind of cosmopolitanism (really pantheism) far different from the personal God of Paul. It was Rome, not Greece, that carried out the moral ideas of Zeno. Man is part of the universe (verse 24) and God created (*epoiēsen*) man as he created (*poiēsas*) the all. *For to dwell* (*katoikein*). Infinitive (present active) of purpose, so as to dwell. *Having determined* (*horisas*). First aorist active participle of *horizō*, old verb to make a horizon as already in 19:42 which see. Paul here touches

God's Providence. God has revealed himself in history as in creation. His hand appears in the history of all men as well as in that of the Chosen People of Israel. *Appointed seasons* (*prostetagmenous kairous*). Not the weather as in 14:17, but "the times of the Gentiles" (*kairoi ethnōn*) of which Jesus spoke (Luke 21:24). The perfect passive participle of *prostassō*, old verb to enjoin, emphasizes God's control of human history without any denial of human free agency as was involved in the Stoic Fate (*Heirmarmenē*). *Bounds* (*horothesias*). Limits? Same idea in Job 12:23. Nations rise and fall, but it is not blind chance or hard fate. Thus there is an interplay betwen God's will and man's activities, difficult as it is for us to see with our shortened vision.

27. *That they should seek God* (*Zētein ton theon*). Infinitive (present active) of purpose again. Seek him, not turn away from him as the nations had done (Rom. 1:18-32). *If haply they might feel after him* (*ei ara ge psēlaphēseian auton*). First aorist active (Aeolic form) optative of *psēlaphaō*, old verb from *psaō*, to touch. So used by the Risen Jesus in his challenge to the disciples (Luke 24:39), by the Apostle John of his personal contact with Jesus (I John 1:1), of the contact with Mount Sinai (Heb. 12:18). Here it pictures the blind groping of the darkened heathen mind after God to "find him" (*heuroien*, second aorist active optative) whom they had lost. One knows what it is in a darkened room to feel along the walls for the door (Deut. 28:29; Job 5:14; 12:25; Isa. 59:10). Helen Keller, when told of God, said that she knew of him already, groping in the dark after him. The optative here with *ei* is due to the condition of the fourth class (undetermined, but with vague hope of being determined) with aim also present (Robertson, *Grammar*, p. 1021). Note also *ara ge* the inferential particle *ara* with the delicate intensive particle *ge*. *Though he is not far from each one of us* (*kai ge ou makran apo henos hekastou hēmōn huparchonta*).

More exactly with B L (*kai ge* instead of *kaitoi* or *kaitoi ge*), "and yet being not far from each one of us," a direct statement rather than a concessive one. The participle *huparchonta* agrees with *auton* and the negative *ou* rather than the usual *mē* with the participle makes an emphatic negative. Note also the intensive particle *ge*.

28. *For in him* (*en autōi gar*). Proof of God's nearness, not stoic pantheism, but real immanence in God as God dwells in us. The three verbs (*zōmen, kinoumetha, esmen*) form an ascending scale and reach a climax in God (life, movement, existence). *Kinoumetha* is either direct middle present indicative (we move ourselves) or passive (we are moved). *As certain even of your own poets* (*hōs kai tines tōn kath' humās poiētōn*). "As also some of the poets among you." Aratus of Soli in Cilicia (ab. B.C. 270) has these very words in his *Ta Phainomena* and Cleanthes, Stoic philosopher (300–220 B.C.) in his *Hymn to Zeus* has *Ek sou gar genos esmen*. In I Cor. 15:32 Paul quotes from Menander and in Titus 1:12 from Epimenides. J. Rendel Harris claims that he finds allusions in Paul's Epistles to Pindar, Aristophanes, and other Greek writers. There is no reason in the world why Paul should not have acquaintance with Greek literature, though one need not strain a point to prove it. Paul, of course, knew that the words were written of Zeus (Jupiter), not of Jehovah, but he applies the idea in them to his point just made that all men are the offspring of God.

29. *We ought not to think* (*ouk opheilomen nomizein*). It is a logical conclusion (*oun*, therefore) from the very language of Aratus and Cleanthes. *That the Godhead is like* (*to theion einai homoion*). Infinitive with accusative of general reference in indirect discourse. *To theion* is strictly "the divine" nature like *theiotēs* (Rom. 1:20) rather than like *theotēs* (Col. 2:9). Paul may have used *to theion* here to get back behind all their notions of various gods to the real nature of God. The Athenians may even have used the term themselves.

After *homoios* (like) the associative instrumental case is used as with *chrusōi, argurōi, lithōi. Graven by art and device of man* (*charagmati technēs kai enthumēseōs anthrōpou*). Apposition with preceding and so *charagmati* in associative instrumental case. Literally, graven work or sculpture from *charassō*, to engrave, old word, but here alone in N.T. outside of Revelation (the mark of the beast). Graven work of art (*technēs*) or external craft, and of thought or device (*enthumēseōs*) or internal conception of man.

30. *The times of ignorance* (*tous chronous tēs agnoias*). The times before full knowledge of God came in Jesus Christ. Paul uses the very word for their ignorance (*agnoountes*) employed in verse 23. *Overlooked* (*huperidōn*). Second aorist active participle of *huperoraō* or *hupereidō*, old verb to see beyond, not to see, to overlook, not "to wink at" of the Authorized Version with the notion of condoning. Here only in the N.T. It occurs in the LXX in the sense of overlooking or neglecting (Psa. 18:62; 55:1). But it has here only a negative force. God has all the time objected to the polytheism of the heathen, and now he has made it plain. In Wisdom 11:23 we have these words: "Thou overlookest the sins of men to the end they may repent." *But now* (*ta nun*). Accusative of general reference, "as to the now things or situation." All is changed now that Christ has come with the full knowledge of God. See also 27:22. *All everywhere* (*pantas pantachou*). No exceptions anywhere. *Repent* (*metanoein*). Present active infinitive of *metanoeō* in indirect command, a permanent command of perpetual force. See on *metanoeō* Acts 2:38 and the Synoptic Gospels. This word was the message of the Baptist, of Jesus, of Peter, of Paul, this radical change of attitude and life.

31. *Inasmuch as* (*kathoti*). According as (*kata, hoti*). Old causal conjunction, but in N.T. only used in Luke's writings (Luke 1:7; 19:9; Acts 2:45; 4:35; 17:31). *Hath appointed a day* (*estēsen hēmeran*). First aorist active indicative of

histēmi, to place, set. God did set the day in his counsel and he will fulfil it in his own time. *Will judge (mellei krinein).* Rather, is going to judge, *mellō* and the present active infinitive of *krinō.* Paul here quotes Psa. 9:8 where *krinei* occurs. *By the man whom he hath ordained (en andri hōi hōrisen).* Here he adds to the Psalm the place and function of Jesus Christ, a passage in harmony with Christ's own words in Matt. 25. *Hōi* (whom) is attracted from the accusative, object of *hōrisen* (first aorist active indicative of *horizō*) to the case of the antecedent *andri.* It has been said that Paul left the simple gospel in this address to the council of the Areopagus for philosophy. But did he? He skilfully caught their attention by reference to an altar to an Unknown God whom he interprets to be the Creator of all things and all men who overrules the whole world and who now commands repentance of all and has revealed his will about a day of reckoning when Jesus Christ will be Judge. He has preached the unity of God, the one and only God, has proclaimed repentance, a judgment day, Jesus as the Judge as shown by his Resurrection, great fundamental doctrines, and doubtless had much more to say when they interrupted his address. There is no room here for such a charge against Paul. He rose to a great occasion and made a masterful exposition of God's place and power in human history. *Whereof he hath given assurance (pistin paraschōn).* Second aorist active participle of *parechō,* old verb to furnish, used regularly by Demosthenes for bringing forward evidence. Note this old use of *pistis* as conviction or ground of confidence (Heb. 11:1) like a note or title-deed, a conviction resting on solid basis of fact. All the other uses of *pistis* grow out of this one from *peithō,* to persuade. *In that he hath raised him from the dead (anastēsas auton ek nekrōn).* First aorist active participle of *anistēmi,* causal participle, but literally, "having raised him from the dead." This Paul knew to be a fact because he himself had seen the Risen

Christ. Paul has here come to the heart of his message and could now throw light on their misapprehension about "Jesus and the Resurrection" (verse 18). Here Paul has given the proof of all his claims in the address that seemed new and strange to them.

32. *The resurrection of the dead* (*anastasin nekrōn*). Rather, "a resurrection of dead men." No article with either word. The Greeks believed that the souls of men lived on, but they had no conception of resurrection of the body. They had listened with respect till Paul spoke of the actual resurrection of Jesus from the dead as a fact, when they did not care to hear more. *Some mocked* (*hoi men echleuazon*). Imperfect active of *chleuazō*, a common verb (from *chleuē*, jesting, mockery). Only here in the N.T. though late MSS. have it in 2:13 (best MSS. *diachleuazō*). Probably inchoative here, began to mock. In contempt at Paul's statement they declined to listen further to "this babbler" (verse 18) who had now lost what he had gained with this group of hearers (probably the light and flippant Epicureans). *But others* (*hoi de*). A more polite group like those who had invited him to speak (verse 19). They were unconvinced, but had better manners and so were in favour of an adjournment. This was done, though it is not clear whether it was a serious postponement or a courteous refusal to hear Paul further (probably this). It was a virtual dismissal of the matter. "It is a sad story—the noblest of ancient cities and the noblest man of history—and he never cared to look on it again" (Furneaux).

33. *Thus Paul went out from among them* (*houtōs ho Paulos exēlthen ek mesou autōn*). No further questions, no effort to arrest him, no further ridicule. He walked out never to return to Athens. Had he failed?

34. *Clave unto him and believed* (*kollēthentes autōi episteusan*). First aorist passive of this strong word *kollaō*, to glue to, common in Acts (5:13; 8:29; 9:26; 10:28). No sermon is a

failure which leads a group of men (*andres*) to believe (ingressive aorist of *pisteuō*) in Jesus Christ. Many so-called great or grand sermons reap no such harvest. *Dionysius the Areopagite (Dionusios ho Areopagitēs).* One of the judges of the Court of the Areopagus. That of itself was no small victory. He was one of this college of twelve judges who had helped to make Athens famous. Eusebius says that he became afterwards bishop of the Church at Athens and died a martyr. *A woman named Damaris (gunē onomati Damaris).* A woman by name Damaris. Not the wife of Dionysius as some have thought, but an aristocratic woman, not necessarily an educated courtezan as Furneaux holds. And there were "others" (*heteroi*) with them, a group strong enough to keep the fire burning in Athens. It is common to say that Paul in I Cor. 2:1-5 alludes to his failure with philosophy in Athens when he failed to preach Christ crucified and he determined never to make that mistake again. On the other hand Paul determined to stick to the Cross of Christ in spite of the fact that the intellectual pride and superficial culture of Athens had prevented the largest success. As he faced Corinth with its veneer of culture and imitation of philosophy and sudden wealth he would go on with the same gospel of the Cross, the only gospel that Paul knew or preached. And it was a great thing to give the world a sermon like that preached in Athens.

CHAPTER XVIII

1. *To Corinth (eis Korinthon)*. Mummius had captured and destroyed Corinth B.C. 146. It was restored by Julius Caesar B.C. 46 as a boom town and made a colony. It was now the capital of the province of Achaia and the chief commercial city of Greece with a cosmopolitan population. It was only fifty miles from Athens. The summit of Acrocorinthus was 1,800 feet high and the ports of Cenchreae and Lechaeum and the Isthmus across which ships were hauled gave it command of the trade routes between Asia and Rome. The temple of Aphrodite on the Acrocorinthus had a thousand consecrated prostitutes and the very name to Corinthianize meant immorality. Not the Parthenon with Athene faced Paul in Corinth, but a worse situation. Naturally many Jews were in such a mart of trade. Philippi, Thessalonica, Beroea, Athens, all had brought anxiety to Paul. What could he expect in licentious Corinth?

2. *Aquila (Akulan)*. Luke calls him a Jew from Pontus, apparently not yet a disciple, though there were Jews from Pontus at the great Pentecost who were converted (2:9). Aquila who made the famous A.D. translation of the O.T. was also from Pontus. Paul "found" (*heurōn*, second aorist active participle of *heuriskō*) though we do not know how. Edersheim says that a Jewish guild always kept together whether in street or synagogue so that by this bond they probably met. *Lately come from Italy (prosphatōs elēluthota apo tēs Italias)*. Second perfect participle of *erchomai*. *Koiné* adverb, here only in the N.T., from adjective *prosphatos (pro, sphaō or sphazō, to kill)*, lately slaughtered and so fresh or recent (Heb. 10:20). *With his wife Priscilla (kai Priskillan gunaika autou)*. Diminutive of *Priska* (Rom.

16:3; I Cor. 16:19). Prisca is a name in the Acilian family and the Prisci was the name of another noble clan. Aquila may have been a freedman like many Jews in Rome. Her name comes before his in verses 18, 26; Rom. 16:3; II Tim. 4:9. *Because Claudius had commanded* (*dia to diatetachenai Klaudion*). Perfect active articular infinitive of *diatassō*, old verb to dispose, arrange, here with accusative of general reference. *Dia* here is causal sense, "because of the having ordered as to Claudius." This was about A.D. 49, done, Suetonius says (*Claudius* C. 25), because "the Jews were in a state of constant tumult at the instigation of one Chrestus" (probably among the Jews about Christ so pronounced). At any rate Jews were unpopular in Rome for Tiberius had deported 4,000 to Sardinia. There were 20,000 Jews in Rome. Probably mainly those implicated in the riots actually left.

3. *Because he was of the same trade* (*dia to homotechnon einai*). Same construction with *dia* as above. *Homotechnon* is an old word (*homos, technē*), though here alone in N.T. Rabbi Judah says: "He that teacheth not his son a trade, doth the same as if he taught him to be a thief." So it was easy for Paul to find a home with these "tentmakers by trade" (*skēnoipoioi tēi technēi*). Late word from *skēnē* and *poieō*, here only in the N.T. They made portable tents of leather or of cloth of goat's hair. So Paul lived in this home with this noble man and his wife, all the more congenial if already Christians which they soon became at any rate. They worked as partners in the common trade. Paul worked for his support elsewhere, already in Thessalonica (I Thess. 2:9; II Thess. 3:8) and later at Ephesus with Aquila and Priscilla (Acts 18:18, 26; 20:34; I Cor. 16:19). They moved again to Rome (Rom. 16:3) and were evidently a couple of considerable wealth and generosity. It was a blessing to Paul to find himself with these people. So he "abode" (*emenen*, imperfect active) with them and "they wrought"

(*ērgazonto*, imperfect middle), happy and busy during week days.

4. *He reasoned* (*dielegeto*). Imperfect middle, same form as in 17:17 about Paul's work in Athens, here only on the Sabbaths. *Persuaded* (*epeithen*). Imperfect active, conative, he tried to persuade both Jews and Greeks (God-fearers who alone would come).

5. *Was constrained by the word* (*suneicheto tōi logōi*). This is undoubtedly the correct text and not *tōi pneumati* of the Textus Receptus, but *suneicheto* is in my opinion the direct middle imperfect indicative, not the imperfect passive as the translations have it (Robertson, *Grammar*, p. 808). Paul held himself together or completely to the preaching instead of just on Sabbaths in the synagogue (verse 4). The coming of Silas and Timothy with the gifts from Macedonia (I Thess. 3:6; II Cor. 11:9; Phil. 4:15) set Paul free from tent-making for a while so that he began to devote himself (inchoative imperfect) with fresh consecration to preaching. See the active in II Cor. 5:14. He was now also assisted by Silas and Timothy (II Cor. 1:19). *Testifying to the Jews that Jesus was the Christ* (*diamarturomenos tois Ioudaiois einai ton Christon Iēsoun*). Paul's witness everywhere (9:22; 17:3). This verb *diamarturomenos* occurs in 2:40 (which see) for Peter's earnest witness. Perhaps daily now in the synagogue he spoke to the Jews who came. *Einai* is the infinitive in indirect discourse (assertion) with the accusative of general reference. By *ton Christon* Paul means "the Messiah." His witness is to show to the Jews that Jesus of Nazareth is the Messiah.

6. *When they opposed themselves* (*antitassomenōn autōn*). Genitive absolute with present middle (direct middle again) of *antitassō*, old verb to range in battle array (*tassō*) face to face with or against (*anti*). In the N.T. only here and Rom. 13:2; James 4:6; I Peter 5:5. Paul's fresh activity roused the rabbis as at Antioch in Pisidia and at Thessalonica

in concerted opposition and railing (blasphemy). *He shook out his raiment (ektinaxamenos ta himatia).* First aorist middle of *ektinassō*, old verb, in the N.T. only here as in 13:51 (middle) and Mark 6:11 = Matt. 10:15 where active voice occurs of shaking out dust also. Vivid and dramatic picture here like that in Neh. 5:13, "undoubtedly a very exasperating gesture" (Ramsay), but Paul was deeply stirred. *Your blood be upon your own heads (To haima humōn epi tēn kephalēn humōn).* As in Ezek. 3:18f. and 33:4, 8f.; II Sam. 1:16. Not as a curse, but "a solemn disclaimer of responsibility" by Paul (Page) as in Acts 20:26. The Jews used this very phrase in assuming responsibility for the blood of Jesus (Matt. 27:25). Cf. Matt. 23:35. *I am clean (katharos egō).* Pure from your blood. Repeats the claim made in previous sentence. Paul had done his duty. *From henceforth (apo tou nun).* Turning point reached in Corinth. He will devote himself to the Gentiles, though Jews will be converted there also. Elsewhere as in Ephesus (19:1-10) and in Rome (Acts 28:23-28) Paul will preach also to Jews.

7. *Titus Justus (Titou Ioustou).* So Aleph E Vulgate, while B has *Titiau Ioustou*, while most MSS. have only *Ioustou*. Evidently a Roman citizen and not Titus, brother of Luke, of Gal. 2:1. We had Barsabbas Justus (Acts 1:23) and Paul speaks of Jesus Justus (Col. 4:11). The Titii were a famous family of potters in Corinth. This Roman was a God-fearer whose house "joined hard to the synagogue" (*ēn sunomorousa tēi sunagōgēi*). Periphrastic imperfect active of *sunomoreō*, a late (Byzantine) word, here only in the N.T., followed by the associative instrumental case, from *sunomoros (sun, homoros* from *homos,* joint, and *horos,* boundary) having joint boundaries, right next to. Whether Paul chose this location for his work because it was next to the synagogue, we do not know, but it caught the attendants at the synagogue worship. In Ephesus when Paul had to leave the synagogue he went to the school house of Tyrannus

(19:9f.). The lines are being drawn between the Christians and the Jews, drawn by the Jews themselves.

8. *Crispus* (*Krispos*). Though a Jew and ruler of the synagogue (cf. 13:15), he had a Latin name. Paul baptized him (I Cor. 1:14) himself, perhaps because of his prominence, apparently letting Silas and Timothy baptize most of the converts (I Cor. 1:14-17). Probably he followed Paul to the house of Titus Justus. It looked like ruin for the synagogue. *With all his house* (*sun holōi tōi oikōi autou*). Another household conversion, for Crispus "believed (*episteusen*) in the Lord with all his house." *Hearing believed and were baptized* (*akouontes episteuon kai ebaptizonto*). Present active participle and imperfect indicatives active and passive, expressing repetition for the "many" others who kept coming to the Lord in Corinth. It was a continual revival after Silas and Timothy came and a great church was gathered here during the nearly two years that Paul laboured in Corinth (possibly A.D. 51 and 52).

9. *Be not afraid, but speak, and hold not thy peace* (*Mē phobou, alla lalei kai mē siōpēseis*). Literally, "stop being afraid (*mē* with present middle imperative of *phobeō*), but go on speaking (present active imperative of *laleō*) and do not become silent (*mē* and first aorist active of *siōpaō*, ingressive aorist)." Evidently there were signs of a gathering storm before this vision and message from the Lord Jesus came to Paul one night. Paul knew only too well what Jewish hatred could do as he had learned it at Damascus, Jerusalem, Antioch in Pisidia, Iconium, Lystra, Derbe, Thessalonica, Beroea. He had clearly moments of doubt whether he had not better move on or become silent for a while in Corinth. Every pastor knows what it is to have such moods and moments. In II Thess. 3:2 (written at this time) we catch Paul's dejection of spirits. He was like Elijah (I Kings 19:4) and Jeremiah (Jer. 15:15ff.).

10. *Because I am with thee* (*dioti egō eimi meta sou*). Jesus

had given this promise to all believers (Matt. 28:20) and here he renews it to Paul. This promise changes Paul's whole outlook. Jesus had spoken to Paul before, on the way to Damascus (9:4), in Jerusalem (22:17f.), in Troas (16:9), in great crises of his life. He will hear him again (23:11; 27:23). Paul knows the voice of Jesus. *No man shall set on thee to harm thee* (*oudeis epithēsetai soi tou kakōsai se*). Future direct middle indicative of *epitithēmi*, old and common verb, here in direct middle to lay or throw oneself upon, to attack. Jesus kept that promise in Corinth for Paul. *Tou kakōsai* is genitive articular infinitive of purpose of *kakoō*, to do harm to. Paul would now face all the rabbis without fear. *I have much people* (*laos estin moi polus*). Dative of personal interest. "There is to me much people," not yet saved, but who will be if Paul holds on. There is the problem for every preacher and pastor, how to win the elect to Christ.

11. *A year and six months* (*eniauton kai mēnas hex*). Accusative of extent of time. How much time before this incident he had been there we do not know. He was in Corinth probably a couple of years in all. His work extended beyond the city (II Cor. 11:10) and there was a church in Cenchreae (Rom. 16:1).

12. *When Gallio was proconsul of Achaia* (*Galliōnos de anthupatou ontos tēs Achaias*). Genitive absolute of present participle *ontos*. Brother of Seneca the Stoic (Nero's tutor) and uncle of Lucan the author of the *Pharsalia*. His original name was M. Annaeus Novatus till he was adopted by Gallio the rhetorician. The family was Spanish. Gallio was a man of culture and refinement and may have been chosen proconsul of Achaia for this reason. Statius calls him "*dulcis Gallio.*" Seneca says of him: *Nemo enim mortalium uni tam dulcis quam hic omnibus* (No one of mortals is so pleasant to one person as he is to all). Luke alone among writers says that he was proconsul, but Seneca speaks of his being in Achaia where he caught fever, a corroboration of Luke.

But now a whitish grey limestone inscription from the Hagios Elias quarries near Delphi (a letter of Claudius to Delphi) has been found which definitely names Gallio as proconsul of Achaia (*authupatos tēs Achaias*). The province of Achaia after various shifts (first senatorial, then imperial) back and forth with Macedonia, in A.D. 44 Claudius gave back to the Senate with proconsul as the title of the governor. It is amazing how Luke is confirmed whenever a new discovery is made. The discovery of this inscription has thrown light also on the date of Paul's work in Corinth as it says that Gallio came in the 26th acclamation of Claudius as Emperor in A.D. 51, that would definitely fix the time of Paul in Corinth as A.D. 50 and 51 (or 51 and 52). Deissmann has a full and able discussion of the whole matter in Appendix I to his *St. Paul. Rose up (katepestēsan).* Second aorist active of *kat-eph-istēmi,* intransitive, to take a stand against, a double compound verb found nowhere else. They took a stand (*estēsan*) against (*kata,* down on, *epi,* upon), they made a dash or rush at Paul as if they would stand it no longer. *Before the judgment seat (epi to bēma).* See on 12:21. The proconsul was sitting in the basilica in the forum or agora. The Jews had probably heard of his reputation for moderation and sought to make an impression as they had on the praetors of Philippi by their rush (*sunepestē,* 16:22). The new proconsul was a good chance also (25:2). So for the second time Paul faces a Roman proconsul (Sergius Paulus, 13:7) though under very different circumstances.

13. *Contrary to the law (para ton nomon).* They did not accuse Paul of treason as in Thessalonica, perhaps Paul had been more careful in his language here. They bring the same charge here that the owners of the slave-girl brought in Philippi (16:21). Perhaps they fear to go too far with Gallio, for they are dealing with a Roman proconsul, not with the politarchs of Thessalonica. The Jewish religion was a *religio licita* and they were allowed to make proselytes,

but not among Roman citizens. To prove that Paul was acting contrary to Roman law (for Jewish law had no standing with Gallio though the phrase has a double meaning) these Jews had to show that Paul was making converts in ways that violated the Roman regulations on that subject. The accusation as made did not show it nor did they produce any evidence to do it. The verb used *anapeithei* means to stir up by persuasion (old verb here only in the N.T.), a thing that he had a right to do.

14. *When Paul was about to open his mouth* (*mellontos tou Paulou anoigein to stoma*). Genitive absolute again. Before Paul could speak, Gallio cut in and ended the whole matter. According to their own statement Paul needed no defence. *Wrong* (*adikēma*). *Injuria*. Old word, a wrong done one. In N.T. only here, Acts 24:20; Rev. 18:5. Here it may mean a legal wrong to the state. *Wicked villainy* (*rhāidiourgēma*). A crime, act of a criminal, from *rhāidiourgos* (*rhāidios*, easy, *ergon*, work), one who does a thing with ease, adroitly, a "slick citizen." *Reason would that I should bear with you* (*kata logon an aneschomēn humōn*). Literally, "according to reason I should have put up with you (or held myself back from you)." This condition is the second class (determined as unfulfilled) and means that the Jews had no case against Paul in a Roman court. The verb in the conclusion (*aneschomēn*) is second aorist middle indicative and means with the ablative *humōn* "I should have held myself back (direct middle) from you (ablative). The use of *an* makes the form of the condition plain.

15. *Questions* (*zētēmata*). Plural, contemptuous, "a parcel of questions" (Knowling). *About words* (*peri logou*). Word, singular, talk, not deed or fact (*ergon, factum*). *And names* (*kai onomatōn*). As to whether "Jesus" should also be called "Christ" or "Messiah." The Jews, Gallio knew, split hairs over words and names. *And your own law* (*kai nomou tou kath' humās*). Literally, "And law that according

to you." Gallio had not been caught in the trap set for him. What they had said concerned Jewish law, not Roman law at all. *Look to it yourselves (opsesthe autoi).* The volitive future middle indicative of *horaō* often used (cf. Matt. 27:4) where an imperative could be employed (Robertson, *Grammar*, p. 874). The use of *autoi* (yourselves) turns it all over to them. *I am not minded (ou boulomai).* I am not willing, I do not wish. An absolute refusal to allow a religious question to be brought before a Roman civil court. This decision of Gallio does not establish Christianity in preference to Judaism. It simply means that the case was plainly that Christianity was a form of Judaism and as such was not opposed to Roman law. This decision opened the door for Paul's preaching all over the Roman Empire. Later Paul himself argues (Rom. 9 to 11) that in fact Christianity is the true, the spiritual Judaism.

16. *He drave them (apēlasen autous).* First aorist active indicative of *apelaunō*, old word, but here alone in the N.T. The Jews were stunned by this sudden blow from the mild proconsul and wanted to linger to argue the case further, but they had to go.

17. *They all laid hold on Sosthenes (epilabomenoi pantes Sōsthenēn).* See 16:19; 17:19 for the same form. Here is violent hostile reaction against their leader who had failed so miserably. *Beat him (etupton).* Inchoative imperfect active, began to beat him, even if they could not beat Paul. Sosthenes succeeded Crispus (verse 8) when he went over to Paul. The beating did Sosthenes good for he too finally is a Christian (I Cor. 1:1), a co-worker with Paul whom he had sought to persecute. *And Gallio cared for none of these things (kai ouden toutōn tōi Galliōni emelen).* Literally, "no one of these things was a care to Gallio." The usually impersonal verb (*melei, emelen,* imperfect active) here has the nominative as in Luke 10:40. These words have been often misunderstood as a description of Gallio's lack of interest in Christian-

ity, a religious indifferentist. But that is quite beside the mark. Gallio looked the other way with a blind eye while Sosthenes got the beating which he richly deserved. That was a small detail for the police court, not for the proconsul's concern. Gallio shows up well in Luke's narrative as a clear headed judge who would not be led astray by Jewish subterfuges and with the courage to dismiss a mob.

18. *Having tarried after this yet many days* (*eti prosmeinas hēmeras hikanas*). First aorist (constative) active participle of *prosmenō*, old verb, to remain besides (*pros* as in I Tim. 1:3) and that idea is expressed also in *eti* (yet). The accusative is extent of time. On Luke's frequent use of *hikanos* see 8:11. It is not certain that this period of "considerable days" which followed the trial before Gallio is included in the year and six months of verse 11 or is in addition to it which is most likely. Vindicated as Paul was, there was no reason for haste in leaving, though he usually left after such a crisis was passed. *Took his leave* (*apotaxamenos*). First aorist middle (direct), old verb, to separate oneself, to bid farewell (Vulgate *valefacio*), as in verse 21 and Mark 6:46. *Sailed thence* (*exeplei*). Imperfect active of *ekpleō*, old and common verb, inchoative imperfect, started to sail. Only Priscilla and Aquila are mentioned as his companions though others may have been in the party. *Having shorn his head* (*keiramenos tēn kephalēn*). First aorist middle (causative) of *keirō*, old verb to shear (sheep) and the hair as also in I Cor. 11:6. The participle is masculine and so cannot refer to Priscilla. Aquila comes next to the participle, but since mention of Priscilla and Aquila is parenthetical and the two other participles (*prosmeinas, apotaxamenos*) refer to Paul it seems clear that this one does also. *For he had a vow* (*eichen gar euchēn*). Imperfect active showing the continuance of the vow up till this time in Cenchreae, the port of Corinth when it expired. It was not a Nazarite vow which could be absolved only in Jerusalem. It is possible that the

hair was only polled or trimmed, cut shorter, not "shaved" (*xuraō* as in 21:24) for there is a distinction as both verbs are contrasted in I Cor. 11:6 (*keirāsthai ē xurāsthai*). It is not clear what sort of a vow Paul had taken nor why he took it. It may have been a thank offering for the outcome at Corinth (Hackett). Paul as a Jew kept up his observance of the ceremonial law, but refused to impose it on the Gentiles.

19. *Came* (*katēntēsan*). Came down, as usual in speaking of coming to land (16:1). *To Ephesus* (*eis Epheson*). This great city on the Cayster, the capital of the Province of Asia, the home of the worship of Diana (Artemis) with a wonderful temple, Paul at last had reached, though forbidden to come on the way out on this tour (16:6). Here Paul will spend three years after his return from Jerusalem. *He left them there* (*kākeinous katelipen autou*). That is, Priscilla and Aquila he left (second aorist active indicative) here (*autou*). But Luke mentions the departure by way of anticipation before he actually went away (verse 21). *But he himself* (*autos de*). Paul again the leading person in the narrative. On this occasion he may have gone alone into the synagogue. *He reasoned* (*dielexato*). Luke's favourite word for Paul's synagogue discourses (17:2, 17; 18:4 which see) as also 19:8, 9.

20. *When they asked him* (*erōtōntōn autōn*). Genitive absolute of present participle of *erōtaō*, old verb to ask a question, common in *Koiné* to make a request as here. *He consented not* (*ouk epeneusen*). First aorist active indicative of *epineuō*, old verb to express approval by a nod, only here in the N.T.

21. *I shall return* (*anakampsō*). Future active indicative of *anakamptō*, old verb to bend back, turn back (Matt. 2:2). *If God will* (*tou theou thelontos*). Genitive absolute of present active participle. This expression (*ean* with subjunctive) occurs also in I Cor. 4:19; 16:7; James 4:15. Such phrases were common among Jews, Greeks, and Romans, and are today. It is simply a recognition that we are in God's hands.

The Textus Receptus has here a sentence not in the best MSS.: "I must by all means keep this feast that cometh in Jerusalem." This addition by D and other documents may have been due to a desire to give a reason for the language in verse 22 about "going up" to Jerusalem. Whether Paul said it or not, it was in the spring when he made this journey with a company of pilgrims probably going to the feast of Pentecost in Jerusalem. We know that later Paul did try to reach Jerusalem for Pentecost (20:16) and succeeded. As the ship was leaving, Paul had to go, but with the hope of returning soon to Ephesus as he did.

22. *He went up and saluted the church* (*anabas kai aspasamenos tēn ekklēsian*). The language could refer to the church in Caesarea where Paul had just landed, except for several things. The going up (*anabas*, second aorist active participle of *anabainō*) is the common way of speaking of going to Jerusalem which was up from every direction save from Hebron. It was the capital of Palestine as people in England today speaking of going up to London. Besides "he went down to Antioch" (*katebē eis Antiocheian*, second aorist active indicative of *katabainō*) which language suits better leaving Jerusalem than Caesarea. Moreover, there was no special reason for this trip to Caesarea, but to Jerusalem it was different. Here Paul saluted the church in the fourth of his five visits after his conversion (9:26; 11:30; 15:4; 18:22; 21:17). The apostles may or may not have been in the city, but Paul had friends in Jerusalem now. Apparently he did not tarry long, but returned to Antioch to make a report of his second mission tour as he had done at the close of the first when he and Barnabas came back (14:26–28). He had started on this tour with Silas and had picked up Timothy and Luke, but came back alone. He had a great story to tell.

23. *Having spent some time* (*poiēsas chronon tina*). Literally, having done some time. How long we do not know,

probably not long. There are those who place the visit of Peter here to which Paul alludes in Gal. 2:11ff. and which we have located while Paul was here the last time (Acts 15:35). *He departed* (*exēlthen*). Thus simply and alone Paul began the third mission tour without a Barnabas or a Silas. *Went through* (*dierchomenos*). Present middle participle, going through. *The region of Galatia and Phrygia* (*tēn Galatikēn chōran kai Phrygian*). See on Acts 16:6 for discussion of this phrase, here in reverse order, passing through the Galatic region and then Phrygia. Does Luke mean Lycaonia (Derbe and Lystra) and Phrygia (Iconium and Pisidian Antioch)? Or does he mean the route west through the old Galatia and the old Phrygia on west into Asia? The same conflict exists here over the South Galatian and the North Galatian theories. Phrygia is apparently distinguished from the Galatic region here. It is apparently A.D. 52 when Paul set out on this tour. *In order* (*kathexēs*). In succession as in 11:4, though the names of the cities are not given. *Stablishing* (*stērizōn*). As he did in the second tour (15:41, *epistērizōn*, compound of this same verb) which see.

24. *Apollos* (*Apollōs*). Genitive -ō Attic second declension. Probably a contraction of *Apollonios* as D has it here. *An Alexandrian* (*Alexandreus*). Alexander the Great founded this city B.C. 332 and placed a colony of Jews there which flourished greatly, one-third of the population at this time. There was a great university and library there. The Jewish-Alexandrian philosophy developed here of which Philo was the chief exponent who was still living. Apollos was undoubtedly a man of the schools and a man of parts. *A learned man* (*anēr logios*). Or eloquent, as the word can mean either a man of words (like one "wordy," verbose) or a man of ideas, since *logos* was used either for reason or speech. Apollos was doubtless both learned (mighty in the Scriptures) and eloquent, though eloquence varies greatly in people's ideas. *Mighty in the Scriptures* (*dunatos ōn en*

tais graphais). Being powerful (*dunatos* verbal of *dunamai* and same root as *dunamis*, dynamite, dynamo) in the Scriptures (in the knowledge and the use of the Scriptures), as should be true of every preacher. There is no excuse for ignorance of the Scriptures on the part of preachers, the professed interpreters of the word of God. The last lecture made to the New Testament English class in Southern Baptist Theological Seminary by John A. Broadus was on this passage with a plea for his students to be mighty in the Scriptures. In Alexandria Clement of Alexandria and Origen taught in the Christian theological school.

25. *Had been instructed in the way of the Lord* (*ēn katēchēmenos tēn hodon tou kuriou*). Periphrastic past perfect passive of *katēcheō*, rare in the old Greek and not in the LXX from *kata* and *ēcheō* (*ēchō*, sound) as in Luke 1:4, to re-sound, to re-echo, to teach by repeated dinning into the ears as the Arabs do now, to teach orally by word of mouth (and ear). Here the accusative of the thing (the word) is retained in the passive like with *didaskō*, to teach (Robertson, *Grammar*, p. 485). *Being fervent in spirit* (*zeōn tōi pneumati*). Boiling (from *zeō*, to boil, old and common verb, in N.T. only here and Rom. 12:11) like boiling water or yeast. The Latin verb *ferveo* means to boil or ferment. Locative case after it. *Taught carefully* (*edidasken akribōs*). Imperfect active, was teaching or inchoative, began teaching, accurately. He taught accurately what he knew, a fine gift for any preacher. *Only the baptism of John* (*monon to baptisma Iōanou*). It was a *baptism of repentance* (marked by repentance) as Paul said (13:24; 19:4), as Peter said (2:38) and as the Gospels tell (Mark 1:4, etc.). That is to say, Apollos knew only what the Baptist knew when he died, but John had preached the coming of the Messiah, had baptized him, had identified him as the Son of God, had proclaimed the baptism of the Holy Spirit, but had not seen the Cross, the Resurrection of Jesus, nor the great Day of Pentecost.

26. *They took him unto them* (*proselabonto*). Second aorist
middle (indirect) indicative of *proslambanō*, old verb, to
their home and heart as companion (cf. the rabbis and the
ruffians in 17:5). Probably for dinner after service. *Expounded* (*exethento*). Second aorist (effective) middle indicative of *ektithēmi* seen already in 11:4, to set forth. *More
carefully* (*akribesteron*). Comparative adverb of *akribōs*.
More accurately than he already knew. Instead of abusing
the young and brilliant preacher for his ignorance they
(particularly Priscilla) gave him the fuller story of the life
and work of Jesus and of the apostolic period to fill up the
gaps in his knowledge. It is a needed and delicate task, this
thing of teaching gifted young ministers. They do not learn
it all in schools. More of it comes from contact with men
and women rich in grace and in the knowledge of God's ways.
He was not rebaptized, but only received fuller information.

27. *Encouraged him* (*protrepsamenoi*). First aorist middle
participle of *protrepō*, old verb, to urge forward, to push on,
only here in the N.T. Since Apollos wanted (*boulomenou
autou*, genitive absolute) to go into Achaia, the brethren
(including others besides Priscilla and Aquila) wrote (*egrap-
san*) a letter of introduction to the disciples in Corinth to
receive him (*apodexasthai auton*), a nice letter of recommendation and a sincere one also. But Paul will refer to this
very letter later (II Cor. 3:1) and observe that he himself
needed no such letter of commendation. The Codex Bezae
adds here that certain Corinthians who had come to Ephesus
heard Apollos and begged him to cross over with them to
Corinth. This may very well be the way that Apollos was
led to go. Preachers often receive calls because visitors from
other places hear them. Priscilla and Aquila were well
known in Corinth and their approval would carry weight.
But they did not urge Apollos to stay longer in Ephesus.
Helped them much (*sunebaleto polu*). Second aorist middle indicative of *sunballō* used in 17:18 for "dispute," old verb to

throw together, in the N.T. always in the active save here in the middle (common in Greek writers) to put·together, to help. *Through grace* (*dia tēs charitos*). This makes sense if taken with "believed," as Hackett does (cf. 13:48; 16:14) or with "helped" (I Cor. 3:10; 15:10; II Cor. 1:12). Both are true as the references show.

28. *Powerfully* (*eutonōs*). Adverb from *eutonos* (*eu*, well, *teinō*, to stretch), well-strung, at full stretch. *Confuted* (*dia-katēlegcheto*). Imperfect middle of the double compound verb *dia-kat-elegchomai*, to confute with rivalry in a contest, here alone. The old Greek has *dielegchō*, to convict of falsehood, but not this double compound which means to argue down to a finish. It is the imperfect tense and does not mean that Apollos convinced these rabbis, but he had the last word. *Publicly* (*dēmosiāi*). See 5:18; 16:37. In open meeting where all could see the victory of Apollos. *Shewing* (*epideiknus*). Present active participle of *epideiknumi*, old verb to set forth so that all see. *By the Scriptures* (*dia tōn graphōn*). In which Apollos was so "mighty" (verse 24) and the rabbis so weak for they knew the oral law better than the written (Mark 7:8-12). *That Jesus was the Christ* (*einai ton Christon Iēsoun*). Infinitive and the accusative in indirect assertion. Apollos proclaims the same message that Paul did everywhere (17:3). He had not yet met Paul, but he had been instructed by Priscilla and Aquila. He is in Corinth building on the foundation laid so well by Paul (I Cor. 3:4-17). Luke has here made a brief digression from the story of Paul, but it helps us understand Paul better. There are those who think that Apollos wrote Hebrews, a guess that may be correct.

CHAPTER XIX

1. *While Apollos was at Corinth* (*en tōi ton Apollō einai en Korinthōi*). Favourite idiom with Luke, *en* with the locative of the articular infinitive and the accusative of general reference (Luke 1:8; 2:27, etc.). *Having passed through the upper country* (*dielthonta ta anōterika merē*). Second aorist active participle of *dierchomai*, accusative case agreeing with *Paulon*, accusative of general reference with the infinitive *elthein*, idiomatic construction with *egeneto*. The word for "upper" (*anōterika*) is a late form for *anōtera* (Luke 14:10) and occurs in Hippocrates and Galen. It refers to the highlands (cf. Xenophon's *Anabasis*) and means that Paul did not travel the usual Roman road west by Colossae and Laodicea in the Lycus Valley, cities that he did not visit (Col. 2:1). Instead he took the more direct road through the Cayster Valley to Ephesus. Codex Bezae says here that Paul wanted to go back to Jerusalem, but that the Holy Spirit bade him to go into Asia where he had been forbidden to go in the second tour (16:6). Whether the upper "parts" (*merē*) here points to North Galatia is still a point of dispute among scholars. So he came again to Ephesus as he had promised to do (18:21). The province of Asia included the western part of Asia Minor. The Romans took this country B.C. 130. Finally the name was extended to the whole continent. It was a jewel in the Roman empire along with Africa and was a senatorial province. It was full of great cities like Ephesus, Smyrna, Pergamum, Thyatira, Sardis, Philadelphia, Laodicea (the seven churches of Rev. 2 and 3), Colossae, Hierapolis, Apamea, to go no further. Hellenism had full sway here. Ephesus was the capital and chief city and was a richer and larger city than Corinth. It was

located at the entrance to the valley of the Maeander to the east. Here was the power of Rome and the splendour of Greek culture and the full tide of oriental superstition and magic. The Temple of Artemis was one of the seven wonders of the world. While in Ephesus some hold that Paul at this time wrote the Epistle to the Galatians after his recent visit there, some that he did it before his recent visit to Jerusalem. But it is still possible that he wrote it from Corinth just before writing to Rome, a point to discuss later. *Certain disciples* (*tinas mathētas*). Who were they? Apollos had already gone to Corinth. They show no connection with Priscilla and Aquila. Luke calls them "disciples" or "learners" (*mathētas*) because they were evidently sincere though crude and ignorant. There is no reason at all for connecting these uninformed disciples of the Baptist with Apollos. They were floating followers of the Baptist who drifted into Ephesus and whom Paul found. Some of John's disciples clung to him till his death (John 3:22–25; Luke 7:19; Matt. 14:12). Some of them left Palestine without the further knowledge of Jesus that came after his death and some did not even know that, as turned out to be the case with the group in Ephesus.

2. *Did ye receive the Holy Spirit when ye believed?* (*ei pneuma hagion elabete pisteusantes?*). This use of *ei* in a direct question occurs in 1:6, is not according to the old Greek idiom, but is common in the LXX and the N.T. as in Luke 13:23 which see (Robertson, *Grammar*, p. 916). Apparently Paul was suspicious of the looks or conduct of these professed disciples. The first aorist active participle *pisteusantes* is simultaneous with the second aorist active indicative *elabete* and refers to the same event. *Nay, we did not so much as hear whether the Holy Spirit was* (*All' oude ei pneuma hagion estin ēkousamen*). The reply of these ignorant disciples is amazing. They probably refer to the time of their baptism and mean that, when baptized, they did not hear whether

(*ei* in indirect question) the Holy Spirit was (*estin* retained as in John 7:39). Plain proof that they knew John's message poorly.

3. *Into what* (*eis ti*). More properly, *Unto what* or *on what basis* (Robertson, *Grammar*, p. 592). Clearly, Paul felt they had received a poor baptism with no knowledge of the Holy Spirit. *John's baptism* (*to Iōanou baptisma*). Last mention of John the Baptist in the N.T. They had been dipped in other words, but they had not grasped the significance of the ordinance.

4. *With the baptism of repentance* (*baptisma metanoias*). Cognate accusative with *ebaptisen* and the genitive *metanoias* describing the baptism as marked by (case of species or genus), not as conveying, repentance just as in Mark 1:4 and that was the work of the Holy Spirit. But John preached also the baptism of the Holy Spirit which the Messiah was to bring (Mark 1:7f. = Matt. 3:11f. = Luke 3:16). If they did not know of the Holy Spirit, they had missed the point of John's baptism. *That they should believe on him that should come after him, that is on Jesus* (*eis ton erchomenon met' auton hina pisteusōsin, tout' estin eis ton Iēsoun*). Note the emphatic prolepsis of *eis ton erchomenon met' auton* before *hina pisteusōsin* with which it is construed. This is John's identical phrase, "the one coming after me" as seen in Mark 1:7 = Matt. 3:11 = Luke 3:16 = John 1:15. It is not clear that these "disciples" believed in a Messiah, least of all in Jesus. They were wholly unprepared for the baptism of John. Paul does not mean to say that John's baptism was inadequate, but he simply explains what John really taught and so what his baptism signified.

5. *The name of the Lord Jesus* (*to onoma ton kuriou Iēsou*). Apollos was not rebaptized. The twelve apostles were not rebaptized. Jesus received no other baptism than that of John. The point here is simply that these twelve men were grossly ignorant of the meaning of John's baptism as regards

repentance, the Messiahship of Jesus, the Holy Spirit. Hence Paul had them baptized, not so much again, as really baptized this time, in the name or on the authority of the Lord Jesus as he had himself commanded (Matt. 28:19) and as was the universal apostolic custom. Proper understanding of "Jesus" involved all the rest including the Trinity (Father, Son, and Holy Spirit). Luke does not give a formula, but simply explains that now these men had a proper object of faith (Jesus) and were now really baptized.

6. *When Paul had laid his hands upon them* (*epithentos autois tou Paulou cheiras*). Genitive absolute of second aorist active participle of *epitithēmi*. This act of laying on of the hands was done in Samaria by Peter and John (8:16) and in Damascus in the case of Paul (9:17) and was followed as here by the descent of the Holy Spirit in supernatural power. *They spake with tongues* (*elaloun glōssais*). Inchoative imperfect, began to speak with tongues as in Jerusalem at Pentecost and as in Caesarea before the baptism. *Prophesied* (*eprophēteuon*). Inchoative imperfect again, began to prophesy. The speaking with tongues and prophesying was external and indubitable proof that the Holy Spirit had come on these twelve uninformed disciples now fully won to the service of Jesus as Messiah. But this baptism in water did not "convey" the Holy Spirit nor forgiveness of sins. Paul was not a sacramentalist.

8. *Spake boldly* (*eparrēsiazeto*). Imperfect middle, kept on at it for three months. Cf. same word in 18:26. *Persuading* (*peithōn*). Present active conative participle of *peithō*, trying to persuade (28:23). Paul's idea of the Kingdom of God was the church of God which he (Jesus, God's Son) had purchased with his own blood (Acts 20:28, calling Christ God). Nowhere else had Paul apparently been able to speak so long in the synagogue without interruption unless it was so at Corinth. These Jews were already interested (18:30).

9. *But when some were hardened* (*hōs de tines esklērunonto*).

Imperfect passive of *sklērunō*, causative like *hiphil* in Hebrew, to make hard (*sklēros*) or rough or harsh (Matt. 25:24). In LXX and Hippocrates and Galen (in medical writings). In N.T. only here and Rom. 9:18 and 4 times in Heb. (3:8, 13, 15; 4:7, 8) quoting and referring to Psa. 95:8 about hardening the heart like a gristle. The inevitable reaction against Paul went on even in Ephesus though slowly. *Disobedient* (*epeithoun*). Imperfect again, showing the growing disbelief and disobedience (*apeithēs*), both ideas as in 14:2; 17:5, first refusal to believe and then refusal to obey. Both *sklērunō* and *apeitheō* occur together, as here, in Ecclus. 30:12. *Speaking evil of the Way* (*kakologountes tēn hodon*). Late verb from *kakologos* (speaker of evil) for the old *kakōs legō*. Already in Mark 7:10; 9:39; Matt. 15:4. Now these Jews are aggressive opponents of Paul and seek to injure his influence with the crowd. Note "the Way" as in 9:2 for Christianity. *He departed from them* (*apostas ap' autōn*). Second aorist active participle of *aphistēmi*, made an "apostasy" (standing off, cleavage) as he did at Corinth (18:7, *metabas*, making a change). *Separated the disciples* (*aphōrisen tous mathētas*). First aorist active indicative of *aphorizō*, old verb to mark limits (horizon) as already in 13:2. Paul himself was a spiritual Pharisee "separated" to Christ (Rom. 1:1). The Jews regarded this withdrawal as apostasy, like separating the sheep from the goats (Matt. 25:32). Paul now made a separate church as he had done at Thessalonica and Corinth. *In the school of Tyrannus* (*en tēi scholēi Turannou*). *Scholē* (our school) is an old word from *schein* (*echō*) to hold on, leisure and then in later Greek (Plutarch, etc.) a place where there is leisure as here. Only this example in the N.T. This is the Greek notion of "school," the Jewish being that of "yoke" as in Matt. 11:29. The name Tyrannus (our tyrant) is a common one. It is an inscription in the Columbarium of the Empress Livia as that of a physician in the court. Furneaux suggests the possibility that a relative of this physician was lecturing on medicine in Ephesus and so as a friend of Luke, the physician, would be glad to help Paul about a place to preach. It was probably a public building or lecture hall with this name whether hired by Paul or loaned to him. The pagan sophists often spoke in such halls. The Codex Bezae adds "from the fifth hour to the tenth" as the time allotted Paul for his work in this hall, which is quite possible, from just before midday till the close of the afternoon (from before the noon meal till two hours before sunset) each day. Here Paul had great freedom and a great hearing. As the church grows there will be other places of meeting as the church in the house of Aquila and Priscilla (I Cor. 16:19).

10. *For two years* (*epi etē duo*). Note *epi* with accusative for extent of time as in verse 8, *epi mēnas treis* and often. But in 20:31 Paul said to the Ephesian elders at Miletus that he laboured with them for the space of "three years." That may be a general expression and there was probably a longer period after the "two years" in the school of Tyrannus besides the six months in the synagogue. Paul may have preached thereafter in the house of Aquila and Priscilla for some months, the "for a while" of verse 22. *So that all they which dwelt in Asia heard* (*hōste pantas tous katoikountas tēn Asian akousai*). Actual result with *hōste* and the infinitive with accusative of general reference as is common (also verse 11) in the *Koinē* (Robertson, *Grammar*, pp. 999f.). Paul apparently remained in Ephesus, but the gospel spread all over the province even to the Lycus Valley including the rest of the seven churches of Rev. 1:11 and chapters 2 and 3. Demetrius in verse 26 will confirm the tremendous influence of Paul's ministry in Ephesus on Asia. Forty years after this Pliny in his famous letter to Trajan from Bithynia will say of Christianity: "For the contagion of this superstition has not only spread through cities, but also through villages and country places." It was during these years in Ephesus

that Paul was greatly disturbed over the troubles in the Corinthian Church. He apparently wrote a letter to them now lost to us (I Cor. 5:9), received messages from the household of Chloe, a letter from the church, special messengers, sent Timothy, then Titus, may have made a hurried trip himself, wrote our First Corinthians, was planning to go after the return of Titus to Troas where he was to meet him after Pentecost, when all of a sudden the uproar raised by Demetrius hurried Paul away sooner than he had planned. Meanwhile Apollos had returned from Corinth to Ephesus and refused to go back (I Cor. 16:12). Paul doubtless had helpers like Epaphras and Philemon who carried the message over the province of Asia, Tychicus, and Trophimus of Asia who were with him on the last visit to Jerusalem (verses 22, 29; 20:4). Paul's message reached Greeks, not merely Hellenists and God-fearers, but some of the Greeks in the upper circles of life in Ephesus.

11. *Special miracles* (*dunameis ou tas tuchousas*). "Powers not the ones that happen by chance," "not the ordinary ones," litotes for "the extraordinary." All "miracles" or "powers" (*dunameis*) are supernatural and out of the ordinary, but here God regularly wrought (*epoiei*, imperfect active) wonders beyond those familiar to the disciples and completely different from the deeds of the Jewish exorcists. This phrase is peculiar to Luke in the N.T. (also 28:2), but it occurs in the classical Greek and in the *Koinê* as in III Macc. 3:7 and in papyri and inscriptions (Deissmann, *Bible Studies*, p. 255). In Samaria Philip wrought miracles to deliver the people from the influence of Simon Magus. Here in Ephesus exorcists and other magicians had built an enormous vogue of a false spiritualism and Paul faces unseen forces of evil. His tremendous success led some people to superstitious practices thinking that there was power in Paul's person.

12. *Handkerchiefs* (*soudaria*). Latin word for *sudor* (sweat). Used in Luke 19:20 and John 11:44; 20:7. In two

papyri marriage-contracts this word occurs among the toilet articles in the dowry (Deissmann, *Bible Studies*, p. 223). *Aprons* (*simikinthia*). Latin word also, *semicinctium* (*semi*, *cingo*). Only here in the N.T. Linen aprons used by servants or artisans (Martial XIV. 153). Paul did manual work at Ephesus (20:34) and so wore these aprons. *Departed* (*apallassethai*). Present passive infinitive with *hōste* for actual result as in verse 10. If one wonders how God could honour such superstitious faith, he should remember that there is no power in superstition or in magic, but in God. If God never honoured any faith save that entirely free from superstition, how about Christian people who are troubled over the number 13, over the moon, the rabbit's foot? The poor woman with an issue of blood touched the hem of Christ's garment and was healed (Luke 8:44–46) as others sought to do (Matt. 14:36). God condescends to meet us in our ignorance and weakness where he can reach us. Elisha had a notion that some of the power of Elijah resided in his mantle (II Kings 2:13). Some even sought help from Peter's shadow (Acts 5:15).

13. *Of the strolling Jews, exorcists* (*tōn perierchomenōn Ioudaiōn exorkistōn*). These exorcists travelled around (*peri*) from place to place like modern Gypsy fortune-tellers. The Jews were especially addicted to such practices with spells of sorcery connected with the name of Solomon (Josephus, *Ant.* VIII. 2.5). See also Tobit 8:1–3. Jesus alludes to those in Palestine (Matt. 12:27 = Luke 11:19). The exorcists were originally those who administered an oath (from *exorkizō*, to exact an oath), then to use an oath as a spell or charm. Only instance here in the N.T. These men regarded Paul as one of their own number just as Simon Magus treated Simon Peter. Only here these exorcists paid Paul the compliment of imitation instead of offering money as Magus did. *To name over* (*onomazein epi*). They heard what Paul said and treated his words as a magic charm or

spell to drive the evil spirits out. *I adjure you by Jesus whom Paul preacheth* (*Horkizō humas ton Iēsoun hon Paulos kērussei*). Note two accusatives with the verb of swearing (cf. Mark 5:7) as a causative verb (Robertson, *Grammar*, p. 483). The papyri furnish numerous instances of *horkizō* in such constructions (Deissmann, *Bible Studies*, p. 281). Note also the article with Jesus, "the Jesus," as if to identify the magic word to the demons with the addition "whom Paul preaches." They thought that success turned on the correct use of the magical formula. The Ephesian mysteries included Christianity, so they supposed.

14. *Seven sons of Sceva* (*Skeuā hepta huioi*). Who this Sceva was we do not know. If a high priest, he was highly connected in Jerusalem (cf. 5:24). Some MSS. have ruler instead of priest. His name may be Latin in origin. *Skeuā* has Doric form of genitive. But that he had seven sons in this degraded business shows how Judaism had fared poorly in this superstitious city. Did they imagine there was special power in the number seven?

15. *Jesus I know* (*ton Iēsoun ginōskō*). "The (whom you mention) Jesus I recognize (*ginōskō*)" and "the (whom you mentioned) Paul I am acquainted with (*ton Paulon epistamai*)." Clear distinction between *ginōskō* and *epistamai*. *But who are ye?* (*humeis de tines este?*). But you, who are you? Emphatic prolepsis.

16. *Leaped on them* (*ephalomenos ep' autous*). Second aorist (ingressive) middle participle of *ephallomai*, old verb to spring upon like a panther, here only in the N.T. *Mastered* (*katakurieusas*). First aorist (effective) active participle of *katakurieuō*, late verb from *kata* and *kurios*, to become lord or master of. *Both* (*amphoterōn*). Papyri examples exist where *amphoteroi* means "all" or more than "two" (Robertson, *Grammar*, p. 745). So here *amphoteroi* includes all seven. "Both" in old English was used for more than two. *So that* (*hōste*). Another example (verses 10, 11) of *hōste* with

the infinitive for result. *Naked* (*gumnous*). Probably with torn garments. *Wounded* (*tetraumatismenous*). Perfect passive participle of *traumatizō*, old verb to wound, from *trauma* (a wound). In the N.T. only here and Luke 20:12.

17. *Was magnified* (*emegaluneto*). Imperfect passive. To make great. It was a notable victory over the powers of evil in Ephesus.

18. *Came* (*ērchonto*). Imperfect middle, kept coming, one after another. Even some of the believers were secretly under the spell of these false spiritualists just as some Christians today cherish private contacts with so-called occult powers through mediums, seances, of which they are ashamed. *Confessing* (*exomologoumenoi*). It was time to make a clean breast of it all, to turn on the light, to unbosom their secret habits. *Declaring their deeds* (*anaggellontes tas praxeis autōn*). Judgment was beginning at the house of God. The dupes (professing believers, alas) of these jugglers or exorcists now had their eyes opened when they saw the utter defeat of the tricksters who had tried to use the name of Jesus without his power. The boomerang was tremendous. The black arts were now laid bare in their real character. Gentile converts had a struggle to shake off their corrupt environment.

19. *Not a few of them that practised curious arts* (*hikanoi tōn ta perierga praxantōn*). Considerable number of the performers or exorcists themselves who knew that they were humbugs were led to renounce their evil practices. The word *perierga* (curious) is an old word (*peri*, *erga*) originally a piddler about trifles, a busybody (I Tim. 5:13), then impertinent and magical things as here. Only two examples in the N.T. It is a technical term for magic as the papyri and inscriptions show. Deissmann (*Bible Studies*, p. 323) thinks that these books here burned were just like the Magic Papyri now recovered from Egypt. *Burned them in the sight of all* (*katekaion enōpion pantōn*). Imperfect active of *kata-*

kaiō. It probably took a good while to do it, burned them completely (up, we say; down, the Greeks say, perfective use of *kata*). These Magical Papyri or slips of parchment with symbols or magical sentences written on them called *Ephesia Grammata* (Ephesian Letters). These Ephesian Letters were worn as amulets or charms. *They brought them together (sunenegkantes)*. Second aorist active participle of *sunpherō*. What a glorious conflagration it would be if in every city all the salacious, blasphemous, degrading books, pamphlets, magazines, and papers could be piled together and burned. *They counted (sunepsēphisan)*. First aorist active indicative of *sunpsēphizō*, to reckon together. In LXX (Jer. 29:49). Only here in N.T. *Sunkatapsēphizō* in 1:26. *Fifty thousand pieces of silver (arguriou muriadas pente)*. Five ten thousand (*muriadas*) pieces of silver. Ephesus was largely Greek and probably the silver pieces were Greek drachmae or the Latin denarius, probably about ten thousand dollars or two thousand English pounds.

20. *Mightily (kata kratos)*. According to strength. Only here in N.T., common military term in Thucydides. Such proof of a change counted. *Grew and prevailed (ēuxanen kai ischuen)*. Imperfect actives, kept growing and gaining strength. It was a day of triumph for Christ in Ephesus, this city of vast wealth and superstition. Ephesus for centuries will be one of the centres of Christian power. Timothy will come here and John the Apostle and Polycarp and Irenaeus.

21. *Purposed in the spirit (etheto en tōi pneumati)*. Second aorist middle indicative for mental action and "spirit" expressed also. A new stage in Paul's career begins here, a new division of the Acts. *Passed through (dielthōn)*. Word (*dierchomai*) used ten times in Acts (cf. 19:1) of missionary journeys (Ramsay). *Macedonia and Achaia (tēn Makedonian kai Achaian)*. This was the way that he actually went, but originally he had planned to go to Achaia (Corinth) and

then to Macedonia, as he says in II Cor. 1:15f., but he had
now changed that purpose, perhaps because of the bad news
from Corinth. Already when he wrote I Corinthians he proposed to go first to Macedonia (I Cor. 16:5-7). He even
hoped to spend the winter in Corinth "if the Lord permit"
and to remain in Ephesus till Pentecost, neither of which
things he did. *I must also see Rome (dei me kai Rōmēn idein).*
This section of Acts begins with Rome in the horizon of
Paul's plans and the book closes with Paul in Rome (Rackham). Here he feels the necessity of going as in Rom. 1:15
he feels himself "debtor" to all including "those in Rome"
(verse 16). Paul had long desired to go to Rome (Rom. 1:10),
but had been frequently hindered (1:13), but he has definitely set his face to go to Rome and on to Spain (15:23-29).
Paley calls sharp attention to this parallel between Acts 19:21
and Rom. 1:10-15 and 15:23-29. Rome had a fascination
for Paul as the home of Aquila and Priscilla and numerous
other friends (Rom. 16), but chiefly as the capital of the
Roman Empire and a necessary goal in Paul's ambition to
win it to Jesus Christ. His great work in Asia had stirred
afresh in him the desire to do his part for Rome. He wrote
to Rome from Corinth not long after this and in Jerusalem
Jesus in vision will confirm the necessity (*dei*) that Paul see
Rome (Acts 23:11).

22. *Timothy and Erastus (Timotheon kai Eraston).* Paul
had sent Timothy to Corinth (I Cor. 4:17) and had requested
kindly treatment of this young minister in his difficult task
of placating the divided church (16:10-11) that he might
return to Paul as he evidently had before Paul leaves Ephesus. He then despatched Titus to Corinth to finish what
Timothy had not quite succeeded in doing with instructions
to meet him in Troas. Now Timothy and Erastus (cf. Rom.
16:23; II Tim. 4:20) go on to Macedonia to prepare the way
for Paul who will come on later. *He himself stayed in Asia
for a while (autos epeschen chronon eis tēn Asian).* Literally,

He himself had additional time in Asia. Second aorist active indicative of *epechō*, old and common idiom, only here in the N.T. in this sense and the verb only in Luke and Paul. The reason for Paul's delay is given by him in I Cor. 16:8f., the great door wide open in Ephesus. Here again Luke and Paul supplement each other. Pentecost came towards the end of May and May was the month of the festival of Artemis (Diana) when great multitudes would come to Ephesus. But he did not remain till Pentecost as both Luke and Paul make plain.

23. *No small stir* (*tarachos ouk oligos*). Same phrase in 12:18 and nowhere else in the N.T. Litotes. *Concerning the Way* (*peri tēs hodou*). See this phrase for Christianity in 9:2; 19:9; 24:22 which see, like the "Jesus Way" of the Indians. There had already been opposition and "stir" before this stage (cf. 19:11–20). The fight with wild beasts in I Cor. 15:32 (whatever it was) was before that Epistle was written and so before this new uproar. Paul as a Roman citizen could not be thrown to wild beasts, but he so pictured the violent opponents of Christ in Ephesus.

24. *Demetrius, a silversmith* (*Dēmētrios argurokopos*). The name is common enough and may or may not be the man mentioned in III John 12 who was also from the neighbourhood of Ephesus. There is on an inscription at Ephesus near the close of the century a Demetrius called *neopoios Artemidos* a temple warden of Artemis (Diana). Zoeckler suggests that Luke misunderstood this word *neopoios* and translated it into *argurokopos*, a beater (*koptō*, to beat) of silver (*arguros*, silver), "which made silver shrines of Artemis" [*poiōn naous (argurous) Artemidos*]. It is true that no silver shrines of the temple have been found in Ephesus, but only numerous terra-cotta ones. Ramsay suggests that the silver ones would naturally be melted down. The date is too late anyhow to identify the Demetrius who was *neopoios* with the Demetrius *argurokopos* who made little silver temples of

Artemis, though B does not have the word *argurous*. The poor votaries would buy the terra-cotta ones, the rich the silver shrines (Ramsay, *Paul the Traveller*, p. 278). These small models of the temple with the statue of Artemis inside would be set up in the houses or even worn as amulets. It is a pity that the Revised Version renders Artemis here. Diana as the Ephesian Artemis is quite distinct from the Greek Artemis, the sister of Apollo, the Diana of the Romans. This temple, built in the 6th century B.C., was burnt by Herostratus Oct. 13 B.C. 356, the night when Alexander the Great was born. It was restored and was considered one of the seven wonders of the world. Artemis was worshipped as the goddess of fertility, like the Lydian Cybele, a figure with many breasts. The great festival in May would offer Demetrius a golden opportunity for the sale of the shrines. *Brought no little business* (*pareicheto ouk oligēn ergasian*). Imperfect middle, continued to bring (furnish, provide). The middle accents the part that Demetrius played as the leader of the guild of silversmiths, work for himself and for them. *Unto the craftsmen* (*tais technitais*). The artisans from *technē* (craft, art). Trade guilds were common in the ancient world. Demetrius had probably organized this guild and provided the capital for the enterprise.

25. *Whom he gathered together* (*hous sunathroisas*). First aorist active participle of *sunathroizō*, old verb to assemble together (*athroos*, a crowd), in the N.T. only here and Acts 12:12. *With the workmen of like occupation* (*kai tous peri ta toiauta ergatas*). "And the workmen concerning such things," apparently those who made the marble and terra-cotta shrines who would also be affected in the same way. It was a gathering of the associated trades, not for a strike, for employer and employees met together, but in protest against the preaching of Paul. *We have our wealth* (*hē euporia hēmin estin*). The wealth is to us (dative of possession). This old word for wealth occurs here alone in the N.T. It is from *eu*

and *poros*, easy to pass through, easy to accomplish, to be well off, wealthy, welfare, weal, well-being, rich. Demetrius appeals to this knowledge and self-interest of the artisans as the basis for their zeal for Artemis, piety for revenue.

26. *At Ephesus* (*Ephesou*). Genitive of place as also with *Asias* (Asia). Cf. Robertson, *Grammar*, pp. 494f. *This Paul* (*ho Paulos houtos*). Contemptuous use of *houtos*. *Hath turned away* (*metestēsen*). Changed, transposed. First aorist active indicative, did change. Tribute to Paul's powers as a preacher borne out by Luke's record in 19:10. There may be an element of exaggeration on the part of Demetrius to incite the workmen to action, for the worship of Artemis was their wealth. Paul had cut the nerve of their business. There had long been a Jewish colony in Ephesus, but their protest against idolatry was as nothing compared with Paul's preaching (Furneaux). *Which are made with hands* (*hoi dia cheirōn ginomenoi*). Note the present tense, made from time to time. No doubt Paul had put the point sharply as in Athens (Acts 17:29). Isaiah (44:9–17) had pictured graphically the absurdity of worshipping stocks and stones, flatly forbidden by the Old Testament (Ex. 20:4; Psa. 135:15–18). The people identified their gods with the images of them and Demetrius reflects that point of view. He was jealous of the brand of gods turned out by his factory. The artisans would stand by him on this point. It was a reflection on their work.

27. *This our trade* (*touto to meros*). Part, share, task, job, trade. *Come into disrepute* (*eis apelegmon elthein*). Not in the old writers, but in LXX and *Koinē*. Literally, reputation, exposure, censure, rejection after examination, and so disrepute. Their business of making gods would lose caste as the liquor trade (still called the trade in England) has done in our day. They felt this keenly and so Demetrius names it first. They felt it in their pockets. *Of the great goddess Artemis* (*tēs megalēs theas Artemidos*). She was generally known as the Great (*hē Megalē*). An inscription found at

Ephesus calls her "the greatest god" (*hē megistē theos*). The priests were eunuchs and there were virgin priestesses and a lower order of slaves known as temple-sweepers (*neōkoroi*, verse 35). They had wild orgiastic exercises that were disgraceful with their Corybantic processions and revelries. *Be made of no account* (*eis outhen logisthēnai*). Be reckoned as nothing, first aorist passive infinitive of *logizomai* and *eis*. *Should even be deposed of her magnificence* (*mellein te kai kathaireisthai tēs megaleiotētos autēs*). Note the present infinitive after *mellein*, ablative case (so best MSS.) after *kathaireō*, to take down, to depose, to deprive of. The word *megaleiotēs* occurs also in Luke 9:43 (the majesty of God) and in II Peter 1:16 of the transfiguration of Christ. It is already in the LXX and Deissmann (*Light from the Ancient East*, p. 363) thinks that the word runs parallel with terms used in the emperor-cult. *All Asia and the world* [*holē* (*hē*) *Asia kai* (*hē*) *oikoumenē*]. See 11:28 for same use of *oikoumenē*. An exaggeration, to be sure, but Pausanias says that no deity was more widely worshipped. Temples of Artemis have been found in Spain and Gaul. *Multitudo errantium non efficit veritatem* (Bengel). Even today heathenism has more followers than Christianity. To think that all this splendour was being set at naught by one man and a despised Jew at that!

28. *They were filled with wrath* (*genomenoi plereis thumou*). Having become full of wrath. *Cried out* (*ekrazon*). Inchoative imperfect, began to cry out and kept it up continuously. Reiteration was characteristic of the orgiastic exercises. The Codex Bezae adds after *thumou* (wrath): *Dramontes eis tēn amphodon* (running into the street), which they certainly did after the speech of Demetrius. *Great is Artemis of the Ephesians* (*Megalē hē Artemis Ephesiōn*). D (Codex Bezae) omits *hē* (the) and makes it read: "Great Artemis of the Ephesians." This was the usual cry of the votaries in their orgies as the inscriptions show, an ejaculatory outcry or prayer instead of an argument as the other MSS. have it.

That is vivid and natural (Ramsay, *Church in the Roman Empire*, pp. 135ff.). Yet on this occasion the artisans were making an argumentative protest and plea against Paul. An inscription at Dionysopolis has "Great is Apollo."

29. *With the confusion* (*tēs sugchuseōs*).   Genitive case after *eplēsthē*. An old word, but in the N.T. only here, from verb *sugcheō*, to pour together like a flood (only in Acts in the N.T.). Vivid description of the inevitable riot that followed "the appearance of such a body in the crowded agora of an excitable city" (Rackham) "vociferating the city's watchword." *They rushed* (*hōrmēsan*). Ingressive aorist active indicative of *hormaō*, old verb for impetuous dashing, a case of mob psychology (mob mind), with one accord (*homothumadon* as in Acts 1:14, etc.). *Into the theatre* (*eis to theatron*). A place for seeing (*theaomai*) spectacles, originally for dramatic representation (Thucydides, Herodotus), then for the spectators, then for the spectacle or show (I Cor. 4:9). The theatre (amphitheatre) at Ephesus can still be traced in the ruins (Wood, *Ephesus*) and shows that it was of enormous size capable of seating fifty-six thousand persons (some estimate it only 24,500). It was the place for large public gatherings of any sort out of doors like our football and baseball parks. In particular, gladiatorial shows were held in these theatres. *Having seized Gaius and Aristarchus men of Macedonia* (*sunarpasantes Gaion kai Aristarchon Makedonas*). See 6:12 for this same verb. They wanted some victims for this "gladiatorial" show. These two men were "Paul's companions in travel" (*sunekdēmous Paulou*), together (*sun*) with Paul in being abroad, away from home or people (*ek-dēmous*, late word, in the N.T. only here and II Cor. 8:19). How the mob got hold of Gaius (Acts 20:4) and Aristarchus (20:4; 27:2; Col. 4:10; Philemon 24) we do not know whether by accidental recognition or by search after failure to get Paul. In Rom. 16:4 Paul speaks of Priscilla and Aquila as those "who for my life laid down their

own necks." Paul lived with them in Ephesus as in Corinth. It is possible that Demetrius led the mob to their house and that they refused to allow Paul to go or to be seized at the risk of their own lives. Paul himself may have been desperately ill at this time as we know was the case once during his stay in Ephesus when he felt the answer of death in himself (II Cor. 1:9) and when God rescued him. That may mean that, ill as he was, Paul wanted to go and face the mob in the theatre, knowing that it meant certain death.

30. *And when Paul was minded to enter in unto the people* (*Paulou de boulomenou eiselthein eis ton dēmon*). Genitive absolute. Plainly Paul wanted to face the howling mob, whether it was the occasion pictured in II Cor. 1:9 or not. "St. Paul was not the man to leave his comrades in the lurch" (Knowling). *Suffered him not* (*ouk eiōn auton*). Imperfect of *eaō*, common verb to allow, what Gildersleeve called the negative imperfect (Robertson, *Grammar*, p. 885), denoting resistance to pressure. The more Paul insisted on going the more the disciples refused to agree to it and they won.

31. *Certain also of the chief officers of Asia* (*tines de kai tōn Asiarchōn*). These "Asiarchs" were ten officers elected by cities in the province who celebrated at their own cost public games and festivals (Page). Each province had such a group of men chosen, as we now know from inscriptions, to supervise the funds connected with the worship of the emperor, to preside at games and festivals even when the temple services were to gods like Artemis. Only rich men could act, but the position was eagerly sought. *Being his friends* (*ontes autōi philoi*). Evidently the Asiarchs had a high opinion of Paul and were unwilling for him to expose his life to a wild mob during the festival of Artemis. They were at least tolerant toward Paul and his preaching. "It was an Asiarch who at Smyrna resisted the cry of the populace to throw Polycarp to the lions" (Furneaux). *Besought him* (*parekaloun auton*). Imperfect active, showing that the

messengers sent had to insist over Paul's protest. "*Not to adventure himself*" (*mē dounai heauton*). It was a hazard, a rash adventure "to give himself" (second aorist active infinitive of *didōmi*). Just this sense of "adventure" with the idiom occurs only here in the N.T., though in Polybius V., 14, 9. But the phrase itself Paul uses of Jesus who gave himself for our sins (Gal. 1:4; I Tim. 2:6; Titus 2:14). It is not the first time that friends had rescued Paul from peril (Acts 9:25, 30; 17:10, 14). The theatre was no place for Paul. It meant certain death.

32. *Some therefore cried one thing and some another* (*alloi men oun allo ti ekrazon*). This classical use of *allos allo* (Robertson, *Grammar*, p. 747) appears also in 2:12; 21:34. Literally, "others cried another thing." The imperfect shows the repetition (kept on crying) and confusion which is also distinctly stated. *For the assembly was in confusion* (*ēn gar hē ekklēsia sunkechumenē*). The reason for the previous statement. Periphrastic past perfect passive of *sugcheō, sugchunō* (-*unnō*), to pour together, to commingle as in verse 29 (*sugchuseōs*). It was not an "assembly" (*ekklēsia, ek, kaleō*, to call out), but a wholly irregular, disorganized mob in a state (perfect tense) of confusion. There was "a lawful assembly" (verse 39), but this mob was not one. Luke shows his contempt for this mob (Furneaux). *Had come together* (*sunelēlutheisan*). Past perfect active of *sunerchomai*. It was an assembly only in one sense. For some reason Demetrius who was responsible for the mob preferred now to keep in the background, though he was known to be the ring-leader of the gathering (verse 38). It was just a mob that shouted because others did.

33. *And they brought Alexander out of the crowd* (*ek de tou ochlou sunebibasan Alexandron*). The correct text (Aleph A B) has this verb *sunebibasan* (from *sunbibazō*, to put together) instead of *proebibasan* (from *probibazō*, to put forward). It is a graphic word, causal of *bainō*, to go, and occurs

in Acts 16:10; Col. 2:19; Eph. 4:16. Evidently some of the
Jews grew afraid that the mob would turn on the Jews as well
as on the Christians. Paul was a Jew and so was Aristarchus,
one of the prisoners. The Jews were as strongly opposed to
idolatry as were the Christians. *The Jews putting him forward* (*probalontōn auton tōn Ioudaiōn*). Genitive absolute
of the second aorist active participle of *proballō*, old verb
to push forward as leaves in the spring (Luke 21:30). In
the N.T. only in these two passages. Alexandria had already
disgraceful scenes of Jew-baiting and there was real peril
now in Ephesus with this wild mob. So Alexander was
pushed forward as the champion to defend the Jews to the
excited mob. He may be the same Alexander the coppersmith who did Paul much evil (II Tim. 4:14), against whom
Paul will warn Timothy then in Ephesus. "The Jews were
likely to deal in the copper and silver required for the shrines,
so he may have had some trade connexion with the craftsmen
which would give him influence" (Furneaux). *Beckoned with
the hand* (*kataseisas tēn cheira*). Old verb *kataseiō*, to shake
down, here the hand, rapidly waving the hand up and down
to get a hearing. In the N.T. elsewhere only in Acts 12:17;
13:16; 21:40 where "with the hand" (*tēi cheiri*, instrumental
case) is used instead of *tēn cheira* (the accusative). *Would
have made a defence unto the people* (*ēthelen apologeisthai tōi
dēmōi*). Imperfect active, wanted to make a defence, tried
to, started to, but apparently never got out a word. *Apologeisthai* (present middle infinitive, direct middle, to defend
oneself), regular word for formal apology, but in N.T. only
by Luke and Paul (twice in Gospel, six times in Acts, and
in Rom. 2:15; II Cor. 12:19).

34. *When they perceived* (*epignontes*). Recognizing, coming
to know fully and clearly (*epi-*), second aorist (ingressive)
active participle of *epiginōskō*. The masculine plural is
left as nominative absolute or *pendens* without a verb. The
rioters saw at once that Alexander was (*estin*, present tense

retained in indirect assertion) a Jew by his features. *All with one voice cried out* (*phōnē egeneto mia ek pantōn krazontōn*). Anacoluthon or construction according to sense. Literally, "one voice arose from all crying." *Krazontōn* agrees in case (ablative) with *pantōn*, but Aleph A have *krazontes*. This loose construction is not uncommon (Robertson, *Grammar*, pp. 436f.). Now at last the crowd became unanimous (one voice) at the sight of a hated Jew about to defend their attacks on the worship of Artemis. The unanimity lasted "about the space of two hours" (*hosei epi hōras duo*), "as if for two hours." Their creed centred in this prolonged yell: "Great is Artemis of the Ephesians" with which the disturbance started (verse 28).

35. *The town-clerk* (*ho grammateus*). Ephesus was a free city and elected its own officers and the recorder or secretary was the chief magistrate of the city, though the proconsul of the province of Asia resided there. This officer is not a mere secretary of another officer or like the copyists and students of the law among the Jews, but the most influential person in Ephesus who drafted decrees with the aid of the *stratēgoi*, had charge of the city's money, was the power in control of the assembly, and communicated directly with the proconsul. Inscriptions at Ephesus give frequently this very title for their chief officer and the papyri have it also. The precise function varied in different cities. His name appeared on the coin at Ephesus issued in his year of office. *Had quieted the multitude* (*katasteilas ton ochlon*). First aorist active participle of *katastellō*, to send down, arrange dress (Euripides), lower (Plutarch), restrain (papyrus example), only twice in the N.T. (here and verse 36, be quiet), but in LXX and Josephus. He evidently took the rostrum and his very presence as the city's chief officer had a quieting effect on the billowy turmoil and a semblance of order came. He waited, however, till the hubbub had nearly exhausted itself (two hours) and did not speak till there was

a chance to be heard. *Saith* (*phēsin*). Historical present for vividness. *How that.* Merely participle *ousan* and accusative *polin* in indirect discourse, no conjunction at all (Robertson, *Grammar*, pp. 1040ff.), common idiom after *ginōskō*, to know. *Temple-keeper* (*neōkoron*). Old word from *neōs* (*naos*), temple, and *koreō*, to sweep. Warden, verger, cleaner of th᷎ temple, a sacristan. So in Xenophon and Plato. Inscriptions so describe Ephesus as *neōkoron tēs Artemidos* as Luke has it here and also applied to the imperial *cultus* which finally had several such temples in Ephesus. Other cities claimed the same honour of being *neōkoros,* but it was the peculiar boast of Ephesus because of the great temple of Artemis. A coin of A.D. 65 describes Ephesus as *neōkoros.* There are papyri examples of the term applied to individuals, one to Priene as *neōkoros* of the temple in Ephesus (Moulton and Milligan, *Vocabulary*). *And of the image which fell down from Jupiter* (*kai tou diopetous*). Supply *agalma* (image), "the from heaven-fallen image." From *Zeus* (*Dios*) and *petō* (*piptō, pipetō*), to fall. Zeus (Jupiter) was considered lord of the sky or heaven and that is the idea in *diopetous* here. The legend about a statue fallen from heaven occurs concerning the statue of Artemis at Tauris, Minerva at Athens, etc. Thus the recorder soothed the vanity (Rackham) of the crowd by appeal to the world-wide fame of Ephesus as sacristan of Artemis and of her heaven-fallen image.

36. *Cannot be gainsaid* (*anantirētōn oun ontōn*). Genitive absolute with *oun* (therefore). Undeniable (*an, anti, rētos*), verbal adjective. Occasionally in late Greek (Polybius, etc.), only here in N.T., but adverb *anantirētōs* in Acts 10:29. These legends were accepted as true and appeased the mob. *Ye ought* (*deon estin*). It is necessary. Periphrastic present indicative instead of *dei* like I Peter 1:6; I Tim. 5:13f. *Be quiet* (*katestalmenous*). Perfect passive participle of *katastellō* (see verse 35). *Rash* (*propetes*). Old adjective from *pro* and *petō*, to fall forward, headlong, precipitate. In

the N.T. only here and II Tim. 3:4, though common in the *Koiné*. Better look before you leap.

37. *Neither robbers of temples* (*oute hierosulous*). Common word in Greek writers from *hieron*, temple, and *sulaō*, to rob, be guilty of sacrilege. The word is found also on inscriptions in Ephesus. The Jews were sometimes guilty of this crime (Rom. 2:22), since the heathen temples often had vast treasures like banks. The ancients felt as strongly about temple-robbing as westerners used to feel about a horse-thief. *Nor blasphemers of our goddess* (*oute blasphēmountas tēn theon hēmōn*). Nor those who blasphemed our goddess. That is to say, these men (Gaius and Aristarchus) as Christians had so conducted themselves (Col. 4:5) that no charge could be placed against them either in act (temple-robbery) or word (blasphemy). They had done a rash thing since these men are innocent. Paul had used tact in Ephesus as in Athens in avoiding illegalities.

38. *Have a matter against any one* (*echousin pros tina logon*). For this use of *echō logon* with *pros* see Matt. 5:32 and Col. 3:13. The town-clerk names Demetrius and the craftsmen (*technitai*) as the parties responsible for the riot. *The courts are open* (*agoraioi agontai*). Supply *hēmerai* (days), court days are kept, or *sunodoi*, court-meetings are now going on, Vulgate *conventus forenses aguntur*. Old adjective from *agora* (forum) marketplace where trials were held. Cf. Acts 17:4. There were regular court days whether they were in session then or not. *And there are proconsuls* (*kai anthupatoi eisin*). Asia was a senatorial province and so had proconsuls (general phrase) though only one at a time, "a rhetorical plural" (Lightfoot). Page quotes from an inscription of the age of Trajan on an aqueduct at Ephesus in which some of Luke's very words occur (*neōkoros, anthupatos, grammateus, dēmos*). *Let them accuse one another* (*egkaleitōsan allēlois*). Present active imperative of *egkaleō* (*en, kaleō*), old verb to call in one's case, to bring a charge

against, with the dative. Luke uses the verb six times in Acts for judicial proceedings (19:38, 40; 23:28, 29; 26:2, 7). The town-clerk makes a definite appeal to the mob for orderly legal procedure as opposed to mob violence in a matter where money and religious prejudice unite, a striking rebuke to so-called lynch-law proceedings in lands today where Christianity is supposed to prevail.

39. *Anything about other matters* (*ti peraiterō*). Most MSS. here have *ti peri heterōn*, but B b Vulgate read *ti peraiterō* as in Plato's *Phaedo*. Several papyri examples of it also. It is comparative *peraiteros* of *pera*, beyond. Note also *epi* in *epizēteite*. Charges of illegal conduct (Page) should be settled in the regular legal way. But, if you wish to go further and pass resolutions about the matter exciting you, "it shall be settled in the regular assembly" (*en tōi ennomōi ekklēsiāi*). "In the lawful assembly," not by a mob like this. Wood (*Ephesus*) quotes an inscription there with this very phrase "at every lawful assembly" (*kata pāsan ennomon ekklēsian*). The Roman officials alone could give the sanction for calling such a lawful or regular assembly. The verb *epiluō* is an old one, but in the N.T. only here and Mark 4:34 (which see) where Jesus privately opened or disclosed the parables to the disciples. The papyri give examples of the verb in financial transactions as well as of the metaphorical sense. The solution will come in the lawful assembly, not in a riot like this. See also II Peter 1:20 where the substantive *epilusis* occurs for disclosure or revelation (prophecy).

40. *For indeed we are in danger to be accused concerning this day's riot* (*kai gar kinduneuomen egkaleisthai staseōs peri tēs sēmeron*). The text is uncertain. The text of Westcott and Hort means "to be accused of insurrection concerning to-day's assembly." The peril was real. *Kinduneuomen*, from *kindunos*, danger, peril. Old verb, but in the N.T. only here and Luke 8:23; I Cor. 15:30. *There being no cause for it* (*mēdenos aitiou huparchontos*). Genitive absolute with

aitios, common adjective (cf. *aitia*, cause) though in N.T. only here and Heb. 5:9; Luke 23:4, 14, 22. *And as touching it (peri hou)*. "Concerning which." But what? No clear antecedent, only the general idea. *Give an account of this concourse (apodounai logon peri tēs sustrophēs tautēs). Rationem reddere.* They will have to explain matters to the proconsul. *Sustrophē* (from *sun*, together, *strephō*, to turn) is a late word for a conspiracy (Acts 23:12) and a disorderly riot as here (Polybius). In Acts 28:12 *sustrephō* is used of gathering up a bundle of sticks and of men combining in Matt. 17:22. Seneca says that there was nothing on which the Romans looked with such jealousy as a tumultuous meeting.

41. *Dismissed the assembly (apelusen tēn ekklēsian)*. The town-clerk thus gave a semblance of law and order to the mob by formally dismissing them, this much to protect them against the charge to which they were liable. This vivid, graphic picture given by Luke has all the earmarks of historical accuracy. Paul does not describe the incidents in his letters, was not in the theatre in fact, but Luke evidently obtained the details from one who was there. Aristarchus, we know, was with Luke in Caesarea and in Rome and could have supplied all the data necessary. Certainly both Gaius and Aristarchus were lively witnesses of these events since their own lives were involved.

CHAPTER XX

1. *After the uproar was ceased* (*meta to pausasthai ton thorubon*). Literally, after the ceasing (accusative of articular aorist middle infinitive of *pauō*, to make cease) as to the uproar (accusative of general reference). Noise and riot, already in Matt. 26:5; 27:24; Mark 5:38; 14:2; and see in Acts 21:34; 24:18. Pictures the whole incident as bustle and confusion. *Took leave* (*aspamenos*). First aorist middle participle of *aspazomai*, old verb from *a* intensive and *spaō*, to draw, to draw to oneself in embrace either in greeting or farewell. Here it is in farewell as in 21:6. Salutation in 21:7, 19. *Departed for to go into Macedonia* (*exēlthen poreuesthai eis Makedonian*). Both verbs, single act and then process. Luke here condenses what was probably a whole year of Paul's life and work as we gather from II Corinthians, one of Paul's "weighty and powerful" letters as his enemies called them (II Cor. 10:10). "This epistle more than any other is a revelation of S. Paul's own heart: it is his spiritual autobiography and *apologia pro vita sua*."

2. *Those parts* (*ta merē ekeina*). We have no way of knowing why Luke did not tell of Paul's stay in Troas (II Cor. 2:12f.) nor of meeting Titus in Macedonia (II Cor. 2:13 to 7:16) nor of Paul's visit to Illyricum (Rom. 15:19f.) to give time for II Corinthians to do its work (II Cor. 13), one of the most stirring experiences in Paul's whole career when he opened his heart to the Corinthians and won final victory in the church by the help of Titus who also helped him round up the great collection in Achaia. He wrote II Corinthians during this period after Titus arrived from Corinth. The unity of II Corinthians is here assumed. Paul probably met Luke again in Macedonia, but all this is passed by

except by the general phrase: "had given them much exhortation" (*parakalesas autous logōi pollōi*). Literally, "having exhorted them (the Macedonian brethren) with much talk" (instrumental case). *Into Greece* (*eis tēn Hellada*). That is, Achaia (18:12; 19:21), and particularly Corinth, whither he had at last come again after repeated attempts, pauses, and delays (II Cor. 13:1). Now at last the coast was clear and Paul apparently had an open door in Corinth during these three months, so completely had Titus at last done away with the opposition of the Judaizers there.

3. *When he had spent three months there* (*poiēsas mēnas treis*). Literally, "having done three months," the same idiom in Acts 14:33; 18:23; James 5:13. During this period Paul may have written Galatians as Lightfoot argued and certainly did Romans. We do not have to say that Luke was ignorant of Paul's work during this period, only that he did not choose to enlarge upon it. *And a plot was laid against him by the Jews* (*genomenēs epiboulēs autōi hupo tōn Ioudaiōn*). Genitive absolute, "a plot by the Jews having come against him." *Epiboulē* is an old word for a plot against one. In the N.T. only in Acts (9:24; 20:3, 19; 23:30). Please note that this plot is by the Jews, not the Judaizers whom Paul discusses so vehemently in II Cor. 10-13. They had given Paul much anguish of heart as is shown in I Cor. and in II Cor. 1-7, but that trouble seems now past. It is Paul's old enemies in Corinth who had cherished all these years their defeat at the hands of Gallio (Acts 18:5-17) who now took advantage of Paul's plans for departure to compass his death if possible. *As he was about to set sail for Syria* (*mellonti anagesthai eis tēn Surian*). The participle *mellonti* agrees in case (dative) with *autōi*. For the sense of intending see also verse 13. *Anagesthai* (present middle infinitive) is the common word for putting out to sea (going up, they said, from land) as in 13:13. *He determined* (*egeneto gnōmēs*). The best MSS. here read *gnōmēs* (predicate ablative of

Ο Παύλος δια τους εν Βεροια;

Εδεξαντο του λογον μετα πολλης προθυμιας
ἡμιεραν δε ωνοι δ̣ε ἑορτας
το καθ ἡμεραν ανακρινοντες τας γραφας
(Ιωαννα) εκκλησιι 17.11

ὁ λογος του Θεου ειναι δυναμις
θεν σωση θεοσ ις ραιθθι

Πληρωθσ εκλησια την ξυγη

source like *epiluseōs*, II Peter 1:20, Robertson, *Grammar*, p. 514), not *gnōmē* (nominative). "He became of opinion." The Jews had heard of Paul's plan to sail for Syria and intended in the hurly-burly either to kill him at the docks in Cenchreae or to push him overboard from the crowded pilgrim ship bound for the passover. Fortunately Paul learned of their plot and so eluded them by going through Macedonia. The Codex Bezae adds here that "the Spirit bade him return into Macedonia."

4. *Accompanied him* (*suneipeto autōi*). Imperfect of *sunepomai*, old and common verb, but only here in the N.T. The singular is used agreeing with the first name mentioned *Sōpatros* and to be supplied with each of the others. Textus Receptus adds here "into Asia" (*achri tēs Asias*, as far as Asia), but the best documents (Aleph B Vulg. Sah Boh) do not have it. As a matter of fact, Trophimus went as far as Jerusalem (Acts 21:29) and Aristarchus as far as Rome (27:2; Col. 4:10). The phrase could apply only to Sopatros. It is not clear though probable that Luke means to say that these seven brethren, delegates of the various churches (II Cor. 8:19-23) started from Corinth with Paul. Luke notes the fact that they accompanied Paul, but the party may really have been made up at Philippi where Luke himself joined Paul, the rest of the party having gone on to Troas (20:5f.). These were from Roman provinces that shared in the collection (Galatia, Asia, Macedonia, Achaia). In this list three were from Macedonia, Sopater of Beroea, Aristarchus and Secundus of Thessalonica; two from Galatia, Gaius of Derbe and Timothy of Lystra; two from Asia, Tychicus and Trophimus. It is a bit curious that none are named from Achaia. Had Corinth failed after all (II Cor. 8, 9) to raise its share of the collection after such eager pledging? Rackham suggests that they may have turned their part over directly to Paul. Luke joined Paul in Philippi and could have handled the money from Achaia.

It was an important event and Paul took the utmost pains to remove any opportunity for scandal in the handling of the funds.

5. *Were waiting for us in Troas* (*emenon hēmās en Troiadi*). Here again we have "us" for the first time since chapter 16 where Paul was with Luke in Philippi. Had Luke remained all this time in Philippi? We do not know, but he is with Paul now till Rome is reached. The seven brethren of verse 4 went on ahead from Philippi to Troas while Paul remained with Luke in Philippi.

6. *After the days of unleavened bread* (*meta tas hēmeras tōn azumōn*). Paul was a Jew, though a Christian, and observed the Jewish feasts, though he protested against Gentiles being forced to do it (Gal. 4:10; Col. 2:16). Was Luke a proselyte because he notes the Jewish feasts as here and in Acts 27:9? He may have noted them merely because Paul observed them. But this passover was a year after that in Ephesus when Paul expected to remain there till Pentecost (I Cor. 16: 8). He was hoping now to reach Jerusalem by Pentecost (Acts 20:16) as he did. We do not know the precise year, possibly A.D. 56 or 57. *In five days* (*achri hēmerōn pente*). Up to five days (cf. Luke 2:37). D has *pemptaioi*, "fifth day men," a correct gloss. Cf. *deuteraioi*, second-day men (Acts 28:13). In Acts 16:11 they made the voyage in two days. Probably adverse winds held them back here. *Seven days* (*hepta hēmeras*). To atone for the short stay in Troas before (II Cor. 2:12f.) when Paul was so restless. Now he preaches a week to them.

7. *Upon the first day of the week* (*en de miāi tōn sabbatōn*). The cardinal *miāi* used here for the ordinal *prōtēi* (Mark 16:9) like the Hebrew *ehadh* as in Mark 16:2; Matt. 28:1; Luke 24:1; John 20:1 and in harmony with the *Koiné* idiom (Robertson, *Grammar*, p. 671). Either the singular (Mark 16:9)*sabbatou* or the plural *sabbatōn* as here was used for the week (sabbath to sabbath). For the first time here we have

services mentioned on the first day of the week though in
I Cor. 16:2 it is implied by the collections stored on that
day. In Rev. 1:10 the Lord's day seems to be the day of
the week on which Jesus rose from the grave. Worship on
the first day of the week instead of the seventh naturally
arose in Gentile churches, though John 20:26 seems to mean
that from the very start the disciples began to meet on the
first (or eighth) day. But liberty was allowed as Paul makes
plain in Rom. 14:5f. *When we were gathered together* (*sun-
ēgmenōn hēmōn*). Genitive absolute, perfect passive participle of *sunagō*, to gather together, a formal meeting of the
disciples. See this verb used for gatherings of disciples in
Acts 4:31; 11:26; 14:27; 15:6, 30; 19:7, 8; I Cor. 5:4. In Heb.
10:25 the substantive *episunagōgēn* is used for the regular
gatherings which some were already neglecting. It is impossible for a church to flourish without regular meetings
even if they have to meet in the catacombs as became necessary in Rome. In Russia today the Soviets are trying to
break up conventicles of Baptists. They probably met on
our Saturday evening, the beginning of the first day at sunset. So these Christians began the day (Sunday) with worship. But, since this is a Gentile community, it is quite
possible that Luke means our Sunday evening as the time
when this meeting occurs, and the language in John 20:19
"it being evening on that day the first day of the week"
naturally means the evening following the day, not the
evening preceding the day. *To break bread* (*klasai arton*).
First aorist active infinitive of purpose of *klaō*. The language
naturally bears the same meaning as in 2:42, the Eucharist
or the Lord's Supper which usually followed the *Agapē*. See
I Cor. 10:16. The time came, when the *Agapē* was no longer
observed, perhaps because of the abuses noted in I Cor.
11:20ff. Rackham argues that the absence of the article
with bread here and its presence (*ton arton*) in verse 11 shows
that the *Agapē* is referred to in verse 7 and the Eucharist

in verse 11, but not necessarily so because *ton arton* may merely refer to *arton* in verse 7. At any rate it should be noted that Paul, who conducted this service, was not a member of the church in Troas, but only a visitor. *Discoursed* (*dielegeto*). Imperfect middle because he kept on at length. *Intending* (*mellō*). Being about to, on the point of. *On the morrow* (*tēi epaurion*). Locative case with *hēmerāi* understood after the adverb *epaurion*. If Paul spoke on our Saturday evening, he made the journey on the first day of the week (our Sunday) after sunrise. If he spoke on our Sunday evening, then he left on our Monday morning. *Prolonged his speech* (*Pareteinen ton logon*). Imperfect active (same form as aorist) of *parateinō*, old verb to stretch beside or lengthwise, to prolong. Vivid picture of Paul's long sermon which went on and on till midnight (*mechri mesonuktiou*). Paul's purpose to leave early next morning seemed to justify the long discourse. Preachers usually have some excuse for the long sermon which is not always clear to the exhausted audience.

8. *Many lights* (*lampades hikanai*). It was dark at night since the full moon (passover) was three weeks behind. These lamps were probably filled with oil and had wicks that flickered and smoked. They would not meet in the dark. *In the upper room* (*en tōi huperōiōi*). As in 1:13 which see.

9. *Sat* (*kathezomenos*). Sitting (present middle participle describing his posture). *In the window* (*epi tēs thuridos*). Old word diminutive from *thura*, door, a little door. Latticed window (no glass) opened because of the heat from the lamps and the crowd. Our window was once spelt *windore* (Hudibras), perhaps from the wrong idea that it was derived from *wind* and *door*. Eutychus (a common slave name) was sitting on (*epi*) the window sill. Ahaziah "fell down through a lattice in his upper chamber" (II Kings 1:2). In the N.T. *thuris* only here and II Cor. 11:33 (*dia thuridos*) through which Paul was let down through the wall in

Damascus. *Borne down with deep sleep* (*katapheromenos hupnōi bathei*). Present passive participle of *katapherō*, to bear down, and followed by instrumental case (*hupnōi*). Describes the gradual process of going into deep sleep. Great medical writers use *bathus* with *hupnos* as we do today (deep sleep). D here has *basei* (heavy) for *bathei* (deep). *As Paul discoursed yet longer* (*dialegomenou tou Paulou epi pleion*). Genitive absolute of present middle participle of *dialegomai* (cf. verse 7) with *epi pleion*. Eutychus struggled bravely to keep awake, vainly hoping that Paul would finish. But he went on "for more." *Being borne down by his sleep* (*katenechtheis apo tou hupnou*). First aorist (effective) passive showing the final result of the process described by *katapheromenos*, finally overcome as a result of (*apo*) the (note article *tou*) sleep (ablative case). These four participles (*kathezomenos, katapheromenos, dialegomenou, katenechtheis*) have no connectives, but are distinguished clearly by case and tense. The difference between the present *katapheromenos* and the aorist *katenechtheis* of the same verb is marked. *Fell down* (*epesen katō*). Effective aorist active indicative of *piptō* with the adverb *katō*, though *katapiptō* (compound verb) could have been used (Acts 26: 14; 28:6). Hobart (*Medical Language of St. Luke*) thinks that Luke shows a physician's interest in the causes of the drowsiness of Eutychus (the heat, the crowd, the smell of the lamps, the late hour, the long discourse). Cf. Luke 22:45. *From the third story* (*apo tou tristegou*). From *treis* (three) and *stegē* (roof), adjective *tristegos* having three roofs. *Was taken up dead* (*ērthē nekros*). First aorist passive indicative of *airō*. Luke does not say *hōs* (as) or *hōsei* (Mark 9:26 as if). The people considered him dead and Luke the physician seems to agree with that view.

10. *Fell on him* (*epepesen autōi*). Second aorist active indicative of *epipiptō* with dative case as Elijah did (I Kings 17:21) and Elisha (II Kings 4:34). *Embracing* (*sunperilabōn*).

Second aorist active participle of *sunperilambanō*, old verb to embrace completely (take hold together round), but only here in the N.T. In Ezra 5:3. *Make ye no ado* (*mē thorubeisthe*). Stop (*mē* and present middle imperative of *thorubeō*) making a noise (*thorubos*) as the people did on the death of Jairus's daughter (Matt. 9:23 *thoruboumenou* and Mark 5:38 *thorubou*) when Jesus asked *Ti thorubeisthe? For his life is in him* (*hē gar psuchē autou en autōi estin*). This language is relied on by Ramsay, Wendt, Zoeckler to show that Eutychus had not really died, but had merely swooned. Paul's language would suit that view, but it suits equally well the idea that he had just been restored to life and so is indecisive. Furneaux urges also the fact that his friends did not bring him back to the meeting till morning (verse 12) as additional evidence that it was a case of swooning rather than of death. But this again is not conclusive as they would naturally not take him back at once. One will believe here as the facts appeal to him.

11. *When he was gone up* (*anabas*). Second aorist active participle in sharp contrast to *katabas* (went down) of verse 10. *Had broken bread* (*klasas ton arton*). Probably the Eucharist to observe which ordinance Paul had come and tarried (verse 7), though some scholars distinguish between what took place in verse 7 and verse 11, needlessly so as was stated on verse 7. *And eaten* (*kai geusamenos*). The word is used in 10:10 of eating an ordinary meal and so might apply to the *Agapē*, but it suits equally for the Eucharist. The accident had interrupted Paul's sermon so that it was observed now and then Paul resumed his discourse. *And had talked with them a long while* (*eph' hikanon te homilēsas*). Luke, as we have seen, is fond of *hikanos* for periods of time, for a considerable space of time, "even till break of day" (*achri augēs*). Old word for brightness, radiance like German *Auge*, English eye, only here in the N.T. Occurs in the papyri and in modern Greek for dawn. This second discourse

lasted from midnight till dawn and was probably more informal (as in 10:27) and conversational (*homilēsas*, though our word homiletics comes from *homileō*) than the discourse before midnight (*dialegomai*, verses 7, 9). He had much to say before he left. *So he departed* (*houtōs exēlthen*). Thus Luke sums up the result. Paul left (went forth) only after all the events narrated by the numerous preceding participles had taken place. Effective aorist active indicative *exelthen*. *Houtōs* here equals *tum demum*, now at length (Acts 27:7) as Page shows.

12. *They brought the lad alive* (*ēgagon ton paida zōnta*). Second aorist active indicative of *agō*. Evidently the special friends of the lad who now either brought him back to the room or (Rendall) took him home to his family. Knowling holds that *zōnta* (living) here is pointless unless he had been dead. He had been taken up dead and now they brought him living. *Not a little* (*ou metriōs*). Not moderately, that is a great deal. Luke is fond of this use of the figure *litotes* (use of the negative) instead of the strong positive (1:5, etc.). D (Codex Bezae) has here instead of *ēgagon* these words: *aspazomenōn de autōn ēgagen ton neaniskon zōnta* (while they were saying farewell he brought the young man alive). This reading pictures the joyful scene over the lad's restoration as Paul was leaving.

13. *To the ship* (*epi to ploion*). Note article. It is possible that Paul's party had chartered a coasting vessel from Philippi or Troas to take them to Patara in Lycia. Hence the boat stopped when and where Paul wished. That is possible, but not certain, for Paul could simply have accommodated himself to the plans of the ship's managers. *To take in Paul* (*analambanein ton Paulon*). So in verse 14. Same use in II Tim. 4:11: "Picking up Mark" (*Markon analabōn*). Assos was a seaport south of Troas in Mysia in the province of Asia. *He had appointed* (*diatetagmenos ēn*). Past perfect periphrastic middle of *diatassō*, old verb to give orders

(military in particular). *To go by land (pezeuein)*. Present active infinitive of *pezeuō*, old verb to go on foot, not on horse back or in a carriage or by ship. Here only in the N.T. It was about twenty miles over a paved Roman road, much shorter (less than half) than the sea voyage around Cape Lectum. It was a beautiful walk in the spring-time and no doubt Paul enjoyed it whatever his reason was for going thus to Assos while the rest went by sea. Certainly he was entitled to a little time alone, this one day, as Jesus sought the Father in the night watches (Matt. 14:23).

14. *Met us (suneballen hēmin)*. Imperfect active where the aorist (*sunebalen*, as C D have it) would seem more natural. It may mean that as soon as (*hōs*) Paul "came near or began to meet us" (inchoative imperfect), we picked him up. Luke alone in the N.T. uses *sunballō* to bring or come together either in a friendly sense as here or as enemies (Luke 14:31). *To Mitylene (eis Mitulēnēn)*. The capital of Lesbos about thirty miles from Assos, an easy day's sailing.

15. *We came over against Chios (katēntēsamen antikrus Chiou)*. Luke uses this *Koiné* verb several times (16:1; 18:19), meaning to come right down in front of and the notion of *anta* is made plainer by *antikrus*, face to face with, common "improper" preposition only here in the N.T. They probably lay off the coast (anchoring) during the night instead of putting into the harbour. The Island of Chios is about eight miles from the mainland. *The next day (tēi heterāi)*. The third day in reality from Assos (the fourth from Troas), in contrast with *tēi epiousēi* just before for Chios. *We touched at Samos (parebalomen eis Samon)*. Second aorist active of *paraballō*, to throw alongside, to cross over, to put in by. So Thucydides III. 32. Only here in the N.T. though in Textus Receptus in Mark 4:30. The word parable (*parabolē*) is from this verb. The Textus Receptus adds here *kai meinantes en Trogulliōi* (and remaining at Trogyllium), but clearly not genuine. In passing from Chios to Samos

they sailed past Ephesus to save time for Pentecost in Jerusalem (verse 16), if in control of the ship, or because the captain allowed Paul to have his way. The island of Samos is still further down the coast below Chios. It is not stated whether a stop was made here or not. *The day after* (*tēi echomenēi*). The day holding itself next to the one before. Note Luke's three terms in this verse (*tēi epiousēi, tēi heterāi, tēi echomenēi*). This would be the fourth from Assos. *To Miletus* (*eis Milēton*). About 28 miles south of Ephesus and now the site is several miles from the sea due to the silt from the Maeander. This city, once the chief city of the Ionian Greeks, was now quite eclipsed by Ephesus.

16. *For Paul had determined* (*kekrikei gar ho Paulos*). Past perfect active (correct text) of *krinō* and not the aorist *ekrine*. Either Paul controlled the ship or the captain was willing to oblige him. *To sail past Ephesus* (*parapleusai tēn Epheson*). First aorist active infinitive of *parapleō*, old verb to sail beside, only here in the N.T. *That he might not have* (*hopōs mē genētai autōi*). Final clause (negative) with aorist middle subjunctive of *ginomai* and dative "that it might not happen to him." *To spend time* (*chronotribēsai*). First aorist active of the late compound verb *chronotribeō* (*chronos*, time, *tribō*, to spend), only here in the N.T. The verb *tribō*, to rub, to wear out by rubbing, lends itself to the idea of wasting time. It was only a year ago that Paul had left Ephesus in haste after the riot. It was not expedient to go back so soon if he meant to reach Jerusalem by Pentecost. Paul clearly felt (Rom. 15) that the presentation of this collection at Pentecost to the Jewish Christians would have a wholesome influence as it had done once before (Acts 11:30). *He was hastening* (*espeuden*). Imperfect active of *speudō*, old verb to hasten as in Luke 2:16; 19:56. *If it were possible for him* (*ei dunaton eiē autōi*). Condition of the fourth class (optative mode), if it should be possible for

him. The form is a remote possibility. It was only some thirty days till Pentecost. *The day of Pentecost (tēn hēmeran tēs pentēkostēs)*. Note the accusative case. Paul wanted to be there for the whole day. See Acts 2:1 for this very phrase.

17. *Called to him (metekalesato)*. Aorist middle (indirect) indicative of *metakaleō*, old verb to call from one place to another (*meta* for "change"), middle to call to oneself, only in Acts in the N.T. (7:14; 10:32; 20:17; 24:25). Ephesus was some thirty miles, a stiff day's journey each way. They would be with Paul the third day of the stay in Miletus. *The elders of the church (tous presbuterous tēs ekklēsias)*. The very men whom Paul terms "bishops" (*episkopous*) in verse 28 just as in Titus 1:5 and 7 where both terms (*presbuterous, ton episkopon*) describe the same office. The term "elder" applied to Christian ministers first appears in Acts 11:30 in Jerusalem and reappears in 15:4, 6, 22 in connection with the apostles and the church. The "elders" are not "apostles" but are "bishops" (cf. Phil. 1:1) and with "deacons" constitute the two classes of officers in the early churches. Ignatius shows that in the early second century the office of bishop over the elders had developed, but Lightfoot has shown that it was not so in the first century. Each church, as in Jerusalem, Philippi, Ephesus, had a number of "elders" ("bishops") in the one great city church. Hackett thinks that other ministers from the neighbourhood also came. It was a noble group of preachers and Paul, the greatest preacher of the ages, makes a remarkable talk to preachers with all the earmarks of Pauline originality (Spitta, *Apostelgeschichte*, p. 252) as shown by the characteristic Pauline words, phrases, ideas current in all his Epistles including the Pastoral (testify, course, pure, take heed, presbyter, bishop, acquire, apparel). Luke heard this address as he may and probably did hear those in Jerusalem and Caesarea (Acts 21 to 26). Furneaux suggests that Luke probably took shorthand notes of the address

since Galen says that his students took down his medical lectures in shorthand: "At any rate, of all the speeches in the Acts this contains most of Paul and least of Luke. . . . It reveals Paul as nothing else does. The man who spoke it is no longer a man of eighteen centuries ago: he is of yesterday; of today. He speaks as we speak and feels as we feel; or rather as we fain would speak and feel." We have seen and listened to Paul speak to the Jews in Antioch in Pisidia as Luke pictures the scene, to the uneducated pagans at Lystra, to the cultured Greeks in Athens. We shall hear him plead for his life to the Jewish mob in Jerusalem, to the Roman governor Felix in Caesarea, to the Jewish "King" Herod Agrippa II in Caesarea, and at last to the Jews in Rome. But here Paul unbosoms himself to the ministers of the church in Ephesus where he had spent three years (longer than with any other church) and where he had such varied experiences of prowess and persecution. He opens his heart to these men as he does not to the average crowd even of believers. It is Paul's *Apologia pro sua Vita*. He will probably not see them again and so the outlook and attitude is similar to the farewell discourse of Jesus to the disciples in the upper room (John 13–17). He warns them about future perils as Jesus had done. Paul's words here will repay any preacher's study today. There is the same high conception of the ministry here that Paul had already elaborated in II Cor. 2:12–6:10 (see my *Glory of the Ministry*). It is a fitting time and occasion for Paul to take stock of his ministry at the close of the third mission tour. What wonders had God wrought already.

18. *Ye yourselves know* (*humeis epistasthe*). Pronoun expressed and emphatic. He appeals to their personal knowledge of his life in Ephesus. *From the first day that* (*apo prōtēs hēmeras aph' hēs*). "From first day from which." He had first "set foot" (*epebēn*, second aorist active indicative of old verb *epibainō*, to step upon or step into) in Ephesus four

years ago in the spring of 51 or 52, but had returned from
Antioch that autumn. It is now spring of 54 or 55 so that
his actual ministry in Ephesus was about two and a half
years, roughly three years (verse 31).

After what manner I was with you (*pōs meth' hūmōn
egenomēn*). Literally, "How I came (from Asia and so was)
with you." Cf. I Thess. 1:5 and II Thess. 2:1–10 where
Paul likewise dares to refer boldly to his life while with them
"all the time" (*ton panta chronon*). Accusative of duration
of time. So far as we know, Paul stuck to Ephesus the whole
period. He had devoted himself consecratedly to the task
in Ephesus. Each pastor is bishop of his field and has a
golden opportunity to work it for Christ. One of the saddest
things about the present situation is the restlessness of
preachers to go elsewhere instead of devoting themselves
wholly to the task where they are. 19. *Serving the Lord* (*dou-
leuōn tōi kuriōi*). It was Paul's glory to be the *doulos* (bond-
slave) as in Rom. 1:1; Phil. 1:1. Paul alone, save Jesus
in Matt. 6:24 and Luke 16:13, uses *douleuō* six times for
serving God (Page). *With all lowliness of mind* (*meta pasēs
tapeinophrosunēs*). Lightfoot notes that heathen writers use
this word for a grovelling, abject state of mind, but Paul
follows Christ in using it for humility, humble-mindedness
that should mark every Christian and in particular the
preacher. *With tears* (*dakruōn*). Construed with *meta*. Paul
was a man of the deepest emotion along with his high intel-
lectuality. He mentions his tears again in verse 31, tears of
sorrow and of anxiety. He refers to his tears in writing the
sharp letter to the church in Corinth (II Cor. 2:4) and in
denouncing the sensual apostates in Phil. 3:18. Adolphe
Monod has a wonderful sermon on the tears of Paul. Consider also the tears of Jesus. *Trials which befell me* (*peiras-
mōn tōn sumbantōn moi*). Construed also with *meta*. Second
aorist active participle of *sunbainō*, to walk with, to go with,
to come together, to happen, to befall. Very common in

this sense in the old Greek (cf. Acts 3:10). *By the plots of the Jews* (*en tais epiboulais tōn Ioudaiōn*). Like the plot (*epiboulē*) against him in Corinth (20:3) as well as the earlier trial before Gallio and the attacks in Thessalonica. In Acts 19:9 Luke shows the hostile attitude of the Jews in Ephesus that drove Paul out of the synagogue to the school of Tyrannus. He does not describe in detail these "plots" which may easily be imagined from Paul's own letters and may be even referred to in I Cor. 4:10; 15:30ff.; 16:9; II Cor. 1:4–10; 7:5; 11:23. In fact, one has only to dwell on the allusions in II Cor. 11 to picture what Paul's life was in Ephesus during these three years. Luke gives in Acts 19 the outbreak of Demetrius, but Paul had already fought with "wild-beasts" there.

20. *How that I shrank not* (*hōs ouden hupesteilamen*). Still indirect discourse (question) after *epistasthe* (ye know) with *hōs* like *pōs* in verse 18. First aorist middle of *hupostellō*, old verb to draw under or back. It was so used of drawing back or down sails on a ship and, as Paul had so recently been on the sea, that may be the metaphor here. But it is not necessarily so as the direct middle here makes good sense and is frequent, to withdraw oneself, to cower, to shrink, to conceal, to dissemble as in Hab. 2:4 (Heb. 10:38). Demosthenes so used it to shrink from declaring out of fear for others. This open candour of Paul is supported by his Epistles (I Thess. 2:4, 11; II Cor. 4:2; Gal. 1:10). *From declaring unto you* (*tou mē anaggeilai humin*). Ablative case of the articular first aorist active infinitive of *anaggellō* with the redundant negative after verbs of hindering, etc. (Robertson, *Grammar*, p. 1094). *Anything that was profitable* (*tōn sumpherontōn*). Partitive genitive after *ouden* of the articular present active participle of *sumpherō*, to bear together, be profitable. *Publicly* (*dēmosiāi*, adverb) *and from house to house* (*kai kat' oikous*). By (according to) houses. It is worth noting that this greatest of preachers preached from house to house and

did not make his visits merely social calls. He was doing kingdom business all the while as in the house of Aquila and Priscilla (I Cor. 16:19).

21. *Testifying* (*diamarturomenos*). As Peter did (Acts 2:40) where Luke uses this same word thoroughly Lucan and Pauline. So again in verses 23 and 24. Paul here as in Rom. 1:16 includes both Jews and Greeks, to the Jew first. *Repentance toward God* (*tēn eis theon metanoian*) *and faith toward our Lord Jesus* (*kai pistin eis ton kurion hēmōn Iēsoun*). These two elements run through the Epistle to the Romans which Paul had recently written and sent from Corinth. These two elements appear in all Paul's preaching whether "to Jews or Gentiles, to philosophers at Athens or to peasants at Lystra, he preached repentance toward God and faith toward the Lord Jesus" (Knowling).

22. *Bound in the spirit* (*dedemenos tōi pneumati*). Perfect passive participle of *deō*, to bind, with the locative case. "Bound in my spirit" he means, as in 19:21, from a high sense of duty. The mention of "the Holy Spirit" specifically in verse 23 seems to be in contrast to his own spirit here. His own spirit was under the control of the Holy Spirit (Rom. 8:16) and the sense does not differ greatly. *Not knowing* (*mē eidōs*). Second perfect active participle of *oida* with *mē*. *That shall befall me* (*ta sunantēsonta emoi*). Articular future active participle of *sunantaō*, to meet with (Acts 10:25), to befall (with associative instrumental case) and compare with *sumbantōn* (befell) in verse 19. One of the rare instances of the future participle in the N.T.

23. *Save that* (*plēn hoti*). The *hoti* clause is really in the ablative case after *plēn*, here a preposition as in Phil. 1:18, this idiom *plēn hoti* occasionally in ancient Greek. *In every city* (*kata polin*). Singular here though plural in *kat' oikous* (verse 20). *Bonds and afflictions* (*desma kai thlipseis*). Both together as in Phil. 1:17; II Cor. 1:8. Literal bonds and actual pressures. *Abide me* (*me menousin*). With the accusa-

tive as in verse 5 (*emenon hēmas*) and nowhere else in the N.T.

24. *But I hold not my life of any account* (*all' oudenos logou poioumai tēn psuchēn*). Neat Greek idiom, accusative *psuchēn* and genitive *logou* and then Paul adds "dear unto myself" (*timian emautōi*) in apposition with *psuchēn* (really a combination of two constructions). *So that I may accomplish my course* (*hōs teleiōsō dromon mou*). Rather, "In order that" (purpose, not result). Aleph and B read *teleiōsō* here (first aorist active subjunctive) rather than *teleiōsai* (first aorist active infinitive). It is the lone instance in the N.T. of *hōs* as a final particle (Robertson, *Grammar*, p. 987). Paul in Acts 13:25 in his sermon at Antioch in Pisidia described John as fulfilling his course and in II Tim. 4:7 he will say: "I have finished my course" (*ton dromon teteleka*). He will run the race to the end. *Which I received from the Lord Jesus* (*hēn elabon para tou kuriou Iēsou*). Of that fact he never had a doubt and it was a proud boast (Gal. 1:1; Rom. 11:13). *The gospel of the grace of God* (*to euaggelion tēs charitos tou theou*). To Paul the gospel consisted in the grace of God. See this word "grace" (*charis*) in Romans and his other Epistles.

25. *And now, behold* (*kai nun, idou*). Second time and solemn reminder as in verse 22. *I know* (*egō oida*). Emphasis on *egō* which is expressed. *Ye all* (*humeis pantes*). In very emphatic position after the verb *opsesthe* (shall see) and the object (my face). Twice Paul will write from Rome (Phil. 2:24; Philemon 22) the hope of coming east again; but that is in the future, and here Paul is expressing his personal conviction and his fears. The Pastoral Epistles show Paul did come to Ephesus again (I Tim. 1:3; 3:14; 4:13) and Troas (II Tim. 4:13) and Miletus (II Tim. 4:20). There need be no surprise that Paul's fears turned out otherwise. He had reason enough for them. *Among whom I went about* (*en hois diēlthon*). Apparently Paul here has in mind others

beside the ministers. They represented the church in Ephesus and the whole region where Paul laboured.

26. *I testify* (*marturomai*). Elsewhere in the N.T. only in Paul's Epistles (Gal. 5:3; Eph. 4:17; I Thess. 2:12). It means "I call to witness" while *martureō* means "I bear witness." *This day* (*en tēi sēmeron hēmerāi*). The today day, the last day with you, our parting day. *I am pure from the blood of all men* (*katharos eimi apo tou haimatos pantōn*). Paul was sensitive on this point as in Corinth (Acts 18:6). It is much for any preacher to claim and it ought to be true of all. The papyri also give this use of *apo* with the ablative rather than the mere ablative after *katharos*.

27. Paul here repeats the very words and idioms used in verse 20, adding "the whole counsel of God" (*pāsan tēn boulēn tou theou*). All the counsel of God that concerned Paul's work and nothing inconsistent with the purpose of God of redemption through Christ Jesus (Page).

28. *Take heed unto yourselves* (*prosechete heautois*). The full phrase had *ton noun*, hold your mind on yourselves (or other object in the dative), as often in old writers and in Job 7:17. But the ancients often used the idiom with *noun* understood, but not expressed as here and Acts 5:35; Luke 12:1; 17:3; 21:34; I Tim. 1:4; 3:8; 4:13. *Epeche* is so used in I Tim. 4:16. *To all the flock* (*panti tōi poimniōi*). Contracted form of *poimenion* = *poimnē* (John 10:16) already in Luke 12:32 and also in Acts 20:29 and I Pet. 5:2, 3. Common in old Greek. *Hath made* (*etheto*). Did make, second aorist middle indicative of *tithēmi*, did appoint. Paul evidently believed that the Holy Spirit calls and appoints ministers. *Bishops* (*episkopous*). The same men termed elders in verse 17 which see. *To shepherd* (*poimainein*). Present active infinitive of purpose of *poimainō*, old verb to feed or tend the flock (*poimnē*, *poimnion*), to act as shepherd (*poimēn*). These ministers are thus in Paul's speech called elders (verse 17), bishops (verse 28), and

shepherds (verse 28). Jesus had used this very word to Peter (John 21:16, twice *boske*, feed, 21:15, 17) and Peter will use it in addressing fellow-elders (I Pet. 5:2) with memories, no doubt of the words of Jesus to him. The "elders" were to watch over as "bishops" and "tend and feed as shepherds" the flock. Jesus is termed "the shepherd and bishop of your souls" in I Peter 2:25 and "the great Shepherd of the sheep" in Heb. 13:20. Jesus called himself "the good Shepherd" in John 10:11. *The church of God* (*tēn ekklēsian tou theou*). The correct text, not "the church of the Lord" or "the church of the Lord and God" (Robertson, *Introduction to Textual Criticism of the N.T.*, p. 189). *He purchased* (*periepoiēsato*). First aorist middle of *peripoieō*, old verb to reserve, to preserve (for or by oneself, in the middle). In the N.T. only in Luke 17:33; Acts 20:28; I Tim. 3:13. The substantive *peripoiēsin* (preservation, possession) occurs in I Peter 2:9 ("a peculiar people" = a people for a possession) and in Eph. 1:14. *With his own blood* (*dia tou haimatos tou idiou*). Through the agency of (*dia*) his own blood. Whose blood? If *tou theou* (Aleph B Vulg.) is correct, as it is, then Jesus is here called "God" who shed his own blood for the flock. It will not do to say that Paul did not call Jesus God, for we have Rom. 9:5; Col. 2:9 and Tit. 2:13 where he does that very thing, besides Col. 1:15–20 and Phil. 2:5–11.

29. *After my departing* (*meta tēn aphixin mou*). Not his death, but his departure from them. From *aphikneomai* and usually meant arrival, but departure in Herodotus IX. 17, 76 as here. *Grievous wolves* (*lukoi bareis*). *Bareis* is heavy, rapacious, harsh. Jesus had already so described false teachers who would raven the fold (John 10:12). Whether Paul had in mind the Judaizers who had given him so much trouble in Antioch, Jerusalem, Galatia, Corinth or the Gnostics the shadow of whose coming he already foresaw is not perfectly clear. But it will not be many

years before Epaphras will come to Rome from Colossae
with news of the new peril there (Epistle to the Colossians).
In writing to Timothy (I Tim. 1:20) Paul will warn him
against some who have already made shipwreck of their
faith. In Rev. 2:2 John will represent Jesus as describing
false apostles in Ephesus. *Not sparing the flock* (*mē pheido-
menoi tou poimniou*). Litotes again as so often in Acts.
Sparing the flock was not the fashion of wolves. Jesus sent
the seventy as lambs in the midst of wolves (Luke 10:3).
In the Sermon on the Mount Jesus had pictured the false
prophets who would come as ravening wolves in sheep's
clothing (Matt. 7:15).

30. *From among your own selves* (*ex humōn autōn*). In
sheep's clothing just as Jesus had foretold. The outcome
fully justified Paul's apprehensions as we see in Colossians,
Ephesians, I and II Timothy, Revelation. False philosophy,
immorality, asceticism will lead some astray (Col. 2:8, 18;
Eph. 4:14; 5:6). John will picture "antichrists" who went
out from us because they were not of us (I John 2:18f.).
There is a false optimism that is complacently blind as well
as a despondent pessimism that gives up the fight. *Perverse
things* (*diestrammena*). Perfect passive participle of *diastrephō*, old verb to turn aside, twist, distort as in Acts 13:8
10. *To draw away* (*tou apospāin*). Articular genitive present
active participle of purpose from *apospao*, old verb used
to draw the sword (Matt. 26:51), to separate (Luke 22:41;
Acts 21:1). The pity of it is that such leaders of dissension
can always gain a certain following. Paul's long residence
in Ephesus enabled him to judge clearly of conditions there.

31. *Wherefore watch ye* (*dio grēgoreite*). Paul has concluded his defence of himself and his warning. Now he ex-
horts on the basis of it (*dio*) because of which thing. The
very command of Jesus concerning the perils before his
return as in Mark 13:35 (*grēgoreite*), the very form (late
present imperative from the second perfect *egrēgora* of

egeirō, to arouse). Stay awake. *I ceased not to admonish* (*ouk epausamēn nouthetōn*). Participle describes Paul, I did not cease admonishing, night and day (*nukta kai hēmeran*, accusative of extent of time, for three years *trietian*, accusative of extent of time also). *Nouthetōn* is from *noutheteō*, to put sense into one. So Paul kept it up with tears (verse 19) if so be he could save the Ephesians from the impending perils. Forewarned is to be forearmed. Paul did his duty by them.

32. *And now* (*kai ta nun*). Same phrase as in verses 22 and 25 save that *idou* (behold) is wanting and the article *ta* occurs before *nun*, accusative of general reference. And as to the present things (or situation) as in 4:29. *I commend* (*paratithemai*). Present middle indicative of *paratithēmi*, old verb to place beside, middle, to deposit with one, to interest as in I Tim. 1:18; II Tim. 2:2. Paul can now only do this, but he does it hopefully. Cf. I Pet. 4:19. *The word of his grace* (*tōi logōi tēs charitos autou*). The instrumentality through preaching and the Holy Spirit employed by God. Cf. Col. 4:6; Eph. 4:29. *Which is able to build up* (*tōi dunamenōi oikodomēsai*). God works through the word of his grace and so it is able to build up (edify); a favourite Pauline word (I Cor. 3:10–14; 3:9; II Cor. 5:1; Eph. 2:20–22; II Tim. 3:15; etc.), and James 1:21. The very words "build" and "inheritance among the sanctified" will occur in Eph. 1:11; 2:30; 3:18 and which some may recall on reading. Cf. Col. 1:12. Stephen in Acts 7:5 used the word "inheritance" (*klēronomian*), nowhere else in Acts, but in Eph. 1:14, 18; 5:5. In Eph. 1:18 the very expression occurs "his inheritance among the saints" (*tēn klēronomian autou en tois hagiois*).

33. *No man's silver or gold or apparel* (*arguriou ē chrusiou ē himatismou oudenos*). Genitive case after *epethumēsa*. One of the slanders against Paul was that he was raising this collection, ostensibly for the poor, really for himself (II Cor. 12:17f.). He includes "apparel" because oriental wealth

consisted largely in fine apparel (not old worn out clothes). See Gen. 24:53; II Kings 5:5; Psa. 45:13f.; Matt. 6:19. Paul did not preach just for money.

34. *Ye yourselves* (*autoi*). Intensive pronoun. Certainly they knew that the church in Ephesus had not supported Paul while there. *These hands* (*hai cheires hautai*). Paul was not above manual labour. He pointed to his hands with pride as proof that he toiled at his trade of tent-making as at Thessalonica and Corinth for his own needs (*chreiais*) and for those with him (probably Aquila and Priscilla) with whom he lived and probably Timothy because of his often infirmities (I Tim. 5:23). *Ministered* (*hupēretēsan*). First aorist active of *hupēreteō*, to act as under rower, old verb, but in the N.T. only in Acts 13:36; 20:34; 24:23. While in Ephesus Paul wrote to Corinth: "We toil, working with our own hands" (I Cor. 4:12). "As he held them up, they saw a tongue of truth in every seam that marked them" (Furneaux).

35. *I gave you an example* (*hupedeixa*). First aorist active indicative of *hupodeiknumi*, old verb to show under one's eyes, to give object lesson, by deed as well as by word (Luke 6:47). *Hupodeigma* means example (John 13:15; James 5:10). So Paul appeals to his example in I Cor. 11:1; Phil. 3:17. *Panta* is accusative plural of general reference (in all things). *So labouring ye ought to help* (*houtōs kopiōntas dei antilambanesthai*). So, as I did. Necessity (*dei*). Toiling (*kopiōntas*) not just for ourselves, but to help (*antilambanesthai*), to take hold yourselves (middle voice) at the other end (*anti*). This verb common in the old Greek, but in the N.T. only in Luke 1:54; Acts 20:35; I Tim. 6:2. This noble plea to help the weak is the very spirit of Christ (I Thess. 5:14; I Cor. 12:28; Rom. 5:6; 14:1). In I Thess. 5:14 *antechesthe tōn asthenountōn* we have Paul's very idea again. Every Community Chest appeal today re-echoes Paul's plea. *He himself said* (*autos eipen*). Not in the Gospels, one

of the sayings of Jesus in current use that Paul had received and treasured. Various other *Agrapha* of Jesus have been preserved in ancient writers and some in recently discovered papyri which may be genuine or not. We are grateful that Paul treasured this one. This Beatitude (on *makarion* see on Matt. 5:3–11) is illustrated by the whole life of Jesus with the Cross as the culmination. Aristotle (Eth. IV. 1) has a saying somewhat like this, but assigns the feeling of superiority as the reason (Page), an utterly different idea from that here. This quotation raises the question of how much Paul personally knew of the life and sayings of Jesus.

36. *He kneeled down* (*theis ta gonata autou*). Second aorist active participle of *tithēmi*, to place. The very idiom used in 7:60 of Stephen. Not in ancient writers and only six times in the N.T. (Mark 15:19; Luke 22:41; Acts 7:60; 9:40; 20:36; 21:5). Certainly kneeling in prayer is a fitting attitude (cf. Jesus, Luke 22:41), though not the only proper one (Matt. 6:5). Paul apparently prayed aloud (*proseuxato*).

37. *They all wept sore* (*hikanos klauthmos egeneto pantōn*). Literally, There came considerable weeping of all (on the part of all, genitive case). *Kissed him* (*katephiloun auton*). Imperfect active of *kataphileō*, old verb, intensive with *kata* and repetition shown also by the tense: They kept on kissing or kissed repeatedly, probably one after the other falling on his neck. Cf. also Matt. 26:49.

38. *Sorrowing* (*odunōmenoi*). Present middle participle of *odunaō*, old verb to cause intense pain, to torment (Luke 16:24), middle to distress oneself (Luke 2:48; Acts 20:38). Nowhere else in N.T. *Which he had spoken* (*hōi eirēkei*). Relative attracted to the case of the antecedent *logōi* (word). Past perfect indicative of *eipon*. *They brought him on his way* (*proepempon auton*). Imperfect active of *propempō*, old verb to send forward, to accompany as in Acts 15:3; 20:38; 21:5; I Cor. 16:6, 11; II Cor. 1:16; Tit. 3:13; III John 6. Graphic picture of Paul's departure from this group of ministers.

CHAPTER XXI

1. *Were parted from them* (*apospasthentas ap' autōn*). First aorist passive participle of *apospaō* same verb as in 20:30 and Luke 22:41. *Had set sail* (*anachthēnai*). First aorist passive of *anagō*, the usual verb to put out (up) to sea as in verse 2 (*anēchthēmen*). *We came with a straight course* (*euthudromēsantes ēlthomen*). The same verb (aorist active participle of *euthudromeō*) used by Luke in 16:11 of the voyage from Troas to Samothrace and Neapolis, which see. *Unto Cos* (*eis tēn Ko*). Standing today, about forty nautical miles south from Miletus, island famous as the birthplace of Hippocrates and Apelles with a great medical school. Great trading place with many Jews. *The next day* (*tēi hexēs*). Locative case with *hēmerāi* (day) understood. The adverb *hexēs* is from *echō* (future *hexō*) and means successively or in order. This is another one of Luke's ways of saying "on the next day" (cf. three others in 20:15). *Unto Rhodes* (*eis tēn Rhodon*). Called the island of roses. The sun shone most days and made roses luxuriant. The great colossus which represented the sun, one of the seven wonders of the world, was prostrate at this time. The island was at the entrance to the Aegean Sea and had a great university, especially for rhetoric and oratory. There was great commerce also. *Unto Patara* (*eis Patara*). A seaport on the Lycian coast on the left bank of the Xanthus. It once had an oracle of Apollo which rivalled that at Delphi. This was the course taken by hundreds of ships every season.

2. *Having found a ship* (*heurontes ploion*). Paul had used a small coasting vessel (probably hired) that anchored each night at Cos, Rhodes, Patara. He was still some four hundred miles from Jerusalem. But at Patara Paul caught a large

358

vessel (a merchantman) that could sail across the open sea. *Crossing over unto Phoenicia (diaperōn eis Phoinikēn)*. Neuter singular accusative (agreeing with *ploion*) present active participle of *diaperaō*, old verb to go between (*dia*) and so across to Tyre. *We went aboard (epibantes)*. Second aorist active participle of *epibainō*.

3. *When we had come in sight of Cyprus (anaphanantes tēn Kupron)*. First aorist active participle of *anaphainō* (Doric form *-phanāntes* rather than the Attic *-phēnantes*), old verb to make appear, bring to light, to manifest. Having made Cyprus visible or rise up out of the sea. Nautical terms. In the N.T. only here and Luke 19:11 which see. *On the left hand (euōnumon)*. Compound feminine adjective like masculine. They sailed south of Cyprus. *We sailed (epleomen)*. Imperfect active of common verb *pleō*, kept on sailing till we came to Syria. *Landed at Tyre (katēlthomen eis Turon)*. Came down to Tyre. Then a free city of Syria in honour of its former greatness (cf. the long siege by Alexander the Great). *There (ekeise)*. Thither, literally. Only one other instance in N.T., 22:5 which may be pertinent = *ekei* (there). *Was to unlade (ēn apophortizomenon)*. Periphrastic imperfect middle of *apophortizō*, late verb from *apo* and *phortos*, load, but here only in the N.T. Literally, "For thither the boat was unloading her cargo," a sort of "customary" or "progressive" imperfect (Robertson, *Grammar*, p. 884). *Burden (gomon)*. Cargo, old word, from *gemō*, to be full. Only here and Rev. 18:11f. in N.T. Probably a grain or fruit ship. It took seven days here to unload and reload.

4. *Having found (aneurontes)*. Second aorist active participle of *aneuriskō*, to seek for, to find by searching (*ana*). There was a church here, but it was a large city and the number of members may not have been large. Probably some of those that fled from Jerusalem who came to Phoenicia (Acts 11:19) started the work here. Paul went also through Phoenicia on the way to the Jerusalem Conference (15:3). As

at Troas and Miletus, so here Paul's indefatigible energy shows itself with characteristic zeal. *Through the Spirit* (*dia tou pneumatos*). The Holy Spirit undoubtedly who had already told Paul that bonds and afflictions awaited him in Jerusalem (20:23). *That he should not set foot in Jerusalem* (*mē epibainein eis Ierosoluma*). Indirect command with *mē* and the present active infinitive, not to keep on going to Jerusalem (Robertson, *Grammar*, p. 1046). In spite of this warning Paul felt it his duty as before (20:22) to go on. Evidently Paul interpreted the action of the Holy Spirit as information and warning although the disciples at Tyre gave it the form of a prohibition. Duty called louder than warning to Paul even if both were the calls of God.

5. *That we had accomplished the days* (*exartisai hēmās tas hēmeras*). First aorist active infinitive of *exartizō*, to furnish perfectly, rare in ancient writers, but fairly frequent in the papyri. Only twice in the N.T., here and II Tim. 3:17. Finish the exact number of days (seven) of verse 4. The accusative of general reference *hēmās* is the usual construction and the infinitive clause is the subject of *egeneto*. *We departed and went on our journey* (*exelthontes eporeuometha*). Sharp distinction between the first aorist active participle *exelthontes* (from *exerchomai*, to go out) and the imperfect middle *eporeuometha* from *poreuō* (we were going on). *And they all, with wives and children, brought us on our way* (*propempontōn hēmās pantōn sun gunaixi kai teknois*). No "and" in the Greek, simply genitive absolute, "They all with wives and children accompanying us," just as at Miletus (20:28), same verb *propempō* which see. The first mention of children in connection with the apostolic churches (Vincent). Vivid picture here as at Miletus, evident touch of an eyewitness. *Till we were out of the city* (*heōs exō tēs poleōs*). Note both adverbial prepositions (*heōs exō*) clear outside of the city.

6. *Beach* (*aigialon*). As in Matt. 13:2 which see. This scene is in public as at Miletus, but they did not care.

Bade each other farewell (*apespasametha allēlous*). First
aorist middle of *apaspazomai*. Rare compound, here alone
in the N.T. Tender scene, but "no bonds of long comrade-
ship, none of the clinging love" (Furneaux) seen at Miletus
(Acts 20:37f.). *Home again* (*eis ta idia*). To their own places
as of the Beloved Disciple in John 19:27 and of Jesus in John
1:11. This idiom in the papyri also.

7. *Had finished* (*dianusantes*). First aorist active participle of *dianuō*, old verb to accomplish (*anuō*) thoroughly
(*dia*), only here in the N.T. *From Tyre* (*apo Turou*). Page
takes (Hackett also) with *katēntēsamen* (we arrived) rather
than with "*ton ploun*" (the voyage) and with good reason:
"And we, having (thereby) finished the voyage, arrived
from Tyre at Ptolemais." Ptolemais is the modern Acre,
called Accho in Judges 1:31. The harbour is the best on the
coast of Palestine and is surrounded by mountains. It is
about thirty miles south of Tyre. It was never taken by
Israel and was considered a Philistine town and the Greeks
counted it a Phoenician city. It was the key to the road
down the coast between Syria and Egypt and had successively the rule of the Ptolemies, Syrians, Romans. *Saluted*
(*aspasamenoi*). Here greeting as in 21:19 rather than farewell
as in 20:1. The stay was short, one day (*hēmeran mian*,
accusative), but "the brethren" Paul and his party found
easily. Possibly the scattered brethren (Acts 11:19) founded
the church here or Philip may have done it.

8. *On the morrow* (*tēi epaurion*). Another and the more
common way of expressing this idea of "next day" besides
the three in 20:15 and the one in 21:1. *Unto Caesarea* (*eis
Kaisarian*). Apparently by land as the voyage (*ploun*)
ended at Ptolemais (verse 7). Caesarea is the political
capital of Judea under the Romans where the procurators
lived and a city of importance, built by Herod the Great
and named in honour of Augustus. It had a magnificent
harbour built. Most of the inhabitants were Greeks. This

is the third time that we have seen Paul in Caesarea, on his journey from Jerusalem to Tarsus (Acts 9:30), on his return from Antioch at the close of the second mission tour (18:22) and now. The best MSS. omit *hoi peri Paulou* (we that were of Paul's company) a phrase like that in 13:13. *Into the house of Philip the evangelist* (*eis ton oikon Philippou tou euaggelistou*). Second in the list of the seven (6:5) after Stephen and that fact mentioned here. By this title he is distinguished from "Philip the apostle," one of the twelve. His evangelistic work followed the death of Stephen (Acts 8) in Samaria, Philistia, with his home in Caesarea. The word "evangelizing" (*euēggelizeto*) was used of him in 8:40. The earliest of the three N.T. examples of the word "evangelist" (Acts 21:8; Eph. 4:11; II Tim. 4:5). Apparently a word used to describe one who told the gospel story as Philip did and may have been used of him first of all as John was termed "the baptizer" (*ho baptizōn*, Mark 1:4), then "the Baptist" (*ho baptistēs*, Matt. 3:1). It is found on an inscription in one of the Greek islands of uncertain date and was used in ecclesiastical writers of later times on the Four Gospels as we do. As used here the meaning is a travelling missionary who "gospelized" communities. This is probably Paul's idea in II Tim. 4:5. In Eph. 4:11 the word seems to describe a special class of ministers just as we have them today. Men have different gifts and Philip had this of evangelizing as Paul was doing who is the chief evangelist. The ideal minister today combines the gifts of evangelist, herald, teacher, shepherd. *"We abode with him"* (*emeinamen par' autōi*). Constative aorist active indicative. *Par autōi* (by his side) is a neat idiom for "at his house." What a joyful time Paul had in conversation with Philip. He could learn from him much of value about the early days of the gospel in Jerusalem. And Luke could, and probably did, take notes from Philip and his daughters about the beginnings of Christian history. It is generally supposed that the "we" sections of Acts represent a travel document by Luke (notes made by him as he journeyed from Troas to Rome). Those who deny the Lukan authorship of the whole book usually admit this. So we may suppose that Luke is already gathering data for future use. If so, these were precious days for him.

9. *Virgins which did prophesy* (*parthenoi prophēteusai*). Not necessarily an "order" of virgins, but Philip had the honour of having in his home four virgin daughters with the gift of prophecy which was not necessarily predicting events, though that was done as by Agabus here. It was more than ordinary preaching (cf. 19:6) and was put by Paul above the other gifts like tongues (I Cor. 14:1–33). The prophecy of Joel (2:28f.) about their sons and daughters prophesying is quoted by Peter and applied to the events on the day of Pentecost (Acts 2:17). Paul in I Cor. 11:5 gives directions about praying and prophesying by the women (apparently in public worship) with the head uncovered and sharply requires the head covering, though not forbidding the praying and prophesying. With this must be compared his demand for silence by the women in I Cor. 14:34–40 and I Tim. 2:8–15 which it is not easy to reconcile. One wonders if there was not something known to Paul about special conditions in Corinth and Ephesus that he has not told. There was also Anna the prophetess in the temple (Luke 2:36) besides the inspired hymns of Elizabeth (Luke 1:42–45) and of Mary (Luke 1:46–55). At any rate there was no order of women prophets or official ministers. There were Old Testament prophetesses like Miriam, Deborah, Huldah. Today in our Sunday schools the women do most of the actual teaching. The whole problem is difficult and calls for restraint and reverence. One thing is certain and that is that Luke appreciated the services of women for Christ as is shown often in his writings (Luke 8:1–3, for instance) before this incident.

10. *As we tarried* (*epimenontōn hēmōn*). Genitive absolute.

Note *epi* (additional) with *menō* as in 12:16. *Many days* (*hēmeras pleious*). More days (than we expected), accusative of time. *A certain prophet named Agabus* (*prophētēs onomati Agabos*). A prophet like the daughters of Philip, mentioned already in connection with the famine predicted by him (Acts 11:28), but apparently not a man of prominence like Barnabas, and so no allusion to that former prophecy.

11. *Coming* (*elthōn*, second aorist active participle of *erchomai*), *taking* (*aras*, first aorist active participle of *airō*, to take up), *binding* (*dēsas*, first aorist active participle of *deō*, to bind). Vivid use of three successive participles describing the dramatic action of Agabus. *Paul's girdle* (*tēn zōnēn tou Paulou*). Old word from *zōnnumi*, to gird. See on 12:8. *His own feet and hands* (*heautou tous podas kai tas cheiras*). Basis for the interpretation. Old Testament prophets often employed symbolic deeds (I Kings 22:11; James 2:2; Jer. 13:1-7; Ezek. 4:1-6). Jesus interpreted the symbolism of Peter's girding himself (John 21:18). *So* (*houtōs*). As Agabus had bound himself. Agabus was just from Jerusalem and probably knew the feeling there against Paul. At any rate the Holy Spirit revealed it to him as he claims. *Shall deliver* (*paradōsousin*). Like the words of Jesus about himself (Matt. 20:19). He was "delivered" into the hands of the Gentiles and it took five years to get out of those hands.

12. *Both we and they of that place* (*hēmeis te kai hoi entopioi*). Usual use of *te kai* (both—and). *Entopioi*, old word, only here in N.T. *Not to go up* (*tou mē anabainein*). Probably ablative of the articular present active infinitive with redundant negative *me* after *parekaloumen* (imperfect active, conative). We tried to persuade him from going up. It can be explained as genitive, but not so likely: We tried to persuade him in respect to not going up. Vincent cites the case of Regulus who insisted on returning from Rome to Carthage to certain death and that of Luther on the way to the Diet of Worms. Spalatin begged Luther not to go on.

Luther said: "Though devils be as many in Worms as tiles upon the roofs, yet thither will I go." This dramatic warning of Agabus came on top of that in Tyre (21:4) and Paul's own confession in Miletus (20:23). It is small wonder that Luke and the other messengers together with Philip and his daughters (prophetesses versus prophet?) joined in a chorus of dissuasion to Paul.

13. *What are you doing weeping?* (*Ti poieite klaiontes?*) Strong protest as in Mark 11:5. *Breaking my heart* (*sunthruptontes mou tēn kardian*). The verb *sunthruptō*, to crush together, is late *Koinē* for *apothruptō*, to break off, both vivid and expressive words. So to enervate and unman one, weakening Paul's determination to go on with his duty. *I am ready* (*Egō hetoimōs echō*). I hold (myself) in readiness (adverb, *hetoimōs*). Same idiom in II Cor. 12:14. *Not only to be bound* (*ou monon dethēnai*). First aorist passive infinitive of *deō* and note *ou monon* rather than *mē monon*, the usual negative of the infinitive because of the sharp contrast (Robertson, *Grammar*, p. 1095). Paul's readiness to die, if need be, at Jerusalem is like that of Jesus on the way to Jerusalem the last time. Even before that Luke (9:51) said that "he set his face to go on to Jerusalem." Later the disciples will say to Jesus, "Master, the Jews were but now seeking to stone thee; and goest thou thither?" (John 11:8). The stature of Paul rises here to heroic proportions "for the name of the Lord Jesus" (*huper tou onomatos tou kuriou Iēsou*).

14. *When he would not be persuaded* (*mē peithomenou autou*). Genitive absolute of the present passive participle of *peithō*. Literally, "he not being persuaded." That was all. Paul's will (*kardia*) was not broken, not even bent. *We ceased* (*hēsuchasamen*). Ingressive aorist active indicative of *hēsuchazō*, old verb to be quiet, silent. *The will of the Lord be done* (*tou kuriou to thelēma ginesthō*). Present middle imperative of *ginomai*. There is a quaint naïveté in this con-

fession by the friends of Paul. Since Paul would not let them have their way, they were willing for the Lord to have his way, acquiescence after failure to have theirs.

15. *We took up our baggage* (*episkeuasamenoi*). First aorist middle participle of *episkeuazō*, old verb to furnish (*skeuos, epi*) with things necessary, to pack up, saddle horses here Ramsay holds. Here only in the N.T. *Went up* (*anebainomen*). Inchoative imperfect active of *anabainō*, we started to go up.

16. *Certain of the disciples* (*tōn mathētōn*). The genitive here occurs with *tines* understood as often in the Greek idiom, the partitive genitive used as nominative (Robertson, *Grammar*, p. 502). *Bringing* (*agontes*). Nominative plural participle agreeing with *tines* understood, not with case of *mathētōn*. *One Mnason of Cyprus, an early disciple, with whom we should lodge* (*par hōi xenisthōmen Mnasōni tini Kupriōi archaiōi mathētēi*). A thoroughly idiomatic Greek idiom, incorporation and attraction of the antecedent into the relative clause (Robertson, *Grammar*, p. 718). *Mnasōni* is really the object of *agontes* or the accusative with *para* or *pros* understood and should be accusative, but it is placed in the clause after the relative and in the same locative case with the relative *hōi* (due to *par'*, beside, with). Then the rest agrees in case with *Mnasōni*. He was originally from Cyprus, but now in Caesarea. The Codex Bezae adds *eis tina kōmēn* (to a certain viliage) and makes it mean that they were to lodge with Mnason at his home there about halfway to Jerusalem. This may be true. The use of the subjunctive *xenisthōmen* (first aorist passive of *xenizō*, to entertain strangers as in Acts 10:6, 23, 32 already) may be volitive of purpose with the relative (Robertson, *Grammar*, pp. 955, 989). The use of *archaiōi* for "early" may refer to the fact that he was one of the original disciples at Pentecost as Peter in 15:7 uses *hēmerōn archaiōn* (early days) to refer to his experience at Ceasarea in Acts 10. "As the number of

the first disciples lessened, the next generation accorded a sort of honour to the survivors" (Furneaux).

17. *When we were come* (*genomenōn hēmōn*). Genitive absolute again, "we having come." *Received* (*apedexanto*). *Apodechomai*, to receive from. This old compound only in Luke in the N.T. *Gladly* (*asmenōs*). Old adverb *hēsmenōs* from *hēdomai*, to be pleased. Here only in the N.T. Perhaps this first glad welcome was from Paul's personal friends in Jerusalem.

18. *The day following* (*tēi epiousēi*). As in 20:15 which see. *Went in* (*eisēiei*). Imperfect active of *eiseimi*, old classic verb used only four times in the N.T. (Acts 3:3; 21:18, 26; Heb. 9:6), a mark of the literary style rather than the colloquial Koiné use of *eiserchomai*. *Together with us to James* (*sun hēmin pros Iakōbon*). So then Luke is present. The next use of "we" is in 27:1 when they leave Caesarea for Rome, but it is not likely that Luke was away from Paul in Jerusalem and Caesarea. The reports of what was done and said in both places is so full and minute that it seems reasonable that Luke got first hand information here whatever his motive was for so full an account of these legal proceedings to be discussed later. There are many details that read like an eye witness's story (21:30, 35, 40; 22:2, 3; 23:12, etc.). It was probably the house of James (*pros* and *para* so used often). *And all the elders were present* (*pantes te paregenonto hoi presbuteroi*). Clearly James is the leading elder and the others are his guests in a formal reception to Paul. It is noticeable that the apostles are not mentioned, though both elders and apostles are named at the Conference in chapter 15. It would seem that the apostles are away on preaching tours. The whole church was not called together probably because of the known prejudice against Paul created by the Judaizers.

19. *He rehearsed* (*exēgeito*). Imperfect middle of *exēgeomai*, old verb to lead out, to draw out in narrative, to recount. So

Paul is pictured as taking his time for he had a great story to tell of what had happened since they saw him last. *One by one* (*kath' hena hekaston*). According to each one (item) and the adverbial phrase used as an accusative after the verb *exēgeito* as Demosthenes does (1265), though it could be like *kath' hena hekastos* in Eph. 5:33. *Which* (*hōn*). Genitive attracted from *ha* (accusative) into the case of the unexpressed antecedent *toutōn*. *God had wrought* (*epoiēsen ho theos*). Summary constative aorist active indicative that gathers up all that God did and he takes pains to give God the glory. It is possible that at this formal meeting Paul observed an absence of warmth and enthusiasm in contrast with the welcome accorded by his friends the day before (verse 17). Furneaux thinks that Paul was coldly received on this day in spite of the generous offering brought from the Gentile Christians. "It looks as though his misgiving as to its reception (Rom. 15:31) was confirmed. Nor do we hear that the Christians of Jerusalem later put in so much as a word on his behalf with either the Jewish or the Roman authorities, or expressed any sympathy with him during his long imprisonment at Caesarea" (Furneaux). The most that can be said is that the Judaizers referred to by James do not appear actively against him. The collection and the plan proposed by James accomplished that much at any rate. It stopped the mouths of those lions.

20. *Glorified* (*edoxazon*). Inchoative imperfect, began to glorify God, though without special praise of Paul. *How many thousands* (*posai muriades*). Old word for ten thousand (Acts 19:19) and then an indefinite number like our "myriads" (this very word) as Luke 12:1; Acts 21:20; Jude 14; Rev. 5:11; 9:16. But it is a surprising statement even with allowable hyperbole, but one may recall Acts 4:4 (number of the men—not women—about five thousand); 5:14 (multitudes both of men and women); 6:7. There were undoubtedly a great many thousands of believers in Jerusalem and all

Jewish Christians, some, alas, Judaizers (Acts 11:2; 15:1, 5). This list may include the Christians from neighbouring towns in Palestine and even some from foreign countries here at the Feast of Pentecost, for it is probable that Paul arrived in time for it as he had hoped. But we do not have to count the hostile Jews from Asia (verse 27) who were clearly not Christians at all. *All zealous for the law* (*pantes zēlōtai tou nomou*). Zealots (substantive) rather than zealous (adjective) with objective genitive (*tou nomou*). The word zealot is from *zēloō*, to burn with zeal, to boil. The Greek used *zēlōtēs* for an imitator or admirer. There was a party of Zealots (developed from the Pharisees), a group of what would be called "hot-heads," who brought on the war with Rome. One of this party, Simon Zelotes (Acts 1:13), was in the number of the twelve apostles. It is important to understand the issues in Jerusalem. It was settled at the Jerusalem Conference (Acts 15 and Galatians 2) that the Mosaic ceremonial law was not to be imposed upon Gentile Christians. Paul won freedom for them, but it was not said that it was wrong for Jewish Christians to go on observing it if they wished. We have seen Paul observing the passover in Philippi (Acts 20:6) and planning to reach Jerusalem for Pentecost (20:16). The Judaizers rankled under Paul's victory and power in spreading the gospel among the Gentiles and gave him great trouble in Galatia and Corinth. They were busy against him in Jerusalem also and it was to undo the harm done by them in Jerusalem that Paul gathered the great collection from the Gentile Christians and brought it with him and the delegates from the churches. Clearly then Paul had real ground for his apprehension of trouble in Jerusalem while still in Corinth (Rom. 15:25) when he asked for the prayers of the Roman Christians (verses 30–32). The repeated warnings along the way were amply justified.

21. *They have been informed concerning thee* (*katēchēthēsan peri sou*). First aorist passive indicative of *katēcheō*. A word

in the ancient Greek, but a few examples survive in the papyri. It means to sound (echo, from *ēchō*, our word) down (*kata*), to resound, re-echo, to teach orally. Oriental students today (Arabs learning the Koran) often study aloud. In the N.T. only in Luke 1:4 which see; Acts 18:25; 21:21; I Cor. 14:19; Gal. 6:6; Rom. 2:18. This oral teaching about Paul was done diligently by the Judaizers who had raised trouble against Peter (Acts 11:2) and Paul (15:1, 5). They had failed in their attacks on Paul's world campaigns. Now they try to undermine him at home. In Paul's long absence from Jerusalem, since 18:22, they have had a free hand, save what opposition James would give, and have had great success in prejudicing the Jerusalem Christians against Paul. So James, in the presence of the other elders and probably at their suggestion, feels called upon to tell Paul the actual situation. *That thou teachest all the Jews which are among the Gentiles to forsake Moses* (*hoti apostasian didaskeis apo Mōuseōs tous kata ta ethnē pantas Ioudaious*). Two accusatives with *didaskeis* (verb of teaching) according to rule. Literally, "That thou art teaching all the Jews among (*kata*) the Gentiles (the Jews of the dispersion as in 2:9) apostasy from Moses." That is the point, the dreadful word *apostasian* (our apostasy), a late form (I Macc. 2:15) for the earlier *apostasis* (cf. II Thess. 2:3 for *apostasia*). "In the eyes of the church at Jerusalem this was a far more serious matter than the previous question at the Conference about the status of Gentile converts" (Furneaux). Paul had brought that issue to the Jerusalem Conference because of the contention of the Judaizers. But here it is not the Judaizers, but the elders of the church with James as their spokesman on behalf of the church as a whole. They do not believe this false charge, but they wish Paul to set it straight. Paul had made his position clear in his Epistles (I Corinthians, Galatians, Romans) for all who cared to know. *Telling them not to circumcise their children* (*legōn mē peritem-*

nein autous ta tekna). The participle *legōn* agrees with "thou" (Paul), the subject of *didaskeis*. This is not indirect assertion, but indirect command, hence the negative *mē* instead of *ou* with the infinitive (Robertson, *Grammar*, p.1046). The point is not that Paul stated what the Jewish Christians in the dispersion do, but that he says that they (*autous* accusative of general reference) are not to go on circumcising (*peritemnein*, present active infinitive) their children. Paul taught the very opposite (I Cor. 7:18) and had Timothy circumcised (Acts 16:3) because he was half Jew and half Greek. His own practice is stated in I Cor. 9:19 ("to the Jews as a Jew"). *Neither to walk after the customs* (*mēde tois ethesin peripatein*). Locative case with infinitive *peripatein*. The charge was here enlarged to cover it all and to make Paul out an enemy of Jewish life and teachings. That same charge had been made against Stephen when young Saul (Paul) was the leader (6:14): "Will change the customs (*ethē* the very word used here) which Moses delivered unto us." It actually seemed that some of the Jews cared more for Moses than for God (Acts 6:11). So much for the charge of the Judaizers.

22. *What is it therefore? (Ti oun estin?).* See this form of question by Paul (I Cor. 14:15, 26). What is to be done about it? Clearly James and the elders do not believe these misrepresentations of Paul's teaching, but many do. *They will certainly hear (pantōs akousontai). Pantōs* is old adverb, by all means, altogether, wholly, certainly as here and 28:4; Luke 4:23; I Cor. 9:10. This future middle of *akouō* is the usual form instead of *akousō*. There was no way to conceal Paul's arrival nor was it wise to do so. B C and several cursives omit *dei plēthos sunelthein* (The multitude must needs come together).

23. *Do therefore this (touto oun poiēson).* The elders had thought out a plan of procedure by which Paul could set the whole matter straight. *We have (eisin hēmin).* "There

are to us" (dative of possession as in 18:10). Apparently members of the Jerusalem church. *Which have a vow on them* (*euchēn echontes aph'*—or *eph' heautōn*). Apparently a temporary Nazarite vow like that in Numb. 6:1–21 and its completion was marked by several offerings in the temple, the shaving of the head (Numb. 6:13–15). Either Paul or Aquila had such a vow on leaving Cenchreae (Acts 18:18). "It was considered a work of piety to relieve needy Jews from the expenses connected with this vow, as Paul does here" (Page). The reading *aph' heautōn* would mean that they had taken the vow voluntarily or of themselves (Luke 12:57; II Cor. 3:5), while *eph' heautōn* means that the vow lies on them still.

24. *These take* (*toutous paralabōn*). Second aorist active participle of *paralambanō*. Taking these alone. *Purify thyself with them* (*hagnisthēti sun autois*). First aorist passive imperative of *hagnizō*, old verb to purify, to make pure (*hagnos*). See the active voice in James 4:8; I Peter 1:22; I John 3:3. It is possible to see the full passive force here, "Be purified." But a number of aorist passives in the *Koinē* supplant the aorist middle forms and preserve the force of the middle (Robertson, *Grammar*, p. 819). That is possible here. Hence, "Purify thyself" is allowable. The word occurs in Numb. 6:1 for taking the Nazarite vow. The point is that Paul takes the vow with them. Note *hagnismou* in verse 26. *Be at charges for them* (*dapanēson ep' autois*). First aorist active imperative of old verb *dapanaō*, to incur expense, expend. Spend (money) upon (*ep'*) them. Ramsay (*St. Paul the Traveller*, etc., p. 310) argues that Paul had use of considerable money at this period, perhaps from his father's estate. The charges for five men would be considerable. "A poor man would not have been treated with the respect paid him at Caesarea, on the voyage, and at Rome" (Furneaux). *That they may shave their heads* (*hina xurēsontai tēn kephalēn*). Note *tēn kephalēn*, the head

(singular). Future middle indicative of *xuraō*, late form for the old *xureō*, to shave, middle to shave oneself or (causative) to get oneself shaved. This use of *hina* with the future indicative is like the classic *hopōs* with the future indicative and is common in the N.T. as in the *Koiné* (Robertson, *Grammar*, p. 984). *And all shall know* (*kai gnōsontai*). This future middle indicative of *ginōskō* (cf. *akousontai* in verse 22) may be independent of *hina* or dependent on it like *xurēsontai*, though some MSS. (H L P) have *gnōsin* (second aorist subjunctive, clearly dependent on *hina*). *Of which* (*hōn*). Genitive plural of the relative *ha* (accusative) object of the perfect passive verb *katēchēntai* (cf. verse 21 *katēchēthēsan*) attracted into the case of the omitted antecedent *toutōn*. The instruction still in effect. *But that thou thyself walkest orderly* (*alla stoicheis kai autos*). *Stoicheis* is an old verb to go in a row (from *stoichos*, row, rank, series), to walk in a line or by rule. In the N.T. only here and Gal. 5:25; Rom. 4:12; Phil. 3:16. The rule is the law and Paul was not a sidestepper. The idea of the verb is made plain by the participle *phulassōn ton nomon* (keeping or observing the law).

25. *We wrote* (*epesteilamen*). First aorist active of *epistellō*, to send to and so to write like our epistle (*epistolē*). Old verb, but in the N.T. only here and Acts 15:20; Heb. 13:22. It is the very word used by James in this "judgment" at the Conference (Acts 15:20, *episteilai*). B D here read *apesteilamen* from *apostellō*, to send away, to give orders. Wendt and Schuerer object to this as a gloss. Rather is it an explanation by James that he does not refer to the Gentile Christians whose freedom from the Mosaic ceremonial law was guaranteed at the Jerusalem Conference. James himself presided at that Conference and offered the resolution that was unanimously adopted. James stands by that agreement and repeats the main items (four: anything sacrificed to idols, blood, anything strangled, fornication, for discussion see

ch. 15) from which they are to keep themselves (direct middle *phulassesthai* of *phulassō*, indirect command after *krinantes* with accusative, *autous*, of general reference). James has thus again cleared the air about the Gentiles who have believed (*pepisteukotōn*, perfect active participle genitive plural of *pisteuō*). He asks that Paul will stand by the right of Jewish Christians to keep on observing the Mosaic law. He has put the case squarely and fairly.

26. *Took the men* (*paralabōn tous andras*). The very phrase used in verse 24 to Paul. *The next day* (*tēi echomenēi*). One of the phrases in 20:15 for the coming day. Locative case of time. *Purifying himself with them* (*sun autois hagnistheis*, first aorist passive participle of *hagnizō*). The precise language again of the recommendation in verse 24. Paul was conforming to the letter. *Went into the temple* (*eisēiei eis to hieron*). Imperfect active of *eiseimi* as in verse 18 which see. Went on into the temple, descriptive imperfect. Paul joined the four men in their vow of separation. *Declaring* (*diaggellōn*). To the priests what day he would report the fulfilment of the vow. The priests would desire notice of the sacrifice. This verb only used by Luke in N.T. except Rom. 11:17 (quotation from the LXX). It is not necessary to assume that the vows of each of the five expired on the same day (Rackham). *Until the offering was offered for every one of them* (*heōs hou prosēnechthē huper henos hekastou autōn hē prosphora*). This use of *heōs hou* (like *heōs*, alone) with the first aorist passive indicative *prosēnechthē* of *prospherō*, to offer, contemplates the final result (Robertson, *Grammar*, pp. 974f.) and is probably the statement of Luke added to Paul's announcement. He probably went into the temple one day for each of the brethren and one for himself. The question arises whether Paul acted wisely or unwisely in agreeing to the suggestion of James. What he did was in perfect harmony with his principle of accommodation in I Cor. 9:20 when no principle was involved. It is charged that here on

this occasion Paul was unduly influenced by considerations of expediency and was willing for the Jewish Christians to believe him more of a Jew than was true in order to placate the situation in Jerusalem. Furneaux calls it a compromise and a failure. I do not so see it. To say that is to obscure the whole complex situation. What Paul did was not for the purpose of conciliating his opponents, the Judaizers, who had diligently spread falsehoods about him in Jerusalem as in Corinth. It was solely to break the power of these "false apostles" over the thousands in Jerusalem who have been deluded by Paul's accusers. So far as the evidence goes that thing was accomplished. In the trouble that comes in Jerusalem and Caesarea the Judaizers cut no figure at all. The Jewish Christians do not appear in Paul's behalf, but there was no opportunity for them to do so. The explosion that came on the last day of Paul's appearance in the temple was wholly disconnected from his offerings for the four brethren and himself. It must be remembered that Paul had many kinds of enemies. The attack on him by these Jews from Asia had no connexion whatever with the slanders of the Judaizers about Paul's alleged teachings that Jewish Christians in the dispersion should depart from the Mosaic law. That slander was put to rest forever by his following the advice of James and justifies the wisdom of that advice and Paul's conduct about it.

27. *The seven days* (*hai hepta hēmerai*). For which Paul had taken the vow, though there may be an allusion to the pentecostal week for which Paul had desired to be present (20:16). There is no necessary connexion with the vow in 18:15. In 24:17 Paul makes a general reference to his purpose in coming to Jerusalem to bring alms and offerings (*prosphoras*, sacrifices). Paul spent seven days in Troas (20:6), Tyre (21:4), and had planned for seven here if not more. It was on the last of the seven days when Paul was completing his offerings about the vows on all five that the incident

occurred that was to make him a prisoner for five years. *When they saw him in the temple* (*theasamenoi auton en tōi hierōi*). First aorist middle participle of *theaomai* (from *thea*, a view, cf. theatre) to behold. In the very act of honouring the temple these Jews from Asia raise a hue and cry that he is dishonouring it. Paul was not known by face now to many of the Jerusalem Jews, though once the leader of the persecution after the death of Stephen and the outstanding young Jew of the day. But the Jews in Ephesus knew him only too well, some of whom are here at the pentecostal feast. They had plotted against him in Ephesus to no purpose (Acts 19:23-41; 20:19), but now a new opportunity had come. It is possible that the cry was led by Alexander put forward by the Jews in Ephesus (19:33) who may be the same as Alexander the coppersmith who did Paul so much harm (II Tim. 4:14). Paul was not in the inner sanctuary (*ho naos*), but only in the outer courts (*to hieron*). *Stirred up all the multitude* (*sunecheon panta ton ochlon*). Imperfect (kept on) active of *suncheō* or *sunchunō* (*-unnō*), to pour together, to confuse as in Acts 2:6; 9:22; 19:31, 32; 21:31 and here to stir up by the same sort of confusion created by Demetrius in Ephesus where the same word is used twice (19:31, 32). The Jews from Ephesus had learned it from Demetrius the silversmith. *Laid hands on him* (*epebalan ep' auton tas cheiras*). Second aorist (ingressive, with endings of the first aorist, *-an*) active indicative of *epiballō*, old verb to lay upon, to attack (note repetition of *epi*). They attacked and seized Paul before the charge was made.

28. *Help* (*boētheite*). Present active imperative of *boētheō*, to run (*theō*) at a cry (*boē*), as if an outrage had been committed like murder or assault. *All men everywhere* (*pantas pantachēi*). Alliterative. *Pantachēi* is a variation in MSS., often *pantachou*, and here only in the N.T. The charges against Paul remind one of those against Stephen (Acts 6:13) in which Paul had participated according to his con-

fession (22:20). Like the charges against Stephen and Jesus before him truth and falsehood are mixed. Paul had said that being a Jew would not save a man. He had taught the law of Moses was not binding on Gentiles. He did hold, like Jesus and Stephen, that the temple was not the only place to worship God. But Paul gloried himself in being a Jew, considered the Mosaic law righteous for Jews, and was honouring the temple at this very moment. *And moreover also he brought Greeks also into the temple (eti te kai Hellēnas eisēgagen eis to hieron)*. Note the three particles (*eti te kai*), *and* (*te*) *still more* (*eti*) *also* or even (*kai*). Worse than his teaching (*didaskōn*) is his dreadful deed: he actually brought (*eisēgagen*, second aorist active indicative of *eisagō*). This he had a right to do if they only went into the court of the Gentiles. But these Jews mean to imply that Paul had brought Greeks beyond this court into the court of Israel. An inscription was found by Clermont-Ganneau in Greek built into the walls of a mosque on the Via Dolorosa that was on the wall dividing the court of Israel from the court of the Gentiles. Death was the penalty to any Gentile who crossed over into the Court of Israel (*The Athenaeum*, July, 1871). *Hath defiled this holy place* (*kekoinōken ton hagion topon touton*). Present perfect active of *koinoō*, to make common (see on 10:14). Note vivid change of tense, the defilement lasts (state of completion). All this is the substance of the call of these shrewd conspirators from Ephesus, Jews (not Jewish Christians, not even Judaizers) who hated him for his work there and who probably "spoke evil of the Way before the multitude" there so that Paul had to separate the disciples from the synagogue and go to the School of Tyrannus (19:9f.). These enemies of Paul had now raised the cry of "fire" and vanish from the scene completely (24:19). This charge was absolutely false as we shall see, made out of inferences of hate and suspicion.

29. *For (gar)*. Luke adds the reason for the wild charges

made against Paul. *They had before seen* (*ēsan proeōrakotes*). Periphrastic past perfect of *prooraō*, old verb to see before, whether time or place. Only twice in the N.T., here and Acts 2:25 quoted from Psa. 15:8. Note the double reduplication in -*eō*- as in Attic (Robertson, *Grammar*, p. 364). *With him in the city Trophimus the Ephesian* (*Trophimon ton Ephesion en tēi polei sun autōi*). The Jews from Asia (Ephesus) knew Trophimus by sight as well as Paul. One day they saw both of them together (*sun*) in the city. That was a fact. They had just seized Paul in the temple (*hieron*). That was another fact. *They supposed* (*enomizon*). Imperfect active of *nomizō*, common to think or suppose. Perfectly harmless word, but they did, as so many people do, put their supposed inference on the same basis with the facts. They did not see Trophimus with Paul now in the temple, nor had they ever seen him there. They simply argued that, if Paul was willing to be seen down street with a Greek Christian, he would not hesitate to bring him (therefore, did bring him, *eisēgagen* as in verse 28) into the temple, that is into the court of Israel and therefore both Paul and Trophimus were entitled to death, especially Paul who had brought him in (if he had) and, besides, they now had Paul. This is the way of the mob-mind in all ages. Many an innocent man has been rushed to his death by the fury of a lynching party.

30. *All the city was shaken* (*ekinēthē hē polis holē*). First aorist passive of *kineō*, common verb for violent motion and emotion. See also 24:5 where the word is used by Tertullus of Paul as the stirrer up of riots! *The people ran together* (*egeneto sundromē tou laou*). Rather, There came a running together (*sun-dromē* from *sun-trechō*) of the people. The cry spread like wildfire over the city and there was a pell-mell scramble or rush to get to the place of the disturbance. *They laid hold on Paul* (*epilabomenoi tou Paulou*). Second aorist middle participle of *epilambanomai* with the genitive (cf. *epebalan* in verse 27). *Dragged* (*heilkon*). Imperfect ac-

tive of *helkō* (and also *helkuō*), old verb to drag or draw. Imperfect tense vividly pictures the act as going on. They were saving the temple by dragging Paul outside. Curiously enough both *epilabomenoi* and *heilkusan* occur in 16:19 about the arrest of Paul and Silas in Philippi. *Straightway the doors were shut (eutheōs ekleisthēsan hai thurai)*. With a bang and at once. First aorist (effective) passive of *kleiō*. The doors between the inner court and the court of the Gentiles. But this was only the beginning, the preparation for the real work of the mob. They did not wish to defile the holy place with blood. The doors were shut by the Levites.

31. *As they were seeking to kill him (zētountōn autōn)*. Genitive absolute of *zēteō*, to seek, without *autōn* (they). This was their real purpose. *Tidings (phasis)*. From *phainō*, to show. Old word for the work of informers and then the exposure of secret crime. In LXX. Here only in the N.T. *Came up (anebē)*. Naturally in the wild uproar. The Roman guard during festivals was kept stationed in the Tower of Antonia at the northwest corner of the temple overlooking the temple and connected by stairs (verse 35). *To the chief captain (tōi chiliarchōi)*. Commander of a thousand men or cohort (Mark 15:16). His name was Claudius Lysias. *Of the band (tēs speirēs)*. Each legion had six tribunes and so each tribune (chiliarch) had a thousand if the cohort had its full quota. See on 10:1; 27:1. The word is the Latin *spira* (anything rolled up). Note the genitive *speirēs* instead of *speiras* (Attic). *Was in confusion (sunchunnetai)*. Present passive indicative of *sunchunnō* (see verse 27, *sunecheon*). This is what the conspirators had desired.

32. *Forthwith (exautēs)*. Common in the Koiné (*ex autēs*, supply *hōras*, hour). *He took (paralabōn)*. See verses 24 and 26. *Centurions (hekatontarchas)*. See on Luke 7:2 for discussion. Plural shows that Lysias the chiliarch took several hundred soldiers along (a centurion with each hundred). *Ran down (katedramen)*. Effective second aorist active in-

dicative of *katatrechō*. From the tower of Antonia, vivid scene. *And they* (*hoi de*). Demonstrative use of *hoi*. The Jewish mob who had begun the work of killing Paul (verse 31). *Left off beating Paul* (*epausanto tuptontes ton Paulon*). The participle with *pauomai* describes what they were already doing, the supplementary participle (Robertson, *Grammar*, p. 1121). They stopped before the job was over because of the sudden onset of the Roman soldiers. Some ten years before in a riot at the passover the Roman guard marched down and in the panic several hundred were trampled to death.

33. *Came near* (*eggisas*). First aorist active participle of *eggizō*, to draw near, *Koiné* verb from *eggus*, near, and common in the N.T. *Laid hold on him* (*epelabeto antou*). See same verb in verse 30. *To be bound* (*dethēnai*). First aorist passive infinitive of *deō* (see verse 11). *With two chains* (*halusesi dusi*). Instrumental case of *halusis*, old word from *a* privative and *luō* (not loosing, i.e. chaining). With two chains as a violent and seditious person, probably leader of a band of assassins (verse 38). See on Mark 5:4. *Inquired* (*epunthaneto*). Imperfect middle of *punthanomai*, old and common verb used mainly by Luke in the N.T. Lysias repeated his inquiries. *Who he was* (*tis eiē*). Present active optative of *eimi* changed from *estin* (present indicative) in the indirect question, a change not obligatory after a past tense, but often done in the older Greek, rare in the N.T. (Robertson, *Grammar*, p. 1043f.). *And what he had done* (*kai ti estin pepoiēkōs*). Periphrastic perfect active indicative of *poieō* here retained, not changed to the optative as is true of *eiē* from *estin* in the same indirect question, illustrating well the freedom about it.

34. *Some shouting one thing, some another* (*alloi allo ti epephōnoun*). Same idiom of *alloi allo* as in 19:32 which see. The imperfect of *epiphōneō*, to call out to, suits well the idiom. This old verb occurs in the N.T. only in Luke and Acts

(already in 12:22). *When he could not know* (*mē dunamenou autou gnōnai*). Genitive absolute of present middle participle of *dunamai* with negative *mē* and second aorist active infinitive of *ginōskō*. *The certainty* (*to asphales*). Neuter articular adjective from *a* privative and *sphallō*, to make totter or fall. Old word, in the N.T. only in Acts 21:34; 22:30; 25:26; Phil. 3:1; Heb. 6:19. *Into the castle* (*eis tēn parembolēn*). *Koinē* word from *paremballō*, to cast in by the side of, to assign soldiers a place, to encamp (see on Luke 19:43). So *parembolē* comes to mean an interpolation, then an army drawn up (Heb. 11:34), but mainly an encampment (Heb. 13:11, 13), frequent in Polybius and LXX. So here barracks of the Roman soldiers in the tower of Antonia as in verse 37; 22:24; 23:10, 16, 32.

35. *Upon the stairs* (*epi tous anabathmous*). From *ana*, up, and *bainō*, to go. Late word, in LXX and *Koinē* writers. In the N.T. only here and verse 40. *So it was* (*sunebē*). Second aorist active of *sumbainō*, to happen (see on 20:19) with infinitive clause as subject here as often in the old Greek. *He was borne* (*bastazesthai auton*). Accusative of general reference with this subject infinitive, present passive of *bastazō*, to take up with the hands, literally as here. *Violence* (*bian*). See on Acts 5:26. *Biazō*, to use force, is from *bia*.

36. *Followed after* (*ēkolouthei*). Imperfect active of *akoluthéō*, was following. Cheated of their purpose to lynch Paul, they were determined to have his blood. *Crying out* (*krazontes*). Construction according to sense, plural masculine participle agreeing with neuter singular substantive *plēthos* (Robertson, *Grammar*, p. 401). *Away with him* (*Aire auton*). The very words used by the mob to Pilate when they chose Barabbas in preference to Jesus (Luke 23:18, *Aire touton*). He will hear it again from this same crowd (Acts 22:22). It is the present imperative (*aire*) as in Luke 23:18, but some may have used the urgent aorist active imperative as also

in the case of Jesus (John 19:15, *āron, āron* with *stauróson* added). Luke does not say that this mob demanded crucifixion for Paul. He was learning what it was to share the sufferings of Christ as the sullen roar of the mob's yells rolled on and on in his ears.

37. *May I say something unto thee?* (*Ei exestin moi eipein ti pros se?*). On this use of *ei* in a direct question see on 1:6. The calm self-control of Paul in the presence of this mob is amazing. His courteous request to Lysias was in Greek to the chiliarch's amazement. *Dost thou know Greek?* (*Hellēnisti ginōskeis?*). Old Greek adverb in -*i* from *Hellēnizō*, meaning "in Greek." "Do you know it in Greek?" In the N.T. only here and John 19:20. *Art thou not then the Egyptian?* (*Ouk ara su ei ho Aiguptios?*). Expects the answer *Yes* and *ara* argues the matter (therefore). The well-known (*ho*) Egyptian who had given the Romans so much trouble. *Stirred up to sedition* (*anastatōsas*). First aorist active participle of *anastatoō*, a late verb from *anastatos*, outcast, and so to unsettle, to stir up, to excite, once known only in LXX and Acts 17:6 (which see); 21:38; Gal. 5:12, but now found in several papyri examples with precisely this sense to upset. *Of the Assassins* (*tōn sikariōn*). Latin word *sicarius*, one who carried a short sword *sica* under his cloak, a cutthroat. Josephus uses this very word for bands of robbers under this Egyptian (*War* II. 17, 6 and 13, 5; *Ant.* XX. 8, 10). Josephus says that there were 30,000 who gathered on the Mount of Olives to see the walls of Jerusalem fall down and not merely 4,000 as Lysias does here. But Lysias may refer to the group that were armed thus (banditti) the core of the mob of 30,000. Lysias at once saw by Paul's knowledge of Greek that he was not the famous Egyptian who led the Assassins and escaped himself when Felix attacked and slew the most of them.

39. *I am* (*Egō men eimi*). In contrast with the wild guess of Lysias Paul uses *men* and *de*. He tells briefly who he is:

a *Jew* (*Ioudaios*) by race, *of Tarsus in Cilicia* (*Tarseus tēs Kilikias*) by country, belonging to Tarsus (this adjective *Tarseus* only here and Acts 9:11), and proud of it, one of the great cities of the empire with a great university. *A citizen of no mean city* (*ouk asēmou poleōs politēs*). Litotes again, "no mean" (*asēmos*, old adjective, unmarked, *a* privative and *sēma*, mark, insignificant, here only in the N.T.). This same litotes used by Euripides of Athens (*Ion* 8). But Paul calls himself a citizen (*politēs*) of Tarsus. Note the "effective assonance" (Page) in *poleōs politēs*. Paul now (*de*) makes his request (*deomai*) of Lysias. *Give me leave* (*epitrepson moi*). First aorist active imperative of *epitrepō*, old and common verb to turn to, to permit, to allow. It was a strange request and a daring one, to wish to speak to this mob howling for Paul's blood.

40. *When he had given him leave* (*epitrepsantos autou*). Genitive absolute of aorist active participle of the same verb *epitrepō*. *Standing on the stairs* (*hestōs epi tōn anabathmōn*). Second perfect active participle of *histēmi*, to place, but intransitive to stand. Dramatic scene. Paul had faced many audiences and crowds, but never one quite like this. Most men would have feared to speak, but not so Paul. He will speak about himself only as it gives him a chance to put Christ before this angry Jewish mob who look on Paul as a renegade Jew, a turncoat, a deserter, who went back on Gamaliel and all the traditions of his people, who not only turned from Judaism to Christianity, but who went after Gentiles and treated Gentiles as if they were on a par with Jews. Paul knows only too well what this mob thinks of him. *Beckoned with the hand* (*kateseise tēi cheiri*). He shook down to the multitude with the hand (instrumental case *cheiri*), while Alexander, Luke says (19:33), "shook down the hand" (accusative with the same verb, which see). In 26:1 Paul reached out the hand (*ekteinas tēn cheira*). *When there was made a great silence* (*pollēs sigēs genomenēs*). Genitive abso-

lute again with second aorist middle participle of *ginomai*, "much silence having come." Paul waited till silence had come. *In the Hebrew language* (*tēi Ebraidi dialektōi*). The Aramaean which the people in Jerusalem knew better than the Greek. Paul could use either tongue at will. His enemies had said in Corinth that "his bodily presence was weak and his speech contemptible" (II Cor. 10:10). But surely even they would have to admit that Paul's stature and words reach heroic proportions on this occasion. Self-possessed with majestic poise Paul faces the outraged mob beneath the stairs.

CHAPTER XXII

1. *Brethren and fathers* (*Andres adelphoi kai pateres*).
Men, brethren, and fathers. The very language used by
Stephen (7:2) when arraigned before the Sanhedrin with
Paul then present. Now Paul faces a Jewish mob on the
same charges brought against Stephen. These words are
those of courtesy and dignity (*amoris et honoris nomina*,
Page). These men were Paul's brother Jews and were (many
of them) official representatives of the people (Sanhedrists,
priests, rabbis). Paul's purpose is conciliatory, he employs
"his ready tact" (Rackham). *The defence which I now
make unto you* (*mou tēs pros humas nuni apologias*). Literally,
My defence to you at this time. *Nuni* is a sharpened form
(by -*i*) of *nun* (now), just now. The term *apologia* (apology)
is not our use of the word for apologizing for an offence, but
the original sense of defence for his conduct, his life. It is an
old word from *apologeomai*, to talk oneself off a charge, to
make defence. It occurs also in Acts 25:16 and then also in
I Cor. 9:3; II Cor. 7:11; Phil. 1:7, 16; II Tim. 4:16; I Peter
3:15. Paul uses it again in Acts 25:16 as here about his defence against the charges made by the Jews from Asia. He
is suspected of being a renegade from the Mosaic law and
charged with specific acts connected with the alleged profanation of the temple. So Paul speaks in Aramaic and re-
cites the actual facts connected with his change from Judaism
to Christianity. The facts make the strongest argument. He
first recounts the well-known story of his zeal for Judaism
in the persecution of the Christians and shows why the
change came. Then he gives a summary of his work among
the Gentiles and why he came to Jerusalem this time. He
answers the charge of enmity to the people and the law and of

desecration of the temple. It is a speech of great skill and force, delivered under remarkable conditions. The one in chapter 26 covers some of the same ground, but for a slightly different purpose as we shall see. For a discussion of the three reports in Acts of Paul's conversion see chapter 9. Luke has not been careful to make every detail correspond, though there is essential agreement in all three.

2. *He spake* (*prosephōnei*). Imperfect active, was speaking. See aorist active *prosephōnēsen* in 21:40. *They were the more quiet* (*mällon pareschon hēsuchian*). Literally, The more (*mällon*) they furnished or supplied (second aorist active indicative of *parechō*) quietness (*hēsuchian*, old word, in the N.T. only here and II Thess. 3:12; I Tim. 2:11ff.). Precisely this idiom occurs in Plutarch (*Cor.* 18) and the LXX (Job 34:29). Knowling notes the fondness of Luke for words of silence (*sigē, sigaō, hēsuchazō*) as in Luke 14:4; 15:26; Acts 11:18; 12:17; 15:12; 21:14, 40. It is a vivid picture of the sudden hush that swept over the vast mob under the spell of the Aramaic. They would have understood Paul's *Koiné* Greek, but they much preferred the Aramaic. It was a masterstroke.

3. *I am a Jew* (*Egō eimi anēr Ioudaios*). Note use of *Egō* for emphasis. Paul recounts his Jewish advantages or privileges with manifest pride as in Acts 26:4f.; II Cor. 11:22; Gal. 1:14; Phil. 3:4–7. *Born* (*gegennēmenos*). Perfect passive participle of *gennaō*. See above in 21:39 for the claim of Tarsus as his birth-place. He was a Hellenistic Jew, not an Aramaean Jew (cf. Acts 6:1). *Brought up* (*anatethrammenos*). Perfect passive participle again of *anatrephō*, to nurse up, to nourish up, common old verb, but in the N.T. only here, 7:20ff., and MSS. in Luke 4:16. The implication is that Paul was sent to Jerusalem while still young, "from my youth" (26:4), how young we do not know, possibly thirteen or fourteen years old. He apparently had not seen Jesus in the flesh (II Cor. 5:16). *At the feet of Gamaliel* (*pros*

tous podas Gamaliēl). The rabbis usually sat on a raised seat with the pupils in a circle around either on lower seats or on the ground. Paul was thus nourished in Pharisaic Judaism as interpreted by Gamaliel, one of the lights of Judaism. For remarks on Gamaliel see chapter 5:34ff. He was one of the seven Rabbis to whom the Jews gave the highest title *Rabban* (our Rabbi). *Rabbi* (my teacher) was next, the lowest being *Rab* (teacher). "As Aquinas among the schoolmen was called *Doctor Angelicus*, and Bonaventura *Doctor Seraphicus*, so Gamaliel was called *the Beauty of the Law*" (Conybeare and Howson). *Instructed (pepaideumenos)*. Perfect passive participle again (each participle beginning a clause), this time of *paideuō*, old verb to train a child (*pais*) as in 7:22 which see. In this sense also in I Tim. 1:20; Tit. 2:12. Then to chastise as in Luke 23:16, 22 (which see); II Tim. 2:25; Heb. 12:6f. *According to the strict manner (kata akribeian)*. Old word, only here in N.T. Mathematical accuracy, minute exactness as seen in the adjective in 26:5. See also Rom. 10:2; Gal. 1:4; Phil. 3:4–7. *Of our fathers (patrōiou)*. Old adjective from *patēr*, only here and 24:14 in N.T. Means descending from father to son, especially property and other inherited privileges. *Patrikos* (patrician) refers more to personal attributes and affiliations. *Being zealous for God (zēlōtēs huparchōn tou theou)*. Not adjective, but substantive *zealot* (same word used by James of the thousands of Jewish Christians in Jerusalem, 21:20 which see) with objective genitive *tou theou* (for God). See also verse 14; 28:17; II Tim. 1:3 where he makes a similar claim. So did Peter (Acts 3:13; 5:30) and Stephen (7:32). Paul definitely claims, whatever freedom he demanded for Gentile Christians, to be personally "a zealot for God" "even as ye all are this day" (*kathōs pantes humeis este sēmeron*). In his conciliation he went to the limit and puts himself by the side of the mob in their zeal for the law, mistaken as they were about him. He was generous surely to interpret their fanatical frenzy as zeal for God. But Paul is sincere as he proceeds to show by appeal to his own conduct.

4. *And I* (*hos*). *I who*, literally. *This Way* (*tautēn tēn hodon*). The very term used for Christianity by Luke concerning Paul's persecution (9:2), which see. Here it "avoids any irritating name for the Christian body" (Furneaux) by using this Jewish terminology. *Unto the death* (*achri thanatou*). Unto death, actual death of many as 26:10 shows. *Both men and women* (*andras te kai gunaikas*). Paul felt ashamed of this fact and it was undoubtedly in his mind when he pictured his former state as "a blasphemer, and a persecutor, and injurious (I Tim. 1:13), the first of sinners" (I Tim. 1:15). But it showed the lengths to which Paul went in his zeal for Judaism.

5. *Doth bear me witness* (*marturei moi*). Present active indicative as if still living. Caiaphas was no longer high priest now, for Ananias is at this time (23:2), though he may be still alive. *All the estate of the elders* (*pan to presbuterion*). All the eldership or the Sanhedrin (4:5) of which Paul was probably then a member (26:10). Possibly some of those present were members of the Sanhedrin then (some 20 odd years ago). *From whom* (*par' hōn*). The high priest and the Sanhedrin. *Letters unto the brethren* (*epistalas pros tous adelphous*). Paul still can tactfully call the Jews his "brothers" as he did in Rom. 9:3. There is no bitterness in his heart. *Journeyed* (*eporeuomēn*). Imperfect middle indicative of *poreuomai*, and a vivid reality to Paul still as he was going on towards Damascus. *To bring also* (*axōn kai*). Future active participle of *agō*, to express purpose, one of the few N.T. examples of this classic idiom (Robertson, *Grammar*, p. 1118). *Them which were there* (*tous ekeise ontas*). *Constructio praegnans*. The usual word would be *ekei* (there), not *ekeise* (thither). Possibly the Christians who had fled to Damascus, and so were there (Robertson, *Grammar*, p. 548). *In bonds* (*dedemenous*). Perfect passive participle of *deō*,

predicate position, "bound." *For to be punished* (*hina timōrēthōsin*). First aorist passive subjunctive of *timōreō*, old verb to avenge, to take vengeance on. In the N.T. only here, and 26:11. Pure final clause with *hina*. He carried his persecution outside of Palestine just as later he carried the gospel over the Roman empire.

6. *And it came to pass* (*egeneto de*). Rather than the common *kai egeneto* and with the infinitive (*periastrapsai*), one of the three constructions with *kai* (*de*) *egeneto* by Luke (Robertson, *Grammar*, pp. 1042f.), followed by *kai*, by finite verb, by subject infinitive as here. *As I made my journey* (*moi poreuomenōi*). To me (dative after *egeneto*, happened to me) journeying (participle agreeing with *moi*). See this same idiom in verse 17. Luke uses *egeneto de* seventeen times in the gospel and twenty-one in the Acts. *Unto Damascus* (*tēi Damaskōi*). Dative after *eggizonti* (drawing nigh to). *About noon* (*peri mesēmbrian*). Mid (*mesos*) day (*hēmera*), old word, in the N.T. only here and 8:26 which see where it may mean "toward the south." An item not in ch. 9. *Shone round about me* (*periastrapsai peri eme*). First aorist active infinitive of *periastraptō*, to flash around, in LXX and late Greek, in the N.T. only here and 9:3 which see. Note repetition of *peri*. *A great light* (*phōs hikanon*). Luke's favourite word *hikanon* (considerable). Accusative of general reference with the infinitive.

7. *I fell* (*epesa*). Second aorist active indicative with -*a* rather than *epeson*, the usual form of *piptō*. *Unto the ground* (*eis to edaphos*). Old word, here alone in N.T. So the verb *edaphizō*, is in Luke 19:44 alone in the N.T. *A voice saying* (*phōnēs legousēs*). Genitive after *ēkousa*, though in 26:14 the accusative is used after *ēkousa*, as in 22:14 after *akousai*, either being allowable. See on 9:7 for discussion of the difference in case. Saul's name repeated each time (9:4; 22:7; 26:14). Same question also in each report: "Why persecuted thou *me*?" (*Ti me diōkeis?*). These piercing words stuck in Paul's mind.

8. *Of Nazareth* (*ho Nazōraios*). The Nazarene, not in 9:5 or 26:15 and here because Jesus is mentioned now for the first time in the address. The form *Nazōraios* as in Matt. 2:23 (which see) is used also in 24:5 for the followers of Jesus instead of *Nazarēnos* as in Mark 1:24, etc. (which see).

9. *But they heard not the voice* (*tēn de phōnēn ouk ēkousan*). The accusative here may be used rather than the genitive as in verse 7 to indicate that those with Paul did not understand what they heard (9:7) just as they beheld the light (22:9), but did not see Jesus (9:7). The difference in cases allows this distinction, though it is not always observed as just noticed about 22:14 and 26:14. The verb *akouō* is used in the sense of understand (Mark 4:33; I Cor. 14:2). It is one of the evidences of the genuineness of this report of Paul's speech that Luke did not try to smooth out apparent discrepancies in details between the words of Paul and his own record already in ch. 9. The Textus Receptus adds in this verse: "And they became afraid" (*kai emphoboi egenonto*). Clearly not genuine.

10. *Into Damascus* (*eis Damaskon*). In 9:6 simply "into the city" (*eis tēn polin*). *Of all things which* (*peri pantōn hōn*). *Hōn*, relative plural attracted to genitive of antecedent from accusative *ha*, object of *poiēsai* (do). *Are appointed for thee* (*tetaktai soi*). Perfect passive indicative of *tassō*, to appoint, to order, with dative *soi*. Compare with *hoti se dei* of 9:6. The words were spoken to Paul, of course, in the Aramaic, Saoul, Saoul.

11. *I could not see* (*ouk eneblepon*). Imperfect active of *emblepō*, I was not seeing, same fact stated in 9:8. Here the reason as "for the glory of that light" (*apo tēs doxēs tou phōtos ekeinou*). *Being led by the hand* (*cheiragōgoumenos*). Present passive participle of *cheiragōgeō*, the same verb used in 9:8 (*cheiragōgountes*) which see. Late verb, in the N.T. only in these two places. In LXX.

12. *A devout man according to the law* (*eulabēs kata ton nomon*). See on 2:5; 8:2; Luke 2:25 for the adjective *eulabēs*. Paul adds "according to the law" to show that he was introduced to Christianity by a devout Jew and no lawbreaker (Lewin).

13. *I looked up on him* (*anablepsa eis auton*). First aorist active indicative and same word as *anablepson* (Receive thy sight). Hence here the verb means as the margin of the Revised Version has it: "I received my sight and looked upon him." For "look up" see John 9:11.

14. *Hath appointed thee* (*proecheirisato*). First aorist middle indicative of *procheirizō*, old verb to put forth into one's hands, to take into one's hands beforehand, to plan, propose, determine. In the N.T. only in Acts 3:20; 22:14; 26:16. Three infinitives after this verb of God's purpose about Paul: *to know* (*gnōnai*, second aorist active of *ginōskō*) his will, *to see* (*idein*, second aorist active of *horaō*) the Righteous One (cf. 3:14), *to hear* (*akousai*, first aorist active of *akouō*) a voice from his mouth.

15. *A witness for him* (*martus autōi*). As in 1:8. *Of what* (*hōn*). Attraction of the accusative relative *ha* to the genitive case of the unexpressed antecedent *toutōn*. *Thou hast seen and heard* (*heōrakas*, present perfect active indicative *kai ēkousas*, first aorist active indicative). This subtle change of tense is not preserved in the English. Blass properly cites the perfect *heōraka* in I Cor. 9:1 as proof of Paul's enduring qualification for the apostleship.

16. *Be baptized* (*baptisai*). First aorist middle (causative), not passive, Get thyself baptized (Robertson, *Grammar*, p. 808). Cf. I Cor. 10:2. Submit yourself to baptism. So as to *apolousai*, Get washed off as in I Cor. 6:11. It is possible, as in 2:38, to take these words as teaching baptismal remission or salvation by means of baptism, but to do so is in my opinion a complete subversion of Paul's vivid and picturesque language. As in Rom. 6:4–6 where baptism is the

picture of death, burial and resurrection, so here baptism pictures the change that had already taken place when Paul surrendered to Jesus on the way (verse 10). Baptism here pictures the washing away of sins by the blood of Christ.

17. *When I had returned* (*moi hupostrepsanti*), *while I prayed* (*proseuchomenou mou*), *I fell* (*genesthai me*). Note dative *moi* with *egeneto* as in verse 6, genitive *mou* (genitive absolute with *proseuchomenou*), accusative of general reference *me* with *genesthai*, and with no effort at uniformity, precisely as in 15:22 and 23 which see. The participle is especially liable to such examples of anacolutha (Robertson, *Grammar*, p. 439).

18. *Saw him saying* (*idein auton legonta*). The first visit after his conversion when they tried to kill him in Jerusalem (9:29). *Because* (*dioti, dia* and *hoti*), *for that*.

19. *Imprisoned and beat* (*ēmēn phulakizōn kai derōn*). Periphrastic imperfect active of *phulakizō* (LXX and late *Koinē*, here alone in the N.T.) and *derō* (old verb to skin, to beat as in Matt. 21:35 which see). *In every synagogue* (*kata tas sunagogas*). Up and down (*kata*) in the synagogues.

20. *Was shed* (*exechunneto*). Imperfect passive of *ekchunnō* (see on Matt. 23:35), was being shed. *Witness* (*marturos*). And "martyr" also as in Rev. 2:13; 17:6. Transition state for the word here. *I also was standing by* (*kai autos ēmēn ephestōs*). Periphrastic second past perfect in form, but imperfect (linear) in sense since *hestōs = histamenos* (intransitive). *Consenting* (*suneudokōn*). The very word used by Luke in Acts 8:1 about Paul. *Koinē* word for being pleased at the same time with (cf. Luke 11:48). Paul adds here the item of "guarding the clothes of those who were slaying (*anairountōn* as in Luke 23:32; Acts 12:2) him" (Stephen). Paul recalls the very words of protest used by him to Jesus. He did not like the idea of running away to save his own life right where he had helped slay Stephen. He is getting on dangerous ground.

21. *I will send thee forth far hence unto the Gentiles* (*Egō eis ethnē makran exapostelō se*). Future active of the double (*ex*, out, *apo*, off or away) compound of *exapostellō*, common word in the Koiné (cf. Luke 24:49). This is a repetition by Jesus of the call given in Damascus through Ananias (9:15). Paul had up till now avoided the word Gentiles, but at last it had to come, "the fatal word" (Farrar).

22. *They gave him audience* (*ēkouon*). Imperfect active, they kept on listening, at least with respectful attention. *Unto this word* (*achri toutou tou logou*). But "this word" was like a spark in a powder magazine or a torch to an oil tank. The explosion of pent-up indignation broke out instantly worse than at first (21:30). *Away with such a fellow from the earth* (*Aire apo tēs gēs ton toiouton*). They renew the cry with the very words in 21:36, but with "from the earth" for vehemence. *For it is not fit* (*ou gar kathēken*). Imperfect active of *kathēkō*, old verb to come down to, to become, to fit. In the N.T. only here and Rom. 1:28. The imperfect is a neat Greek idiom for impatience about an obligation: It was not fitting, he ought to have been put to death long ago. The obligation is conceived as not lived up to like our "ought" (past of owe). See Robertson, *Grammar*, p. 886.

23. *As they cried out* (*kraugazontōn autōn*). Genitive absolute with present active participle of *kraugazō*, a rare word in the old Greek from *kraugē* (a cry). See on Matt. 12:19. Two other genitive absolutes here, *rhiptountōn* (throwing off, present active participle, frequent active variation of *rhiptō*) and *ballontōn* (present active participle of *ballō*, flinging). These present participles give a lively picture of the uncontrolled excitement of the mob in their spasm of wild rage.

24. *That he be examined by scourging* (*mastixin anetazesthai auton*). The present passive infinitive of *anetazō* in indirect command after *eipas* (bidding). This verb does not occur in the old Greek (which used *exetazō* as in Matt. 2:8), first

in the LXX, in the N.T. only here and verse 29, but Milligan and Moulton's *Vocabulary* quotes an Oxyrhynchus papyrus of A.D. 127 which has a prefect using the word directing government clerks to "examine" (*anetazein*) documents and glue them together into volumes (*tomoi*). The word was evidently in use for such purposes. It was a kind of "third degree" applied to Paul by the use of scourges (*mastixin*), instrumental plural of *mastix*, old word for whip, as in Heb. 11:36. But this way of beginning an inquiry by torture (inquisition) was contrary to Roman law (Page): *Non esse a tormentis incipiendum, Divus Augustus statuit. That he might know* (*hina epignōi*). Final clause with *hina* and second aorist active subjunctive of *epignōskō* (full knowledge). Lysias was as much in the dark as ever, for Paul's speech had been in Aramaic and this second explosion was a mystery to him like the first. *They so shouted* (*houtōs epephōnoun*). Imperfect active progressive imperfect had been so shouting.

25. *When they had tied him up* (*hōs proeteinan auton*). First aorist active indicative of *proteinō*, old verb to stretch forward, only here in the N.T. Literally, "When they stretched him forward." *With the thongs* (*tois himasin*). If the instrumental case of *himas*, old word for strap or thong (for sandals as Mark 1:7, or for binding criminals as here), then Paul was bent forward and tied by the thongs to a post in front to expose his back the better to the scourges. But *tois himasin* may be dative case and then it would mean "for the lashes." In either case it is a dreadful scene of terrorizing by the chiliarch. *Unto the centurion that stood by* (*pros ton hestōta hekatontarchon*). He was simply carrying out the orders of the chiliarch (cf. Matt. 27:54). Why had not Paul made protest before this? *Is it lawful?* (*ei exestin?*). This use of *ei* in indirect questions we have had before (1:6). *A Roman and uncondemned* (*Romaion kai akatakriton*). Just as in 16:37 which see. Blass says of Paul's question: *Interrogatio subironica est confidentiae plena.*

26. *What art thou about to do?* (*Ti melleis poiein?*). On the point of doing, sharp warning.

27. *Art thou a Roman?* (*Su Romaios ei?*). *Thou* (emphatic position) a Roman? It was unbelievable.

28. *With a great sum* (*pollou kephalaiou*). The use of *kephalaiou* (from *kephalē*, head) for sums of money (principal as distinct from interest) is old and frequent in the papyri. Our word capital is from *caput* (head). The genitive is used here according to rule for price. "The sale of the Roman citizenship was resorted to by the emperors as a means of filling the exchequer, much as James I. made baronets" (Page). Dio Cassius (LX., 17) tells about Messalina the wife of Claudius selling Roman citizenship. Lysias was probably a Greek and so had to buy his citizenship. *But I am a Roman born* (*Egō de kai gegennēmai*). Perfect passive indicative of *gennaō*. The word "Roman" not in the Greek. Literally, "But I have been even born one," (i.e. born a Roman citizen). There is calm and simple dignity in this reply and pardonable pride. Being a citizen of Tarsus (21:39) did not make Paul a Roman citizen. Tarsus was an *urbs libera*, not a *colonia* like Philippi. Some one of his ancestors (father, grandfather) obtained it perhaps as a reward for distinguished service. Paul's family was of good social position. "He was educated by the greatest of the Rabbis; he was at an early age entrusted by the Jewish authorities with an important commission; his nephew could gain ready access to the Roman tribune; he was treated as a person of consequence by Felix, Festus, Agrippa, and Julius" (Furneaux).

29. *Departed from him* (*apestēsan ap' autou*). Second aorist active indicative (intransitive) of *aphistēmi*, stood off from him at once. *Was afraid* (*ephobēthē*). Ingressive aorist passive indicative of *phobeomai*, became afraid. He had reason to be. *That he was a Roman* (*hoti Romaios estin*). Indirect assertion with tense of *estin* retained. *Because he had bound him* (*hoti auton ēn dedekōs*). Causal *hoti* here after

declarative *hoti* just before. Periphrastic past perfect active of *deō*, to bind.

30. *To know the certainty* (*gnōnai to asphales*). Same idiom in 21:34 which see. *Wherefore he was accused* (*to ti kategoreitai*). Epexegetical after *to asphales*. Note article (accusative case) with the indirect question here as in Luke 22:1, 23, 24 (which see), a neat idiom in the Greek. *Commanded* (*ekeleusen*). So the Sanhedrin had to meet, but in the Tower of Antonia, for he brought Paul down (*katagagōn*, second aorist active participle of *katagō*). *Set him* (*estēsen*). First aorist active (transitive) indicative of *histēmi*, not the intransitive second aorist *estē*. Lysias is determined to find out the truth about Paul, more puzzled than ever by the important discovery that he has a Roman citizen on his hands in this strange prisoner.

CHAPTER XXIII

1. *Looking steadfastly (atenisas)*. See on this word 1:10; 3:12; 6:15; 7:55; 13:9. Paul may have had weak eyes, but probably the earnest gaze was to see if he recognized any faces that were in the body that tried Stephen and to which he apparently once belonged. *I have lived before God (pepoliteumai tōi theōi)*. Perfect middle indicative of *politeuō*, old verb to manage affairs of city (*polis*) or state, to be a citizen, behave as a citizen. In the N.T. only here and Phil. 1:27. The idea of citizenship was Greek and Roman, not Jewish. "He had lived as God's citizen, as a member of God's commonwealth" (Rackham). God (*theōi*) is the dative of personal interest. As God looked at it and in his relation to God. *In all good conscience unto this day (pasēi suneidēsei agathēi achri tautēs tēs hēmeras)*. This claim seems to lack tact, but for brevity's sake Paul sums up a whole speech in it. He may have said much more than Luke here reports along the line of his speech the day before, but Paul did not make this claim without consideration. It appears to contradict his confession as the chief of sinners (I Tim. 1:13–16). But that depends on one's interpretation of "good conscience." The word *suneidēsis* is literally "joint-knowledge" in Greek, Latin (*conscientia*) and English "conscience" from the Latin. It is a late word from *sunoida*, to know together, common in O.T., Apocrypha, Philo, Plutarch, New Testament, Stoics, ecclesiastical writers. In itself the word simply means consciousness of one's own thoughts (Heb. 10:2), or of one's own self, then consciousness of the distinction between right and wrong (Rom. 2:15) with approval or disapproval. But the conscience is not an infallible guide and acts according

397

to the light that it has (I Cor. 8:7, 10; I Peter 2:19). The conscience can be contaminated (Heb. 10:22, evil *ponērās*). All this and more must be borne in mind in trying to understand Paul's description of his motives as a persecutor. Alleviation of his guilt comes thereby, but not removal of guilt as he himself felt (I Tim. 1:13-16). He means to say to the Sanhedrin that he persecuted Christians as a conscientious (though mistaken) Jew (Pharisee) just as he followed his conscience in turning from Judaism to Christianity. It is a pointed disclaimer against the charge that he is a renegade Jew, an opposer of the law, the people, the temple. Paul addresses the Sanhedrin as an equal and has no "apologies" (in our sense) to make for his career as a whole. The golden thread of consistency runs through, as a good citizen in God's commonwealth. He had the consolation of a good conscience (I Peter 3:16). The word does not occur in the Gospels and chiefly in Paul's Epistles, but we see it at work in John 8:9 (the interpolation 7:53 to 8:11).

2. *Ananias (Hananias).* Not the one in Luke 3:2; John 18:13; Acts 4:7, but the son of Nebedaeus, nominated high priest by Herod, King of Chalcis, A.D. 48 and till A.D. 59. He was called to Rome A.D. 52 to answer "a charge of rapine and cruelty made against him by the Samaritans, but honourably acquitted" (Page). Though high priest, he was a man of bad character. *Them that stood by him (tois parestōsin autōi).* Dative case of second perfect participle of *paristēmi,* to place, and intransitive. See the same form in verse 4 (*parestōtes*). *To smite him on the mouth (tuptein autou to stoma).* See on 12:45; and 18:17. Cf. the treatment of Jesus (John 18:22). Ananias was provoked by Paul's self-assertion while on trial before his judges. "The act was illegal and peculiarly offensive to a Jew at the hands of a Jew" (Knowling). More self-control might have served Paul better. Smiting the mouth or cheek is a peculiarly irritating offence and one not uncommon among the Jews

and this fact gives point to the command of Jesus to turn the other check (Luke 6:29 where *tuptō* is also used).

3. *Thou whited wall* (*toiche kekoniamene*). Perfect passive participle of *koniaō* (from *konia*, dust or lime). The same word used in Matt. 23:27 for "whited sepulchres" (*taphoi kekoniamenoi*) which see. It is a picturesque way of calling Ananias a hypocrite, undoubtedly true, but not a particularly tactful thing for a prisoner to say to his judge, not to say Jewish high priest. Besides, Paul had hurled back at him the word *tuptein* (*smite*) in his command, putting it first in the sentence (*tuptein se mellei ho theos*) in strong emphasis. Clearly Paul felt that he, not Ananias, was living as a good citizen in God's commonwealth. *And sittest thou to judge me?* (*Kai su kathēi krinōn me?*) Literally, "And thou (being what thou art) art sitting (*kathēi*, second person singular middle of *kathēmai*, late form for *kathēsai*, the uncontracted form) judging me." Cf. Luke 22:30. *Kai su* at the beginning of a question expresses indignation. *Contrary to the law* (*paranomōn*). Present active participle of *paranomeō*, old verb to act contrary to the law, here alone in the N.T., "acting contrary to the law."

4. *Of God* (*tou theou*). As God's representative in spite of his bad character (Deut. 17:8f.). Here was a charge of irreverence, to say the least. The office called for respect.

5. *I wist not* (*ouk ēidein*). Second past perfect of *oida* used as an imperfect. The Greek naturally means that Paul did not know that it was the high priest who gave the order to smite his mouth. If this view is taken, several things may be said by way of explanation. The high priest may not have had on his official dress as the meeting was called hurriedly by Lysias. Paul had been away so long that he may not have known Ananias on sight. And then Paul may have had poor eyesight or the high priest may not have been sitting in the official seat. Another way of ex-

plaining it is to say that Paul was so indignant, even angry,
at the command that he spoke without considering who it
was that gave the order. The Greek allows this idea also.
At any rate Paul at once recognizes the justice of the point
made against him. He had been guilty of irreverence against
the office of high priest as the passage from Ex. 22:18 (LXX)
shows and confesses his fault, but the rebuke was deserved.
Jesus did not threaten (I Peter 2:23) when smitten on the
cheek (John 18:22), but he did protest against the act and
did not turn the other cheek.

6. *But when Paul perceived* (*gnous de ho Paulos*).   Per-
ceiving (second aorist ingressive of *ginōskō*).   Paul quickly
saw that his cause was ruined before the Sanhedrin by his
unwitting attack on the high priest.   It was impossible to
get a fair hearing.   Hence, Vincent says, "Paul, with great
tact, seeks to bring the two parties of the council into col-
lision with each other."   So Alford argues with the motto
"divide and conquer."   Farrar condemns Paul and takes
24:21 as a confession of error here, but that is reading into
Paul's word about the resurrection more than he says.
Page considers Luke's report meagre and unsatisfactory.
Rackham thinks that the trial was already started and that
Paul repeated part of his speech of the day before when
"the Sadducees received his words with ostentatious scepti-
cism and ridicule: this provoked counter-expressions of
sympathy and credulity among the Pharisees."   But all
this is inference.   We do not have to adopt the Jesuitical
principle that the end justifies the means in order to see
shrewdness and hard sense in what Paul said and did.   Paul
knew, of course, that the Sanhedrin was nearly evenly
divided between Pharisees and Sadducees, for he himself
had been a Pharisee. *I am a Pharisee, a son of Pharisees*
(*Egō Pharisaios eimi huios Pharisaiōn*).   This was strictly
true as we know from his Epistles (Phil. 3:5). *Touching the
hope and resurrection of the dead I am called in question* (*peri*

elpidos kai anastaseōs nekrōn krinomai). This was true also and this is the point that Paul mentions in 24:21. His failure to mention again the fact that he was a Pharisee throws no discredit on Luke's report here. The chief point of difference between Pharisees and Sadducees was precisely this matter of the resurrection. And this was Paul's cardinal doctrine as a Christian minister. It was this fact that convinced him that Jesus was the Messiah and was "the very centre of his faith" (Page) and of his preaching. It was not a mere trick for Paul to proclaim this fact here and so divide the Sanhedrin. As a matter of fact, the Pharisees held aloof when the Sadducees persecuted Peter and the other apostles for preaching resurrection in the case of Jesus and even Gamaliel threw cold water on the effort to punish them for it (Acts 5:34–39). So then Paul was really recurring to the original cleavage on this point and was able to score a point against the Sadducees as Gamaliel, his great teacher, had done before him. Besides, "Paul and Pharisaism seem to us such opposite ideas that we often forget that to Paul Christianity was the natural development of Judaism" (Page). Paul shows this in Gal. 3 and Rom. 9–11.

7. *When he had so said* (*touto autou lalountos*). Genitive absolute of present participle (Westcott and Hort) rather than aorist (*eipontos*). While he was saying this. *A dissension* (*stasis*). This old word for standing or station (Heb. 9:8) from *histēmi*, to place, we have seen already to mean insurrection (Acts 19:40 which see). Here it is strife as in 15:2. *Was divided* (*eschisthē*). See on 14:4.

8. *There is no resurrection, neither angel, nor spirit* (*mē einai anastasin mēte aggelon mēte pneuma*). Infinitive with negative *mē* in indirect assertion. These points constitute the chief doctrinal differences between the Pharisees and the Sadducees. *Both* (*amphotera*). Here used though three items of belief are mentioned as in 19:16 where the seven sons of Sceva are thus described. This idiom is common

enough in papyri and Byzantine Greek (Robertson, *Grammar*, p. 745).

9. *Strove* (*diemachonto*). Imperfect middle of *diamachomai*, old Attic verb, to fight it out (between, back and forth, fiercely). Here only in the N.T. It was a lively scrap and Luke pictures it as going on. The Pharisees definitely take Paul's side. *And what if a spirit hath spoken to him or an angel?* (*ei de pneuma elalēsen autōi ē aggelos?*). This is aposiopesis, not uncommon in the N.T., as in Luke 13:9; John 6:62 (Robertson, *Grammar*, p. 1203). See one also in Ex. 32:32.

10. *When there arose a great dissension* (*pollēs tēs ginomenēs staseōs*). Present middle participle (genitive absolute). Literally, "dissension becoming much." *Lest Paul should be torn in pieces by them* (*mē diaspasthēi ho Paulos*). First aorist passive subjunctive of *diaspaō*, to draw in two, to tear in pieces, old verb, in the N.T. only here and Mark 5:4 of tearing chains in two. The subjunctive with *mē* is the common construction after a verb of fearing (Robertson, *Grammar*, p. 995). *The soldiers* (*to strateuma*). The army, the band of soldiers and so in verse 27. *To go down* (*kataban*). Second aorist active participle of *katabainō*, having gone down. *Take him by force* (*harpasai*). To seize. The soldiers were to seize and save Paul from the midst of (*ek mesou*) the rabbis or preachers (in their rage to get at each other). Paul was more of a puzzle to Lysias now than ever.

11. *The night following* (*tēi epiousēi nukti*). Locative case, on the next (following) night. *The Lord* (*ho kurios*). Jesus. Paul never needed Jesus more than now. On a previous occasion the whole church prayed for Peter's release (12:5), but Paul clearly had no such grip on the church as that, though he had been kindly welcomed (21:18). In every crisis Jesus appears to him (cf. Acts 18:9). It looked dark for Paul till Jesus spoke. Once before in Jerusalem Jesus spoke words of cheer (22:18). Then he was told to

leave Jerusalem. Now he is to have "cheer" or "courage" (*tharsei*). Jesus used this very word to others (Matt. 9:2, 22; Mark 10:49). It is a brave word. *Thou hast testified* (*diemarturō*). First aorist middle indicative second person singular of *diamarturomai*, strong word (see on 22:18). *Must thou* (*se dei*). That is the needed word and on this Paul leans. His hopes (19:21) of going to Rome will not be in vain. He can bide Christ's time now. And Jesus has approved his witness in Jerusalem.

12. *Banded together* (*poiēsantes sustrophēn*). See on 19:40 (riot), but here conspiracy, secret combination, binding together like twisted cords. *Bound themselves under a curse* (*anethematisan heautous*). First aorist active indicative of *anathematizō*, a late word, said by Cremer and Thayer to be wholly Biblical or ecclesiastical. But Deissmann (*Light from the Ancient East*, p. 95) quotes several examples of the verb in an Attic cursing tablet from Megara of the first or second century A.D. This proof shows that the word, as well as *anathema* (substantive) from which the verb is derived, was employed by pagans as well as by Jews. Deissmann suggests that Greek Jews like the seven sons of Sceva may have been the first to coin it. It occurs in the LXX as well as Mark 14:71 (which see and Luke 21:5); Acts 23:12, 14, 21. They placed themselves under an anathema or curse, devoted themselves to God (cf. Lev. 27:28f.; I Cor. 16:22). *Drink* (*pein = piein*). Second aorist active infinitive of *pinō*. For this shortened form see Robertson, *Grammar*, p. 343. *Till they had killed* (*heōs hou apokteinōsin*). First aorist active subjunctive of *apokteinō*, common verb. No reason to translate "had killed," simply "till they should kill," the aorist merely punctiliar action, the subjunctive retained instead of the optative for vividness as usual in the *Koinē* (Robertson, *Grammar*, pp. 974–6). Same construction in verse 14. King Saul took an "anathema" that imperilled Jonathan (I Sam. 14:24). Perhaps the forty felt

that the rabbis could find some way to absolve the curse if they failed. See this verse repeated in verse 21.

13. *More than forty* (*pleious tesserakonta*). Without "than" (*ē*) as in verse 21 and 24:11 and often in the ancient Greek. *Conspiracy* (*sunōmosian*). Old word from *sunomnumi*, to swear together. Only here in the N.T.

14. *Came to the chief priests and the elders* (*proselthontes tois archiereusin kai tois presbuterois*). The Sanhedrin, just as Judas did (Luke 22:4). *With a great curse* (*anathemati*). This use of the same word as the verb repeated in the instrumental case is in imitation of the Hebrew absolute infinitive and common in the LXX, the very idiom and words of Deut. 13:15; 20:17, an example of translation Greek, though found in other languages (Robertson, *Grammar*, p. 531). See on Luke 21:5 for the distinction between *anathema* and *anathēma*. Jesus had foretold: "Whoso killeth you will think that he doeth God service" (John 16:2).

15. *Ye* (*humeis*). Emphatic. *Signify* (*emphanisate*). First aorist active imperative of *emphanizō*. Make plain from *emphanēs*, chiefly in Acts. Repeated in verse 22. The authority is with the chiliarch not with the Sanhedrin, but he had appealed to the Sanhedrin for advice. *As though ye would judge of his case more exactly* (*hōs mellontas diaginōskein akribesteron ta peri autou*). *Hōs* with the participle gives the alleged reason as here. So also in verse 20. *Diagnoskō*, old verb to distinguish accurately, only here in N.T. and 24:22. *Or ever come near* (*pro tou eggisai auton*). "Before the coming near as to him." *Pro* and the genitive of the articular infinitive of *eggizō* with accusative of general reference. *We are ready to slay him* (*hetoimoi esmen tou anelein auton*). Genitive of purpose of the articular infinitive after the adjective *hetoimoi* (Robertson, *Grammar*, p. 1061). *Anelein*, second aorist active of *anaireō*.

16. *Their lying in wait* (*tēn enedran*). Old word from *en* (in) and *hedra* (seat), ambush. In N.T. only here and 25:3.

Accusative object of *akousas*. *He came (paragenomenos)*.
Second aorist middle participle of *paraginomai*. It may
mean, "having come upon them" and so discount their
plot, a graphic touch. Vincent thinks that some Pharisee,
since Paul was a Pharisee and so a member of the "guild,"
told his nephew of the plot. Perhaps, and perhaps not.
Told Paul (apēggeilen tōi Paulōi). This nephew is not known
otherwise. He may be a student here from Tarsus as Paul
once was. Anyhow he knows what to do when he catches
on to the conspirators. He had enough address to get into
the barracks where Paul was. He ran the risk of death if
discovered.

17. *Called unto him (proskalesamenos)*. First aorist participle indirect middle, calling to himself. Paul laid his plans
as energetically as if Jesus had not promised that he would
see Rome (23:11). *Bring (apage)*. "Take away."

18. *Paul the prisoner (ho desmios Paulos)*. Bound (*desmios*) to a soldier, but not with two chains (21:33), and with
some freedom to see his friends as later (28:16), in military
custody (*custodia militaris*). This was better than *custodia
publica* (public custody), the common prison, but more
confining. *Who hath something to say to thee (echonta ti
lalēsai soi)*. Same idiom as in verse 17 and in 19, but *lalēsai*
here instead of *apaggeilai*.

19. *Took him by the hand (epilabomenos tēs cheiros autou)*.
Kindly touch in Lysias, *ut fiduciam adolescentis confirmaret*
(Bengel). Note genitive with the second aorist middle (indirect, to himself) of *epilambanō* as in Luke 8:54 with *kratēsas*
which see. How old the young man (*neanias*) was we do not
know, but it is the very word used of Paul in 7:58 when he
helped in the killing of Stephen, a young man in the twenties
probably. See also 20:9 of Eutychus. He is termed *neaniskos*
in verse 22. *Asked him privately (kat' idian epunthaneto)*.
Imperfect middle, began to ask (inchoative).

20. *The Jews (hoi Ioudaioi)*. As if the whole nation was in

the conspiracy and so in verse 12. The conspirators may have belonged to the Zealots, but clearly they represented the state of Jewish feeling toward Paul in Jerusalem. *Have agreed* (*sunethento*). Second aorist middle indicative of *suntithēmi*, old verb to join together, to agree. Already this form in Luke 22:5 which see. See also John 9:22; Acts 24:9. *To bring down* (*hopōs katagagēis*). Very words of the conspirators in verse 15 as if the young man overheard. Second aorist active subjunctive of *katagō* with *hopōs* in final clause, still used, but nothing like so common as *hina* though again in verse 23 (Robertson, *Grammar*, p. 985). *As though thou wouldest inquire* (*hōs mellōn punthanesthai*). Just as in verse 15 except that here *mellōn* refers to Lysias instead of to the conspirators as in verse 15. The singular is used by the youth out of deference to the authority of Lysias and so modifies a bit the scheming of the conspirators, not "absurd" as Page holds.

21. *Do not therefore yield unto them* (*Su oun mē peisthēis autois*). First aorist passive subjunctive of *peithō*, common verb, here to be persuaded by, to listen to, to obey, to yield to. With negative and rightly. Do not yield to them (dative) at all. On the aorist subjunctive with *mē* in prohibitions against committing an act see Robertson, *Grammar*, pp. 851-4. *For there lie in wait* (*enedreuousin gar*). Present active indicative of *enedreuō*, old verb from *enedra* (verse 16), in the N.T. only here and Luke 11:54 which see. *Till they have slain him* (*heōs hou anelōsin auton*). Same idiom as in verse 12 save that here we have *anelōsin* (second aorist active subjunctive) instead of *apokteinōsin* (another word for kill), "till they slay him." *Looking for the promise from thee* (*prosdechomenoi tēn apo sou epaggelian*). This item is all that is needed to put the scheme through, the young man shrewdly adds.

22. *Tell no man* (*mēdeni eklalēsai*). Indirect command (*oratio obliqua*) after *paraggeilas* (charging) with first aorist

active infinitive of *eklaleō* (in ancient Greek, but here only in N.T.), but construction changed to direct in rest of the sentence (*oratio recta*) as in 1:4, "that thou hast signified these things to me" (*hoti tauta enephanisas pros eme*). Same verb here as in verse 15. This change is common in the N.T. (Robertson, *Grammar*, p. 1047).

23. *Two* (*tinas duo*). "Some two" as in Luke 7:19, indicating (Page) that they were not specially chosen. *Soldiers* (*stratiōtas*), *horsemen* (*hippeis*), *spearmen* (*dexiolabous*). The three varieties of troops in a Roman army like the cohort of Lysias (Page). The *stratiōtai* were the heavy-armed legionaries, the *hippeis* belonged to every legion, the *dexiolaboi* were light-armed supplementary troops who carried a lance in the right hand (*dexios*, right, *lambanō*, to take). Vulgate, *lancearios*. *At the third hour of the night* (*apo tritēs hōras tēs nuktos*). About nine in the evening.

24. *Provide beasts* (*ktenē parastēsai*). Change from direct to indirect discourse just the opposite of that in verse 22. *Beasts* (*ktenē*). For riding as here or for baggage. See on Luke 10:34. Asses or horses, but not war-horses. Since Paul was chained to a soldier, another animal would be required for baggage. It was also seventy miles and a change of horses might be needed. The extreme precaution of Lysias is explained in some Latin MSS. as due to fear of a night attack with the result that he might be accused to Felix of bribery. Luke also probably accompanied Paul. *To bring safe* (*hina diasōsōsin*). Final clause with *hina* and the first aorist active subjunctive of *diasōzō*, old verb, to save through (*dia*) to a finish. Eight times in the N.T. (Matt. 14:36; Luke 7:3; Acts 23:24; 27:43, 44; 28:1, 4; I Peter 3:20). *Unto Felix the governor* (*pros Phēlika ton hēgemona*). Felix was a brother of Pallas, the notorious favourite of Claudius. Both had been slaves and were now freedmen. Felix was made procurator of Judea by Claudius A.D. 52. He held the position till Festus succeeded him after complaints by

the Jews to Nero. He married Drusilla the daughter of
Herod Agrippa I with the hope of winning the favour of the
Jews. He was one of the most depraved men of his time.
Tacitus says of him that "with all cruelty and lust he
exercised the power of a king with the spirit of a slave." The
term "governor" (*hēgemōn*) means "leader" from *hēgeomai*,
to lead, and was applied to leaders of all sorts (emperors,
kings, procurators). In the N.T. it is used of Pilate (Matt.
27:2), of Felix, (Acts 23:24, 26, 33; 24:1), of Festus (26:30).

25. *And he wrote* (*grapsas*). First aorist active participle
of *graphō*, agreeing with the subject (Lysias) of *eipen* (said)
back in verse 23 (beginning). *After this form* (*echousan ton
tupon touton*). Textus Receptus has *periechousan*. The use
of *tupon* (type or form) like *exemplum* in Latin (Page who
quotes Cicero *Ad Att.* IX. 6. 3) may give merely the purport
or substantial contents of the letter. But there is no reason
for thinking that it is not a genuine copy since the letter
may have been read in open court before Felix, and Luke
was probably with Paul. The Roman law required that a
subordinate officer like Lysias in reporting a case to his
superior should send a written statement of the case and it
was termed *elogium*. A copy of the letter may have been
given Paul after his appeal to Caesar. It was probably
written in Latin. The letter is a "dexterous mixture of
truth and falsehood" (Furneaux) with the stamp of genuineness. It puts things in a favourable light for Lysias and makes
no mention of his order to scourge Paul.

26. *Most excellent* (*kratistōi*). See on Luke 1:3 to Theophilus though not in Acts 1:1. It is usual in addressing men of
rank as here, like our "Your Excellency" in 24:3 and Paul
uses it to Festus in 26:25. *Greeting* (*chairein*). Absolute
infinitive with independent or absolute nominative (*Klaudios
Lusias*) as is used in letters (Acts 15:23; James 1:1) and in
countless papyri (Robertson, *Grammar*, p. 1092).

27. *Was seized* (*sullēmphthenta*). First aorist passive par-

ticiple of *sullambanō*. *Rescued him having learned that he was a Roman* (*exeilamen mathōn hoti Romaios estin*). Wendt, Zoeckler, and Furneaux try to defend this record of two facts by Lysias in the wrong order from being an actual lie as Bengel rightly says. Lysias did rescue Paul and he did learn that he was a Roman, but in this order. He did not first learn that he was a Roman and then rescue him as his letter states. The use of the aorist participle (*mathōn* from *manthanō*) after the principal verb *exeilamen* (second aorist middle of *exaireō*, to take out to oneself, to rescue) can be either simultaneous action or antecedent. There is in Greek no such idiom as the aorist participle of subsequent action (Robertson, *Grammar*, pp. 1112–14). Lysias simply reversed the order of the facts and omitted the order for scourging Paul to put himself in proper light with Felix his superior officer and actually poses as the protector of a fellow Roman citizen.

28. *To know* (*epignōnai*). To know fully, *epi*, second aorist active infinitive. *They accused him* (*enekaloun autōi*). Imperfect active indicative, were accusing him (dative), repeating their charges.

29. *Concerning questions of their law* (*peri zētēmata tou nomou autōn*). The very distinction drawn by Gallio in Corinth (Acts 18:14f.). On the word see on 15:2. *But to have nothing laid to his charge worthy of death or of bonds* (*mēden de axion thanatou ē desmōn echonta enklēma*). Literally, "having no accusation (or crime) worthy of death or of bonds." This phrase here only in the N.T. *Egklēma* is old word for accusation or crime from *egkaleō* used in verse 28 and in the N.T. only here and 25:16. Lysias thus expresses the opinion that Paul ought to be set free and the lenient treatment that Paul received in Caesarea and Rome (first imprisonment) is probably due to this report of Lysias. Every Roman magistrate before whom Paul appears declares him innocent (Gallio, Lysias, Felix, Festus).

30. *When it was shown to me that there would be a plot* (*mēnutheisēs moi epiboulēs esesthai*). Two constructions combined; genitive absolute (*mēnutheisēs epiboulēs*, first aorist passive participle of *mēnuō*) and future infinitive (*esesthai* as if *epiboulēn* accusative of general reference used) in indirect assertion after *mēnuō* (Robertson, *Grammar*, p. 877). *Charging his accusers also* (*paraggeilas kai tois katēgorois*). First aorist active participle of *paraggellō* with which compare *mathōn* above (verse 27), not subsequent action. Dative case in *katēgorois*. *Before thee* (*epi sou*). Common idiom for "in the presence of" when before a judge (like Latin *apud*) as in 24:20, 21; 25:26; 26:2. What happened to the forty conspirators we have no way of knowing. Neither they nor the Jews from Asia are heard of more during the long five years of Paul's imprisonment in Caesarea and Rome.

31. *As it was commanded them* (*kata to diatetagmenon autois*). "According to that which was commanded them," perfect passive articular participle of *diatassō*. *By night* (*dia nuktos*). Through the night, travelling by night forty miles from Jerusalem to Antipatris which was founded by Herod the Great and was on the road from Jerusalem to Caesarea, a hard night's ride.

33. *And they* (*hoitines*). Which very ones, the cavalry, the horsemen of verse 31. *Delivered* (*anadontes*). Second aorist active participle of *anadidōmi*, old verb to give up, to hand over, here only in the N.T. *Presented Paul also* (*parestēsan kai ton Paulon*). First aorist active (transitive, not second aorist intransitive) indicative of *paristēmi*, common verb to present or place beside. What would Paul's friends in Caesarea (Philip and his daughters) think of the prophecy of Agabus now so quickly come true.

34. *When he had read it* (*anagnous*). Second aorist active participle of *anaginōskō*, to know again, to read. *Of what province he was* (*ek poias eparcheias estin*). Tense of *estin* (is) retained in indirect question. *Poias* is strictly "of what

kind of" province, whether senatorial or imperial. Cilicia, like Judea, was under the control of the propraetor of Syria (imperial province). Paul's arrest was in Jerusalem and so under the jurisdiction of Felix unless it was a matter of insurrection when he could appeal to the propraetor of Syria.

35. *I will hear thy cause* (*diakousomai*). "I will hear thee fully" (*dia*). *When—are come* (*paragenōntai*). Second aorist middle subjunctive of *paraginomai* with temporal conjunction *hotan*, indefinite temporal clause of future time (Robertson, *Grammar*, p. 972), "whenever thine accusers come." *In Herod's palace* (*en tōi praitōriōi*). The Latin word *praetorium*. The word meant the camp of the general, then the palace of the governor as here and Matt. 27:27 which see, and then the camp of praetorian soldiers or rather the praetorian guard as in Phil. 1:13.

CHAPTER XXIV

1. *And with an Orator, one Tertullus (kai rhētoros Tertullou tinos)*. A deputation of elders along with the high priest Ananias, not the whole Sanhedrin, but no hint of the forty conspirators or of the Asian Jews. The Sanhedrin had become divided so that now it is probably Ananias (mortally offended) and the Sadducees who take the lead in the prosecution of Paul. It is not clear whether after five days is from Paul's departure from Jerusalem or his arrival in Caesarea. If he spent nine days in Jerusalem, then the five days would be counted from then (verse 11). The employment of a Roman lawyer (Latin *orator*) was necessary since the Jews were not familiar with Roman legal procedure and it was the custom in the provinces (Cicero *pro Cael.* 30). The speech was probably in Latin which Paul may have understood also. *Rhētōr* is a common old Greek word meaning a forensic orator or advocate but here only in the N.T. The Latin *rhetor* was a teacher of rhetoric, a very different thing. Tertullus is à diminutive of Tertius (Rom. 16:22). *Informed (enephanisan)*. Same verb as in 23:15, 22, somewhat like our modern "indictment," certainly accusations "against Paul" *(kata tou Paulou)*. They were down on Paul and the hired barrister was prosecuting attorney. For the legal form see *Oxyrhynchus Papyri*, Vol. II., p. 162, line 19.

2. *When he (Paul) was called (klēthentos autou)*. Genitive absolute (as so often in Acts) with first aorist passive participle of *kaleō*. *Seeing that by thee we enjoy much peace (pollēs eirēnēs tugchanontes dia sou)*. Literally, obtaining much peace by thee. A regular piece of flattery, *captatio benevolentiae*, to ingratiate himself into the good graces of the governor. Felix had suppressed a riot, but Tacitus (*Ann.* XII. 54)

declares that Felix secretly encouraged banditti and shared
the plunder for which the Jews finally made complaint to
Nero who recalled him.   But it sounded well to praise Felix
for keeping peace in his province, especially as Tertullus
was going to accuse Paul of being a disturber of the peace.
And that by thy providence (kai dia tēs pronoias). Forethought,
old Greek word from *pronoos* (*pronoeō* in I Tim. 5:8; Rom.
12:17; II Cor. 8:21), in N.T. only here and Rom. 13:14.
"Providence" is Latin *Providentia* (foreseeing, *provideo*).
Roman coins often have *Providentia Caesaris*. Post-Augustan
Latin uses it of God (*Deus*).   *Evils are corrected for this
nation (diorthōmatōn ginomenōn tōi ethnei toutōi).* Genitive
absolute again, *ginomenōn*, present middle participle describing the process of reform going on for this nation (dative
case of personal interest). *Diorthōma* (from *diorthoō*, to set
right) occurs from Aristotle on of setting right broken limbs
(Hippocrates) or reforms in law and life (Polybius, Plutarch).
"Reform continually taking place for this nation."   Felix
the Reform Governor of Judea! It is like a campaign speech,
but it doubtless pleased Felix.

3. *In all ways and in all places (pantēi te kai pantachou).*
Pantēi, old adverb of manner only here in N.T.   *Pantachou*
also old adverb of place, several times in N.T.   But these
adverbs most likely go with the preceding clause about
"reforms" rather than as here translated with "we accept"
(*apodechometha*).   But "with all gratitude" (*meta pasēs
eucharistias*) does naturally go with *apodechometha*.

4. *That I be not further tedious unto thee (hina mē epi pleion
se enkoptō).* Koiné verb (Hippocrates, Polybius) to cut in on
(or into), to cut off, to impede, to hinder.   Our modern
telephone and radio illustrate it well.   In the N.T. (Acts
24:4; I Thess. 2:18; Gal. 5:7; Rom. 15:22; I Peter 3:7). "That
I may not cut in on or interrupt thee further (*epi pleion*) in
thy reforms." Flattery still.   *Of thy clemency (tēi sēi epiei-
keiāi).*   Instrumental case of old word from *epieikēs* and this

from *epi* and *eikos* (reasonable, likely, fair). "Sweet Reasonableness" (Matthew Arnold), gentleness, fairness.   An *epieikēs* man is "one who makes reasonable concessions" (Aristotle, *Eth.* V. 10), while *dikaios* is "one who insists on his full rights" (Plato, *Leg.* 757 D) as translated by Page. *A few words* (*suntomōs*). Old adverb from *suntemnō*, to cut together (short), abbreviate.   Like *dia bracheōn* in Heb. 13:22.   In N.T. only here and Mark 16 (shorter conclusion).

5. *For we have found* (*heurontes gar*). Second aorist active participle of *heuriskō*, but without a principal verb in the sentence.   Probably we have here only a "summary of the charges against Paul" (Page). *A pestilent fellow* (*loimon*). An old word for pest, plague, pestilence, Paul the pest.   In N.T. only here and Luke 21:11 (*loimoi kai limoi*, pestilences and famines) which see.   Latin *pestis*.   Think of the greatest preacher of the ages being branded a pest by a contemporary hired lawyer. *A mover of insurrections* (*kinounta staseis*). This was an offence against Roman law if it could be proven. "Plotted against at Damascus, plotted against at Jerusalem, expelled from Pisidian Antioch, stoned at Lystra, scourged and imprisoned at Philippi, accused of treason at Thessalonica, haled before the proconsul at Corinth, cause of a serious riot at Ephesus, and now finally of a riot at Jerusalem" (Furneaux).   Specious proof could have been produced, but was not.   Tertullus went on to other charges with which a Roman court had no concern (instance Gallio in Corinth). *Throughout the world* (*kata tēn oikoumenēn*). The Roman inhabited earth (*gēn*) as in 17:6. *A ringleader of the sect of the Nazarenes* (*prōtostatēn tēs tōn Nazōraiōn haireseōs*). *Prōtostatēs* is an old word in common use from *prōtos* and *histēmi*, a front-rank man, a chief, a champion.   Here only in the N.T.   This charge is certainly true.   About "sect" (*hairesis*) see on 5:17.   *Nazōraioi* here only in the plural in the N.T., elsewhere of Jesus (Matt. 2:23; 26:71; Luke 18:37; John 18:5, 7; 19:19; Acts 2:22; 3:6; 4:10; 6:14; 22:8; 26:9).

The disciple is not above his Master. There was a sneer in the term as applied to Jesus and here to his followers.

6. *Assayed to profane* (*epeirasen bebēlōsai*). A flat untruth, but the charge of the Asian Jews (21:28-30). *Verbum optum ad calumnian* (Bengel). *We seized* (*ekratēsamen*). As if the Sanhedrin had arrested Paul, Tertullus identifying himself with his clients. But it was the mob (21:28-31) that attacked Paul and Lysias who rescued him (21:32ff.).

7. This whole verse with some words at the end of verse 6 and the beginning of verse 8 in the Textus Receptus ("And would have judged according to our law. But the chief captain Lysias came upon us, and with great violence took him away out of our hands, commanding his accusers to come unto thee") is absent from Aleph A B H L P 61 (many other cursives) Sahidic Bohairic. It is beyond doubt a later addition to the incomplete report of the speech of Tertullus. As the Revised Version stands, verse 8 connects with verse 6. The motive of the added words is clearly to prejudice Felix against Lysias and they contradict the record in Acts 21. Furneaux holds them to be genuine and omitted because contradictory to Acts 21. More likely they are a clumsy attempt to complete the speech of Tertullus.

8. *From whom* (*par' hou*). Referring to Paul, but in the Textus Receptus referring to Lysias. *By examining him thyself* (*autos anakrinas*). Not by torture, since Paul was a Roman citizen, but by hearing what Paul has to say in defence of himself. *Anakrinō* is to examine thoroughly up and down as in Luke 23:14.

9. *Joined in the charge* (*sunepethento*). Second aorist middle indicative of *sunepitithēmi*, old verb, double compound, to place upon (*epi*) together with (*sun*), to make a joint attack, here only in the N.T. *Affirming* (*phaskontes*). Alleging, with the accusative in indirect assertion as in 25:19; Rom. 1:22 (nominative with infinitive, Robertson, *Grammar*, p. 1038). *Were so* (*houtōs echein*), "held thus," common idiom.

10. *When the governor had beckoned to him* (*neusantos autōi tou hēgemonos*). Genitive absolute again with first aorist active participle of *neuō*, to give a nod, old word, in N.T. only here and John 13:24. "The governor nodding to him." *Forasmuch as I know* (*epistamenos*). Knowing, from *epistamai*. *That thou hast been of many years a judge* (*ek pollōn etōn onta se kritēn*). The participle in indirect assertion after *epistamenos* (Robertson, *Grammar*, p. 1041). Paul goes as far as he can in the way of a compliment. For seven years Felix has been governor, *onta* being a sort of progressive present participle with *ek pollōn etōn* (Robertson, *Grammar*, p. 892). *Cheerfully* (*euthumōs*). Old adverb from *euthumos* (*eu* and *thumos*, good spirit), here only in N.T. *Make my defence* (*apologoumai*). Old and regular word for this idea as in Luke 21:14 which see.

11. *Seeing that thou canst take knowledge* (*dunamenou sou epignōnai*). Genitive absolute again. The same word and form (*epignōnai*) used by Tertullus, if in Greek, in verse 8 to Felix. Paul takes it up and repeats it. *Not more than twelve days* (*ou pleious hēmerai dōdeka*). Here *ē* (than) is absent without change of case to the ablative as usually happens. But this idiom is found in the *Koiné* (Robertson, *Grammar*, p. 666). *Since* (*aph' hēs*). Supply *hēmeras*, "from which day." *To worship* (*proskunēsōn*). One of the few examples of the future participle of purpose so common in the old Attic.

12. *Disputing* (*dialegomenon*). Simply conversing, discussing, arguing, and then disputing, common verb in old Greek and in N.T. (especially in Acts). *Stirring up a crowd* (*epistasin poiounta ochlou*). *Epistasis* is a late word from *ephistēmi*, to make an onset or rush. Only twice in the N.T., II Cor. 11:28 (the pressure or care of the churches) and here (making a rush of a crowd). The papyri give examples also for "onset." So Paul denies the two charges that were serious and the only one that concerned Roman law (insurrection).

13. *Prove* (*parastēsai*). First aorist active infinitive of *paristēmi*, to place beside. They have made "charges," mere assertions. They have not backed up these charges with proof, "nor can they," says Paul. *Now* (*nuni*). As if they had changed their charges from the cries of the mob in Jerusalem which is true. Paul has no hired lawyer to plead for him, but he has made a masterly plea for his freedom.

14. *I confess* (*homologō*). The only charge left was that of being a ringleader of the sect of the Nazarenes. This Paul frankly confesses is true. He uses the word in its full sense. He is "guilty" of that. *After the Way* (*kata tēn hodon*). This word Paul had already applied to Christianity (22:4). He prefers it to "sect" (*hairesin* which means a choosing, then a division). Paul claims Christianity to be the real (whole, catholic) Judaism, not a "sect" of it. But he will show that Christianity is not a deviation from Judaism, but the fulfilment of it (Page) as he has already shown in Gal. 3 and Rom. 9. *So serve I the God of our fathers* (*houtōs latreuō tōi patrōiōi theōi*). Paul has not stretched the truth at all. He has confirmed the claim made before the Sanhedrin that he is a spiritual Pharisee in the truest sense (23:6). He reasserts his faith in all the law and the prophets, holding to the Messianic hope. A curious "heretic" surely! *Which these themselves also look for* (*hēn kai autoi houtoi prosdechontai*). Probably with a gesture towards his accusers. He does not treat them all as Sadducees. See Titus 2:13 for similar use of the verb (*prosdechomenoi tēn makarian elpida*, looking for the happy hope).

15. *That there shall be a resurrection* (*anastasin mellein esesthai*). Indirect assertion with infinitive and accusative of general reference (*anastasin*) after the word *elpida* (hope). The future infinitive *esesthai* after *mellein* is also according to rule, *mellō* being followed by either present, aorist, or future infinitive (Robertson, *Grammar*, pp. 870, 877, 878). *Both of the just and the unjust* (*dikaiōn te kai adikōn*). Apparently

at the same time as in John 5:29 (cf. Acts 17:31f.). Gardner
thinks that Luke here misrepresents Paul who held to no
resurrection save for those "in Christ," a mistaken interpretation of Paul in my opinion. The Talmud teaches the
resurrection of Israelites only, but Paul was more than a
Pharisee.

16. *Herein* (*en toutōi*). His whole confession of belief in
verses 14 and 15. *Do I also exercise myself* (*kai autos askō*).
"Do I also myself take exercise," take pains, labour, strive.
Old word in Homer to work as raw materials, to adorn by
art, then to drill. Our word ascetic comes from this root,
one who seeks to gain piety by rules and severe hardship.
Paul claims to be equal to his accusers in efforts to please
God. *Void of offence* (*aproskopon*). This word belongs to the
papyri and N.T. (only in Paul), not in the ancient writers.
The papyri examples (Moulton Milligan, *Vocabulary*) use
the word to mean "free from hurt or harm." It is *a* privative
and *proskoptō* (to cut or stumble against). Page likes "void
of offence" since that can be either active "not stumbling"
as in Phil. 1:10 or passive "not stumbled against" as in I
Cor. 10:32 (the first toward God and the second toward
men), the only other N.T. examples. Hence the word here
appears in both senses (the first towards God, the second
towards men). Paul adds "alway" (*dia pantos*), a bold claim
for a consistent aim in life. "Certainly his conscience acquitted him of having caused any offence to his countrymen" (Rackham). Furneaux thinks that it must have been
wormwood and gall to Ananias to hear Paul repeat here the
same words because of which he had ordered Paul to be
smitten on the mouth (23:1f.).

17. *After many years* (*di' etōn pleionōn*). "At an interval
(*dia*) of more (*pleionōn*) years" (than a few, one must add),
not "after many years." If, as is likely Paul went up to
Jerusalem in Acts 18:22, that was some five years ago and
would justify "*pleionōn*" (several years ago or some years

ago). *To bring alms (eleēmosunas poiēsōn)*. Another (see *proskunēsōn* in verse 11) example of the future participle of purpose in the N.T. These "alms" (on *eleēmosunas* see on Matt. 6:1, 4 and Acts 10:2, common in Tobit and is in the papyri) were for the poor saints in Jerusalem (I Cor. 16:1–4; II Cor. 8 and 9; Rom. 15:26) who were none the less Jews. "And offerings" *(kai prosphoras)*. The very word used in 21:26 of the offerings or sacrifices made by Paul for the four brethren and himself. It does not follow that it was Paul's original purpose to make these "offerings" before he came to Jerusalem (cf. 18:18). He came up to worship (verse 11) and to be present at Pentecost (20:16).

18. *Amidst which (en hais)*. That is, "in which offerings" (in presenting which offerings, 21:27). *They found me* (my accusers here present, *heuron me*), *purified in the temple (hēgnismenon en tōi hierōi)*. Perfect passive participle of *hagnizō* (same verb in 21:24, 26) state of completion of the Jewish sacrifices which had gone on for seven days (21:27), the very opposite of the charges made. *With no crowd (ou meta ochlou)*. "Not with a crowd" till the Asiatic Jews gathered one (21:27). *Nor yet with tumult (oude meta thorubou)*. They made the tumult (27:30), not Paul. Till they made the stir, all was quiet.

19. *But certain Jews from Asia (tines de apo tēs Asias Ioudaioi)*. No verb appears in the Greek for these words. Perhaps he meant to say that "certain Jews from Asia charged me with doing these things." Instead of saying that, Paul stops to explain that they are not here, a thoroughly Pauline anacoluthon (II Cor. 7:5) as in 26:9. "The passage as it stands is instinct with life, and seems to exhibit the abruptness so characteristic of the Pauline Epistles" (Page). *Who ought to have been here before thee (hous edei epi sou pareinai)*. This use of *epi* with genitive of the person is common. The imperfect indicative with verbs of necessity and obligation to express failure to live up to it is common

in Greek (Robertson, *Grammar*, pp. 919–21). "The accusers who were present had not witnessed the alleged offence: those who could have given evidence at first-hand were not present" (Furneaux). There was no case in a Roman court. These Asiatic Jews are never heard of after the riot, though they almost succeeded in killing Paul then. *If they had aught against me* (*ei ti echoien pros eme*). A condition of the fourth class or undetermined with less likelihood of being determined (*ei* with the optative, Robertson, *Grammar*, p. 1021). This is a "mixed condition" (*op. cit.*, p. 1022) with a conclusion of the second class.

20. *These men themselves* (*autoi houtoi*). Since the Asiatic Jews are not present and these men are. *Wrong doing* (*adikēma*). Or misdeed. Old word from *adikeō*, to do wrong. In the N.T. only here and Acts 18:14; Rev. 18:5. Paul uses "*adikēma*" from the standpoint of his accusers. "To a less sensitive conscience his action before the Sanhedrin would have seemed venial enough" (Furneaux). *When I stood* (*stantos mou*). Genitive absolute, second aorist active participle of *histēmi* (intransitive), "when I took my stand." *Before the council* (*epi tou sunedriou*). Same use of *epi* with genitive as in verse 19.

21. *Except it be* (*ē*). Literally, "than," but after interrogative *ti* = *ti allo* "what else than." *For this one voice* (*peri mias tautēs phōnēs*). The normal Greek idiom with the attributive use of *houtos* calls for the article before *mias*, though some inscriptions show it as here (Robertson, *Grammar*, p. 702). *That* (*hēs*). Genitive of the relative attracted to the case of the antecedent *phōnēs*. *I cried* (*ekekraxa*). Reduplicated aorist as is usual with this verb in the LXX (Judges 3:15). Robertson, *Grammar*, p. 348. *Touching* (*peri*). Concerning (around, about). *I am called in question* (*krinomai*). As in 23:6. *Before you* (*eph' humōn*). Same idiom as in verses 19 and 20.

22. *Having more exact knowledge* (*akribesteron eidōs*).

"Knowing" (second perfect active participle of *oida*) "more accurately" (comparative of adverb *akribōs*). More accurately than what? Than the Sanhedrin supposed he had "concerning the Way" (*ta peri tēs hodou*, the things concerning the Way, common in Acts for Christianity). How Felix had gained this knowledge of Christianity is not stated. Philip the Evangelist lived here in Caesarea and there was a church also. Drusilla was a Jewess and may have told him something. Besides, it is wholly possible that Felix knew of the decision of Gallio in Corinth that Christianity was a *religio licita* as a form of Judaism. As a Roman official he knew perfectly well that the Sanhedrin with the help of Tertullus had failed utterly to make out a case against Paul. He could have released Paul and probably would have done so but for fear of offending the Jews whose ruler he was and the hope that Paul (note "alms" in verse 17) might offer him bribes for his liberty. *Deferred them* (*anebaleto autous*). Second aorist middle indicative of *anaballō*, old verb (only here in N.T.) to throw or toss up, to put back or off, in middle to put off from one, to delay, to adjourn. Felix adjourned the case without a decision under a plausible pretext, that he required the presence of Lysias in person, which was not the case. Lysias had already said that Paul was innocent and was never summoned to Caesarea, so far as we know. Since Paul was a Roman citizen, Lysias could have thrown some light on the riot, if he had any. *Shall come down* (*katabēi*). Second aorist active subjunctive of *katabainō*. *I will determine your matter* (*diagnōsomai ta kath' humās*). Future middle of *diaginōskō*, old and common verb to know accurately or thoroughly (*dia*). In the N.T. only here (legal sense) and 23:15. "The things according to you" (plural, the matters between Paul and the Sanhedrin).

23. *And should have indulgence* (*echein te anesin*). From *aniēmi*, to let loose, release, relax. Old word, in the N.T. only here and II Thess. 1:7; II Cor. 2:13; 7:5; 8:13. It is the

opposite of strict confinement, though under guard, "kept in charge" (*tēreisthai*). *Forbid* (*kōluein*). To hinder "no one of his friends" (*mēdena tōn idiōn*). No one of Paul's "own" (cf. 4:23; John 1:11) or intimates. Of these we know the names of Luke, Aristarchus, Trophimus, Philip the Evangelist.

24. *With Drusilla his wife* (*sun Drousillēi tēi idiāi gunaiki*). Felix had induced her to leave her former husband Aziz, King of Emesa. She was one of three daughters of Herod Agrippa I (Drusilla, Mariamne, Bernice). Her father murdered James, her great-uncle Herod Antipas slew John the Baptist, her great-grandfather (Herod the Great) killed the babes of Bethlehem. Perhaps the mention of Drusilla as "his own wife" is to show that it was not a formal trial on this occasion. Page thinks that she was responsible for the interview because of her curiosity to hear Paul. *Sent for* (*metepempsato*). First aorist middle of *metapempō* as usual (Acts 10:5).

25. *Was terrified* (*emphobos genomenos*). Ingressive aorist middle of *ginomai*, "becoming terrified." *Emphobos* (*en* and *phobos*) old word, in the N.T. only Luke 24:5; Acts 10:5; 24:25; Rev. 11:13 . Paul turned the tables completely around and expounded "the faith in Christ Jesus" as it applied to Felix and Drusilla and discoursed (*dialegomenou autou*, genitive absolute) concerning "righteousness" (*dikaiosunēs*) which they did not possess, "self-control" or temperance (*egkrateias*) which they did not exhibit, and "the judgment to come" (*tou krimatos tou mellontos*) which was certain to overtake them. Felix was brought under conviction, but apparently not Drusilla. Like another Herodias her resentment was to be feared (Knowling). *Go thy way for this time* (*to nun echon poreuou*). The ancient Greek has this use of *to nun echon* (Tobit 7:11) in the accusative of time, "as for the present or holding the now." *When I have a convenient season* (*kairon metalabōn*). Second aorist active

participle of the old verb *metalambanō*, to find a share in, to obtain. It was his "excuse" for dodging the personal turn that Paul had given.

26. *He hoped withal* (*hama kai elpizōn*). "At the same time also hoping." Paul had mentioned the "alms" (24:17) and that excited the avarice of Felix for "money" (*chrēmata*). Roman law demanded exile and confiscation for a magistrate who accepted bribes, but it was lax in the provinces. Felix had doubtless received them before. Josephus (*Ant.* XX. 8, 9) represents Felix as greedy for money. *The oftener* (*puknoteron*). Comparative adverb of *puknos*, old word, in N.T. only here and Luke 5:33 which see and I Tim. 5:23. Kin to *pugmē* (Mark 7:3) which see from *pukō*, thick, dense, compact. Paul kept on not offering a bribe, but Felix continued to have hopes (present tense *elpizōn*), kept on sending for him (present tense *metapempomenos*), and kept on communing (imperfect active *hōmilei* from *homileō*, old word as in Acts 20:11 and Luke 24:14, which see, only N.T. examples of this word). But he was doomed to disappointment. He was never terrified again.

27. *But when two years were fulfilled* (*dietias de plērōtheisēs*). Genitive·absolute first aorist passive of *pleroō*, common verb to fill full. *Dietia*, late word in LXX and Philo, common in the papyri, in N.T. only here and Acts 28:30. Compound of *dia*, two (*duo*, *dis*) and *etos*, year. So Paul lingered on in prison in Caesarea, waiting for the second hearing under Felix which never came. Caesarea now became the compulsory headquarters of Paul for two years. With all his travels Paul spent several years each at Tarsus, Antioch, Corinth, Ephesus, though not as a prisoner unless that was true part of the time at Ephesus for which there is some evidence though not of a convincing kind. We do not know that Luke remained in Caesarea all this time. In all probability he came and went with frequent visits with Philip the Evangelist. It was probably during this period that Luke secured

the material for his Gospel and wrote part or all of it before going to Rome. He had ample opportunity to examine
the eyewitnesses who heard Jesus and the first attempts at
writing including the Gospel of Mark (Luke 1:1-4). *Was
succeeded by* (*elaben diadochon*). Literally, "received as successor." *Diadochos* is an old word from *diadechomai*, to receive in succession (*dia, duo,* two) and occurs here alone in
the N.T. Deissmann (*Bible Studies*, p. 115) gives papyri
examples where *hoi diadochoi* means "higher officials at the
court of the Ptolemies," probably "deputies," a usage growing out of the "successors" of Alexander the Great (Moulton
and Milligan's *Vocabulary*), though here the original notion
of "successor" occurs (cf. Josephus, *Ant.* XX. 8, 9). Luke
does not tell why Felix "received" a successor. The explanation is that during these two years the Jews and the Gentiles
had an open fight in the market-place in Caesarea. Felix put
the soldiers on the mob and many Jews were killed. The
Jews made formal complaint to the Emperor with the result that Felix was recalled and Porcius Festus sent in his
stead. *Porcius Festus* (*Porkion Phēston*). We know very
little about this man. He is usually considered a worthier
man than Felix, but Paul fared no better at his hands and
he exhibits the same insincerity and eagerness to please the
Jews. Josephus (*Ant.* XX. 8, 9) says that "Porcius Festus
was sent as a successor to Felix." The precise year when this
change occurred is not clear. Albinus succeeded Festus by
A.D. 62, so that it is probable that Festus came A.D. 58 (or
59). Death cut short his career in a couple of years though
he did more than Felix to rid the country of robbers and
sicarii. Some scholars argue for an earlier date for the recall of Felix. Nero became Emperor Oct. 13, A.D. 54. Pop-
paea, his Jewish mistress and finally wife, may have had
something to do with the recall of Felix at the request of the
Jews. *Desiring to gain favour with the Jews* (*thelōn te charita
katathesthai tois Ioudaiois*). Reason for his conduct. Note

second aorist (ingressive) middle infinitive *katathesthai* from *katatithēmi*, old verb to place down, to make a deposit, to deposit a favour with, to do something to win favour. Only here and 25:9 in N.T., though in some MSS. in Mark 15:46. It is a banking figure. *Left Paul in bonds* (*katelipe ton Paulon dedemenon*). Effective aorist active indicative of *kataleipō*, to leave behind. Paul "in bonds" (*dedemenon*, perfect passive participle of *deō*, to bind) was the "deposit" (*katathesthai*) for their favour. Codex Bezae adds that Felix left Paul in custody "because of Drusilla" (*dia Drousillan*). She disliked Paul as much as Herodias did John the Baptist. So Pilate surrendered to the Jews about the death of Jesus when they threatened to report him to Caesar. Some critics would date the third group of Paul's Epistles (Philippians, Philemon, Colossians, Ephesians) to the imprisonment here in Caesarea, some even to one in Ephesus. But the arguments for either of these two views are more specious than convincing. Furneaux would even put II Tim. 4:9–22 here in spite of the flat contradiction with Acts 21:29 about Trophimus being in Jerusalem instead of Miletus (II Tim. 4:20), a "mistake" which he attributes to Luke! That sort of criticism can prove anything.

CHAPTER XXV

1. *Having come into the province* (*epibas tēi eparcheiāi*). Second aorist active participle of *epibainō*, to set foot upon. Literally, "Having set foot upon his province." *Eparcheia* is a late word for province, in N.T. only here and 23:34. Judea was not strictly a province, but a department (Page) of the province of Syria which was under a *propraetor* (*legatus Caesaris*) while Judea was under a *procurator* (*epitropos*). *After three days* (*meta treis hēmeras*). So in Acts 28:17 in Rome. That is on the third day, with a day of rest in between. Precisely the language used of the resurrection of Jesus "after three days" = "on the third day." So by common usage then and now.

2. *The principal men* (*hoi prōtoi*). The first men, the leading men of the city, besides the chief priests. In verse 15 we have "the chief priests and the elders." These chief men among the Jews would desire to pay their respects to the new Procurator on his first visit to Jerusalem. There was another high priest now, Ishmael in place of Ananias. *Informed him against Paul* (*enephanisan autōi kata tou Paulou*). "This renewal of the charge after two years, on the very first opportunity, is a measure, not only of their unsleeping hatred, but of the importance which they attached to Paul's influence" (Furneaux). *Besought* (*parekaloun*). Imperfect active, kept on beseeching as a special favour to the Jews.

3. *Asking favour against him* (*aitoumenoi charin kat' autou*). A favour to themselves (middle voice), not to Paul, but "against" (*kat'*, down, against) him. *That he would send for* (*hopōs metapempsētai*). First aorist middle subjunctive of *metapempō* (see 24:24, 26) with final particle *hopōs* like *hina*. Aorist tense for single case. *Laying wait* (*enedran poiountes*).

See on 23:16 for the word *enedra*. Old idiom (Thucydides) for laying a plot or ambush as here. Only these two uses of *enedra* in N.T. Two years before the Sanhedrin had agreed to the plot of the forty conspirators. Now they propose one on their own initiative. *On the way* (*kata tēn hodon*). Down along, up and down along the way. Plenty of opportunity would occur between Caesarea and Jerusalem for ambush and surprise attacks.

4. *Howbeit* (*men oun*). No antithesis expressed, though Page considers *de* in verse 6 to be one. They probably argued that it was easier for one man (Paul) to come to Jerusalem than for many to go down there. But Festus was clearly suspicious (verse 6) and was wholly within his rights to insist that they make their charges in Caesarea where he held court. *Was kept in charge* (*tēreisthai*). Present passive infinitive of *tēreō* in indirect assertion. *Hoti* with finite verb is more common after *apokrinomai*, but the infinitive with the accusative of general reference is proper as here (Robertson, *Grammar*, p. 1036). *Shortly* (*en tachei*). In quickness, in speed. Old and common usage, seen already in Luke 18:8; Acts 12:7; 22:18. Festus is clearly within his rights again since his stay in Caesarea had been so brief. He did go down in "eight or ten days" (verse 6). Luke did not consider the matter important enough to be precise.

5. *Them therefore which are of power among you* (*hoi oun en humin dunatoi*). "The mighty ones among you," "the men of power" (*dunatoi*) and authority, "the first men," the Sanhedrin, in other words. Note change here by Luke from indirect discourse in verse 4, to direct in verse 5 (*phēsin*, says he). *Go down with me* (*sunkatabantes*). Double compound (*sun, kata*) second aorist active participle of *sunkatabainō*. It was a fair proposal. *If there is anything amiss in the man* (*ei ti estin en tōi andri atopon*). Condition of the first class, assuming that there is (to be courteous to them), but not committing himself on the merits of the case. *Atopon*

is an old word, specially common in Plato, meaning "out of place." In N.T. only here and Luke 23:41 which see; Acts 28:6; II Thess. 3:2. Note present tense active voice of *katēgoreitōsan* (imperative) of *katēgoreō*, repeat their accusations.

6. *On the morrow* (*tēi epaurion*). Locative case of the article with *hēmerāi* understood (*epaurion*, adverb, to-morrow). Festus lost no time-for the chief men had come down with him. *Sat on the judgment seat* (*kathisas epi tou bēmatos*). A legal formality to give weight to the decision. Ingressive aorist active participle. For this use of *bēma* for judgment seat see on Matt. 27:19; John 19:13; Acts 12:21; 18:12; 25:10, 17. Same phrase repeated in 25:17. *To be brought* (*achthēnai*). First aorist passive infinitive of *agō* after *ekeleusen* (commanded). Same words repeated in 25:17 by Festus.

7. *When he was come* (*paragenomenou autou*). Genitive absolute of common verb *paraginomai* (cf. 24:24). *Which had come down* (*hoi katabebēkotes*). Perfect active participle of *katabainō*. They had come down on purpose at the invitation of Festus (verse 5), and were now ready. *Stood round about him* (*periestēsan auton*). Second aorist (ingressive) active (intransitive) of *periistēmi*, old verb, "Took their stand around him," "*periculum intentantes*" (Bengel). Cf. Luke 23:10 about Christ. They have no lawyer this time, but they mass their forces so as to impress Festus. *Bringing against him* (*katapherontes*). Bearing down on. See on 20:9 and 26:10, only N.T. examples of this ancient verb. *Many and grievous charges* (*polla kai barea aitiōmata*). This word *aitiōma* for old form *aitiama* is found in one papyrus (Moulton and Milligan's *Vocabulary*) in sense of "blame." But the charges were no "heavier" than those made by Tertullus (24:5–8). Paul's reply proves this and they were also probably on court record (Furneaux). See this adjective *barus* (heavy) used with *lukoi* (wolves) in

20:29. *Which they could not prove* (*ha ouk ischuon apodeixai*). Imperfect active of *ischuō*, to have strength or power as in 19:16, 20. Repetition and reiteration and vehemence took the place of proof (*apodeixai*, first aorist active infinitive of *apodeiknumi*, to show forth, old verb, in N.T. only here, Acts 2:22 which see and I Cor. 4:9).

8. *While Paul said in his defence* (*tou Paulou apologoumenou*). Genitive absolute again, present middle participle of *apologeomai*, old verb to make defence as in 19:33; 24:10; 26:1, 2. The recitative *hoti* of the Greek before a direct quotation is not reproduced in English. *Have I sinned at all* (*ti hēmarton*). Constative aorist active indicative of *hamartanō*, to miss, to sin. The *ti* is cognate accusative (or adverbial accusative). Either makes sense. Paul sums up the charges under the three items of law of the Jews, the temple, the Roman state (Caesar). This last was the one that would interest Festus and, if proved, would render Paul guilty of treason (*majestas*). Nero was Emperor A.D. 54–68, the last of the emperors with any hereditary claim to the name "Caesar." Soon it became merely a title like Kaiser and Czar (modern derivatives). In Acts only "Caesar" and "Augustus" are employed for the Emperor, not "King" (*Basileus*) as from the time of Domitian. Paul's denial is complete and no proof had been presented. Luke was apparently present at the trial.

9. *Desiring to gain favour with the Jews* (*thelōn tois Ioudaiois charin katathesthai*). Precisely the expression used of Felix by Luke in 24:27 which see. Festus, like Felix, falls a victim to fear of the Jews. *Before me* (*ep' emou*). Same use of *epi* with the genitive as in 23:30; 24:19, 21. Festus, seeing that it was unjust to condemn Paul and yet disadvantageous to absolve him (Blass), now makes the very proposal to Paul that the rulers had made to him in Jerusalem (verse 3). He added the words "*ep' emou*" (before me) as if to insure Paul of justice. If Festus was unwilling to give Paul

justice in Caesarea where his regular court held forth, what
assurance was there that Festus would give it to him at
Jerusalem in the atmosphere of intense hostility to Paul?
Only two years ago the mob, the Sanhedrin, the forty conspirators had tried to take his life in Jerusalem. Festus had
no more courage to do right than Felix, however plausible
his language might sound. Festus also, while wanting Paul
to think that he would in Jerusalem "be judged of these
things before me," in reality probably intended to turn
Paul over to the Sanhedrin in order to please the Jews,
probably with Festus present also to see that Paul received
justice (*me presente*). Festus possibly was surprised to find
that the charges were chiefly against Jewish law, though
one was against Caesar. It was not a mere change of
venue that Paul sensed, but the utter unwillingness of
Festus to do his duty by him and his willingness to con-
nive at Jewish vengeance on Paul. Paul had faced the mob
and the Sanhedrin in Jerusalem, two years of trickery at
the hands of Felix in Caesarea, and now he is confronted
by the bland chicanery of Festus. It is too much, the last
straw.

10. *I am standing before Caesar's judgment-seat* (*Hestōs epi
tou bēmatos Kaisaros eimi*). Periphrastic present perfect
indicative (*hestōs eimi*), second perfect participle *hestōs* of
histēmi (intransitive). Paul means to say that he is a Roman
citizen before a Roman tribunal. Festus was the representative of Caesar and had no right to hand him over to a Jewish
tribunal. Festus recognized this by saying to Paul "wilt
thou" (*theleis*). *Where I ought to be judged* (*hou me dei
krinesthai*). Rather, "Where I must be judged," for *dei*
expresses necessity (it is necessary). Paul exposes the conduct of Festus with merciless precision. *As thou also very
well knowest* (*hōs kai su kallion epiginōskeis*). "As thou also
dost understand (hast additional knowledge, *epiginōskeis*)
better" (than thou art willing to admit). That this is

Paul's meaning by the use of the comparative *kallion* (positive *kalōs*) is made plain by the confession of Festus to Agrippa in verse 18. Paul says that Festus knows that he has done no wrong to the Jews at all (*ouden ēdikēka*) and yet he is trying to turn him over to the wrath of the Jews in Jerusalem.

11. *If I am a wrong-doer* (*ei men oun adikō*). Condition of the first class with *ei* and the present active indicative of *adikeō* (*a* privative and *dikē*): "If I am in the habit of doing injustice," assuming it to be true for the sake of argument. *And have committed anything worthy of death* (*kai axion thanatou pepracha*). Same condition with the difference in tense (*pepracha*, perfect active indicative) of a single case instead of a general habit. Assuming either or both Paul draws his conclusion. *I refuse not to die* (*ou paraitoumai to apothanein*). Old verb to ask alongside, to beg from, to deprecate, to refuse, to decline. See on Luke 14:18f. Josephus (*Life*, 29) has *thanein ou paraitoumai*. Here the articular second aorist active infinitive is in the accusative case the object of *paraitoumai*: "I do not beg off dying from myself." *But if none of these things is* (*ei de ouden estin*). *De* here is contrasted with *men* just before. No word for "true" in the Greek. *Estin* ("is") in the Greek here means "exists." Same condition (first class, assumed as true). *Whereof these accuse me* (*hōn houtoi katēgorousin mou*). Genitive of relative *hōn* by attraction from *ha* (accusative with *katēgorousin*) to case of the unexpressed antecedent *toutōn* ("of these things"). *Mou* is genitive of person after *katēgorousin*. *No man can give me up to them* (*oudeis me dunatai autois charisasthai*). "Can" legally. Paul is a Roman citizen and not even Festus can make a free gift (*charisasthai*) of Paul to the Sanhedrin. *I appeal unto Caesar* (*Kaisara epikaloumai*). Technical phrase like Latin *Caesarem appello*. Originally the Roman law allowed an appeal from the magistrate to the people (*provocatio ad populum*), but the emperor repre-

sented the people and so the appeal to Caesar was the right
of every Roman citizen. Paul had crossed the Rubicon on
this point and so took his case out of the hands of dilatory
provincial justice (really injustice). Roman citizens could
make this appeal in capital offences. There would be expense connected with it, but better that with some hope than
delay and certain death in Jerusalem. Festus was no better
than Felix in his vacillation and desire to curry favour with
the Jews at Paul's expense. No doubt Paul's long desire to
see Rome (19:21; Rom. 15:22–28) and the promise of Jesus
that he would see Rome (Acts 23:11) played some part in
Paul's decision. But he made it reluctantly for he says in
Rome (Acts 28:19): "I was constrained to appeal." But
acquittal at the hands of Festus with the hope of going to
Rome as a free man had vanished.

12. *When he had conferred with the council* (*sunlalēsas
meta tou sumbouliou*). The word *sumboulion* in the N.T.
usually means "counsel" as in Matt. 12:14, but here alone
as an assembly of counsellors or council. But the papyri
(Milligan and Moulton's *Vocabulary*) furnish a number of
instances of this sense of the word as "council." Here it
apparently means the chief officers and personal retinue of
the procurator, his assessors (*assessores consiliarii*). These
local advisers were a necessity. Some discretion was allowed
the governor about granting the appeal. If the prisoner were
a well-known robber or pirate, it could be refused. *Thou hast
appealed unto Caesar* (*Kaisara epikeklēsai*). The same
technical word, but the perfect tense of the indicative.
Unto Caesar thou shalt go (*epi Kaisara poreusēi*). Perhaps
the volitive future (Robertson, *Grammar*, p. 874). Bengel
thinks that Festus sought to frighten Paul with these words.
Knowling suggests that "they may have been uttered, if
not with a sneer, yet with the implication 'thou little knowest
what an appeal to Caesar means.'" But embarrassment
will come to Festus. He has refused to acquit this prisoner.

Hence he must formulate charges against him to go before Caesar.

13. *When certain days were passed* (*Hēmerōn diagenomenon*). Genitive absolute of *diaginomai*, to come between, "days intervening." *Agrippa the King* (*Agrippas ho basileus*). Agrippa II son of Agrippa I of Acts 12:20–23. On the death of Herod King of Chalcis A.D. 48, Claudius A.D. 50 gave this Herod Agrippa II the throne of Chalcis so that Luke is correct in calling him king, though he is not king of Judea. But he was also given by Claudius the government of the temple and the right of appointing the high priest. Later he was given also the tetrarchies of Philip and Lysanias. He was the last Jewish king in Palestine, though not king of Judea. He angered the Jews by building his palace so as to overlook the temple and by frequent changes in the high priesthood. He made his capital at Caesarea Philippi which he called Neronias in honour of Nero. Titus visited it after the fall of Jerusalem. *Bernice* (*Bernikē*). He was her brother and yet she lived with him in shameful intimacy in spite of her marriage to her uncle Herod King of Chalcis and to Polemon King of Cilicia whom she left. Schuerer calls her both a Jewish bigot and a wanton. She afterwards became the mistress of Titus. *Arrived at Caesarea* (*katēntēsan eis Kaisarian*). Came down (first aorist active of *katantaō*) to Caesarea from Jerusalem. *And saluted Festus* (*aspasamenoi ton Phēston*). The Textus Receptus has *aspasomenoi* the future participle, but the correct text is the aorist middle participle *aspasamenoi* which cannot possibly mean subsequent action as given in the Canterbury Revision "and saluted." It can only mean contemporaneous (simultaneous) action "saluting" or antecedent action like the margin "having saluted." But antecedent action is not possible here, so that simultaneous action is the only alternative. It is to be noted that the salutation synchronized with the arrival in Caesarea (note *kata*, down, the effec-

tive aorist tense), not with the departure from Jerusalem, nor with the whole journey. Rightly understood the aorist participle here gives no trouble at all (Robertson, *Grammar*, pp. 861–3).

14. *Tarried* (*dietribon*). Imperfect active of *diatribō*, common verb for spending time (Acts 12:19, etc.). *Many days* (*pleious hēmeras*). More days (than a few). Accusative case for extent of time. *Laid Paul's case* (*anetheto ta kata ton Paulon*). Second aorist middle indicative of *anatithēmi*, old verb to set before, to place up, as if for consultation in conference. Only twice in N.T. here and Gal. 2:2. The motive of Festus is not given, though it was natural enough in view of the quandary of Festus about Paul (the things about Paul) and Agrippa's interest in and responsibility for Jewish worship in the temple in Jerusalem. It is quite possible that Festus had a bit of *ennui* over the visit of these Jewish dignitaries as "more days" went by. Hence the tone of Festus about Paul in this proposal for the entertainment of Agrippa and Bernice is certainly one of superficial and supremely supercilious indifference. *Left a prisoner* (*katalelimmenos desmios*). Perfect passive participle of *kataleipō*, to leave behind. Paul is one of Felix's left overs (left behind), a sort of "junk" left on his hands. This cowardly Roman procurator thus pictures the greatest of living men and the greatest preacher of all time to this profligate pair (brother and sister) of sinners. Undoubtedly today in certain circles Christ and his preachers are held up to like contempt.

15. *Informed* (*enephanisan*). Same word as in 23:15, 22; 25:2 which see. *Asking for sentence against him* (*aitoumenoi kat' autou katadikēn*). Only N.T. example of this old word (penalty, fine, condemnation) from *kata* and *dikē* (justice against).

16. *It is not the custom of the Romans* (*hoti ouk estin ethos Rōmaiois*). If a direct quotation, *hoti* is recitative as in Authorized Version. Canterbury Revision takes it as indirect

discourse after *apekrithēn* (I answered), itself in a relative clause (*pros hous*) with the present tense (*estin*, is) preserved as is usual. There is a touch of disdain (Furneaux) in the tone of Festus. He may refer to a demand of the Jews before they asked that Paul be brought to Jerusalem (25:3). At any rate there is a tone of scorn towards the Jews. *Before that the accused have* (*prin ē ho katēgoroumenos echoi*). This use of the optative in this temporal clause with *prin ē* instead of the subjunctive *an echēi* is in conformity with literary Greek and occurs only in Luke's writings in the N.T. (Robertson, *Grammar*, p. 970). This sequence of modes is a mark of the literary style occasionally seen in Luke. It is interesting here to note the succession of dependent clauses in verses 14 to 16. *The accusers face to face* (*kata prosōpon tous katēgorous*). Same word *katēgoros* as in 23:30, 35; 25:18. This all sounds fair enough. *And have had opportunity to make his defence concerning the matter laid against him* (*topon te apologias laboi peri tou egklēmatos*). Literally, "And should receive (*laboi* optative for same reason as *echoi* above, second aorist active of *lambanō*) opportunity for defence (objective genitive) concerning the charge" (*egklēmatos* in N.T. only here and 23:19 which see).

17. *When they were come together here* (*sunelthontōn enthade*). Genitive absolute of second aorist active participle of *sunerchomai*, but without *autōn* (they), merely understood. *Delay* (*anabolēn*). Old word from *anaballō*, only here in N.T.

18. *Brought* (*epheron*). Imperfect active of *pherō*, referring to their repeated charges. *Of such evil things as I supposed* (*hōn egō hupenooun ponērōn*). Incorporation of the antecedent *ponērōn* into the relative clause and change of the case of the relative from the accusative *ha* object of *hupenooun* to the genitive like *ponērōn* (Robertson, *Grammar*, p. 719). Note the imperfect active *hupenooun* of *huponoeō* to emphasize Festus's state of mind about Paul before the trial. This

old verb only three times in the N.T. (here, Acts 13:25 which see; 27:27).

19. *But had* (*de eichon*). Descriptive imperfect active of *echō* and *de* of contrast (but). *Concerning their own religion* (*peri tēs idias deisidaimonias*). See on 17:22 for discussion of this word. Festus would hardly mean "superstition," whatever he really thought, because Agrippa was a Jew. *And of one Jesus* (*kai peri tinos Iēsou*). This is the climax of supercilious scorn toward both Paul and "one Jesus." *Who was dead* (*tethnēkotos*). Perfect active participle of *thnēskō* agreeing with *Iēsou* (genitive). As being dead. *Whom Paul affirmed to be alive* (*hon ephasken ho Paulos zēin*). Imperfect active of *phaskō*, old form of *phēmi* to say, in the N.T. only here and Acts 24:9; Rom. 1:22. Infinitive *zēin* in indirect discourse with *hon* (whom) the accusative of general reference. With all his top-loftical airs Festus has here correctly stated the central point of Paul's preaching about Jesus as no longer dead, but living.

20. *Being perplexed* (*aporoumenos*). Present middle participle of the common verb *aporeō* (*a* privative and *poros* way), to be in doubt which way to turn, already in Mark 6:20 which see and Luke 24:4. The Textus Receptus has *eis* after here, but critical text has only the accusative which this verb allows (Mark 6:20) as in Thucydides and Plato. *How to inquire concerning these things* (*tēn peri toutōn zētēsin*). Literally, "as to the inquiry concerning these things." This is not the reason given by Luke in verse 9 (wanting to curry favour with the Jews), but doubtless this motive also actuated Festus as both could be true. *Whether he would go to Jerusalem* (*ei bouloito poreuesthai eis Ierosoluma*). Optative in indirect question after *elegon* (asked or said) imperfect active, though the present indicative could have been retained with change of person: "Dost thou wish, etc.," (*ei boulēi, etc.*). See Robertson, *Grammar*, pp. 1031, 1044. This is the question put to Paul in verse 9 though *theleis* is there used.

21. *When Paul had appealed* (*tou Paulou epikalesamenou*). Genitive absolute with first aorist middle participle of *epikaleomai*, the technical word for appeal (verses 11 and 12). The first aorist passive infinitive *tērēthēnai* (to be kept) is the object of the participle. *For the decision of the emperor* (*eis tēn tou Sebastou diagnōsin*). *Diagnōsin* (cf. *diagnōsomai* 24:22, I will determine) is the regular word for a legal examination (*cognitio*), thorough sifting (*dia*), here only in N.T. Instead of "the Emperor" it should be "the Augustus," as *Sebastos* is simply the Greek translation of *Augustus*, the adjective (Revered, Reverent) assumed by Octavius B.C. 27 as the *agnomen* that summed up all his various offices instead of *Rex* so offensive to the Romans having led to the death of Julius Caesar. The successors of Octavius assumed *Augustus* as a title. The Greek term *Sebastos* has the notion of worship (cf. *sebasma* in Acts 17:25). In the N.T. only here, verse 25, and 27:1 (of the legion). It was more imposing than "Caesar" which was originally a family name (always official in the N.T.) and it fell in with the tendency toward emperor-worship which later played such a large part in Roman life and which Christians opposed so bitterly. China is having a revival of this idea in the insistence on bowing three times to the picture of Sun-Yat-Sen. *Till I should send him to Caesar* (*heōs an anapempsō auton pros Kaisara*). Here *anapempsō* can be either future indicative or first aorist subjunctive (identical in first person singular), aorist subjunctive the usual construction with *heōs* for future time (Robertson, *Grammar*, p. 876). Literally, "send up" (*ana*) to a superior (the emperor). Common in this sense in the papyri and *Koinē* writers. Here "Caesar" is used as the title of Nero instead of "Augustus" as *Kurios* (Lord) occurs in verse 26.

22. *I also could wish* (*eboulomēn kai autos*). The imperfect for courtesy, rather than the blunt *boulomai*, I wish, I want. Literally, "I myself also was wishing" (while you were

talking), a compliment to the interesting story told by Festus. The use of *an* with the imperfect would really mean that he does not wish (a conclusion of the second class condition, determined as unfulfilled). *An* with the optative would show only a languid desire. The imperfect is keen enough and yet polite enough to leave the decision with Festus if inconvenient for any reason (Robertson, *Grammar*, pp. 885–7). Agrippa may have heard much about Christianity.

23. *When Agrippa was come and Bernice* (*elthontos tou Agrippa kai tēs Bernikēs*). Genitive absolute, the participle agreeing in number and gender (masculine singular, *elthontos*) with *Agrippa*, *Bernikēs* being added as an afterthought. *With great pomp* (*meta pollēs phantasias*). *Phantasia* is a *Koiné* word (Polybius, Diodorus, etc.) from the old verb *phantazō* (Heb. 12:21) and it from *phainō*, common verb to show, to make an appearance. This is the only N.T. example of *phantasia*, though the kindred common word *phantasma* (appearance) occurs twice in the sense of apparition or spectre (Matt. 14:26; Mark 6:49). Herodotus (VII. 10) used the verb *phantazō* for a showy parade. Festus decided to gratify the wish of Agrippa by making the "hearing" of Paul the prisoner (verse 22) an occasion for paying a compliment to Agrippa (Rackham) by a public gathering of the notables in Caesarea. Festus just assumed that Paul would fall in with this plan for a grand entertainment though he did not have to do it. *Into the place of hearing* (*eis to akroatērion*). From *akroaomai* (to be a hearer) and, like the Latin *auditorium*, in Roman law means the place set aside for hearing, and deciding cases. Here only in the N.T. Late word, several times in Plutarch and other *Koiné* writers. The hearing was "semi-official" (Page) as is seen in verse 26. *With the chief captains* (*sun te chiliarchois*). Chiliarchs, each a leader of a thousand. There were five cohorts of soldiers stationed in Caesarea. *And the principal men of the city* (*kai andrasin tois kat' exochēn*). The use of *kat' exochēn*,

like our French phrase *par excellence*, occurs here only in the
N.T., and not in the ancient Greek, but it is found in inscriptions of the first century A.D. (Moulton and Milligan's
Vocabulary). *Exochē* in medical writers is any protuberance
or swelling. Cf. our phrase "outstanding men." *At the
command of Festus (keleusantos tou Phēstou).* Genitive absolute again, "Festus having commanded."

24. *Which are here present with us (hoi sunparontes hēmin).*
Present articular participle of *sunpareimi* (only here in N.T.)
with associative instrumental case *hēmin*. *Made suit to me
(enetuchon moi).* Second aorist active indicative of *entug-
chanō*, old verb to fall in with a person, to go to meet for
consultation or supplication as here. Common in old Greek
and *Koiné*. Cf. Rom. 8:27, 34. See *enteuxis* (petition) I Tim.
2:1. Papyri give many examples of the technical sense of
enteuxis as petition (Deissmann, *Bible Studies*, p. 121).
Some MSS. have plural here *enetuchon* rather than the
singular *enetuchen*. *Crying (boōntes).* Yelling and demand-
ing with loud voices. *That he ought not to live any longer (mē
dein auton zēin mēketi).* Indirect command (demand) with
the infinitive *dein* for *dei* (it is necessary). The double negative (*mē—mēketi*) with *zēin* intensifies the demand.

25. *But I found (egō de katelabomēn).* Second aorist
middle of *katalambanō*, to lay hold of, to grasp, to comprehend as in 4:13; 10:34. *That he had committed nothing worthy
of death (mēden axion auton thanatou peprachenai).* Perfect
active infinitive of *prassō* in indirect assertion with negative
mē and accusative *auton* of general reference, the usual
idiom. Verse 25 repeats the statement in verse 21, perhaps
for the benefit of the assembled dignitaries.

26. *No certain thing (asphales ti — ou).* Nothing definite
or reliable (*a* privative, *sphallō*, to trip). All the charges of
the Sanhedrin slipped away or were tripped up by Paul.
Festus confesses that he had nothing left and thereby con-
victs himself of gross insincerity in his proposal to Paul in

verse 9 about going up to Jerusalem. By his own statement
he should have set Paul free. The various details here bear
the marks of the eyewitness. Luke was surely present and
witnessed this grand spectacle with Paul as chief performer.
Unto my lord (*tōi kuriōi*). Augustus (Octavius) and Tiberius
refused the title of *kurios* (lord) as too much like *rex* (king)
and like master and slave, but the servility of the subjects
gave it to the other emperors who accepted it (Nero among
them). Antoninus Pius put it on his coins. Deissmann
(*Light from the Ancient East*, p. 105) gives an ostracon dated
Aug. 4, A.D. 63 with the words "in the year nine of Nero
the lord" (*enatou Nerōnos tou kuriou*). Deissmann (*op. cit.,*
pp. 349ff.) runs a most interesting parallel "between the cult
of Christ and the cult of Caesar in the application of the
term *kurios*, lord" in ostraca, papyri, inscriptions. Beyond
a doubt Paul has all this fully in mind when he says in I Cor.
12:3 that "no one is able to say *Kurios Iēsous* except in the
Holy Spirit" (cf. also Phil. 2:11). The Christians claimed this
word for Christ and it became the test in the Roman persecutions as when Polycarp steadily refused to say "Lord
Caesar" and insisted on saying "Lord Jesus" when it meant
his certain death. *Before you* (*eph' humōn*). The whole
company. In no sense a new trial, but an examination in
the presence of these prominent men to secure data and to
furnish entertainment and pleasure to Agrippa (verse 22).
Especially before thee (*malista epi sou*). Out of courtesy. It
was the main reason as verse 22 shows. Agrippa was a Jew
and Festus was glad of the chance to see what he thought
of Paul's case. *After examination had* (*tēs anakriseōs genomenēs*). Genitive absolute, "the examination having taken
place." *Anakrisis* from *anakrinō* (cf. 12:19; 24:8; 28:18)
is a legal term for preliminary examination. Only here in the
N.T. Inscriptions and papyri give it as examination of
slaves or other property. *That I may have somewhat to write*
(*hopōs schō ti grapsō*). Ingressive aorist subjunctive *schō*

(may get) with *hopōs* (final particle like *hina*). *Ti grapsō* in indirect question after *schō* is either future indicative or aorist subjunctive (Robertson, *Grammar*, p. 1045). Festus makes it plain that this is not a "trial," but an examination for his convenience to help him out of a predicament.

27. *Unreasonable* (*alogon*). Old word from *a* privative and *logos* (reason, speech). "Without reason" as of animals (Jude 10; II Peter 2:12), "contrary to reason" here. These the only N.T. instances and in harmony with ancient usage. *In sending* (*pemponta*). Note accusative case with the infinitive *sēmānai* though *moi* (dative) just before. Cf. same variation in 15:22f.; 22:17. *Signify* (*sēmānai*). First aorist active infinitive (not *sēmēnai*, the old form) of *sēmainō*, to give a sign (*sēmeion*). *The charges* (*tas aitias*). This naïve confession of Festus reveals how unjust has been his whole treatment of Paul. He had to send along with the appeal of Paul *litterae dimissoriae* (*apostoli*) which would give a statement of the case (Page).

CHAPTER XXVI

1. *Thou art permitted (epitrepetai soi)*. Literally, It is permitted thee. As if Agrippa were master of ceremonies instead of Festus. Agrippa as a king and guest presides at the grand display while Festus has simply introduced Paul. *For thyself (huper seautou)*. Some MSS. have *peri* (concerning). Paul is allowed to speak in his own behalf. No charges are made against him. In fact, Festus has admitted that he has no real proof of any charges. *Stretched forth his hand (ekteinas tēn cheira)*. Dramatic oratorical gesture (not for silence as in 12:17; 13:16) with the chain still upon it (verse 29) linking him to the guard. First aorist active participle of *ekteinō*, to stretch out. *Made his defence (apologeito)*. Inchoative imperfect of *apologeomai* (middle), "began to make his defence." This is the fullest of all Paul's defences. He has no word of censure of his enemies or of resentment, but seizes the opportunity to preach Christ to such a distinguished company which he does with "singular dignity" (Furneaux). He is now bearing the name of Christ "before kings" (Acts 9:15). In general Paul follows the line of argument of the speech on the stairs (chapter 22).

2. *I think myself happy (hēgēmai emauton makarion)*. See on Matt. 5:3 for *makarios*. Blass notes that Paul, like Tertullus, begins with *captatio benevolentiae*, but *absque adulatione*. He says only what he can truthfully speak. For *hēgēmai* see Phil. 3:7; I Tim. 6:1 (perfect middle indicative of *hēgeomai*), I have considered. *That I am to make my defence (mellōn apologeisthai)*. Literally, "being about to make my defence." *Whereof I am accused (hōn egkaloumai)*. Genitive with *egkaloumai* as in 19:40 or by attraction from accusative of relative (*ha*) to case of antecedent (*pantōn*).

3. *Especially because thou art expert* (*malista gnōstēn onta se*). Or like the margin, "because thou art especially expert," according as *malista* is construed. *Gnōstēn* is from *ginōskō* and means a knower, expert, connoisseur. Plutarch uses it and Deissmann (*Light*, etc., p. 367) restores it in a papyrus. Agrippa had the care of the temple, the appointment of the high priest, and the care of the sacred vestments. But the accusative *onta se* gives trouble here coming so soon after *sou* (genitive with *epi*). Some MSS. insert *epistamenos* or *eidōs* (knowing) but neither is genuine. Page takes it as "governed by the sense of thinking or considering." Knowling considers it an anacoluthon. Buttmann held it to be an accusative absolute after the old Greek idiom. *Tuchon* is such an instance though used as an adverb (I Cor. 16:6). It is possible that one exists in Eph. 1:18. See other examples discussed in Robertson's *Grammar*, pp. 490f. *Customs and questions* (*ethōn te kai zētēmatōn*). Both *consuetudinum in practicis* and *quaestionum in theoreticis* (Bengel). Agrippa was qualified to give Paul an understanding and a sympathetic hearing. Paul understands perfectly the grand-stand play of the whole performance, but he refused to be silent and chose to use this opportunity, slim as it seemed, to get a fresh hearing for his own case and to present the claims of Christ to this influential man. His address is a masterpiece of noble apologetic. *Patiently* (*makrothumōs*). Adverb from *makrothumos*. Only here in the N.T., though *makrothumia* occurs several times. Vulgate has *longanimiter*. Long spirit, endurance, opposite of impatience. So Paul takes his time.

4. *My manner of life* (*tēn men oun biōsin mou*). With *men oun* Paul passes from the *captatio benevolentiae* (verses 1 and 2) "to the *narratio* or statement of his case" (Page). *Biōsis* is from *bioō* (I Peter 4:2) and that from *bios* (course of life). This is the only instance of *biōsis* yet found except the Prologue (10) of Ecclesiasticus and an inscription given in Ramsay's *Cities and Bishoprics of Phrygia*, Vol. II, p. 650.

Know (*isāsi*). Literary form instead of the vernacular *Koiné* *oidasin*. Paul's early life in Tarsus and Jerusalem was an open book to all Jews.

5. *Having knowledge of me from the first* (*proginōskontes me anōthen*). Literally, "knowing me beforehand" (both *pro* and *anōthen*), from the beginning of Paul's public education in Jerusalem (Knowling). Cf. II Peter 3:17. *If they be willing to testify* (*ean thelōsin marturein*). Condition of third class (*ean* and subjunctive). A neat turning of the tables on the distinguished audience about Paul's Jerusalem reputation before his conversion. *After the straitest sect* (*tēn akribestatēn hairesin*). This is a true superlative (not elative) and one of the three (also *hagiōtatos*, Jude 20, *timiōtatos* Rev. 18:12; 21:11) superlatives in -*tatos* in the N.T. (Robertson, *Grammar*, pp. 279f., 670), though common enough in the LXX and the papyri. *Hairesin* (choosing) is properly used here with Pharisees (Josephus, *Life*, 38). *Religion* (*thrēskeias*). From *thrēskeuō* and this from *thrēskos* (James 1:26), old word for religious worship or discipline, common in the papyri and inscriptions (Moulton and Milligan's *Vocabulary*) for reverent worship, not mere external ritual. In N.T. only here, James 1:26f.; Col. 2:18. *I lived a Pharisee* (*ezēsa Pharisaios*). Emphatic position. Paul knew the rules of the Pharisees and played the game to the full (Gal. 1:14; Phil. 3:5f.). The Talmud makes it plain what the life of a Pharisee was. Paul had become one of the leaders and stars of hope for his sect.

6. *And now* (*kai nun*). Sharp comparison between his youth and the present. *To be judged for the hope* (*ep' elpidi — krinomenos*). The hope of the resurrection and of the promised Messiah (13:32). Page calls verses 6 to 8 a parenthesis in the course of Paul's argument by which he shows that his life in Christ is a real development of the best in Pharisaism. He does resume his narrative in verse 9, but verses 6 to 8 are the core of his defence already presented in Gal. 3

and Rom. 9 to 11 where he proves that the children of faith
are the real seed of Abraham.

7. *Our twelve tribes* (*to dōdekaphulon hēmōn*). A word
found only here in N.T. and in Christian and Jewish writings, though *dōdekamēnon* (twelve month) is common in the
papyri and *dekaphulos* (ten tribes) in Herodotus. Paul's
use of this word for the Jewish people, like James 1:1 (*tais
dōdeka phulais*, the twelve tribes), shows that Paul had no
knowledge of any "lost ten tribes." There is a certain national pride and sense of unity in spite of the dispersion
(Page). *Earnestly* (*en ekteneiāi*). A late word from *ekteinō*,
to stretch out, only here in N.T., but in papyri and inscriptions. Page refers to Simeon and Anna (Luke 2:25-28)
as instances of Jews looking for the coming of the Messiah.
Note the accusative of *nukta kai hēmeran* as in 20:31. *Hope
to attain* (*elpizei katantēsai*). This Messianic hope had been
the red thread running through Jewish history. Today, alas,
it is a sadly worn thread for Jews who refuse to see the Messiah in Jesus. *I am accused by Jews* (*egkaloumai hupo Ioudaiōn*). The very word used in 23:28 (*enekaloun*) which see,
and by Jews of all people in the world whose mainspring
was this very "hope." It is a tremendously effective turn.

8. *Incredible with you* (*apiston par' humin*). This old
word *apiston* (*a* privative and *pistos*) means either unfaith-
ful (Luke 12:46), unbelieving (John 20:27), or unbelievable
as here). Paul turns suddenly from Agrippa to the audience
(*par' humin*, plural), most of whom were probably Gentiles
and scouted the doctrine of the resurrection as at Athens
(17:32). *If God doth raise the dead* (*ei ho theos nekrous egeirei*).
Condition of the first class assuming that God does raise
dead people. Only God can do it. This rhetorical question
needs no answer, though the narrative resumed in verse 9
does it in a way.

9. *I verily thought with myself* (*egō men oun edoxa emautōi*).
Personal construction instead of the impersonal, a touch

of the literary style. Paul's "egoism" is deceived as so often happens. *I ought* (*dein*). Infinitive the usual construction with *dokeō*. Necessity and a sense of duty drove Paul on even in this great sin (see on 23:1), a common failing with persecutors. *Contrary* (*enantia*). Old word (adjective), over against, opposite (Acts 27:4), then hostile to as here.

10. *I both shut up many* (*pollous te katekleisa*). Effective aorist active of *katakleiō*, old word to shut down like a trap door, in N.T. only here and Luke 3:20. Double use of *te* (both—and). *Having received authority from the chief priests* (*tēn para tōn archiereōn exousian labōn*). "The authority," he says. Paul was the official persecutor of the saints under the direction of the Sanhedrin. He mentions "chief priests" (Sadducees), though a Pharisee himself. Both parties were co-operating against the saints. *And when they were put to death* (*anairoumenōn te autōn*). Genitive absolute with present passive participle of *anaireō*. *I gave my vote against them* (*katēnegka psēphon*). "I cast down my pebble" (a black one). The ancient Greeks used white pebbles for acquittal (Rev. 2:17), black ones for condemnation as here (the only two uses of the word in the N.T.). Paul's phrase (not found elsewhere) is more vivid than the usual *katapsēphizō* for voting. They literally cast the pebbles into the urn. Cf. *sumpsēphizō* in Acts 19:19, *sugkatapsephizo* in Acts 1:26. If Paul's language is taken literally here, he was a member of the Sanhedrin and so married when he led the persecution. That is quite possible, though he was not married when he wrote I Cor. 7:7f., but a widower. It is possible to take the language figuratively for approval, but not so natural.

11. *Punishing* (*timōrōn*). Old word *timōreō* originally to render help, to succor (*timōros*, from *timē* and *ouros*), then to avenge (for honour). In N.T. only here and 22:5. *I strove to make them blaspheme* (*ēnagkazon blasphēmein*). Conative imperfect active of *anagkazō*, old verb from *anagkē*

(necessity, compulsion). The tense, like the imperfect in Matt. 3:14; Luke 1:59, leaves room to hope that Paul was not successful in this effort, for he had already said that he brought many "unto death" (22:4). *I persecuted (ediōkon).* Imperfect active again, repeated attempts. The old verb *diōkō* was used to run after or chase game and then to chase enemies. The word "persecute" is the Latin *persequor*, to follow through or after. It is a vivid picture that Paul here paints of his success in hunting big game, a grand heresy hunt. *Even unto foreign cities (kai eis exō poleis).* We know of Damascus, and Paul evidently planned to go to other cities outside of Palestine and may even have done so before the fateful journey to Damascus.

12. *Whereupon (en hois).* "In which things" (affairs of persecution), "on which errand." Cf. 24:18. Paul made them leave Palestine (11:19) and followed them beyond it (9:2). *With the authority and commission (met' exousias kai epitropēs).* Not merely "authority" (*exousia*), but express appointment (*epitropē*, old word, but here only in N.T., derived from *epitropos*, steward, and that from *epitrepō*, to turn over to, to commit).

13. *At midday (hēmeras mesēs).* Genitive of time and idiomatic use of *mesos*, in the middle of the day, more vivid than *mesēmbrian* (22:6). *Above the brightness of the sun (huper tēn lamprotēta tou hēliou).* Here alone not in Acts 9 or 22, though implied in 9:3 and 22:6, "indicating the supernatural character of the light" (Knowling). Luke makes no effort to harmonize the exact phrases here with those in the other accounts and Paul here (verse 16) blends together what Jesus said to him directly and the message of Jesus through Ananias (9:15). The word *lamprotēs*, old word, is here alone in the N.T. *Shining round about me (perilampsan me).* First aorist active participle of *perilampō*, common Koiné verb, in N.T. only here and Luke 2:9.

14. *When we were all fallen (pantōn katapesontōn hēmōn).*

Genitive absolute with second aorist active participle of *katapiptō*. *In the Hebrew language* (*tēi Ebraidi dialektōi*). Natural addition here, for Paul is speaking in Greek, not Aramaic as in 22:2. *It is hard for thee to kick against the goad* (*sklēron soi pros kentra laktizein*). Genuine here, but not in chapters 9 and 22. A common proverb as Aeschylus *Ag.* 1624: *Pros kentra mē laktize*. "It is taken from an ox that being pricked with a goad kicks and receives a severer wound" (Page). Cf. the parables of Jesus (Matt. 13:35). Blass observes that Paul's mention of this Greek and Latin proverb is an indication of his culture. Besides he mentions (not invents) it here rather than in chapter 22 because of the culture of this audience. *Kentron* means either sting as of bees (II Macc. 14:19) and so of death (I Cor. 15:55) or an iron goad in the ploughman's hand as here (the only two N.T. examples). Note plural here (goads) and *laktizein* is present active infinitive so that the idea is "to keep on kicking against goads." This old verb means to kick with the heel (adverb *lax*, with the heel), but only here in the N.T. There is a papyrus example of kicking (*laktizō*) with the feet against the door.

16. *Arise and stand* (*anastēthi kai stēthi*). "Emphatic assonance" (Page). Second aorist active imperative of compound verb (*anistēmi*) and simplex (*histēmi*). "Stand up and take a stand." *Have I appeared unto thee* (*ōphthēn soi*). First aorist passive indicative of *horaō*. See on Luke 22:43. *To appoint thee* (*procheirisasthai se*). See 3:30 and 22:14 for this verb. *Both of the things wherein thou hast seen me* (*hōn te eides me*). The reading *me* (not in all MSS.) makes it the object of *eides* (didst see) and *hōn* is genitive of *ha* (accusative of general reference) attracted to the case of the unexpressed antecedent *toutōn*. Paul is thus a personal eyewitness of the Risen Christ (Luke 1:1; I Cor. 4:1; 9:1). *And of the things wherein I will appear unto thee* (*hōn te ophthēsomai soi*). Here again *hōn* is genitive of the accusa-

tive (general reference) relative *ha* attracted to the case of
the antecedent *toutōn* or *ekeinōn* as before. But *ophthēsomai*
is first future passive of *horaō* and cannot be treated as
active or middle. Page takes it to mean "the visions in which
I shall be seen by you," the passive form bringing out the
agency of God. See those in Acts 18:9; 23:11; II Cor. 12:2.
The passive voice, however, like *apekrithēn* and *ephobēthēn*,
did become sometimes transitive in the *Koinē* (Robertson,
Grammar, p. 819).

17. *Delivering thee (exairoumenos se)*. Present middle participle of *exaireō*, old verb and usually so rendered, but the
old Greek also uses it for "choose" as also in LXX (Isa.
48:10). The papyri give examples of both meanings and
either makes good sense here. God was continually rescuing
Paul "out of the hands of Jews and Gentiles and Paul was
a chosen vessel" (9:15). Modern scholars are also divided.

18. *To open (anoixai)*. First aorist active infinitive of
purpose. *That they may turn (tou epistrepsai)*. Another infinitive of purpose first aorist active (genitive case and articular), epexegetic to *anoixai*. *That they may receive (tou labein)*.
Another genitive articular infinitive of purpose subordinate
(epexegetic) to *tou epistrepsai*. *Sanctified by faith in me
(hēgiasmenois pistei tēi eis eme)*. Perfect passive participle
of *hagiazō*, instrumental case of *pistei*, article before *eis eme*
("by faith, that in me"). These important words of Jesus to
Paul give his justification to this cultured audience for his
response to the command of Jesus. This was the turning
point in Paul's career and it was a step forward and upward.

19. *Wherefore (hothen)*. This relatival adverb (cf. 14:26;
28:13) gathers up all that Paul has said. *I was not disobedient
(ouk egenomēn apeithēs)*. Litotes again, "I did not become
(second aorist middle indicative of *ginomai*) disobedient"
(*apeithēs*, old word already in Luke 1:17). *Unto the heavenly
vision (tēi ouraniōi optasiāi)*. A later form of *opsis*, from

optazō, in LXX, and in N.T. (Luke 1:22; 24:23; Acts 26:19; II Cor. 12:1). Only time that Paul uses it about seeing Christ on the Damascus road, but no reflection on the reality of the event.

20. *But declared* (*alla apēggellon*). Imperfect active of *apaggellō*, repeatedly. *Throughout all the country of Judea* (*pāsan te tēn chōran tēs Ioudaias*). The accusative here in the midst of the datives (*tois en Damaskōi, Ierosolumois, tois ethnesin*) seems strange and Page feels certain that *eis* should be here even though absent in Aleph A B. But the accusative of extent of space will explain it (Robertson, *Grammar*, p. 469). *Doing works worthy of repentance* (*axia tēs metanoias erga prassontas*). Accusative case of present active participle *prassontas* because of the implied *autous* with the present infinitive *metanoein* (repent) and *epistrephein* (turn), though the dative *prassousin* could have been used to agree with *ethnesin* (Gentiles). Cf. Matt 3:8 for similar language used of the Baptist. Paul, the greatest of theologians, was an interesting practical preacher.

21. *Assayed to kill me* (*epeirōnto diacheirisasthai*). Conative imperfect middle of *peiraō*, the old form of the later *Koiné peirazō* so common in the *Koiné*, but in N.T. here only. Some MSS. have it in Acts 9:26 and Heb. 4:15. The old verb *diacheirizō*, to take in hand, middle to lay hands on, to slay, occurs in N.T. only here and 5:30 which see.

22. *Having therefore obtained* (*oun tuchōn*). Second aorist active participle of old verb *tugchanō*. *The help that is from God* (*epikourias tēs apo tou theou*). Old word from *epikoureō*, to aid, and that from *epikouros*, ally, assister. Only here in N.T. God is Paul's ally. All of the plots of the Jews against Paul had failed so far. *I stand* (*hestēka*). Second perfect of *histēmi*, to place, intransitive to stand. Picturesque word (Page) of Paul's stability and fidelity (cf. Phil. 4:1; Eph. 6:13). *Both to small and great* (*mikrōi te kai megalōi*). Dative

singular (rather than instrumental, taking *marturoumenos* middle, not passive) and use of *te kai* links the two adjectives together in an inclusive way. These two adjectives in the singular (representative singular rather than plural) can apply to age (young and old) or to rank (Rev. 11:18) as is specially suitable here with Festus and Agrippa present. In Acts 8:10 (Heb. 8:11) the phrase explains *pantes* (all). *Saying nothing but what* (*ouden ektos legōn hōn*). "Saying nothing outside of those things which." The ablative relative *hōn* is attracted into the case of the unexpressed antecedent *toutōn* and so ablative after *ektos* (adverbial preposition common in LXX, the papyri. In N.T. here and I Cor. 6:18; 15:27; II Cor. 12:2f.). Cf. Luke 16:29 about Moses and the prophets.

23. *How that the Christ must suffer* (*ei pathētos ho Christos*). Literally, "if the Messiah is subject to suffering." *Ei* can here mean "whether" as in Heb. 7:15. This use of a verbal in *-tos* for capability or possibility occurs in the N.T. alone in *pathētos* (Robertson, *Grammar*, p. 157). This word occurs in Plutarch in this sense. It is like the Latin *patibilis* and is from *paschō*. Here alone in N.T. Paul is speaking from the Jewish point of view. Most rabbis had not rightly understood Isa. 53. When the Baptist called Jesus "the Lamb of God" (John 1:29) it was a startling idea. It is not then "must suffer" here, but "can suffer." The Cross of Christ was a stumbling-block to the rabbis. *How that he first by the resurrection of the dead* (*ei prōtos ex anastaseōs nekrōn*). Same construction with *ei* (whether). This point Paul had often discussed with the Jews: "whether he (the Messiah) by a resurrection of dead people." Others had been raised from the dead, but Christ is the first (*prōtos*) who arose from the dead and no longer dies (Rom. 6:19) and proclaims light (*phōs mellei kataggellein*). Paul is still speaking from the Jewish standpoint: "is about to (going to) proclaim light." See verse 18 for "light" and Luke 2:32. *Both to the people*

and to the Gentiles (tōi te laōi kai tois ethnesin). See verse 17. It was at the word Gentiles *(ethnē)* that the mob lost control of themselves in the speech from the stairs (22:21f.). So it is here, only not because of that word, but because of the word "resurrection" *(anastasis).*

24. *As he thus made his defence (tauta autou apologoumenou).* Genitive absolute again with present middle participle. Paul was still speaking when Festus interrupted him in great excitement. *With a loud voice (megalēi tēi phōnēi).* Associative instrumental case showing manner (Robertson, *Grammar,* p. 530) and the predicate use of the adjective, "with the voice loud" (elevated). *Thou art mad (mainēi).* Old verb for raving. See also John 10:20; Acts 12:15; I Cor. 14:23. The enthusiasm of Paul was too much for Festus and then he had spoken of visions and resurrection from the dead (verse 8). "Thou art going mad" (linear present), Festus means. *Thy much learning doth turn thee to madness (ta polla se grammata eis manian peritrepei).* "Is turning thee round." Old verb *peritrepō,* but only here in N.T. Festus thought that Paul's "much learning" (= "many letters," cf. John 7:15 of Jesus) of the Hebrew Scriptures to which he had referred was turning his head to madness (wheels in his head) and he was going mad right before them all. The old word *mania* (our mania, frenzy, cf. maniac) occurs here only in N.T. Note unusual position of *se* between *polla* and *grammata* (Robertson, *Grammar,* pp. 418, 420)

25. *But speak forth (alla apophtheggomai).* Verb for dignified and elevated discourse, a word from the literary *Koinē,* not the vernacular. In N.T. only here and 2:4, 14 which see. It occurs three times in Vettius Valens in a "mantic" sense. Paul was not ruffled by the rude and excited interruption of Festus, but speaks with perfect courtesy in his reply "words of truth and soberness." The old word *sōphrosunē* (soundness of mind) from *sōphrōn* (and that from *sōs* and

phrēn) is directly opposed to "madness" (*mania*) and in N.T. occurs only here and I Tim. 2:15.

26. *For the king knoweth of these things* (*epistatai gar peri toutōn ho basileus*). *Epistatai* (present middle probably Ionic form of *ephistēmi*) is a literary word and suits well here (cf. 24:10). *Freely* (*parrēsiazomenos*). Present middle participle, speaking fully, making a clean breast of it. From *parrēsia* (*pan, rhēsis*) (cf. 13:46). *Is hidden from him* (*lanthanein auton*). Escapes his notice. Infinitive in indirect discourse after *peithomai* (I am persuaded).

27. *I know that thou believest* (*oida hoti pisteueis*). Paul had "cornered" Agrippa by this direct challenge. As the Jew in charge of the temple he was bound to confess his faith in the prophets. But Paul had interpreted the prophets about the Messiah in a way that fell in with his claim that Jesus was the Messiah risen from the dead. To say, "Yes" would place himself in Paul's hands. To say "No" would mean that he did not believe the prophets. Agrippa had listened with the keenest interest, but he slipped out of the coils with adroitness and a touch of humour.

28. *With but little persuasion thou wouldest fain make me a Christian* (*en oligōi me peitheis Christianon poiēsai*). The Authorized rendering is impossible: "Almost thou persuadest me to be a Christian." *En oligōi* does not mean "almost." That would require *oligou, par' oligon*, or *dei oligou*. It is not clear, however, precisely what *en oligōi* does mean. It may refer to time (in little time) or a short cut, but that does not suit well *en megaloi* in verse 29. Tyndale and Crammer rendered it "somewhat" (in small measure or degree). There are, alas, many "somewhat" Christians. Most likely the idea is "in (or with) small effort you are trying to persuade (*peitheis*, conative present active indicative) me in order to make me a Christian." This takes the infinitive *poiēsai* to be purpose (Page renders it by "so as") and thus avoids trying to make *poiēsai* like *genesthai* (become).

The aorist is punctiliar action for single act, not "perfect." The tone of Agrippa is ironical, but not unpleasant. He pushes it aside with a shrug of the shoulders. The use of "Christian" is natural here as in the other two instances (11:26; I Peter 4:16).

29. *I would to God* (*euxaimēn an tōi theōi*). Conclusion of fourth-class condition (optative with *an*), undetermined with less likelihood, the so-called potential optative (Robertson, *Grammar*, p. 1021). Polite and courteous wish (first aorist middle optative of *euchomai*). *Whether with little or with much* (*kai en mikrōi kai en megalōi*). Literally, "both in little and in great," or "both with little and with great pains" or "both in some measure and in great measure." Paul takes kindly the sarcasm of Agrippa. *Such as I am* (*toioutous hopoios kai egō eimi*). Accusative *toioutous* with the infinitive *genesthai*. Paul uses these two qualitative pronouns instead of repeating the word "Christian." *Except these bonds* (*parektos tōn desmōn toutōn*). Ablative case with *parektos* (late preposition for the old *parek*). Paul lifts his right manacled hand with exquisite grace and good feeling.

30. *Rose up* (*anestē*). Second aorist active of *anistēmi* (intransitive), agreeing only with "the king" (*ho basileus*). The entertainment was over.

31. *They spake one to another* (*elaloun pros allēlous*). Imperfect active, describing the eager conversation of the dignitaries about Paul's wonderful speech. *Nothing worthy of death or bonds* (*ouden thanatou ē desmōn axion*). This is the unanimous conclusion of all these dignitaries (Romans, Jews, Greeks) as it was of Festus before (25:25). But Paul had not won any of them to Christ. The conclusion leaves Festus in a predicament. Why had he not set Paul free before this?

32. *This man might have been set at liberty* (*Apolelusthai edunato ho anthrōpos houtos*). Conclusion of the second class

condition (determined as unfulfilled) without *an* as in 24:19 because of *edunato* (verb of possibility, Robertson, *Grammar*, p. 1014). Note perfect passive infinitive *apolelusthai* from *apoluō*. He certainly "could have been set free." Why was it not done? *If he had not appealed unto Caesar* (*ei mē epekeklēto Kaisara*). Condition of the second class with the past perfect middle indicative (*op. cit.*, p. 1015) of *epikaleō* (cf. 25:11f.). But Paul *only* appealed to Caesar after Festus had tried to shift him back to Jerusalem and had refused to set him free in Caesarea. Festus comes out with no honour in the case. Since Agrippa was a favourite at court perhaps Festus would be willing to write favourably to Caesar.

CHAPTER XXVII

1. *That we should sail* (*tou apoplein hēmās*). This genitive articular infinitive with *ekrithē* like the LXX construction translating the Hebrew infinitive construct is awkward in Greek. Several similar examples in Luke 17:1; Acts 10:25; 20:3 (Robertson, *Grammar*, p. 1068). Luke alone uses this old verb in N.T. He uses nine compounds of *pleō*, to sail. Note the reappearance of "we" in the narrative. It is possible, of course, that Luke was not with Paul during the series of trials at Caesarea, or at least, not all the time. But it is natural for Luke to use "we" again because he and Aristarchus are travelling with Paul. In Caesarea Paul was the centre of the action all the time whether Luke was present or not. The great detail and minute accuracy of Luke's account of this voyage and shipwreck throw more light upon ancient seafaring than everything else put together. Smith's *Voyage and Shipwreck of St. Paul* is still a classic on the subject. Though so accurate in his use of sea terms, yet Luke writes like a landsman, not like a sailor. Besides, the character of Paul is here revealed in a remarkable fashion. *They delivered* (*paredidoun*). Imperfect active *ōmega* form rather than the old *-mi* form *paredidosan* as in 4:33, from *paradidōmi*. Perhaps the imperfect notes the continuance of the handing over. *Certain other prisoners* (*tinas heterous desmōtas*). Bound (*desmōtas*) like Paul, but not necessarily appellants to Caesar, perhaps some of them condemned criminals to amuse the Roman populace in the gladiatorial shows, most likely pagans though *heterous* does not have to mean different kind of prisoners from Paul. *Of the Augustan band* (*speirēs Sebastēs*). Note Ionic genitive *speirēs*, not *speiras*. See on Matt. 27:1; Acts 10:1. *Cohortis*

Augustae. We do not really know why this cohort is called "Augustan." It may be that it is part of the imperial commissariat (*frumentarii*) since Julius assumes chief authority in the grain ship (verse 11). These legionary centurions when in Rome were called *peregrini* (foreigners) because their work was chiefly in the provinces. This man Julius may have been one of them.

2. *In a ship of Adramyttium* (*ploiōi Hadramuntēnōi*). A boat belonging to Adramyttium, a city in Mysia in the province of Asia. Probably a small coasting vessel on its way home for the winter stopping at various places (*topous*). Julius would take his chances to catch another ship for Rome. The usual way to go to Rome was to go to Alexandria and so to Rome, but no large ship for Alexandria was at hand. *We put to sea* (*anēchthēmen*). First aorist passive of *anagō*, usual word in Luke. *Aristarchus, a Macedonian of Thessalonica, being with us* (*ontos sun hēmin Aristarchou Makedonos Thessalonikeōs*). Genitive absolute. Ramsay suggests that Luke and Aristarchus accompanied Paul as his slaves since they would not be allowed to go as his friends. But Luke was Paul's physician and may have gained permission on that score.

3. *The next day* (*tēi heterāi*). Locative case with *hēmerāi* understood. *We touched* (*katēchthēmen*). First aorist passive of *katagō*, the usual term for "coming down" from the seas as *anagō* above (and verse 4) is for "going up" to sea. So it *looks* to sailors. Sidon was 67 miles from Caesarea, the rival of Tyre, with a splendid harbour. The ship stopped here for trade. *Treated Paul kindly* (*philanthrōpōs tōi Paulōi chrēsamenos*). "Using (*chrēsamenos*, first aorist middle participle of *chraomai*, to use) Paul (instrumental case used with this verb) kindly" (*philanthrōpōs*, "philanthropically," adverb from *phil-anthrōpos*, love of mankind). He was kindly to Paul throughout the voyage (verse 43; 28:16), taking a personal interest in his welfare. *Refresh himself* (*epimeleias*

tuchein). Second aorist active infinitive of *tugchanō* (to obtain) with the genitive *epimeleias*, old word from *epimelēs*, careful, only here in the N.T. Whether it was mere hospitality we do not know. It may have been medical attention required because of Paul's long confinement. This is Paul's first visit to Sidon, but Christians were already in Phoenicia (11:19) and so Paul had "friends" here.

4. *We sailed under the lee of Cyprus* (*hupepleusamen tēn Kupron*). First aorist active indicative of *hupopleō*, to sail under. Cyprus was thus on the left between the ship and the wind from the northwest, under the protection of Cyprus. *Because the winds were contrary* (*dia to tous anemous einai enantious*). The articular infinitive after *dia* and the accusative of general reference (*anemous*) with predicate accusative (*enantious*, facing them, in their very teeth if they went that way). The Etesian winds were blowing from the northwest so that they could not cut straight across from Sidon to Patara with Cyprus on the right. They must run behind Cyprus and hug the shore of Cilicia and Pamphylia.

5. *When we had sailed across* (*diapleusantes*). First aorist active participle of *diapleō* (another compound of *pleō*). *The sea which is off Cilicia and Pamphylia* (*to pelagos to kata tēn Kilikian kai Pamphulian*). *Pelagos* is properly the high sea as here. In Matt. 18:6 (which see) Jesus uses it of "the depth of the sea." Only these examples in the N.T. The current runs westward along the coast of Cilicia and Pamphylia and the land would protect from the wind. *We came to Myra of Lycia* (*katēlthamen eis Murra tēs Lukias*). Literally, "We came down." This town was two and a half miles from the coast of Lycia. The port Andriace had a fine harbour and did a large grain business. No disciples are mentioned here nor at Lasea, Melita, Syracuse, Rhegium.

6. *Sailing for Italy* (*pleon eis tēn Italian*). This was the opportunity for which Lysias had been looking. So he put (*enebibasen*, first aorist active of *embibazō*, to cause to enter.

Cf. *epibantes* in verse 2) prisoners and soldiers on board. This was a ship of Alexandria bound for Rome, a grain ship (38) out of its course because of the wind. Such grain ships usually carried passengers.

7. *When we had sailed slowly* (*braduploountes*). Present active participle of *braduploeō* (*bradus*, slow, *plous*, voyage). Literally, "sailing slowly," not "having or had sailed slowly." Only here and in Artemidorus (sec. cent. A.D.). It may mean "tacking" before the wind. Polybius uses *tachuploeō*, to sail swiftly. *Many days* (*en hikanais hēmerais*). See on Luke 7:6 for *hikanos*. Literally, "in considerable days." *With difficulty* (*molis*). Used in old Greek, like *mogis* (Luke 9:39) from *molos*, toil (see Acts 14:18). *Over against Cnidus* (*kata tēn Knidon*). "Down along Cnidus." A hundred and thirty miles from Myra, the southwest point of Asia Minor and the western coast. Here the protection of the land from the northwest wind ceased. *The wind not further suffering us* (*mē proseōntos hēmās tou anemou*). Genitive absolute with present active participle of *proseaō*, one of the few words still "not found elsewhere" (Thayer). Regular negative *mē* with participles. They could not go on west as they had been doing since leaving Myra. *We sailed under the lee of Crete* (*hupepleusamen tēn Krētēn*). See under verse 4. Instead of going to the right of Crete as the straight course would have been they sailed southwest with Crete to their right and got some protection against the wind there. *Over against Salmone* (*kata Salmōnēn*). Off Cape Salmone, a promontory on the east of the island.

8. *Coasting along* (*paralegomenoi*). Present middle participle of *paralegō*, to lay beside, not from *legō*, to collect or *legō*, to say. Diodorus Siculus uses *paralegomai* in precisely this sense of coasting along, like Latin *legere oram*. In N.T. only here and verse 13. *Fair Havens* (*Kalous Limenas*). This harbour is named Kalus Limeonas, a small bay two miles east of Cape Matala. It opens to the East and South-

east, but is not fit to winter in. This harbour would protect them for a time from the winds. *The city of Lasea* (*polis Lasea*). Neither Lasea nor Fair Havens is mentioned by any ancient writer, two of the hundred cities of Crete.

9. *Where much time was spent* (*Hikanou chronou diagenomenou*). Genitive absolute again with second aorist middle participle of *diaginomai*, to come in between (*dia*). "Considerable time intervening," since they became weatherbound in this harbour, though some take it since they left Caesarea. *And the voyage was now dangerous* (*kai ontos ēdē episphalous*). Genitive absolute, "and the voyage being already (*ēdē* = Latin *jam*) dangerous" (old word from *epi* and *sphallō*, to trip, to fall, and so prone to fall, here only in N.T.). *Because the Fast was now already gone by* (*dia to kai tēn nēsteian ēdē pareleluthenai*). Accusative (after *dia*) of the articular infinitive perfect active of *parerchomai*, to pass by, with the accusative of general reference (*nēsteian*, the great day of atonement of the Jews, Lev. 16:29ff.) occurring about the end of September. The ancients considered navigation on the Mediterranean unsafe from early October till the middle of March. In A.D. 59 the Fast occurred on Oct. 5. There is nothing strange in Luke using this Jewish note of time as in 20:6 though a Gentile Christian. Paul did it also (I Cor. 16:8). It is no proof that Luke was a Jewish proselyte. We do not know precisely when the party left Caesarea (possibly in August), but in ample time to arrive in Rome before October if conditions had been more favourable. But the contrary winds had made the voyage very slow and difficult all the way (verse 7) besides the long delay here in this harbour of Fair Havens. *Paul admonished them* (*pareinei ho Paulos*). Imperfect active of *paraineō*, old word to exhort from *para* and *aineō*, to praise (3:8), only here and verse 22 in N.T. It is remarkable that a prisoner like Paul should venture to give advice at all and to keep on doing it (imperfect tense inchoative, began to admonish

and kept on at it). Paul had clearly won the respect of the centurion and officers and also felt it to be his duty to give this unasked for warning. *I perceive* (*theōrō*). Old word from *theoros*, a spectator. See Luke 10:18. Paul does not here claim prophecy, but he had plenty of experience with three shipwrecks already (II Cor. 11:25) to justify his apprehension. *Will be* (*mellein esesthai*). Infinitive in indirect assertion followed by future infinitive after *mellein* in spite of *hoti* which would naturally call for present indicative *mellei*, an anacoluthon due to the long sentence (Robertson, *Grammar*, p. 438). *With injury* (*meta hubreōs*). An old word from *huper* (above, upper, like our "uppishness") and so pride, insult, personal injury, the legal word for personal assault (Page). Josephus (*Ant.* III. 6, 4) uses it of the injury of the elements. *Loss* (*zēmian*). Old word, opposite of *kerdos*, gain or profit (Phil. 3:7f.). Nowhere else in N.T. *Lading* (*phortiou*). Diminutive of *phortos* (from *pherō*, to bear) only in form. Common word, but in N.T. only here in literal sense, as metaphor in Matt. 11:30; 23:4; Luke 11:46; Gal. 6:5. *But also of our lives* (*alla kai tōn psuchōn*). Common use of *psuchē* for life, originally "breath of life" (Acts 20:10), and also "soul" (14:2). Fortunately no lives were lost, though all else was. But this outcome was due to the special mercy of God for the sake of Paul (verse 24), not to the wisdom of the officers in rejecting Paul's advice. Paul begins now to occupy the leading rôle in this marvellous voyage.

11. *Gave more heed* (*mallon epeitheto*). Imperfect middle of *peithō*, to yield to (with the dative case). The "Frumentarian" centurion ranked above the captain and owner. As a military officer the centurion was responsible for the soldiers, the prisoners, and the cargo of wheat. It was a government ship. Though the season was not advanced, the centurion probably feared to risk criticism in Rome for timidity when the wheat was so much needed in Rome

(Knowling). *To the master* (*tōi kubernētēi*). Old word from *kubernaō*, to steer, and so steersman, pilot, sailing-master. Common in this sense in the papyri. In N.T. only here and Rev. 18:17. *And to the owner of the ship* (*kai tōi nauklērōi*). Old word compounded of *naus* and *klēros* and used for owner of the ship who acted as his own skipper or captain. The papyri examples (Moulton and Milligan's *Vocabulary*) all have the meaning "captain" rather than "owner."

12. *Because the haven was not commodious to winter in* (*aneuthetou tou limenos huparchontos pros paracheimasian*). Genitive absolute again present tense of *huparchō*: "The harbour being unfit (*aneuthetou*, this compound not yet found elsewhere, simplex in Luke 9:62; 14:35; Heb. 6:7) for wintering" (*paracheimasia*, only here in N.T., but in Polybius and Diodorus, in an inscription A.D. 48, from *paracheimazō*). *The more part advised* (*hoi pleiones ethento boulēn*). Second aorist middle indicative of *tithēmi*, ancient idiom with *boulēn*, to take counsel, give counsel. Lysias held a council of the officers of the ship on the issue raised by Paul. *If by any means they could reach Phoenix and winter there* (*ei pōs dunainto katantēsantes eis Phoinika paracheimasai*). The optative *dunainto* (present middle of *dunamai*) here with *ei* is a condition of the fourth class with the notion of purpose implied and indirect discourse (Robertson, *Grammar*, p. 1021). "We vote for going on the chance that we may be able" (Page). Phoenix is the town of palms (John 12:13), the modern Lutro, the only town in Crete on the southern coast with a harbour fit for wintering, though Wordsworth and Page argue for Phineka which suits Luke's description better. The verb *paracheimazō*, to winter, is from *para* and *cheimōn* (see also 28:11). Used in several *Koinē* writers. *Looking northeast and southeast* (*bleponta kata liba kai kata chōron*). There are two ways of interpreting this language. *Lips* means the southwest wind and *chōros* the northwest wind. But what is the effect of *kata* with these words? Does

it mean "facing" the wind? If so, we must read "looking southwest and northwest." But *kata* can mean down the line of the wind (the way the wind is blowing). If so, then it is proper to translate "looking northeast and southeast." This translation suits Lutro, the other suits Phoenike. Ramsay takes it to be Lutro, and suggests that sailors describe the harbour by the way it looks as they go into it (the subjectivity of the sailors) and that Luke so speaks and means Lutro which faces northeast and southeast. On the whole Lutro has the best of the argument.

13. *When the south wind blew softly* (*hupopneusantos notou*). Genitive absolute with aorist active participle of *hupopneō*, old verb to blow under, then to blow gently, here only in N.T. "A south wind having blown gently," in marked contrast to the violent northwest wind that they had faced so long. They were so sure of the wisdom of their decision that they did not even draw up the small boat attached by a rope to the vessel's stern (verse 16). It was only some forty miles to Lutro. *Their purpose* (*tēs protheseōs*, set before them, from *protithēmi*), genitive after *krateō* (*kekratēkenai*, perfect active infinitive in indirect discourse). *They weighed anchor* (*ārantes*). First aorist active participle of *airō*, old verb used in technical sense with *tas agkuras* (anchors) understood as in Thucydides I. 52; II. 23, "having lifted the anchors." Page takes it simply as "moving." *Sailed along Crete* (*parelegonto tēn Krētēn*). Imperfect middle. See verse 8, "were coasting along Crete." *Close in shore* (*āsson*). Comparative adverb of *agki*, near, and so "nearer" to shore. Only here in N.T.

14. *After no long time* (*met' ou polu*). Litotes again. *Beat down from it* (*ebalen kat' autēs*). Second aorist active indicative of *ballō*, to throw. Here "dashed" (intransitive). *Autēs* is in the ablative, not genitive case, beat "down from it" (Crete), not "against it or on it." (Robertson, *Grammar*, p. 606). *Autēs* cannot refer to *ploion* (boat) which is neuter.

So the ablative case with *kata* as in Mark 5:13, Homer also. The Cretan mountains are over 7,000 feet high. *A tempestuous wind which is called Euraquilo* (*anemos tuphōnikos ho kaloumenos Eurakulōn*). *Tuphōn = Tuphōs* was used for the typhoon, a violent whirlwind (*turbo*) or squall. This word gives the character of the wind. The *Eurakulōn* (reading of Aleph A B against the Textus Receptus *Eurokludōn*) has not been found elsewhere. Blass calls it a hybrid word compounded of the Greek *euros* (east wind) and the Latin *aquilo* (northeast). It is made like *euronotos* (southeast). The Vulgate has *euroaquilo*. It is thus the east north east wind. Page considers Euroclydon to be a corruption of Euraquilo. Here the name gives the direction of the wind.

15. *When the ship was caught* (*sunarpasthentos tou ploiou*). Genitive absolute again with first aorist passive of *sunarpazō*, old word, in N.T. only Luke 8:29; Acts 6:12; 19:29, and here. Graphic picture as if the ship was seized by a great monster. *Face the wind* (*antophthalmein tōi anemōi*). Dative case with the vivid infinitive of *antophthalmeō* from *antophthalmos*, looking in the eye, or eye to eye (*anti*, facing and *opthalmos*, eye). Eyes were painted on the prows of vessels. The ship could not face the wind enough to get to Phoenix. Modern sailors talk of sailing into the eye of the wind. We were not able to look the wind in the eye. *Koinē* verb used by Polybius. Some MSS. have it in Acts 6:11, but only here in N.T. In Wisdom of Sol. 12:14 it is used of a prince who cannot look God in the face. Clement of Rome 34 uses it of an idle workman not able to look his employer in the face (Milligan and Moulton's *Vocabulary*). *We gave way* (*epidontes*). Second aorist active participle of *epididōmi*, giving way to the wind. *Were driven* (*epherometha*). Imperfect passive of *pherō*, "we were being borne along." We "scudded before the gale" (Page). "The suddenness of the hurricane gave no time to furl the great mainsail" (Furneaux).

16. *Running under the lee of* (*hupodramontes*). Second aorist active participle of *hupotrechō*. Same use of *hupo* as in *hupepleusamen* (verses 4, 8) for "under the lee", under the protection of. *Nēsion* is diminutive of *nēsos*, a small island. The MSS. vary between Cauda (B) and Clauda (Aleph). *To secure the boat* (*perikrateis genesthai tēs skaphēs*). "To become masters (*perikrateis* from *peri* and *kratos*, power over, found in Susannah and ecclesiastical writers, and here only in N.T.) of the boat ("dug out," like Indian boats, literally, from *skaptō*, to dig, old word, here only in N.T. and verses 30, 32). The smooth water behind the little island enabled them to do this. *When they had hoisted it up* (*hēn ārantes*). "Which (the little boat) having hoisted up (*arantes*, verse 13)." Even so it was "with difficulty" (*molis*). Perhaps the little boat was waterlogged. *Used helps* (*boētheiais echrōnto*). Imperfect middle of *chraomai* with instrumental case. The "helps" were ropes or chains, no doubt. *Undergirding the ship* (*hupozōnnuntes to ploion*). Present active participle of *hupozōnnumi*. Old verb, here only in N.T. Probably cables (*hupozōmata*) or ropes were used under the hull of the ship laterally or even longitudinally, tightly secured on deck. This "frapping" was more necessary for ancient vessels because of the heavy mast. The little island made it possible to do this also. *Lest we be cast upon the Syrtis* (*mē eis tēn Surtin ekpesōsin*). Final clause after verb of fearing (*phoboumenoi*) with *mē* and the second aorist active subjunctive of *ekpiptō*, old verb to fall out or off, to be cast away. So here and verses 26, 29, a classical use of the verb for a ship driven out of its course on to shoals or rocks (Page who cites Xenophon, *Anab.* VII. 5, 12). The Syrtis was the name for two quicksands between Carthage and Cyrenaica, this clearly being the Syrtis Major most dangerous because of the sandbanks (*surtis*, from *surō*). The wind would drive the ship right into this peril if something were not done. *They lowered the gear* (*chalasantes to skeuos*). First aorist

active participle of *chalaō* (cf. Luke 5:4 for lowering the nets). *Skeuos* means vessel or gear. They slackened or reduced sail, especially the mainsail, but leaving enough to keep the ship's head as close to the wind as was practicable. *So were driven* (*houtōs epheronto*). Imperfect passive indicative again as in verse 15 with the addition of *houtōs* (thus). The ship was now fixed as near to the wind (E N E) as possible (seven points). That would enable the ship to go actually W by N and so avoid the quicksands. J. Smith has shown that, a day being lost around Cauda, the ship going 36 miles in 24 hours in 13 days would make 468 miles. The Island of Malta (Melita) is precisely in that direction (W by N) from Cauda and is 480 miles. Page sees a difficulty about this explanation of the steady drift of the ship in the word *diapheromenon* in verse 27, but that was at the end of the drifting and the varied winds could have come then and not before. The whole narrative as explained carefully in Smith's *Voyage and Shipwreck of St. Paul* is a masterpiece of precise and accurate scholarship. A résumé of his results appears in my *Luke the Historian in the Light of Research*.

18. *As we laboured exceedingly with the storm* (*sphodrōs cheimazomenōn hēmōn*). Genitive absolute with present passive participle of *cheimazō*, old verb to afflict with a tempest (*cheima*, stormy weather), to toss upon the waves, here alone in N.T. *They began to throw overboard* (*ekbalēn epoiounto*). Literally, "They began to make (inchoative imperfect middle of *poieō*) a casting out" (*ekbolēn* from *ekballō*, to cast out, old word, only here in N.T.). Cf. Latin *jacturam facere*. This to lighten the ship by throwing overboard the cargo. The grain in the ship would shift and make it list and so added to the danger. *They cast out* (*eripsan*). Third person plural aorist active of *riptō*, not *eripsamen* as Textus Receptus. *With their own hands* (*autocheires*). Old word (*autos*, *cheir*) but here alone in N.T. Vivid and graphic touch by Luke who, of course, watched every movement day by day.

The tackling (tēn skeuēn). The furniture of the ship that could be spared. It was becoming desperate.

20. *When neither sun nor stars shone upon us (mēte hēliou mēte astrōn epiphainontōn).* Genitive absolute again. *For many days (epi pleionas hēmeras).* For more days than a few. *No small tempest (cheimonos ouk oligou).* Litotes again. *All hope that we should be saved was now taken away (loipon periēireito elpis pāsa tou sōzesthai hēmās).* "For the rest (or future) there began to be taken from around us (*periēireito* inchoative imperfect and see use of the verb in II Cor. 13:16 of the veil) all hope of the being saved so far as we were concerned." Despair was beginning to settle like a fog on all their hopes. Had Paul lost hope?

21. *When they had been long without food (pollēs te asitias huparchousēs).* Genitive absolute, the old word *asitia* from *asitos* (verse 33) *a* privative and *sitos*, food, here alone in N.T. Literally, "There being much abstinence from food." They had plenty of grain on board, but no appetite to eat (seasickness) and no fires to cook it (Page). "Little heart being left for food" (Randall). Galen and other medical writers use *asitia* and *asitos* for want of appetite. *Stood forth (statheis).* As in 1:15; 2:14; 17:22. Pictorial word (Page) that sets forth the vividness and solemnity of the scene (Knowling). *Ye should have hearkened unto me (edei men peitharchēsantas moi).* Literally, "It was necessary for you hearkening unto me not to set sail (mē anagesthai)." It was not the "I told you so" of a small nature, "but a reference to the wisdom of his former counsel in order to induce acceptance of his present advice" (Furneaux). The first aorist active participle is in the accusative of general reference with the present infinitive *anagesthai*. *And have gotten this injury and loss (kerdēsai te tēn hubrin tautēn kai tēn zēmian).* This Ionic form *kerdēsai*(from *kerdaō*) rather than *kerdēnai* or *kerdānai* is common in late Greek (Robertson, *Grammar*, p. 349). The Revised Version thus carries over the negative

mē to this first aorist active infinitive *kerdēsai* from *kerdaō* (cf. on Matt. 16:26). But Page follows Thayer in urging that this is not exact, that Paul means that by taking his advice they ought to have escaped this injury and loss. "A person is said in Greek 'to gain a loss' when, being in danger of incurring it, he by his conduct saves himself from doing so." This is probably Paul's idea here.

22. *And now* (*kai ta nun*). Accusative plural neuter article of general reference in contrast with *men* in verse 21. Paul shows modesty (Bengel) in the mild contrast. *No loss of life* (*apobolē psuchēs oudemia*). Old word from *apoballō*, to throw away, only twice in N.T. Romans 11:15 (rejection) and here. He had foretold such loss of life as likely (verse 10), but he now gives his reason for his changed view.

23. *For there stood by me* (*parestē gar moi*). Second aorist active (intransitive) indicative of *paristēmi* with the locative case (beside me). The very form used by Paul of his trial (II Tim. 4:17) when "the Lord stood by me" (*ho de kurios moi parestē*) when others deserted him. This angel of the God whom Paul serves (in distinction from the heathen gods) is the reason for Paul's present confidence.

24. *Thou must stand before Caesar* (*Kaisari se dei parastēnai*). Note the same *dei* (must) as in 23:11 when Jesus appeared to Paul in Jerusalem and the same verb *parastēnai* (second aorist active infinitive) used in verse 23. *Hath granted thee* (*kecharistai soi*). Perfect middle indicative of *charizomai* and that from *charis*, a gift or grace. The lives of those that sailed with Paul God had spared as a gift (*charis*) to Paul.

25. *Wherefore be of good cheer* (*dio euthumeite*). God had spoken. That was enough. This old verb from *euthumos* in the N.T. only here, verse 25, and James 5:13. See the adjective 27:36. *For I believe God* (*pisteuō gar tōi theōi*). This is Paul's reason for his own good cheer and for his exhortation to confidence in spite of circumstances so untoward. Paul

had doubtless prayed for his own life and for the lives of all.
He was sure that he was to bear his witness in Rome.

26. *We must be cast* (*dei hēmās ekpesein*). It is necessary
for us to fall out (*ekpesein*, second aorist active infinitive of
ekpiptō). It was not revealed to Paul what island it would
be.

27. *As we were driven to and fro* (*diapheromenōn hēmōn*).
Genitive absolute with present passive participle of *diapherō*,
old verb to bear different ways (*dia = duo*, two), this way
and that. Continued to be tossed to and fro in the rough
seas. It would seem so to those on board. It does not necessarily mean that the wind had changed. The fourteenth
night is reckoned from the time they left Fair Havens. *In
the sea of Adria* (*en tōi Hadriāi*). Not the Adriatic Sea as we
now call the sea between Italy and the mainland of Illyricum,
but all the lower Mediterranean between Italy and Greece.
Luke's usage is like that of Strabo. *Surmised* (*hupenooun*).
Imperfect active indicative of *huponoeō*, inchoative, began
to suspect. *That they were drawing near to some country*
(*prosagein tina autois chōran*). Infinitive with accusative
of general reference in indirect assertion. *Prosagō* is here
used intransitively and Luke writes from the sailor's standpoint that a certain land was drawing near to them (*autois*,
dative). The sailors heard the sound of breakers and grew
uneasy.

28. *They sounded* (*bolisantes*). First aorist active participle
of *bolizō* rare verb only here and in Eustathius who says it
was familiar in ancient Greek. Apparently from *bolis*, a mis-
sile or dart, and so to throw down the lead into the sea, to
heave the lead, to take soundings. The inscriptions give
bolimos for "leaden." *Twenty fathoms* (*orguias eikosi*). This
old word, from *oregō*, to stretch, means the distance from
one outstretched middle finger tip to the other likewise outstretched. *After a little space* (*brachu diastēsantes*). Literally,
"standing apart a little" (second aorist active participle of

diistēmi), that is, the ship going a short distance further on. A ship today approaching St. Paul's Bay by the rocky point of Koura would pass first twenty, then fifteen fathoms (Furneaux).

29. *Lest haply we should be cast ashore on rocky ground* (*mē pou kata tracheis topous ekpesōmen*). The usual construction after a verb of fearing (*mē* and the aorist subjunctive *ekpesōmen*). Literally, "Lest somewhere (*pou*) we should fall out down against (*kata*) rocky places." The change in the soundings made it a very real fear. *Tracheis* (rough) is old adjective, but in the N.T. only here and Luke 3:5 (from Isa. 40:4). *Four anchors* (*agkuras tessaras*). Old word from *agkē*. In N.T. only in this chapter, with *rhiptō* here, with *ekteinō* in verse 30, with *periaireō* in verse 40; and Heb. 6:19 (figuratively of hope). *From the stern* (*ek prumnēs*). Old word, but in N.T. only in Mark 4:38; here and 41 in contrast with *prōira* (prow). The usual practice was and is to anchor by the bows. "With a view to running the ship ashore anchoring from the stern would, it is said, be best" (Page). Nelson is quoted as saying that he had been reading Acts 27 the morning of the Battle of Copenhagen (April, 1801) where he anchored his ships from the stern. *Wished for the day* (*euchonto*). Imperfect middle, kept on praying for "day to come" (*hēmeran genesthai*) before the anchors broke under the strain of the storm or began to drag. If the ship had been anchored from the prow, it would have swung round and snapped the anchors or the stern would have faced the beach.

30. *The sailors* (*tōn nautōn*). Old word from *naus* (ship), in N.T. only here, verse 30, and Rev. 18:17. *Were seeking* (*zētountōn*). Genitive absolute again with present active participle of *zēteō* to seek. *Had lowered* (*chalasantōn*). Aorist active participle of *chalazō*. *Under colour* (*prophasei*). Possibly the same word as "prophecy" (from *pro-phēmi*, to speak forth), but here pretence, pretext, although it may

come from *prophainō*, to show forth. The use here is an old one and appears also in Mark 12:40; Luke 20:47; I Thess. 2:5; Phil. 1:18. *As though* (*hōs*). The alleged reason, a common Greek idiom with *hōs* and the participle (Robertson, *Grammar*, p. 966). Here with *mellontōn*. *From the foreship* (*ek prōirēs*). Old word for prow of the ship. In the N.T. only here and verse 41. Note here *ekteinein* (lay out, stretch out) rather than *rhipsantes* (casting) in verse 29, for they pretended to need the small boat to stretch out or lay out the anchors in front.

31. *Except these abide in the ship* (*Ean mē houtoi meinōsin en tōi ploiōi*). Condition of the third class (undetermined, but with hope, etc.). Paul has no hesitancy in saying this in spite of his strong language in verse 24 about God's promise. He has no notion of lying supinely down and leaving God to do it all. Without the sailors the ship could not be properly beached.

32. *The ropes* (*ta schoinia*). Diminutive of *schoinos*, old word, but in N.T. only here and John 2:15. Paul is now saviour of the ship and the soldiers quickly cut loose the skiff and "let her fall off" (*eiasan autēn ekpesein*) rather than be the means of the escape of the sailors who were needed. This dastardly scheme of the sailors would have brought frightful loss of life.

33. *While the day was coming on* (*achri hou hēmera ēmellen ginesthai*). More likely here *achri hou* (for *achri toutou hōi*) with the imperfect *ēmellen*, has its usual meaning, "until which time day was about to come on (*ginesthai*, present middle infinitive, linear action)." That is Paul kept on exhorting or beseeching (*parekalei*, imperfect active) them until dawn began to come on (cf. verse 39 when day came). In Heb. 3:13 *achri hou* with the present indicative has to mean "so long as" or while, but that is not true here (Robertson, *Grammar*, p. 975). See on Acts 2:46 for the same phrase for partaking food (*metalambanō trophēs*, genitive case) as

also in 27:34. Paul wanted them to be ready for action when day really came. "Fourteenth day" repeated (verse 27), only here in the accusative of duration of time (*hēmeran*). It is not clear whether the "waiting" (*prosdokōntes*, present active participle predicate nominative complementary participle after *diateleite*, Robertson, *Grammar*, p. 1121) means fourteen days of continuous fasting or only fourteen successive nights of eager watching without food. Galen and Dionysius of Halicarnassus employ the very idiom used here by Luke (*asitos diateleō*). *Having taken nothing* (*mēthen proslabomenoi*). Second aorist middle participle of *proslambanō* with the accusative *mēthen* rather than the more usual *mēden*. Probably Paul means that they had taken no regular meals, only bits of food now and then.

34. *For this is for your safety* (*touto gar pros tēs humeteras sōtērias huparchei*). Note *sōtēria* in sense of "safety," literal meaning, not spiritual salvation. This is the only instance in the N.T. of the use of *pros* with the ablative meaning "from the side of" your safety, though a classic idiom (Robertson, *Grammar*, p. 623), an example of Luke's literary style. *Perish* (*apoleitai*). Future middle (intransitive) of *apollumi* (*-uō*), to destroy. So the oldest MSS. rather than *peseitai* from *piptō*, to fall. This proverbial expression occurs also in Luke 21:18 which see and in I Sam. 14:45; II Sam. 14:11; I King, 1:52.

35. *Gave thanks to God* (*eucharistēsen tōi theōi*). First aorist active indicative of *eucharisteō* from which our word "Eucharist" comes. It was saying grace like the head of a Hebrew family and the example of Paul would encourage the others to eat. Probably Paul, Luke, and Aristarchus had memories of the Lord's supper (Acts 2:42) while to others it was only an ordinary meal (Luke 24:30).

36. *Then were they all of good cheer* (*euthumoi de genomenoi*). More exactly, "Then all becoming cheerful," because of Paul's words and conduct. *Took food* (*proselabonto trophēs*).

Partitive genitive here (some food), not accusative as verse 33. Paul's courage was contagious.

37. *Two hundred three-score and sixteen souls* (*diakosiai hebdomēkonta hex*). The Vatican Manuscript (B) has *hōs* in place of *diakosiai* (two hundred) which Westcott and Hort put in the margin. But Alford is probably correct in suggesting that the scribe of B wrote *hōs* by repeating the omega in *ploiōi* with *s* = 200 (Greek numeral). If the number 276 seems large, it is to be remembered that we do not know the size of the ship. Josephus (*Life*, 3) says that there were 600 on the ship that took him to Italy. The grain ships were of considerable size. The number included sailors, soldiers, and prisoners. A muster or roll call may have been made.

38. *When they had eaten enough* (*koresthentes trophēs*). First aorist passive of *korennumi*, old verb to satisfy, to satiate, with the genitive. Literally, "Having been satisfied with food." Here only in the N.T. *They lightened* (*ekouphizon*). Inchoative imperfect active, began to lighten. Old verb from *kouphos* and originally to be light, but transitive to lighten, as here, from Hippocrates on. *Throwing out the wheat* (*ekballomenoi ton siton*). The cargo of wheat. The second *ekbolē* (verse 18) or casting out and overboard which was only partially done at first.

39. *They knew not* (*ouk epeginōskon*). Imperfect active of *epiginōskō*, to recognize. Probably conative, tried to recognize and could not (Conybeare and Howson). The island was well-known (28:1, *epegnōmen*), but St. Paul's Bay where the wreck took place was some distance from the main harbour (Valetta) of Melita (Malta). *They perceived* (*katenooun*). Imperfect active of *katanoeō*, gradually perceived after some effort as in 11:16. This beach seemed their only hope. *They took counsel* (*ebouleuonto*). Imperfect middle showing the process of deliberation and doubt. The bay "having a beach" (*echonta aigialon*) is a phrase found in Xenophon's *Anabasis* VI. 4, 4. *Whether they could drive* (*ei dunainto*

eksōsai). This use of the optative with *ei* in questions of this sort (implied indirect) is a neat Greek idiom (Robertson, *Grammar*, p. 1021). B C Bohairic read *eksōsai* (first aorist active infinitive of *eksōzō*),to save out (so Westcott and Hort), instead of *exōsai* (from *exōtheō*, to push out, as Textus Receptus).

40. *Casting off* (*perielontes*). Second aorist active of *periaireō*. Literally, "Having taken away from around," that is all four anchors from around the stern. Cf. the other verbs with *agkuras* in verse 29 and 30. *They left them in the sea* (*eiōn eis tēn thalassan*). Imperfect active of *eaō*, either descriptive or inchoative. They let the anchors go and the ropes fell down into the sea. *At the same time loosing the bands of the rudders* (*hama anentes tas zeuktērias tōn pēdaliōn*). On the use of *hama* with the participle, old Greek idiom see Robertson, *Grammar*, p. 1139. The second aorist active participle of *aniēmi*, to relax, loosen up. Old verb, in N.T. Acts 16:26; 27:40; Eph. 6:9; Heb. 13:5. Thayer notes that *zeuktērias* (bands) occurs nowhere else, but several papyri use it of yokes and waterwheels (Moulton and Milligan's *Vocabulary*). The word for rudders (*pēdalion*) is an old one (from *pēdon*, the blade of an oar), but in the N.T. only here and James 3:4. Page notes that the ancient ships had a pair of paddle rudders like those of the early northmen, one on each quarter. The paddle rudders had been fastened while the ship was anchored. *Hoisting up the foresail to the wind* (*eparantes ton artemōna tēi pneousēi*). Supply *aurāi* (breeze) after *pneousēi* (blowing). It is not clear what "sail" is meant by "*artemōna*." No other example in Greek is known, though the scholiast to Juvenal XII. 68 explains *velo prora suo* by *artemone solo*. Hence "foresail" is probably correct. *They made for the beach* (*kateichon eis ton aigialon*). Imperfect active of *katechō*, to hold down, perhaps inchoative. "They began to hold the ship steadily for the beach."

41. *But lighting upon* (*peripesontes de*). Second aorist ac-

tive participle of *peripiptō*, old verb to fall into and so be encompassed by as in Luke 10:30; James 1:2. There is a current on one side of St. Paul's Bay between a little island (Salmonetta) and Malta which makes a sand bank between the two currents. Unexpectedly the ship stuck in this sandbar. *Where two seas met* (*dithalasson*). Used in Strabo and Dio Chrysostom for divided seas (*dis, thalassa*). *They ran the vessel aground* (*epekeilan tēn naun*). First aorist active indicative of old verb *epikellō*, to run a ship ashore. Only here in N.T. Here also we have the only N.T. use of *naus* for ship (from *naō, neō*, to swim) so common in ancient Greek. Our word navy is from this word through the Latin. *Struck* (*ereisasa*). First aorist active participle of *ereidō*, old verb to fix firmly. Only here in N.T. *Unmoveable* (*asaleutos*). From *a* privative and *saleuō* to shake. Old word. In N.T. only here and Heb. 12:28. *Began to break up* (*elueto*). Inchoative imperfect passive of the old verb *luō*, to loosen. The prow was stuck in the sand-bar, and the stern was breaking to pieces by the opposing waves lashing on both sides. It was a critical moment.

42. *Counsel was to kill* (*boulē egeneto hina—apokteinōsin*). The soldiers did not relish the idea of the escape of the prisoners. Hence there came this "counsel" (*boulē*). Regular Greek idiom for purpose (*hina* and aorist active subjunctive of *apokteinō*, to kill). Soldiers were responsible for the lives of prisoners (Acts 12:19). *Swim out* (*ekkolumbēsas*). First aorist active participle of *ekkolumbaō*, old verb to swim out and so away. *Escape* (*diaphugēi*). Second aorist (effective) active subjunctive of *diapheugō*, to make a clean (*dia*) escape.

43. *To save Paul* (*diasōsai ton Paulon*). Effective first aorist active infinitive of *diasōzō*. And no wonder for the centurion knew now how much they all owed to Paul. *Stayed them from their purpose* (*ekōleusen autous tou boulēmatos*.) Ablative case of *boulēma* after *ekōleusen* (from *kōleuō*, to hinder, common verb). *And get first to land* (*prōtous*

eis tēn gēn exienai). This classic verb *exeimi* occurs four times
in Acts (13:42; 17:15; 20:7; 27:32) and nowhere else in the
N.T. It was a wise command.

44. *Some on planks* (*hous men epi sanisin*). Common
Greek idiom (*hous men—hous de*) for "some—some."
The only N.T. instance of the old Greek word *sanis* for
board or plank. The breaking of the ship gave scraps of
timber which some used. *They all escaped safe* (*pantas
diasōthēnai*). First aorist passive infinitive of *diasōzō* (the
very word used for the desire of the centurion about Paul)
with accusative of general reference, the clause being subject
of *egeneto*. So Luke in this marvellous narrative, worthy of
any historian in any age, shows how Paul's promise was fulfilled (verse 24). Paul the prisoner is the hero of the voyage
and shipwreck, a wonderful example of God's providential
care.

CHAPTER XXVIII

1. *Then we knew* (*tote epegnōmen*). Second aorist (ingressive) active indicative of *epiginōskō*. Then we recognized. See 27:39. *Was called* (*kaleitai*). Present passive indicative retained in indirect discourse. *Melita* (*Melitē*). Not *Miletenē* as only B reads, a clerical error, but retained in the text of Westcott and Hort because of B. Page notes that the island was Malta as is shown from the name, the location, the presence of a ship from Alexandria bound for Rome wintering there (verse 11), and the mention of Syracuse as the next stop after leaving (verse 12).

2. *The barbarians* (*hoi barbaroi*). The Greeks called all men "barbarians" who did not speak Greek (Rom. 1:14), not "barbarians" in our sense of rude and uncivilized, but simply "foreign folk." Diodorus Siculus (V. 12) says that it was a colony of the Phoenicians and so their language was Punic (Page). The word originally meant an uncouth repetition (*barbar*) not understood by others (I Cor. 14:11). In Col. 3:11 Paul couples it with Scythian as certainly not Christian. These are (with verse 4 below) the only N.T. instances. *Showed us* (*pareichan*). Imperfect active of *parechō* with -*an* instead of -*on* as *eichan* in Mark 8:7 (Robertson, *Grammar*, p. 339). It was their habit on this occasion, Luke means, they kept on showing. *No common kindness* (*ou tēn tuchousan philanthrōpian*). The old word *philanthrōpia* (*philos*, *anthrōpos*), love of mankind, occurs in the N.T. only here and Titus 3:4 (adverb in 27:3). See on 19:11 for this use of *ou tēn tuchousan*, "not the kindness that happens every day." They were not "wreckers" to take advantage of the calamity. *They kindled a fire* (*hapsantes puran*). The only N.T. example and verse 3 of the old word *pura* (from *pur*, fire), a pile of burning fuel (sticks). First aorist active participle

of *haptō*, to set fire to, to kindle. Cf. *anaptō* in Luke 12:49.
Received us all (*proselabonto pantas hēmās*).   Second aorist
middle (indirect indicative of *proslambanō*.   They took us
all to themselves (cf. Acts 18:26).   *The present* (*ton ephestōta*).
Second perfect active participle (intransitive) of *ephistēmi*,
"the rain that stood upon them" (the pouring rain).   Only
in Luke and Paul in N.T.

3. *When Paul had gathered* (*sustrepsantos tou Paulou*).
Genitive absolute with first aorist active participle of *sus-
trephō*, old verb to twist or turn together or roll into a bundle.
In N.T. only here and Matt. 17:22.   *A bundle of sticks* (*phruganōn ti plēthos*).   "Some multitude (or pile) of dry twigs"
(*phruganōn* from *phrugō* or *phrussō*, to dry.   Only here in
N.T.).   *Laid* (*epithentos*).   So genitive absolute again with
second aorist active participle of *epitithēmi*, to place upon.
Few things show Paul to better advantage than this incident.
By reason of the heat (*apo tēs thermēs*).   Old word, only here
in N.T.   Ablative case with *apo* (from the heat).   The viper
was in a state of torpor in the bundle of sticks.   The heat
wakened him.   *A viper* (*echidna*).   The old word used by the
Baptist of the Pharisees (Matt. 3:7 = Luke 3:7) and by
Jesus also (Matt. 12:34; 23:33).   It is objected that there
is little wood in the island today and no vipers, though
Lewin as late as 1853 believes that he saw a viper near St.
Paul's Bay.   But the island now has 1,200 people to the
square mile and snakes of any kind have a poor chance.
The viper has also disappeared from Arran as the island
became more frequented (Knowling).   Ramsay thinks that
the small constrictor (*Coronella Austriaca*) which still exists
in the island may be the "viper," though it has no poison
fangs, but clings and bites.   The natives thought that it was
a poisonous viper.   *Fastened on his hand* (*kathēpse tēs cheiros
autou*).   First aorist active indicative of *kathaptō*, to fasten
down on with the genitive case.   Old verb, here only in N.T.
Cf. Mark 16:18.

4. *The beast* (*to thērion*). Diminutive of *thēr* and so little beast. See on Mark 1:13. Aristotle and the medical writers apply the word to venomous serpents, the viper in particular (Knowling), as Luke does here. Vincent calls attention to the curious history of our word "*treacle*" for molasses (Latin *theriaca*) from *thēriakē*, an antidote made from the flesh of vipers. Coverdale translates Jer. 8:22: "There is no more treacle in Gilead." Jeremy Taylor: "We kill the viper and make treacle of him." *Hanging from his hand* (*kremamenon ek tēs cheiros autou*). Vivid picture of the snake dangling from Paul's hand. Present middle participle of *kremamai*, late form for *kremannumi*, to hang up, to suspend (cf. Gal. 3:13). *No doubt* (*pantōs*). Literally, By all means, old adverb. Cf. 21:22; Luke 4:23; I Cor. 9:22. Only by Luke and Paul in the N.T. "They *knew* that he was a prisoner being taken to Rome on some grave charge, and *inferred* that the charge was murder" (Page). *Though he hath escaped* (*diasōthenta*). First aorist passive participle of *diasōzō* (same verb used in 24:43, 44 and 28:1), so-called concessive use of the participle (Robertson, *Grammar*, p. 1129). *Yet Justice* (*dikē*). An abstraction personified like the Latin *Justitia* (Page). The natives speak of *Dikē* as a goddess, but we know nothing of such actual worship in Malta, though the Greeks worshipped abstractions as in Athens. *Hath not suffered* (*ouk eiasen*). Did not suffer. They look on Paul as a doomed man as good as dead. These people thought that calamity was proof of guilt, poor philosophy and worse theology.

5. *Shook off* (*apotinaxas*). First aorist active participle of *apotinassō*, to shake off. Rare word (Euripides, Galen, LXX). In N.T. only here and Luke 9:5.

6. *But they expected* (*hoi de prosedokōn*). Imperfect active, were expecting, continued to expect. *That he would have swollen* (*auton mellein pimprasthai*). More exactly, "Expecting him to be about (or that he was about) to swell up." *Pimprasthai* is present middle infinitive from *pimprēmi*, to

blow, to burn, to inflame, to cause to swell. *Prēthō*, to swell, seems connected and both use the aorist *eprēsa*. Our word "inflammation" likewise means a burning and a swelling. This verb is a common medical term used as Luke has it. It occurs here only in N.T. *Or fallen down dead suddenly* (*ē katapiptein aphnō nekron*). Rather, "or was about to fall down dead suddenly." The two common results of a bite by a viper or other poisonous snake, both medical terms used by Luke. *But when they were long in expectation* (*epi polu de autōn prosdokōntōn*). Genitive absolute. "But while they were expecting for much time." *Nothing amiss come to him* (*mēden atopon eis auton ginomenon*). "Nothing out of place coming to him" (present middle participle). *Mēden* the usual negative of the participle and the accusative case the object of *theōrountōn* (genitive absolute). *Changed their minds* (*metabalomenoi*). Aorist middle (direct) participle of *metaballō*, old verb to turn about or around, turning themselves about, changing their minds. Plato uses this very verb in middle voice for changing the mind. *That he was a god* (*auton einai theon*). Accusative and infinitive in indirect discourse. At Lystra Paul was first received as a god (Mercury) and then they stoned him to kill him (Acts 14:11, 19). So fickle is popular favour.

7. *To the chief man of the island* (*tōi prōtōi tēs nēsou*). An official title correct in Malta (Ramsay, *St. Paul*, p. 343). An inscription in Malta calls Prudens "Primate of the Maltese" (*prōtos Melitaiōn*). Here it is plainly a title and not the common use seen in 13:50; 25:2; 28:17. *Publius* (*Popliōi*). This Greek name (*praenomen*) can be derived either from *Popilius* or *Publius* (cf. *publicus* for *populicus* from *populus*). *Entertained us* (*exenisen hēmās*). Paul and his companions (Luke and Aristarchus). Was Julius included? On *xenizō* see Acts 10:23. *Courteously* (*philophronōs*). This old adverb from *philophrōn* (*philos*, *phrēn*, friendly mind) occurs here alone in the N.T. In a kindly

or friendly manner, all the more so because of the original suspicion of Paul as a criminal.

8. *Lay* (*katakeisthai*). Common verb for the sick (Mark 1:30; John 5:6). *Sick* (*sunechomenon*). "Held together." Common verb again for the sick as in Luke 4:38. *Of fever* (*puretois*). Instrumental case, and plural "fevers," medical term for intermittent attacks of fever (Demosthenes, Lucian, medical writers). *Dysentery* (*dusenterioi*). Instrumental case also. Late form of the older *dusenteria* and only here in N.T. Our very word *dysentery*. Another medical term of which Luke uses so many. Hippocrates often mentions these two diseases together. *Laying his hands on him healed him* (*epitheis tas cheiras autoi iasato auton*). Either like the laying on of hands in James 5:14, the gift of healing (I Cor. 12:9f.), or the tender interest of Jesus when he took hold of the hand of Peter's mother-in-law (Mark 1:31). Ramsay argues that *iaomai* is employed here of the miraculous healing by Paul while *therapeuō* is used of the cures by Luke the physician (verse 9). This is a general distinction and it is probably observed here, but in Luke 6:18 (which see) both verbs are employed of the healings by Jesus. *Came and were healed* (*proserchonto kai etherapeuonto*). Imperfect middle and imperfect passive. A regular stream of patients came during these months. Luke had his share in the honours, "us" (*hēmās*), and no doubt his share in the cures. *With many honours* (*pollais timais*). Instrumental case. The word was often applied to payment for professional services as we today speak of an honorarium. *They put on board* (*epethento*). Second aorist middle indicative of *epitithēmi*, to put on. The idea of "on board" is merely suggested by *anagomenois* (when we sailed) "the things for our needs" (*ta pros tas chreias*).

11. *Which had wintered* (*parakecheimakoti*). Perfect active participle of *paracheimazō*, to pass the winter. Old verb, in N.T. only 27:12; 28:11; I Cor. 16:6; Titus 3:12. The loca-

tive case agreeing with *ploiōi*. Navigation in the Mediterranean usually opened up in February (always by March), spring beginning on Feb. 9 (Page). *Whose sign was the Twin Brothers* (*parasēmōi Dioskourois*). The word *parasēmōi* can be either a substantive (as Revised Version has it) or an adjective "marked by the sign," examples of both uses common in ancient Greek. *Dioskourois* is in apposition with *parasēmōi*. The word means the twin sons (*kouros* or *koros*) of Zeus (*Dios*, genitive of *Zeus*) and Leda, viz., Castor and Pollux. The Attic used the dual, *tō Dioskorō*. Castor and Pollux were the tutelary deities of sailors whose figures were painted one on each side of the prow of the ship. This sign was the name of the ship. So they start in another grain ship of Alexandria bound for Rome.

12. *Touching* (*katachthentes*). First aorist passive participle of *katagō*, to go down to land, just the opposite of *anēchthēmen* in verse 11 from *anagō*, to go up to sea. *At Syracuse* (*eis Surakousas*). The chief city of Sicily and eighty miles from Malta. Perhaps open weather and a southerly wind helped them across. Here it was that Alcibiades wrecked the power and glory of Athens. Why the ship spent three days we do not know.

13. *We made a circuit* (*perielthontes*). Second aorist active of *perierchomai*, to go around, old verb, already in 19:13. See also Heb. 11:37; I Tim. 5:13. But Westcott and Hort read *perielontes* after Aleph B (from *periaireō*) as in 27:40, though here it could only mean casting loose, for which no other authority exists. At any rate the ship had to tack to reach Rhegium and was not able to make a straight course (*enthudromeō*, 16:11). Rhegium (*Rhēgion*) is from *rhēgnumi*, to break off, the place where the land breaks off, the southern entrance to the straits of Messina. *A south wind sprang up* (*epigenomenou notou*). Genitive absolute again, and for all the world like that fatal south wind in 27:13, but with no bad results this time, though the weather was plainly treach-

erous at this early season. *On the second day* (*deuteraioi*). This is the classical use of the predicate adjective, "We second day men" as in Luke 24:22; John 11:39; Phil. 3:5 instead of the adverb (Robertson, *Grammar*, p. 657). *To Puteoli* (*eis Potiolous*). It was 182 miles from Rhegium and would require 26 hours (Page). It was eight miles northwest from Neapolis (Naples) and the chief port of Rome, the regular harbour for the Alexandrian ships from Rome. Portions of the great mole are said to be still visible.

14. *Where we found brethren* (*hou heurontes adelphous*). Possibly from Alexandria, but, as Blass observes, it is no more strange to find "brethren" in Christ in Puteoli when Paul arrives than in Rome. There was a large Jewish quarter. *Seven days* (*hēmeras hepta*). Accusative of extent of time. Paul and his party remained so long at the urgent request of the brethren. He was still a prisoner, but clearly Julius was only too glad to show another courtesy to Paul to whom they all owed their lives. It was 130 miles by land from Puteoli to Rome over one of the great Roman roads. *And so we came to Rome* (*kai houtōs eis tēn Romēn ēlthamen*). So at last. Luke is exultant as Page observes: *Paulus Romae captivus: triumphus unicus.* It is the climax of the book of Acts (19:21; 23:11), but not the close of Paul's career. Page rightly remarks that a new paragraph should begin with verse 15, for brethren came from Rome and this part of the journey is touched with the flavour of that incident. The great event is that Paul reached Rome, but not as he had once hoped (Rom. 15:22–29).

15. *When they heard of us* (*akousantes ta peri hēmōn*). How "they heard the things concerning us" we do not know. Good news had its way of travel even before the days of telegraph, telephone, daily papers. Possibly Julius had to send on special couriers with news of his arrival after the shipwreck. Possibly some of the brethren in Puteoli at once (beginning of the week) sent on news to the brethren in

Rome. The church in Rome had long ago received Paul's letter from Corinth at the hands of Phoebe. *To meet us* (*eis apantēsin hēmin*). Idiomatic phrase, "for meeting with us" (associative instrumental case). *Koiné* word *apantēsis* from verb *apantaō*, to meet, in N.T. only here; Matt. 25:6; I Tim. 4:17. Use after *eis* rather than infinitive like a translation Hebraism (Robertson, *Grammar*, p. 91). *As far as the Market of Appius* (*achri Appiou Phorou*). The Forum of Appius, 90 miles from Puteoli, 40 from Rome, on the great Appian Way. The Censor Appius Claudius had constructed this part of the road, B.C. 312. Paul probably struck the Appian Way at Capua. Portions of this great stone highway are still in use. If one wishes to tread where Paul trod, he can do it here. Appii Forum had a bad reputation, the haunt of thieves, thugs, and swindlers. What would this motley crowd think of Paul chained to a soldier? *Three Taverns* (*Triōn Tabernōn*). Genitive case after *achri* like *Appiou Phorou*. About 30 miles from Rome. *Tres Tabernae*. *Whom* (*hous*). Two groups of the disciples came (one Gentile, one Jewish, Rackham thinks), one to Appii Forum, the other to Three Taverns. It was a joyous time and Julius would not interfere. *Took courage* (*elabe tharsos*). The old substantive *tharsos* is here alone in the N.T. Jesus himself had exhorted Paul to be of good courage (*tharsei* Acts 23:11) as he had done the disciples (John 16:33). Paul had passed through enough to cause depression, whether he was depressed or not, but he deeply appreciated this kindly sympathy.

16. *Paul was suffered to abide by himself* (*epetrapē tōi Paulōi menein kath' heauton*). Second aorist passive of *epitrepo*, to permit or allow. Literally, "It was permitted to Paul to abide by himself." Some late documents (Textus Receptus) here add: "The centurion delivered the prisoners to the captain of the guard" (or the *stratopedarch*). This officer used to be considered Burrus who was Prefect of the

Praetorian Guard A.D. 51–62. But it is by no means certain that Julius turned the prisoners over to this officer. It seems more likely that Julius would report to the captain of the Peregrini. If so, we may be sure that Julius would give a good report of Paul to this officer who would be kindly disposed and would allow Paul comparative freedom (living by himself, in his lodging, verse 23, his own hired house verse 30, though still chained to a soldier). *With the soldier that guarded him* (*sun tōi phulassonti auton stratiōtēi*). Probably a new soldier every day or night, but always with this soldier chained to his right hand day and night. Now that Paul is in Rome what can he do for Christ while he awaits the outcome of his own appeal to Nero?

17. *Those that were the chief of the Jews* (*tous ontas tōn Ioudaiōn prōtous*). This use of *prōtos* for the leading men of a city or among the Jews we have already had in 13:50; 25:2; Luke 19:47. Literally, "Those that were first among the Jews." The position of the participle *ontas* between the article and the adjective *prōtous* is regular (Robertson, *Grammar*, p. 777). *When they were come together* (*sunelthontōn autōn*). Genitive absolute again. Paul could not go to the synagogue, as his custom was, being a bound prisoner. So he invited the Jewish leaders to come to his lodging and hear his explanation of his presence in Rome as a prisoner with an appeal to Caesar. He is anxious that they may understand that this appeal was forced upon him by Festus following Felix and not because he has come to make an attack on the Jewish people. He was sure that false reports had come to Rome. These non-Christian Jews accepted Paul's invitation. *Nothing against* (*ouden enantion*). Adjective here as in 26:9, not preposition as in 7:10; 8:32. From *en* and *antios* (*anti*), face to face. Concessive participle *poiēsas* as in verse 4 (*diasōthenta*) which see. *Yet was I delivered prisoner from Jerusalem into the hands of the Romans* (*desmios ex Ierosolumōn paredothēn eis tas cheiras tōn Rom-*

aiōn). This condensed statement does not explain how he "was delivered," for in fact the Jews were trying to kill him when Lysias rescued him from the mob (22:27–36). The Jews were responsible for his being in the hands of the Romans, though they had hoped to kill him first.

18. *When they had examined me* (*anakrinantes me*). First aorist active participle of *anakrinō*, the same verb used already in 24:8; 25:6, 26 of the judicial examinations by Felix and Festus. *Desired* (*eboulonto*). Imperfect middle of attempted action or picture of their real attitude. This is a correct statement as the words of both Felix and Festus show. *Because there was* (*dia to — huparchein*). Accusative case with *dia* (causal use) with the articular infinitive, "Because of the being no cause of death in me" (*en emoi*, in my case, *aitia*, usual word for crime or charge of crime).

19. *When the Jews spake against it* (*antilegontōn tōn Ioudaiōn*). Genitive absolute again, *antilegontōn* (*antilegō*) common verb for speaking against as in 13:45. *Clementer dicit* (Bengel). "The word is a mild one to describe the bitter enmity of the Jews" (Knowling). *I was constrained* (*ēnagkasthēn*). "I was compelled," first aorist passive indicative of *anagkazō*, the very word used of Paul's efforts to get the Christians to blaspheme (26:11) which see. Paul was compelled to appeal to Caesar (see 25:11 and 12 for this phrase), unless Paul was willing to be the victim of Jewish hate when he had done no wrong. *Not that I had aught to accuse my nation of* (*ouch hōs tou ethnous mou echōn ti katēgorein*). This use of *hōs* with a participle (*echōn*) is common in Greek for the alleged reason. The genitive case with the infinitive *katēgorein* is regular. Paul says *ethnos* instead of *laos* as in 24:17; 26:4.

20. *Did I intreat* (*parekalesa*). Did I invite you. *Because of the hope of Israel* (*heineken tēs elpidos tou Israel*). Genitive with preposition *heineken*. The hope of the Messiah is his point as in 26:6. *I am bound with this chain* (*tēn halusin tau-*

tēn perikeimai). This old verb means to lie around as in Luke 17:2; Heb. 12:1. But it is also used as the passive of *peritithēmi*, to place around with the accusative of *peritithēmi* retained. It is a transitive passive. Paul does not lie around the chain, but the chain lies around him, a curious reversal of the imagery (Robertson, *Grammar*, p. 815).

21. *Letters* (*grammata*). Official documents from the Sanhedrin about the charges against Paul. *Any harm of thee* (*ti peri sou ponēron*). *Evil* (*ponēron*). The three aorists (*edexametha, apēggeilen, elalēsen*) cover the past. These Jews do not mean to say that they had never heard of Paul. It is hardly likely that they had heard of his appeal to Caesar, "for how could the news have reached Rome before Paul?" (Page).

22. *But we desire* (*axioumen de*). Old verb *axioō*, to deem worthy, to think right or proper as in 15:38 which see. They think it only fair to hear Paul's side of his case. *Concerning this sect* (*peri tēs haireseōs tautēs*). Paul had identified Christianity with Judaism (verse 20) in its Messianic hope. The language seems to imply that the number of Christians in Rome was comparatively small and mainly Gentile. If the edict of Claudius for the expulsion of the Jews from Rome (Acts 18:2) was due to disturbance over Christ (*Chrēstus*), then even in Rome the Jews had special reason for hostility towards Christians. *Everywhere spoken against* (*pantachou antilegetai*). Cf. verse 19. The line of cleavage between Jew and Christian was now sharply drawn everywhere.

23. *Appointed* (*taxamenoi*). First aorist middle participle of *tassō*. Formal arrangement as in Matt. 28:16 when Jesus appointed the mountain for his meeting in Galilee. *In great number* (*pleiones*). Comparative of *polus*, "more than a few." *Expounded* (*exetitheto*). Imperfect middle of *ektithēmi*, to set forth, as in 11:4; 18:26. He did it with detail and care and spent all day at it, "from morning till evening" (*apo prōi heōs hesperas*). In N.T. only here, 4:3 and Luke

24:29, though common word. *Persuading them concerning Jesus* (*peithōn autous peri tou Iēsou*). Conative present active participle, trying to persuade. It was only about Jesus that he could make good his claim concerning the hope of Israel (verse 20). It was Paul's great opportunity. So he appealed both to Moses and to the prophets for proof as it was his custom to do.

24. *Some believed* (*hoi men epeithonto*). Imperfect passive indicative of *peithō*. More exactly, "some began to be persuaded" (inchoative). *Some disbelieved* (*hoi de ēpistoun*). Imperfect active of *apisteō*, to disbelieve, continued to disbelieve. It is usually so.

25. *When they agreed not* (*asumphōnoi ontes*). Old adjective, only here in N.T., double compound (*a* privative, *sum*, *phōnē*), without symphony, out of harmony, dissonant, discordant. It was a triumph to gain adherents at all in such an audience. *They departed* (*apeluonto*). Imperfect middle (direct) indicative, "They loosed themselves from Paul." Graphic close. *After that Paul had spoken one word* (*eipontos tou Paulou rhēma hen*). Genitive absolute. One last word (like a preacher) after the all day exposition. *Well* (*kalōs*). Cf. Matt. 14:7; Mark 7:6, 9 (irony). Here strong indignation in the very position of the word (Page). *To your fathers* (*pros tous pateras humōn*). So Aleph A B instead of *hēmōn* (our) like Stephen in 7:52 whose words Paul had heard. By mentioning the Holy Spirit Paul shows (Knowling) that they are resisting God (7:52).

26. *Say* (*eipon*). Second aorist active imperative instead of the old form *eipe*. The quotation is from Isa. 6:9 and 10. This very passage is quoted by Jesus (Matt. 13:14 and 15 = Mark 4:12 = Luke 8:10) in explanation of his use of parables and in John 12:40 the very point made by Paul here, "the disbelief of the Jews in Jesus" (Page). See on Matthew for discussion of the language used. Here the first time ("go to this people and say.") does not occur in

Matthew. It is a solemn dirge of the doom of the Jews for their rejection of the Messiah foreseen so long ago by Isaiah.

28. *This salvation (touto to sōtērion)*. Adjective from *sōtēr* (Saviour), saving, bringing salvation. Common in the old Greek. The neuter as here often in LXX (as Psa. 67:2) as substantive like *sōtēria* (cf. Luke 3:6). *They will also hear (autoi kai akousontai)*. *Autoi* as opposed to the rejection by the Jews, "vivid and antithetical" (Page).

30. *Two whole years (dietian holēn)*. Only here in N.T. and 24:27 which see. During these busy years in Rome Paul wrote Philippians, Philemon, Colossians, Ephesians, Epistles that would immortalize any man, unless, forsooth, one or more of them was written from Ephesus or Caesarea, which has not yet been proven. *In his own hired dwelling (en idiōi misthōmati)*. Old word, here only in N.T., that which is hired for a price (from *misthoō* and that from *misthos*, hire). *Received (apedecheto)*. Imperfect middle of *apodechomai*, received from time to time as they came, all that came *(eisporeuomenous)* from time to time. *Preaching (kerussōn)*, teaching *(didaskōn)*, the two things that concerned Paul most, doing both as if his right hand was not in chains, to the amazement of those in Rome and in Philippi (Phil. 1:12–14). *None forbidding him (akōlutōs)*. Old adverb from *a* privative and the verbal adjective *kōlutos* (from *kōluō*, to hinder), here only in the N.T. Page comments on "the rhythmic cadence of the concluding words." Page rejects the notion that the book is an unfinished work. It closes with the style of a concluded work. I agree with Harnack that Luke wrote the Acts during this period of two years in Rome and carried events no further because they had gone no further. Paul was still a prisoner in Rome when Luke completed the book. But he had carried Paul to "Rome, the capital of the world, *Urbi et Orbi*" (Page). The gospel of Christ has reached Rome. For the fate of Paul we must turn elsewhere. But Luke had the presence of Paul while

he carried the Acts to its triumphant conclusion. Ramsay can give a good deal in proof of his claim that Luke is the greatest of all historians. Beyond a doubt his rank is high and the world can never repay its debt to this cultured physician who wrote the Gospel and the Acts.